W9-BCG-673

Measurement and Evaluation in Psychology and Education

Measurement and Evaluation in Psychology and Education

THIRD EDITION

ROBERT L. THORNDIKE

Richard March Hoe Professor of Psychology and Education
Teachers College
Columbia University

ELIZABETH HAGEN

Professor of Psychology and Education
Teachers College
Columbia University

JOHN WILEY & SONS, INC.

NEW YORK · LONDON · SYDNEY · TORONTO

Library of Congress Catalog Card Number: 69-19091
SBN 471 86363 7

10 9 8 7 6 5

Printed in the United States of America

Preface

Preparing a new edition of a book gives the authors an opportunity to achieve two main objectives. On the one hand, they can bring their work up to date, adding a consideration of new developments with respect to both the technology of their field and the problems of focal concern. On the other, they can rework those aspects of their presentation that their own experience or the reactions of others have suggested could be improved. In this, our third edition, we have tried to do both of these things.

The basic structure of the book remains unchanged from the previous editions because we have found it serviceable and it has been well received by our colleagues. However, we have made one or two shifts in the order of chapters in order to achieve what seems a smoother sequence, and we have completely rewritten the present chapters 3, 4, 9, 16, and 17. We believe our present treatment will be clearer and more teachable, and we feel that a few useful new ideas have been introduced.

In a general introductory text, one is faced with a conflict as to how fully one should document the points that one is trying to make. On the one hand, frequent citations of sources can be distracting and not very meaningful to the beginning student. On the other, there will be some who will wish to examine at first hand the evidence on which an assertion is made. We have tried to add a number of recent references, but have avoided the burden of long lists of citations, especially of relationships that have been repeatedly found over the years.

We have, of course, included discussion of some of the interesting new tests, as we have retained material on the established tools of our trade. We have also considered some of the problems in the use of tests that have been in the public eye in the recent past—problems of invasion of privacy, of test fairness to minority groups, of use of multivariate procedures in guidance and classification.

The tests that we describe in any detail in the book remain only samples of the array of perhaps 2000 published test devices available to the potential user at this time. A number of others are described in brief annotations in Appendix IV. We continue in the belief that an introductory text in measurement should focus on teaching the student how to find the tests he needs; how to evaluate them once he has found them; how to use and how *not* to use them once he has selected one or more that fit his purposes. It is in the hope that it may help achieve these goals that we offer this third edition to our colleagues, to their students, and to ours.

Robert L. Thorndike
Elizabeth P. Hagen

Contents

Measurement and Evaluation in Psychology and Education

CHAPTER 1

Historical and Philosophical Orientation

ooooooooooooooooooooooooooooooooooooooooooooooooooooooooooooooooooooooooooooooooooooooooooooooooooooooooooooooo

WHEN Johnny was two years old, mama was concerned because he didn't seem to be talking quite as well as he should, so she took him to a psychologist for an "IQ test." In the kindergarten that he went to, reading readiness tests were routinely given toward the end of the year. He had a reading achievement test at the end of the first and again at the end of the second grade. Each year from grades 3 to 6 he was tested with a standardized achievement test battery, and, in grades 4 and 6, he received a scholastic aptitude test. In the ninth grade, an inventory of interests was administered to all students in his class. In grade 11 and again in grade 12, scholastic aptitude tests to assess promise for collegiate education were Johnny's lot, and he also took a battery of vocational aptitude tests to help guide him in an occupational choice. But he enlisted in the Navy, where he found still another battery of ability and interest tests awaiting him at the Navy Reception Center.

This may seem a test-ridden life, but it is not an unrealistic picture of the youngster growing up in the United States of today. The number and type of test will vary somewhat from person to person, but tests and testing are practically universal experiences, and have an important role to play in the life of practically everyone. In view of the prevalence of educational and psychological testing in present-day America, it is sometimes hard to realize how very new this field is. But testing is a phenomenon of the twentieth century. In 1900 there was nothing remotely resembling educational or psychological measurement as we know it today. In schools the homemade essay examination ruled supreme. The worker in the mental hospital or clinic had some simple tests that he could use, but had to rely largely upon his personal accumulated experience to provide standards of performance. Selecting a man for a job depended largely upon the whim of the person who happened to talk to the applicant. Uniform, standardized tests played no part in either the practical affairs of the day or in the emerging science of psychology. They simply didn't exist.

Early Educational Testing

The appraisal of educational achievement in the United States before 1850 had relied very largely upon oral examination. The teacher or visiting examiner asked a question. The designated pupil undertook to answer it. The questioner arrived at an immediate subjective evaluation of the answer. The method was burdensome and inefficient, since only one pupil could be tested at a time. And since different pupils were asked different questions, the answers to which were evaluated subjectively by the examiner, there was no comparability from pupil to pupil either in the task or in the evaluation of it.

During the latter half of the nineteenth century, oral examinations by boards of visitors were replaced by set written examinations as a basis for promotion or admission to an academy or college. Outside examination in turn yielded to evaluation by the classroom teacher. Whether carried out by an outside examiner or by a teacher, however, the technique was that of the essay examination, in which a pupil responded in his own words to a question set by the examiner.

The written examination had advantages over the oral examination of (1) presenting the same tasks to each member of the group and (2) letting each pupil work for the full examination period. However, though the task was made uniform, at least for the members of a given class, appraisal of each individual's response to the task remained highly subjective, depending upon the standards and prejudices of the particular scorer. As we shall see in Chapter 3, great variations were found in the *scoring* of a particular paper. Only since 1900 has there been any general development of objectively scored tests in which a preestablished key can be routinely and uniformly applied to the responses made by each pupil. Only since 1900 has the idea emerged of a general norm of performance for an age or grade, with which the performance by any class or any individual may be compared.

The Beginnings of Psychological Measurement

Psychology in 1850 was still in large measure a part of philosophy. Courses dealing with man and his actions were presented under the title "Moral Philosophy," and discussed in an armchair fashion the nature of the Mind and the Soul. Psychology was almost entirely nonexperimental, and the idea that one could measure in quantitative terms the speed of responding, the amount of forgetting, or the level of intelligence would have been received in most quarters with hostility or, more probably, ignored as not worthy of rebuttal. The nearest approaches to psychological measurement were a few scattered experiments by physicists and physiologists on the measurement of the ability to make sensory discriminations and the speed of simple elementary responses.

By 1900 psychology had felt the impact of the physical and biological sciences and was striving mightily to become a science itself. It was shaking off the ties that bound it to philosophy and forming new alliances with the biological sciences. It had adopted the experimental method and was measurement-conscious. The basic tool of experimentation is measurement, and psychology was expanding its measurement techniques in all directions. The record since 1900 is the record of the attempt to expand and adapt measurement techniques to cover all aspects of human behavior.

Three main streams combined to yield the vigorous measurement movement in psychology and its spread through education. Some of the flavor and some of the emphasis have come from each stream. These were (1) the physiological and experimental psychology that had its main growth in Germany in the nineteenth century, (2) Darwinian biology, and (3) the clinical concern for the maladjusted and underdeveloped individual.

Beginnings of Experimental Psychology

The modern scientific era was first ushered into the physical sciences in the seventeenth and eighteenth centuries. Scientific interest and method soon spread over to the biological sciences, and by the early nineteenth century experimental physiology was a center of active research interest in the experimental laboratories in Germany and other European countries. Experimental physiologists became interested in the operation of the senses, studying intensively seeing, hearing, and the other senses. Physiologists also became interested in measuring the speed of simple motor responses.

In 1879 the first laboratory for experimental psychology was established by Wilhelm Wundt at Leipzig. Early experimental psychologists were interested in many of the same measurements that had concerned the physiologists. These were measures of seeing, hearing, feeling, and speed of response. But gradually they extended their concern to more clearly psychological matters, such as measurement of perceptual span—the amount that the individual can "take in" at once, of rate of learning, of the timing of complex mental tasks, and so forth.

One area of particular interest for its contribution to the broad field of psychological and educational measurement was that known as *psychophysics*. The experimental psychologist was much interested in exploring the relationship between physical stimulus intensities, for example, of light wave or of sound wave, and the experienced intensity of the resulting sensation. The designing of effective experimental procedures for studying these problems gave rise to a set of techniques that have proved adaptable to a wide range of problems of psychological measurement.

From experimental psychology came a legacy of respect for careful experimental method and precision of technique, a number of experimental designs, and statistical techniques that could be carried over to more general psychological and educational measurement problems.

Early Study of Individual Differences

A second stream contributing to psychological measurement was Darwinian biology. In 1859 Darwin brought out his *Origin of Species*. The basic concern in Darwin's work was with variation among the members of a species, that is, individual differences. Darwin's work was followed up in England and applied to distinctively human affairs, particularly by Sir Francis Galton. Whereas German psychology had focused on finding the general facts true of all people, Galton became interested primarily in the differences among people. Stimulated by Darwin to study the inheritance of traits, he gathered data both on physical and on psychological characteristics. The study of these individual differences required better statistical tools, and the British group, under the leadership of Karl Pearson, developed improved techniques for analyzing and describing the patterns of individual differences.

These, then, were the two main contributions of the British group to the growth of psychological measurement: a deep concern for studying the differences among people as interesting and significant facts and the invention of appropriate statistical techniques and tools for carrying out this study.

Clinical Study of Deviates

During this same period, a third stream was gathering strength. This was concern for the individual who was not functioning successfully. Humanitarian concern for the insane, the feebleminded, and the general misfit led in the nineteenth century to active research and investigation aimed toward understanding their condition and improving their lot. This clinical interest in the maladjusted individual was particularly strong in France, and it was here that it bore fruit for the field of measurement. As psychologists worked with these unfortunate deviates, the need became more and more apparent for some uniform way of expressing the degree of their defect, particularly in the mental sphere. It was in this context of concern for the child who was not getting along in school that Binet and his colleagues developed the series of intellectual tasks that ultimately grew into the whole array of measures of intelligence.

Synthesis in the United States

By the early years of the present century, all these streams of influence had made themselves felt in the United States. James McKeen Cattell had taken his graduate work in psychology in Germany with Wundt, where he had received a good grounding in quantitative and experimental psychology. But he had also been exposed to the work of Galton and had developed a lasting interest in individual differences and statistical method. When he returned to the United States in 1888, he began an investigation of individual differences in the simple sensory and motor performances that were being measured in German psychological laboratories. He studied the relationship between these performances and academic success.

E. L. Thorndike was a student of Cattell's just before the turn of the century and became a focal influence in the spread and development of standardized educational tests. Both his own work and that of a large group of students at Teachers College, Columbia University rapidly spread the gospel of objective measurement in education.

The work of Binet was eagerly seized upon in this country. His tests were translated and produced in several versions, of which by far the most influential became the *Stanford-Binet* first produced by Lewis Terman in 1916. The testing movement seemed especially suited to the temper of this country and took hold here with a vigor and enthusiasm unequaled elsewhere.

Measurement in the Twentieth Century

The first 60 years of the twentieth century may conveniently be divided into four equal parts, so far as the recent history of psychological and educational measurement is concerned. We may designate the period from 1900 to 1915 the pioneering phase. This was the period of exploration and initial development of methods. It saw the emergence of the first Binet intelligence scales and their American revisions. Standardized achievement tests in different subjects began to appear, exemplified by Stone's arithmetic tests, Buckingham's spelling tests, and Trabue's language tests. Thorndike developed his first handwriting scale. Otis and others were initiating work on group tests of intelligence.

The next 15 years, 1915 to 1930, can perhaps be called the "boom" period in test development. The pioneers had shown the way, and in the hands of enthusiastic followers tests multiplied like rabbits. Standardized tests were developed for all the school skills and for the content areas of the school program. Achievement batteries made their appearance. Starting with *Army Alpha* of World War I, group intelligence tests were produced in great numbers. Also starting with a wartime product, the *Woodworth Personal Data Sheet,* a whole line of personality questionnaires and inventories came into being.

The rapid development of testing instruments and methods was pushed by a group of enthusiasts. They were converts who had "gotten the word." Their enthusiasm was contagious and extended not only to the production of tests but also to their use. Tests of intelligence and achievement were administered widely and somewhat indiscriminately. Test results were often accepted unhesitatingly and uncritically and served as the basis for a variety of frequently unjustified judgments and actions with respect to individuals. In the expansive flood of enthusiasm for objective measurement, some enthusiasts were not inclined to be critical of their instruments or the interpretation of results from them. Many sins were committed in the name of measurement by uncritical test users.

After a while the pendulum began to swing back. More and more sharply voiced criticisms of objective tests and of the uses made of such tests began to be heard. Heredity-environment discussions became acrimonious. The use of test scores as a basis for classroom grouping became the subject of bitter attack. Criticism was directed at specific tests in terms of their limited scope and their emphasis upon restricted and traditional objectives. It was also directed at the whole underlying philosophy of quantification and the use of numbers to express psychological qualities.

The critical attack had the healthy effect of forcing the test enthusiasts themselves to become more critical of their assumptions and procedures and to broaden their approach to the whole problem of psychological and educational appraisal. From about 1930 to 1945 may be considered a period of critical appraisal, devoted to taking stock, broadening techniques and delimiting interpretations. It was a period in which the center of attention shifted from "measuring" a limited range of academic skills to "evaluating" achievement of the whole range of educational objectives. It was a period in which the holistic, global projective methods of personality appraisal came to the fore.

It is difficult to view with any perspective at all events that have taken place as recently as the 1950's. History may eventually characterize the period quite differently than do we, standing so close to it. However, we will venture to predict that the period from 1945 to 1960 will be characterized as the period of test batteries and testing programs. Partly as a result of their successful use in World War II, integrated aptitude batteries for educational and personnel use multiplied during this period. And the large-scale external testing programs, such as those administered by the College Entrance Examination Board, though stemming from much earlier in the century, expanded in size and multiplied in numbers at a striking rate. We have experienced a second boom period—not so much in test development and construction, as in test administration and use. The mid-twentieth century is a period in which standardized testing is a widely experienced and widely accepted phenomenon of our American culture.

Finally, we may sense in the past few years the swing to a second cycle of criticism. In an age of computerized technology, when an individual is identified by number—social security number, draft board number, student number—rather than by name, there is a resurgence of reaction against quantification and the use of numbers to express psychological assessments. Subscribing to an egalitarian philosophy, which is sometimes carried to the extreme of denying the existence of individual differences, many thoughtful people are concerned over the social implications of testing programs for our society.

Is the amount of testing, especially for college admissions, a burden upon the pupil and the schools? Do standardized tests penalize the creative individual? Do present instruments, especially self-report inventories, represent an unwarranted invasion of privacy? Are employment tests discriminatory, eliminating potentially good employees from limited cultural backgrounds? These are some of the questions being raised insistently at the present time.

Under these circumstances it is particularly important that construction, use, and interpretation of these instruments be well understood by teachers, guidance workers, and psychologists for whom they are daily tools of the trade. It is also important that the phenomenon of standardized testing be understood by the citizens who are exposed to it in their search for employment for themselves or education for their children. Therefore, let us try at this point to formulate a philosophy of measurement that will take into account the lessons of the past, and will serve to guide our attack on measurement problems and our use of measurement techniques in the years ahead.

PHILOSOPHICAL ORIENTATION

In education and in psychology we are concerned with human beings. Sometimes we are concerned with them as specific individuals, as when we want to know why Mary is having so much difficulty in learning to do long division. Sometimes we are concerned with them as specific groups of individuals, as when we inquire whether the children in class A can read as well as those in class B. Sometimes we are concerned with them as general representatives of mankind, as when we try to determine whether children with high verbal intelligence tend to show more or less signs of emotional disturbance than children of average intellectual ability.

Knowledge as a Guide to Action

In practically all of education and in much of psychology, our concern about individuals is to *do* something about them, individually or collectively. Insofar as education is a science, it is an applied science, and in psychology, too, the applied aspects bulk large in the present scene. The educator or the practical psychologist is continually faced with the necessity of arriving at some decision as to a course of action. He must decide what to do about an individual or individuals, or he must help the person himself decide what to do. He must decide in which grade to place a child or what special instruction to provide for him. He must reach a diagnosis of a child with a reading disability, with a view to recommending treatment. He must recommend whether or not to employ a job applicant. He must help a student decide whether to plan for college and, if so, what sort of program to take and what type of job to aim for. The educator or psychologist wants each one of these decisions to be a sound and well-conceived one.

Our basic assumption is that *sound decisions arise out of relevant knowledge* of the individual or individuals. We assume that the more we know about a person that relates to our present decision, and the more accurately we know it, the more likely we are to arrive at a sound decision about him or a wise plan of action for him. By the same token, we assume that the more relevant and accurate information we can provide the individual about himself, the more likely he is to arrive at a sound decision on his own problem. It may be necessary for us to qualify this assumption as we proceed. There may be limits on the amount and kind of information that can be used in a particular situation. We shall indicate that knowledge in and of itself is not wisdom. But in its general form the assumption is basic not only to educational and psychological measurement but also to all science. We assume basically that knowledge is good, that knowledge is power, that knowledge is the basis for effective handling of the problems that confront us from day to day. This is a basic tenet of our faith.

THE ESSENTIALS OF MEASUREMENT

To "know" a person really means to be able to describe him accurately and fully. But any description is selective. We cannot describe everything about a person, so we must choose for description those attributes that are relevant to our present concerns. We may be content to describe him roughly and qualitatively, or we may try to describe him more precisely and in quantitative terms. The more we try to make our description precise and quantitative, the more we get involved in measurement.

Measurement in any field always involves three common steps: (1) identifying and defining the quality or attribute that is to be measured, (2) determining a set of operations by which the attribute may be made manifest and perceivable, and (3) establishing a set of procedures or definitions for translating observations into quantitative statements of degree or amount. An understanding of each of these steps and of the difficulties that it presents provides a sound foundation for understanding the procedures and problems of measurement in psychology and education.

Identifying and Defining the Attribute

We never measure a thing or a person. Measurement is always of a quality or attribute of the thing or person. We undertake to measure the *length* of the table, the *temperature* of the blast furnace, the *durability* of the auto tire, the *flavor* of the cigarette, the *intelligence* of the school child, the *emotional maturity* of the adolescent. When we deal with the simplest physical attributes, such as length, it rarely occurs to us to wonder about the meaning or definition of the attribute. A clear meaning for length was established long ago in the history of both the race and the individual. Though mastery of concepts of "long" and "short" may represent significant accomplishments in the life of the preschool child, the concepts are automatic and axiomatic in adult society. We all know what we mean by *length.* However, this is not true of all physical attributes. What do we mean by *durability* in an auto tire? Do we mean resistance to wear and abrasion from contact with the road? Do we mean resistance to puncture by pointed objects? Do we mean resistance to deterioration and decay with the passage of time? Or do we mean some combination of these three and possibly other elements? Until we can reach some agreement as to what we mean by *durability,* we can make no progress toward measuring it. To the extent that we disagree on what *durability* means, we will disagree on what procedures are appropriate for measuring it, and if we use different procedures, we will disagree in the value that we get as representing the durability of a particular brand of tire.

The problem of reaching agreement as to what a given concept means is even more acute when we start to consider those attributes with which the psychologist or educator is concerned. What do we mean by intelligence? What kinds of behavior shall we characterize as intelligent? Shall the concept refer primarily to dealing with ideas and abstract concepts, or shall it include dealing with things—with concrete objects? Shall it refer primarily to behavior in novel situations, or shall it include response in familiar and habitual settings? Shall it refer to speed and fluency of response, or to level of complexity of reaction without regard to time? We all have a general idea as to what we mean when we characterize behavior as intelligent, but you can see that there are many specific points on which we may disagree as we try to make our definition precise. This is true of almost all psychological concepts—some more than others—and the first problem that the psychologist or educator faces as he tries to measure the attributes that he is interested in is that of arriving at a clear, precise, and generally accepted definition of the attribute that he proposes to measure.

Of course, we also face a prior question. We must decide which attributes it is relevant and important to measure if our description is to be useful for our present needs. A description may fail to be useful for the need at hand because we choose irrelevant features to describe. Thus, in describing a painting we might report its height, its breadth, and its weight. We might report these with great precision. If our concern were to crate the picture for shipment, these might be just the items of information we would need. On the other hand, if our purpose was that of characterizing the painting as a work of art, our description would be worthless. The attributes of the picture we had described would be essentially irrelevant to its quality as a work of art.

Similarly, a description of a person may be of little value for our purpose if we choose the wrong things to describe. Thus, a company selecting employees to become truck drivers might test their verbal comprehension and ability to solve quantitative problems, getting very accurate measures of these functions. It is likely, however, that information on these factors would help little in identifying men who would have low accident records and be steady and dependable on the job. Other factors, such as eye-hand coordination, depth perception, and freedom from uncontrolled aggressive impulses might prove much more relevant to the tasks and pressures that a truck driver faces.

Again, we have known a high school music teacher who tested very thoroughly his pupils' knowledge of such facts as who wrote the Emperor Concerto and whether andante is faster than allegro, getting a very dependable appraisal of their information about music and musicians, without presenting them with a single note of actual music, a single theme or melody, a single interpretation or appraisal of living music. As an appraisal of musical appreciation his test seemed to us almost worthless because it was using bits of factual knowledge *about* music and composers in place of any indication of progress in the appreciation of music itself.

Determining a Set of Operations to Expose the Attribute to View

The second aspect of measurement is finding or inventing a set of operations that will isolate the attribute in which we are interested and display it to us. Once again, the operations for measuring the length of an object such as a table were laid down in the early history of mankind. We convey them to the child early in elementary school. The ruler, the yardstick, the tape measure are uniformly accepted as appropriate instruments, and laying them along the object as an appropriate procedure for displaying to our eye the length of the table, desk, or other object we are studying. But the operations for measuring length or distance are not always so simple. By what operations do we measure the distance from New York to Chicago? From the earth to the sun? From the solar system to the giant spiral nebula in Andromeda? How shall we measure the length of a tuberculosis bacillus or the diameter of a neuron? Physical science has progressed by developing instruments that extend the capabilities of our senses and indirect procedures that make accessible to us amounts too great or too small for the simple direct approach of laying a measuring stick along the object. The operations for measuring length or distance have become indirect, elaborate, and increasingly precise. And they are accepted because they give results that are consistent, verifiable, and useful.

Turning to the example of durability of an auto tire, we can see that the operations for eliciting or displaying that attribute will depend upon and interact with the definition that we have accepted for it. If our definition is in terms of resistance to abrasion, we need to develop some standard and uniform procedure for applying an abrasive force to the specimen and gauging the rate at which the rubber wears away—some standardized simulated road test. If we have indicated puncture resistance as the central concept, we need a way of applying graduated puncturing forces. If our definition has been in terms of deterioration from sun, oil, and other destructive agents, our procedure must expose the specimens to these agents and must provide some index of the loss of strength or resilience that results. If our definition incorporates more than one aspect, then each must be incorporated, with appropriate weight, in our assessment.

The definition of an attribute and the operations for eliciting it interact. On the one hand, the definition we have set up determines what we will accept as relevant and reasonable operations. Conversely, the operations we are able to devise to elicit or display the attribute constitute in a very practical sense the definition of the attribute. We speak of an "operational definition." What we are saying is that the set of procedures we are willing to accept as showing the durability of an auto tire become the effective definition of durability so far as we are concerned.

The history of psychological and educational measurement during this century has been in large part the history of invention of instruments and procedures for eliciting, in a standard way and under uniform conditions, the behaviors that serve as indicators of the relevant attributes of persons. Thus, the series of tasks devised by Binet and his successors constitute operations for eliciting behavior that is indicative of intelligence, and the Stanford-Binet and other tests have come to provide operational definitions of intelligence. The fact that there is no single universally accepted test, and that different tests vary somewhat in the tasks they include and in the order in which they rank people is evidence that we do not have complete consensus as to what intelligence is on the one hand, or what the appropriate procedures are for eliciting it on the other. And this lack of consensus is generally characteristic of the "state of the art" so far as psychological and educational measurement are concerned. There is enough ambiguity in our definitions on the one hand, and enough variety in the instruments we have devised to elicit the relevant behaviors on the other, so that different measures of what alleges to be the same trait may rank persons quite differently. Consider, for example, the rubric "citizenship," which appears as a trait to be rated on a number of school report cards. What does good citizenship mean in a school child? How well can we agree in defining it? And once we have had a try at defining it, what operations can we devise to assess its presence or absence?

Quantifying the Attribute in Units of Degree or Amount

The third step, once we have accepted a set of operations for eliciting an attribute, is to express the result of those operations in quantitative terms. We ask the question, "How many or how much?" In the case of the length of a table the question becomes "How many inches?" The inch represents a basic unit, and we can demonstrate that any inch equals any other by laying them side by side and seeing their equality. This is the direct and straightforward proof of equality for some of the simplest physical measures. For other measuring devices, such as the thermometer, equality of units rests upon a *definition*. Thus, we define equal increases in temperature as corresponding to equal amounts of expansion of a volume of mercury. Long experience with this definition has shown it to be a useful one because it gives results that relate in an orderly and meaningful way to many other physical measures.

None of our psychological attributes have units whose equality can be demonstrated by direct comparison, in the way that the equality of inches or pounds can. How shall we demonstrate that arithmetic problem X is equal, in amount of arithmetical ability that it represents, to arithmetic problem Y? How can we show that one symptom of anxiety is equal to another anxiety indicator? Thus, for the qualities with which the psychologist or educator is concerned, we always have to fall back upon some definition to provide units and quantification. Most frequently, we call one task successfully completed—a word defined, an arithmetic problem solved, or an analogy made—equal to any other task in the series successfully completed, and count the total number of successes for an individual. The raw score of tasks done correctly is converted into some statement about the age or grade group that a person matches, or about his standing within such a group by procedures discussed more fully in Chapter 7. This type of a count of tasks successfully completed or of choices of a certain type provides a plausible and manageable definition of amount, but we have no really adequate evidence of the equivalence of different test tasks, or different questionnaire responses. By what right do we treat a number series item such as "1 3 6 10 15 ____ ____" as showing the same amount of intellectual ability as, for example, a verbal analogies item such as "Hot is to cold as wet is to ____________?"

Thus, the definition of equivalent tasks, and consequently of units for psychological tests is rather shaky at best. When we have to deal with a teacher's rating of a child's cooperativeness or a supervisor's evaluation of an employee's initiative, for example, where some set of categories such as "superior," "very good," "good," "satisfactory," and "unsatisfactory" is used, the meaningfulness of the units in which these ratings are expressed is even more suspect.

In psychological and educational measurement, we encounter problems in relation to all three of the steps that have just been set forth. First, we have problems in selecting the attributes with which to be concerned and in defining them clearly, unequivocally, and in terms upon which all can agree. Even for something as straightforward as "reading ability" we can get a range of interpretation. To what extent should a definition include each of the following?

1. Speed of reading.
2. Mechanics of converting visual symbols to sounds.
3. Getting direct literal meanings from a text.
4. Drawing inferences that go beyond what is directly stated.
5. Being aware of the author's bias or point of view.

As we deal with more complex and intangible concepts, such as cooperativeness, anxiety, adjustment, or rigidity, we may expect even more diversity in definition.

Second, we encounter problems in devising procedures to elicit the relevant attributes. For some psychological attributes, we have been fairly successful in setting up operations that call upon the individual to display the attribute, and permit us to observe it under uniform and standardized conditions. This holds true primarily for the domain of abilities, where standardized tests have been assembled through which the examinee is called upon, for instance, to read with understanding, to perceive quantitative relationships, or to identify correct forms of English expression. But there are many attributes with which we have been clearly less successful. By what standard operations can we elicit, in a form in which we can assess it, a potential employee's initiative, a school pupil's anxiety, or a soldier's suitability for combat duty? With continued research and with improved ingenuity we may hope to devise improved operations for making certain of these qualities manifest. But one suspects that there are many psychological qualities for which the identification of suitable measurement operations will always remain a problem.

Finally, even our best psychological units of measure leave something to be desired. Units are set equal by definition. The definition may have a certain amount of plausibility, but the equality of units cannot be established in any fundamental sense. So the addition, subtraction, and comparison of scores will always be somewhat suspect. Furthermore, the precision with which the attribute is assessed—the reliability from one occasion to another or from one appraiser to another—is often discouragingly low.

Criticisms of Psychological and Educational Measurement

Certainly, our present ability truly to *measure* many of the attributes of persons that appear to be relevant and important for making decisions about them and planning actions with respect to them leaves much to be desired. However, while recognizing this fact we must also appreciate that enormous strides have been made since 1900 toward more objective and more accurate appraisals of human beings. The fact that we are limited in some directions does not lessen the value of increased precision wherever such increased precision has been achieved. While keeping a critical eye upon the limitations of measurement procedures, we should still use them for all they are worth in increasing the accuracy of our information about students, employees, or clients.

Though instruments for psychological and educational measurement have proliferated, and their use has become widespread through the United States, and to a somewhat lesser extent in many other countries, the enterprise of measuring the abilities and attributes of man has come in for a good deal of criticism from a variety of sources. Educational philosophers, humanists, scholars in certain disciplines, and even politicians have voiced hostility and concern. In part, the criticisms have been directed at the basic logic of measurement of man. These criticisms have focused on the limitations that we have just been discussing, as well as other problems concerning the equivalence of units and scores, problems we shall consider briefly in a later chapter. In part, however, the criticisms have been directed at the effects that the measurement procedures have had upon our society, and especially upon our schools. The following types of criticisms have been made:

1. Standardized measurement procedures have fostered undemocratic attitudes and methods. An early focus of this criticism was on the use of tests of intelligence or achievement to form homogeneous classroom groups. More recently, concern has centered on the appropriateness of the tests and norms for use with socially deprived and minority groups.

2. It has been contended that standardized tests have tended to freeze school curricula and to prevent experiment and change, in that the standardized educational tests have typically lagged behind the progress of educational thought and practice.

3. The limited scope of many standardized tests has been pointed out, and it has been indicated that they appraise only a part of the changes in children that schools should be interested in producing.

4. Achievement tests have been alleged to reward the person who has partial or superficial knowledge and to penalize the person who is really expert in the subject, since the ablest student is said to see qualifications and exceptions to the formulation of the item that make him question the generally accepted answer.

5. Psychological tests (especially those that delve into personality and temperament) have been viewed as an unwarranted invasion of individual privacy. They are used to delve into personal matters that may be of no legitimate concern to the inquirer, especially if he uses the information for selfish and personal ends.

There has been at least a germ of truth in each of these criticisms. Some of them we shall consider in more detail in later chapters. The criticisms make it clear that there are hazards and pitfalls in an attempt to measure man. The hazards lie partly in poor technique and partly in misuse of the information that the techniques provide. Any new tool presents problems. We have to know how to sharpen it and how to use it.

It cannot be too much emphasized that measurement at best provides only information, not judgment. A test will yield only a score, not the conclusion to be drawn from that score. The information provided in a test score is not a substitute for insight. This information is the raw material with which insight must work, in the clinic, in the classroom, and in the research laboratory. Experience, training, and basic sagacity must provide the insight that will take the available data about an individual or group, know how much faith to place in them and what meaning to give them, and draw from them a sound conclusion or plan for action.

Furthermore, it should be emphasized that the information that *any* measurement procedure gives is limited. It is limited by the nature of the measurement instrument itself. The typical intelligence test, for example, samples certain types of performances with abstract ideas expressed in symbolic form. It is not a measure of the general worth of the individual, of his ability to acquire mechanical skills or artistic techniques, or of his integrity and dependability as a member of society. The information is limited by the conditions under which the procedure is applied. Thus, an intelligence test given to an emotionally disturbed and resistant child may give a very inadequate picture of what that same child could do if the disturbing influences were removed and the resistance overcome. Learning to use measurement results wisely is in part learning what information a particular device does and does not provide and in part learning under what circumstances that information is likely to be trustworthy. Throughout this book there will be recurring attempts to guide that learning.

SUMMARY STATEMENT

We can summarize much of the foregoing discussion on a working philosophy of measurement in the following four points:

1. The process of measurement is secondary to that of defining objectives. The ends to be achieved must first be formulated clearly. Then measurement procedures can be sought as tools for appraising the extent to which those ends have been achieved.
2. Much of educational and psychological measurement is, and will probably remain, at a relatively low level of elegance and precision. We must recognize this fact, using the best procedures available to us, but always treating the resulting score as a tentative hypothesis rather than as an established conclusion.
3. The more elegant procedures of formal test and measurement must be supplemented by the cruder procedures of informal observation, anecdotal description, and rating if we are to obtain a description of the individual that is usefully complete and comprehensive.
4. No amount of ingenuity in developing improved procedures for measuring and appraising the individual will ever eliminate the need to *interpret* the results from those procedures. Measurement procedures are only tools. Insight and skill are required in the use of such tools. The sharper and more varied the tools, the more skill it takes to use them most effectively.

QUESTIONS AND EXERCISES

1. The development of objective and standardized tests has proceeded faster and further in the United States than in any other country. What factors do you see as contributing to this?

2. Try to talk to a student from some foreign country and find out what examinations are like and how they are used in his country. What differences do you find, as compared with the United States? What are the advantages and disadvantages of each system?

3. In many graduate and professional schools, oral examinations are still used in examining candidates for higher degrees. What are the advantages and disadvantages of this type of examination?

4. From your reading or from your personal experience, give one or more concrete examples of the *misuse* or *misinterpretation* of the results from standardized tests.

5. How universally acceptable is the statement "knowledge is good" in the field of education and applied psychology? What objections would you have to this statement, or what limitations would you place upon it?

6. Your textbook states that "to know an individual means to be able to describe him accurately and fully." What would be central in such a description for:

   a. A fourth-grade girl having difficulty with arithmetic.
   b. An eighth-grade boy who has been picked up for throwing rocks through the school windows.
   c. A recent high-school graduate who is being considered for a job as receptionist.

7. Taking one of the attributes named below, indicate what would be involved in (1) defining the attribute, (2) setting up procedures to make it observable, and (3) quantifying it.

   a. Scientific thinking.
   b. "Good citizenship" in a fourth-grade pupil.
   c. Sociability.
   d. Competence as an automobile driver.

8. In discussing the structure of American society, three different points of view have been expressed: (1) the egalitarian, which affirms that all men are equal, (2) the aristocratic, which asserts that the members of the upper class are inherently superior to the members of the lower class, and (3) the open competitive, which states that in each generation a talented elite exists not depending on family background. How would each of these philosophies influence an individual's attitude toward tests?

9. With current computer facilities, it would be possible for a city or school system to maintain a complete "data bank," containing all the school grades, test scores, and other information that the school had gathered on each pupil during his school years. The information could be made available to his present teachers or guidance counselor, or to other appropriate individuals. What values and what problems do you see in such an enterprise?

SUGGESTED ADDITIONAL READING

Adkins, D. C. Measurement in relation to the educational process. In J. T. Flynn and H. Garber (Eds.), *Assessing behavior: Readings in educational and psychological measurement*. Reading, Massachusetts: Addison-Wesley, 1967. Pp. 35–53.

Anastasi, A. Psychology, psychologists, and psychological testing. In N. E. Gronlund (Ed.), *Readings in measurement and evaluation*. New York: Macmillan, 1968. Pp. 436–453.

Carter, L. F., Brim, O. G., Stalnaker, J. M., & Messick, S. Psychological tests and public responsibility. *American Psychologist*, 1965, **20**, 123–142.

Dingle, H. Basic problems of measurement. In J. T. Flynn and H. Garber (Eds.), *Assessing behavior: Readings in educational and psychological measurement*. Reading, Massachusetts: Addison-Wesley, 1967. Pp. 1–7.

DuBois, P. H. A test-dominated society: China 1115 B.C.–1905 A.D. In A. Anastasi (Ed.), *Testing problems in perspective*. Washington, D.C.: American Council on Education, 1966. Pp. 29–36.

Englehart, M. D. & Thomas, M. Rice as the inventor of the comparative test. *Journal of Educational Measurement*, 1966, **3**, 141–145.

Goslin, D. A. *The Search for ability: Standardized testing in social perspective*. New York: Russell Sage Foundation, 1963.

Montgomery, R. J. *Examinations*. Pittsburgh: University of Pittsburgh Press, 1967.

Thorndike, R. L. Educational decisions and human assessment. *Teachers College Record*, 1964, **66**, 103–112.

CHAPTER 2

Overview of Measurement Methods

ooooooooooooooooooooooooooooooooooooooooooooooooooooooooooooooooooooooooooooooooooooooooooooooooooooooooooooooooooooooo

DURING the present century techniques for appraising the individual have been developed in great variety, and they have been applied to many aspects of his abilities and personality. Specific techniques will be discussed in detail in later chapters. The present chapter is devoted to a general overview, mapping out some of the main landmarks of the whole domain.

APPRAISAL BY TESTS VERSUS APPRAISAL BY OBSERVATION IN NATURAL SITUATIONS

Attempts to appraise and describe a person can be grouped into two main categories: those that depend upon setting up special test situations and those that depend upon observing behavior in the actual naturally occurring situations of life. The usual earmarks of a test are that (1) it occurs at a specified time and place, (2) it consists of a set of tasks uniform for each person tested, and (3) it is seen as a test situation by the person being appraised. By contrast, evaluation based upon the naturally occurring situations of life is likely to (1) extend over an indefinite period, (2) be based upon situations that vary from person to person, and (3) not be perceived as a test by the person being appraised. The distinction between test situations and natural life situations is not an entirely sharp and clear-cut one, and we will have occasion to consider some in-between cases. However, it is usually clear whether we are dealing with a test as such or with observations under the natural conditions of life.

In thinking about the evaluation and measurement of man, we are likely to think primarily of tests narrowly defined, for example, a test of arithmetic, a test of scholastic aptitude, or a test of auditory acuity. But we must remember that many of the important appraisals we make of people have always been, and will continue to be, based on observations of them as they live from day to day. Appraisals of the nursery-school child's insecurity in relation to other children, of the 10-year-old's cooperativeness, or of the junior executive's initiative will almost necessarily be based upon observations of him over a period of time as he functions in his natural social group. Evaluations based on these observations have serious limitations. We are likely to find little uniformity from person to person in either the situations observed or the standards of judgment of the observers. But for some kinds of behavior we have no adequate tests to substitute for observations of natural situations—and very likely never will have.

Any complete picture of evaluation procedures must, therefore, pay attention both to test techniques and to devices for improving the observation of naturally occurring behavior. We will tend to prefer test situations where suitable ones can be devised. The examiner has more control over the situation, since he can present the same tasks or questions to everyone in the same way. He can usually get more precise results from a test and results that depend less upon the particular person making the appraisal. However, we must recognize that many significant aspects of individual behavior, by their very nature, defy reduction to a neat test. These can be appraised validly only as the individual functions in a natural life situation.

Of course, not all tests are perfectly frank and aboveboard. We shall have occasion to consider various types of test instruments in which the characteristics appraised are not those that the test seems to be getting at. Outstanding in this group are the so-called *projective tests* discussed in Chapter 15. What purports to be a test of "imagination" may in fact be directed at revealing anxieties, tensions, and inner emotional conflicts. Or a test of arithmetic computation may be rigged to yield a measure of cheating. But these are exceptions to the general rule that in a test the person knows that he is being tested and knows *what* is being tested.

TWO FORMS OF TESTS

Within a defined test setting we may again recognize an important distinction, which depends upon whether the examinee leaves a permanent record of his behavior or whether it must be observed "on the wing" as it takes place. The first situation is represented by any test, such as one of reading comprehension, in which the examinee marks his answers on a paper. The marks are then permanently recorded and can be scored at leisure. The second type of test would be encountered in an appraisal of oral reading, for example, where errors are noted by the listener as they occur or the quality is judged by the listener as the reader speaks.

In this comparison, again, the advantages with respect to reliability and objectivity usually fall on the side of the test that gives a permanent record, the test with answers on an answer sheet or a definite product produced. It is hard to observe and record behavior accurately as it is taking place. Inaccuracies and biases tend to creep in. The observer is hurried; his attention lapses. Consequently, in developing testing devices the tendency has been to make them of the sort that leaves a permanent record.

But young children cannot read or write, and many others are handicapped in a test that requires them to do so. Again, some types of performances, such as speaking or singing, are not readily reduced to a usable permanent record. It is also true that sometimes we are interested not merely in *what* a person does but also in *how* he does it. If a child gets the right answer for 6×7, does he get it quickly or slowly? Surely or with fumbling? By automatic habituation of the correct answer or by counting up from 6×6? The process does not show in the written answer but can sometimes be observed if the child answers the problem orally or "thinks out loud."

There are test situations, therefore, in which we shall have to depend upon observations of the behavior as it takes place rather than upon scoring the written record. These test situations pose special problems. Observers must be taught what to look for. They must be taught what responses to record and how to record them. They must be trained in standards of judgment, so that the pronunciation that they accept as right, for example, will also be one accepted as right by other observers. It is for this type of test that special training of examiners is usually required.

EXTERNAL OBSERVERS VERSUS SELF-OBSERVATION

As we move out of a test setting into observation of the individual's behavior in the natural situations of life, two distinct options are again open to us. We may rely upon some outsider to observe the person's behavior, someone such as his teacher, his employer, a friend, or a member of his family. Or we can ask him to report on his *own* characteristics as *he* sees them. These provide two quite different views of the individual, the one from the outside, the other from the inside.

The outside view is filtered through the biases and limited contacts of a particular outsider. The teacher, for example, sees only one side of the youngster—the school side that is turned toward him. Furthermore, he sees it colored by his own prejudices and limitations. What he sees as "cooperation" may from another viewpoint appear to be docility; what he considers "insubordination" may appear to another to be independence.

The self-picture is limited by the reporter's lack of self-understanding and unwillingness to reveal himself to the watching world. We do not know ourselves perfectly. Some of our limitations, our petty meannesses and evasions, our weak and sensitive spots, we cannot face and admit even to ourselves. Still other shortcomings we recognize but are unwilling to acknowledge to an outsider.

Sometimes one set of limitations will seem more serious, sometimes the other. If a person is applying for a job he very much wants, we will probably feel that we can put more trust in the evaluations of outsiders than in his self-evaluation. He has too much at stake in the impression he makes. On the other hand, if he has come to us for help and guidance, his own more intimate self-picture may provide a better basis for counseling with him than will the impressions of an outsider. We shall need to become acquainted with evaluation instruments of both types.

PLANNED VERSUS RETROSPECTIVE OBSERVATION

When we rely upon observations, either by the subject himself or by others observing him from outside, we may call for new observations made specially for us, or we may fall back upon the informal and undirected observations that have occurred in the past. Suppose we are studying the individual's tendency to become angry. We might ask him to keep track of all the times he got mad during the following week, noting down the circumstances for each anger episode, that is, when it occurred, what precipitated it, what he did, etc. This would be an example of planned self-observation. By contrast, a second possibility would be to give him a list of situations that tend to annoy or irritate people. We might then ask him to look into himself and judge how readily he had tended to get angry at people who push in front in line, at being called by the wrong name, at being called down for something he did, and so forth. The self-observations would now be retrospective. If an outsider—say, a teacher—were doing the job, he might be asked to note down times during a specified period when he saw the particular pupil push, hit, or talk sharply to another. Or he might be asked to think back over his contacts with the child and rate him on a scale ranging from "exceptionally calm and even-tempered" to "flares up and gets angry at the slightest provocation."

Again, there are advantages and disadvantages to both the planned and the retrospective type of observation. A major difficulty with systematic planned observations is that they are laborious and time-consuming. It takes a great deal of time and a high level of observer cooperation to get the necessary observations made. Partly because of this, the observations are likely to cover a limited time period and therefore to represent a rather meager sample of the individual's behavior. However, when observations are of actual current behavior, they tend to be more objective and less influenced by biases and the selective effects of memory than retrospective reports. The retrospective observations called for in self-report inventories and in rating scales have been widely used because of their administrative simplicity and because they summarize concisely the whole history of self-observation or contact with the person rated. But this type of summarizing judgment gives the biases of the respondent the fullest chance to express themselves.

OBSERVATION AND TEST COMBINED—THE SITUATIONAL TEST

As we noted earlier, some behavior in test situations leaves no record behind but must be observed as it occurs. Here we have something of a hybrid involving both observation and test. The observer notes the specific errors a child makes when he reads aloud or his hesitations and false starts in spelling a word. Sometimes the "test" may involve a much more complex and total situation and more subtle types of behavior. In many of these "tests," the person being observed may not realize what is being observed (or even that he is being observed). So, if we want to appraise the individual's tendency to get angry, we may put him in a standard anger-producing situation. For example, we may give him a job to do and two intentionally stupid assistants who keep making mistakes and getting in the way. Insofar as we are able to present each subject with the same task, we have a test situation. But we must depend upon the observations and judgments of outsiders to evaluate his behavior.

These complexly structured lifelike situations, which strive for the uniformity of a test situation and yet for the naturalness of real-life events, may be called *situational tests.* They represent a compromise between the objectivity and standardization of the testing approach and the naturalness of a real-life situation. This approach presents interesting possibilities for getting at types of behavior that do not readily lend themselves to the conventional types of testing.

The problems involved in devising situational tests are very great. These tests call for elaborate staging if the naturalness of real life is to be maintained. The need, at least to some extent, to deceive the examinee as to what is being assessed raises both practical problems of maintaining the "security" of the test and ethical problems of invasion of privacy. And there are further problems in getting satisfactory observations of the behavior and adequate reports of those observations. For these reasons, situational tests have not been widely used. But they present an interesting, and still only partly explored type of tool.

FUNCTIONS FOR WHICH MEASUREMENT HAS BEEN UNDERTAKEN

Broadly speaking, psychologists and educators have been interested in measuring in two general areas, what a person *can* do and what he *will* do. Measures of the first sort are measures of *ability*. In our discussion we will divide ability measures into measures of *aptitude* and measures of *achievement*. Again, roughly speaking, an aptitude test undertakes to measure what a person *could learn* to do, whereas an achievement test measures what he *has learned* to do.

The distinction between aptitude tests and achievement tests is far from a clear one, because we often use what a person has learned as a cue to what he can learn. Thus, a measure of the amount of knowledge of mechanical devices a person has gained in the past may be one of the most accurate indicators of the amount of further knowledge of things mechanical he will acquire in the future. The clearest distinction between aptitude and achievement tests lies in the direction of our interest. In an aptitude test, our interest is to predict what the individual *can learn* or develop into in the future; in the achievement test our interest is in what he *has learned* in the past.

Measures of the second major category—of what the person *will* do—correspond to the area we may roughly label *personality* measurement. "What the person will do" is a somewhat broad and loose definition of personality. It is also a somewhat external one. That is, we have indicated a concern for what a person *does* rather than for how he feels or what his inner urges and conflicts are. We may be interested in those to a degree. But, so far as a testing or observational procedure is concerned, it is always based on what a person does—how he acts, what answers he marks, or what he says. His actions are the basic material that we study.

In the long run, we study his actions in the present so as to be able to predict something about him in the future. We want to predict whether he will graduate from college, whether he will be happy and persist in a sales job, whether he will behave in a more socially acceptable fashion after a particular type of therapy. For such prediction and understanding we are likely to find it helpful to group our observations of specific actions into clusters that seem to belong together. And these "constructs" that we use to tie together the observations that we make may often imply something "inside" the individual—an interest, an attitude, a need, a conflict. But these terms referring to the inner life of the individual represent inferences that we make as a way of structuring and organizing our observations of behavior. We cannot *see* a strong need for approval. What we observe is that a child often brings things into class, attempts to monopolize discussions, buys candy for other children, and tries to worm his way into social groups in the playground. We may *infer* a need for approval as a common underlying factor giving unity to the various behaviors, but what we observe is a series of actions.

THE CONCEPT OF TRAIT

To speak of a person as "cheerful," as "sociable," or as "introverted" implies that his behavior shows a consistency over time and place, and that we recognize certain behaviors as belonging together as a unified aspect of this person. For this cluster of related behaviors we often use the term "trait." *

Evidence for a trait is often largely intuitive. That is, the term "sociable" has come to signify to us a range of behaviors that we have sensed as belonging together which involve seeking out the companionship of others, indicating satisfaction with the companionship of others, participating in activities involving others, choosing free-time activities that bring one into a group, and so forth. We sense that some persons tend to show this behavior with a consistently high frequency, whereas others are consistently more often solitary in their pursuits. Evidence for a trait may also be statistical using the methods of correlation (Chapter 5) and of factor analysis (Chapter 11). We verify, through analysis of the data on groups of persons, that certain behaviors do tend to "hang together," so that if the person exhibits one he is likely to exhibit the other.

* Although psychologists have used a number of other terms, including hexis, syndrome, and type to apply to behavioral clusters of different degrees of generality.

This focus, around which an array of behaviors are found to cluster, provides an empirical definition of a trait.

Some traits, especially in the ability domain, are quite tightly knit and coherent—as verbal ability and numerical ability. Others are more loosely defined and diffuse—for example, honesty or impulsiveness. As a consequence, our ability to predict from one specific situation to a somewhat different one is relatively good in the first instance, relatively poor in the second.

We must remember that a trait is *not* something that exists as a separate entity in the person whom we are studying. A trait is a *construct*. It is a conception that we invent to organize and give coherence and meaning to the separate behaviors that we observe. And though the varied behaviors that we include as evidences of a common trait *tend* to go together, this tendency is neither perfect nor universal. Though there is a nucleus of consistency in action and in feeling, a haze of inconsistency surrounds it. Thus, for each trait name we must ask whether the gain from labeling a cluster of somewhat related behaviors more than makes up for ignoring the individuality that makes each act distinct and somewhat different from the others.

Aspects of Personality

It will be convenient to use a number of terms to refer to certain fractions or aspects of personality that we may wish to evaluate. These terms and the meanings that attach to them are discussed briefly below.

CHARACTER. Character traits are aspects of individual behavior to which a definite social value has been attached. Honesty, cooperativeness, thrift, kindliness, and loyalty are all labels for social virtues. Educational and religious organizations have always been concerned with the inculcation of such virtues. Based on this concern there have been developed a number of evaluation procedures that we shall refer to as measures of character.

ADJUSTMENT. Educators and psychologists have long been concerned with the concept of adjustment. The mental hygiene approach as applied both in and out of school has striven to develop "well-adjusted personalities." Maladjustment is recognized in individuals who fail to fit into the social group or who appear to live unhappy and unproductive lives. As with character, degree of adjustment represents a social judgment, and what is conceived to be well-adjusted behavior varies from one culture to another, depending upon what is normal for that culture. Normal behavior in our competitive, acquisitive society might seem pathological if transferred to a South Sea island. Adjustment will mean, then, behavior patterns that enable the person to get along in and be comfortable in his social setting—typically, the setting of middle-class, twentieth-century American-European culture. We shall encounter a group of instruments designed to evaluate deviations from this norm—the tendency to show maladjusted behavior or behavior typical of people who do not get on happily and successfully in our culture.

TEMPERAMENT. From early days observers of human nature have noted conspicuous differences in energy level, prevailing mood, and general style of life. Literary men and men of science alike have proposed systems for classifying temperaments. Hippocrates, for example, proposed that men could be divided into the sanguine (energetic and cheerful), choleric (energetic and irascible), phlegmatic (sluggish and placid), and melancholic (sluggish and sad), and proposed physiological bases for these distinctions. There have been many other classifications before and since. Appraisals of such dimensions as these we shall speak of as measures of temperament.

INTEREST. The individual makes a variety of choices with respect to the activities in which he engages. He shows preferences for some, aversion to others. Appraising these tendencies to seek or avoid particular activities constitutes the domain of interest measurement.

ATTITUDE. The individual responds with enthusiasm and aversion not only toward activities but also to social groups, social institutions, and the other aspects of his world. These reactions, with their various ramifications, constitute the individual's constellation of attitudes. Various devices have been developed for evaluating these prejudices pro and con, and these constitute the field of attitude measurement.

CONCLUDING STATEMENT

In summary, then, approaches to the measurement of the individual cover a great diversity both of methods and of content areas. Variations of method may be represented by the following outline:

I. *Test methods,* involving a defined task and testing period.
   A. Permanent record or product available for scoring or analysis.
   B. Process must be observed and evaluated as it occurs.

II. *Observational methods,* in which behavior is observed in the natural situations of life.
   A. *Self-observation,* in which the individual reports on his own reactions, as far as he is aware of them.
      1. Planned observations, planned in advance to cover a specified period.

2. Retrospective observation, based on present memory and evaluation of past reactions.

B. *Observation by an outsider,* in which relative, employer, teacher, etc., reports on the individual's reactions.

1. Planned observations.
2. Retrospective observations.

III. *Mixed methods,* characterized by some of the aspects of a test but also relying upon observation and evaluation of observed behavior.

Advantages and problems of these approaches have been sketched in but will need to be considered in more detail as specific methods are elaborated in later chapters.

Aspects of the individual for which evaluation procedures have been developed and in which we shall be interested include the following:

I. *Abilities,* evidences of what the individual *can* do if he tries.

A. *Aptitudes,* performances serving as indicators of what he can learn to do.

B. *Achievements,* performances used to show what he has already learned to do.

II. *Personality variables,* indications of what an individual *will* do, of how he will respond to the events and pressures of life.

A. *Character,* certain qualities defined by society as estimable or the reverse.

B. *Adjustment,* degree of ability to fit into and live happily in the culture in which one is placed.

C. *Temperament,* qualities relating to energy level, mood, and style of life.

D. *Interests,* activities that are sought or avoided.

E. *Attitudes,* reactions for or against the people, the phenomena, and the concepts that make up society.

This analysis of aspects of the individual is neither complete nor detailed. However, it serves to indicate the range of measures with which we shall be concerned in the following chapters.

QUESTIONS AND EXERCISES

1. It would generally be agreed that personality measures are less satisfactory than measures of aptitude or achievement. What factors give rise to this?

2. How would you fit each of the following into the classification of measurement methods given in the chapter?

a. Anecdotal records kept by a teacher, describing behavior in his classroom.
b. An autobiography written by a pupil for a high-school counselor.
c. An individual intelligence test in which both questions and answers are given orally.
d. A Boy Scout's record of "good deeds," kept over a two-week period and reported to his Scoutmaster.

3. Illustrate, from your reading or experience, each of the categories of measurement methods in the outline on pp. 27–28.

4. How would you fit each of the following into the outline of aspects of the individual to be evaluated, given on p. 28?

a. Observations of how well a high-school student gets along with adults.
b. A pupil's expression of his preferences for books in an annotated list of titles.
c. A kindergarten child's performance on a test of readiness to learn reading.
d. A pupil's performance on an English test, used to place him in the appropriate section.
e. Ratings of a pupil on his loyalty to his friends.

5. From your reading or personal experience, give an illustration of measurement procedures for each of the aspects of the individual identified in the outline on p. 28.

6. A class has just finished a unit on nutrition, and the teacher wishes to evaluate the effectiveness of the unit. Which of the methods outlined on pp. 27–28 might she use? What would be the advantages and limitations of each?

7. The term "honesty" is sometimes used with the implication that this is a trait that characterizes an individual. What are the values and what are the problems in thinking of "honesty" in these terms?

SUGGESTED ADDITIONAL READING

Allport, G. W. Traits revisited. In J. T. Flynn and H. Garber (Eds.), *Assessing behavior: Readings in educational and psychological measurement.* Reading, Massachusetts: Addison-Wesley, 1967. Pp. 328–348.

CHAPTER 3

Planning a Test

oooooooooooooooooooooooooooooooooooooooooooooooooooooooooooooooooooooooooooooooooooooooooooooooooooooo

In this book dealing with educational and psychological measurement procedures, we have elected to start with a consideration of the teacher's own tests. We have done this for several reasons. In the first place, informal test making is an operation that is familiar to every teacher, and the outcomes of such test making are familiar to every student. In the second place, because the teacher-made test is so widely used and has such an important place in evaluating student achievement, it strongly influences students' views toward tests and test taking specifically and toward education generally. In the third place, the techniques of testing available to every teacher form the backbone of standardized tests of achievement and of aptitude. Furthermore, the quality of the items on a standardized test and the adequacy of the coverage of a standardized test are judged by precisely the same standards that apply to teacher-made tests.

THE ROLE OF TEACHER-MADE TESTS

Evaluation * of pupil progress is a major aspect of the teacher's job. A good picture of where the pupil is and of how he is progressing is fundamental to effective teaching by the teacher and to effective learning by the pupil. To

* The term "evaluation" as we use it here is closely related to measurement. It is in some respects more inclusive, including informal and intuitive judgments of pupil progress. It also includes more definitely the aspect of valuing—of saying what is desirable and good. Good measurement techniques provide the solid foundation for sound evaluation, whether of a single pupil or of a total curriculum.

evaluate the range of outcomes in which a modern school is interested—understanding as well as knowledge, appreciation as well as skill, ability to apply as well as to reproduce, attitudes and interests as well as achievements—the teacher must call upon a variety of types of appraisal. He must observe the student in the classroom, laboratory, and in other settings. He must size up the student in conference, interview, and informal discussion. He must rate the work produced in the laboratory or shop and appraise the quality of assignments done outside of school. He must also make use of classroom tests. Some of the objectives of his teaching can be measured efficiently, realistically, and completely by paper-and-pencil tests; some can be measured only partially by such means, while some cannot be measured at all in this way. But, in an educational setting, tests loom large in a child's life. As the child progresses through school, tests assume a greater and greater importance to him. For both the child and the teacher, the testing situation frequently becomes the prime basis for evaluation of progress.

The evaluation procedures the teacher uses with his group serve a number of functions. We will identify four, commenting briefly on each of them. All of the procedures that a teacher develops for pupil evaluation may serve these functions, but we shall be concerned with pointing out how they may be served by the more formal instruments called "tests."

Motivation

Anyone who has worked in an educational setting or any parent has heard children say, "I can't go out now. I've got to study for a test." Frequently in a school setting one hears teachers instruct students, "Be sure to read this assignment tonight and do your homework. Tomorrow I am going to give you a test on this material." Both of these comments indicate that students and teachers view tests as having a strong motivating function. To some degree, varying from pupil to pupil and from class to class, tests determine when students study, what they study, and how they study. Well-constructed examinations can give students an opportunity to test out their knowledge and with prompt and constructive feedback can motivate students to improve on their performance. Tests that are poorly constructed or used punitively can just as effectively discourage the students or misdirect their learning.

Diagnosis and Instruction

A classroom teacher planning a particular unit of instruction based on knowledge and skills that students are expected to have mastered previously needs to know whether the students have in fact learned the underlying material.

To ascertain this, the teacher can give a test before beginning the new instruction. If the prerequisite skills are not available, review and remedial work may be needed before moving ahead. Again it is sometimes wise for the teacher to determine whether the students already have developed to a satisfactory level the knowledge and skills that are included in his plans for teaching. If they have, he can eliminate the material from his plans and move on to some other topic. In both of these situations, the teacher would be using a pretest to help him plan for efficient instruction.

During the instructional process, the teacher frequently observes that some students are not making satisfactory progress. A test constructed to reveal weaknesses of the student can help the teacher locate the sources of difficulty from which constructive action can be taken. This type of test is called a diagnostic test. Finally, the good teacher wants to know after a period of instruction how successful he has been in achieving his instructional objectives. A carefully constructed test covering all the important objectives of instruction that can be measured by a test can yield information on this point. After the test is given, the teacher can analyze it, item by item, to determine which items were correctly answered by the majority of students and which were missed by a large number of the students. For example, suppose a teacher were interested both in increasing the fund of knowledge of seventh-grade students in the area of health and in increasing their ability to apply principles of health in everyday situations. If a test emphasizing both of these processes is given to students and the majority of the students answer the items on recall of information correctly but get the application items wrong, then the teacher can begin looking at the materials and procedures he has used to determine why such a result was obtained.

Tests become especially important in programs of individualized instruction, such as the Oak Leaf program or PLAN currently being developed for Westinghouse Learning Corporation. To the extent that each child is proceeding through instructional units individually at his own rate, end-of-unit tests provide the main guidance to pupil and teacher on whether he has mastered the unit and should move ahead to new material, or whether he needs to be looped back to a review program elaborating material that he has already studied.

Defining Teaching Objectives

The evaluation procedures that a teacher uses in the classroom should be directed not only toward obtaining evidence on the important objectives of instruction but also toward making clear to students what skills, abilities, and knowledge are important in the subject matter area. From the primary grades to graduate school, students frequently ask, "Should I learn this? Is it going to be on the test?" The frequency of the question indicates that students view the test situation as being an extremely important guide as to what does and does not need to be learned. Several studies (Lawrence, 1963; Pfeifer, 1965; Scannell and Steelwagen, 1960) have shown that the majority of items on teacher-made tests (as many as 98 percent in one study) required only rote recall of very specific information whereas the majority of the objectives formulated by these teachers were concerned with skills of application, analysis, and synthesis. Although the studies cited did not determine what students were studying in these classes, one can surmise that students were concentrating on rote memory rather than on the more complex skills to which the teachers gave lip service.

Differentiation and Certification of Pupils

The teacher has a responsibility for appraising the individual differences among students in their achievement of various educational objectives. He must pass on to the next teacher a report of these differences, either in the form of a mark or a specific recommendation, if the school is to provide an optimum learning environment for each child. At the secondary school level, particularly, the teacher is responsible for certifying whether the student has reached a level of achievement in an area adequate for entry into college or an occupation. Decisions about permitting students to pursue certain courses of study in high school, about admitting students to college, and about selecting students for certain occupations depend very largely upon judgments recorded by previous teachers concerning the competence of each student. The information on which these judgments are based is provided in considerable measure by tests.

In view of the many functions that evaluation instruments serve and in view of the disservice that may be done to a student by poorly conceived or executed instruments, it is important that the teachers' evaluation devices be well made and be used appropriately. In this chapter and the next one, we will be concerned with teacher-made tests and ways of improving them to make them more effective evaluation devices. Consideration of other evaluation devices such as observational procedures and ratings will be given in later chapters.

PLANNING THE TEST

Over the past ten years, we have had occasion to examine hundreds of teacher-made tests collected from all levels of education and from many different school systems. Others have published studies of the quality of teacher-made tests. Both the results of the published studies and of our examination indicate that teacher-made tests generally are quite defective evaluation devices. The most common faults of these tests are given below.

1. The tests do not cover the range of objectives specified by teachers. Most teachers espouse objectives covering a wide variety of mental skills ranging from simple recall to application and synthesis of knowledge. The tests, however, measure primarily simple recall. Published studies and our examination indicate that from 90 to 95 percent of all items on teacher-made tests require only rote recall of specific information.

2. The content tends toward the trivial. By limiting themselves to the specific and the factual, test makers automatically eliminate much that is important. And difficulty is often achieved by including that which is obscure and trivial, rather than by requiring a synthesis of the broad, important aspects of the field.

3. The type of test exercise that the teacher uses is poorly adapted to appraising the mental process or content that the test is supposed to measure. Often the teacher includes a number of different item types not because each is especially effective for assessing certain objectives, but just to achieve a diversity of format.

4. The questions that teachers write for tests are ambiguous. The wording is unclear, or the task is incompletely specified so that the questions require students to enter into a guessing game or to use extrasensory perception to determine what the teacher is asking and wants for an answer.

5. The characteristics of the test are inappropriate for the purpose for which the teacher wants to use the results. As a matter of fact, seldom does the teacher explicitly state the purpose for which he is constructing the test or for which he wants to use the results.

Weaknesses 1, 2, 3, and 5 generally result from the failure to plan adequately for the test before one starts to construct questions. Too often a teacher suddenly realizes that it is time to give a test, sits down to write items with the idea of producing a certain number of items, and never does plan a test that truly reflects his teaching emphasis. To plan for a test adequately requires that the teacher state explicitly the purpose for which the test is to be constructed, define in operational terms the objectives that are to be measured by the test, determine the content to be covered by the test, and decide upon the relative importance of each of the objectives and each area of content to be reflected in the test. Any test represents a sample of all possible questions that could be asked in a particular area of study. The purpose of the test plan is to make sure that the sample of questions truly reflects the objectives and emphasis of teaching. In the remainder of this chapter we will discuss the different steps in planning a test; in the next chapter we will discuss the writing of different kinds of test items to help teachers overcome weakness number 4 above. The purpose of giving tests has already been discussed on pages 31–33. Although it is true that teachers may often be interested in having a test serve more than one purpose, it is likely that each test has a primary purpose. It is this primary purpose that should be central in the teacher's mind as he plans for the test.

Defining Objectives

The first and most important step in planning a test is to define the objectives of instruction. In almost all educational settings one finds statements of the aims and goals of the institution. These are usually very general and global statements which are supposed to serve as an overall frame of reference for developing curricula, for organizing learning experiences, and for selecting teaching methods. Within this broad framework, the teacher is responsible for developing his instructional objectives for a particular group of individuals in a particular area of study. Although a teacher can turn to curriculum guides, yearbooks of his national association, the taxonomies of educational objectives developed by Bloom (1956) and Krathwohl (1964), and many other sources for help in identifying appropriate objectives, the ultimate responsibility for selecting objectives suitable for the group of students that he is teaching and stating the objectives in such a way that they can guide instruction and evaluation rests with the classroom teacher.

The majority of statements of objectives written by teachers are too vague and global to be useful as a guide to evaluation or teaching. To serve this purpose, a set of objectives should have the following characteristics:

1. Objectives should be stated in terms of student behavior, not in terms of learning activities or purposes of the teacher. For example, "Observes bacteria through a microscope" is not a satisfactory statement of an objective. This describes a learning activity. Why does a teacher want the students to observe bacteria? An analysis of the activities and contents of the course of study in which the objective appears indicates that the teacher wants the student to know the characteristics of organisms that cause diseases, and that observation of bacteria is incidental to this objective. It would be better to state the objective as, "Recalls characteristics of organisms that cause diseases."

2. Objectives should begin with an active verb that indicates the behavior that

a student should show in dealing with content. This format tends to guarantee a focus on the student and what he does. The objective should not consist of a list of content. For example, the statement "Scurvy, beriberi, rickets, and pellagra are caused by a lack of vitamins in the body" is a statement of content not a statement of an objective. The objective should be stated, "Identifies certain disease conditions that are caused by lack of vitamins."

3. Objectives should be stated in terms of *observable* changes in student behavior. For example, an objective formulated as, "Always practices good health habits to prevent the spread of disease" is not stated in observable terms. The inclusion of "always" in the formulation means that it is impossible to gather the evidence needed to judge the achievement of the students. One cannot *always* observe a student. Another example is the statement, "Does his share to create good emotional atmosphere during meals at home." The behavior specified in this statement occurs in a situation outside of school in which the teacher would be unable to observe the student. It is unlikely that he is going to be able to get relevant evidence on the achievement of the objective. Another example is the statement, "Feels secure in making wise choices of food." In this statement, "feels secure" is unobservable; it is a covert characteristic of a student. One cannot observe a feeling of security. One can only observe behavior and perhaps make inferences about the security of the student.

4. Objectives should be stated precisely using terms that have uniform meaning. For example, in the objective, "Understands the responsibility of the community in control of communicable disease" the word "understands" means different things to different people. To one teacher it may mean that the students can name the different agencies in the community that have responsibility for controlling communicable disease. To another it may mean that the student, given a novel problem concerning communicable disease, can identify the appropriate community agency or agencies and indicate the services or actions to be expected from these agencies.

5. Objectives should be unitary; each statement should relate to only one process. For instance, the objective, "Knows elementary principles of immunization and accepts immunization willingly," contains two processes, a cognitive process of recall of information and an affective process of acceptance of an action. The two processes are quite different and require different evaluative procedures to obtain relevant evidence on their achievement. If both are important instructional objectives, then they should be stated as two separate objectives.

6. Objectives should be stated at an appropriate level of generality. On the one hand, the statement of an objective should not be so general and global as to be meaningless nor on the other hand should the statements be so narrow and

specific that the educational process seems to be made up of isolated bits and pieces. In the latter case, an adequate list of objectives becomes too long and too unwieldy to use effectively. For example, the objective, "Knows nutrition" is too vague to serve any useful purpose. On the other hand, a series of statements such as "Identifies the function of proteins in the body," "Identifies the function of fats in the body," "Identifies the function of carbohydrates in the body," "Identifies the function of vitamins in the body," not only becomes boring to read but is also unnecessarily specific. At an appropriate level of generality, all the specific statements could be combined into one statement that reads, "Identifies the function of the five classes of nutrients in the body."

7. Objectives should represent intended direct outcomes of a planned series of learning experiences. For example, it is obvious that one would never write as an educational objective for eighth graders "Increases in height" simply because health instruction is not directed toward making eighth graders taller. However, it is common to find statements of objectives that deal with attitudes in programs in which no particular instructional effort is given to the development of attitudes.

8. Objectives should be realistic in terms of the time available for teaching and the characteristics of the students. An example of an unrealistic objective would be, "Understands the reasons why people become drug addicts." This is unrealistic simply because no one knows why people become drug addicts; therefore it is impossible to teach toward this objective.

Another example of an objective that would be an unrealistic one for eighth graders reads, "Understands the principles of immunization." The principles of immunization are extremely complex and understanding of the nature of immunization is probably beyond the experience level of the students in the eighth grade. The objective should be reexamined and probably recast in the form of knowing the different kinds of immunization or of knowing the methods that have been developed for immunizing against disease.

Let us look at an actual example of a set of objectives that were prepared for a six-week unit in nutrition for an eighth-grade class. In Figure 3.1, column 1 gives the objectives as they appeared in the teacher's course outline, column 2 indicates the weakness, if any, of each objective and column 3 suggests revisions for the objectives where they are needed.

As one can see, the objectives as originally written have many faults. The revised list of objectives provides a better guide both for teaching and evaluation. The revisions in the objectives were made after studying the detailed curriculum guide. Objectives that were eliminated were ones for which no specific learning experiences were provided in that curriculum guide.

Objective as Originally Written in Curriculum Guide	Comment	Suggested Revision
1. Knows terms and vocabulary used in nutrition.	1. "Knows" is vague. At what level is the student supposed to know these?	1. Recalls or recognizes terms and vocabulary.
2. Has a rudimentary knowledge of food nutrients and their functions.	2. What is a "rudimentary knowledge"? What kind of behavior does a student show who has a "rudimentary knowledge"?	2. Recalls or recognizes essential food nutrients and their functions in the body.
3. Values the health protection provided by good dietary habits.	3. "Value" is vague. How does this objective differ from numbers 7, 9, 11, and 13?	3 (a) Identifies good sources of various food nutrients. (b) Identifies effects of poor diets.
4. Understands the digestive process.	4. "Understands" is vague. How does a student show he understands?	4. (a) Identifies parts of digestive system. (b) Identifies process of digestion for each nutrient. (c) Recognizes factors that interfere with digestion.
5. Plans meals and snacks using principles of good nutrition.	5. Well-stated objective. Desired student behavior is clear. Stated at an appropriate level of generality.	5. No revisions
6. Realizes that food patterns differ in various parts of U.S.A. and world.	6. "Realizes" is vague. Objective is too specific.	6. (a) Identifies factors that influence kinds and amounts of food that people eat.
7. Is willing to choose an adequate diet.	7. Willingness to do something is covert. One can observe whether a student does something, but not his willingness to do it.	7. Chooses adequate lunch in school cafeteria.

8. Understands that the daily food guide is based on scientific research.	8. The last part of the objective is a specific fact. What is there to "understand"? Essential part of objective is included in 12.	8. Eliminate objective.
9. Uses information about nutrition every day.	9. Doesn't everyone? More of a fond hope than an objective. See comment on number 3.	9. Eliminate objective.
10. Persuades other members of his family to develop good nutritional habits.	10. Is this reasonable? How would one obtain evidence on the achievement of the objective? Is this a direct outcome of teaching?	10. Eliminate objective.
11. Recognizes flaws in his diet and desires to eliminate them.	11. Double objective. Contains two different behaviors. First part of objective is restatement of 2 and 5. Second part is stated in 7.	11. Eliminate objectives.
12. Is aware that advertisements and statements concerning foods are not always based on facts.	12. "Is aware of" is vague. What behaviors should the student exhibit?	12. (a) Distinguishes statements about foods and diets that are based on good scientific evidence from those that are not. (b) Identifies authoritative sources of information about foods and diets.
13. Appreciates being healthy	13. Appreciates is vague. What behavior is a student to show when he appreciates being healthy? How do you teach a student to appreciate being healthy?	13. Eliminate objective.

Fig. 3.1 Objectives for unit on nutrition.

Specifying Content to be Covered

The second step in planning a test is to specify the content to be covered. The content is important because it is the vehicle through which the process objectives are to be achieved. An outline of the content could be prepared based on the appropriate sections of the textbook or curriculum guide or the teacher could merely indicate the content to be covered by marking the appropriate sections in the textbook.

Preparing the Test Blueprint

The content and a statement of process objectives represent the two dimensions into which a test plan should be fitted. These two dimensions need to be put together to see which objectives especially relate to which segments of content and to provide a complete framework for the development of the test. In planning for the *total* evaluation of a unit the teacher would be well advised to make a blueprint covering *all* objectives and to add a column to the blueprint indicating the method or methods to be used in evaluating student progress toward achieving each objective. However, in making a blueprint for a *test*, only those objectives that can be assessed either wholly or in part by a paper-and-pencil test should be included.

In a list of objectives, any objective that calls for only cognitive processes can be appraised by a paper-and-pencil test. These are objectives that specify such processes as recalling, recognizing, identifying, defining, applying, analyzing, synthesizing, generalizing, predicting, or evaluating. In the list of revised objectives in Fig. 3.1, all the revised objectives except number 7 can be evaluated by a paper-and-pencil test. Objective number 7 in Fig. 3.1 cannot be measured by a paper-and-pencil test because it involves the actual act of choosing food. The extent to which objective 7 has been achieved can be determined only by systematic observation of students in the school cafeteria. Examples of other types of objectives that cannot be assessed by paper-and-pencil tests are those that involve affective behaviors, such as interests, and attitudes, that is, feelings of favorableness or unfavorableness toward an object, group, or institution. This type of objective would need to be evaluated through self-report or observation. The teacher should remember that no single test or evaluation device can measure all the objectives he is trying to achieve.

Figure 3.2 shows a blueprint for a final examination in health for an eighth-grade class. As it has been prepared, with the specification calling for 60 items, this illustration is based on a decision that the test is to be a short-answer or objective test with a large number of separate items. It is especially for this type of test that a formal blueprint is useful. However, the choice of 5 or 6 items for an essay test can also be improved by the kind of thinking that goes into the formulation of a blueprint. The issues that are involved in the decision about type of test exercise to use are considered later (pages 67–72).

In the blueprint, the process objectives for the unit in nutrition as well as for the other units have been listed in the left-hand column. The titles of each of the three units have been entered as headings on the other columns. Each box or cell under the unit headings contains content entries that relate to the objective opposite the cell. The complete blueprint specifies the content deemed important by the teacher and indicates what the student is supposed to be able to do with that content.

The preparation of such a two-dimensional outline is an exacting and time-consuming task. The busy classroom teacher may often fall short of achieving such a complete analysis. There is no question, however, that attempting the analysis will go far toward clarifying the objectives of a particular unit and toward guiding not only the preparation of a sound test but also the teaching of the unit itself. It is also true that once such a complete blueprint has been prepared it can be used until the curriculum or teaching emphasis is changed.

Examination of the blueprint at this point should make clear to the reader that any test can be only a sample of student behaviors related to the content covered in class. First, the objectives included in the blueprint represent only those objectives that are suitable for appraisal by a paper-and-pencil test. Second, the entries in the cells under each area of content are examples representing only part of the total content. Third, there is an unlimited number of questions that could be written for the material that is included in the blueprint. The time available for testing in the usual school setting is limited; one can ask only a relatively small number of all the possible questions. If the test is to reflect accurately and truly the teacher's emphasis in teaching, then the test maker must choose carefully the sample of items to represent the domain being assessed.

To complete the test plan so that it will be an adequate guide for constructing a test that will truly represent the teaching emphasis, the teacher must arrive at some answer to each of the following questions before starting to write the exercises for the test.

1. What relative emphasis should each of the content areas and each of the process objectives receive on the test? In other words, what proportion of all the items on the test should be written for each content area and, within each content area, for each process objective?
2. What type or types of items would be most appropriate to use on the test?

Process Objectives	A. Nutrition 40%	B. Communicable Diseases 40%	C. Noncommunicable Diseases 20%	Number of Items
	CONTENT AREAS			
1. Recognizes terms and vocabulary	Nutrients, Vitamins, Enzymes, Metabolism, Oxidation, Incomplete protein, Complete protein, Amino acids, Glycogen, Carbohydrate	Immunity, Virus, Pathogenic, Carrier, Incubation period, Epidemic, Endemic, Antibodies, Protozoa	Goiter Deficiency diseases Diabetes Cardiovascular diseases Caries	
20%	4 or 5 items	4 or 5 items	2 or 3 items	12
2. Identifies specific facts	Nutrients essential to health Good sources of food nutrients Parts of digestive system Process of digestion of each nutrient Sources of information about foods and nutrition	Common communicable diseases Incidence of various diseases Methods of spreading disease Types of immunization Symptoms of common communicable diseases	Specific diseases caused by lack of vitamins Specific disorders resulting from imbalance in hormones Incidence of noncommunicable diseases Common noncommunicable diseases of adolescents and young adults	
30%	7 or 8 items	7 or 8 items	3 or 4 items	18

3. Identifies principles, concepts, and generalizations	Bases of well-balanced diet Enzyme reactions Transfer of materials between cells Cell metabolism Functions of nutrients in body	Basic principles underlying control of disease Actions of antibiotics Body defenses against disease Immune reactions in body	Pressure within cardiovascular system Control of diabetes Inheritance of abnormal conditions Abnormal growth of cells	
30%	7 or 8 items	7 or 8 items	3 or 4 items	18
4. Evaluates health information and advertisements	Analyzes food and diet advertisements Interprets labels on foods Identifies good sources of information about foods and diets	Distinguishes between adequate and inadequate evidence for medicines Identifies misleading advertisements for medications	Identifies errors or misleading information in health material Identifies appropriate source of information for health problems	
10%	2 or 3 items	2 or 3 items	1 or 2 items	6
5. Applies principles and generalizations to novel situations	Identifies well-balanced diet Computes calories needed for weight-gaining or weight-losing diet Predicts consequences of changes in enzymes on digestive system Identifies services and protection provided by the Federal Food and Drug Act	Recognizes conditions that are likely to result in increase of communicable disease Identifies appropriate methods for sterilizing objects Gives appropriate reasons for regulations, processes, or treatments	Predicts consequences of changes in secretion of certain hormones Predicts probability of inheriting abnormal conditions	
10%	2 or 3 items	2 or 3 items	1 or 2 items	6
Number of items	24	24	12	60
Total time for test—90 minutes			Total number of items—60	

Fig. 3.2 Blueprint for final examination in health for eighth grade.

3. How long should the test be? How many questions or items should the total test have? How many items should be written for each cell of the blueprint?

4. What should the difficulty of the items be to achieve adequately the purpose of the test?

DETERMINING RELATIVE EMPHASIS OF CONTENT AREAS AND PROCESS OBJECTIVES. The proportion of test questions on each content area should correspond to the proportionate emphasis given to the topic in class, and the proportion of items calling for each process objective should correspond to the importance the teacher considers that process to have for the level of students he has been teaching. The decisions made by the teacher in allocating the questions on a test are necessarily subjective ones. As stated before, the basic principle underlying these decisions is that the test should maintain the same balance in relative emphasis on both content and mental process that the teacher has been trying to achieve through his instruction. Allocation of differing numbers of items to different topics and process objectives is one way (and the most desirable way) of weighting topics and objectives differentially in the test.

Weighting of both the content areas and the process objectives is done initially by assigning percentages to each content area and to each process objective in such a way that the total of the percentages across the content areas adds up to 100 percent and the total of the percentages for the process objectives also adds up to 100 percent. In the blueprint shown in Figure 3.2, the test maker decided that topic A, Nutrition, should receive a weight of 40 percent; topic B, Communicable Disease, should also receive a weight of 40 percent; topic C, Noncommunicable Disease, should receive a weight of 20 percent. Since 5 weeks of instructional time were spent on topic A and also on topic B and only 2 weeks were spent on topic C, the allocation of weights corresponds roughly to teaching time.

For the process objectives in Figure 3.2, the teacher decided that 20 percent of all the items should be allocated to objective 1, 30 percent each to objective 2 and objective 3 and 10 percent each to objective 4 and objective 5. These allocations imply that the teacher has emphasized in his teaching those objectives that relate to remembering or recalling terms, specific facts, principles, concepts and generalizations. In other words, he has been concerned primarily with increasing the fund of knowledge that the student has at his command and has given less attention to the ability of the students to use the information in novel situations. If the allocation of items to the process objectives truly reflects the teacher's emphasis in teaching, then the allocation is appropriate. We might take issue with the teacher's emphasis in teaching but, given that emphasis, we cannot say that the allocation of test items is inappropriate.

DETERMINING THE TYPE OR TYPES OF ITEMS TO BE USED. There are a number of different types of items that can be used on a teacher-made test. The different types of items can be placed in two major categories: (1) the type in which the student supplies his own answer, and (2) the type in which the student selects his answer from the answer choices supplied by the test maker. Examples of type 1 are the essay question requiring an extended answer from the student; the short-answer question requiring no more than one or two sentences for an answer; and the completion item requiring only a word or phrase for an answer. Examples of type 2 are the alternate-response item such as the true-false statement; the multiple-choice item; and the matching item.

The decision as to which type of item to use depends to a large extent upon the process objective to be measured. Other factors that can influence the decision are the content and the skill of the teacher in constructing the different types. The characteristics, advantages, and disadvantages of the different types of items are discussed at length on pages 50–70.

DETERMINING THE TOTAL NUMBER OF ITEMS FOR THE TEST. The test maker must now decide upon the total number of items for the test. If the teacher decides to use the essay type of exercise calling for extended answers, the number of questions will necessarily be limited. The more elaborate the answer, the fewer the questions, so that a 40-minute test in high school might have 3 or 4 questions each calling for an answer of a page or two, while a 3-hour examination in graduate school might still present no more than 3 or 4 questions, but calling for very extended answers. The balance of this section assumes that the test maker has decided to use short-answer or objective items, and considers the number of items within this context.

The total number of items included in a test should be large enough to provide an adequate sample of student behavior across content areas and across process objectives. The larger the number of content areas and process objectives to be measured by a test, the longer the test needs to be. A weekly quiz can be a short test because both the content and objectives to be tested are rather limited, whereas a six-week test or final examination needs to have a larger number of items because there are more content areas and more objectives to be covered in the test.

The time available for testing is a practical factor that limits the number of items on a test. Most teacher-made tests should be power tests, not speed tests; that is, there should be enough time so that at least 80 percent of the students can attempt to answer every item. There are few subject areas in which speed of answering is a relevant aspect of achievement. The primary purpose of an achievement test is to determine the range of information that a student has and his ability to apply his knowledge in novel situations, not to determine how fast he can work. Some teachers think that speed of performance has a high positive relationship to level of performance. The research evidence on this point is scanty but one study showed that the highest scores on a final examination were obtained by those who turned their papers in first and last (Briggs and Johnson, 1942).

The number of test items that can be asked in a given amount of time depends upon many different factors such as:

1. The type of items used on the test. A short-answer item in which a student has to write his answer is likely to require more time than a true-false or multiple-choice item in which a student is only required to write or mark a number or letter to indicate his answer.

2. The age and educational level of the student. Students in the primary grades whose skills of reading and writing are just beginning to develop require more time per test item than do older students who have well-developed skills in these areas. Young children also do not have the ability to attend to the same task for very long periods of time. Therefore testing time should be less for them, and this further reduces the number of items.

3. The ability level of students. High-ability students not only have better developed reading and writing skills than low-ability students but also generally have better command of the subject matter and better skills of problem solving. As a rule, high-ability students can answer more questions per unit of testing time than low-ability students of the same age and grade.

4. The length and complexity of the item. If test items are based on a reading passage, tabular material, map or graph, time must be allowed for reading and examining the stimulus material. The more stimulus material of this type that is used on a test, the fewer the number of items that can be asked in a given amount of time.

5. The type of process objective being tested. Items that require only the recall of knowledge can be answered more quickly than those that require the application of knowledge to a new situation.

6. The amount of computation or quantitative thinking required by the item. Most individuals work more slowly when dealing with quantitative materials than when dealing with verbal materials; therefore, if the items require mathematical computation the time allotted per item must be longer than for a purely verbal item.

It is impossible to give hard and fast rules about the number of items to be included in a test for a given amount of testing time. As a teacher becomes familiar with the kinds of students he usually has in class, he will be able to judge the number of items he can include in a given amount of time while still having a power test. As a rough rule of thumb, the typical student might require from 30 to 45 seconds to read and attempt to answer a simple factual type multiple-choice or true-false item and from 75 to 100 seconds to read and attempt a fairly complex multiple-choice item requiring problem solving. The total amount of time required for a number of items sufficient to provide adequate coverage of the blueprint may sometimes be more than a single class period. The most satisfactory solution to this problem is to break the test up into two or more separate subtests that can be given on successive days.

For the illustrative final examination in health for the eighth grade, the teacher had 90 minutes of testing time. Keeping in mind all of the factors mentioned above, the teacher decided that he would have 60 questions on the test. Now he should go back to the blueprint to determine how many items should be written for each cell in the blueprint. The first thing to do is to determine the total number of items for each content area and for each process objective. The blueprint in Figure 3.2 specifies that 40 percent of the items or 24 items ($.40 \times 60$) should be on topic A, 40 percent or 24 items on topic B, and 20 percent or 12 items on topic C. These numbers are entered in the bottom row of the blueprint. The percentage assigned to each process objective is multiplied by the total number of items to determine the number of items that should be written to measure each process. When this is done, one gets the numbers that are entered in the extreme right-hand column of the blueprint.

To determine the number of items in each cell of the blueprint, one multiplies the total number of items in a content area by the percentage assigned to the objective in each row. For example, to determine the number of items for the first cell under topic A, Nutrition, we multiply 24 by 0.2 (20 percent) which gives 4.8 items. Since the number 4.8 is between 4 and 5, we can note that we should have either 4 or 5 items covering this content and this objective. The other cells in the blueprint are filled in by the same process. However, it must be recognized that certain process outcomes may be primarily related to certain aspects of content. Thus, in a social studies examination an objective related to map reading might be testable primarily in a content unit on natural resources rather than one on human resources. This may lead the test maker to modify the cell entries so as to adjust to these particular congruences of content and process. Furthermore, it is probably desirable to indicate a range of items for each cell, as was done in our example, in order to provide flexibility if difficulty is encountered in writing acceptable items for certain cells. The number of items planned for each cell is to be thought of as a guide, not as a straight jacket.

When one is writing the items for a test, it is best to write each one on a separate 5×8 card or slip of paper. This will make it easier to revise, discard, or rearrange the items for the test. After all the items have been constructed, the teacher should make a final check by sorting the items according to the blueprint cells to make sure that the test matches the blueprint.

DETERMINING THE APPROPRIATE LEVEL OF DIFFICULTY OF THE ITEMS. The final decision to be made in the preliminary planning for a test concerns the desired difficulty of the test items. Once again, difficulty implies something different for an essay test calling for an extended answer than for a short-answer or objective test. A question that is of appropriate difficulty for an essay examination, as such examinations are typically used, is one for which each member of the class can produce some kind of an answer showing at least minimal awareness of the issues, and one that elicits responses varying in completeness, thoughtfulness, and quality of organization of ideas. In the case of an objective item, difficulty takes on a sharper definition, and may be defined as the percentage of examinees who get the item right. For example, if a particular item on a test is answered correctly by 40 percent of all the students who take the test, we say the item has a 40 percent difficulty. The most suitable average difficulty and spread of difficulty of test items is dependent in large part upon the purpose of the test. When the test is being designed to measure *mastery* of the basic essentials in an area, the questions should be limited to those basic essentials. If a unit has been well taught, all the items may then turn out to be very easy for the group. On such a test, a teacher may well expect to have perfect or near perfect scores for most of his students with only a few of the students, or none, missing any given item. For this type of test a large number of perfect scores gives the desired information, that the students have indeed learned the basic essentials in the area. On a diagnostic test, the purpose of which is to locate isolated individuals who are having special difficulty, it is also reasonable to expect a large number of perfect scores or near perfect scores and very few relatively low scores. On the other hand, let us consider a test that is given before starting on a new area of instruction by a teacher who wants to find out whether some students already have the skills and knowledge that he plans to teach. If he gives them a pretest on what he plans to teach he really does not expect the students to know the material, so he would expect a large number of zero or near zero scores; in other words, he would expect the tests to be very difficult for the students.

On mastery tests, on diagnostic tests, or on pretests before instruction, we are not concerned about spreading people out. Even if everyone gets a perfect score or if everyone gets a zero score, these scores give us the information that we sought from the test. On the other hand, when the purpose of the test is to discriminate levels of achievement of different members of the group, that is, to serve as a basis for ranking or grading, then we want the test to yield a spread of scores. We want to be able to separate the really high achiever from the next highest achiever and the really low achiever from the next to the lowest achiever.

We do not want anyone to get a perfect score on such a test because then we cannot be sure we have gotten adequate measure of how much he can do. However, we would not want to get zero or chance level scores from any person because then we would not have gotten down to his level. On such a test, we would not want an item that everyone got right or an item that everyone got wrong simply because neither of these items contributes to making discriminations among students according to their level of achievement.

Usually when we talk about difficulty of a test, we talk about it in terms of average difficulty. For example, suppose we made up a test of 50 items and gave this test to a group of students. Assume that when we scored the papers we found that the average score for all the students who took the test was 25 items right. Since the average score for the group of students was 25 out of 50 we would say that the test had an average difficulty of 50 percent (25/50 = 50 percent). When one uses this method to express difficulty in operational terms, that is, the percent of all students getting an item right, the following chart has been found to provide a good rule-of-thumb guide for the test maker to shoot at in preparing tests made up of different types of items (Lord, 1952).

Type of Item	*Average Difficulty (Percent Correct)*
Completion type items and short-answer items	50
Five-choice multiple-choice	70
Four-choice multiple-choice	74
Three-choice multiple-choice	77
True-false or two-choice items	85

These percentages allow for the possibility of getting right answers by guessing, and for the typical finding that very difficult items are often ambiguous and nondiscriminating as between the more and the less able students. To follow through our example, suppose we had 50 items on a test and they were all completion type items. We would want the average score for the class to be about 25. If the 50 items were five-choice multiple-choice items, then we would want the average score of the class to be about 35. If, on the other hand, the 50 items were true-false items, we would want the average score on the test to be 42 or 43. The percentages shown in the table sometimes bother teachers who are accustomed to thinking of "passing" scores or "failing" scores in terms of the percentage of the items that a student gets right on a test. The above suggestions have nothing to do with passing or failing; assigning marks or grades to students is an entirely different problem and will be taken up in a later chapter. The percentages that are suggested here will tend to yield a set of test scores that will be maximally useful to a teacher if he wants to discriminate levels of achievement among his students.

In the process of achieving the average difficulty level that is wanted on a test, the teacher is likely to produce some hard items that are passed by as few as 30 or 40 percent of pupils (assuming a four-choice item) and some easy ones that are passed by 85 to 90 percent. One would hope that many of the items would approach the desired average level of 74 percent, and they should be written with that goal in mind. However, it is much more important that the items provide a good coverage of content and objectives and that each item be one that is passed more often by able than by less able students (a matter that will be considered in Chapter 4) than that any particular spectrum of item difficulties be maintained.

In summary, then, the test plan at this stage includes:

1. An outline of content and process objectives.
2. Specific suggestions of what might be covered under each combination of content and process objective.
3. An allocation of percents of the total test by content area and by process objective and an estimate of the total number of items.
4. The number of items to be written for each cell of the blueprint.
5. Specifications for the spread of item difficulties.

The next task is to prepare the actual test items. In the remainder of this chapter we will discuss the different types of items and their advantages and disadvantages. In Chapter 4 we will provide guides for writing the different types of items.

DISTINCTIVE CHARACTERISTICS OF FREE-RESPONSE ITEMS AND STRUCTURED-RESPONSE ITEMS

As indicated earlier, the items on teacher-made tests may be divided into two broad categories, the free-answer type of item and the structured-answer type of item. The free-answer type of item may be further subdivided into the extended free-answer or essay item and the restricted free-answer item that takes the form of a short answer or a sentence completion. The structured-response item may be one in which a student chooses one from among three, four, or five answer choices, an item having two answer choices such as true-false, or a matching type of item. Each type of item has its own distinctive characteristics and its own advantages and limitations. No one item type can be used for everything. The goal is to learn the distinctive characteristics of the various types of items and to use each in ways that maximize its advantages and minimize its weaknesses.

The Essay Test

The essay test consists of questions such as the ones below.

1. An article on health used the phrase "inborn errors of metabolism." In your own words explain what the phrase means and give one example of an inborn error of metabolism.
2. A girl fifteen years old is five feet two inches tall and weighs 160 pounds. She is very much overweight, looks unattractive, and wants to lose weight. Outline a plan for her to follow in attacking her weight problem. Be specific in the steps you propose for her and give reasons for each step in the plan.
3. During spring of almost every year the area where a primitive tribe lives is flooded. The people must leave their homes and move to higher ground until the water recedes. After the people move back to their homes there is an outbreak of typhoid fever and amebic dysentery of epidemic proportions. Explain why the epidemic occurs each year. What is the most appropriate and immediate action that could be taken to prevent the epidemic from occurring?
4. In 1960 an insecticide was discovered that killed 90 percent of the insects that were responsible for spreading a certain kind of disease. In 1968 the same insecticide was completely ineffective in killing the same kind of insects. Explain what probably happened between 1960 and 1968 to produce this result.

The essential characteristics of the task set by an essay test are that each student:

1. Organizes his own answers with a minimum of constraint.
2. Uses his own words and his own style of writing (usually his own handwriting).
3. Answers a small number of questions.
4. Produces answers having all degrees of completeness and accuracy.

In these characteristics lie both the strengths and the weaknesses of the essay examination. Let us consider each one in turn.

THE STUDENT ORGANIZES HIS OWN ANSWERS. A well-prepared essay question requires that the student:

1. Determine what the problem is that is being presented.
2. Review the body of knowledge that he has and select those facts, principles, or ideas that are relevant to the problem.
3. Relate these to one another and organize them into a coherent whole.
4. Produce his answer.

The essay question can give the student the opportunity to show either how logical or how innovative and original he can be in attacking a problem provided that the question has been appropriately worded to bring out these responses. The potential of the essay question for eliciting these integrated responses from the student and for providing the student with an opportunity to show original thinking makes it a valuable tool both for teaching and for evaluation. Unfortunately most essay questions on teacher-made tests are not constructed to elicit these kinds of responses. In addition, the judgments that are made of the student's answers are too undependable to justify much confidence in the scores obtained. In the next chapter, we shall consider ways of writing essay questions to maximize the unique contribution to the essay type question and ways of improving the scoring to make the results more dependable.

The distinctive characteristics of essay questions mentioned in the previous paragraph have led people, particularly classroom teachers, to claim advantages for them that are not supported by evidence. The fact that a student must recall his answer to an essay question rather than recognize the answer has led some to claim that the essay test measures a higher level mental process. Implicit in this kind of claim is the idea that the student must have real mastery of the subject to achieve well on an essay test, whereas a student who knows very little can score high on an objective type test such as a multiple-choice test. In general, empirical evidence does not support this point of view. The relationships between different types of achievement measures are always positive, in that students who do well on one type of measure tend, on the average, to do well on others. Of course, the relationship is not perfect, and discrepancies do occur. However, these arise in considerable measure from the lack of precision of the essay examination. Thus, in one study of essay writing carried out by the College Entrance Examination Board (Godshalk, 1966) it was found that a set of objective tests of correctness and effectiveness of expression predicted scores on an extended and carefully judged series of essays *almost* as well as the stability of the essay score would permit, and that a writing sample added on only a trifling amount of new information about the pupils. This is only one instance, and the same situation may not hold true in a subject matter area. However, a number of studies comparing short free-answer tests with tests based on recognition items indicate that the rank order of pupils remains approximately the same no matter which form of test is used. In other words, the student who is a good recaller of knowledge is a good recognizer of knowledge whereas a student who is a poor recaller of knowledge is also a poor recognizer of knowledge. Studies with students in the United States have shown that putting a question in a free-answer form makes the question somewhat more difficult than having it in a multiple-choice or other objective form. However, in Great Britain, it was found that the free-answer type of question was easier for students than the objective type question. There is no evidence to establish that a free-answer type of test requires either a different mental process or a higher level mental process than does the structured-answer type of question.

Among the claims made for the essay test is that it can measure student attitudes and methods of thinking. Although modifying student attitudes may be a relevant objective of the school experience, it is difficult to conceive of a student revealing his true attitudes in an answer to an essay examination. He is more likely to express the attitudes that he feels the teacher wants him to have. There is no evidence to show that one can get a dependable measure of attitude from the analysis of this kind of written material. As for revealing the student's method of thinking, one must remember that the answer to an essay test is a product both of the student's thinking and of the student's writing. The answer is not a sample of the student's thinking but the results of interactions of the previously mentioned two factors. Again, there is no evidence to support the point that a dependable analysis can be made of the styles of student thinking or methods of student thinking from this kind of written material.

IN PRODUCING THE ANSWER THE STUDENT USES HIS OWN WORDS, HIS OWN STYLE OF WRITING, AND USUALLY HIS OWN HANDWRITING. Partisans of the essay test claim that the fact that the student must write out his answer is an invaluable contribution to the student's education. College teachers and high school teachers as well as other critics of education contend that students going through the schools of the United States today do not learn to write because the essay test is no longer used. There are two wrong assumptions in this criticism: (1) students learn to write by taking essay tests and (2) essay tests are not used in public education. Neither of these has any basis in fact. Goslin (1967), in a survey of educational testing sponsored by the Russell Sage Foundation, found that most teachers in secondary school used both essay tests and objective tests. There is also no evidence to show that students have learned to write better by taking essay type examinations. The time pressures of the essay examination, where one has little opportunity to think about his writing or to edit his output, interfere with getting an adequate sample of the student's writing ability. It is more likely that people have learned to write poorly under the pressures of an essay examination than to write well. There is also another idea implicit in the claims about writing on essay tests; namely that the quality of writing can be dependably judged by the reader. There is an extensive literature on the agreement among judges of the quality of English compositions. The literature quite clearly shows that there is a marked disagreement among different readers of a composition about the quality of the writing. For example, in a study conducted by the Educational Testing Service (Diederich 1961), each student's composition received a full range of scores from failure to excellent.

When one is testing in a subject matter area, differences in the writing ability of the students enters in as a source of contamination that makes it difficult to separate competence in the subject matter area from competence in written expression. Studies of the grading of the answers to essay type examinations (Gosling, 1966; Scannell and Marshall, 1966; Marshall, 1967) have quite clearly shown that the score a student receives can be affected by his skill in written expression, his spelling, his conformity to rules of grammar, and the quality of his handwriting. If a student knows nothing, or very little, in a subject matter area but has a high degree of skill in written expression, he can clothe his ideas in words that make a favorable impression on some readers (that is, bluff), and get a high mark even though he really knows little or nothing. On the other hand, a student who knows the same amount but is poor in written expression is likely to get a failing mark. The differences between the two students are not due to differences in subject matter competence but are due to differences in written expression that are really irrelevant to the judgments that the teacher wants to make about the subject matter area. Scannell and Marshall have studied the influence of spelling errors and errors in English usage on teacher's judgments of the quality of an answer to an essay question on a test of social studies. In these studies, the introduction of errors in spelling, punctuation, and English usage resulted in lower ratings for the answer even though the raters were instructed to ignore such errors. The spelling errors had a more detrimental effect upon the student scores than any other type of error.

The quality of the student's handwriting also affects his score on an essay type of test. As a matter of fact, students sometimes actually use the quality of handwriting to obscure their lack of knowledge. This is called the scrawl or ink blot technique of hiding ignorance. That is, the student writes very clearly when he is sure of his knowledge, then either writes illegibly or carefully makes a blot over the material where he is less sure of himself. On the other hand, when the reader of an essay has difficulty in deciphering a student's handwriting, he may become annoyed and assign a lower rating than the answer really deserves.

The remarks in the previous paragraph should not be construed to mean that writing ability, spelling ability, or ability to use the correct forms of the English language are skills that can be ignored in schools. They are very important objectives of schooling and efforts should be made to develop the student's skills in these areas. The point at issue here is whether possession or lack of this type of skill should be allowed to influence the judgment of the competence of the person in a content field such as science or social studies.

THE TEST IS LIMITED TO A SMALL NUMBER OF QUESTIONS. When the individual must organize and compose an answer of some length to an essay question, the number of questions is inevitably limited. The time required to answer a single question makes it impossible to include more than five or ten questions in even a fairly lengthy test. This tends to result in what we might call a lumpy sampling of what the student knows. We sink four or five big shafts into the mine of knowledge that the student possesses. If these happen to hit pay-dirt, a student does well, but if they hit the gaps in his knowledge, he does poorly. With this small number of items, chance is likely to play a relatively large part. We may get a very unfair sample of the student's knowledge. Of course, it is possible to use the free-answer type of question which requires a restricted answer of no more than a brief paragraph, and thus increase the number of questions that can be asked within a given amount of testing time. However, an answer as short as this loses, to some extent, the unique advantages of the extended-answer essay question.

Oddly enough, there are teachers who claim that they really get an extremely large sample of a student's behavior in an essay test. Their claim is based on the fact that they ask very general questions such as "Discuss nutrition" or "Discuss communicable diseases." What the teachers appear to forget is that the time available to the student to answer the question is limited. In that limited time he can only select certain aspects of the knowledge that he possesses and put these down for the teacher to review. If his selection happens to hit the aspects that the teacher considers important, he is likely to get a good mark on the test. On the other hand, if his selection is different than that which the teacher deemed important, then he is likely to get a poor mark. If about fifteen minutes has been allotted for each essay question, then only a fifteen minute sample of the student's behavior has been obtained, and much of that fifteen minutes has been devoted to the mechanics of writing rather than to thinking. From the two questions that we have cited, the teacher obtains only two samples of the student's behavior limited by time and by the selection that the student chances to have made, not an extremely large sample of behavior.

ANSWERS ARE OF ALL DEGREES OF CORRECTNESS. The bugaboo of the essay examination is the laborious and subjective operation of evaluating the answers. That it is laborious any teacher who has ever graded a set of essay papers for even a middle-sized class can testify. That the grading is subjective and relatively undependable has been shown by a number of separate studies.

Consider the following answers written by two eighth-grade students to the question "Compare the powers and organization of the central government under the Articles of Confederation with the powers and organization of our own central government today."

Student A

Our government today has a president, a house of representatives, and a senate. Each state has two senators but the number of representatives is different for each state. This is because of compramise at the Constitutional Convention. The Articles of Confederation had only a Congress and each state had delegates in it and had one vote. This Congress couldn't do much of anything because all the states had to say it was alright. Back then Congress couldn't make people obey the law and there wasn't no supreme court to make people obey the law. The Articles of Confederation let Congress declare war, make treaties, and borrow money and Congress can do these things today. But Congress then really didn't have any power, it had to ask the states for everything. Today Congress can tell the states what to do and tax people to raise money they don't have to ask the states to give them money. Once each state could print its own money if it wanted to but today only the U.S. Mint can make money.

Student B

There is a very unique difference between the Central Government under the Articles of Confederation and the National Government of today. The Confederation could not tax directly where as the National Government can. The government of today has three different bodies—Legislative, Judicial, and Executive branches. The Confederation had only one branch which had limited powers. The confederate government could not tax the states directly or an individual either. The government of today, however, has the power to tax anyone directly and if they don't respond, the government has the right to put this person in jail until they are willing to pay the taxes. The confederation government was not run nearly as efficiently as the government of today. While they could pass laws (providing most of the states voted with them) the confederate government could not enforce these laws, (something which the present day can and does do) they could only hope and urge the states to enforce the laws.

These two answers together with three other answers written by students in the same class were given to two groups of graduate students in courses in measurement or evaluation. Both groups of students were provided with a model answer to the question and given the following instructions:

Instructions: The essay question was a part of a social studies test consisting of fifty objective items and one essay question. The students were given 25 minutes to write their answers to the essay question. You have been given the answers written by five of the students. The class that these five students were in was a heterogeneous one. Twenty-five points is the maximum score for the question. Please grade each paper using the model answer provided. The grade is to reflect completeness and accuracy of the answer—not quality of English expression, spelling, or grammar.

Suppose that *you* grade these two answers in accordance with the instructions given above before you read any further. Record the scores that you would give the answers.

Now look at Table 3.1, which shows the scores actually given to all five answers, including these two. Every one of the answers receives scores spreading over about 20 points of the possible range of 25. Any one of the papers might have gotten a score as high as 18; any one might have gotten a score as low as 5. The responses of students A and B were judged to be outstandingly good by some raters, poor by others. The inconsistency of the judgments is demonstrated most forcefully. A single rating of any one of these papers tells us very little about how that same paper will be rated by someone else. Why is this? What makes the appraisal of an essay response so undependable?

Let us admit to start with that the dice were somewhat loaded against the graders in this little experiment. Most of them were not social studies teachers, though the majority had had some teaching experience. (Previous experience

TABLE 3.1 GRADES GIVEN TO FIVE ANSWERS TO ESSAY QUESTIONS

Score	Student A	Student B	Student C	Student D	Student E
25	6	5	..	6	..
24	2	2	..	4	..
23	4	3	..	4	..
22	3	9	2	5	..
21	8	2	..	4	..
20	32	21	6	24	..
19	6	1	..	3	..
18	14	11	3	12	1
17	6	8	3	2	1
16	4	2	2	4	..
15	23	23	18	34	4
14	4	1	3	5	..
13	2	2	3	2	1
12	4	13	9	7	6
11	1	3	6	1	2
10	6	11	33	4	25
9	1	4	9	1	5
8	..	6	9	3	6
7	2	3	3	..	..
6	..	..	3	3	16
5	3	..	11	2	50
4	..	..	1	1	7
3	..	1	3	..	15
2	...	..	1	..	1
1	..	..	..	..	..
0	..	..	2	..	1

has indicated that social studies teachers will show about as much variation.) Furthermore, they had not taught the class, and did not know anything about the general level of performance in this and similar groups.

One major reason for the wide range of scores found in Table 3.1 is that different raters maintained very different standards for rating *all* the papers. Different raters used quite different parts of the scale of scores. Though it was most common for a rater to spread his scores between about 5 and 20, a few awarded no grade higher than 10 to *any* of the answers while others assigned no grades below 15. These last two groups were operating in entirely different score ranges and showed no overlap. The best for one group was lower than the poorest for the other. Judges differed not only in the average level at which they rated the papers, but also in how much they spread out their scores. Some were very "conservative," bunching all their ratings close together, while others tended to spread them widely over the whole range. Such differences in grading standards are very real in actual school situations—as every student knows—and provide one main source for inconsistency in grading essay responses.

However, the judges were also not very consistent in the rank order in which they arranged the 5 papers. In Table 3.2 we have shown how often each paper was ranked first, how often second, and so on. (Tie ranks have been indicated as 1.5, 2.5, etc.) In this table we see that every one of the 5 answers was ranked first by somebody, and every answer was either last or tied for last. There is some consensus that student E wrote the poorest answer and student C the next poorest, but practically no agreement as to the relative standing of the other three. Students A, B, or D could easily have been judged best of the group or only average. Thus, there is not only a marked difference in *absolute* standard from judge to judge, but also inconsistency in the *relative* judgment of one paper in comparison with the others.

TABLE 3.2 RANK ORDER ASSIGNED TO EACH OF FIVE ESSAY QUESTIONS

Rank	Student A	Student B	Student C	Student D	Student E
1	44	29	2	33	1
1.5	13	12	1	11	..
2	28	23	8	31	1
2.5	12	10	5	17	..
3	24	32	19	23	..
3.5	1	6	9	5	3
4	3	16	55	9	11
4.5	3	1	18	1	20
5	1	1	13		94

Inconsistency in relative judgment is characteristic not only of different raters but also of the same rater at different times. Thus, when the evaluation class was asked to grade the papers a second time 3 weeks later (without advance notice that this was to be done), a third of the ratings differed from the original rating by 5 points or more (out of the possible range of 25 points). Only a third of the papers kept the same rank in the group of 5 on the second grading.

The results that we have presented illustrate the situation that commonly prevails in evaluating essay responses. A study by Coffman and Kurfman (1968) on scoring the essay examinations of the College Entrance Examination Board Advanced Placement Test in social studies showed that the judges differed markedly in the ratings that they assigned on the average to the answers to an essay question. Some of the judges were consistently high raters; some were consistently low raters. The same study showed that all judges tended to give lower ratings on the second day of scoring than they did on the first day. Other studies have shown that if the scoring of papers requires five days, on the last day the agreement of judges as to the quality of papers is much lower than on the previous days. The studies by Scannell and Marshall (1966) and Marshall (1967) show that spelling and grammatical errors in writing differentially affect the judgment by different judges of the quality of the answer to an essay question. The low level of agreement in judging the quality of an answer to an essay question weakens the value of this type of question in obtaining accurate measurements of the level of achievement of students. An unknown part of the differences in score level among students is attributable to the idiosyncrasies or instability of the judges rather than to real differences among students in the attribute being measured.

We should mention here that it is possible to obtain greater agreement among raters in their judgments of the quality of answers to essay questions. Generally, a higher degree of accuracy in judging the quality of answers requires multiple judges, a good training program for the judges, good supervision of judges, and improved construction of the question posed to the student. We shall consider methods of improving the scoring of essay questions in Chapter 4.

Restricted-Response Type of Question

The restricted-response type of question is somewhere in between the extended-answer essay question and the question providing a completely structured response, and has some of the characteristics of the essay question and some of the characteristics of the objective question. It has sometimes been referred to as a semiobjective question. The most commonly used types are the short-answer question and the completion question. Examples of the short-answer question are:

Give an example of an antibiotic.

What is an enlargement of the thyroid gland in a human being called?

Why should someone who has a sore on his lips that does not heal within a reasonable length of time see a doctor?

If frozen foods have been thawed, they should not be frozen again. Why?

What unit is used to measure the fuel value of a food?

Examples of the completion type item are:

Fresh tomatoes are a good source of Vitamin ______.

The enzyme, ptyalin, acts on the class of food substances called ______.

The unit used to measure the fuel value of a food is called ______.

There is one other type of restricted-response question that has been used primarily to test effectiveness of written expression. It requires essentially that students edit materials. A good example of this type of item is the Interlinear Exercise that was, for a number of years, included in certain editions of the College Entrance Examination Board English Composition Test. A part of this test together with the directions is given below.

C E E B Interlinear Exercise

(Suggested time: 30 minutes)

Directions: Reprinted below is a poorly written passage. You are to treat it as though it were the first draft of a composition of your own, and revise it so that it conforms with standard formal English. Wide spaces have been left between the lines so that you may write in the necessary improvements. Do not omit any ideas and do not add any ideas not now present. However, you may change any word that you think expresses an idea inexactly, and you may omit words, phrases, or sentences that are unnecessary.

You are not expected to rewrite the whole passage. Trying to do so will not only waste your time but will also cause you to miss many of the specific errors you are expected to correct. Much of the passage is satisfactory as it stands. Leave such parts alone and concentrate on finding weak places that need changing.

In general, corrections should be made by crossing out the word, phrase, or mark of punctuation you wish to change and writing your own version above it. Any clear method of indicating changes is satisfactory, however. Simply make sure that what you intend is clear.

The compact form of the housefly is a patent model of Nature's most effective germ-dispensing device and a superb example of the mechanism which is so intricate that produces the activity of the tiniest insects. Its wings are attached to the dusty-gray mid-body. Which has four dark stripes running back along the top, and they give it great freedom. At one time it was assumed by the generality of people that these houseflies never traveled more than only short distances which was disproved by a scientist carrying out a simple experiment who shook up a number of flies in a bag. This bag contained colored chalk. Then the insects which were marked by the chalk were liberated. Observers within twenty-four hours reported that the flies had traveled as far if not farther than a dozen miles from the point where they started away from. . . .

The distinctive characteristics of the task set by the restricted free-response type of question are as follows.

1. The student is presented with a problem or question that is quite specific.
2. He produces his own answer, in his own words, and usually in his own handwriting.
3. He answers a relatively large number of questions.
4. He produces answers that for certain questions can be classified categorically as right or wrong and for other questions vary in completeness and accuracy.

Let us examine these characteristics in detail to see how they contribute to the advantages and disadvantages of this type of question.

THE PROBLEM OR QUESTION IS QUITE SPECIFIC. The specificity of the question posed to the student limits his freedom in answering the question. The freedom that a student has in answering a restricted free-response type of question is much less than that for answering an essay type question but more than that for answering a structured-response type of question. The amount of freedom that the student has in answering depends, of course, upon the question posed. The student has more freedom in supplying an answer to "Give an example of an antibiotic" than in supplying an answer to "What is an enlargement of the thyroid gland in a human being called?" The specificity of the question sacrifices the main feature of the essay question, the requirement that the examinee produce an organized answer in which he relates, evaluates, and integrates a number of facts and ideas. However, the restricted-response type of question because of its free-answer aspect still has some potential for measuring originality of response provided that the question is worded to elicit original responses.

The highly specific nature of the task presented in a short-answer or completion item seriously limits the range of objectives for which these item types can effectively be used. They lend themselves well to the testing of specific information—names, dates, definitions—but are poorly adapted to assessing inference, application, or problem solving except for quantitative problems. The item types are not very versatile, and if used to the exclusion of other item types are likely to bias the sampling of learning objectives assessed by the teacher.

THE ANSWER IS IN THE STUDENT'S OWN WORDS AND HANDWRITING. Although the restricted-response type of question does not make as great demands on the verbal fluency and the skill of expression of the student as does the essay question, it still demands that the student produce his own answer. Teachers frequently demand that the student use complete sentences in answering a short-answer type of question and reduce the marks of students whose sentence structure does not please them, thus introducing considerations of grammar into a test of content. Since the student writes out his own answer, his spelling and the legibility of his handwriting may also affect the teacher's judgment of the quality of the answer.

ANSWERS A RELATIVELY LARGE NUMBER OF QUESTIONS. Because of the brevity of the answer required for the restricted-response type of question, the number of questions of this type that can be included in a test is greater than that for the essay test. For example, in a 50-minute testing period about 20 or 25 short-answer or completion items can be answered by a high school freshman whereas in that time only three of four essay questions can be answered. The larger number of questions enables one to obtain a more representative sample of content than can be obtained in the essay test.

ANSWERS MAY SOMETIMES BE CATEGORICALLY CLASSIFIED AS RIGHT OR WRONG OR MAY VARY IN ACCURACY. The time required to score the answers to a number of restricted-response questions is shorter than that required for evaluating answers to essay questions but usually longer than for the structured-response questions. How accurately and dependably the answers can be judged depends to a large extent upon the nature of the questions asked. For example, a completion item asking the student to name the year that a particular historical event occurred could be scored unequivocally as right or wrong. Some completion or short-answer questions appear as though they have unequivocally right or wrong answers but one runs into difficulty as to what allowances, if any, should be made for misspelling. For example, suppose as an answer to the question, "What is an enlargement of the thyroid gland in a human being called?" the teacher received the following answers: (1) goiter; (2) goter; (3) gorter; (4) garter; (5) guttr; (6) Adam's apple. The first answer is clearly correct and the sixth is clearly wrong but what about the other four? The teacher may insist that the spelling be accurate in order to receive any credit for answering the question—but can the teacher state with any degree of confidence that the other four students did not know the answer to the question?

The more freedom in answering a restricted-response question that a student has, the more difficult the answer is to score. Sometimes difficulty in scoring arises because of ambiguities in the question and at other times from the way the student has expressed his answer. For example, consider the question "Give one important reason why young people should not begin to smoke cigarettes." The desired answer to the question was that there appears to be a relationship between cigarette smoking and lung cancer. But suppose the following answers were given by students: (1) It's an expensive habit; (2) It will become a habit that you can't break; and (3) It causes lung disease. Are these answers right or wrong? The original question is vague and ambiguous in the use of the word "*important*." The student who gave answer number 1 interpreted importance from the standpoint of economics and the student giving answer number 2 interpreted importance from the standpoint of establishing and changing habitual behavior patterns. Answer number 3 lacks precision; should it be given credit?

As a rule, the scoring of a short-answer or completion type of question must be done by someone who is competent in the subject area. Equally competent judges may arrive at different scores for the same paper but usually the differences on the short-answer or completion type questions are not as great as those on the essay test. However, the fact that there is variation among judges scoring the test means that some of the differences in score among students will be due to idiosyncrasies of the person doing the scoring rather than to real differences among the students in the attribute that the test is supposed to measure.

The Structured-Response or Objective Item

The structured-response item provides or should provide both a specific problem and a limited set of choices from which the student must select his answer. The correct or desired answer, usually only one, is determined when the test item is written. These types of items are usually called *objective* items. The word "objective" refers only to the scoring of answers; the choice of content and coverage of an objective test is as subjective as for an essay test. For some objective items there is also subjective judgment involved in the original decision as to which answer choice shall be scored as the correct or best answer. The common types of objective items are the alternate-response question such as the true-false item; the multiple-choice item; and the matching item. Examples of each kind of item are given below.

Alternate-response

T F Mumps is caused by a virus.

Multiple-choice

A vegetarian diet that includes neither animal flesh nor animal products is likely to be severely deficient in

A. starch.
B. sugar.
C. fat.
* D. protein.

Matching

Column I Disease	*Column II Cause of Disease*
(F) Measles	A. Bacteria
(D) Hemophilia	B. Dietary deficiency
(C) Ringworm of scalp	C. Fungus
(E) Malaria	D. Hereditary defects
	E. Protozoa
	F. Virus

The essential characteristics of the task set by an objective test are that the examinee:

1. Operates within a completely structured situation.
2. Selects his answer from a limited number of answer choices supplied by the test constructor.
3. Responds to each of a large sample of items.
4. Receives a score for each answer according to a predetermined key.

These characteristics contribute to advantages and disadvantages of the objective item that are the reverse of those for the free-answer type of question. Let us look at each one in detail.

THE TASK IS COMPLETELY STRUCTURED. Both the problem presented to the student and his choice of answer are completely structured. The student has little or no freedom to define the problem for himself and to organize and present his answer. On the debit side, this means that the objective item cannot measure originality of response or the ability to integrate various ideas or concepts from one or more content areas into an organized whole. The requirement that the problem be stated precisely and that there be a clearly "right" or "best" answer also makes the objective item a somewhat unsatisfactory type of question for dealing with controversial issues. On the credit side, the structured nature of the objective item assures that each student deals with the same problem and permits the examiner to break a complex skill or process into its component parts to obtain measures of both very specific and more general responses of the student. There are two major advantages that result: (1) comparable measures are obtained on all students, and (2) the results of the test can provide more diagnostic information about the student. In a well-made objective test, each student can be required to respond to all aspects of a complex area, whereas in many essay test situations, he can devote his entire attention to the one or two aspects of the area that he knows well and ignore entirely or give relatively little attention to other aspects.

THE STUDENT SELECTS HIS ANSWER FROM A LIMITED NUMBER OF GIVEN ANSWER CHOICES. In the objective item, the student's choice of answers is limited to those provided by the test constructor. Where the answer choices are provided, the student is required to recognize rather than recall the correct answer. We have discussed whether the recognition and recall of answers represent different mental processes in connection with the essay test on page 52. The amount of recall required by a well-constructed multiple-choice item is often underestimated by critics of this type of item. When the multiple-choice item presents a novel problem to the student, the student frequently has to recall definitions of terms, specific facts, and principles before he is able to choose the correct answer.

When the student must choose his answer from among the answer choices supplied by the test constructor, he can be expected to get some answers right by guessing. Guessing becomes a serious problem on objective tests when there are only two answer choices, when the test is very short, when the items on the test are too difficult for the examinees, when the test is highly speeded, and when the test items are poorly constructed. The problem of guessing can be controlled by using items with four or five answer choices, by giving long tests instead of short ones, by constructing items of appropriate difficulty, by giving enough time for all examinees to complete the test, and by making sure that all items have really attractive error choices.

Another criticism that has been made of the objective test is that items appear in which among the answer choices provided either none is correct or several can be considered correct, and yet the student is instructed to choose only one answer. Because of this, say the critics, the objective type of item may reward the superficial thinker or the student who knows the least and penalize the deep thinker or the student who knows the most. None of the critics offers any solid evidence that the most able students are in fact penalized. It is true, that many teacher-made tests contain objective items that are very poorly constructed but they also contain free-answer items that are poorly constructed. If the statement of the critics were true, then one would expect that students who score high on an objective test would rank low on teacher's judgment of achievement or on other measures of achievement. However, this is not true; there is, instead, a high, positive relationship between performance on an objective test and other judgments of achievement.

Another objection that is raised by teachers and others to the objective test is that seeing false statements in a true-false test or wrong answers on a multiple-choice test may lead the student to learn the incorrect response rather than the correct one. Very little research has been done on this point, but a study by Preston (1965) revealed that there was a slightly greater tendency for students to be conditioned by selecting the correct response on a multiple-choice test than by selecting the wrong response. Preston's study has some deficiencies; however, it seems unlikely that a student will fix a wrong response more strongly in his mind by reading it on an objective test than by writing a wrong answer to a free-response type of item.

THE SAMPLE OF ITEMS IS LARGE. Since each item is brief, many items can be included. These can be spread more evenly over the topics to be covered and a more representative sampling can be obtained. This reduces the role of luck, of the individual just happening to have reviewed a particular topic. As a consequence of the inclusion of many separate items, the score from a well-made objective test is likely to be more accurate than that from an essay test, so that two separate tests of an individual based on the same content areas will rank him at more nearly the same place in his group.

EACH ITEM HAS A PREDETERMINED KEY. The key is established once and for all by the test maker at the time the test items are written. This means that scoring the test is a routine clerical task and can be done by a person who knows nothing about the subject matter of the test or even by one of the electrical test-scoring machines on the market. The saving in time in scoring the test is very substantial, but it must be remembered that much of that saving will have been used up in preparing the test. Writing clear and unambiguous objective test items is a fairly demanding literary task.

The economy in scoring time is less important than the uniformity in evaluating answers that results. The score will be the same whoever scores the test, once the key has been agreed upon. The score will be the same no matter who it was that chose the answers. Teacher's pet or hellion, Spencerian specialist or scribbler, if they choose the same answer they get the same score.

EFFECTIVE USE AND SUMMARY COMPARISON OF ITEM TYPES

From the previous discussion it should be quite clear that neither the free-answer question nor the objective item is free from faults. All types of items have advantages and disadvantages. The most voluble critics of tests have recently focused their attention on the objective type item and seem largely to have ignored the deficiencies of essay tests. Since, in the objective type of item, both the problem posed to the students and the answer choices are open to view, it is a much easier type of test to criticize. Many essay type questions are written in such a vague way that each reader can interpret the question in any way that he wishes and he usually does not know what is being valued in the answers. One really cannot judge the adequacy of an essay question unless he knows what is being valued in the answer.

In the classroom, the teacher will find that he needs to use all kinds of items to evaluate adequately the objectives of instruction. The choice of item types will depend in part upon theoretical considerations and in part upon practical considerations. The test constructor should consider each of these carefully, make his decision on which type of item to use on rational rather than emotional grounds, and be fully aware of both the advantages and disadvantages that are inherent in his final choice.

The theoretical issues that should be considered in making a choice of item type should take precedence over the practical considerations. There are four important theoretical considerations in choosing the type of item.

1. The adequacy of the item type in eliciting the student behavior that we are trying to measure on the test.

2. The degree of precision needed in the results of the test to achieve the purpose for which the test was given.

3. The freedom from irrelevant sources of variation that is desired in the test results.

4. Appropriateness to the age and developmental level of the students being tested.

Adequacy in Eliciting Desired Student Behavior

Each item on a test should be written so that it elicits the type of student response that we are trying to measure. If we want to measure how well a student can deal with a problem that requires him to select, relate, and organize his knowledge, to create essentially new patterns, and to use language to express his ideas, then we must present him with a novel problem in the form of an extended-answer essay type of question. If we want to determine how original or innovative he can be in his responses, we must use a free-response type of item. If we are interested in determining the fund of knowledge that an individual has, or his ability to apply his knowledge to solve problems, or his ability to interpret or analyze or evaluate, it is possible to use either a free-answer type of question or a structured-response type of question. However, we should prefer the structured-response or objective question because this item type is more efficient and more dependable than the free-response type of item.

Degree of Precision Needed in Results

As we have mentioned previously, classroom tests are given to serve many purposes. If the test is given to provide the student with an opportunity to try out his knowledge and to motivate him to improve, then the results do not have to be highly accurate. If the test is given to determine whether individuals or groups of individuals in the classroom need additional help or reteaching, we can use tests of moderate accuracy quite well because the classroom teacher can easily adjust for incorrect decisions as he works with children. In these two situations the low level of precision of the free-response type of item can be tolerated. However, when test results are being used to assign grades to students or to make decisions about admission of students to programs or institutions or to place students, we want to be sure that we have as accurate and dependable a measure of the level of students as possible. In these kinds of situations, the decision that is reached may have profound implications for the future of the individual. Once the decision has been made, it becomes extremely difficult, if not impossible, to change the effects of the decision. In these situations, we should use the objective type of item for two reasons: (1) a large number of items can be included in the test, leading to a more adequate sampling of relevant student behavior, and (2) the scoring of the answers is more accurate and dependable.

Freedom from Irrelevant Sources of Variation

When we are trying to measure the extent to which students have achieved the objectives of instruction that are specific to a subject matter area, such as science, we would like to get scores that reflect *only* the differences between students in their achievement of these objectives and that are free from differences among students in general writing ability, or spelling ability, or general reading ability. No item type is completely free from all these irrelevant factors; however, the objective item does not require the student to write and is free from most of them. General reading ability does enter into the performance on an objective test. If a student cannot read the question, he cannot answer it. However, it is possible to hold down the reading difficulty level on an objective test and to minimize this as a source of irrelevant differences among students. There is no way to eliminate writing skill, spelling, or penmanship from the group administered free-answer test.

Age and Developmental Level of Students

Students in the elementary grades are typically limited both in their writing and reading skills. For this reason, the extended-answer essay type question is very inappropriate for them. The restricted-answer free-response question and the various forms of objective items are more appropriate.

There are a number of situations in testing in which, after considering all the theoretical issues, the test constructor still has a choice between the free-answer type of question and the objective type of question. In these situations, practical considerations may determine which type of question is used. Among the practical considerations that influence the decision are the following ones.

1. Time available for constructing items and time available for scoring the test.
2. Number of people to be tested.
3. Method of administering the test.
4. Skill in writing different types of items.

Time Available for Constructing Items and Scoring the Test

Free-answer questions (both essay and short-answer or completion) usually can be written more quickly than can the objective type questions. Furthermore, fewer free-answer type of questions than objective questions need to be written for a given amount of testing time. On the other hand, the scoring of free-answer items, particularly essay items, requires a large amount of time. If time for constructing the test items is very limited and the scores on the test are not needed immediately, a free-answer type of test may be more practical. But it should be pointed out that if one considers the total time required for constructing the test items and for scoring the test, then the free-answer type of test represents no saving of time over the objective type of test unless the number of people tested is very small. It should also be emphasized that making good tests of *any* kind requires considerable thought and effort; no one can expect to write good test items if he dashes off the questions a half hour before the test is to be given.

Number of People To Be Tested

A person highly skilled in item writing can spend anywhere from three to five hours in constructing a fifty-item multiple-choice test in a subject matter area. A less highly skilled person could spend even more time. When the number of people to be tested is small, that is, only 20 to 25, and the test is not going to be reused, then the free-answer type of test is likely to be more practical. As the number of examinees increases, the balance shifts toward the objective test. If the same test is to be used with other groups and there is a possibility that there will be communication between the groups, a common free-answer type of test with a small number of items is a poor choice because the questions can be remembered and passed on to other individuals who will take the test later.

Method of Administering the Test

In some schools, there are limited facilities for running off copies of a test. In that case a set of essay questions or short answer questions written on the blackboard is a practical solution. Blackboard space is usually too limited to present an objective test, particularly a multiple-choice test.

It is possible to administer a set of test items orally, though the procedure can hardly be recommended for a class group. Differences in tempo among students in deciding upon an answer and in recording it make for problems, and it becomes difficult for the examiner to keep good control of the testing situation. Items to be administered orally need to be structurally simple, and short-answer, completion, or true-false items seem to fit best. Multiple-choice questions are often too complex to follow well orally, and there is rarely any advantage in trying to dictate essay questions.

Skill in Writing Different Types of Items

The different kinds of test items present different kinds of problems to the would-be item writer. Generally, classroom teachers encounter more difficulty in constructing good multiple-choice items than in constructing good restricted free-response items. Many teachers have much more confidence in their skill in judging the adequacy of an answer to an essay question than in constructing good objective questions. That this confidence is frequently misplaced has been pointed out in previous sections on the essay test. Skill in writing any kind of test item can be developed with appropriate instruction and practice and with willingness to invest the necessary amount of time in test construction. On the other hand, if a classroom teacher is highly skilled in writing a particular kind of test item, he should probably use that type as much as possible. The teacher, though, should make sure that he is as skillful as he thinks he is.

The issues that we have been discussing in Chapter 3 are summarized in Table 3.3. In the column for each item type, "+ +" indicates the test item is

TABLE 3.3 SUMMARY OF EVALUATION OF TEST TYPES

Factor	Essay	Short Answer or Completion	Objective
Can measure ability to solve novel problems	++	+	++
Can measure ability to organize, integrate, or synthesize	++	+	− −
Can measure originality or innovative approaches to problems	++	+	− −
Can isolate specific abilities in subject area from general skills of writing, spelling, and language usage	− −	−	++
Has potential value for diagnosis	− −	+	++
Can sample adequately the objectives of instruction	− −	−	++
Can sample adequately the content of instruction	− −	−	++
Is free from opportunities for guessing answer	++	++	− −
Gives consistent scores from scorer to scorer	− −	−	++
Is accurate in differentiating levels of competency among examinees	− −	−	++
Can be scored by unskilled clerk or machine	− −	−	++
Can be scored quickly	− −	−	++
Takes little time for writing items	+	+	−

superior in relation to the factor; "+" indicates a slight advantage; "–" indicates a slight disadvantage; and "– –" indicates a marked disadvantage.

The table shows quite clearly that each item type has its advantages and disadvantages. To take advantage of the potential of each item type requires careful construction of the items.

SUMMARY STATEMENT

Evaluation of pupil achievement is one of the teacher's important responsibilities. In view of the many functions that tests serve in motivating and directing learning, and in view of the disservice that may be done the pupil from poorly conceived or executed evaluation instruments, it is important that the teacher's evaluation devices be well thought out and well made. Both written tests and a variety of informal appraisals are needed to evaluate completely the objectives of the modern curriculum.

For any type of written test, it is desirable to have a definite plan in advance of preparing the test items. The development of such a plan requires an analysis of the outcomes one is trying to achieve in the teaching of a particular course or unit and of the significant segments of content through which those objectives are to be realized. A statement of objectives useful for guiding the construction of test items must be phrased in terms of pupil behaviors—specific things that the pupil is supposed to be able to do—rather than in broad generalizations. In addition, the plan should include the allocation of test items among the content areas and objectives, the types of items to be used, the total number of items in the test, and specifications for the spread of item difficulties.

Both essay and objective tests should be used to evaluate pupil achievement. The essay test is easier to prepare and has certain advantages in appraising ability to recall information, select relevant material, and organize it into an integrated answer. However, the objective test has marked advantages in freedom from such irrelevant factors as quality of handwriting or of English usage, in breadth of sampling of the desired outcomes of teaching, and in ease and objectivity of scoring.

QUESTIONS AND EXERCISES

1. Prepare a statement of the objectives for a course, or a unit within a course, that you are teaching or plan to teach.

2. Which of the objectives in Question 1 could be measured effectively by a written test? Which only partially or not at all? Why is a written test inadequate for these? How might these objectives best be appraised?

3. Based on the objectives identified in the first part of Question 2 and a course outline, prepare a blueprint for a test to evaluate the unit or course.

4. In a junior high school, one teacher takes complete responsibility for preparing the common final examination for all the classes in general science. He makes the examination up without consulting the other teachers. What advantages and disadvantages do you see in this procedure? How could it be improved?

5. One objective that is often proposed for the social studies program in the secondary school is to increase the pupil's "critical reaction to the news in different news media." How could the formulation of this objective be improved so that progress toward it could be measured?

6. The following were included in a school system's formulation of the objectives of a unit on health. Criticize each of these, revising it if there are ways in which it could be improved.

a. Makes posters illustrating good health habits.
b. Demonstrates health consciousness.
c. Points out relationships between improvements in sanitation and drop in occurrence of disease.
d. Appreciates the critical role of bacteria for sickness and health.
e. Shows knowledge of and a lasting improvement in health habits.

7. Students are sometimes heard to remark: "You can't get a good mark on Miss X's tests unless you really know Miss X." What does this remark imply about Miss X's tests?

8. On p. 71 is a list of factors that have been presented as favoring either essay, short answer, or objective tests. Do you agree with the classification given there? Which are the most important factors? What other points should be considered in deciding which type of test to use for the final examination in a particular course?

9. Look at the blueprint for the examination on a unit on health that appears on pp. 42–43. For which of the cells in this blueprint would it be appropriate to use (a) extended-response exercises, (b) restricted-response exercises, and (c) structured-response items? What factors influenced your decisions?

REFERENCES

Balch, J. The influence of the evaluating instrument on students' learning. *American Educational Research Journal,* 1964, **1** (3), 169–182.

Bloom, B. (Ed.) *Taxonomy of educational objectives, Handbook I: Cognitive domain.* New York: Longmans, Green & Co., 1956.

Briggs, A. & Johnson, D. M. A note on the relation between persistence and achievement on the final examination. *Journal of Educational Psychology,* 1942, **33,** 623–627.

Coffman, W. E. & Kurfman, D. A comparison of two methods of reading essay examinations. *American Educational Research Journal,* 1968, **5,** 99–107.

Diederich, P. G. Factors in the judgment of writing ability. *Educational Testing Service Research Bulletin 61–65.* Princeton: Educational Testing Service, 1961.

Godshalk, F. I., Swineford, F., & Coffman, W. E. *The measurement of writing ability.* New York: College Entrance Examination Board, 1966.

Goslin, D. A. *Teachers and Testing.* New York: Russell Sage Foundation, 1967. Pp. 122–125.

Gosling, G. W. H. *Marking English compositions.* Victoria, Australia: Australian Council for Educational Research, 1966. Ch. 3.

Krathwohl, D. R., Bloom, B. S., & Masia, B. B. *Taxonomy of educational objectives, the classification of educational goals, Handbook II: Affective domain.* New York: David McKay, 1964.

Lawrence, G. D. Analysis of teacher-made tests in social studies according to the *Taxonomy of educational objectives. Clarmontiana Collection,* 1963.

Lord, F. M. The relation of the reliability of multiple-choice tests to the distribution of item difficulties. *Psychometrika,* 1952, **17,** 181–194.

Marshall, J. C. Composition errors and essay examination grades reexamined. *American Educational Research Journal,* 1967, **4** (4), 375–386.

Pfeiffer, I. & Davis, O. L., Jr. Teacher-made examinations: What kinds of thinking do they demand? *Bulletin of the National Association of Secondary School Principals,* 1965, **49,** 1–10.

Preston, R. C. The multiple-choice test as an instrument in perpetuating false concepts. *Educational and Psychological Measurement,* 1965, **25** (1), 111–116.

Sax, G. & Collet, L. S. An empirical comparison of the effects of recall and multiple-choice tests on student achievement. *Journal of Educational Measurement,* 1968, **5,** 169–173.

Scannell, D. P. & Marshall, J. C. The effect of selected composition errors on grades assigned essay examinations. *American Educational Research Journal,* 1966, **3** (2), 125–130.

Scannell, D. P. & Steelwagen, W. R. Teaching and testing for degrees of understanding. *California Journal of Instructional Improvement,* 1960, **3** (1).

Standlee, L. S. & Popham, W. J. Quizzes' contribution to learning. *Journal of Educational Psychology,* 1960, **51** (6), 322–325.

SUGGESTED ADDITIONAL READING

Ashburn, R. R. An experiment in the essay-type question. In C. I. Chase and H. G. Ludlow (Eds.), *Reading in educational and psychological measurement.* Boston: Houghton Mifflin, 1966. Pp. 291–295.

Ballinger, S. E. Of testing and its tyranny. In C. I. Chase and H. G. Ludlow (Eds.), *Readings in educational and psychological measurement.* Boston: Houghton Mifflin, 1966. Pp. 32–39.

Berg, H. D. (Ed.) *Evaluation in social studies,* Thirty-Fifth Yearbook of the National Council for the Social Studies. Washington, D.C.: National Council for the Social Studies, 1965. Chapters 1, 2, 9.

Dressel, P. L. Measurement and evaluation of instructional objectives. In N. E. Gronlund (Ed.), *Readings in measurement and evaluation.* New York: Macmillan, 1968. Pp. 11–17.

Dunnette, M. D. Critics of psychological tests: Basic assumptions: How good? In J. T. Flynn and H. Garber (Eds.), *Assessing behavior: Readings in educational and psychological measurement.* Reading, Massachusetts: Addison-Wesley, 1967. Pp. 132–141.

Ebel, R. L. The social consequences of educational testing. In C. I. Chase and H. G. Ludlow (Eds.), *Readings in educational and psychological measurement.* Boston: Houghton Mifflin, 1966. Pp. 26–31.

French, J. W. Schools of thought in judging excellence of English themes. In A. Anastasi (Ed.), *Testing problems in perspective.* Washington, D.C.: American Council on Education, 1966. Pp. 587–596.

Hubbard, J. P. Programmed testing in the examinations of the National Board of Medical Examiners. In A. Anastasi (Ed.), *Testing problems in perspective.* Washington, D.C.: American Council on Education, 1966. Pp. 195–207.

Lindvall, C. M. (Ed.) *Defining educational objectives.* Pittsburgh: University of Pittsburgh Press, 1964.

Page, E. B. Grading essays by computer. In N. E. Gronlund (Ed.), *Readings in measurement and evaluation.* New York: Macmillan, 1968. Pp. 402–412.

Sanders, N. M. *Classroom questions. What kinds?* New York: Harper & Row, 1966.

Starch, D. & Elliott, E. C. The reliability of grading work in English, mathematics and history. In D. A. Payne and R. F. McMorris (Eds.), *Educational and psychological measurement.* Waltham, Massachusetts: Blaisdell, 1967. Pp. 54–59.

Tyler, R. W. What testing does to teachers and students. In A. Anastasi (Ed.), *Testing problems in perspective.* Washington, D.C.: American Council on Education, 1966. Pp. 46–52.

CHAPTER 4

Preparing Test Exercises

INTRODUCTION

ONCE the basic planning for a test has been completed, the teacher must prepare the test, administer and score it, and analyze the results. Preparation of the test includes writing the items or questions, writing directions for the examinees, and reproducing the test in a form suitable for administration. After the test has been given, it must be scored and the results reported and interpreted to the students. Often a classroom teacher stops here; but if he does, he will fail to derive all the possible benefits from the time he has invested in constructing the test. He should go one step further and make a systematic analysis of the results. Procedures for analyzing the questions and answers on a test have been most fully worked out for the objective types of test item, but it is possible, although more difficult and time consuming, to analyze the results of free-answer tests. This kind of analysis will provide data useful in helping the teacher to improve the questions on future tests and to identify aspects of his teaching that have been effective or ineffective for the class as a whole.

The most time-consuming and difficult aspect of preparing classroom tests is constructing the test questions. Writing good questions is an art. It is a little like writing a good sonnet and a little like baking a good cake. The operation is not quite as free and fanciful as writing the sonnet, but not quite as standardized as baking the cake. It lies somewhere in between. So a discussion of item writing lies somewhere between the exhortation to the poet to go forth and express himself and the warning to the neophyte cook to follow the recipe precisely. The point we wish to make is that there is no exact science of test construction. Most of the guides and maxims that we shall offer have not been tested out by controlled scientific experimentation. Instead, they represent a distillation of practical experience and professional judgment. As with the recipe in the cookbook, if they are carefully followed the final product can usually be depended on to be good; if they are judiciously seasoned with a pinch of imagination and a dash of originality the final product is likely to be excellent.

In this chapter, we shall consider the construction of the different types of tests and the scoring and analysis of the results.

There are a few general admonitions that apply more or less equally to all kinds of test exercises, and these can be stated first. They represent practices that are followed quite automatically by professional test makers, and can be applied, though less formally and elaborately, to the test-making activities of the classroom teacher.

1. *Keep the test plan or blueprint in mind, and probably in view, as test exercises are written.* The blueprint represents your master plan and should be readily available to guide the specific tasks of item writing and review.

2. *Draft the test exercises some time in advance,* put them on the back burner for a few days, and then review them. It is amazing how often a statement or question that seemed perfectly clear as it was written turns out to be ambiguous or to have alternate meanings when it is reexamined after a lapse of time.

3. *Have the test exercises examined and critiqued by one or more colleagues.* Where this can be done, it is preferable to a personal review. A completely fresh reading by another person will elicit a wide assortment of questions and suggestions. If possible, the reviewer should select or provide answers to the questions (without seeing your key), so that you can check to be sure that there is agreement on the answer.

4. *Prepare a surplus of test exercises.* Then, if some do not stand up under further scrutiny there will still be enough. Again, a surplus will give some freedom for adjusting the composition of the test to match the blueprint.

IMPROVING ESSAY TESTS

The major advantage of the essay type of question lies in its potential for measuring the student's abilities to organize, integrate, and synthesize his knowledge; to use his information to solve novel problems and to be original or innovative in his approaches to problem situations. To realize this potential requires that each question be carefully phrased so that it will require the student to reveal these kinds of abilities. Merely casting a question in essay form does not automatically insure that these abilities will be assessed.

Look at the following two essay questions, A and B.

Question A

What methods have been used in the United States to prevent and control communicable diseases?

Question B

TABLE 1 CAUSES OF DEATH AND RATE FOR EACH IN 1900 AND 1967

Cause of Death	Death Rate per 100,000 People	
	1900	1967
1. Pneumonia	175.4	21.8
2. Diarrhea and enteritis	139.9	2.0
3. Diseases of the heart	137.4	399.9
4. Cancer	64.0	160.9
5. Diphtheria	40.3	0.02

Examine the data provided in the table shown above.

Explain how changes in knowledge, in medical practice, and in the conditions of life in the United States between 1900 and 1967 account for the changes in death rate shown in the table.

To answer question A, the student need only recall information and write it down in much the same form in which it was presented in the textbook or in class. On the other hand, question B requires that the student recall something about the characteristics of each of the diseases and disease conditions, and about methods of transmission or conditions that affect incidence of disease. He must then relate these to such things as immunization, chemotherapy, improvements in sanitation, and the increasing proportion of older people in the population. Question B seems more clearly appropriate for an essay question.

To realize the value of the essay question for appraising the ability to use information, to organize materials, or to use language effectively depends not only upon writing questions appropriate to elicit these abilities but also upon being able to structure the situation so that other factors do not obscure the desired appraisal. In the typical essay examination differences in knowledge of basic factual material hide differences in ability to use and organize those facts and time pressures often militate against the student's producing his best writing.

The "open-book" examination has been suggested as one means of partially evening out differences in factual knowledge. In this form of examination, the students have access to any data in their texts or their notes. Realistically, one cannot expect to wash out all differences in knowledge by an "open-book" examination. The able student knows what to look for in the book and where to find it; the poor one can spend a whole period aimlessly leafing through the pages. However, there seem to be other advantages to the "open-book" examination. Feldhusen (1961) reported that college students who were given "open-book" examinations felt that this type of examination was more effective in promoting learning, reducing worry and tenseness about the examination, and reducing cheating. He also reported that, although students spent less time memorizing factual material in preparing for an "open-book" than for a closed-book examination, they spent as much or more time on general review of the material.

The time pressures of the typical essay testing situation can be eased by assigning essay questions as an out-of-class examination or by having very liberal time limits. If the former is done, one not only minimizes time pressures but also gains the advantages of the "open-book" examination. Under these conditions, the student has time not only to write carefully but also to edit his writing, and the teacher can get samples of his best writing under optimal conditions. An out-of-class examination does introduce other problems such as the possibility of help from parents or others. We can never be sure how much the final product is a result of the student's own efforts and how much should be attributed to others. Because of this, some essay testing must continue to be done under supervised conditions, but the out-of-class essay examination can be a valuable teaching device.

Writing the Essay Questions

The following suggestions are presented as guides to writing more effective essay questions.

1. *Have clearly in mind what mental processes you want the student to use in answering before starting to write the question.* The teacher or test constructor must understand as fully as possible the kinds of student responses that represent the ability or abilities he is trying to measure before he can determine the kinds of stimulus material he needs to elicit those responses. For example, a teacher who wants to use the essay question to evaluate eighth graders' ability to think critically about health information may identify as evidence of critical thinking

the abilities to evaluate the adequacy of an authority, to recognize bias or emotional factors in the presentation, to distinguish between verifiable and unverifiable data, to recognize the adequacy of data, to check statements against other known data, and to determine whether data support the conclusion. Once he has decided that these competencies should be appraised, he can then select, adapt, or create stimulus materials that will require the student to display these abilities.

2. *Use novel material or novel organization of material in phrasing essay questions.* Generally speaking, we want the essay question to appraise the student's ability to use his information. To determine whether a student can do this, we must put him in a situation where he must do more than merely reproduce the material as it has appeared in the text or in the classroom lecture and discussion. Questions A and B on page 78 are good illustrations of this point. Question A does not require the student to use information but merely to reproduce it, whereas question B does require him to use it.

3. *Start essay questions with such words or phrases as "Compare," "Contrast," "Give the reasons for," "Give original examples of," "Explain how," "Predict what would happen if," "Criticize," "Differentiate," "Illustrate."* The use of words or phrases such as these, combined with novel material, will help to present tasks requiring the student to select, organize, and use his knowledge. Don't start essay questions with such words as "what," "who," "when," and "list" since these words tend to lead to tasks requiring only the reproduction of information.

4. *Write the essay question in such a way that the task is clearly and unambiguously defined for each examinee.* We want the score that a student gets to be a reflection of how well he can do a specified task, not of how well he can figure out what the task is that he is supposed to do. And, too, in large-scale testing programs we want the task to be perceived in the same way by all paper graders, so that a student's score will be affected as little as possible by who scores his paper. Luck in guessing what is wanted for an answer and disagreements in the quality of answers produced can be reduced by writing essay questions that set a clearly defined task for the examinee.

Thus, a question such as "Discuss the organizations that contribute to the health of the community," is global, vague, and ambiguous. First, what is meant by the word "discuss"? Does it imply listing organizations and their activities? Criticism and evaluation of what they do? Identification of gaps in the organizational structure? Second, does the teacher expect the student to consider only government organizations or does he expect the student to consider the whole gamut of public and private organizations that contribute to the health of a community? Third, what does the teacher mean by "contribute to the health of the community"? Does he want the student to confine his answer to the kinds of contributions that involve enforcement of health regulations, direct treatment of illness and preventive medicine or does he want the student to include contributions through education and research? The question as written requires that the student guess what the teacher wanted for an answer and his score is likely to depend on how lucky he was in his guess.

A better way to phrase the question so that each examinee will interpret it the same way would be:

> Using tuberculosis as an example, indicate how each of the following organizations could be expected to contribute to the prevention of the disease or the cure or care of persons with the disease.
>
> (a) Local and state health departments
> (b) United States Public Health Service
> (c) Department of Agriculture
> (d) The National Tuberculosis Association
> (e) The American Public Health Association

The question as it has been rephrased provides for a more common basis for response without sacrificing the freedom of the student in answering the question. (The revised question also clearly indicates that the task will be difficult for the typical eighth-grade student in terms of whom the blueprint on pp. 42–43 was conceived.)

5. *A question dealing with a controversial issue should ask for and be evaluated in terms of the presentation of evidence for a position, rather than the position taken.* On many issues that individuals and society face there are no generally agreed-upon answers. Yet, these controversial issues constitute much of what is genuinely vital in education. In these areas, it is not defensible to demand that a student accept a specific conclusion or solution. However, it is reasonable to appraise him on how well he knows, can marshall, and can utilize the evidence upon which a specific conclusion is based. Thus, the question "What laws should Congress pass to improve the medical care of all citizens in the United States?" has no generally accepted answer. But one could reasonably ask a student to respond to such a question as the following: "It has been suggested that the cost of all medical care provided by physicians and the cost of all medications be borne by funds provided by the federal government. Do you agree or disagree? Support your position with logical arguments." In this type of question, the teacher should *not* grade the student on the position he takes but only on the basis of how well he defends or supports his position.

6. *Be sure the essay question asks for the behavior that you really want the student to display.* Teacher-made essay tests quite frequently have questions

such as "Give your best definition of good health"; "What do you think is the difference between active and passive immunity?"; "In your opinion what factors have contributed to the decreasing number of cases of diphtheria between 1900 and 1967 in the United States?" Usually, in these questions the teacher is not interested in what the student's opinion is but in whether the student knows the factual material. The questions should be rewritten to read, "Define good health"; "Explain the differences between active and passive immunity"; "What factors have contributed to the decreasing number of cases of diphtheria in the United States between 1900 and 1967?" (When this is done, it becomes clear that the questions are too factual in nature to be good essay questions.)

7. *Adapt the length and complexity of the answer to the maturity level of the students.* Though at all levels the distinctive value of the essay question lies in its ability to require the respondent to select and organize his own ideas in his own way, the organization and expression that one can reasonably expect an elementary school or junior high school pupil to produce is quite restricted in amount and conceptual level. A question such as that on p. 78 may be too elaborate, too conceptually sophisticated, and too long for such a group. The essay questions on p. 51 appear to be more appropriate for the typical eighth grader.

Preparing the Essay Test for Use

To make the most of essay questions as indicators of student achievement certain precautions should be taken. In addition to the suggestions on p. 77 that are general to all types of tests, the following merit consideration.

1. *Be sure that the students do not have too many or too lengthy questions to answer in the time available.* The number of questions that can be included in an essay test depends upon the complexity and length of the desired answer, the grade and ability level of the students, and the time available for testing. An essay test should not be a test of speed of writing. Good essay questions demand that the student analyze the question carefully, decide what is and what is not required for an answer, think about the most appropriate way of organizing the answer, and then write it. These processes take time and the more complex the question, the longer the required time. The typical student in the eighth grade is likely to need 20 to 25 minutes to write an adequate answer to either question B on p. 78 or the revised question on p. 81. In many classroom tests, three to five such questions or one complex essay question and 40 or 50 objective questions are given for a 35 or 40 minute testing period. This practice may encourage both sloppy thinking and sloppy writing on the part of the student.

2. *If several essay questions are to be given, try to have a range of complexity and difficulty in the questions.* Most classroom tests are given for the purpose of differentiating among students as to their degree of mastery of the material taught. If all the essay questions are difficult and complex, some of the less able students will be unable to produce an acceptable answer to any of them. On the other hand, if all the questions are simple and easy, we will have an inadequate measure of what the better students can do. By varying the complexity and difficulty of the questions, the teacher can obtain information on both the least and most able students.

3. *In most classroom tests, require all students to answer the same questions.* When an essay test is being used to appraise achievement of the objectives of a common program of instruction, each student should be required to answer the same questions. Giving a choice of questions reduces the common basis upon which different individuals may be compared. It adds one further source of variability to the subjectivity and inaccuracy that already exist in essay tests.

There are, of course, circumstances when a choice among questions is desirable. This is the case primarily when different students have studied different things or when the instructional objectives have been different for different students. Under these conditions, students can be expected to have different areas of competence. Thus, in statewide or national testing programs, such as the College Entrance Examination Board's Advanced Placement Tests that are given to pupils from schools all over the country, a choice of questions is reasonable and appropriate.

4. *Write a set of general directions for the test.* On many essay tests given in the classroom, the questions are prefaced only by the statement "Answer the following questions." This statement is inadequate to provide direction for the student in answering the questions. A good set of directions for an essay test should include statements covering (a) the general plan the student should use in taking the test; (b) the form in which the answer should be written, that is, connected prose or outline form; (c) the general criteria that will be used in evaluating the answers; and (d) the time available for taking the test.

5. *Specify the point value for each question on the test.* If more than one essay question is used on a test or if an essay question is combined with a set of objective items, the teacher should inform the student of the point value of the questions. Any allocation of points among questions is essentially arbitrary. However, when the questions on an essay test vary in complexity and consequently in time to answer adequately, it seems reasonable that the more complex questions should carry a higher point value than the simpler questions. By assigning different point values for different questions, the teacher can help the student judge the

relative complexity of the questions, thereby enabling him to allocate his time more wisely.

Scoring Essay Tests

Adequate appraisal of student achievement with an essay test requires not only well-formulated questions but also sound and consistent judgment of the quality of the answers. In Chapter 3 (pp. 53 to 54) we discussed various factors that bias the judgment of the quality of answers to essay questions. Essentially the problem in obtaining accurate and dependable scoring of answers centers on maintaining consistent standards for all students regardless of who scores the paper or when the paper is scored.

Research on the scoring of essays has been limited, and much of what there is has been concerned with the essay as a sample of writing rather than as an answer to a specific substantive problem. Recently, interest has focused upon comparison of a holistic with an analytic method of reading. In the holistic method, the reader concentrates on getting a general, unanalyzed impression of the quality of the essay, and records this general impression. In the analytical method, the scorer is given several distinct aspects of the specimen that are to be looked for (for example, completeness of evidence, logicality of organization, effectiveness of expression, correctness of English usage) and is required to produce a judgment with respect to each. It has been commonly stated that the analytical method provides a better basis for maintaining a consistent standard from paper to paper and from reader to reader, but studies (Gosling, 1966) have not been consistent in showing this to be true. Sometimes the analytic method has given more consistent results and sometimes there has been no difference, but consistently the analytic method has been found to be more laborious and time consuming, and consistently the differences in severity from reader to reader have been large in relation to any influence of method of reading.

When large numbers of papers are read holistically, the procedure has sometimes been adopted of providing standard sample essays as anchor points to define the scoring scale that is being used. Specimen papers are selected that have been read by several judges and judged to be, for example, clearly below average, average, and clearly above average. One or more papers may be used to represent each level. These are reproduced and made available to all paper readers, who familiarize themselves with them. Each student's answer is then read and assigned to the category of the paper that it most nearly matches. With samples at three quality levels, it is even possible to sort the answers into seven piles representing seven categories of quality, as shown below.

Pile

1 X_1
2 Above average sample
3 X_2
4 Average sample
5 X_3
6 Below average sample
7 X_4

For example, if a student's answer seems better than the average sample but not as good as the above average, he would be placed between those two samples in the space marked X_2. Score values can be assigned to each category on the scale and the student would be awarded the score that his answer most nearly matches. A classroom teacher could select the anchor samples from the group taking the test, but the method is not very feasible for small groups.

The research evidence on scoring essay tests is quite consistent on one point; namely, the sum of the ratings assigned by several raters to an essay question represents a more precise estimate of the student's true ability in the attribute being appraised by an essay question than does the rating by a single individual. In the typical school setting, it is extremely difficult, if not impossible, to have answers to essay questions read by more than one person, so the classroom teacher who reads and rates answers to essay questions by himself should be extremely cautious about the actions he takes on the basis of the score and should make every effort to supplement essay tests with more precise measures of student achievement.

Formal research provides little systematic guidance for improving the scoring of essay tests, but the following suggestions are offered, stemming from accumulated professional experience. These suggestions should help the teacher to maintain a more consistent standard for judging the answers across all students, make him more consciously aware of the basis for his ratings, thereby enabling him to feed back more specific comments to the student on his performance, and help him to reduce irrelevant factors that might influence his judgment of the quality of the answers.

1. *Decide in advance what qualities are to be considered in judging the adequacy of the answer. If more than one distinct quality is to be appraised, make separate evaluations of each.* In an essay in a subject matter field such as science or social studies, the teacher is generally trying to appraise the achievement of objectives that are directly and explicitly related to the content area, such as knowledge of facts, principles, and theories of the content area and the applica-

tion and development of these to novel situations and problems; he may also wish to appraise the development of generalized skills of writing such as logical organization, English usage, and spelling. These two dimensions are quite different and should be rated separately and reported to the student separately. There are two reasons for this: (1) to enable the teacher to make a judgment of the extent to which the student is achieving the distinctive objectives of the content subject and (2) to reveal to the student whether any deficiency in answering the question is due to weakness in subject matter or weakness in written expression or both.

2. *Prepare an answer guide or model answer in advance showing what points should be covered.* This should help to provide a common frame of reference for evaluating each paper and is especially important if the scoring of the papers is spread across a number of different days. After the preliminary guide has been prepared, it should be checked against a sample of student responses. No ratings should be given to this sample of papers; the purpose of this step is to determine the adequacy of the scoring guide. If the check reveals that students have consistently interpreted the question differently from the way the teacher had intended or have responded to the question at a consistently lower level than the scoring guide, then the specifications of what represents an acceptable answer should be revised to correspond more closely to the performance. Teachers frequently object to this procedure as representing a lowering of educational standards, but it is not. In the majority of cases, differences between the original scoring guide and students' answers are due to lack of clarity in the original question or unrealistic expectations on the part of the teacher of what students can do within the limits of the testing time.

3. *Read all answers to one question before going on to the next.* Reading the answers for the same question for all examinees before going on to the next question accomplishes two purposes: (1) the teacher can maintain a more uniform set of standards of grading across papers and (2) the teacher is less likely to be influenced in his judgment of the quality of the answer to another question by how the student has answered the previous one.

4. *After scoring the answer to one question for all papers, shuffle or rearrange the papers before starting to score the next question.* In the last analysis, judgments of the quality of answers to essay questions are relative, not absolute. The teacher's rating of a particular paper can be influenced by the quality of the answer in the paper that he has just finished reading. For example, suppose Gus wrote an outstanding answer for every question and Max wrote an average answer for every question. If the teacher reads Max's average answer immediately after Gus's outstanding one, Max's answer may appear poorer to the teacher than it actually is. To prevent Max's paper from being systematically downgraded because it follows an outstanding paper, the papers should be shuffled or re-

arranged so that the answers to the different questions are read in a different sequence.

5. *Grade the papers as nearly anonymously as possible.* The less one knows about *who* wrote an answer, the more objectively he can judge *what* was written. The criteria of quality for answers to an essay question should be applied uniformly to all students who take the test. Some teachers object to this for heterogeneous classes because they think the indices of quality should be adjusted for different levels of ability. Adjustments for individual differences should *not* be made at the point of scoring a test; these should be made at an earlier point where objectives, content, and learning experiences can be differentiated for various ability levels. If this differentiation is done, then the teacher will need to develop separate tests for each instructional group or else include a range of questions that cover the differentiated curriculum.

6. *Write comments and correct errors on answers to essay questions.* As we pointed out in Chapter 3, p. 31, a test is most effective for motivation and learning where students get prompt, specific information on their strengths and weaknesses. If the teacher makes a tally of the types of comments and types of errors, he will also gain valuable information to judge the effectiveness of his teaching. Writing comments and correcting errors are time-consuming activities, but from an instructional viewpoint one essay question that is carefully read and commented upon is worth much more than 4 or 5 questions that are cursorily read without comment.

IMPROVING RESTRICTED-RESPONSE TESTS

The restricted-response exercise can be in the form of a question (short-answer) or of a statement with blanks to fill in (completion). Generally these two forms are interchangeable, that is, the same problem could be presented either as a question or as a statement to be completed. To be classified as a restricted-response item, the question or statement must be answerable with a word, a date, a number or a phrase, a list of several words, or at most with no more than two or three sentences. The advantages and disadvantages of the item type have been discussed in Chapter 3, pp. 59–63. The restricted-response question is not very flexible and should be used sparingly on teacher-made tests. Items of this type are best suited for testing knowledge of vocabulary, names or dates, simple comprehension of concepts, and ability to solve quantitative problems. Quantitative problems that yield a specific numerical solution are "short-answer" by their very nature.

Though short-answer questions have a simple, straightforward structure, there are still many bad exercises of this type written by teachers. The most common faults found in teacher-made items are ambiguity of meaning, lack of precision in stating the question, and triviality of the content being measured. When constructing completion items, teachers too frequently lift a sentence from a textbook and remove one or two words. This practice is undesirable for two reasons: (1) a sentence out of context loses much of its meaning and (2) too great a premium is placed on rote memorization of textbook material. In the section that follows we will provide some guidelines for improving the construction of short-answer and completion items.

Writing Restricted-Response Questions

1. *Be sure that each item deals with important content; do not measure trivia.* The information that a student is required to recall on a test should be important in the area. Avoid the type of item that could quite justifiably be answered, "Who cares?" Ask yourself in each case whether knowing or not knowing the answer would make a significant difference in the individual's competence in the area being appraised. Both the examples of poor questions given below are measuring trivial information but both appeared in a teacher-made test on health in the eighth grade. No revision is suggested for the items since the information called for could be of no significance in an eighth grader's understanding of health or health practices.

Example

Poor: Short answer: How many cases of smallpox occurred in the United States in 1950? (*Answer:* 39)

Poor: Completion: In 1965, only 1 out of (10) Americans provided for adequate dental care.

2. *Be sure the question or statement poses a specific problem to the examinee.* A short-answer question or completion item should be written in such a way that a student who knows the material will know what the desired answer is. Look at the examples of short-answer and completion items labeled poor. For both of the questions, the answer desired was nicotine. However, as the questions are written many words or phrases other than nicotine would be factually correct and reasonably sensible, that is, chlorophyll, pigments, veins, moisture, starch, cells, leaf tissue, poison. The problem needs to be more specifically defined as is done in the revised statements.

Example

Poor: Short answer: What does the tobacco leaf contain? (Nicotine.)
Completion: The tobacco leaf contains (nicotine).

Better: Short answer: What is the name of the poisonous substance found in tobacco leaves? (Nicotine.)

Completion: The poisonous substance found in tobacco leaves is named (nicotine).

3. *Be sure that the answer that the student is required to produce is factually correct.* Look at the poor examples given below. The answer the test maker wanted was cirrhosis of the liver, but alcohol per se does *not cause* cirrhosis of the liver; it is the nutritional deficiency that is frequently associated with excessive drinking of alcohol that leads to cirrhosis of the liver.

Example

Poor: Short answer: What organic disease of the liver is caused by alcohol? (Cirrhosis of the liver.)

Completion: Alcohol causes an organic disease called (cirrhosis) of the liver.

Better: Short answer: What organic disease of the liver is common among people who drink large amounts of alcohol and have inadequate diets? (Cirrhosis of the liver.)

Completion: People who drink large amounts of alcohol and have inadequate diets frequently suffer from an organic disease called (cirrhosis) of the liver.

4. *Be sure the language used in the question is precise and accurate in relation to the subject matter area being tested.* The sample completion item appeared on an eighth-grade health test. From a biological standpoint, the statement is imprecise in calling genes "particles" and inaccurate in using the adjectives "strong" and "weak" instead of "dominant" and "recessive." The revision of the question shows how it could have been stated in a more precise way without giving the answer away.

Example

Poor: Some of the small particles inside chromosomes are stronger than others. These stronger ones are said to be (dominant) while the weaker ones are said to be (recessive).

Better: A mother has type A blood and a father has type O blood. Four children are born in the family, all of whom have type A blood. From this one would conclude that the genes for type A blood are (dominant) to those of type O.

5. *If the problem requires a numerical answer, indicate the units in which it is to be expressed.* This will simplify the problem of scoring and will remove one source of ambiguity in the examinee's answer. In the poor example below, the answer can be given as 4 cups, 2 pints or 1 quart and if the student does not designate the units in which he is expressing his answer, the teacher may have difficulty in determining whether the student really knows the answer.

Example

Poor: What is the recommended daily minimum requirement of milk for a 14-year-old boy?

Better: The minimum daily requirement of milk for a 14-year-old boy is (4) cups.

6. *In a completion item, omit only key words.* The blank in a completion item should require the student to supply a fact or term that is important in the area being appraised. Do not leave the verb out of a completion statement unless the purpose of the item is to measure knowledge of verb forms. In the sample item, the teacher should decide whether he wants to test for knowledge of the word "glycogen," of the place where excess glucose is stored in the body, or of a function of the liver and write the item accordingly.

Example

Poor: The liver (stores) excess glucose as glycogen.

Better: In normal body metabolism, excess glucose in the blood is stored in the liver in the form of (glycogen).

7. *In an achievement test, do not leave too many blanks in a completion statement.* Overmutilation of a statement reduces the task of the examinee to a guessing game. Overly mutilated statements may be appropriate when one is trying to appraise creativity or originality with words but not when one is trying to appraise factual knowledge.

Example

Poor: The ___(1)___ whose primary ___(2)___ is ___(3)___ are the ___(4)___. (*Answer:* 1, teeth; 2, function; 3, cutting; 4, incisors.)

Better: The teeth whose primary function is cutting are called the (incisors).

8. *In a completion item, put blanks near the end of the statement rather than at the beginning.* The student should know what question he is being asked before he encounters the blank.

Example

Poor: The __________ gland is an example of an endocrine gland.

Better: An example of an endocrine gland is the __________ gland.

Preparing the Test for Use

The main objectives to be sought in preparing a restricted-answer test for administration are that the test format be easy for examinees to understand and follow and that the responses be convenient for the test maker to score. Some suggestions that will help to achieve these ends are given below.

1. *If both completion and short-answer questions are used on the same test, put items of the same type together.* Each type of question requires a different set of directions and a somewhat different mental set on the part of the students.

2. *Have students write their answers on a separate answer sheet.* Students should have ample space for recording their answers. Since the size of handwriting varies with different students, it is very difficult to judge how much space each will need. The teacher will also find it easier to score papers if the answers are recorded in a uniform manner. For short-answer questions, blue books or blank sheets of paper can be used and the students can be instructed to number their answers to correspond to the question. For completion items, an answer sheet can be dittoed or mimeographed containing the number of each question with a line extending from the number on which the student can record his answer.

3. *Write a set of directions for each item type that is used on the test.* The directions should be simple but complete. They should include such things as how and where the student is to record his answers, the score value of each question and whether spelling will be considered in judging the adequacy of the answer. For quantitative problems, the student should be instructed as to whether he is to show all of his work or merely record the answer. For short-answer questions, the student should be instructed whether his answers must be written in complete sentences.

4. *So far as possible, group items dealing with the same content or skill together.* If this is done, it may help to reduce the feeling that the test is made up of unrelated bits and pieces. The examinee will also be able to concentrate on a single area of content at a time rather than having to shift back and forth among areas of content. Furthermore, the teacher will have an easier job of analyzing the test results for the group or for the individual since he will be able to see at a glance whether the errors are more frequent in one content area than another.

Scoring the Test

1. *Check the answer key against a sample of papers before scoring any paper.* Checking the prepared key against a few papers, preferably of those who are known to be good students, may disclose one or more items to which students have consistently given a response different from that in the key. This may arise either from a clerical error in preparing the key or from an interpretation of the question by students that differs from the one the instructor had intended. When

this occurs, and if the alternate interpretation is defensible, the key should be corrected or extended to include the variant. In an item such as, "Give an example of a communicable disease," a number of answers could be correct. Sometimes in making the original key, the teacher does not think of some possible answers, and the key may need to be extended as scoring proceeds.

2. *If spelling and sentence structure, as well as accuracy of content, are to be scored, provide a separate score for each.* This is the same point that was made in relation to the essay test on pp. 85–86.

3. *Correct errors and make comments on each question as it is scored or provide a complete set of answers for each student when the papers are returned.* This practice provides better direction to students' learning from a test and has also been shown to increase motivation for student learning.

4. *Generally speaking, score each question either right or wrong and assign equal weight to each question.* A well-written restricted-response question will pose a very specific problem to the student and should be scored either 0 for wrong or 1 for correct. Awarding partial credits creates difficulties in scoring. The issue of partial credit generally arises in those questions presenting a quantitative problem or in completion questions that include more than one blank. Although awarding partial credit for correct method of work in a quantitative problem or for correctly filling some of the blanks in a completion item may make for happier relations with students, it contributes little or nothing to the measurement effectiveness of a test.

The practice of having some questions count more in the total than others on a purely arbitrary basis contributes nothing to the test and increases scoring difficulties. If the teacher believes that some content or some skills are more important than others, he should have more questions based on that content or requiring that skill (see Chapter 3, pp. 44 to 47).

Analyzing the Results of the Test

To obtain maximum value from the test, the teacher should make a tally of the kinds of errors that students make on the test. The summary could then be used to plan instructional activities for the class as a whole or for groups of individuals.

The teacher should also check the adequacy of the questions to determine their difficulty and their ability to discriminate between those students who know the most and those who know the least. The procedures for doing this kind of analysis are similar for those for the objective test and will be discussed on pp. 124 to 127.

IMPROVING STRUCTURED-RESPONSE TESTS

The structured-response item is one in which the examinee must choose his answer from the options supplied by the test maker rather than producing it himself. The type of item is usually called an objective item. The form of objective items may be alternate-response such as true-false, multiple-choice with three to five answer choices, or matching. The general advantages and disadvantages of objective items have been discussed on pp. 63 to 67.

Objective items, particularly multiple-choice, can be used to appraise a wide variety of educational objectives. They are efficient and, minute for minute, yield scores that are more dependable than those from free-response questions. However, the advantages of objective items can be achieved only if they are well constructed. In the following sections, we will first present suggestions that apply to almost any type of objective item, and then consider different item types, indicating the specific virtues and limitations of that type of item and giving suggestions for writing and editing.

General Suggestions for Writing Objective Items

1. *Keep the reading difficulty and vocabulary level of the test item as simple as possible.* Ordinarily we do not want involved sentence structure or unnecessarily difficult words to interfere with a student's showing what he knows. Where technical vocabulary has been taught in a course and knowledge of that vocabulary is one of the objectives of instruction, it may appropriately be used, but obscure general vocabulary should be avoided. In the poor example below, which had been written for eighth graders, the sentence posing the question is unnecessarily wordy and complex and the words "promiscuous," "pernicious," and "deleterious" are unnecessarily difficult for this age level.

Example

Poor: The promiscuous use of sprays, oils, and antiseptics in the nose during acute colds is a pernicious practice because it may have a deleterious effect on

A. the sinuses.
B. red blood cells.
C. white blood cells.
D. the olfactory nerve.

Better: Frequent use of sprays, oils, and antiseptics in the nose during acute colds may result in

A. spreading the infection to the sinuses.
B. damage to the olfactory nerve.
C. destruction of white blood cells.
D. congestion of the mucous membranes in the nose.

2. *Be sure the item has a correct or best answer on which experts would agree.* Ordinarily statements of a controversial nature do not make good objective items, though there are instances where knowledge of different viewpoints on controversial issues may be important. When this is the case, the item should clearly state whose opinion or what authority is to be used as the basis for answering. The student should not be placed in the position of having to endorse a particular opinion or viewpoint as an indisputable fact.

Example

Poor: T F Alcoholism is a disease.
Better: T F According to your textbook, alcoholism is a disease.

3. *Be sure each item deals with an important aspect of the content area, and not with trivia.* Each item on a test should appraise command of an important aspect of the content of the subject area or the ability to use significant content. Sometimes teachers try to increase the difficulty of a test by basing items on obscure or trivial detail such as the content of the third footnote on page 90 in the textbook. The first poor example below, written for an eighth-grade health test, asks for an utterly trivial, specific detail, knowledge of which could not possibly make any significant difference in an eighth grader's competence in health. Example 2 says nothing; it is an example of lifting a statement from the textbook and the best answer to it is "Ho-hum, who cares?"

Example 1

Poor: In 1967, the death rate from accidents of all types per 100,000 population in the age group 15–24 was

A. 59.0
B. 59.1
C. 59.2
D. 59.3

Better: In 1967, the leading cause of death in the age group 15–24 was

A. respiratory diseases.
B. cancer.
C. accidents.
D. rheumatic heart disease.

Example 2

Poor: T F The manufacture of prescription drugs is a highly scientific industry.

4. *Be sure that each item is independent. The answer to one item should not be required as a condition for solving the next item.* Every individual should have a fair chance at each item as it comes. Thus, in the example shown below, the person who does not know the answer to the first question is in a very weak position in answering the second one.

Example

Poor: 1. Scurvy is caused by the lack of

A. vitamin A.
B. vitamin B_1.
C. vitamin B_{12}.
D. vitamin C.

2. A good source of this vitamin is

A. orange juice.
B. cod-liver oil.
C. liver.
D. whole rice.

5. *Avoid trick and catch questions in an achievement test.* Objective items tend to be trick items when the student has to pick one word or number out of a sentence that appears to be focusing on an entirely different point. In the poor example below, the item is keyed false because the immunizing agent for diphtheria is either a toxoid or an antitoxin, not a vaccine. However, the statement conveys the idea that the student is to react to the effectiveness of immunization procedures against diphtheria. If the purpose of the item is to test whether a student knows the correct use of the word "vaccine," the item should be rephrased as indicated. Trick questions are likely to mislead the better student who attempts to focus on the meaning of the statement rather than checking each word.

Example

Poor: T F The use of diphtheria vaccine has contributed to the decline in death rate from this disease between 1900 and 1968.

Better: T F The immunizing material used to prevent diphtheria is called a vaccine.

6. *Be sure that the problem posed is clear and unambiguous.* This is a general admonition, somewhat like "Sin no more!" and it may be no more effective. However, it is certainly true that ambiguity of statement and meaning is the most pervasive fault in objective test items.

Example 1

Poor: T F Diabetes develops after forty.

The statement was keyed true, but what does it mean? Does it mean "only after forty years of age" or does it mean "more frequently after forty"? What does "develop" mean in this context? One can obtain data on the relative frequency of diagnosis of diabetes in people of different ages but the time of diagnosis and the time of development are not the same. What kind of diabetes is the item writer referring to—diabetes mellitus or diabetes insipidus or some other form? These kinds of questions are likely to trouble the student who knows the most and not the ill-informed student. The item cannot be revised to make it an adequate item and should be dropped from the test.

Example 2

Poor: Which of the following substances is most essential to man?

A. Protein
B. Water
C. Vitamins
D. Minerals

The keyed answer to the question was B, but all of the substances are essential to man. The examinee has to guess what the item writer meant by "most essential" in order to answer the question. In this question, the item writer was trying to determine whether the students knew that a healthy man could survive for a fairly long time without food but could survive only for a few days without replenishing water lost from the body. The revised question tests for this knowledge with greater clarity.

Example

Better: A healthy man is marooned on a deserted island. To survive the man would need to find *almost immediately* a source of

A. protein to maintain body cells.
B. water to drink.
C. vitamins to maintain body metabolism.
D. carbohydrates or fats to supply energy.

Writing Alternate-Response Items

Any item or question for which a student is given two choices from which to select an answer is an alternate-response item. For example, the item frequently used on classroom tests to appraise knowledge of verb forms such as "Neither John nor Jim (a) has (b) have enough money to buy a ring," is an alternate-response item. However, the most widely used item of this type is the one that presents a declarative statement and requires the examinee to indicate whether it is true or false.

The true-false item has had wide popularity in teacher-made tests, probably in large part because it seems so easy to prepare. But this facility is misleading, because it is achieved at the cost of producing many bad items. The true-false item is best suited for assessing knowledge of facts that are unequivocally true or false. It is particularly well-suited to situations in which there exist only two contrasting options, for example, bacteria that may be either pathogenic or non-pathogenic, diseases that may be either communicable or noncommunicable. But only a small fraction of the knowledge in a field is of this type, and much that fits the pattern is relatively unimportant. Consequently many of the items that appear in tests either strain to cast a debatable matter into a format of universal truth or else deal with facts that, while unequivocal, are of marginal importance. Since the statement that constitutes an item typically appears in isolation, out of context, no frame of reference is provided within which the truth or falsity of the statement can be judged, and this aggravates the problem faced by the student, and perhaps especially the more able student.

A quite different type of problem arises from the large role that can be played by guessing and "luck" with two-choice items. Because the pupil has a 50 percent chance of getting the answer right by guessing on a true-false test, this format yields less accurate information about a student per item than do other forms of item, and many more items are needed to provide an equally precise appraisal of students' competence. Thus true-false tests should have a relatively large number of questions, and there should be time enough for all pupils to read and respond to all of them.

In a later section, we will discuss variations that have been used to make the item type more effective in appraising achievement, but the more immediate problem is the writing of good true-false items.

1. *Be sure that the item as written can be unequivocally classified as either true or false.* Each statement should be true enough or false enough that experts would unanimously agree on the answer. Many statements that are supposed to be true cause difficulty because the well-informed person can think of a number of exceptions or reasons why the statement is not universally true. Look at the poor example below. Although the statement is keyed true, the student with the most information knows that penicillin is effective against certain types of pneumonia but not other types. Such a student might well mark the statement false. The revised statement removes the ambiguity.

Example

Poor: T F Penicillin is an effective drug for the treatment of pneumonia.

Better: T F Penicillin is an effective drug for the treatment of streptococcal pneumonia.

2. *Avoid the use of "specific determiners."* Statements that include such words as "all," "never," "no," "always," or other all-inclusive terms represent such broad generalizations that they are likely to be false. Qualified statements involving such terms as "usually," "sometimes," "under certain conditions," "may be," are likely to be true. The test-wise student knows this and will use such cues to get credit for knowledge he does not possess. "All" or "no" may sometimes be used to advantage in *true* statements where the use of the specific determiner will lead to the wrong number.

Example

Poor: T F All bacteria cause disease.

Better: T F All pathogenic bacteria are parasites.

3. *Avoid ambiguous and indefinite terms of degree or amount.* Expressions such as "frequently," "greatly," "to a considerable degree," and "in most cases," are not interpreted in the same way by everyone who reads them. An item in which the answer depends on guessing what the item writer had in mind is likely to be unsatisfactory and frustrating to students. In the poor example, the student may be troubled by "frequently" because the method is used extensively today only for fruits.

Example

Poor: T F Drying is frequently used to preserve foods.

Better: T F Fruits can be preserved by drying.

4. *Avoid the use of negative statements and particularly double negatives.* Wason (1961) working with adults, and Zern (1967) working with elementary school children, have both shown that time required to answer a negatively phrased item is longer than for an equivalent positively phrased item and that more errors are made to negatively phrased items. Both investigators used pairs of statements such as "36 is not an even number" and "36 is an odd number." The negative statement requires a rather involved, reverse process of reasoning to untangle its meaning and is semantically more difficult. In addition, students under time pressures of the examination can easily overlook the negative. Double negatives can be particularly difficult.

Example 1

Poor: T F Resistance to smallpox obtained through the use of smallpox vaccine is not called active immunity.

Better: T F Resistance to smallpox obtained through the use of smallpox vaccine is called passive immunity.

Example 2

Poor: T F Tuberculosis is not a noncommunicable disease.

Better: T F Tuberculosis is a communicable disease.

5. *As a rule, limit true-false statements to a single idea.* Complex statements that include more than one idea are frequently difficult to read and comprehend. A statement that contains one true idea and one false idea borders on the category of trick items. Such an item tends to be a measure of reading skills rather than knowledge of the content area. Complex statements can be used if the student's attention is directed toward the one part of the statement that he is to judge to be true or false.

Example

Poor: T F Bleeding of the gums is associated with gingivitis which can be cured by the sufferer himself by brushing his teeth daily.

Better: T F Daily brushing of the teeth will cure gingivitis.

6. *Keep true and false statements approximately equal in length.* On a teacher-made test there is a tendency for true statements to be longer than false ones. Generally, the greater length of true statements is due to the need to include qualifications and limitations to make the statement unequivocally true. An occasional long true statement is not serious if it is matched by an occasional long false one, and there is no consistent difference in length between the two categories of statements.

VARIATIONS OF TRUE-FALSE ITEMS. Several variations have been introduced in an attempt to improve true-false items. Most of these try to accomplish one or more of the following: (1) reduce the ambiguity of the items; (2) reduce the effects of guessing on the scores; (3) provide more specific information as to how much a student knows. The three most frequently used variations are described below.

1. *Underlining a word or clause in the statement.* This is the simplest variation and is intended to reduce ambiguity by focusing the attention of the examinee on the important part of the statement. Two examples are given below.

Example

1. T F Malaria is transmitted by the Anopheles mosquito.

2. T F If foods are frozen, then harmful bacteria in them will be killed.

The instructions for such items should clearly indicate that the student is to judge the truth or falsity of the underlined portion in relation to the rest of the statement. Use of underlining permits the use of more complex statements.

2. *Requiring students to correct false statements.* A student who correctly marks a false statement as false may have made a lucky guess, but he may also have chosen the answer on the basis of misinformation. For example, in the item, "Insulin is secreted by the pituitary gland," a student could mark it false because he thinks insulin is secreted by the adrenal glands. In this case, his incorrect information leads him to a correct answer. To make sure that the student knows the true facts underlying a false statement and to reduce guessing, the student can be instructed to provide the correct answer whenever he marks a statement false. This works well when combined with the underlining described in the first variation, but is likely to be difficult to score if no constraints are introduced in the item. Our example can be corrected by changing insulin to one of the pituitary hormones, by changing "is secreted" to "is not secreted," by changing "the pituitary gland" to "an endocrine gland" or "the pancreas." It seems unnecessary to mention that, if this variation is used, all statements, true or false, must have underlined portions. The part of the statement that is underlined should be the specific content that the teacher is trying to appraise. Thus, in the example, if the teacher were trying to determine whether the student knew the name of a hormone secreted by the pituitary gland, he should underline the word "insulin." If the teacher were interested in determining whether the student knew the name of the gland that secretes insulin, he should underline "the pituitary gland."

3. *Basing true-false items on specific stimulus material provided for the student.* The true-false item tends to be most effective and most useful when it is based on some given stimulus material such as a chart, map, graph, table, or reading passage. In this situation, the student is instructed to respond to the item only in terms of the given material; therefore, he usually has a better defined frame of reference in terms of which to judge the truth or falsity of the statement. This type of true-false item can be effectively used to appraise comprehension, interpretation, extrapolation, and logical reasoning if appropriate stimulus material is used and items are written to elicit these abilities. An example of this item type is given below.

Example

Directions: The pie graph below shows how each dollar for medical care is spent. Look at the graph carefully. Statements are given below the graph. Read each statement carefully.

Mark T, if the data in the graph support the statement.

Mark F, if the data in the graph contradict the statement or no data are provided in the graph to either support or contradict the statement.

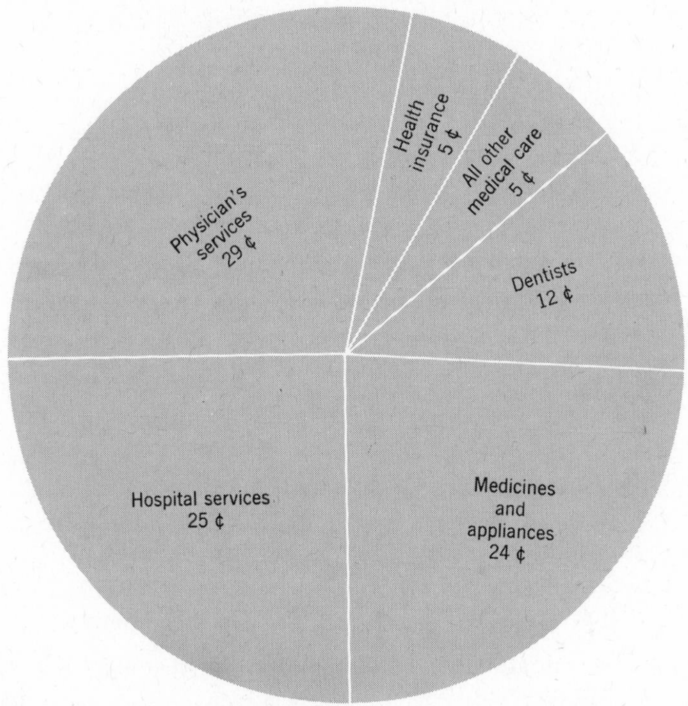

(T) 1. More of the medical care dollar is spent for physicians' services than for any other one category of expense.

(F) 2. Few Americans have health insurance.

(F) 3. Americans spend 24 cents out of every dollar they make on medicines and appliances.

(T) 4. Hospital and physician's services together account for slightly more than half of the money spent for medical care.

(T) 5. Less money is spent on dental care than on physicians' services.

(F) 6. About 25 percent of the medical care dollar is spent on nursing service in hospitals.

This form of item is sometimes made more complex by requiring the student to answer in four or five categories such as "definitely true"; "probably true";

"insufficient data to determine whether it is true or false"; "probably false"; and "definitely false." In this format the item becomes a multiple-choice item rather than a true-false item.

4. *Grouping short true-false items under a common question or statement heading.* Two examples of this variation are given below.

Example

Directions: Place a T in front of each choice that is a correct answer to the question. Put an F in front of each choice that is NOT a correct answer to the question.

A. Which of the following diseases are caused by viruses?

(T) 1. Chicken pox	(T) 5. Measles
(F) 2. Diphtheria	(T) 6. Mumps
(T) 3. Influenza	(F) 7. Tuberculosis
(F) 4. Malaria	(F) 8. Typhoid fever

B. A girl, 14 years old, ate the following food during a 24 hour period.

Breakfast	*Lunch*	*Dinner*
Cup of black coffee	1 glass coca cola (8 oz.)	Roast rib of beef (9 oz.)
	1 hamburger (4 oz.) with bun	Mashed potatoes (½ cup)
	French fried potatoes—20 pieces	Milk—1 glass (8 oz.)
		Apple pie—1 piece

In which of the following was her diet deficient?

(T) 1. Calcium	(F) 5. Niacin
(F) 2. Calories	(F) 6. Protein
(F) 3. Carbohydrates	(T) 7. Vitamin A
(T) 4. Iron	(T) 8. Vitamin C

The format of this variation looks like a multiple-choice item, but the task for the student is to judge whether each choice is true or false in relation to the original question; therefore it is basically a series of true-false items. The variation can be an efficient way to test for knowledge of categories, classifications or characteristics, and for simple applications. It is particularly effective for testing a particular part of a topic in depth. The format reduces the reading load for the student and the question serves as a frame of reference for judging truth or falsity, thus removing some of the ambiguity in true-false statements.

Writing Multiple-Choice Items

The multiple-choice item is the most flexible of the objective item types. It can be used to appraise the achievement of any of the educational objectives that can be measured by a paper-and-pencil test except those relating to skill in written expression and originality. An ingenious and talented item writer can construct multiple-choice items that require not only the recall of knowledge but also the use of skills of comprehension, interpretation, application, analysis, or synthesis to arrive at the keyed answer.

The multiple-choice item consists of two parts: the stem, which presents the problem, and the list of possible answers or options. In the standard form of the item, one of the options is the correct or best answer and the others are misleads or foils or distractors. The stem of the item may be presented either as a question or as an incomplete statement. The form of the stem apparently makes no difference in the overall effectiveness of the item (Dunn and Goldstein, 1959) as long as the stem presents a clear and specific problem to the examinee.

The number of options used in the multiple-choice question differs on different tests, and there is no real reason why it cannot vary for items in the same test. An item must have at least three answer choices to be classified as a multiple-choice item and the typical pattern is to have four or five answer choices to reduce the probability of guessing the answer. A distinction should be made between the number of options written for a multiple-choice item and the number of effective or functioning options that the item has. In the poor example below, written for an eighth-grade test on health, the item will really function as a two-choice item because no one is likely to choose option A or D. The revised item still presents four answer choices but is now likely to really function as a four-choice question because options A and D have been made more reasonable.

Example

Poor: About how many calories are recommended daily for a girl, age 14, height 62 in., weight 103 lbs, moderately active?

A. 0
B. 2,000
C. 2,500
D. 30,000

Better: About how many calories are recommended daily for a girl, age 14, height 62 in., weight 103 lbs, moderately active?

A. 1,500
B. 2,000
C. 2,500
D. 3,000

The revised item will probably be more difficult than the original one because the options are closer together in value. The difficulty of a multiple-choice item depends upon the process called for in the item as well as the closeness of the options. Consider the set of three items shown below, all relating to the meaning of the term "fortified food." We can predict that version I will be relatively easy, version II somewhat more difficult, and version III still more difficult. In version I, the stem is a direct copy of the definition of "fortified food" in the textbook and the misleads are not terms used to indicate the addition of nutrients to foods. The difference between I and II is that the stem of II recasts the textbook definition into a novel form and calls for a different mental process than I. The difference between II and III is in the closeness of the options.

Version I

When a nutrient has been added that is not present in the natural food, the food is said to be

A. fortified.
B. processed.
C. pasteurized.
D. refined.

Version II

In the processing of milk for sale, Vitamin D concentrate has been added to provide at least 400 U.S.P. units per quart. The carton can then legally state that the milk is

A. fortified.
B. processed.
C. pasteurized.
D. refined.

Version III

In the processing of milk for sale, Vitamin D concentrate has been added to provide at least 400 U.S.P. units per quart. The carton can then legally state that the milk is

A. fortified.
B. enriched.
C. irradiated.
D. restored.

Good multiple-choice questions take time and skill to construct. One way to cut down on the time is to draw from existing pools of items; selected references to collections of items in different content areas are provided at the end of the chapter. A step-by-step analysis of the process of constructing multiple-choice items is provided in the booklet, "Multiple-Choice Questions; A Close Look" (Educational Testing Service, 1963). On the following pages a series of suggestions are given for improving both the stem and the options of multiple-choice questions.

1. *Be sure the stem of the item clearly formulates a problem.* The stem should be worded so that the student clearly understands what problem or question is

being asked before he reads the answer choices. Look at the poor example below. When one finishes reading the stem, he knows only that the item is related to a part of the pancreas. He has no idea what the problem is until he reads each of the options. The answer choices that are provided are heterogeneous in content, that is, one relates to structure, one to function, one to permanence, and one to location. The poor item is really nothing more than four true-false items with the words "The cell islets of the pancreas" in common. The revised item provides both a more clearly formulated problem in the stem and a more homogeneous set of answer choices.

Example

Poor: The cell islets of the pancreas

A. contain ducts.
B. produce insulin.
C. disappear as one grows older.
D. are located around the edge of the pancreas.

Better: The cell islets of the pancreas secrete the substance called

A. trypsin.
B. insulin.
C. secretin.
D. adrenalin.

2. *Include as much of the item as possible in the stem and keep options as short as possible.* In the interests of economy of space, economy of reading time, and clear statement of the problem, try to word and arrange the item so that the answer choices can be kept relatively short. If the same words and phrases are repeated in all or most of the options, as in the poor example below, rewrite the stem to include the repetitious material if it is needed to make the item clear. Answer choices that are long in relation to the stem frequently occur because of failure to formulate a problem clearly in the stem.

Example

Poor: The term "empty-calorie" food designates

A. a food that has few essential nutrients but high caloric value.
B. a food that has neither essential nutrients nor caloric value.
C. a food that has both high nutritive value and high caloric value.
D. a food that has high nutritive value but low caloric value.

Better: The term "empty-calorie" is applied to foods that are

A. low in nutrients, high in calories.
B. low both in nutrients and calories.
C. high both in nutrients and calories.
D. high in nutrients, low in calories.

3. *Include in the stem only the material needed to make the problem clear and specific.* Items with long, wordy stems containing material that is irrelevant to the problem are likely to reduce the effectiveness and efficiency of the test. First, the added material increases the reading load of the test, thus making it more difficult to separate generalized skill in reading from competence specific to the subject matter area. Second, it increases reading time at the expense of answering time, making the test inefficient. The practice of including irrelevant material in the stem, as in the poor example below, appears to be a result of the teacher's misinterpretation of the idea that tests should teach as well as test. Tests teach as well as test when they (1) reflect accurately the objectives of instruction; (2) pose clear and meaningful questions or problems; and (3) are commented on specifically and returned promptly to the students; not when new material or review material is introduced in the test item.

If the purpose of the test item is to appraise whether the examinee can differentiate data necessary to solve a problem or support an argument from those that are either unnecessary or irrelevant, then one would have to include extra data in posing the problem. In this instance, though, the extra material is central to the process being measured; therefore it would not be irrelevant.

Example

Poor: Cells of one kind belong to a particular group performing a specialized duty. We call this group of cells a tissue. All of us have different kinds of tissues in our bodies. Which of the following would be classified as epithelial tissue?

A. Tendons
B. Adenoids and tonsils
C. Mucous membranes
D. Cartilage

Better: Which of the following would be classified as epithelial tissue?

A. Tendons
B. Adenoids and tonsils
C. Mucous membranes
D. Cartilage

4. *Use the negative only sparingly in the stem of an item.* Negative stems when combined with the answer choices can present difficult reading problems to students. (See the example on page 112 and material on negatives in true-false items on page 98.) Negative items also provide the teacher with little information concerning the positive knowledge that a student has.

There are times when it is important for the student to know the exception or to be able to detect errors. For these purposes, a few items with the words "not" or "except," in the stem may be justified, particularly when overinclusion is a common error for students. When a negative word is used in a stem, it should be underlined and/or capitalized to call the student's attention to it.

The poor example below was written to measure whether students knew the function of the semicircular canals, but the item as written does not measure this aspect of the student's knowledge. The revised example measures more directly what the teacher wanted to test for. The second "better" example shows a more appropriate use of the negative stem because (1) the most common error made by students about the duties of the Food and Drug Administration is to include inspection of meat which is the duty of the Department of Agriculture; and (2) it would be difficult to get three plausible misleads if the item were stated in positive form.

Example

Poor: Which of the following structures of the ear is *NOT* concerned with hearing?

A. Eardrum
B. Oval window
C. Semicircular canals
D. Cochlea

Better: 1. Which one of the following structures of the ear helps to maintain balance?

A. Eardrum
B. Oval window
C. Semicircular canals
D. Cochlea

2. Which one of the following activities is *NOT* the responsibility of the Food and Drug Administration?

A. Inspection of warehouses storing food for interstate shipment.
B. Inspection of slaughter houses that ship meat across state lines.
C. Initiation of court action to remove an adulterated food from the market.
D. Testing samples of foods for interstate sale.

5. *Use novel material in formulating problems to measure understanding or ability to apply principles.* Most teacher-made tests focus too closely on rote memory of the text or material presented in the classroom and neglect measurement of the ability to use information. The multiple-choice item is well adapted to measuring understanding but a novel situation must be presented to the student if more than rote memory is to be required to answer the question. The second and third variations of the example on p. 104 illustrate an attempt to move away from the form in which the concept was stated in an eighth-grade text on

health. Two examples are given below to illustrate how an item can be structured to appraise ability to use information.

Example

Rote memory: 1. Which of the following foods will yield the largest number of calories when metabolized in the body?

A. 1 gram of fat
B. 1 gram of sugar
C. 1 gram of starch
D. 1 gram of protein

Application: Which of the following would result in the greatest reduction of calories if it were eliminated from the daily diet?

A. 1 tablespoon of butter
B. 1 tablespoon of granulated sugar
C. 1 slice of white, enriched bread
D. 1 boiled egg

Rote memory: 2. Death from pneumonia and influenza is most frequent among

A. infants and aged people.
B. infants and elementary school children.
C. teenagers and aged people.
D. teenagers and young adults.

Interpretation: Look at the graph below which shows the death rate from disease A by age group.

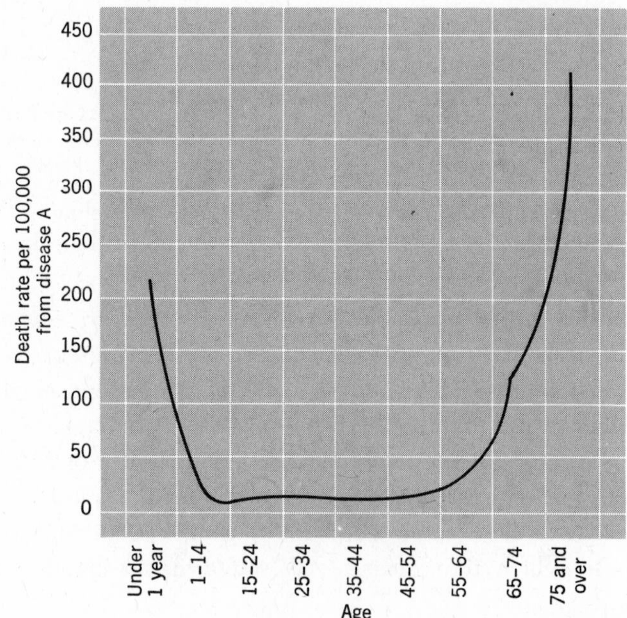

Which of the following diseases could be disease A?

A. Pneumonia
B. Cancer
C. Tuberculosis
D. Heart disease

6. *Be sure that there is one and only one correct or clearly best answer.* In the typical multiple-choice item, the examinee is instructed to choose one and only one answer. Having instructed the examinee to choose *the* answer that is best, the test constructor is obligated to provide one and only one for each item. This seems obvious, but many items on classroom tests either have two or more equally good answers or no good answer. Thus in the following example, B was keyed as the correct answer but there is also a large element of correctness for C, D and E. The revised version eliminates this fault but will probably be an easy item.

Example

Poor: A color-blind boy inherits the trait from a

A. male parent.
B. female parent.
C. maternal grandparent.
D. paternal grandparent.
E. remote ancestor.

Better: A color-blind boy most probably inherited the trait from his

A. father.
B. mother.
C. paternal grandfather.
D. paternal grandmother.

In addition to making sure that there is *only* one correct best answer, the item writer should see to it that the one answer is unequivocally right. It is his responsibility to use his very best scholarship, as well as his skill in phrasing stem and answer choices, to produce a problem and answer with which experts in the field will agree.

7. *Be sure wrong answer choices are plausible.* One of the major advantages of the multiple-choice item is that it can require the examinee to select his answer from among three, four, or five answer choices, thus reducing the chance of guessing the answer. However, the wrong answer choices must be ones that will attract examinees who have no or only partial information. To accomplish this, the wrong answer choices should be logically consistent with the stem and should represent common errors made by students at a particular grade or ability level. This is related to the point made on pp. 103–104 about difficulty.

In the first poor example, options A and C are compounds, not elements, and thus not logically consistent with the stem. In the second poor example options C and D are very implausible.

Example

Poor: 1. Which of the following elements is found in proteins but not in carbohydrates or fats?

A. Carbon dioxide
B. Oxygen
C. Water
D. Nitrogen

2. The gas that is formed in the cells after the oxidation of food and taken to the lungs and expelled is

A. oxygen.
B. carbon dioxide.
C. helium.
D. chlorine.

8. *Be sure no unintentional clues to the correct answer are given.* Inexperienced test constructors frequently give away the correct answer to an item or give clues that permit the examinee to eliminate one or more of the wrong answer choices from consideration. Dunn and Goldstein (1959) have shown that items containing irrelevant cues or specific determiners, correct answers consistently longer than incorrect answers, and grammatical inconsistencies between the stem and the options are easier than items without these faults. Chase (1964) demonstrated that examinees can learn to use length of option as a cue to the correct answer, and Wahlstrom and Boersma (1960) have shown that ninth graders can be taught to use various item writing faults to improve their scores on multiple-choice tests.

Examples of some types of unintentional cues are given below. Number 1 is an example of a clang association, that is, a repetition of a word or phrase or sound in the keyed answer and stem. Number 2 contains specific determiners that have the same effect in multiple-choice options as in true-false statements (see p. 98). In number 3, the keyed answer is much longer than the other options. Number 4 is an example of one kind of grammatical inconsistency in which the word "a" in the stem implies a singular word but options A and C are both plural.

The revised items show how each of these faults can be corrected to make the item potentially more effective in measuring knowledge rather than test-wiseness.

Example

Poor: 1. Clang association
The function of the platelets in the blood is to help in

A. carrying oxygen to the cells.
B. carrying food to the cells.
C. clotting of the blood.
D. fighting disease.

2. Specific determiners
Which of the following is characteristic of anaerobic bacteria?

A. They never live in soil.
B. They can live without molecular oxygen.
C. They always cause disease.
D. They can carry on photosynthesis.

3. Length cues
The term "side effect" of a drug refers to

A. additional benefits from the drug.
B. the chain effect of drug action.
C. the influence of drugs on crime.
D. any action of a drug in the body other than the one the doctor wanted the drug to have.

4. Grammatical inconsistency
Penicillin is obtained from a

A. bacteria.
B. mold.
C. coal-tars.
D. tropical tree.

Better: 1. Which of the following structures in the blood help in forming blood clots?

A. Red blood cells
B. Lymphocytes
C. Platelets
D. Monocytes

2. The *one* characteristic that distinguishes *all* anaerobic bacteria is their ability to

A. withstand extreme variation in air temperature.
B. live without molecular oxygen.
C. live as either saprophytes or parasites.
D. reproduce either in living cells or non-living culture media.

3. Which of the following, if it occurred, would be a side-effect of aspirin for a man who had been taking two aspirin tablets every three hours for a heavy cold and slight fever?

A. Normal body temperature
B. Reduction in frequency of coughing
C. Easier breathing
D. Ringing in the ears

4. Penicillin is obtained from

A. bacteria.
B. molds.
C. coal tars.
D. tropical trees.

9. *Use the option "none of these" or "none of the above" only when the keyed answer can be classified unequivocally as right or wrong.* This type of option has been used by experienced test writers on tests of spelling, mathematics, and study skills. In these types of tests, an absolutely correct answer can be given. On other types of tests, where the student is to choose the best answer and where the keyed answer is the best answer but not necessarily absolutely correct, the use of "none of these" or "none of the above" is inappropriate.

Teachers tend to use this type of option indiscriminately. On teacher-made tests, the option frequently fails to make any sense because it does not complete the stem grammatically, as shown in the item below which appeared on a tenth grade biology test.

Example

Poor: Of the following the one that is *never* a function of the stem of plants is

A. conduction.
B. food storage.
C. photosynthesis.
D. support.
E. none of the above.

Not only is the option "none of the above" in the poor example inconsistent grammatically with the stem, but it is also logically inconsistent with the stem. Option E does not name a function of the plant and the double negative effect of the option and the "never" in the stem makes comprehension of the meaning of the item difficult. There is no way of revising the item to make it better since any function of a plant is performed by the stem in some plant.

Some studies of the use of "none of these" as an option have indicated that use of the option makes items more difficult and more discriminating [Boynton (1950), Hughes and Trimble (1965)], but other studies have failed to confirm this finding [Wesman and Bennett (1946), Rimland (1960)].

If "none of these" or its equivalent is used as an option in items requiring quantitative solutions or in spelling tests, it should be used as frequently for the correct option as any other answer choice and the stem of the item should be phrased as a question. On these kinds of tests, the option functions best if it is used as the correct answer on some of the easier items at the beginning of the test to reinforce the instructions that "none of the above" is sometimes the correct answer.

The poor example given below represents a poor use of the "none of the above" option in an item calling for a numerical answer because only approximations are given rather than exact quantities. Although option B was keyed as the correct answer, option E is the better answer since the estimates of the blood volume for an average adult range from a low of 10 pints to a high of 16 pints. One could also raise the issue of the importance of a junior high school student's knowing this particular fact.

Example

Poor: How many pints of blood does a normal human adult of average weight have?

A. 3 pints
B. 13 pints
C. 30 pints
D. 50 pints
E. None of the above

Better: Approximately what percent of the body weight of a healthy human adult is blood?

A. 3 to 5 percent
B. 8 to 9 percent
C. 12 to 15 percent
D. 20 to 25 percent

10. *Avoid the use of "all of these" or "all of the above" in the typical multiple-choice item.* Usually when the option "all of these" is used on teacher-made tests, it is the correct answer. Items using this option tend to be somewhat easy because the examinee can get the item correct even though he has only partial information. Look at the poor example below. Assume that the student has been instructed to mark only one answer and that he thinks that only age and weight are used to compute basal energy requirements. He must mark D for his answer; thus he gets credit for having complete information even though he does not. In the revised version, he must have full information to arrive at the keyed answer.

The option "all of these," is much more effective if it is used in the variation of the complex multiple-choice item described in the next section.

Example

Poor: Which of the following factors must be considered in computing basal energy requirements?

A. Age
B. Height
C. Weight
D. All of the above

Better: Which of the following factors must be considered in computing basal energy requirements?

A. Weight only
B. Age only
C. Height and weight only
D. Age and weight only
E. Age, height, and weight

VARIATIONS OF MULTIPLE-CHOICE ITEMS. A number of variations of the standard multiple-choice items have been used on tests. Gerberich (1960) gives illustrations of most of these variations. One commonly used variation is the matching item that will be discussed in a separate section. In this section, we will discuss two variations that are used frequently.

1. *Complex multiple-choice item.* This variation gets its name from the format and the combinations of options that are used as answer choices. The variation is most effective when it is used to appraise knowledge of or ability to apply or interpret multiple causation, effects, functions or uses. Example 1 illustrates an effective use of the item type because it requires the student to discriminate between both the kind of food and the kind of commerce that come under the jurisdiction of the Food and Drug Administration. Hughes and Trimble (1965) have shown that this type of item is both more difficult and more discriminating than the typical form of multiple-choice item that tests for the same knowledge.

Example 2 represents a poor use of the complex multiple-choice item and several faults of item construction. Although there are multiple signs of impaired circulation, the options are short, therefore the knowledge could be tested more efficiently in the usual format as in the item on p. 114. The technical faults of the item are as follows: (1) no specific problem is presented to the examinee; (2) signs numbered 1, 2, and 3 are used in all the answer choices so that the student is required only to determine whether numbers 4 and 5 are correct; (3) the method of presenting choices (contrast between option C and options B and D) is varied which creates unnecessary difficulty for the student.

The complex multiple-choice item should be used very sparingly on teacher-made tests.

Example 1

1. Look at each of the food processing or producing activities below.

   1. A housewife makes jellies and sells them in her home town.
   2. A butcher makes scrapple and pork sausage and sells them only in the state of Maryland.
   3. A food processor makes jellies in California and sells them in New York.
   4. A slaughter house in Chicago ships meats to all states.
   5. A citrus grower produces oranges in Florida and ships them to all Eastern states.

Which of the above would be subject to the regulations and supervision of the federal Food and Drug Administration?

A. 2 and 4 only
B. 3 and 5 only
C. 3, 4, and 5 only
D. 1, 3, and 5 only
E. All of them

Example 2

Poor: If a bandage or cast on the arm is too tight, it may interfere with the circulation in the arm. Signs of interference with circulation include

1. cold.
2. blanching.
3. numbness.
4. swelling.
5. loss of motion.

A. All of these
B. 1, 2, 3 and 4
C. All except 5
D. 1, 2, 3 and 5

2. *Use of paired statements as stimuli.* This variation is illustrated below.

Example

Directions: Items 1 through 3 are based on pairs of statements. Read each statement carefully. On your answer sheet, mark:

A. If the amount in statement I is greater than that in statement II.
B. If the amount in statement II is greater than that in statement I.
C. If the amount in statement I is equal to that in statement II.

(B) 1. I Caloric value of 1 tablespoon of cane sugar.
II Caloric value of 1 tablespoon of butter.

(A) 2. I The daily requirement of calories for a male lumberjack, 73 inches tall, weight 190 lbs, age 25.
II The daily requirement of calories for a male office clerk, 73 inches tall, weight 190 lbs, age 25.

(A) 3. I The daily requirement of iron for a 16-year-old girl.
II The daily requirement of iron for a 16-year-old boy.

The paired item format is an efficient and effective way of measuring judgment of relative amounts or quantities, relative effects of changing conditions, or relative chronology. This format should preferably be used for content having established quantitative values. For example, the use of the pair of statements: "(I) The number of hours of sleep needed by a 14-year-old boy and (II) The number of hours of sleep needed by a 30-year-old man," would be undesirable because there is no empirically determined value for the number of hours of sleep required for any age group.

Writing Matching Items

The characteristic that distinguishes the matching item from the ordinary multiple-choice item is that there are several problems whose answers must be drawn from a single list of possible answers. The matching item has most frequently been used to measure factual information such as meanings of terms, dates of events, the achievements of men, symbols for chemical elements, and authors of books. Effective matching items can be constructed by basing the set of items on a chart, map, diagram, or drawing. Features of the figure can be numbered and the examinee can be asked to match names, functions, etc., with the numbers on the figure. This method of constructing matching items is particularly useful in tests dealing with study skills, science, or technology, for example, identification of cell structures on a biology test.

Matching items on teacher-made tests usually have many technical faults and as a result tend to be relatively superficial measurement devices. Look at the sample matching exercise on the next page, which appeared on a test in health and hygiene for an eighth-grade class.

This example illustrates most of the common mistakes made in preparing matching items. First, the directions are vague; they do not specify the basis for matching. Second, the set of stimuli is too heterogeneous for a good matching exercise. How many answer choices in Column II are logically possible answers for the first statement in Column I? For the second? The statements in Column I have very little in common except that they relate to teeth and dental health in general. Third, the set is too long and the answer choices in Column II are not arranged in any systematic order. Even if the examinee knows the answer to a statement, he has to search through the entire list in Column II to find it, which is time consuming. Fourth, some of the entries are vague; for example, 9, 11, and 12 in Column I and I, L, and M in Column II. The vagueness makes it difficult to justify the answer keyed as correct by the teacher; furthermore,

Example

Poor: Directions: Place the correct letter to the left of each number. Use each letter only once.

	Column I	*Column II*
(P)	1. Number of permanent teeth	A. Malocclusion
(I)	2. Vitamin D	B. Tear and rip food
(N)	3. Vitamin C	C. Trench mouth
(K)	4. Enamel	D. Straightening teeth
(O)	5. Bleeding gums	E. Jawbone socket
(C)	6. Vincent's Angina	F. Contains nerves and blood vessels
(D)	7. Orthodontia	G. Grind food
(E)	8. Alveolus	H. Crown
(A)	9. Lower jaw protuding	I. Sunshine
(F)	10. Pulp	J. Cleaning device
(M)	11. Acid	K. Hardest substance
(L)	12. Low percentage of decay	L. Primitives
(B)	13. Cuspids	M. Decay
(G)	14. Molars	N. Citrus fruits
(H)	15. Visible part of tooth	O. Gingivitis
(J)	16. Dental floss	P. 32

Note. The "correct" answers are those designated by the teacher who constructed the exercise.

the accuracy of number 12 can be questioned. Fifth, there are 16 statements in Column I and 16 answer choices in Column II. If the student knows 15, he automatically gets the sixteenth correct.

The guides for writing good matching items are given below.

1. *Keep the set of statements in a single matching exercise homogeneous.* They should all be parts of a tooth or all be diseases of the teeth and gums or all methods of promoting good oral hygiene. A homogeneous set will require the student to make finer discriminations to arrive at a correct answer.

2. *Keep the set of items relatively short.* One reason for keeping the set short is that the statements are more likely to be homogeneous in content. The second reason is that a short answer list puts less of a clerical burden on the examinee.

3. *If the two columns differ in length of statements, have the students choose answers from the column with the least reading load.* The reason for this suggestion is that the answer column will be read several times by the student and it takes less time to read short statements than long ones.

4. *Use a heading for each column that accurately describes its content.* A descriptive heading helps to define the task for the examinee. If the test

constructor is unable to identify a heading that specifically defines the content, then he probably has a heterogeneous collection of items.

5. *Have more answer choices than the number of statements to be answered unless answer choices can be used more than once.* The larger number of answer choices reduces the probability of guessing the answer or obtaining automatic credit as in the poor example.

6. *Arrange the answer choices in a logical order if one exists.* If a student knows the answer, he should be able to find it easily. Arranging names in alphabetical order or dates in chronological order reduces the time required to find the answer.

7. *Specify in the directions the basis for matching and whether answer choices can be used more than once.* This will tend to reduce ambiguity and to result in a more uniform task for all examinees.

A variation of the matching exercise is the classification type or master list. This variation can be used quite effectively to appraise application, comprehension or interpretation. It is an efficient way of exploring range of mastery of a concept or related set of concepts. An illustration of this type of exercise is given below.

Example—Master Matching

Instructions: Below are given four kinds of appeals that advertisers of health and beauty products make.

A. Appeal to fear or a sense of insecurity.

B. Appeal to snobbery or identification with a particular, small group or individual.

C. Appeal to desire to be like others, to join the "bandwagon."

D. Appeal to authority.

Statements 1 to 6 are advertisements of imaginary products. Read each statement carefully. For each statement, mark the letter of the appeal that is being used. Answer choices may be used more than once.

(A) 1. Don't let iron-tired blood get you down. Keep your verve and vivacity. Take Infantol.

(D) 2. Research shows Lucy's Little Lethal Pills are 10 times more effective than ordinary pain-killers.

(B) 3. Dutchess Poorhouse, the international beauty, bathes her face twice a day with Myrtle's Turtle Oil.

(B) 4. Men, are you tired of a woman's deodorant? Be a man. Use No-Sweat. Leave the weaker stuff to the weaker sex.

(B) 5. At $1,629.21 the Inside Jogger is not for everyone. Only a select few can be proud owners of one! Are you one of these?

(C) 6. Be one of the crowd. Drink and serve Popsie's Cola.

Preparing the Objective Test for Use

Objective tests, particularly multiple-choice tests, should be reproduced in some way so that each student has his own copy. Oral administration of objective tests is not satisfactory. Many schools have a spirit duplicator or "Ditto" machine that is adequate for reproducing tests for groups of moderate size. For large groups, mimeographing is preferable. More important than the process of duplication is the quality of work, both in organizing the layout of the test and in typing up the master copy. The most important points to consider in arranging the items of the test will be discussed in the paragraphs that follow.

1. *Arrange items on the test so that they are easy to read.* In the interest of the person taking the test, items should not be crowded together on the test paper. Multiple-choice questions are easier to read if each response option is on a separate line. Having part of an item on one page and part on the next page should be avoided since such an arrangement may confuse the students. If several items all refer to a single diagram or chart, try to arrange the test so that the diagram or chart and all of the items are on the same page.

2. *Plan the layout of the test so that a separate answer sheet can be used to record answers.* Consideration should be given to the convenience of the student in recording his answers and to the convenience of the person scoring the test. An objective test can be scored much more quickly and efficiently if the answers are recorded on a separate answer sheet. Many teachers feel that the use of a separate answer sheet makes the test-taking task more difficult for students. However, even third-grade students can very quickly be taught to use a separate answer sheet and usually have little or no difficulty in using one. Many standardized achievement tests use separate answer sheets with little or no difficulty at the third-grade level. The use of a separate answer sheet represents a test-taking skill that should be taught to students and practice in the skill should be provided early in the school program. Part of a homemade answer sheet that is adaptable to both true-false and multiple-choice items is shown in Fig. 4.1 on p. 120.

3. *Group items of the same format (true-false, multiple-choice or matching) together.* Each different kind of objective item requires a different set of directions. Grouping items of the same format together makes it possible to write a concise and clear set of directions that will apply throughout that part of the test. The different kinds of items also require different response sets or approaches to the item on the part of the student. The student is better able to maintain an appropriate response set or approach if the items of the same type are grouped together.

Course ______________________ Name ______________________

Exam ______________________ Date ______________________

Instructions: Read the directions on the test sheet carefully, and follow them exactly. For each test item, mark your choice for the correct answer by blocking out the letter which corresponds to the best answer for the test item.

Item	Answer	Item	Answer	Item	Answer
1	A B C D E	26	A B C D E	51	A B C D E
2	A B C D E	27	A B C D E	52	A B C D E
3	A B C D E	28	A B C D E	53	A B C D E
4	A B C D E	29	A B C D E	54	A B C D E

Fig. 4.1 Part of a homemade answer sheet.

4. *Within item type, group items dealing with the same content together.* This practice will help reduce the feeling that the test lacks unity or coherence and will encourage a more integrated approach to the items on the part of the student. It will also help both the student and the teacher to see strong and weak points of the student in dealing with the content.

5. *Arrange items so that difficulty progresses from easy to hard.* This is most important when testing time is limited so that some items on the test will not be attempted by all students. Those unattempted items should be the more difficult ones that the examinee would not have been likely to answer correctly even if he had reached them. On power tests, this kind of arrangement is supposed to have some psychological advantages in encouraging students, particularly young children and the less able student, to continue to attempt the items on the test rather than giving up. However, the practice is supported by professional judgment rather than by empirical evidence.

6. *Write a set of specific directions for each item type.* A good set of directions will provide information about how the examinee is to record his answers, the basis on which he is to select his answers, and the scoring procedures that will be used.

For a test made up of multiple-choice items that will not be corrected for guessing and for which separate answer sheets are used, one might use the following set of directions.

> *Directions:* Read each item and decide which choice *best* completes the statement or answers the question.
>
> Mark your answers on the separate answer sheet. Do *not* mark them on the

test booklet. Indicate your answer by blacking out on the answer sheet the letter corresponding to your choice. That is, if you think that choice B is the best answer to item 1, black out the B in the row after No. 1 on your answer sheet.

Your score will be the number of right answers, so it will be to your advantage to answer every question, even if you are not sure of the right answer.

Be sure your name is on your answer sheet.

For a test made up of true-false questions in which answers are to be recorded on the test paper and the total score will be corrected for guessing, the following set of directions could be used.

Directions: Read each of the following statements carefully.

If all or any part of the statement is false, circle the F in front of the statement.

If the statement is completely true, circle the T in front of the statement.

Your score will be the number of right answers minus the number of wrong answers, so *do not guess blindly.* If you are not reasonably sure of an answer, omit the question.

Be sure your name is on your test.

7. *Be sure that one item does not provide cues to the answer of another item or items.* Unless one is very careful in assembling items for a test, the answer to an item may be given away by a previous item. All of the items that are finally selected should be carefully checked because it is possible for a true-false or completion item to give clues to the answer of a multiple-choice item or vice-versa. Thus, in the example, the true-false item provides a cue to the answer to the objective item.

Example

1. T̲ F The spores of the bacteria causing botulism are present in soil and air.

2. Which of the following bacteria form spores?

A. Staphlococcus causing "food poisoning."
B̲. Bacillus causing botulism.
C. Bacillus causing typhoid fever.
D. Pneumococcus causing pneumonia.

8. *Be sure that the correct responses form essentially a random pattern.* Some classroom teachers attempt to make their job of scoring easier by establishing a regular pattern of correct answers. For example, on a true-false test they will use a repetitive pattern such as T, T, F, F, F or on a multiple-choice test a pattern such as A, C, B, D. When this is done, some test-wise students soon discover the pattern and use it as a means of answering items that they really do not know. On four-option multiple-choice tests, sometimes the correct answers appear much more frequently in the second and third positions than in the first and last positions. It is desirable on a multiple-choice test to have the correct answer in each of the possible response positions about the same percentage of

time. For example, on a four-option multiple-choice test of 50 items, each response position should contain the keyed answer in not less than 10 nor more than 15 items.

Scoring the Objective Test

A basic decision that needs to be made before the test is given is whether a correction for guessing will be used. Students should be told whether the correction will be used because it may influence their strategy in taking the test. Test experts are not in complete agreement about the usefulness of the correction for guessing.

It is well known that there are marked differences among examinees in their tendency to guess on an objective test when they are not sure of the answer. These differences in willingness to guess introduce some variation in scores that is not related to real differences in achievement among students. One intended purpose of instructing examinees not to guess and of imposing a penalty for wrong answers is to try to make the guessing behavior more alike for all examinees.

Waters (1967) studied the effects of different scoring formulas on the number of items omitted on a test. The scoring formulas used were rights only, rights − ¼ wrong, rights − wrongs, rights − 2 × wrongs, and rights − 4 × wrongs. He found that the number of omits did increase as the penalty for wrong answers increased, but that the examinees with the more severe scoring penalties did not omit as many items as they should have if they were to achieve the highest score. He also found that the average number of items right was about the same for all scoring patterns. It appears that neither the instruction not to guess with a threat of penalty for wrong answers nor the instruction to answer every question whether you are sure of the answer or not make people behave the same way on an objective test. The probability of taking a risk appears to depend as much on the person's personality as on the test directions.

The formula for correction for guessing that is generally used is

$$\text{Corrected score} = R - \frac{W}{n-1}$$

where R is the number of questions answered correctly;
W is the number of questions answered incorrectly;
n is the number of answer choices for an item.

Note that questions for which examinees do not give an answer, that is, omits, do not count in this formula for guessing. On a true-false test where there are only two possible answers, $n - 1$ in the formula becomes $2 - 1$, or 1, and the correction for guessing is the number of right answers minus the number of wrong answers.

The two examples below, one based on a true-false test and one on a multiple-choice test, illustrate how the formula works.

Example 1

		Student Performance		
Type of test	n	R	W	*Omits*
True-false	2	48	20	7

$$\text{Corrected score} = 48 - \frac{20}{2-1} = 48 - \frac{20}{1} = 28$$

Example 2

		Student Performance		
Type of test	n	R	W	*Omits*
Multiple choice	5	48	20	7

$$\text{Corrected score} = 48 - \frac{20}{5-1} = 48 - \frac{20}{4} = 43$$

The above formula assumes (1) that a person either knows the right answer or else guesses, that is, that he never responds on the basis of misinformation, and (2) that all choices are equally attractive to a person who does not know the answer. These assumptions are rarely justified. On the one hand, a good item writer formulates misleads so as to capitalize on the misconceptions of the poorly informed. On the other hand, the person with partial information or with some shrewdness about objective items can often eliminate one or two options from consideration. The correction formula is, therefore, at best a rough and approximate adjustment that can compensate for gross differences in readiness to mark items.

Guessing on tests presents the most serious problem in tests that are highly speeded or that have items with only two answer choices. The scores obtained from such tests will probably be more dependable if they are corrected for guessing. In multiple-choice tests that have four or five answer choices and liberal enough time limits to permit all or most examinees to attempt every item, a score that is simply the number of right answers is quite satisfactory and there is little or no gain from correcting for guessing.

There have been a number of suggestions made for more complex scoring patterns for objective tests, particularly multiple choice items. Most of these increase scoring time and to some extent test-taking time. Some of these appear to produce small gains in precision of measurement per item, but it is not clear that they provide a gain per minute of testing time. Readers who are interested in these variations are referred to references (Ebel, 1965; Davis, 1959; Combs et al, 1955) at the end of the chapter.

Analyzing and Using the Results of Objective Tests

An analysis of the responses the pupils made to the items on the test can serve two important purposes. In the first place, the test results provide a diagnostic technique for studying the learnings of the class and the failures to learn and for guiding further teaching and study. In the second place, the responses of pupils to the separate items and a review of the items in the light of these responses provide a basis for preparing better tests another year.

The basic analysis that is needed is a tabulation of the responses that have been made to each item on the test. We need to know how many pupils got each item right, how many chose each of the possible wrong answers, and how many omitted the item. It helps our understanding of the item if we have this information for the upper and lower fractions of the group, and perhaps also for those in the middle. From this type of tabulation, we can answer such questions as the following for each item:

1. How hard is the item?
2. Does it distinguish between the better and poorer students?
3. Do all the options attract responses, or are there some that are so unattractive that they might as well not be included?

A simple form can be prepared for recording the responses to each item, like that shown in Fig. 4.2. This can be put on a separate card for each item, and then the information can be accumulated in a permanent item file. This form is planned for a multiple-choice item with as many as five choices but can be used for true-false items by using only the A and B columns.

To illustrate the type of information that is provided by an item analysis, we present below certain items from a social studies test, together with the analysis of responses for each item. This test was given in 1960 to 100 high-school seniors who had had a course in current American problems. There were 95 items on the test. The highest score on the test was 85 and the lowest score was 14. The test papers were arranged in order of total score starting with the score of 85 and ending with the score of 14. The top 25 papers were selected to represent the upper group (score range 59 to 85) and the last 25 papers were selected to represent the lower group (score range 14 to 34). The count of responses is

Item: Which one of the following states was formed from the Northwest Territory?

A. Indiana
B. Iowa
C. Montana
D. Oregon

	Option					
	A	B	C	D	E	Omit
Upper 25%	10					
Middle 50%	17		1	2		
Lower 25%	5	1	1	3		

Fig. 4.2 Form for recording item-analysis data.

based on the 25 cases from the top and the 25 cases from the bottom of the group. The responses made to each item by each individual in the upper and lower groups were tallied to give the frequency of choosing each option. These frequencies are shown on the right. The correct option is underlined. Each item is followed by a brief discussion of the item data.

Item 1

"Everyone's switching to Breath of Spring Cigarettes!" is an example of the propaganda technique called

	Upper	*Lower*
A. glittering generality.	0	2
B. bandwagon.	25	20
C. testimonial.	0	2
D. plain folk.	0	1
(Omit)	0	0

This is an easy item, since all 25 in the upper group and 20 in the lower group get it right. However, it does differentiate in the desired direction, since what errors there are fall in the lower group. The item is also good in that all of the wrong answer choices are functioning; i.e., each wrong answer has been chosen by one or more persons in the lower group. Two or three easy items like this would be good "ice-breakers" with which to start a test.

Item 2

There were no federal income taxes before 1913 because prior to 1913

	Upper	*Lower*
A. the federal budget was balanced.	3	5
B. regular property taxes provided enough revenue to run the government.	9	15
<u>C.</u> a tax on income was unconstitutional.	13	0
D. the income of the average worker in the U.S. was too low to be taxed.	0	5
(Omit)	0	0

This was a difficult item but a very effective one. That it was difficult is shown by the fact that only 13 out of 50 got it right. That it was effective is shown by the fact that all 13 getting the item right were in the upper group. All of the wrong options attracted some choices in the lower group and all of the wrong options attracted more of the lower group than the higher group. Incidentally, an item such as this shows how faulty the idea of "blind guessing" often is when an item is effectively written. In this item, the majority of the lower group concentrated upon one particular wrong option that was particularly plausible and appealing.

Item 3

Under the "corrupt practices act" the national committee of a political party would be permitted to accept a contribution of

	Upper	*Lower*
A. $10,000 from Mr. Jones.	15	6
B. $1,000 from the ABC Hat Corporation.	4	6
<u>C.</u> $5,000 from the National Association of Manufacturers.	2	6
D. $500 from union funds of a local labor union.	4	7
(Omit)	0	0

This item turned out poorly. First, the item was very difficult; only 8 out of the 50 or 16 percent of the students got it right. Second, the item is negatively discriminating, that is, correct answers were more frequent in the lower group than in the upper group. There are two possible explanations for the item analysis data: (1) the item was ambiguous especially for students who knew the most or (2) the students have not learned the provisions of the "corrupt practices act." There are two things that point to the second as the more probable explanation, the concentration of responses of the upper group at option A and the apparently random responses of the lower group that indicate random guessing. In order to arrive at the correct answer to the item the student would have to know (1) the limit placed on contributions to the national committee of a political party, (2) who is forbidden to make contributions, and (3) what kind of organization the National Association of Manufacturers is. The teacher would have to discuss the item with the class to determine where the difficulty lies but one might guess that it is points 1 and 3 that are causing difficulty in the upper group.

Item 4

The term "easy money" as used in economics means

	Upper	*Lower*
<u>A.</u> the ability to borrow money at low interest rates.	21	17
B. dividends that are paid on common stocks.	0	0
C. money that is won in contests.	0	0
D. money paid for unemployment compensation.	4	8
(Omit)	0	0

This item shows some discrimination in the desired direction (21 versus 17), but the differentiation is not very sharp. The response pattern is one that is quite common. Only two of the four choices are functioning at all. Nobody selects either the B or C choices. If we wished to use this item again, we might try substituting "wages paid for easy work" for option B and "Money given to people on welfare" for option C. The repeat of the word "easy" in option B and the idea of getting money for not working in option C might make the item more difficult and more discriminating.

Item statistics such as these can be used not only for evaluating the items but to guide review and restudy of the material with a class. The items that prove difficult for the class as a whole provide leads for further exploration. Discussion of these items with the class should throw light on the nature of the misunderstanding. The misunderstanding may in some cases be cleared up by brief further discussion, although in some cases a fuller review of the topic may be indicated. It is desirable, if local policies permit, to let pupils have their answer sheets and a copy of the test and to make the answer key available to them, so that they can themselves use the test as a guide to review and clarification of the points they missed. An examination should teach as well as test.

SUMMARY

The most difficult and demanding aspect of preparing good classroom tests is writing the test questions. In preparing a classroom test, the teacher can use essay questions, short-answer or completion questions, true-false or multiple-choice or matching items. The choice of item type should be made on the basis of the objective or process to be appraised by the item. If possible, the questions and items for the test should be prepared well in advance of time for testing and reviewed and edited before they are used on a test.

Often the questions and items on the classroom test do not appraise the abilities, skills, and knowledge that the teacher intended because of ambiguity and other faults in the item. Suggestions for writing all kinds of items to improve the accuracy and dependability of teacher made tests are given in the chapter. Some of the suggestions are based on empirical evidence but most of them represent the professional judgment of experts in measurement.

Adequate appraisal of student achievement through the use of essay questions requires not only well-formulated questions but also sound and consistent judgment of the quality of the answers. Essentially, the problem in obtaining accurate and dependable scoring of answers centers on maintaining consistent standards for all students regardless of who scores the paper or when the paper is scored. Suggestions are given in the chapter for improving scoring.

Although there is an unfortunate tendency for writers of objective items to concentrate on factual, often trivial, information, ability to understand, interpret, and apply can also be tested by items that follow this format. For the measurement of understanding, it is often desirable to describe a fairly complex problem situation or to present a fairly full set of data and to organize a set of related questions about the problem or data. Illustrations have been provided in this chapter.

In preparing the objective test for use, items should be grouped so as to emphasize relationships and to provide a general progression from easy to more difficult. Answer sheets and scoring stencils facilitate scoring. The issue of correction for guessing should be resolved in advance, and examinees should be told what procedure will apply.

Test results can be analyzed with profit to guide (1) further teaching and review and (2) the construction of additional tests in later years. Students should receive prompt and specific feedback on their performance on a test in order to promote learning.

QUESTIONS AND EXERCISES

1. Criticize the following features of an essay test planned for a ninth-grade social studies class:

   a. There will be 10 questions on the test.
   b. Each student will answer any 5.
   c. Each question will have a value of 20 points.
   d. One point will be taken off for each misspelled word and each grammatical error.
   e. A 5-point bonus will be given for neatness.
   f. Time for the test will be 40 minutes.

2. Criticize each of the following essay questions:

   a. Instead of talking just about France's industry and agriculture alone, we talked about them as part of the Common Market. What are the advantages to France as a member of the Common Market? What products, raw materials, and agricultural products does France contribute to the Common Market? (9th grade Social Studies)
   b. What should scientists do to make sure that scientific discoveries are used for the benefit of mankind rather than for the destruction of mankind? (8th grade Science)
   c. Select a character from a novel or short story that you have read this year. Give the name of the character and the title and author of the work in which he appeared. In a well-written paragraph, explain how this character has influenced your life. (12th grade English Literature)
   d. Discuss essay-type tests. (College Undergraduate class in Tests and Measurements)

3. For what types of objectives would an open-book multiple-choice examination be most appropriate? What would be the advantages and disadvantages of such an examination, as compared with the usual multiple-choice examination?

4. In appraising the fund of knowledge that a student has at his command, a teacher could use either completion items or multiple-choice items. To what factors should the teacher give major consideration in arriving at his final decision?

5. In what ways should a multiple-choice item designed to appraise understanding or application of a principle differ from one designed to appraise memory of the principle?

6. For which of the following tests would it be important to correct scores for guessing? Give the reason or reasons for your decision.

   a. A 100-item true-false test. All students answered all questions.
   b. A 70-item multiple-choice test of spatial relations. Each item has five answer choices. For each item, one or more than one answer choice may be correct. All students answered all questions.

c. A 50-item multiple-choice test with four answer choices, one of which is the keyed answer. Only forty percent of the examinees completed all items.
d. A 60-item multiple-choice test with four answer choices, one of which is the keyed answer. Ninety percent of the students answered all items.

7. What are the arguments for and against returning major examination papers to students?

8. A college teacher has given an objective test to a large class, scored the papers, and entered the scores in the class record book. What further steps might the teacher take before returning the papers to the students? Why?

9. Collect some examples of poor items you have seen on tests. Indicate what is wrong with each item.

10. Construct four multiple-choice items designed to measure understanding or application in some subject area in which you are interested.

11. Prepare a short objective test for a small unit that you are teaching or plan to teach. Indicate the objectives that you are trying to evaluate with each item. (Use the blueprint from question 3, p. 73, if one is available.)

REFERENCES

Boynton, M. Inclusion of "None of These" makes spelling items more difficult. *Educational and Psychological Measurement,* 1950, **10**, 431–432.

Chase, C. I. Relative length of options and response set in multiple-choice items. *Journal of Educational Measurement,* 1964, **1**, 38. (Abstract)

Coffman, W. & Kurfman, D. A comparison of two methods of reading essay examinations. *American Educational Research Journal,* 1968, **5**, 99–107.

Coombs, C. H., Milholland, J. E., & Womer, F. B. The assessment of partial knowledge. *Educational and Psychological Measurement,* 1955, **16**, 13–37.

Davis, F. B. Estimation and use of scoring weights for each choice in multiple-choice test items. *Educational and Psychological Measurement,* 1959, **19**, 291–298.

Dunn, T. F. & Goldstein, L. G. Test difficulty, validity, and reliability as functions of selective multiple-choice item construction principles. *Educational and Psychological Measurement,* 1959, **19**, 171–179.

Ebel, R. L. Confidence weighting and test reliability. *Journal of Educational Measurement,* 1965, **2**, 49–57.

Educational Testing Service, Test Development Division. *Multiple-choice questions: A close look.* Princeton, New Jersey: Educational Testing Service, 1963.

Feldhusen, J. F. An evaluation of college students' reactions to open book examinations. *Educational and Psychological Measurement,* 1961, **21**, 637–646.

Gerberich, J. R. *Specimen objective test items: A guide to achievement test construction.* New York: Longmans, Green and Co. (David McKay), 1956.

Gosling, G. W. H. *Marking English compositions.* Victoria, Australia: Australian Council for Educational Research, 1966. Pp. 22–37.

Hughes, H. H. & Trimble, W. E. The use of complex alternatives in multiple-choice items. *Educational and Psychological Measurement,* 1965, **25,** 117–126.

Rimland, B. The effects of varying time limits and of using right answer not given in experimental forms of the U.S. Navy Arithmetic Test. *Educational and Psychological Measurement,* 1960, **20,** 533–539.

Wason, P. Response to affirmative and negative binary statements. *British Journal of Psychology,* 1961, **52,** 133–142.

Wahlstrom, M. & Boersma, F. J. The influence of test-wiseness upon achievement. *Educational and Psychological Measurement,* 1968, **28,** 413–420.

Waters, L. K. Effect of perceived scoring formula on some aspects of test performance. *Educational and Psychological Measurement,* 1967, **27,** 1005–1010.

Wesman, A. G. & Bennett, G. K. The use of "None of These" as an option in test construction. *Journal of Educational Psychology,* 1946, **37,** 533–539.

Zern, D. Effects of variations in question phrasing on true-false answers by grade-school children. *Psychological Reports,* 1967, **20** (2), 527–533.

SUGGESTED ADDITIONAL READING

Anderson, H. R. & Lindquist, E. F. Revised by Harriet Stull. *Selected test items in American history: Bulletin No. 6.* Washington, D.C.: National Council for the Social Studies, 1964.

Anderson, H. R. & Lindquist, E. F. Revised by David K. Heenan. *Selected test items in world history, Third Edition: Bulletin No. 9.* Washington, D.C.: National Council for the Social Studies, 1960.

Berg, H. D. (Ed.) *Evaluation in social studies,* Thirty-Fifth Yearbook of the National Council for the Social Studies. Washington, D.C.: National Council for the Social Studies, 1965. Chapters 3, 4, 5, 7, 8, 10.

Commission on English. *End-of-year examinations in English for college-bound students grades 9–12.* Princeton, New Jersey: College Entrance Examination Board, 1963.

Commission on Undergraduate Education in the Biological Sciences. *Testing and evaluation in the biological sciences.* Washington, D.C.: Commission on Undergraduate Education in the Biological Sciences, 1967.

Feldhusen, J. F. Student perceptions of frequent quizzes and post-mortem discussions of tests. *Journal of Educational Measurement,* 1964, **1,** 51–54.

Graesser, R. F. Guessing on multiple-choice tests. *Educational and Psychological Measurement,* 1958, **18,** 617–620.

Hedges, W. D. *Testing and evaluation for the sciences in the secondary school.* Belmont, California: Wadsworth, 1966.

Horn, J. L. Some characteristics of classroom examinations. *Journal of Educational Measurement,* 1966, **3,** 293–294.

Jackson, R. A. Guessing and test performance. *Educational and Psychological Measurement,* 1955, **15,** 74–79.

Kalish, R. A. An experimental evaluation of the open book examination. *Journal of Educational Psychology,* 1958, **49,** 200–204.

Kurfman, D. *Teacher-made test items in American history: Emphasis junior high school: Bulletin Number 40.* Washington, D.C.: National Council for the Social Studies, 1968.

Lado, R. *Language testing: The construction and use of foreign language tests.* New York: McGraw-Hill, 1961.

Morse, H. T. & McCune, G. H. *Selected items for the testing of study skills and critical thinking, Fourth Edition: Bulletin No. 15.* Washington, D.C.: National Council for the Social Studies, 1964.

Nelson, C. H. *Improving objective tests in science.* Washington, D.C.: National Science Teachers Association, 1967.

The National Council of Teachers of Mathematics. *Evaluation in mathematics,* Twenty-Sixth Yearbook. Washington, D.C.: The National Council of Teachers of Mathematics, 1961.

Sassenrath, J. M. & Garverick, C. M. Effects of differential feedback from examinations on retention and transfer. *Journal of Educational Psychology,* 1965, **56,** 259–263.

Sax, G. & Cromack, T. R. The effects of various forms of item arrangements on test performance. *Journal of Educational Measurement,* 1966, **3,** 309–311.

CHAPTER 5

Elementary Statistical Concepts

INTRODUCTION

In its various forms, measurement results in classification, rankings, or scores. Any attempt to describe, summarize, or compare results for individuals or for groups calls for numerical treatment. The branch of arithmetic and mathematics that deals with the analysis of sets of scores for groups of individuals is known as statistics. Every user of tests and measurement devices needs at least a consumer's understanding of the basic objectives and techniques of descriptive statistics. This is a book on measurement, not a statistics textbook. Discussion of statistics as such is limited to this one chapter. It cannot be expected that study of it will make the reader an accomplished statistician. This chapter points out to the novice some basic types of questions that the statistician tries to answer, and introduces him to the simplest tools used to answer them.

Suppose you have prepared tests in reading, arithmetic, and spelling and given them to the pupils in two sixth grades in your school. You have scored the papers and entered the names and scores on a record sheet for the two classes. Table 5.1 on pages 134–135 shows what the record sheet might contain. Now, what questions might you ask the data to answer? Before reading further, suppose you study the set of scores and jot down on a piece of scrap paper the questions that come to *your* mind in connection with these scores. See how many of the question types you can anticipate.

TABLE 5.1 RECORD SHEET FOR SIXTH GRADES AT SCHOOL X

Name	Test Scores		
	Reading	Arithmetic	Spelling
1. Carol A.	32	3	27
2. Mary B.	27	27	26
3. Ruby C.	31	9	23
4. Alice D.	36	18	32
5. Theresa E.	47	21	38
6. Ida F.	42	24	38
7. Vivian G.	22	4	13
8. Grace H.	50	42	46
9. Opal I.	20	18	12
10. Ursula J.	37	2	36
11. Beatrice K.	25	10	21
12. Karen L.	37	13	30
13. Susan M.	28	20	18
14. Jane N.	34	15	32
15. Dorothy O.	31	19	28
16. Frances P.	21	2	17
17. Elizabeth Q.	35	48	30
18. Pearl R.	59	41	54
19. Joan S.	44	41	39
20. Nancy T.	32	40	28
21. Judith U.	56	24	54
22. Edith V.	38	24	37
23. Louise W.	38	18	30
24. Helen X.	29	12	24
25. Martha Y.	24	26	22
26. Doris Z.	36	12	28
27. James A.	36	29	33
28. Albert B.	21	16	13
29. Donald C.	27	7	24
30. Peter D.	37	29	31
31. Samuel E.	46	36	37
32. George F.	33	10	31
33. Roger G.	17	14	14
34. Newton H.	35	18	30
35. Karl I.	30	12	25
36. Isidore J.	22	30	17
37. John K.	43	9	37
38. Benjamin L.	31	15	29
39. Theodore M.	50	38	48
40. Michael N.	34	20	27
41. Herman O.	30	15	29
42. Charles P.	52	39	47

TABLE 5.1 (*Continued*)

Name	Test Scores		
	Reading	Arithmetic	Spelling
43. Patrick Q.	40	33	33
44. William R.	42	6	33
45. Martin S.	17	26	17
46. Frank T.	32	20	23
47. Ralph U.	38	20	30
48. Thomas V.	29	29	33
49. Henry W.	36	25	44
50. Oscar X.	43	19	45
51. Edward Y.	27	19	35
52. Leonard Z.	39	19	44

A first, rather general question you might ask is: What is the general pattern of the set of scores? How do they "run"? What do they "look like"? How can we picture the set of reading scores, for example, so that we can get an impression of the group as a whole? To answer this question we will need to consider simple ways of tabulating and graphing a set of scores.

A second question that will almost certainly arise is: What is this group like, on the average? In general, have they done as well on the test as some other sixth-grade group? What is the typical level of performance in the group? All these questions call for some single score to represent the group as a whole, some measure of the middle of the group. To answer this question we shall need to become acquainted with statistics developed to represent the average or typical score.

Third, in order to describe your group you might feel a need to describe the extent to which the scores spread out away from the average value. Are all the children in the group about the same, so that the same materials and procedures would be suitable for all? If not, how widely do they spread out on a given test? How does this group compare with other classes with respect to the *spread* of scores? This calls for a study of measures of variability.

Fourth, you might ask how a particular individual stands on some one test. Thus, you might want to know whether James A. had done well or poorly on the arithmetic test, and if you decided that his score was a good score you might want some way of saying just how good it was. You might ask whether James A. did better in reading or in arithmetic. To answer this question you would need a common yardstick in terms of which to express performance in two quite different areas. One need, then, is for some uniform way of expressing and interpreting the performance of an individual. How does he stand, relative to his group?

A fifth query is of this type: To what extent did those who excelled in reading also excel in arithmetic? To what extent do these two abilities go together in the same individuals? Is the individual who is superior in one likely also to be superior in the other? To measure this going-togetherness we shall need to become acquainted with measures of *correlation.*

The following sections of this chapter will be devoted to illustrating and discussing the routines that statistics has developed for answering these questions. There are many other questions that may arise with respect to a set of data. The most important ones concern the drawing of general conclusions from data on a limited group. Thus, one sample of fifty boys may have surpassed a sample of fifty girls from the same school on a history test. This is a *descriptive* fact true of these particular boys and girls. What we would like to know is whether we can safely conclude that the *total population of boys* from which this sample was drawn would surpass the *total population of girls* on this same test. This is a problem of *inference.* Problems of statistical inference make up the bulk of advanced statistical work, but we cannot go into them here.

WAYS OF TABULATING AND PICTURING A SET OF SCORES

In Table 5.1 we showed a record sheet on which test scores for 52 sixth-grade pupils had been recorded. Let us look at the scores in the column headed Reading and consider how they could be rearrranged so as to give us a clearer picture of how the pupils did on the reading test.

The simplest rearrangement would be merely to arrange them in order from highest to lowest. We would then have something that looked like this:

59	43	37	34	30	22
56	42	37	33	29	22
52	42	36	32	29	21
50	40	36	32	28	21
50	39	36	32	27	20
47	38	36	31	27	17
46	38	35	31	27	17
44	38	35	31	25	
43	37	34	30	24	

This arrangement gives a somewhat better picture of the way the scores fall. We can see the highest and lowest scores at a glance, i.e., 59 and 17. It is also easy to see that the middle person in the group falls somewhere in the mid-thirties. We can see by inspection that roughly half the scores fall between 30 and 40. But this simple rearrangement of scores still has too much detail for us to see the general pattern clearly. It is also not a convenient form to use in computing. We need to condense it into a more compact form.

Preparing a Frequency Distribution

A further step in organizing the scores for presentation is to prepare what is termed a *frequency distribution.* This is a table showing how often each score occurred. Each score value is listed, and the number of times it occurred is shown. A portion of the frequency distribution for the reading test is shown in Table 5.2. However, Table 5.2 is still not a very good form for reporting our facts. The table is too long and spread out. We have shown only part of it. The whole table would take 43 lines. It would have a number of zero entries. There would be marked ups and downs from one score to the next.

In order to improve the form of presentation further, scores are often *grouped*

TABLE 5.2 FREQUENCY DISTRIBUTION OF READING SCORES

(Ungrouped Data)

Test Score	Frequency
59	1
58	0
57	0
56	1
55	0
54	0
53	0
52	1
51	0
50	2
.	.
.	.
.	.
20	1
19	0
18	0
17	2

TABLE 5.3 FREQUENCY DISTRIBUTION OF READING SCORES

(Grouped Data)

Score Interval	Tallies	Frequency
58–60	/	1
55–57	/	1
52–54	/	1
49–51	//	2
46–48	//	2
43–45	///	3
40–42	///	3
37–39	~~////~~ //	7
34–36	~~////~~ ///	8
31–33	~~////~~ //	7
28–30	~~////~~	5
25–27	////	4
22–24	///	3
19–21	///	3
16–18	//	2

together into broader categories. In our example, we will group together three adjacent scores, so that each grouping includes three points of score. When we do this, our set of scores is represented as shown in Table 5.3 This provides a fairly compact table showing how many persons there are in each group or *class interval.* Thus, we have eight persons in the interval 34–36. We do not know how many of them got 34's, how many 35's, and how many 36's. We have lost this information in the grouping. We assume that they are evenly divided. In most cases, there is no reason to anticipate that any one score will occur more often than any other and this assumption is a sound one, so the gains in compactness and convenience of presentation more than make up for any slight inaccuracy introduced by this grouping.*

In a practical situation, we always face the problem of deciding how broad the groupings should be, that is, whether to group by 3's, 5's, 10's, or some other grouping. The decision is a compromise between losing detail from our data, on the one hand, and obtaining a convenient, compact, and smooth representation of our results, on the other. A broader interval loses more detail but condenses the data into a more compact picture. A practical rule of thumb is to choose a class interval that will divide the total score range into roughly 15 groups.

* In some special types of social statistics, such as reports of income, certain values are more likely than others, i.e., $2,000, $3,000, $5,000, etc. Special precautions are necessary in grouping material of this type. In particular, one should strive to get popular values near the *middle* of a class interval.

Thus, in our example the highest score was 59 and the lowest was 17. The range of scores is 59 − 17 = 42. Dividing 42 by 15, we get 2.8. The nearest whole number is 3, and so we group our data by 3's. In addition to the "rule of 15," we also find that intervals of 5, 10, and multiples of 10 make convenient groupings. Since the purpose of grouping scores is to make a convenient representation, factors of convenience enter as a major consideration.

It should be noted that sometimes there is no need to group data into broader categories. If the original scores cover a range of no more than, say, 20 points, grouping may not be called for.

In practice, when we are tabulating a set of data, deciding on the size of the score interval is the *first* step. Next we set up the score intervals, as shown in the left-hand column of Table 5.3. Each individual is then represented by a tally mark, as shown in the middle column. (It is easier to keep track of the tallies if every fifth tally is a diagonal line across the preceding four.) The column headed Frequency is gotten by counting the number of tallies in each score interval.

Graphic Representation

It is often helpful to translate the facts of Table 5.3 into a pictorial representation. A common type of graphic representation, which is called a *histogram,* is shown in Fig. 5.1. This can be thought of, somewhat grimly, as "piling up the bodies." The score intervals are shown along the horizontal base-line (abscissa). The vertical height of the pile (ordinate) represents the number of cases. The diagram indicates that there are two "bodies" piled up in the interval

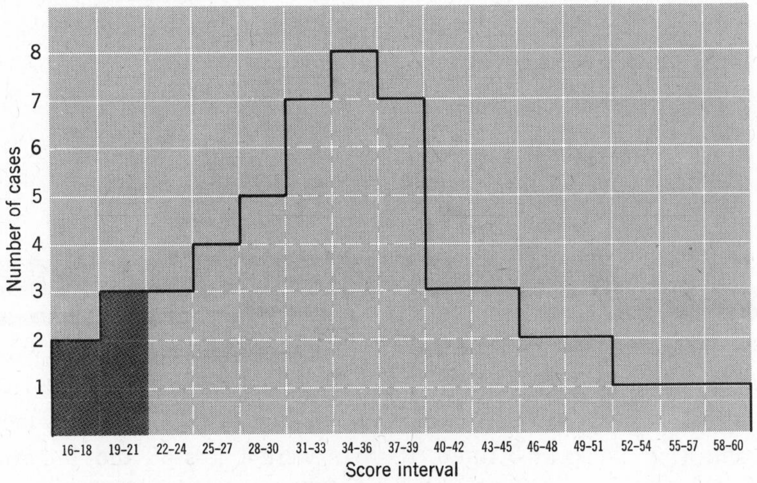

Fig. 5.1 Histogram of reading scores.

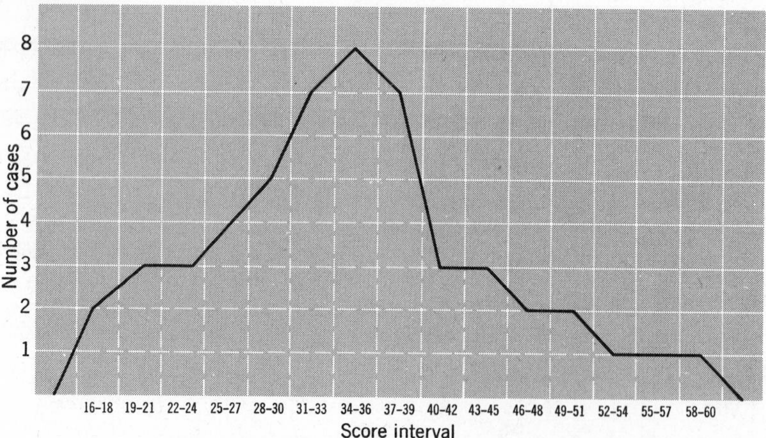

Fig. 5.2 Frequency polygon of reading scores.

16–18, three in the interval 19–21, and so forth. This figure gives a clear picture of how the cases pile up, with most of them in the 30's and a long low pile running up to the high scores.

Another way of picturing the same data is by preparing a *frequency polygon.* This is shown in Fig. 5.2. Here we have plotted a point at the midpoint of each of our score intervals. The height at which we have plotted the point corresponds to the number of cases, or frequency (f), in the interval. These points have been connected, and the jagged line provides a somewhat different picture of the same set of data illustrated in Fig. 5.1. The polygon permits the data to be seen more clearly when two different groups are included in a single chart. Otherwise, the choice between the two is a matter of personal aesthetics, since the two are interchangeable ways of showing the same facts.

MEASURES OF CENTRAL TENDENCY

We often need a statistic to represent the typical, or average, or middle score of a group of scores. A very simple way of identifying the typical score is to pick out the score that occurs most frequently. This is called the *mode.* If we examine the array of scores on p. 136, we see that the score 36 occurs 4 times and is the mode for this set of data. We can also note another fact. The score values 38, 37, 32, 31, and 27 each occur 3 times. If there were 1 less 36 and 1 more 27, for example, the mode would shift by 9 points. The mode is sensitive to such minor changes in the data and is therefore a crude and not very useful indicator of the typical score. In Table 5.3, where we have the grouped frequency distribution, the *modal interval* is the interval 34–36. This is as closely as we can identify the mode for data presented in this way.

Median

A much more useful way of representing the typical or average score is to find the value on the score scale that separates the top half of the group from the bottom half. This is called the *median.* In our example, in which there are 52 cases, this means separating the top 26 from the bottom 26 pupils. The required value can be estimated from the scores shown in Table 5.3. Starting with the lowest score, we count up until we have the necessary 26 cases. The "counting up" is best done in a systematic way, as shown in Table 5.4. Table 5.4 shows the cumulative frequencies as well as the frequency in each interval. Each entry in the column labeled Cumulative Frequency shows the total number having a score equal to or less than the highest score in that interval. That is, there are 5 cases scoring at or below 21, 8 scoring at or below 24, 12 scoring at or below 27, and so forth. As indicated, we wish to identify the point below which 50 percent of the cases fall. Since 50 percent of 52 = 26, we must identify the point below which 26 pupils fall.

TABLE 5.4 FREQUENCY DISTRIBUTION AND CUMULATIVE FREQUENCIES FOR READING SCORES

Score Interval	Frequency	Cumulative Frequency
58–60	1	52
55–57	1	51
52–54	1	50
49–51	2	49
46–48	2	47
43–45	3	45
40–42	3	42
37–39	7	39
34–36	8	32
31–33	7	24
28–30	5	17
25–27	4	12
22–24	3	8
19–21	3	5
16–18	2	2

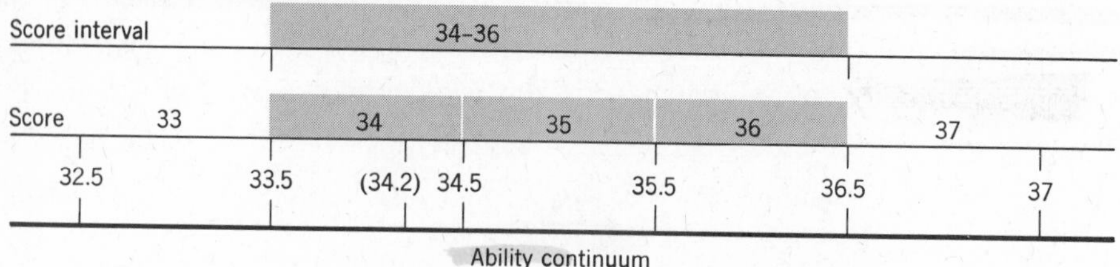

Fig. 5.3 Relation between scores and ability continuum.

We note that 24 individuals have scores of 33 or below. We need to include 2 more cases to obtain the required 26 cases. Note that in the next score interval (34–36) there are 8 individuals. We require only $\frac{2}{8}$ or $\frac{1}{4}$ of these individuals. Now how shall we think of these cases being spread out over the score interval 34–36? As we indicated on p. 138, a reasonable assumption is that they are spread out evenly over the interval. Then to include $\frac{1}{4}$ of the scores, we would have to go $\frac{1}{4}$ of the way up from the bottom of the interval toward the top.

At this point, we must define what we mean by a score of 34. First, let us note that although test scores go by jumps of 1 unit, i.e., 34, 35, 36, we consider the underlying ability to have a continuous distribution taking all intermediate values. This is illustrated in Fig. 5.3. The heavy line represents the continuum of ability. We will define "34" as meaning closer to 34 than to either 33 or 35. Thus, in Fig. 5.3, 34 is represented as extending from 33.5 to 34.5. Although somewhat arbitrary, this definition of a score is a reasonable one, and is accepted by most statistics textbooks. The class interval 34–36 is really to be thought of as extending from 33.5 to 36.5, as shown in the figure. We do not get scores lying *between* 33 and 34—not because those levels of ability do not exist, but just because our measuring instrument does not register any values between 33 and 34.

Since we require $\frac{1}{4}$ of the cases in the interval 34–36, we must go $\frac{1}{4}$ of the way from $33\frac{1}{2}$ to $36\frac{1}{2}$, that is, we have $\frac{1}{4}(36\frac{1}{2} - 33\frac{1}{2}) = \frac{1}{4} \times 3 = \frac{3}{4} = 0.75$. We must add 0.75 to the value $33\frac{1}{2}$, which is the borderline between the 2 intervals. The median for this set of scores is $33.5 + 0.75 = 34.25$.

To compute the median, then:	*In our example:*
1. Calculate the number of cases that represents 50 percent of the total group.	1. 50 percent of 52 is 26.
2. Starting with the lowest score interval, accumulate the scores up through each score interval.	2. The cumulative frequencies, as shown in Table 5.4, are 2, 5, 8, 12, 17, etc.
3. Find the interval for which the cumulative frequency is just less than the required number of cases.	3. In our example, the cumulation through the 31–33 interval is 24.

To compute the median, then:	*In our example:*
4. Find the score distance to be added to the top of this interval, in order to include the required number of cases, by the following operation: $\left(\frac{\text{No. of added cases needed}}{\text{No. of cases in next interval}}\right)\left(\begin{matrix}\text{No. of points}\\ \text{in interval}\end{matrix}\right)$	4. $(2/8)(3) = 0.75$.
5. Add this amount to the upper limit of the interval identified in 3 to give the median.	5. $33.5 + 0.75 = 34.25$.

Percentiles

The same procedure may be used to find the score below which any other percentage of the group falls. These values are all called *percentiles.* The median is the 50th percentile, that is, the score below which 50 percent of individuals fall. If we want to find the 25th percentile, we must find the score below which 25 percent of the cases fall. Twenty-five percent of 52 is 13. Thirteen cases take us through the interval 25–27, and include 1 of the 5 cases in the 28–30 interval. So the 25th percentile is computed to be $27.5 + (1/5)3 = 27.5 + 0.6 = 28.1$.

As another illustration, consider the 85th percentile. We have $(.85)(52) = 44.2$. Since 42 cases carry us to the top of the 40–42 interval, and there are 3 cases in the next interval, we have for the 85th percentile $42.5 + [(44.2–42)/3](3) = 44.7$. Other percentiles can be found in the same way. Percentiles have many uses, especially in connection with test norms and the interpretation of scores.

Arithmetic Mean

Another frequently used statistic for representing the middle of a group is the familiar "average" of everyday experience. Since the statistician speaks of all measures of central tendency as averages, he identifies this one as the *arithmetic mean.* This is simply the sum of a series of scores divided by the number of scores. Thus, the arithmetic mean of 4, 6, and 7 is

$$\frac{4 + 6 + 7}{3} = 5.67$$

In our example, we can add together the scores of all 52 individuals in our group. This gives us 1,798. Dividing by 52, we get 34.58 for the "average" or arithmetic mean for this group.

Adding together all the scores and dividing by the number of cases is the straightforward way of computing the arithmetic mean. If the group is fairly

TABLE 5.5 FREQUENCY DISTRIBUTION OF READING SCORES SHOWING STEPS IN CALCULATING ARITHMETIC MEAN AND STANDARD DEVIATION

Score Interval	Frequency f	x'	fx'	$f(x')^2$
58–60	1	8	8	64
55–57	1	7	7	49
52–54	1	6	6	36
49–51	2	5	10	50
46–48	2	4	8	32
43–45	3	3	9	27
40–42	3	2	6	12
37–39	7	1	7	7
			+61	
34–36	8	0	0	0
31–33	7	−1	−7	7
28–30	5	−2	−10	20
25–27	4	−3	−12	36
22–24	3	−4	−12	48
19–21	3	−5	−15	75
16–18	2	−6	−12	72
			−68	
Sum	52		−7	535

small, and especially if an adding machine is available, it may be the best way. However, it can be rather laborious, especially with a large group. More efficient computing procedures are available, based on the frequency distribution given in Table 5.3. These calculations are based on a type of "trial balance." Picking a score interval that looks to be about in the middle of the group, we sum the plus and minus deviations from this starting place. An adjustment based on the excess of plus or minus deviations is applied to this starting place to give the value for the mean. The application of this procedure to the reading test data is shown in Table 5.5, and the steps are outlined below.

Sequence of Steps	*In Symbolism* *	*Illustrative Example*
1. Choose some interval for the arbitrary starting place or "origin." The midpoint of this arbitrarily chosen interval (A) is called "zero" in our calculations.	A	$A = 35$ For X = 34–36, $x' = 0$

* A list of common statistical symbols and their meanings is given at the end of the chapter. Reference to these definitions may help in reading the remainder of the chapter.

Sequence of Steps	*In Symbolism*	*Illustrative Example*
2. Call the next higher interval +1, the one above that +2, etc., and the ones below −1, −2, etc.	x'	Thus, 37–39 is called +1, 40–42 is called +2, etc., as shown in the column headed x' in Table 5.5
3. For each row, multiply the number of cases (frequency) by the number of steps (x') above or below the chosen origin.	fx'	Thus, $1 \times 8 = 8$, $1 \times 7 = 7$, etc., as shown in the column headed fx' in Table 5.5
4. Sum the values in the fx' column, taking account of the plus and minus signs. (Mistakes will be avoided if the plus entries are summed separately, the minus entries summed, and the two part sums combined to give the final total.)	$\Sigma fx'$	$\Sigma f(x')+ = +61$ $\Sigma f(x')- = -68$ $\Sigma f(x') = -7$
5. Sum the frequencies in the column headed Frequency (or f) to give the total number of cases in the group. This is usually labeled N.	$\Sigma f = N$	$\Sigma f = 52$
6. Divide the sum of fx' values by N to get the average of the deviations from the arbitrary origin (in interval units).	$\frac{\Sigma fx'}{N}$	$\frac{-7}{52} = -0.135$
7. Multiply by the size of the interval to express the deviation in score units.	$i\left(\frac{\Sigma fx'}{N}\right)$	$3\left(\frac{-7}{52}\right) = 3(-0.135) = -0.405$
8. Add the result to the value of the arbitrary origin.	$A + i\left(\frac{\Sigma fx'}{N}\right)$	$35 + (-0.405) = 34.595$ or 34.60

Summarizing all the steps, we may say:

$$\text{Mean} = (\text{Interval})\left(\frac{\text{Sum of } fx'}{N}\right) + \text{Arbitrary Origin}$$

or in our example:

$$\text{Mean} = 3\left(\frac{-7}{52}\right) + 35 = 34.60$$

Starting where we did, the minus deviations slightly overbalanced the plus ones. There was an excess of 7 on the minus side. Our starting point was a little too high. We had to shift it down $\frac{7}{52}$ of 1 interval or $\frac{7}{52} \times 3$ points of score to find a true balance point. Since the middle of our zero interval corresponded to a score of 35, we had to move down $^{21}/_{52}$ points below 35 to get the true balance point, the correct arithmetic mean.

The value 34.60 that we got in this way is almost the same as the 34.58 that resulted from adding all the scores together and dividing by the number of cases. The correspondence is usually not perfect, due to slight inaccuracies involved in grouping our scores into classes in the frequency distribution, but the values obtained by the two methods will always agree closely. When we work with the frequency distribution it makes no difference which interval we use for our starting point. Barring mistakes in arithmetic, we will always get identically the same result.

The arithmetic mean and the median do not correspond exactly, but usually they will not differ greatly. In this example, the values are 34.60 and 34.25, respectively. The mean and median will differ substantially only when the set of scores is very "skewed," that is, there is a piling up of scores at one end and a long tail at the other. Figure 5.4 shows three distributions differing in amount and direction of skewness. The top figure is positively skewed, that is, has a tail running up into the high scores. We get a distribution like this for income in the United States, since there are many people with small and moderate incomes and only a few with very large incomes. The center figure is negatively skewed. A distribution like this would result if a class was given a very easy test, which resulted in a piling up of perfect and near-perfect scores. The bottom figure is symmetrical and is not skewed in either direction. Many physical and psychological variables give such a symmetrical distribution. In the many distributions that are approximately symmetrical either mean or median will serve equally well to represent the average of the group, but with skewed distributions the median generally seems preferable. It is less affected by a few cases out in the long tail.

MEASURES OF VARIABILITY

When describing a set of scores, it is often significant to report how *variable* the scores are, how much they spread out from high to low scores. For example, two groups of children, both with a median age of 10 years, would represent quite different educational situations if one had a spread of ages from 9 to 11 while the other ranged from 6 to 14. A measure of this spread is an important statistic for describing a group.

A very simple measure of variability is the *range* of scores in the group. This is simply the difference between the highest and the lowest score. In our reading

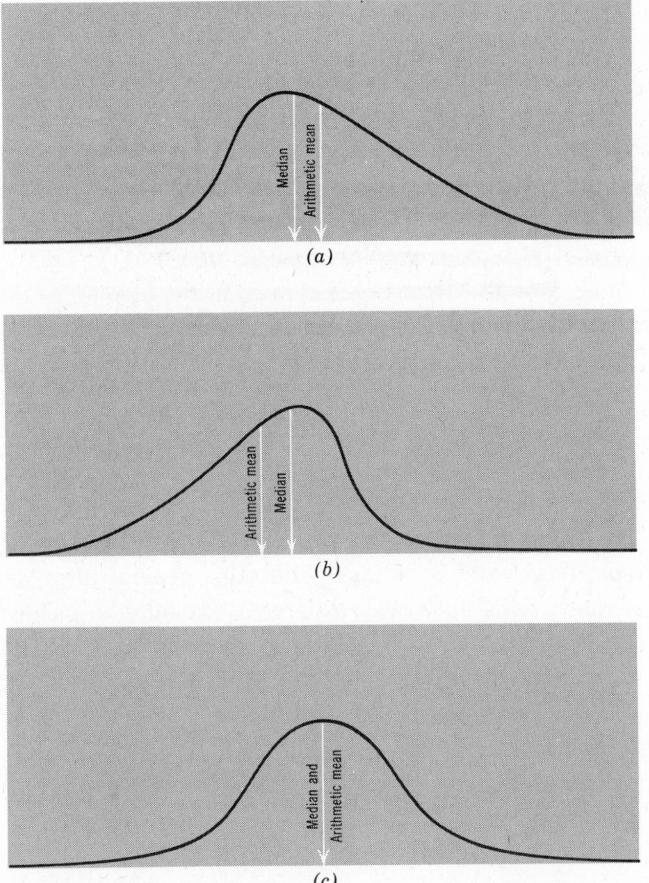

Fig. 5.4 Frequency distributions differing in skewness. (*a*) Positively skewed; (*b*) Negatively skewed; (*c*) Symmetrical.

test example it is 59 − 17 = 42. However, the range depends only upon the two extreme cases in the total group. This makes it very undependable, since it can be changed a good bit by the addition or omission of a single extreme case.

Semi-interquartile Range

A better measure of variability is the range of scores that includes a specified part of the total group—usually the middle 50 percent. The middle 50 percent of the cases in a group are the cases lying between the 25th and 75th percentiles.

We can compute these two percentiles, following the procedures outlined on pp. 142–143. For our example, the 25th percentile was computed to be 28.1. If we calculate the 75th percentile, we will find that it is 39.5. The distance between the 25th and 75th percentiles is thus seen to be 11.4 points of score.

The 25th and 75th percentiles are called *quartiles,* since they cut off the bottom quarter and the top quarter of the group respectively. The score distance between them is called the *interquartile range.* A statistic that is often reported as a measure of variability is the *semi-interquartile range* (Q). This is half of the interquartile range. It is the average distance from the median to the 2 quartiles, that is, it tells how far the quartile points lie from the median, on the average. In our example, the semi-interquartile range is

$$Q = \frac{39.5 - 28.1}{2} = 5.7$$

If the scores spread out twice as far, Q would be twice as great; if they spread out only half as far, Q would be half as large. Two distributions that have the same mean, same total number of cases, and same general form, and that differ only in that one has a variability twice as large as the other are shown in Fig. 5.5.

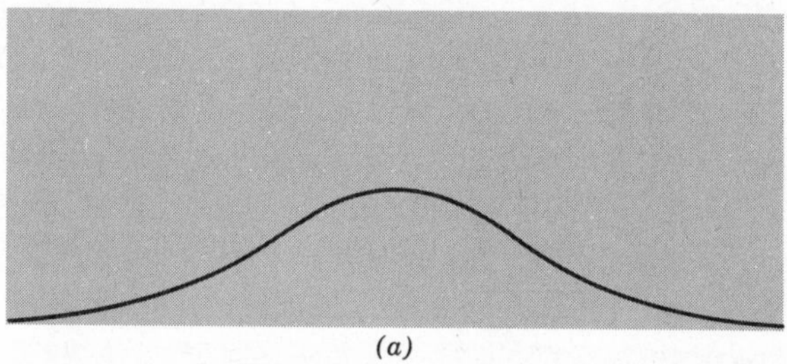

(*a*)

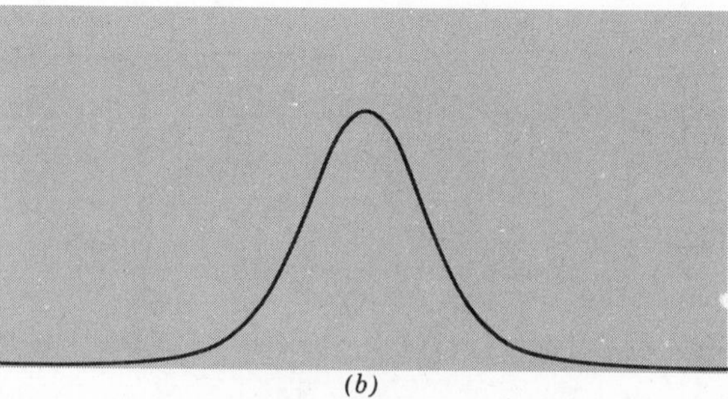

(*b*)

Fig. 5.5 Two distributions differing only in variability. (*a*) Large variability; (*b*) Small variability.

Standard Deviation

The semi-interquartile range belongs to the same family of statistics as the median. Its computation is based upon percentiles. There are also measures of variability that belong to the family of the arithmetic mean and are based upon score deviations. Suppose we had four scores of 4, 5, 6, and 7 respectively. Adding these together and dividing by the number of scores we get

$$\frac{4+5+6+7}{4} = \frac{22}{4} = 5.5$$

This gives us the arithmetic mean. But now we ask how widely these scores spread out around that mean value. Suppose we find the difference between each score and the mean, i.e., we subtract 5.5 from each score. We then have -1.5, -0.5, 0.5, and 1.5. These represent *deviations* of the scores from the mean. The bigger the deviations, the more variable the set of scores. What we require is some type of average of these deviations to give us an overall measure of variability.

If we simply sum the above four deviation values, we find that they add up to zero. This is necessarily so. We defined the arithmetic mean as the point around which the plus and minus deviations exactly balance. We shall have to do something else. The procedure that statisticians have devised for handling the plus and the minus signs is to square all the deviations. (A minus times a minus is a plus.) An average of these squared deviations is obtained by summing them and dividing by the number of cases. To compensate for squaring the individual deviations, the square root of this average value is computed. The resulting statistic is called the *standard deviation* (*SD* or *s*). It is the square root * of the average of the squared deviations from the mean. For our little example of 4 cases, the calculations are as follows:

$$SD = \sqrt{\frac{(-1.5)^2 + (-0.5)^2 + (0.5)^2 + (1.5)^2}{4}}$$

$$= \sqrt{\frac{2.25 + 0.25 + 0.25 + 2.25}{4}} = \sqrt{\frac{5.00}{4}}$$

$$= \sqrt{1.25} = 1.12$$

* The steps for computing the square root are shown in Appendix I.

Standard Deviation Computed from Frequency Distribution

The standard deviation may also be computed from the grouped frequency distribution. The necessary steps have been carried out in Table 5.5. Take special note of the column headed $f(x')^2$. Each entry in this column represents the number of cases (f) multiplied by the square of the deviation (x') of that score interval from the arbitrary origin. The sum of the values in this column gives a sum of squared deviations, but these deviations are around our arbitrary origin and are expressed in interval units. Several adjustments are necessary to express the deviations in *score* units and in terms of the *true* arithmetic mean. The steps are outlined below.

1. Carry out the operations for computing the arithmetic mean, as described on pp. 144–145.
2. In addition, prepare the column headed $f(x')^2$. Each entry in this column is the frequency (f) times the square of the deviation value (x'). However, this last column can be computed most simply by multiplying together the entries in the two preceding columns, i.e., x' times fx'. Note that all the signs in this column are positive, since a minus times a minus gives a plus.

	In Symbolism	*Illustrative Example*
3. Get the sum of the $f(x')^2$ column.	$\Sigma f(x')^2$	535
4. Divide this sum by the number of cases.	$\frac{\Sigma f(x')^2}{N}$	$\frac{535}{52} = 10.288$
5. Divide the sum of the fx' column by the number of cases.	$\frac{\Sigma fx'}{N}$	$\frac{-7}{52} = -0.135$
6. Square the value obtained in 5 above.	$\left(\frac{\Sigma fx'}{N}\right)^2$	$\left(\frac{-7}{52}\right)^2 = (-0.135)^2 = 0.018$
7. Subtract the value in 6 from that in 4.	$\frac{\Sigma f(x')^2}{N} - \left(\frac{\Sigma fx'}{N}\right)^2$	$\frac{535}{52} - \left(\frac{-7}{52}\right)^2 = 10.288 - 0.018 = 10.270$
8. Take the square root of the value in 7.	$\sqrt{\frac{\Sigma f(x')^2}{N} - \left(\frac{\Sigma fx'}{N}\right)^2}$	$\sqrt{10.270} = 3.20$
9. Multiply by the number of score points in each class interval.	$i\sqrt{\frac{\Sigma f(x')^2}{N} - \left(\frac{\Sigma fx'}{N}\right)^2}$	$3(3.20) = 9.60$

Presenting all the computations for our example in summary form, using the formula given in step 9 above, we have

$$SD = 3\sqrt{\frac{535}{52} - \left(\frac{-7}{52}\right)^2} = 9.60$$

Interpreting the Standard Deviation

It is almost impossible to say in any simple words what the standard deviation *is* or what it corresponds to in pictorial or geometric terms. Primarily, it is a statistic that characterizes a distribution of scores. It increases in direct proportion as the scores spread out more widely. The larger the standard deviation, the wider the spread of scores. A student sometimes asks: But what is a small standard deviation? What is a large one? There is really no answer to this question. Suppose that for some group the standard deviation of weights is 10. Is this large or small? It depends on whether we are talking about ounces, or pounds, or kilograms. It depends upon whether we are dealing with the weights of mice, or men, or mammoths.

"Large" and "small" have primarily relative meaning—that is, larger or smaller than that found for some other group or some other test. We do have one reference point with which it is sometimes useful to compare the standard deviation. This is the mean. The ratio 100(Standard Deviation)/Mean is called the *coefficient of variation*, and is sometimes used to compare variability of different groups and measures. It is useful for attributes like height and weight, for which we know that a zero score represents "just none of" the quality in question. It is much less meaningful for most psychological and educational variables in which a zero score does not correspond in any real way to zero ability.

The standard deviation gets its most clear-cut meaning for one particular type of distribution of scores. This distribution is called the "normal" distribution. It is defined by a particular mathematical equation, but to the everyday user it is defined approximately by its pictorial qualities. The "normal" curve is a symmetrical curve having a bell-like shape. That is, most of the cases pile up in the middle score values; as one goes away from the middle in either direction the pile drops off, first slowly and then more rapidly, and the cases tail out to relatively long tails on either end. An illustration of a typical normal curve is shown in Fig. 5.6 on page 152. This curve is the normal curve that best fits the reading test data we have been using as an illustration. It has the same mean, standard deviation, and total area (number of cases) as the reading test data. The histogram of reading test scores appears in light dotted lines, so one can see how closely the curve fits the actual tests scores.

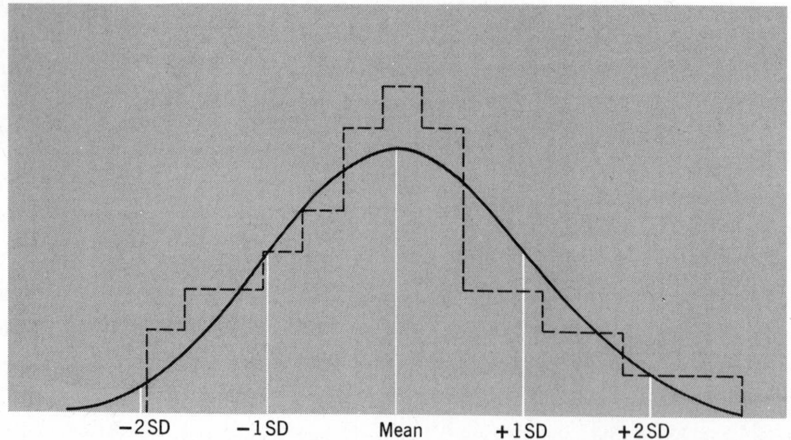

Fig. 5.6 Example of a normal curve (fitted to reading-test data).

For the normal curve, there is an exact mathematical relationship between the standard deviation and the proportion of cases. The same proportion of cases will always be found within the same standard deviation limits. This relationship is shown in Table 5.6. Thus, in *any* normal curve about two-thirds (68.2 percent) of the cases will fall between +1 and −1 standard deviation from the mean. Approximately 95 percent will fall between +2 and −2 standard deviations from the mean, and very nearly all the cases will fall between +3 and −3 standard deviations from the mean. An individual who gets a score 1 standard deviation above the mean will surpass 84 percent of the group, that is, he will surpass the 50 percent who fall below the mean and the 34 percent who fall between the mean and +1 standard deviation.

This unvarying relationship of the standard deviation unit to the arrangement

TABLE 5.6 PROPORTION OF CASES FALLING WITHIN CERTAIN SPECIFIED STANDARD DEVIATION LIMITS FOR A NORMAL DISTRIBUTION

Limits within Which Cases Lie	Percent of Cases
Between the mean and *either* +1.0 *SD* or −1.0 *SD*	34.1
Between the mean and *either* +2.0 *SD* or −2.0 *SD*	47.7
Between the mean and *either* +3.0 *SD* or −3.0 *SD*	49.9
Between +1.0 and −1.0 *SD*	68.2
Between +2.0 and −2.0 *SD*	95.4
Between +3.0 and −3.0 *SD*	99.8

of scores in the normal distribution gives the standard deviation a type of *standard* meaning. It becomes a yardstick in terms of which different groups may be compared or the status of a given individual may be evaluated. Although the relationship of the standard deviation unit to the score distribution does not hold *exactly* in distributions other than the normal distribution, frequently the distribution of test scores or other measures approaches the normal curve closely enough so that the standard deviation continues to have very nearly the same meaning.

The meaning of being a given number of standard deviations above or below the mean may be expressed in terms of the percent of cases in the group whom the individual surpasses. A short table showing the percent of cases falling below different standard deviation values on the normal curve is given in Appendix II. This table makes it easy to translate any score, expressed in standard deviation units, into the equivalent percentile on a normal curve. Thus, consider the set of reading test scores for which we computed the mean and standard deviation to be 34.6 and 9.6 respectively. Suppose a person had a score of 48. Since the mean of the group is 34.6, he falls $48 - 34.6 = 13.4$ points above the mean of the group. The 13.4 points by which he surpasses the mean is equal to $13.4/9.6 = 1.4$ standard deviations. He is 1.4 standard deviations above the mean. We might expect him to surpass approximately 92 percent of the cases in our group. (An actual count shows that this score is better than $^{47}/_{52} = 90.4$ percent of the scores in our set of data.)

A score expressed in standard deviation units has much the same meaning from one set of scores to another. Thus, if a boy falls half a standard deviation above the mean of his group in arithmetic and three fourths of a standard deviation above in reading we can describe him as better in reading than in arithmetic. If he was half a standard deviation above the group mean when he was in arithmetic in grade 3, but is only a quarter of a standard deviation above now in grade 6, we may say that he has dropped back in his arithmetic performance relative to his group. The standard deviation provides a unit in terms of which scores can be directly compared from one test to another or from one time to another.

In summary, the statistics most used for describing the variability of a set of scores are the semi-interquartile range and the standard deviation. The semi-interquartile range is based upon percentiles, i.e., the 25th and 75th percentiles, and is commonly used when the median is being used as a measure of the middle of the group. The standard deviation is a measure of variability that goes with the arithmetic mean. It is useful in the field of tests and measurements primarily as providing a standard unit of measure having comparable meaning from one test to another.

INTERPRETING THE SCORE OF AN INDIVIDUAL

The problems of interpreting the score for an individual will be treated more fully in Chapter 7, when we turn to test norms and units of measure. It will suffice now to indicate that the two sorts of measures we have just been considering, that is, percentiles and standard deviation units, each give us a framework in which we can view the performance of a specific person. Thus, referring to the example we worked out, if a new boy in the class got a score of 48 on the reading test we could say either

1. That he surpassed 90 percent of the group, that is, that he fell at the 90th percentile, or
2. That he fell 1.4 standard deviations above the mean.

Either statement gives his score meaning in relation to his group; he is well above average being surpassed by only about a tenth of the group. Since they are based on the same score, they are two ways of saying the same thing. Each has certain advantages, which we will examine more carefully in Chapter 7.

MEASURES OF RELATIONSHIP

We look now for a statistic to express the relationship between two sets of scores. Thus, in our illustration we have a reading score and an arithmetic score for each pupil. To what extent did those pupils who did well in arithmetic also do well on the reading test? In this case, we have two scores for each individual. We can picture these scores by a plot in two dimensions. This is shown in Fig. 5.7. The first person in our group, Carol A., had a score on the reading test of 32 and a score on the arithmetic test of 3. Her scores are represented by the X in Fig. 5.7, plotted at 32 on the vertical or reading scale and at 3 on the horizontal or arithmetic scale. There is a dot to represent each other child's scores.

When a child who does well in reading also does well in arithmetic, we will find his scores represented by a dot in the upper right-hand part of our picture. A child who does poorly on both tests will fall at the lower left. Where good score on one test goes with poor score on the other, we will find the points falling in the other corners, i.e., upper left and lower right. Inspection of Fig. 5.7 reveals some tendency for the scores to splatter out in the lower-left to upper-

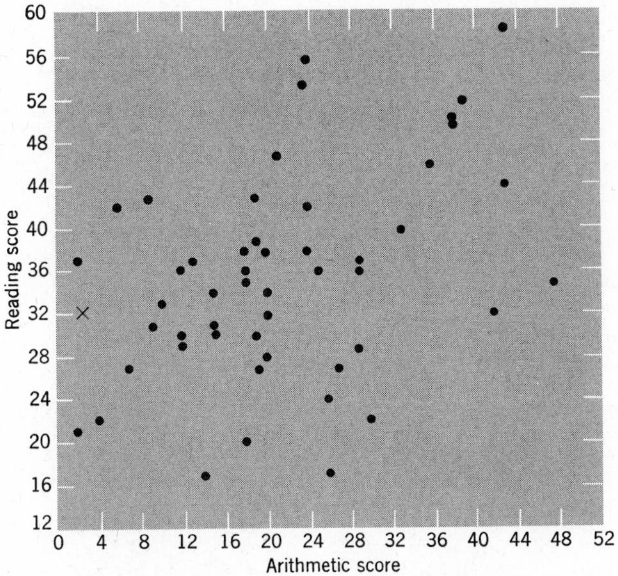

Fig. 5.7 Plot of reading versus arithmetic scores.

right direction, that is, from low-low to high-high. But there are many exceptions. The relationship is far from perfect. It is a matter of degree. We need some type of statistical index to express this degree of relationship.

As an index of this degree of relationship, a statistic known as the *correlation coefficient* can be computed. (The symbol r is used to designate this coefficient.) This coefficient can take values ranging from $+1$ through zero to -1. A correlation of $+1$ signifies that the person who had the highest score on one test also had the highest score on the other, the next highest on one was the next highest on the other, and so on, exactly in parallel through the whole group. A correlation of -1 means that the scores go in exactly the reverse direction, that is, the person highest on one is lowest on the other, next highest on one is next lowest on the other, etc. A zero correlation represents a complete lack of relationship. In-between values of r represent tendencies for relationship to exist but with many discrepancies.

Figure 5.8 on page 156 illustrates four different levels of relationship. In box A the correlation is zero, and the points scatter out in a pattern that is just about circular. All combinations are found—high-high, low-low, high-low, and low-high. Box B corresponds to a correlation of $+.30$. You can see a barely perceptible trend for the points to group in the low-low and high-high direction. The tendency is more marked in box C, which represents a correlation of $+.60$. In box D, which

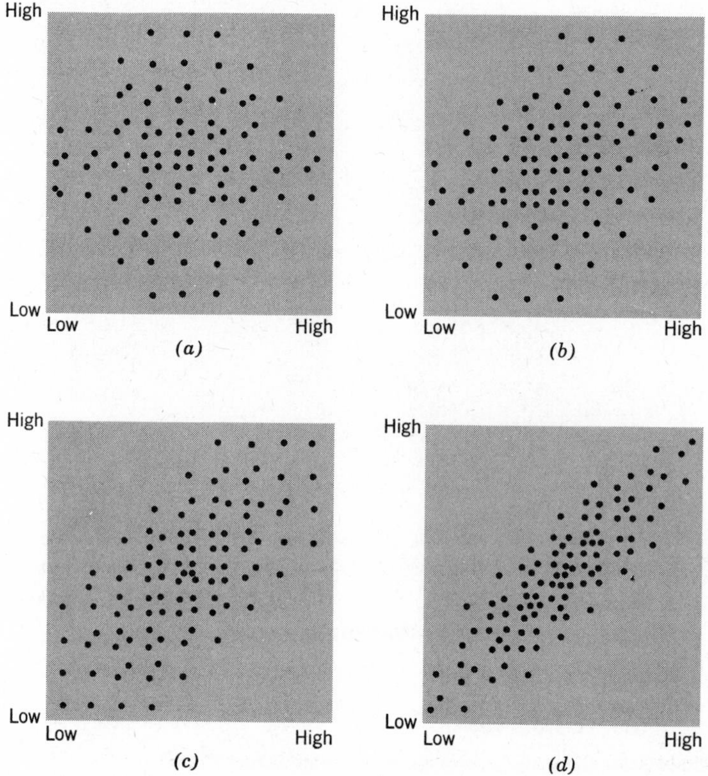

Fig. 5.8 Distribution of scores for representative values of correlation coefficient. (*a*) Correlation of .00; (*b*) Correlation of .30; (*c*) Correlation of .60; (*d*) Correlation of .90.

portrays a correlation of +.90, the trend is much more marked. Note that if the correlation were −.90 the scattering of the points would be just the same, but the swarm of dots would fall along the other diagonal—from lower right-hand corner to upper left-hand corner. But even with as high a correlation as this, the scores spread out quite a bit and do not lie directly on the line from low-low to high-high. We may note in passing that the scores plotted in Fig. 5.7 correspond to a correlation coefficient of +.46. Procedures for computing the correlation coefficient are outlined in Appendix III for those readers who wish to carry out the calculations with a numerical example.

There are three important settings in which correlation coefficients will be encountered in connection with tests and measurements. The first situation is one in which we are trying to determine how precise and consistent a measurement procedure is. Thus, if we wanted to know how consistent a measure of speed we get from a 50-yard dash, we could have each child run the distance twice, perhaps on successive days. The correlation of his two scores would give us information on the precision or reliability of this measure of running speed. The second situation is one in which we are studying the relationship between two different measures, often in order to evaluate one as a predictor of the other. Thus, we might want to study a scholastic aptitude test as a predictor of college grades. The correlation of test with grades would give an indication of the test's usefulness as a predictor.

The third situation is more purely descriptive. We often are interested in the relationships between variables just in order to understand better how behavior is organized. What correlations do we find between measures of verbal and of spatial abilities? How close is the relationship between interest in mechanical jobs and comprehension of mechanical devices? Is rate of physical development related to rate of intellectual development? Many research problems in human behavior can only, or best be studied by observing relationships as they develop in a natural setting.

We face the problem, in each case, of evaluating the correlation we obtain. Suppose the two sets of 50-yard dash scores yield a correlation of .80. Is this satisfactory or not? Suppose the aptitude test correlates .60 with college grades. Shall we be pleased * or discouraged?

The answer lies in part in the plots of Fig. 5.8. Clearly, the higher the correlation, the more closely one variable goes with the other. If we think of discrepancies away from the diagonal line from low-low to high-high as "errors," the errors become smaller as the correlation becomes larger. But, these discrepancies are still discouragingly large for even a rather substantial correlation coefficient, for example, box C in Fig. 5.8. We must always be aware of these discrepancies and realize that with a correlation such as .60 between an aptitude test and school grades there will be a number of children whose school performance differs a good deal from what we have predicted from the test.

However, everything is relative, and any given correlation coefficient must be interpreted in comparison to values that are commonly obtained. Table 5.7 on page 158 contains a number of correlations that have been reported for different types of variables. The nature of the scores being correlated is described and the coefficient reported. An examination of this table will provide some initial background for interpreting correlation coefficients. The coefficient will gradually

* The wording of this statement implies that we want correlations to be high. When a correlation expresses the reliability or consistency of a test, or its accuracy in predicting an outcome of interest to us, it is certainly true that the higher the correlation is, the more pleased we are. In other contexts, however, "bigness" need not correspond to "goodness," and we may not have any preference as to the size of a correlation or may even prefer a low one.

TABLE 5.7 CORRELATION COEFFICIENTS FOR SELECTED VARIABLES

Variables	Correlation Coefficient
Heights of identical twins	.95
Intelligence test scores of identical twins	.88
Reading test scores grade 3 versus grade 6	.80
Rank in high school class versus teachers' rating of work habits	.73
Height versus weight of 10-year-olds	.60
Arithmetic computation test versus nonverbal intelligence test (grade 8)	.54
Height of brothers, adjusted for age	.50
Intelligence test score versus parental occupational level	.30
Strength of grip versus speed of running	.16
Height versus Binet IQ	.06
Ratio of head length to width versus intelligence	.01
Armed Forces Qualification Test scores of recruits versus number of school grades repeated	−.27
Artist interest versus banker interest	−.64

take on added meaning as the reader encounters coefficients of different sizes in his reading about and work with tests.

SUMMARY STATEMENT

We opened this chapter by pointing out the various kinds of questions we might wish to answer by referring to a set of test scores. Let us look at these questions again and see what answers we have offered for them.

1. *How do our scores "run"; what do they "look like"?* To answer this question, we can arrange our scores into a frequency distribution (Table 5.3) or plot them in a histogram (Fig. 5.1).

2. *What score is typical of the group; represents the middle of the group?* To represent the middle of the group we may calculate the median—the 50th percentile (pp. 141–143), or the arithmetic mean—the common average (pp. 143–145).

3. *How widely spread out are the scores; how much do they scatter?* To represent the spread of scores statisticians have developed (1) the semi-interquartile range, half the distance between the 25th and 75th percentile (pp. 147–148), and (2) the standard deviation (pp. 149–151), a type of average of the deviations of the scores away from the average.

4. *How are we to determine what the score of an individual means—whether it is high or low?* Though this problem is left for fuller discussion in Chapter 7, we have seen that the individual score takes on meaning as it is translated into a percentile rank, the percent of the group he beat, or into a standard score, how many standard deviations above or below the mean he fell (p. 154).

5. *To what extent do two sets of scores go together; to what extent are the same individuals high or low on both?* A measure of relationship is given by the correlation coefficient, a numerical index of "going-togetherness" (pp. 154–158). This index is important as describing the precision or reliability of a test, as describing the accuracy with which a test score predicts some other factor, such as school grades or job success, and as describing the organization of traits in the individual.

STATISTICAL SYMBOLS

The student who reads test manuals, books dealing with tests, or articles about testing in the educational journals will encounter a number of conventional symbols to refer to statistical concepts or operations. Some of the commonest are defined below. This table of definitions should help in reading later chapters of this book, as well as outside references.

Symbol	*Definition*
N	The total number of cases in the group.
f	Frequency. The number of cases with a specific score or in a particular class interval.
X	A raw score on some measure.
x	A deviation score, indicating how far the individual falls above or below the mean of the group.
x'	A deviation score from some arbitrary reference point, often expressed in interval units.
i	The number of points of score in one class interval.
$\overline{X}$ or M	The mean of the group.
Md	The median of the group.
Q_1	The lower quartile, the 25th percentile.
Q_3	The upper quartile, the 75th percentile.
Q	The semi-interquartile range. Half the difference between Q_3 and Q_1.
P	A percentile.
A subscript	Modifies a symbol and tells which specific individual or value is referred to, e.g., P_{10} is the 10th percentile, X_j is the raw score of person j.
SD or s	Standard deviation of a set of scores.
σ	Standard deviation in the *population*, though sometimes used to refer to the particular sample.

Symbol	*Definition*
p	Percent of persons getting a test item correct.
q	Percent of persons getting a test item wrong ($p + q = 100$).
r	A coefficient of correlation.
r_{11}	A reliability coefficient. The correlation between two equivalent test forms or two administrations of a test.
Σ	"Take the sum of."

QUESTIONS AND EXERCISES

1. For each of the sets of scores indicated below, select what appears to you to be the most suitable class interval, and set up a form for tallying the scores:

Test	*Number of Cases*	*Range of Scores*
Arithmetic	84	8 to 53
Reading comprehension	57	15 to 75
Interest inventory	563	68 to 224

2. In each of the following distributions, indicate (a) the size of the class interval, (b) the midpoint of the intervals shown, and (c) the real limits of the intervals (i.e., the dividing lines between them).

(1)	(2)	(3)
4–7	17–19	50–59
8–11	20–22	60–69
12–15	23–25	70–79
.	.	.
.	.	.
.	.	.

3. Using the spelling scores given in Table 5.1 on pp. 134–135, make a frequency distribution and a histogram. Compute the median and the upper and lower quartiles. Compute the arithmetic mean and standard deviation.

4. In the Bureau of Census reports the *median* is used in reporting average income. Why is it used, rather than the arithmetic mean?

5. A 50-item vocabulary test given to 150 pupils yielded scores ranging from 18 to 50. Ninety-seven fell between 40 and 50. What would this distribution of scores look like? What could you say about the suitability of the test for the group? What measure of central tendency would be most suitable? Why? What measure of variability would you probably use?

6. A high-school teacher gave two sections of a mathematics class the same test. Results were as follows:

	Section A	*Section B*
Median	64.6	64.3
Mean	65.0	63.2
75th percentile	69.0	70.0
25th percentile	61.0	54.0
Standard deviation	6.0	10.5

From these data, what can you say about the two classes? What implications do the data have for teaching the two groups?

7. A test in biology given to 2500 tenth- and eleventh-grade students had a mean of 52 and a standard deviation of 10.5. How many standard deviations above or below the mean would the following pupils fall?

Alice	48	Henry	60	John	31
Willard	56	Jane	36	Oscar	84

8. If the distribution in the previous example was approximately normal, about what percent of the group would each of these pupils surpass?

9. Assuming that the scores are normally distributed, what proportion of cases would fall below each of the following scores for a test that has a mean of 72 and a standard deviation of 12?

a. 64 b. 75 c. 89

10. Explain the meaning of each of the following correlation coefficients:

a. The correlation between scores on a reading test and on a group intelligence test is +.78.
b. Ratings of pupils on "good citizenship" and on "aggressiveness" show a correlation of −.56.
c. The correlation between height and score on an achievement test is .02.

SUGGESTED ADDITIONAL READING

Gourevitch, V. P. *Statistical methods: A problem-solving approach.* Boston: Allyn & Bacon, 1965.

Guilford, J. P. *Fundamental statistics in psychology and education.* (4th ed.) New York: McGraw-Hill, 1965.

Walker, H. M. & Lev, J. *Elementary statistical methods.* (Rev. ed.) New York: Holt, 1958.

Weinberg, G. H. & Schumaker, J. A. *Statistics, an intuitive approach.* Belmont, California: Wadsworth, 1962.

CHAPTER 6

Qualities Desired in Any Measurement Procedure

WHENEVER a worker in psychology or education desires to measure some quality in a group or individual, he faces the problem of choosing the best instrument for his purpose. Ordinarily, there will be several tests or testing procedures that have been developed for, or that seem to be at least possibilities for, his purpose. He must choose among these. He is also probably interested in determining not only which is the best procedure but how well it satisfies his needs by some absolute standard. On what grounds can he make his choice or his appraisal?

There are many specific considerations entering into the evaluation of a test, but we shall consider them here under three main headings. These are, respectively, validity, reliability, and practicality. Validity refers to the extent to which a test measures what we actually wish to measure. Reliability has to do with accuracy and precision of a measurement procedure. Indices of reliability give an indication of the extent to which a particular measurement is consistent and reproducible. Practicality is concerned with a wide range of factors of economy, convenience, and interpretability that determine whether a test is practical for widespread use. These three aspects of test evaluation will be considered in detail in the following sections.

VALIDITY

The first and foremost question to be asked with respect to any testing procedure is: How valid is it? When we ask this question, we are inquiring whether the test measures what we want it to measure, all of what we want it to measure, and nothing but what we want it to measure.

When we apply a steel tape measure to the top of a desk to determine its length, we have no doubt that the tape does in fact measure the length of the desk and will directly serve our purpose, which may be to determine whether the desk will fit between two windows in our room. Long experience with this type of measuring instrument has confirmed beyond a shadow of doubt its validity as a tool for measuring length.

Suppose now that we give a test of reading achievement to a group of children. This test requires the children to select certain answers to a series of questions about reading passages and to make little pencil marks on an answer sheet. We count the number of pencil marks made in the predetermined right places and give the child as a score the number of his right answers. We call this score his reading comprehension. But the score itself is not the comprehension. It is the *record* of a *sample* of behavior. Any judgment regarding comprehension is an inference from this number which is the number of allegedly correct answers. Its validity is not self-evident but is something we must establish on the basis of adequate evidence.

Consider again the typical personality inventory that endeavors to provide an appraisal of "emotional adjustment." In this type of inventory, the respondent marks a series of statements about feeling or behavior as being characteristic of him or not characteristic of him. On the basis of various types of procedures, which we shall consider in detail in Chapter 12, certain responses are keyed as indicative of emotional maladjustment. A score is obtained by seeing how many of these responses an individual selects. But making certain marks on a piece of paper is a good many steps removed from actually exhibiting emotional disturbance. We must find some way of establishing the extent to which the performance on the test actually corresponds to the quality of behavior in which we are directly interested. How can we determine the validity of such a measurement procedure?

Types of Evidence of Validity

A test may be thought of as corresponding to some aspect of human behavior in any one of three senses. The terms that have been adopted to designate these senses are (1) content validity, (2) criterion-related validity, and (3) construct validity. Let us explore each of these three, so that we may understand clearly what is involved in each case, and for what kinds of tests each of the three is relevant.

CONTENT VALIDITY. Consider a test that has been prepared to measure achievement in using the English language. How can we tell how well the test does in fact measure that achievement? First, we must reach some agreement as to the skills, knowledge, and understanding that comprise correct and effective use of English, and that have been the objectives of language instruction. Then we must examine the test to see what skills, knowledge, and understanding it calls for. Finally, we must match the analysis of *test content* against the analysis of *course content* and instructional objectives and see how well the former represents the latter. To the extent that our objectives, which we have accepted as goals for the course, are represented in the test, the test is valid.

Since the analysis is essentially a rational and judgmental one, this is sometimes spoken of as *rational or logical validity*. The term *content validity* is also used, since the analysis is largely in terms of the test content. However, we should not think of content too narrowly, because we may be interested in *process* as much as in simple content. Thus, in the field of English expression we might be concerned on the one hand with such "content" elements as the rules and principles for capitalization, use of commas, or spelling words with "ei" and "ie" combinations. But we might also be interested in such "process" skills as arranging ideas in a logical order, writing sentences that present a single unified thought, or picking the most appropriate word to convey the desired meaning. In a sense, *content* is what the pupil works with; *process* is what he does with it.

The problem of appraising content validity is closely parallel to the problem of preparing the blueprint for a test, as discussed in Chapter 3, and then building a test to match the blueprint. A teacher's own test has content validity to the extent that a wise and thoughtful analysis of course objectives has been made in the blueprint, and care, skill, and ingenuity have been exercised in building test items to match that blueprint. A standardized test may be shown to have validity for a particular school or a particular curriculum insofar as the content of that test corresponds to and represents the objectives accepted in that school or that curriculum.

It should be clear that rational or content validity, is important primarily for measures of achievement. When we wish to appraise a test of reading comprehension, of biology, or of American history, we can really do so only by asking: How well do the tasks of this test represent what we consider to be important outcomes in this area of instruction? How well do these tasks represent what the best and most expert judgment would consider to be important knowledge and skills? If the correspondence is good, we consider the test valid; if poor, the validity must be deemed to be low.

The responsible maker of a test for publication and widespread use goes to considerable pains to determine the widely accepted goals of instruction in the field in which his test is to be built. There are many types of sources to which he may, and often does resort. These include, among others: (1) the more widely used textbooks in the field, (2) recent courses of study for the large school units, that is, states, counties, and city systems, (3) reports of special study groups, often appearing in yearbooks of one or another of the educational societies, (4) groups of teachers giving instruction in the course, (5) specialists in universities, cities, and state departments concerned with the training or supervision of teachers in the field.

Gathering information from these sources the test maker develops the blueprint for his test, and in terms of this blueprint he prepares his test items. Because of variations from community to community, no published test can be made to fit exactly the content or objectives of every local course of study. In this sense, a test developed on a national basis is always less valid for a specific community than an equally workmanlike test tailored specifically to the local situation. However, the well-made commercial test takes the common components that appear repeatedly in different textbooks and courses of study and builds a test around them. It represents the common core that is central in the different specific local patterns.

It should be clear from what has just been said that the relationship between teaching and testing is typically intimate. Test content is drawn from what has been taught, or what is proposed to be taught. The instructional program is the original source of test materials. Sometimes the thinking in a test may lead the thinking underlying a local course of study, as when a group of specialists have been brought together to design a test corresponding to some emerging trend in education. Sometimes the test may lag behind, as when the test is based on the relatively conventional objectives emphasized in established textbooks. But usually test content and classroom instruction are in close relationship to one another, and the test may be appraised by how faithfully it corresponds to the significant goals of instruction.

To appraise the validity of a test as representing curricular objectives, there is no substitute for a careful and detailed examination of the actual test tasks. A test may be labeled "Mathematical Concepts," and call for nothing but knowledge of the definitions of terms. A test of reading comprehension may only call for answers to questions concerning specific details that appear in the passage. It is the tasks presented by the items that really define what a test is measuring, and one who would judge the validity of its content for his curriculum must take a hard look at the individual items.

CRITERION-RELATED VALIDITY. Frequently, we are interested in using a test to predict some specific future outcome. We use a scholastic aptitude test to predict how likely the high school student is to be successful in college X, where success is represented at least approximately by grade-point average. We use an employment test to pick machine operators who are likely to be successful employees, as represented by some such criterion as high production with little spoilage and low personnel turnover. For this purpose, we care very little what a test looks like.* We are interested only in the degree to which it correlates with some chosen criterion measure of job success. Thus, some other measure (often, but not necessarily, one maturing at a later point in time) is taken as the criterion of "success," and we judge a test in terms of its relationship to that criterion. The higher the correlation, the better the test.

Our evaluation of a test as predicting is primarily an empirical and statistical evaluation, and this aspect of validity has sometimes been spoken of as *empirical* or statistical validity. The basic procedure is to give the test to a group who are entering some job or training program, to follow them up later and get for each one some criterion measure of success on the job or in the training program, and then to compute the correlation between test score and criterion measure of success. The higher the correlation, the more effective the test as a predictor.

This relationship can also be pictured in various ways. For example, the bar chart in Fig. 6.1 shows the percentage of persons failing pilot training at each of nine score levels on a predictor-test battery. Examination of the chart shows a steady increase in the percent failing training as we go from the high to the low scores. The relationship pictured in this chart corresponds to a correlation coefficient of .49.

THE PROBLEM OF THE CRITERION. We said above that predictive validity can be estimated by determining the correlation between test scores and a suitable criterion measure of success on the job. The joker here is the phrase "suitable criterion measure." One of the most difficult problems that the personnel psychologist or educator faces is that of locating or creating a satisfactory measure of job success to serve as a criterion measure for test validation. It may appear to the student that it should be a simple matter to decide upon some measure of

* This is not entirely true. What a test "looks like" may be of importance in determining its acceptability and reasonableness to those who will be tested. Thus, a group of would-be pilots may be more ready to accept an arithmetic test dealing with wind drift and fuel consumption than they would the same essential problems phrased in terms of costs of crops or of recipes for baking cakes. This appearance of reasonableness is sometimes spoken of as "face validity."

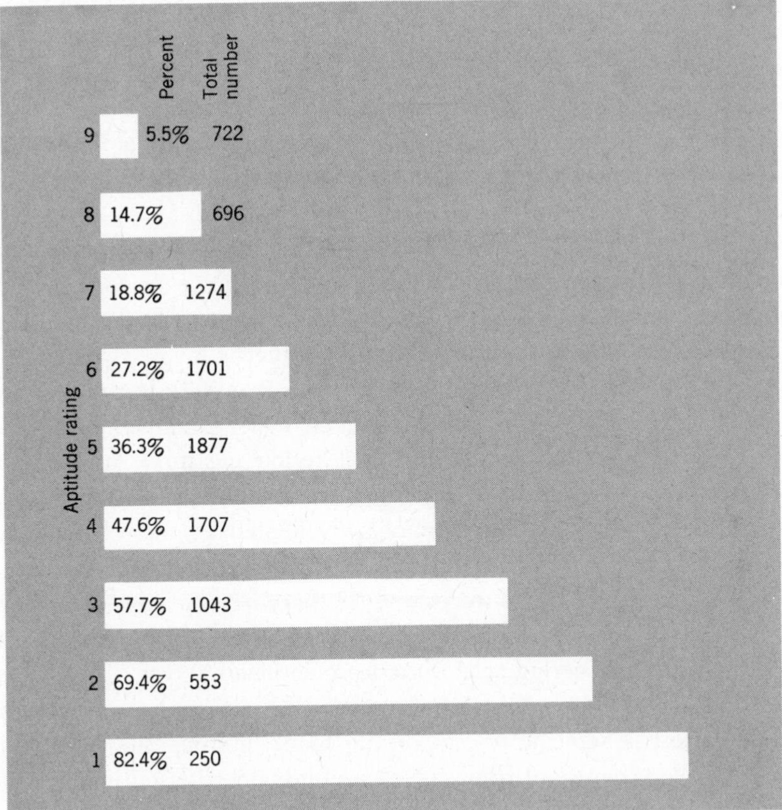

Fig. 6.1 Percent of cadets eliminated from pilot training at each aptitude level. The correlation coefficient for these data is .49.

rate of production or some type of rating by superiors. It may also seem that this measure, once decided upon, should be obtainable in an easy and straightforward fashion. Unfortunately, this is not so. Finding or developing acceptable criterion measures usually involves the research worker in the field of tests and measurements in a number of troublesome problems.

Difficulties in obtaining satisfactory criterion measures arise from a variety of sources. There are many types of jobs, such as those of physician, teacher, secretary, or stock clerk, that yield no objective record of performance or production. But even when such records are available, they are often influenced by a variety of factors outside the worker's control. Thus, the production record of a weaver may depend not only upon his own skill in threading or adjusting the loom, but also on the condition of the equipment, the adequacy of the lighting where he must work, or the color of the thread he must weave. The sales of an insurance agent are not only a function of his own effectiveness as a salesman but also of the territory in which he must work and the supervision and assistance he receives. The problems of effective rating of personnel are discussed in detail in Chapter 13. It suffices to indicate here that ratings are often unstable and influenced by many factors other than the proficiency of the person being rated.

There are always many criterion measures that might be obtained and used for validating a selection test. In addition to quantitative performance records and subjective ratings, which have already been mentioned, we might use later tests of proficiency. This is the type of situation that is involved when a college entrance mathematics test is validated in terms of its ability to predict later performance on a comprehensive examination on college mathematics. Here the comprehensive examination serves as the criterion measure. Another common type of criterion is grades in some type of educational or training program. Thus, tests for the selection of engineers may be validated against course grades in engineering school.

All criterion measures are only partial in that they measure only a part of success on the job or only the preliminaries to actual job performance. This last is true of the engineering school grades mentioned above. They represent a relatively immediate but quite partial criterion of success as an engineer. The ultimate criterion is some appraisal of the man's lifetime success in his profession. In the very nature of things, such an ultimate criterion is inaccessible to us and we must be satisfied with substitutes for it. These substitutes are only partial and are never completely satisfactory. Our problem is always to choose the most satisfactory measure or combination of measures from among those that it appears feasible to obtain. We are faced, then, with the problem of deciding which of several criterion measures is most satisfactory. How shall we arrive at this decision?

QUALITIES DESIRED IN A CRITERION MEASURE. There are four qualities that we desire in a criterion measure. In order of their importance they are (1) relevance, (2) freedom from bias, (3) reliability, and (4) availability.

We judge a criterion to be relevant to the extent that standing on the criterion measure is determined by the same factors that determine success on the job. In appraising the relevance of a criterion, we are thrown back once again upon rational considerations. There is no empirical evidence that will tell us how relevant freshman grade-point average is, for example, as an indicator of having achieved the objectives of the Supercolossal University. For achievement tests we found it necessary to rely upon the best available professional judgment to determine whether the content of the test accurately represented our objectives.

In the same way, with respect to a criterion measure it is also necessary to rely upon professional judgment to provide the appraisal of the degree to which any available partial criterion measure is relevant to the ultimate criterion of success in an educational program or in a job.

A second factor important in a criterion measure is that of freedom from bias. By this we mean that the measure should provide each person with the same opportunity to make a good score. Examples of biasing factors are such things as variation in wealth from one district to another in our previous example of the insurance salesman, variation in the quality of equipment and conditions of work of a factory worker, variation in generosity of the bosses rating private secretaries, or variation in the skill of teachers instructing pupils in different classes. We can see that it will be difficult to get meaning from the relationship of test results to a criterion score if that score depends upon factors in the conditions of work rather than factors in the individual worker.

The topic of reliability will be discussed in general terms later in this chapter. As it applies to the criterion scores, the problem is merely this: a measure of success on the job must be stable or reproducible if it is to be predicted by any type of test device. If the criterion performance is one that jumps around from day to day so that the person who shows high job performance one week may show low job performance the next, then there is no possibility of finding a test that will predict it. A measure that is fundamentally unstable itself cannot be predicted by anything else.

Finally, in the choice of criterion measure one always encounters practical problems of convenience and availability. How long is it going to take to get a criterion score for each individual? How much is it going to cost? Though a personnel research program can often afford to spend a substantial part of its effort in getting good criterion data, there is always a practical limit. Any choice of a criterion measure must take this practical limit into account.

THE INTERPRETATION OF VALIDITY COEFFICIENTS. Suppose that we have gathered test and criterion scores for a group of individuals and computed the correlation between them. Perhaps our predictor is a scholastic aptitude test, and the criterion is an average of college freshman grades. How shall we now decide whether the test is a good predictor?

Obviously, other things being equal, the higher the correlation, the better. In one sense, our basis for evaluating any one predictor is in relation to other possible prediction procedures. Does test A yield a higher or lower validity coefficient than other tests? Than other types of information, such as high-school grades or rating by school principals? We will look with favor on any measure whose validity for a particular criterion is higher than that of measures previously available to us.

TABLE 6.1 VALIDITY OF SELECTED TESTS AS PREDICTORS OF CERTAIN EDUCATIONAL AND VOCATIONAL CRITERIA

Predictor Test	Criterion Variable	Validity Coefficient
Lorge-Thorndike Intelligence Test (Verbal)	*Iowa Tests of Basic Skills (Total Score—Gr. 4)*	.78
American College Testing Program Test Index	College Grades—English	.54
	College Grades—Math	.44
Seashore Tonal Memory Test	Performance test on stringed instrument	.28
Short Employment Test		
Word Knowledge Score	Production index—80 bookkeeping machine operators	.10
Word Knowledge Score	Job grade—106 stenographers	.53
Arithmetic Skill Score	Production index—80 bookkeeping machine operators	.26
Arithmetic Skill Score	Job grade—106 stenographers	.60
Differential Aptitude Tests (Grade 8)		
Verbal Reasoning	English grades 3½ years later	.57
Space Relations	English grades 3½ years later	.01
Mechanical Reasoning	English grades 3½ years later	.17

Some representative validity coefficients are exhibited in Table 6.1. These give some picture of the size of correlation that has been obtained in previous work of different kinds. The investigator concerned with a particular course of study or a particular job criterion will, of course, need to become intimately acquainted with validities previously found for this particular criterion.

The usefulness of a test as a predictor depends not only on how well it correlates with a criterion, but also on how much *new* information it gives. Thus, the *Differential Aptitude Tests' Verbal Reasoning Test* correlates on the average .48 with high-school English grades, and the test of sentence usage correlates .51 with the same grades. But the two tests have an intercorrelation of .62. They overlap and, in part at least, the information each test provides is the same as that provided by the other test. The net result is that pooling information from the two tests can give a validity coefficient of no more than .55. If the two tests were uncorrelated, each giving evidence completely independent of the other, the combination of the two tests would give a validity coefficient of .70.*

* Statistical procedures have been developed that enable us to determine the best weighing to give the two or more predictors and to calculate the correlation that will result from this combination. The procedures for computing the weights for the separate components (called regression weights) and the correlation (multiple correlation) resulting from them are beyond the scope of this discussion but will be found in standard statistics texts.

Clearly, the higher the correlation between a test or other predictor and a criterion, the more pleased we shall be. But in addition to this relative standard, we should like some absolute one. How high must the validity coefficient be for the test to be useful? What is a "satisfactory" validity? This is a little bit like asking, "How high is up?" However, we can try to give some sort of answer.

To an organization using a test as a basis for deciding whether to hire a particular job applicant or admit a particular student, the significant question is: How much more often will we make the right decision on whom to hire or admit if we use this test than if we operate on a purely chance basis or on the basis of some already available but less valid measure? The answer to this question depends in considerable measure on the proportion of individuals who must be accepted. A selection procedure can do much more for us if we need to accept only the individual who appears to be the best one in every ten applicants than if we must accept nine out of ten. However, to provide a specific example, let us assume that we will accept half of the applicants. Let us examine Table 6.2.

TABLE 6.2 TWO BY TWO TABLE OF TEST AND JOB SUCCESS

		Performance on the Job		
		Bottom Half "Failures"	Top Half "Successes"	
Score on Selection Test	Top Half (accepted)			100
	Bottom Half (rejected)			100
		100	100	200

The model is set up to show 200 persons in all, 100 in the top half on the test and 100 in the top half on the job. If there were absolutely no relationship between test and job, there would be 50 persons in each of the four cells of the table. The success ratio would be 50 in 100 for those accepted, and also for those rejected. There would be no difference between the two and the correlation would be zero.

Table 6.3 on page 172 shows the percent of correct choices (that is, "successes") among those accepted for correlations of different sizes. The improvement in our "batting average" as the correlation goes up is shown in the table. Thus, for a correlation of .40 we will pick right 63.1 percent of the time; with a correlation of .80 our percentage will be 79.5, and so forth.

TABLE 6.3 PERCENT OF CORRECT ASSIGNMENTS WHEN 50 PERCENT OF GROUP MUST BE SELECTED

Validity of Selection Procedure	Percent of Correct Choices
.00	50.0
.20	56.4
.40	63.1
.50	66.7
.60	70.5
.70	74.7
.80	79.5
.90	85.6

The table shows not only our accuracy for any given correlation but our gain in accuracy if we raise the validity of our predictor. Thus, if we were able to replace a predictor with a validity of .40 by one with a validity of .60, we would increase our percent of correct decisions from 63.1 to 70.5. All these percentages refer, of course, to the ground rules set in the previous paragraph. However, Table 6.3 gives a fairly representative basis for understanding the effects of a selection program from the point of view of the employing or certifying agency.

In many selection situations, the gain can be crudely translated into a dollars-and-cents saving. Thus, if it costs a company $500 to employ and train a new worker up to the point of useful productivity, a selection procedure that raised the percent of successes from 56.4 to 63.1 would yield a saving in wasted training expenses alone of $3,350 per 100 men tested. This takes no account of the possibility that the test-selected men might also be *better* workers after they had completed their training. This gain would have to be balanced, of course, against any increase of cost in the new selection procedure.

Another way of appraising the practical significance of a correlation coefficient, and one that is perhaps more meaningful from the point of view of the person being tested, is shown in Table 6.4. The rows in the little tables represent the fourths of a group of applicants, potential students or employees, with respect to a predictor test. The columns indicate the percent of cases falling in each fourth on the criterion score. Look at the little table in Table 6.4 corresponding to a validity coefficient of .50. We see that of those who fall in the lowest fourth on our predictor 480 out of 1,000 or 48.0 percent fall in the lowest fourth on the criterion score, 27.9 percent in the next lowest fourth, 16.8 percent in the next to highest fourth, and 7.3 percent in the highest fourth. The diagonal entries represent cases that fall in the same fourth on both predictor and criterion. The further we get from the diagonal, the greater the discrepancy between prediction and outcome.

This table emphasizes not so much the gain from using the predictor test as the variation in job success of those who are similar in predictor scores. From the point of view of schools or employers, the important thing is the improved percentage of accuracy illustrated in Table 6.3. Dealing in large numbers, they can count on gaining from any predictor that is more valid than the procedure currently in use. From the point of view of the single individual, the many marked discrepancies between predicted and actual success shown in Table 6.4 may seem at least as important. If he has done poorly on the test, an applicant

TABLE 6.4 ACCURACY OF PREDICTION FOR DIFFERENT VALUES OF THE CORRELATION COEFFICIENT (1,000 cases in each row or column)

$r = .00$

Quarter on Predictor	Quarter on Criterion 4th	3rd	2nd	1st
1st	250	250	250	**250**
2nd	250	250	**250**	250
3rd	250	**250**	250	250
4th	**250**	250	250	250

$r = .60$

Quarter on Predictor	Quarter on Criterion 4th	3rd	2nd	1st
1st	45	141	277	**537**
2nd	141	264	**318**	277
3rd	277	**318**	264	141
4th	**537**	277	141	45

$r = .40$

Quarter on Predictor	Quarter on Criterion 4th	3rd	2nd	1st
1st	104	191	277	**428**
2nd	191	255	**277**	277
3rd	277	**277**	255	191
4th	**428**	277	191	104

$r = .70$

Quarter on Predictor	Quarter on Criterion 4th	3rd	2nd	1st
1st	22	107	270	**601**
2nd	107	270	**353**	270
3rd	270	**353**	270	107
4th	**601**	270	107	22

$r = .50$

Quarter on Predictor	Quarter on Criterion 4th	3rd	2nd	1st
1st	73	168	279	**480**
2nd	168	258	**295**	279
3rd	279	**295**	258	168
4th	**480**	279	168	73

$r = .80$

Quarter on Predictor	Quarter on Criterion 4th	3rd	2nd	1st
1st	6	66	253	**675**
2nd	66	271	**410**	253
3rd	253	**410**	271	66
4th	**675**	253	66	**6**

may be less impressed by the fact that the *probability* is that he will be below average on the job than by the fact that he *may* do very well. He may always be the exception.

There are several factors that tend to distort validity coefficients, and complicate their interpretation. One is unreliability of the predictor and of the criterion that is being predicted. The effect of this is discussed on pp. 198 and 199. The other is restriction of the range of ability in the group by some type of preselection. This effect will be discussed further in Chapter 19 on pp. 631–632. Low reliability on the one hand or preselection on the other will tend to lower the values that are obtained for validity coefficients.

One further point can well be emphasized in conclusion. Validity is always specific to a particular curriculum or a particular job. When an author or publisher claims that his test is valid, it is always appropriate to ask: Valid for what? A test in social studies that accurately represents the content and objectives of one program of instruction may be quite inappropriate for the program in a different community. The test must always be evaluated against the objectives of a specific program of instruction. Again, a test quite valid for picking department store sales clerks who will be pleasant to customers, informed about their stock, and accurate in financial transactions may be entirely useless in identifying effective insurance salesmen who will go out and find or create new business. Validity must always be evaluated in relation to a situation as similar as possible to the one in which the measure is to be used.

For what kinds of tests is criterion-related validity important? Clearly, this kind of validity is most important for a test that is to be used to predict outcomes that are represented by clear-cut criterion measures. The more readily we can identify performance criteria that unquestionably represent the end results that we are interested in, the more we will be prepared to rely upon the evidence from correlations between our test and the measures of that criterion to guide our decision on whether to use the test. There are two elements in this statement —prediction and clear-cut criterion measures. The main limitation, within the prediction context, is the adequacy of the available criterion measures.

CONSTRUCT VALIDITY. Sometimes we ask, with respect to a psychological test, neither "How well does this test predict job success?" nor "How well does this test represent our curriculum?", but "What does this test *mean* or *signify*?" What does the score tell us about an individual? Does it correspond to some meaningful trait or construct * that will help us in understanding him? For this

* The term "construct" is used in psychology to refer to something that is not observable, but is literally *constructed* by the investigator to summarize or account for the regularities or relationships that he observes in behavior. Thus, most names of traits refer to constructs. We speak of a person's "sociability" as a way of summarizing observed consistency in his past behavior and of organizing a prediction of how he will act on future occasions.

question of whether the test tells us something meaningful about people the term *construct* validity has been used.

Let us examine one specific testing procedure and see how its validity as a measure of a useful psychological quality or construct was studied. McClelland (1953) developed a testing procedure to appraise the individual's need or motivation to achieve—to succeed and do well. The test used pictures like those in the *Thematic Apperception Test* (see Chapter 15). The individual was called upon to make up a story about each picture, telling what was happening and how it turned out. A scoring system was developed for these stories, based on counting the frequency with which themes of accomplishment, mastery, success, and achievement appeared in the story material. Thus, each individual received a score representing the strength of his motivation to achieve. Now, how are we to determine whether this measure has validity in the sense of truthfully describing a meaningful aspect of the individual's make-up? Let us see how McClelland and his co-workers proceeded.

In essence, the investigators proceeded to ask: "With what should a measure of achievement motivation be related?" They made a series of predictions. Some of the predictions were as follows:

1. Those high on achievement motivation should do well in college, in relation to their scholastic aptitude.
2. Achievement motivation should be higher for students just after they have been taking tests described to them as measuring their intelligence.
3. Those high on achievement motivation should complete more items on a motivated speeded test.
4. Achievement motivation should be higher for children of families emphasizing early independence.

Each of these predictions was based on a sort of "theory of human behavior." Thus, academic achievement is seen as a combination of ability and effort. Presumably those with higher motivation to achieve will exert more effort and will, ability being equal, achieve higher grades. A similar chain of reasoning lies back of each of the other predictions.

In general, McClelland found that most of his predictions were supported by the experimental results. The fact that the test scores were related to a number of other events in the way that was predicted from a rational analysis of the trait that the test was presumably measuring lent support to the validity of the test procedure as measuring a meaningful trait or construct, whose essential characteristics are fairly well summarized by the label "achievement motivation."

A great many psychological tests, and, to a lesser extent, some educational tests, are intended to measure general traits or qualities of the individual. Verbal reasoning, spatial visualizing, sociability, introversion, mechanical interest are all designations of traits or constructs. Tests of these functions are valid insofar as they behave in the way that such a trait should reasonably be expected to behave.

A "theory" about a trait will lead to predictions of the following types that can be subjected to empirical verification.

1. *Predictions about correlations.* The nature of the trait, and, therefore, of valid measures of it, will indicate that it should be related to certain other measures. These other measures may be already accepted measures of the function in question. Thus, many subsequent group intelligence tests have been validated in part by their correlations with earlier tests, especially with the individually administered *Stanford-Binet.* Or the other measures may be ones with which the trait should logically be related. Thus, intelligence tests have been validated, in part, through their correlation with success in school; measures of mechanical aptitude, by their correlation with rated proficiency in mechanical jobs.

One way of studying the constructs or attributes that a test measures is to study jointly the intercorrelations of this test and a number of others. The patterning of these correlations makes it possible to see which tests are measuring some common factor. An examination of the tests clustering together in a single factor may serve to clarify the nature and meaning of the factor. However, this internal or "factorial validity" still seems to need evidence of relationship to life events outside the tests themselves if the factor is to have much substance and vitality.

2. *Predictions about group differences.* A "theory" will often suggest that certain kinds of groups should score especially high or low on the trait, and consequently on a test of it. Thus, it seems reasonable that a group of salesmen should be high on a measure of "ascendance," and that a group of librarians should be low. We would probably predict that children of professional and business parents would be more ascendant than those whose parents were in clerical or semiskilled occupations. For any given trait, our general knowledge of our society and the groups within it will suggest an array of group differences that seem to "make sense." Applying a test to these groups, the investigator finds out how consistently his predictions are borne out.

3. *Predictions about response to experimental treatments or interventions.* A "theory" may imply that the expression of a human characteristic will be modified as a result of certain experimental conditions or treatments. Thus, one could reasonably predict that anxiety would increase just before a person was to undergo a minor operation. Rate of flicker fusion * has been proposed as an

* The rate at which alternation of black and white stimulation fuses into a steady gray.

indicator of anxiety level. In one study (Buhler, 1953) it was found that, as predicted, the flicker fusion threshold was lower before the operation than after when the anxiety had presumably relaxed.

For any test that presumes to measure a trait or quality, we can formulate a network of theory, leading to definite predictions. These predictions can be tested. Insofar as they are borne out, the validity of the test as a measure of the trait or construct is supported. Insofar as the predictions fail to be verified, we are led to doubt the validity of our test, or our theorizing, or both.

Evidence of validity is, as we have seen, partly rational and partly empirical. Rational consideration of what is measured takes the center of the stage when we are considering an end product—either a test that is serving to describe an individual's past learning or some indicator that we are accepting as a criterion measure. Again, the elaboration of a "theory" by which we decide how to test out the validity of a measure of a psychological construct is also a rational exercise. By contrast, when we use a test as a selection device to predict some accepted criterion measure, validation becomes primarily statistical. And checking out the "theory" that we have built up for a measure of some construct is also an empirical undertaking. Judgment and evidence join together in the validation enterprise.

RELIABILITY

The second question we raise with respect to a measurement procedure is: How reliable is it? We are now asking not what it measures but how accurately it measures whatever it does measure. What is the precision of our resulting score? How accurately will it be reproduced if we measure the individual again?

Suppose we were to test all the boys in a school class today and again tomorrow to see how far each can throw a football. We mark a starting line on the field, give a pupil one of the old footballs that the physical education department has for team practice, send an assistant out to mark where the ball hits, and tell the boy to throw the ball as far as he can. With a steel tape, we measure the distance from the starting line to where our assistant marked the fall of the ball. We have each boy make a throw today and then make a throw again tomorrow.

When we compare the two scores for a boy, we will find they are rarely exactly the same. The two throws differ. Most of the differences will be fairly small, but some will be moderately large, and a few will be quite large. These differences show that one throw is not perfectly reliable as a measure of the boy's "throwing ability." Results are, to some degree, inconsistent from one day's throw to the next. Why?

We can identify three classes of reasons for inconsistency between a throw today and a throw tomorrow.

1. *The person may actually have changed* from one day to the next. On one day, he may be more rested than he was on the other. On one day, he may have been motivated to try harder on the task. He may even have gotten some special coaching from his father between the two tests. If the interval between the two tests is months rather than days, there may have been very real physical growth, and growth that differed from boy to boy between the two testings. Our example has been of changes affecting physical performance, but it is easy to think of similar categories of change that would apply to a test of mental ability or to a self-report inventory dealing with mood or with interests.

2. *The task may have been different* for the two measurements. For example, the ball used one day may have been tightly inflated, whereas the other day it may have been a somewhat squashy one that permitted a somewhat different grip. Or one day the examiner may have permitted the boys to take a run up to the release line, whereas the examiner on the second day may have allowed only a couple of steps. And these variations may have helped some boys more than others. In paper-and-pencil tests, we often use one form of the test upon one occasion and a parallel form on the second occasion. The specific items are then different, and some pupils may happen to be better able to handle one sampling of tasks, while others are better at the second sampling.

3. *The limited sample of behavior* will have resulted in an unstable and undependable score. Even if we had each boy make two throws with the same ball and same instructions, with only a five-minute rest in between, the two distances would rarely come out to be the same. A single throw is a meager sample of behavior. That sample, and the evaluation of it are subject to all sorts of "chance" influences. Maybe the boy's finger slipped. Maybe he got mixed up in the coordination of his legs and arm. Maybe the ball was held a little too far forward or a little too far back. Maybe the scorer was looking the other way when the ball landed. Maybe there was a gust of wind just as he threw. Maybe any one of a hundred things—some favorable, some unfavorable. These all add up to the end result that a small sample of behavior does not provide a stable and dependable characterization of the individual—whether the sample be of footballs thrown for distance or of sentences read for understanding.

There are two ways in which we can express the reliability or precision of a set of measurements, or, from the reverse point of view, the variation within the set. One approach indicates directly the amount of variation within a set of repeated measurements of a single individual. If we could have Johnny throw the football 200 times (assuming for the present that this could be done without introducing effects of fatigue or practice), we would get a frequency distribution of distances thrown. This frequency distribution has an average value, which we can think of as approximating the "true" distance that Johnny can throw a football. It also has a standard deviation describing the spread or scatter of these distances. We shall call this variation the *standard error of measurement,* since it is the standard deviation of the "errors" of measuring his distance of throw.

With psychological data, we can rarely actually make a whole series of measurements on each individual. There *are* practice and fatigue effects; besides, time does not permit the giving of 200 reading tests or 200 interest inventories. Often we are fortunate if we can get *two* scores for each individual. But if we have a pair of measurements for each individual we can make an estimate of what the scattering of scores would have been if we had made the measurements again and again.

Reliable measurement also implies that the individual stays in about the same place in his group. The boy who scores highest on the football throwing test the first time should also be one of the highest the next time, and each person in the group should stay in about the same position. We have already seen that the correlation coefficient provides us with a statistical index of the extent to which two things go together, high with high and low with low. If the two things we are correlating happen to be two applications of the same measure, the resulting correlation provides an indicator of reliability. We can designate it a *reliability coefficient.* The characteristics of the coefficient are those that we have already seen in Chapter 5 and in our discussion of validity. But the relationship now before us is that of two measurements with the same measuring instrument. The more nearly the scores are reproduced the second time, the higher the correlation and the more reliable the test.

A measure is reliable, then, to the extent that an individual remains nearly the same in repeated measurements—nearly the same as represented by a low standard error of measurement or by a high reliability coefficient. But what exact type of data do we need in order to get an appropriate estimate of this degree of stability or precision in measurement? We shall consider three distinct possibilities, noticing their similarities and differences and evaluating the advantages and disadvantages of each.

1. Repetition of the same test or measure.
2. Administration of a second "equivalent" form of the test.
3. Subdivision of the test into two or more equivalent fractions.

Let us examine each of these in turn.

Retest with the Same Test

If we wish to find how reliably we can evaluate an individual's football throw, we can have him tested twice. It may be a reasonable precaution to have the two measures taken independently by two persons. We don't want the experimenter's recollection of the first score to color the second score. It may be desirable to have the two testings done on different days. That depends on what we are interested in. If we want to know how accurately a single throw (or possibly a single set of throws) characterizes a person at one specific point in time, the two measurements should be carried out one right after the other. Then we know that the *person* has stayed the same and that the only source of variation or "error" is in the operation of measuring him. If we want to know how precisely a given measurement characterizes a person from day to day—how closely we can predict his score next week from what he does today, it would be appropriate to measure him on two separate occasions. Now we are interested in *variation of the individual* as well as *variation due to the operation of measurement.*

Sometimes we are interested in variation of the individual; sometimes we are not. We may ask: How accurately does our measurement characterize S at this moment of time? Or we may ask: How accurately does our measure of S today describe him as he will be tomorrow, or next week, or next month? Both are sensible questions. But they are not the same question. The data we must gather to answer one are different from the data we need to answer the other.

To study the reliability of such a physical characteristic of a person as height or weight, repetition of the measurement is a straightforward and satisfactory operation. It appears satisfactory and applicable also with some simple aspects of behavior, such as speed of reaction or the type of motor skill that is exemplified by the football throw. But suppose now we are interested in the reliability of a test of reading comprehension. Let us assume that the test is made up of six reading passages with ten questions on each. We administer the test once and then immediately administer it again. What happens? Certainly, the child is not going to have to reread all the material he has just read. He may do so in part, but to a considerable extent his answers the second time will involve merely remembering what answer he had chosen the time before and marking it again. If he had not been able to finish the first time, he will now be able to work ahead and spend most of his time on new material. These same effects will hold true to some degree even over a longer period of time. Clearly, this sort of test given a second time does not present the same task that it did the first time.

There is a second consideration entering into the repetition of such a test as a reading comprehension test. Suppose that one of the five passages in the test was about baseball and that a particular boy was an expert on baseball. The passage would then be especially easy for him, and he would in effect get a bonus of several points. The test would overestimate his general level of reading ability. But note that it would do it consistently on both testings if the material remained the same. The error for individual S would be a *constant error* in the two testings. Since it would affect both his scores in the same way, it would make the test look reliable rather than unreliable.

In such an area of ability as reading, we must recognize the possibility that an individual does not perform uniformly well throughout the whole area. His specific interests, experiences, and background give him strengths and weaknesses. A particular test is *one sample* from the whole area. How well individual S does on the test, relative to other persons, is likely to depend in some degree upon the particular sample of tasks chosen to represent the area of ability or personality we are trying to appraise. If the sample remains the same for both measurements, his behavior will stay more nearly the same than if the sample of tasks is varied.

Note that so far we have identified three main sources of variation in performance that will tend to reduce the precision of a particular score as a description of an individual:

1. Variation in response to the test at a particular moment in time.
2. Variation in the individual from time to time.
3. Variation arising out of the particular sample of tasks chosen to represent an area of behavior.

Retesting the individual with identically the same test can be arranged to reflect the first two types of "error," but this procedure cannot evaluate the effects of the third type. In addition, there may be the memory and practice effects to which we referred above.

Parallel Test Forms

Concern about this third source of variation, variation arising because of the necessity of choosing a particular sample of tasks to represent a whole area of behavior, leads us to another set of procedures for evaluating reliability. If the sampling of items may be a significant source of "error," and if, as is usually the case, we want to know with what accuracy we may generalize from the specific score based on one sample of tasks to the area of behavior it is supposed to represent, we must develop some procedures that take account of this variation due to the sample of tasks. We may do this by correlating two equivalent forms of a test.

Equivalent forms of a test should be thought of as forms built according to the same specifications but composed of separate samples from the defined area of behavior. Thus, two equivalent reading tests should contain reading passages and questions of the same difficulty. The same sorts of questions should be asked, that is, the same balance of specific fact and general idea questions. The same types of passages should be represented, that is, expository, argumentative, aesthetic. But the specific passages and questions should be different.

If we have two forms of a test, we may give each pupil first one form and then the other. They may follow each other immediately if we are not interested in stability over time, or may be separated by an interval if we are. The correlation between the two forms will provide an appropriate reliability coefficient. If a time interval has been allowed between the testings, all three sources of variation will have had a chance to get in their effects—variation arising from the measurement itself, variation in the individual over time, and variation due to the sample of tasks.

To ask that a test yield consistent results under these conditions is the most rigorous standard we can set for it. And if we want to use our test results to generalize about what Johnny will do on other tasks of this general sort next week and next month, then this is the appropriate standard by which to evaluate a test. For most educational situations, this *is* the way we want to use test results, and so evidence based on equivalent test forms should usually be given the most weight in evaluating the reliability of a test.

The use of two parallel test forms provides a very sound basis for estimating the precision of a psychological or educational test. This procedure does, however, raise some practical problems. It demands that two parallel forms of a test be available and that time be allowed for administering two separate tests. Sometimes no second form of a test exists, or no time can be found for a second testing. To administer a second separate test is often likely to represent a somewhat burdensome demand upon available resources. These practical considerations of convenience and expediency have made test makers receptive to procedures that extract an estimate of reliability from administration of only one form of a test. However, such procedures are compromises at best. The correlation between two parallel forms, usually administered with a lapse of several days or weeks in between, represents the preferred procedure for estimating reliability.

Subdivided Test

The most widely used procedure for estimating reliability from a single testing divides a particular test up into two presumably equivalent halves. The half-tests may be assembled on the basis of careful examination of the content and difficulty of each item, making a systematic effort to balance out the content and difficulty level of the two halves. A simpler procedure, which is often relied upon to give equivalent halves, is to put alternate items into the two half-tests, that is, to put all the odd-numbered items in one half-test and all the even-numbered items in the other. This is usually a sensible procedure, since items of similar form, content, or difficulty are likely to be grouped together in a test. For a reasonably long test, say, of 60 items or more, splitting the test up in this way will tend to balance out factors of item form, content covered, and difficulty level. The two half-tests will have a good probability of constituting "equivalent" tests, as these are defined in the preceding section.

The procedures we are discussing now divide the test in half only for scoring, not for administration. That is, a single test is given at a single sitting and with a single time limit. However, two separate scores are derived—one by scoring the odd-numbered items and one by scoring the even-numbered items. The correlation between these two scores provides a measure of the accuracy with which the test is measuring the individual.

However, it must be noted that the computed correlation is between two half-length tests. This value is not directly applicable to the full-length test, which is the actual instrument prepared for use. In general, the larger the sample of a person's behavior we have, the more reliable the measure will be. The more behavior we record, the less our measure will depend upon chance elements in behavior of the individual or in the particular sampling of tasks. Single lucky answers or momentary lapses of attention will be more nearly evened out.

Where the two halves of the test, which gave the scores actually correlated, are equivalent, we can get an unbiased estimate of total-test reliability from the correlation between the two half-tests. This estimate is given by the formula

$$r_{11} = \frac{2r_{\frac{1}{2}\frac{1}{2}}}{1 + r_{\frac{1}{2}\frac{1}{2}}} \tag{1}$$

where r_{11} is the estimated reliability of the full-length test,

$r_{\frac{1}{2}\frac{1}{2}}$ is the actual correlation between two half-length tests.

Thus, if the correlation between the two halves of a test is .60, formula 1 would give

$$r_{11} = \frac{2(0.60)}{1 + 0.60} = \frac{1.20}{1.60} = .75$$

This formula, referred to generally as the Spearman-Brown Prophecy Formula from its function and the names of its originators, makes it possible for us to compute an estimate of reliability from a single administration of a single test.

The appealing convenience of the split-half procedure has led to its wide use. Many test manuals will be found to report this type of reliability coefficient and no other. Unfortunately, this coefficient has several types of limitations, which we must now examine.

First, when we have extracted two scores from a single testing, both scores necessarily represent the individual as he is at the same moment of time. Even events lasting only a few minutes will affect both scores about equally. In other words, variation of the individual from day to day cannot be reflected in this type of reliability coefficient. It can only give evidence as to the precision with which we can appraise him at a specific moment in time.

A second factor will sometimes make two half-tests more alike than would be true of separate parallel forms. If the test includes groups of items based on common reference material, that is, reading items based on a single passage, science items referring to a single described experiment, etc., performance on all of these items will depend to some extent on the common act of comprehending the reference materials. Thus, the examinee who succeeds on one item of the set is likely to succeed on the others. The items are not experimentally independent. If we divide such sets of items between the two half-tests, as would happen in an odd-even reliability coefficient, we will produce a spurious and inflated resemblance between the two halves. With such materials the appropriate procedure, rarely used, is to assign alternate *sets* of items to the two half-length tests. If correlation between two half-length tests is to provide an appropriate estimate of the reliability of the full test, the two halves should be experimentally independent and equivalent. That is, there should be no undue overlap of items in one test with items in the other, and each half-test should be built to the same specifications as the whole test.

Third, a split-half reliability coefficient becomes meaningless when a test is highly speeded. Suppose we have a test of simple arithmetic, made up of 100 problems like $3 + 5 = ?$, and that the test is being used with adults with a 2-minute time limit. We will get wide differences in score on such a test, but the differences will be primarily differences in speed. Errors will be a minor factor. The person who gets a score of 50 will very probably have attempted just 50 items, *and of these 25 will be odd and 25 will be even.* In other words, the two halves of the test will appear perfectly consistent, because opportunity to attempt items is automatically balanced out for the two half-tests.

Few tests depend as completely upon speed as does the one that we have chosen to illustrate our point. However, many involve some degree of speeding. This speed factor tends to inflate estimates of reliability based on the split-half procedure. The amount of overestimation depends upon the degree to which the test is speeded, being greater for those tests in which speed plays a greater role. However, speed enters in sufficiently generally so that split-half estimates of reliability should always be discounted somewhat. Test users should demand that commercial publishers provide reliability estimates based on parallel forms of the test.

Reliability Estimated from Item Statistics

The teacher or investigator who makes much use of tests and who reads extensively in test manuals will encounter one other type of procedure for estimating test reliability from a single test administration. This procedure, also named for its originators, yields what is referred to as a Kuder-Richardson reliability coefficient. The essential assumption in the procedure is that the items within one form of a test have as much in common with one another as do the items in that one form with the corresponding items in a parallel or equivalent form. This means that the items in a test are homogeneous in the sense that every item measures the same general factors of ability or personality as do the others. If this assumption is sound, the Kuder-Richardson procedure leads to a reliability estimate that has essentially the same interpretation as the odd-even coefficient we have just considered. The Kuder-Richardson estimate likewise (1) takes no account of variation in the individual from time to time, and (2) is inappropriate for speeded tests. Within these two limitations, it provides a conservative estimate of the split-half type of reliability.*

* A widely used form of the Kuder-Richardson procedure (their Formula 20) takes the form

$$r_{11} = \left(\frac{n}{n-1}\right)\left(\frac{s_t^2 - \Sigma pq}{s_t^2}\right)$$

where r_{11} is the estimate of reliability.
n is the number of items in the test.
s_t is the standard deviation of the test.
Σ means "take the sum of" and covers the n items.
p is the percent passing a particular item.
q is the percent failing the same item.

A formula involving simpler calculations (their Formula 21), which yields a reasonably close but conservative approximation to the above, is

$$r_{11} = \frac{n}{n-1}\left[1 - \frac{M_t\left(1 - \frac{M_t}{n}\right)}{s_t^2}\right]$$

where M_t is the mean score of the group and the other symbols have the same meaning as given above.

Comparison of Methods

A summary comparison of the different procedures for estimating reliability is given in Table 6.5. This shows four factors that may make a single test score an inaccurate picture of the individual's usual performance. The table shows which of the sources of "error" are reflected in each of the procedures for estimating reliability we have discussed. In general, the more X's there are in a column, the more conservative (that is, lower) estimate of a test's reliability we will get. It can be seen that the different procedures are not equivalent. Only administration of parallel test forms with a time interval between permits all sources of variation to have their effects. Each of the other methods masks some source of variation that may be significant in the actual use of tests. Retesting with the same identical test neglects variation arising out of the sample of items. Whenever all the testing is done at one point in time, variation of the individual from day to day is neglected. When the testing is done as a unit with a single time limit, variation in speed of responding is neglected. The facts brought out in this table should be borne in mind in evaluating reliability data found in a test manual or in the report of a research study.

TABLE 6.5 SOURCES OF VARIATION REPRESENTED IN DIFFERENT PROCEDURES FOR ESTIMATING RELIABILITY

	Experimental Procedure for Estimating Reliability					
Sources of Variation	Immediate Retest, Same Test	Retest after Interval, Same Test	Parallel Test Form without Time Interval	Parallel Test Form with Time Interval	Odd-Even Halves of Single Test	Kuder-Richardson Analysis, Single Test
How much the score can be expected to fluctuate owing to:						
Variations arising within the measurement procedure itself	X	X	X	X	X	X
Changes in the individual from day to day		X		X		
Changes in the specific sample of tasks			X	X	X	X
Changes in the individual's speed of work	X	X	X	X		

Interpretation of Reliability Data

Analysis of data obtained from a general intelligence test for elementary-school children has yielded a reliability coefficient of .85. How shall we interpret this result? What does it mean concerning the precision of an individual's score? Should we be pleased or dissatisfied to get a coefficient of this size?

We have already tried to give some content and meaning to correlation coefficients in Fig. 5.8 and in Tables 5.7, 6.1, 6.3 and 6.4. These have shown typical values of the correlation coefficient, the scatter of scores for representative correlations, and the accuracy of prediction with correlations of different sizes. A further contribution to the interpretation of test reliability is found in the relationship between the reliability coefficient and the standard error of measurement.

It will be remembered that the standard error of measurement is an estimate of the standard deviation that would be obtained for a series of measurements of the same individual. (It is assumed that he is not changed by being measured.) The standard error of measurement can be calculated from the reliability coefficient by the formula

$$s_m = s_t \sqrt{1 - r_{11}} \qquad (2)$$

where s_m is the standard error of measurement.
s_t is the standard deviation of test scores.
r_{11} is the reliability coefficient.

Suppose that our test has a reliability of .85 and a standard deviation of 15 points. Then we have

$$s_m = 15\sqrt{1 - .85} = 15\sqrt{.15} = 5.7$$

In this instance, a set of measures of some one person would have a standard deviation of 5.7 points. Remember that a fairly uniform proportion of observations fall within any given number of standard deviation units from the mean. Certain values for this relationship were given in Table 5.6. This table shows that for a normal curve 31.8 percent of cases, or about 1 in 3, differ from the mean by more than 1 standard deviation; 4.6 percent by more than 2 standard deviations. Applying this to the case in which the standard error of our measurements is 5.7 points, we could say that there is about 1 chance in 3 that a score that we get for an individual differs from his "true" score by as much as 5.7 points (1 standard error of measurement). There is about 1 chance in 20 that it differs by as much as 11.4 points (2 standard errors of measurement).

The values shown above are fairly representative of what might be found for intelligence quotients from one of the commercially distributed group intelligence tests applied to children in the upper elementary grades. Note that even with this relatively high reliability coefficient, appreciable errors of measurement are possible in at least a minority of cases. With a standard deviation of 15 or 16, shifts of 5 or 10 points from one testing to another can be expected fairly frequently just because of errors of measurement. Anyone who is impressed by and tries to interpret an IQ difference of 5 points between two persons or two testings of the same person has been fooled into thinking the test has a precision that it simply does not possess. Further testing could perfectly well reverse the result. Any test score or comparison of test scores must be made with acute awareness of the standard error of measurement.

The manner in which the standard error of measurement is related to the reliability coefficient is shown in Table 6.6. We note that the magnitude of errors decreases as the reliability increases, but also that errors of appreciable size can still be found even with reliability coefficients of .90 or .95. In interpreting the score of an individual, it is the standard error of measurement that must be kept in mind. A range extending from 2 standard errors of measurement above the obtained score to 2 below will produce a band within which we can be reasonably sure (19 chances in 20) that the individual's true score lies. Thus, in the case of the intelligence test described in previous paragraphs, we can think of a test IQ of 90 as meaning rather surely an IQ lying between about 80 and 100. If we think in those terms, we shall be much more discreet in interpreting and using test results.

TABLE 6.6 STANDARD ERROR OF MEASUREMENT FOR DIFFERENT VALUES OF RELIABILITY COEFFICIENT

	Standard Error of Measurement	
Reliability Coefficient	General Expression	When S_t * = 10
.50	.71 S_t *	7.1
.60	.63 S_t	6.3
.70	.55 S_t	5.5
.80	.45 S_t	4.5
.85	.38 S_t	3.8
.90	.32 S_t	3.2
.95	.22 S_t	2.2
.98	.14 S_t	1.4

* S_t signifies the standard deviation of the test.

When interpreting the test score of an individual, it is desirable to think in terms of the standard error of measurement and to be somewhat humble and tentative in drawing conclusions from that test score. But for making comparisons between tests and for a number of types of test analysis, the reliability coefficient will be more useful. Where measures are expressed in different units, as height in inches and weight in pounds, the reliability coefficient provides the only possible basis for comparison. Since the competing tests in a given field, such as primary reading, are likely to use types of scores that are not really comparable, the reliability coefficient will usually represent the only satisfactory basis for test comparison. *Other things being equal,* the test with the higher reliability coefficient is to be preferred, that is, the test that provides a more consistent ranking of the individual within his group.

The other things that may not be equal are primarily considerations of validity and practicality. Validity, insofar as we can appraise it, is the crucial test of a measurement procedure. Reliability is important only as a necessary condition for a measure to have validity. The ceiling for the possible validity of a test is set by its reliability. A test must measure *something* before it can measure what we want it to measure. A measuring device with a reliability of .00 is reflecting nothing but chance factors. It does not correlate with itself and cannot correlate with anything else.

The theoretical ceiling for the correlation between any two measures is the square root of the product of their reliabilities. Thus, if a selection test has a reliability of .80 and a set of supervisory ratings has a reliability of .50, the theoretical maximum for the correlation between the two is $\sqrt{(.80)(.50)} = \sqrt{.40} = .63$. Clearly, here the limit on prediction is set more by the low reliability of the criterion measure than of the predictor test—and this is often the situation that we face. But if the reliability of the test had been only .40, by contrast, the ceiling on the prediction would now be a correlation of .45. Often, there is not too much that we can do about the reliability of a criterion variable, except to get information about it, but we can assure reasonable reliability in predictor tests.

The converse of the relationship we have just presented does not follow. A test may measure with the greatest precision and still have no validity for our purposes. Thus, we can measure head size with a good deal of accuracy, but the measure is still useless as an indicator of intelligence. Validity is something over and beyond mere accuracy of measurement.

Considerations of cost, convenience, etc. may also sometimes lead to a decision to use a less reliable test. We may accept a less reliable 40-minute test in preference to a more reliable 3-hour one because the 3 hours of testing time is too much of a burden in view of the purpose the test is designed to serve.

Within the limitations discussed in the preceding paragraphs, we shall prefer the more reliable test. There are several factors that must be taken into account, however, before we can fairly compare the reliability coefficients of two or more different tests. These will be discussed in the paragraphs that follow.

1. *Range of the group.* The reliability coefficient indicates how consistently a test places each individual relative to the others in the group. When there is little shifting from test to retest or form A to form B, the reliability coefficient is high and vice versa. But the extent to which individuals will switch places depends on how closely similar they are. It does not take very accurate testing to differentiate the reading ability of second graders from that of seventh graders. But to place each second grader accurately within his own class is much more demanding.

If children from several different grades are pooled together, we may expect a much higher reliability coefficient. For example, the manual for the *Otis Quick-Scoring Mental Ability Test—Beta* reported alternate-forms reliabilities for single grade groups ranging from .65 to .87. The average value was .78. But pooling the complete range of grades (4–9), the reliability coefficient was reported as .96. These data are all for the same test. They reflect the same precision. Yet the coefficient for the combined groups is strikingly higher. Similar data were reported for the *Durrell-Sullivan Reading Achievement Test.* The data in this case involved a range of four grades—from grade three through grade six. Reliability coefficients were split-half reliabilities based on a single testing. In the case of the *Word Meaning Test,* the average coefficient for a single grade was .93, whereas the correlation for all four grades together was .97. For the test of *Paragraph Meaning* the corresponding values were .87 and .94.

In evaluating a reported reliability coefficient, the range of ability in the group tested must be taken into account. If the reliability coefficient is based upon a combination of age or grade groups, it must usually be sharply discounted, as can be seen above. But even in less extreme cases, account must be taken of the variability of talent within the group. Reliabilities for age groups will tend to be somewhat higher than for grade groups, because an age group will usually contain a greater spread of talent than a single grade. A sample made up of children from a wide range of socio-economic levels will tend to yield higher reliabilities than a very homogeneous one. In comparing different tests, one must take account of the type of sample on which the reliability data were based, insofar as this can be determined from the reported facts, and judge more severely the test whose reliability is based on the more heterogeneous group.

2. *Level of ability in the group.* Precision of measurement by a test may be related to the ability level of the persons being measured. However, no simple rule can be formulated for stating the nature of this relationship. It depends upon the way in which the particular test was built. For those people for whom the test is very hard, so that they are doing a large amount of guessing, accuracy is likely to be low. At the other extreme, if a test is very easy for a group, so that all of them can do most of the items very easily, it may be expected to be ineffective in discriminating among the members of the group. When everyone can do the easy items, it is as if we had shortened the test to just the few harder items that some can do and some cannot.

It is possible, also, that a test may vary in accuracy at different intermediate difficulty levels. The meticulous test constructor will report the standard error of measurement for his test at different score levels. When separate values of the standard error of measurement are reported in the manual, they provide a basis for evaluating the precision of the test for different types of groups. They permit a more appropriate estimate of the accuracy of a particular individual's score. Each individual's score can be interpreted in relation to the standard error of measurement for scores of that level. For example, the Lorge-Thorndike Intelligence Test, Verbal Level A, for which results are expressed as deviation IQ's, reports the standard error of measurement at different raw score levels as follows:

Raw Score	*Standard Error in IQ Units*
15	4.1
25	3.9
35	3.0
45	2.4
55	2.9
65	3.1
75	3.4

This test measures those pupils who get about half of the 100 items right a good deal more accurately (when the measures are expressed in equal-sized standard deviation units) than those who succeed with only a few items or with almost all. This result was produced intentionally, by including many items of moderate difficulty that discriminate degrees of ability in the middle range and relatively few very easy or very hard items. In effect, a longer test is operating for pupils in the middle range than at the extremes, and the result is more accurate measurement of this large middle group.

3. *Length of test.* As we saw on p. 183 in discussing the split-half reliability coefficient, test reliability depends on the length of the test. If one can assume that the quality of the test items and the nature of the examinees remain the

same, then the relationship of reliability to length can be expressed by a simple formula. The formula is

$$r_{nn} = \frac{nr_{11}}{1 + (n - 1)r_{11}} \tag{3}$$

where r_{nn} is the reliability of a test n times as long as the original test.
r_{11} is the reliability of the original test.
n is, as indicated, the factor by which the length of the test is increased.

This is a more general form of formula 1 found on p. 183.

Suppose we have a spelling test made up of 20 items that has a reliability of .50. We want to know how reliable the test will be if it is lengthened to contain 100 items comparable to the original 20. The answer is

$$r_{nn} = \frac{5(.50)}{1 + 4(.50)} = \frac{2.50}{3.00} = .83$$

As the length of the test is increased, the chance errors of measurement more or less cancel out; score comes to depend more and more completely upon the characteristics of the person being measured; and a more accurate appraisal of him is obtained.

Of course, how much we can lengthen a test is limited by a number of practical considerations. It is limited by the amount of time available for testing. It is limited by factors of fatigue and boredom on the part of examinees. It is sometimes limited by our inability to construct more equally good test items. But within these limits, reliability can be increased as needed by lengthening the test.

One special type of lengthening is represented by increasing the number of raters who rate an individual or a product he has produced. When the unreliability of an assessment is due in part to the inconsistency with which a sample of behavior is judged, this source of unreliability can often be reduced by increasing the number of judges. If several judges are available of equal competence with the materials to be rated, or equal familiarity with the ratee if the ratings are of a person, then a pooling of their ratings will produce a composite that is more reliable, and the increase is found to be described approximately by formula 3 above. For example, if a typical pair of judges evaluating samples of writing show a correlation of 0.40, then the pooled rating of three judges could be expected to correlate with three others as follows:

$$\frac{3(.40)}{1 + 2(.40)} = \frac{1.20}{1.80} = 0.67$$

TABLE 6.7 COMPARISON OF RELIABILITY COEFFICIENTS OBTAINED FROM EQUIVALENT FORMS AND FROM FRACTIONS OF A SINGLE TEST

Test	Alternate Forms	Single Test
Lorge-Thorndike Intelligence Tests		
Verbal test–Level C	.91	.94
Nonverbal test–Level C	.87	.94
Iowa Tests of Basic Skills		
Arithmetic test–Grade 5	.87	.90
Spelling–Grade 5	.86	.90
Gates-MacGinitie Reading Test–Survey D		
Vocabulary–Grade 4	.85	.88
Comprehension–Grade 4	.83	.94

4. *Operations used for estimating.* How high a value will be obtained for the reliability coefficient depends also upon which of the several possible sets of experimental operations is used to estimate the reliability. We saw in Table 6.5 that the different procedures treat different sources of variation in different ways, and that it is only the use of parallel forms of a test with a period intervening that includes all four sources of variation in "error." That is, this procedure of estimating reliability represents a more exacting definition of the test's ability to reproduce the same score. The individual must then show consistency both from one sample of tasks to another and from one day to another. We have gathered together a few examples that show reliability coefficients for the same test when these were computed by two different procedures. These are shown in Table 6.7.

The two procedures compared in Table 6.7 are correlation of alternate forms and correlation of half-tests made up from a single form. It will be noted that the alternate-forms correlation is lower in every case. This is consistent with our earlier discussion, in which we pointed out that the alternate-forms procedure constitutes a more demanding test of an instrument's precision. The difference between the two procedures varies from test to test, being as small as .03 in one instance and as large as .11 in another. But in every instance, it is necessary to discount the odd-even correlation.

How High Must the Reliability of a Measurement Be?

Obviously, other things being equal, the more reliable a measuring procedure is, the better satisfied we are with it. A question that is often raised is: What is the *minimum* reliability that is acceptable? Actually, there is no general answer to this question. If we *must* make some decision or take some course of action with respect to an individual, we will do so in terms of the best information we have, however unreliable it may be, provided only that the reliability is better than zero. (Of course, here as always the crucial consideration is the validity of the measure.) The appraisal of any new procedure must always be in terms of other procedures with which it is in competition. Thus, a high-school mathematics test with a reliability coefficient of .80 would look relatively unattractive if tests with reliabilities of .85 to .90 were already available. On the other hand, a procedure for judging "leadership" that had a reliability of no more than .60 might look very attractive if the alternative were a set of uncontrolled ratings having a reliability of .45 to .50.

Although we cannot set an absolute minimum for the reliability of a measurement procedure, we can indicate the level of reliability that is required to enable us to achieve specified levels of accuracy in describing an individual or a group. Suppose that we have given a test to two individuals, and that individual A fell at the 75th percentile of the group while individual B fell at the 50th percentile. What is the probability that A would still surpass B if they were tested again? In Table 6.8 the probability is shown for different values of the reliability coefficient. Thus, where the correlation is .00, there is exactly a fifty-fifty chance that the order of our two individuals will be reversed. When the correlation is

TABLE 6.8 PERCENT OF TIMES DIRECTION OF DIFFERENCE WILL BE REVERSED IN SUBSEQUENT TESTING FOR SCORES FALLING AT 75TH AND 50TH PERCENTILE

	Percent of Reversals with Repeated Test		
Reliability Coefficient	Scores of Single Individuals	Means of Groups of 25	Means of Groups of 100
.00	50.0	50.0	50.0
.40	40.3	10.9	0.7
.50	36.8	4.6	0.04
.60	32.5	1.2	
.70	27.1	0.1	
.80	19.7		
.90	8.7		
.95	2.2		
.98	0.05		

.50, the probability of a reversal is more than 1 in 3. For a correlation of .90, there is still 1 chance in 12 that we will get a reversal on repetition of the testing. To have 4 chances in 5 that our difference will stay in the same direction, we require a reliability of about .80.

Table 6.8 also shows the situation when we are comparing two groups—for groups of 25 or of 100. For example, if in class A of 25 pupils, the average fell at the 75th percentile of some larger reference group, whereas in class B the average fell at the 50th percentile, what is the probability that we would get a reversal if the testing were repeated? Here we still have a fifty-fifty chance in the extreme case in which the reliability coefficient is .00. However, the security of our conclusion increases much more rapidly with groups than with individuals as the reliability of the test becomes greater. With a reliability of .50 the probability of a reversal is already down to 1 in 20 for groups of 25, to 1 in 2,500 for groups of 100. With a correlation of .70 the probability is only 1 in 1,000 for groups of 25 and is vanishingly small for groups of 100. Thus, a test with relatively low reliability will permit us to make useful studies of and draw accurate conclusions about groups, especially groups of substantial size, but quite high reliability is required if we are to speak with confidence about individuals.

Reliability of Difference Scores

Sometimes we are less interested in single scores than we are in the relationship between scores taken in pairs. Thus, we may be concerned with the differences between scholastic aptitude and reading achievement in a group of pupils, or we may wish to study gains in reading from an initial test given in October to a later test given the following May. In these illustrations, the significant fact for each individual is the difference between two scores. We must inquire how reliable our estimates of these differences are, knowing the characteristics of the two component tests.

It is, unfortunately, true that the appraisal of the difference between two tests usually has substantially lower reliability than the reliabilities of the two tests taken separately. This is due to two factors: (1) the errors of measurement in both separate tests affect the difference score, and (2) whatever is common to both measures is canceled out in the difference score. We can illustrate the situation by a diagram (see Fig. 6.2 on p. 196).

Each bar in Fig. 6.2 represents performance * on a test, broken up into a number of parts to represent the factors producing this performance. The first bar

* More precisely, variance in performance.

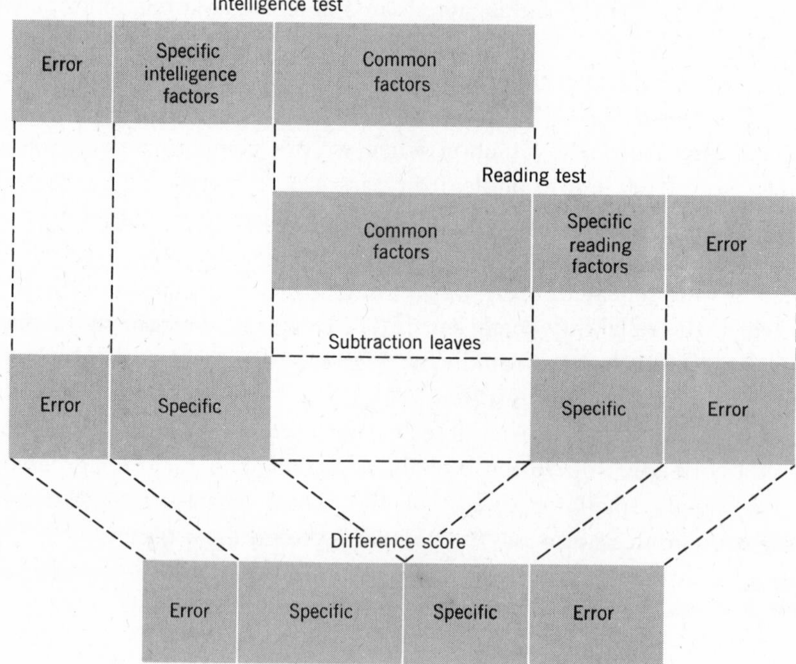

Fig. 6.2 Nature of a difference score.

represents an intelligence test, and the second a reading test. Notice that we have divided reading performance into three parts. One part, labeled "common factors," is a complex of general intellectual abilities that operate both in the reading and the scholastic aptitude test. A second part, labeled "specific reading factors," is abilities that appear only in the reading test. The third part, labeled "error," is chance error of measurement. Three similar parts are indicated for the intelligence test.

Now examine the third bar representing difference score—that is, reading score expressed in some type of standard-score units minus intelligence test score expressed in those same units. In this bar, the common factor has disappeared. It appeared with one sign in the reading test and the reverse sign in the intelligence test, and thus canceled out. Only the specific factors and the errors of measurement remain. These are the factors that determine the difference score. And the errors of measurement bulk relatively much larger in this third bar. In the limit, where two tests measured exactly the same common factors, only the errors of measurement would remain in the difference scores, and the differences would have exactly zero reliability.

The reliability of the difference between two measures expressed in standard scores can be obtained by a fairly simple formula, which reads

$$r_{Diff.} = \frac{\frac{r_{11} + r_{22}}{2} - r_{12}}{1 - r_{12}}$$

where r_{11} is the reliability of one measure.
r_{22} is the reliability of the other measure.
r_{12} is the correlation between the two measures.

Thus, if the reliability of test A is .80, the reliability of test B is .90, and the correlation of A and B is .60, for the reliability of the difference score we have

$$r_{Diff.} = \frac{\frac{.80 + .90}{2} - .60}{1 - .60}$$

$$= \frac{.25}{.40} = .62.$$

In Table 6.9 the value of $r_{Diff.}$ is shown for various combinations of values of $(r_{11} + r_{22})/2$ and r_{12}. Thus, if the average of the reliabilities of two tests $[(r_{11} + r_{22})/2]$ is .80, the reliability of the difference score is .80 when the two tests have zero intercorrelation, is .60 when the intercorrelation is .50, and is .00 when the intercorrelation is .80. It is clear that, as soon as the correlation between the two tests begins to approach the average of their separate reliability coefficients, the reliability of the difference score drops very rapidly.

TABLE 6.9 RELIABILITY OF A DIFFERENCE SCORE

Correlation between Two Tests (r_{12})	Average of Reliability of Two Tests $\left(\frac{r_{11} + r_{22}}{2}\right)$					
	.50	.60	.70	.80	.90	.95
.00	.50	.60	.70	.80	.90	.95
.40	.17	.33	.50	.67	.83	.92
.50	.00	.20	.40	.60	.80	.90
.60		.00	.25	.50	.75	.88
.70			.00	.33	.67	.83
.80				.00	.50	.75
.90					.00	.50
.95						.00

The low reliability that tends to characterize difference scores is something to which the psychologist and educator must always be sensitive. It becomes a problem whenever he wishes to use test patterns for diagnosis. Thus the judgment that Herbert's reading lags behind his scholastic aptitude is a judgment that must be made a good deal more tentatively than a judgment about either his IQ or his reading grade taken separately. The conclusion that Mary has improved in reading more than Jane must usually be a more tentative judgment than that Mary is now a better reader than Jane. Any difference needs to be interpreted in the light of the standard error of measurement of that difference.*

Many differences will be found to be quite small relative to their standard error, and consequently quite undependable. The interpretation of profiles and of gain scores are places where this caution especially applies.

Effects of Unreliability on Correlation Between Variables

There is one further effect of unreliability that merits brief attention here because it affects our interpretation of the correlations between different measures. Let us think of a measure of reading comprehension and one of arithmetic reasoning. In each of these tests, the individual differences in score are due in part to "true" ability and in part to chance "errors of measurement." But if the errors of measurement are really chance matters, the reading test errors and the arithmetic test errors must be uncorrelated. There is no relationship between one toss of a coin and a later toss of a coin. So we have these uncorrelated errors in the total score. This means that they must water down any correlation that exists between the true scores. That is, the actual scores are a combination of true score and error, so the correlation between actual scores is a compromise between the correlation of the underlying true scores and the .00 correlation that characterizes the errors.

We would often like to extract an estimate of the correlation between the underlying true scores from our obtained data in order to understand better how much the functions involved have in common. Fortunately, we can do this quite simply. Such an estimate is provided by the formula

$$r_{1\infty 2\infty} = \frac{r_{12}}{\sqrt{r_{11}r_{22}}} \qquad (4)$$

where $r_{1\infty 2\infty}$ is the correlation of the underlying "true" scores.

r_{12} is the correlation of the obtained scores.

r_{11} and r_{22} are the reliabilities of the two measures in question.

* The standard error of measurement of a difference is roughly equal to $\sqrt{S^2_{m_1} + S^2_{m_2}}$, where S_{m_1} is the standard error of measurement of one test and S_{m_2} is the standard error of measurement of the other.

Thus, if the correlation between the reading test and arithmetic test was found to be .56, and the reliability coefficients of the tests were respectively .71 and .90, we have

$$r_{1_\infty 2_\infty} = \frac{.56}{\sqrt{(.71)(.90)}} = .70$$

Our estimate is that the correlation between error-free measures of arithmetic and reading would be .70. In thinking of these two *functions*, it would be appropriate to think of the correlation as .70 rather than .56, though the *tests* correlate only .56.

FACTORS MAKING FOR PRACTICALITY IN ROUTINE USE

Though validity and reliability may be all important in measures that are to be used for special research purposes, when a test is to be used in classrooms throughout a school or school system a number of down-to-earth practical considerations must also be taken into account. It is easy for the administrator to pay too much attention to small financial savings or to economies of time that make it possible to fit a test into the standard class period with no shifting of schedules, but, nevertheless, these factors of economy and convenience are real considerations. Furthermore, there are other factors relating to the readiness with which the tests may be given, scored, and interpreted that bear more importantly on the use that will be made of the tests and the soundness of the conclusions that will be drawn from them.

Economy

The practical significance of dollar savings does not need to be emphasized. Dollars are of very real significance for any educational or industrial enterprise. Economy in the case of tests depends in part on cost per copy. It depends in part on the possibility of using the test booklets over again. In the upper elementary grades and beyond, it is feasible to administer a test using a separate answer sheet. Such a separate answer sheet permits reuse of the test booklets. If a test will be used in successive years or if testing can be scheduled so that different classes or schools can be tested on successive days, an important economy can be effected by using the same test booklet over again several times.

A second aspect of economy is saving of time in test administration. However, this is often false economy. We saw in the previous section that the reliability of a test depends on its length. As far as testing time is concerned, we get about what we give. Some tests may be a little more efficiently designed, so that they give a little more reliable measure per minute of testing time, but, by and large, any reduction in testing time will be accomplished at the price of loss in the precision or the breadth of our appraisal.

A third, and quite significant aspect of economy is ease of scoring. The clerical work of scoring a battery of tests by hand can become either burdensome if it is done by the already busy teacher, or expensive if it is carried out by clerical help hired especially for the purpose. As a result, test users are relying more and more upon mechanized scoring, and test publishers are producing tests that can be processed by the more and more sophisticated equipment that is being developed. The test user has the option of hand-scoring his own tests, of setting up his own mechanized scoring unit, or of sending tests to one of the test scoring services that specialize in high-speed test processing.

There are several test-scoring services that provide very efficient test scoring and reporting. The basic equipment consists of a photoelectric document reader combined with a digital computer. The document reader responds to marks on an answer sheet, or sometimes on an actual test booklet.

The use of a separate answer sheet is familiar to most American college graduates, who have taken a variety of tests during their educational careers. But separate answer sheets are not satisfactory for young children. The complications of finding an answer in the test booklet, keeping the code letter of the chosen answer in mind while the proper place is located on the answer sheet, and then marking in the proper spot on the answer sheet are too much for children in the primary grades. Current equipment makes it possible to use a booklet for these levels and either to slice the bound edge off the test booklet and run the separate pages through the scanner, or to print the test in a fanfold booklet that can be unfolded and run through the scanner as a unit.

In large-volume scoring services, the information from the optical scanner is fed into a digital computer where it is compared with a key that has been recorded in the memory of the computer. One or more scores are determined and printed out on a record form or pressure-sensitive label. The computer can also be programmed to produce various statistics such as class means, school system means and standard deviations, and local percentiles. Thus, the scoring service provides not only test scores for individuals, but the complete range of statistical information about the test results that are of interest to the local school system.

A local school system cannot support the elaborate equipment that we have just been describing. However, there are several optical scanner-scorer devices available for rent or purchase by city or state school systems that handle quite a volume of scoring. These will scan an answer sheet (not a booklet), and will either print a score upon it or prepare a punched-card record that can be subsequently processed in data processing equipment.

Thus a test that is to be economical for use in large-scale testing programs will be produced in format for scoring by the different types of scanning and scoring equipment. Almost any type of separate answer sheet can be hand-scored relatively efficiently by using an overlay stencil. Some test publishers supply plastic overlay stencils for this purpose. Others use a special type of answer sheet made up of two sheets fastened together, the back one carbon-covered. The key is printed on the back of the first sheet, and as the examinee marks the front, the carbon-backing transfers his marks to the back of the sheet, where the number falling in the printed key spaces can be counted. In some special types of tests the answers are marked by pushing a pin through the answer sheet at the locations corresponding to the choices that are to be marked. Again, the key is printed on the inside of a complex answer form, and the test is scored by counting the number of pinpricks falling within circles printed on the answer form.

The potential test purchaser will want to determine what types of answer forms and what scoring services are available for any test that he is considering using.

Features Facilitating Test Administration

In evaluating the practical usability of a test, one factor to be taken into account is the ease of administration. A test that can be handled adequately by the regular classroom teacher with no more than a session or so of special briefing is much more readily fitted into a testing program than a test requiring specially trained administrators. Several factors contribute to the ease of giving and taking a test.

1. A test is easy to give if it has clear, full instructions. The instructions for the administrator should be written out substantially word for word, so that all the examiner must do is read them and follow them. Instructions for the examinee should also be complete and should provide appropriate practice exercises. The amount of practice that should be provided depends upon how novel the test task is likely to be for those being tested. Where it is a familiar type of task or a simple and straightforward instruction, no more than a single example will be needed. However, for an unusual item format or test task more practice will be desirable.

2. A test is easy to give if the number of units to be separately timed is few, and close timing is not critical. Timing a number of brief subtests to a fraction of a minute is a bothersome undertaking, and the timing is likely to be inaccurate unless a stop watch is available for each tester. Some tests have as many as eight

or ten parts, each taking only 2 or 3 minutes. A test made up of three or four parts, with time limits of 5, 10, or more minutes for each, will be easier to use.

3. The layout of the test items on the page has a good deal to do with the ease of taking the test. Items in which response options are all run together on the same line, items with small or illegible pictures or diagrams, items that are crowded together, and items that run over from one page to the next all make difficulty for the examinee. Print and pictures should be large and clear. Response options should be well separated from one another. All parts of an item and all items referring to a single figure, problem, or reading passage should appear on the same page or double-page spread. Shortcomings on any of these points represent black marks against a test as far as ease of taking it is concerned.

Features Facilitating Interpretation and Use of Scores

It seems axiomatic, though the point is sometimes overlooked, that a test is given to be used. If the score is to be used, it must be interpreted and given meaning. The author and publisher of the test have the responsibility of providing the user with information that permits him to make a sound appraisal of the test in relation to his needs and to give appropriate meaning to the score of an individual. This they do primarily through the *test manual* and other collateral materials that are prepared to accompany the test. What may the test user reasonably expect to find in the manual for a test, together with its supporting materials? We have outlined below the aids we believe the test user should expect.

1. *A statement of the functions the test was designed to measure and of the general procedures by which it was developed.* This is the author's statement of what he considers the test to be valid for and the evidence that proper steps have been taken to achieve that validity. Particularly for achievement tests, in which we are concerned primarily with content and process validity, the author should tell us the procedures by which he arrived at his choice of content or his analysis of the functions being measured. If he is unwilling to expose his thinking to our critical scrutiny, we may perhaps be skeptical of the thoroughness or profundity of that thinking.

Procedures involve not only the rational procedures by which range of content or types of objective were selected, but also the empirical procedures by which items were tried out and screened for final inclusion in the test.

2. *Detailed instructions for administering the test.* We have discussed in an earlier section the need for this aid to uniform and easy administration by the teachers or others who will have to use the test.

3. *Scoring keys and specific instructions for scoring the test.* The problems of scoring have also been discussed, under the heading of economy. The manual and supporting materials should provide detailed instructions as to how the score is to be computed, how errors are to be treated, and how part scores are to be combined into a total score. Scoring keys and stencils should be planned to facilitate as much as possible the onerous task of scoring.

4. *Norms for appropriate reference groups,* together with information as to how they were obtained and instructions for their use. Chapter 7 will be devoted to a full consideration of types of test norms and their use. It will, therefore, be sufficient at this time to point out the responsibility of the test producer to develop suitable norms for the groups with which his test is to be used. General norms are a necessity, and norms suitable for special types of communities, special occupational groups, and other more limited subgroups will add to the usefulness of a test in many cases.

5. *Evidence as to the reliability of the test.* This evidence should indicate not only the bald reliability statistics but also the operations used to obtain the reliability estimates and the descriptive and statistical characteristics of each group on which reliability data are based. If a test is available in more than one form, it is highly desirable that the producers report the correlation between the two forms, in addition to any data that were derived from a single testing. If the test yields part scores, and particularly if it is proposed that any use be made of these part scores, reliability data should be reported for the separate part scores. It is good procedure for the author to report standard errors of measurement as well as reliability coefficients. An author who indicates what the standard error of measurement is at each of a number of score levels is particularly to be commended, since this information shows over what range of scores the test maintains its accuracy.

6. *Evidence on the intercorrelations of subscores.* If the test provides several subscores, the manual should provide evidence on the intercorrelations of these. This is important in guiding the interpretation of the subscores and, particularly, in judging how much confidence to place in *differences* between the subscores. If the scores are correlated to a substantial degree, measuring much the same things, the differences between them will be largely meaningless and uninterpretable.

7. *Evidence on the relationships of the test to other factors.* In so far as the test is to be used as a predictive device, correlations with criterion measures constitute the essential evidence on how well it does in fact predict. Full information should be provided on the nature of the criterion variables, the group for which data are available, and the conditions under which the data were obtained. Only then can the reader fairly judge the validity of the test as a predictor.

It will often be desirable to report correlations with other measures of the same function as collateral evidence bearing on the validity of the test. Thus, correlations with individual intelligence test score are relevant in the case of a group intelligence measure.

Finally, indications of the relationship of test score to age, sex, type of community, socio-economic level, and similar facts about the individual or the group are often helpful. They provide a basis for judging how sensitive the measure is to the background of the group and to circumstances of their life and of their education.

8. *Guides for using the test and for interpreting results obtained with it.* The developers of a test presumably know how it is reasonable for the test to be used and the results from it to be evaluated. They are specialists in that test. For the test to be most useful for others, especially the teacher with limited specialized training, suggestions should be given of ways in which the test results may be used for diagnosing individual and group weaknesses, forming class groupings, organizing remedial instruction, counseling with the individual, or whatever other activities may appropriately be based on that particular type of instrument.

GUIDE FOR EVALUATING A TEST

As a help to the potential test user, we end this chapter with a guide for evaluating a test. The guide consists of a series of questions, based in large part on the *Standards for Educational and Psychological Tests and Manuals* prepared by a joint committee from the American Psychological Association (1966), together with the American Educational Research Association and the National Council on Measurement in Education. The complete *Standards* will well repay careful study by the journeyman test user.

The reader will note that many of the questions in the guide relate to the availability and adequacy of reporting of information about the test. There is an implied, though not explicitly stated, second question as a sequel to many sections of the guide, especially those relating to validity and reliability. This is: "Given that the information is provided, how satisfactory does the test appear to be, in comparison with others as well as by absolute standards, for the use that I want to make of it?" A number of the questions refer to the adequacy of norms and converted scores. These are matters that are considered in the following chapter. Readers will find it profitable to review this portion of the guide after reading Chapter 7.

General Identifying Information

1. What is the name of the test?
2. Who are its authors—by name and position if that information is available.
3. Who publishes the test, and when was it published?
4. What does it cost?
5. How long does it take to administer?

Information About the Test

1. Is there a manual for the test (or other similar source) that is designed to provide the information that a potential user needs?

2. How recently has the test been revised? How recently has the test manual been revised? Has as much as ten years elapsed since revision in either case?

Aids to Interpreting Test Results

1. Do the test, manual, record forms, and accompanying materials guide users toward sound and correct interpretation of the test results?

2. Does the manual provide a clear statement of the purposes and applications for which the test is intended?

3. Does the manual provide a clear statement of the qualifications needed to administer the test and interpret it properly?

4. Are the statements in the manual that express relationships presented in quantitative terms, so that the reader can tell how much precision or confidence to attach to them?

Validity

1. Does the manual report evidence on the validity of the test for each type of inference for which the test is recommended?

2. Does the manual *avoid* referring to correlations between item and total test score as evidence of validity?

3. If the test is designed to be a sample of a specified domain of behaviors (that is, an achievement test), does the manual define the domain clearly and indicate the procedures for sampling from that domain?

4. Where criterion-related validity is involved, does the manual describe criterion variables clearly, comment on their adequacy, and indicate what aspects of the criterion performance are *not* adequately reflected in these measures?

5. Are the samples used for estimating criterion-related validity adequately described, and are they appropriate to the purpose?

6. Are statistical analyses for criterion-related validity presented in a form that permits the reader to judge the degree of confidence that can be placed in inferences about individuals?

7. If the test is designed to measure a theoretical construct (that is, trait of ability, temperament, or attitude), is the proposed interpretation clearly stated, and differentiated from alternate theoretical interpretations? Is the evidence to support this interpretation clearly and fully presented?

In summary, to what extent does the evidence with respect to validity justify the uses of the test suggested in the manual, or the use that you would want to make of the test results?

Reliability

1. Does the manual present data adequate to permit the reader to judge whether scores are sufficiently dependable for the recommended uses?

2. Are the samples on which reliability data were obtained sufficiently well described so that the user can judge whether the data apply to his situation?

3. Are the reliability data presented in the conventional statistics of product-moment reliability coefficients and standard errors of measurement?

4. If more than one form of the test was produced, are data provided to establish comparability of the several forms?

5. If the test purports to measure a generalized homogeneous trait, is evidence reported on the internal consistency (interitem or interpart correlations) of the parts that make up the test?

6. Does the test manual provide data on the stability of test performance over a period of time?

In summary, to what extent do the reliability data provided in the manual justify the uses for the results suggested by the authors or the use that you would want to make of the test results?

Administration and Scoring

1. Are the directions for administration sufficiently full and clear so that the administrator will be able to duplicate the conditions under which the norms were established and reliability and validity data were obtained?

2. Are the procedures for scoring set forth clearly and in detail, in such a way as to maximize scoring efficiency and minimize the likelihood of scoring error?

Scales and Norms

1. Are the scales used for reporting scores clearly and carefully described, so that the test interpreter will fully understand them and be able to communicate the interpretation to an examinee?

2. If more than one form is available, including revised forms, are tables available showing equivalent scores on the different forms?

3. Does the manual discuss the possible value of local norms, and provide any help in preparing local norms?

4. Are norms reported in the manual that are in appropriate form, usually standard scores or percentile ranks in appropriate reference groups?

5. Are the populations to which the norms refer clearly defined and described, and are they populations with which most users can appropriately compare their data?

QUESTIONS AND EXERCISES

1. If the College Entrance Examination Board were developing a general survey test in science for high-school seniors, what might they do to establish the validity of the test?

2. What type of validity is indicated by each of the following statements which might be found in a test manual?

   a. Scores on Personality Test X correlated +.43 with teachers' ratings of adjustment.
   b. The objectives to be appraised by Reading Test Y were rated for importance by 150 classroom teachers.
   c. Scores on Clerical Aptitude Test Z correlated +.57 with supervisors' ratings after 6 months on the job.
   d. Intelligence Test W gives scores that correlate +.69 with *Stanford-Binet* IQ.
   e. Achievement Battery V is based on an analysis of 50 widely used texts and 100 courses of study from all parts of the U.S.

3. Comment on the statement "The classroom teacher is the only one who can judge the validity of a standardized achievement test for his class."

4. Look at the manuals of two or three tests of different types. What evidence on validity is presented? How adequate is it for each test?

5. Using Table 6.4 on p. 173, determine what percent of those selected would be above average on the job if a selection procedure with a validity of .40 were used and only the top quarter were accepted for the job. What percent would be above average if the top three-quarters were selected? What would the two percents be if the validity were .50? What does a comparison of the four percentages bring out?

6. Air Force personnel psychologists are doing research on the selection of jet-engine mechanics. What might they use as criterion measures of success as a mechanic? What are the advantages and limitations of each possible measure?

7. What advantages and disadvantages do school grades have as criterion measures?

8. A test manual contains the following statement: "The validity of test X is shown by the fact that it correlates .80 with the *Stanford-Binet*." What additional information is needed to evaluate this assertion?

9. Look at the evidence presented on reliability in the manuals of two or three tests. How adequate is it? What are its shortcomings?

10. The manual for test T presents reliability data based on (a) retesting with the same test form a week later, (b) correlating odd with even items, and (c) correlating form A with form B, the two forms being given a week apart. Which procedure may be expected to yield the *lowest* coefficient? Why? Which to yield the most *useful* estimate of reliability? Why?

11. A student has been given the *Stanford-Binet Intelligence Test* four different times during his school career, and his cumulative record card shows the following IQ's: 98, 107, 101, and 95. What significance should be attached to the fluctuations in IQ?

12. A school plans to give form A of a reading test in October and form B in May, in order to study individual differences in improvement during the year. The reliability of each form of the test is known to be about .85 for a grade group. The correlation between the two forms turned out to be .80. How much confidence can be placed in the individual differences in amount gained? What factors other than real differences in learning can account for individual differences in gain?

13. You are considering three reading tests for use in your school. As far as you can judge, the three are equally valid. The reliability of each is reported to be .90. What else would you need to know to make a choice among the tests?

14. Examine several tests of intelligence or of achievement that would be suitable for a class you are teaching or might teach. Write an evaluation of one of these tests, following the guide on pp. 204–207.

REFERENCES

American Psychological Association. *Standards for educational and psychological tests and manuals.* Washington, D.C.: American Psychological Association, 1966.

Buhler, R. A. Flicker fusion threshold and anxiety level. Unpublished doctoral dissertation, Columbia University, 1953.

McClelland, D. and others. *The achievement motive.* New York: Appleton-Century-Crofts, 1953.

SUGGESTED ADDITIONAL READING

Anastasi, A. Some current developments in the measurement and interpretation of test validity. In A. Anastasi (Ed.), *Testing problems in perspective.* Washington, D.C.: American Council on Education, 1966. Pp. 307–317.

Payne, D. A. & McMorris, R. F. (eds.) Defining and assessing test validity. *Educational and psychological measurement.* Waltham, Massachusetts: Blaisdell, 1967. Pp. 76–122.

Seashore, H. G. Methods of expressing test scores. *Test Service Bulletin No. 48.* New York: Psychological Corp., 1955.

Thorndike, R. L. Reliability. In A. Anastasi (Ed.), *Testing problems in perspective.* Washington, D.C.: American Council on Education, 1966. Pp. 284–291.

CHAPTER 7

Norms and Units for Measurement

THE NATURE OF A SCORE

JOHNNY got a score of 15 on his spelling test. What does that mean, and how should we interpret it?

Actually, as it stands it has no meaning at all and is completely uninterpretable. At the most superficial level, we don't even know whether this represents a perfect score, that is, 15 out of 15, or a very low percent of the possible, that is, 15 out of 50. But even supposing we do know that it is 15 out of 20, or 75 percent, what then?

Look at Table 7.1. This shows two 20-word spelling tests. A score of 15 would have vastly different meaning if it were on test A than on test B. A person who got only 15 right on test A would not be outstanding in a second- or third-grade class. Try test B out on some friends or classmates. You will probably not find many of them who can spell 15 of these words correctly. When this test was given to a class of graduate students, only 22 percent of them spelled 15 of the words correctly. A score of 15 on test B is a good score among graduate students of education.

As it stands, then, a score of 15 words right, or even of 75 percent of the words

TABLE 7.1 TWO 20-WORD SPELLING TESTS

Test A	Test B
bar	baroque
cat	catarrh
form	formaldehyde
jar	jardiniere
nap	naphtha
dish	discernible
fat	fatiguing
sack	sacrilegious
rich	ricochet
sit	citrus
feet	feasible
act	accommodation
rate	inaugurate
inch	insignia
rent	deterrent
lip	eucalyptus
air	questionnaire
rim	rhythm
must	ignoramus
red	accrued

right, can have no meaning or significance. It gets meaning only as we have some standard with which to compare it.

In the usual classroom test, the standard operates indirectly and imperfectly, partly through the teacher's choice of tasks to make up the test and partly through his standards for evaluating the responses. Thus, the teacher picks tasks to make up the test that he considers to be appropriate to represent the learnings of his group. No teacher in his right mind would give test A to a high-school group or test B to third graders. Where the responses vary in quality, as in essay examinations, the teacher sets a standard for grading that corresponds to what he considers it reasonable to expect from a group like his. Quite different answers to the question "What were the causes of the War of 1812?" would be expected from a ninth grader and from a college history major.

However, the inner standard of the individual teacher is very subjective, inaccurate, and unstable. Furthermore, it provides no basis for comparing different classes or different areas of ability. Such a yardstick can give no answers to such questions as: Are the children in school A better in reading than those in school B? Is Mary better in reading than in arithmetic? Is Johnny doing as well in algebra as we should expect? We need some broader, more uniform, objective, and stable standard of reference if we are to be able to interpret psychological and educational measurements.

Let us take a look at our tests A and B from another angle. Suppose, now, that we were to combine them into a single 40-word test and to give that test to 20 pupils in each grade from second through twelfth. What would we find? We would soon see that above the second or third grade almost everybody would get the first 20 words right. But until we got well up the grade ladder, children would get very few of the second set. It doesn't take much gain in spelling ability to improve from a score of 10 to one of 20 on this combined test, but to improve from 20 up to a score of 30 represents quite a respectable accomplishment. The two 10-point gains don't begin to be equal. The units from 0 to 40 on our scale of scores cannot be considered equal units, then. We have a rubber yardstick that has been stretched out at some points and squeezed in at others.

There is one further point that we should make about the spelling scores. Let us consider test B, since the point will be most clearly and obviously true for this test. A person who fails to get any of the items right on test B cannot be said to fall at an absolute zero of spelling ability. Actually, he may be able to spell hundreds, possibly thousands, of words. So a person who gets 10 words right on test B doesn't demonstrate twice as much spelling ability as a person who gets only 5 right. The difference may actually correspond to an increment in "spelling vocabulary" from 10,000 to 12,000 words. On this test, as in an iceberg, the great bulk of what we are examining lies below "sea level" and can't be seen. We cannot guarantee that even test A gets down to a true zero point. In fact, it would be hard to say what a real zero point is in spelling ability.

TYPES OF NORMS

We must look, then, for some better type of unit in which to express test results than a raw count of units of score or a crude percentage of the possible score. We would like the units to have the following properties.

1. Uniform meaning from test to test, so that a basis of comparison is provided through which we may compare different tests—for example, different reading tests, a reading test with an arithmetic test, or an achievement test with a scholastic aptitude test.

2. Units of uniform size, so that a gain of 10 points on one part of the scale signifies the same thing as a gain of 10 points on any other part of the scale.

3. A true zero point of "just none of" the quality in question, so that we can legitimately think of scores as representing "twice as much as" or "two-thirds as much as."

The different types of norms that have been developed for tests represent marked progress toward the first two of the above objectives. The third can probably never be reached for the traits with which psychological and educational measurement is concerned. We can put five 1-pound loaves of bread on one side of a pair of scales, and they will balance the contents of a 5-pound bag of flour poured into the other. "No weight" is *truly* "no weight," and units of weight can be added together. But we don't have that type of zero point or that way of adding together in the case of educational and psychological measurement. If you put together two morons, you will not get a genius, and a pair of bad spellers cannot jointly win a spelling bee.

Basically, a raw point score can be given meaning only by referring it to some type of group or groups. A score is not high or low, good or bad in any absolute sense; it is higher or lower, better or worse than other scores. There are two general ways in which we may relate a person's score to a more general framework. One way is to compare him with a graded series of groups and see which one he matches. Each group in the series usually represents a particular school grade or a particular chronological age. The other way is to find where, in a particular group, he falls in terms of the percent of the group he surpasses or in terms of the group's mean and standard deviation. Thus, we find four main patterns for interpreting the score of an individual. These are shown schematically in Table 7.2. We shall consider each in turn, evaluating its advantages and disadvantages.

TABLE 7.2 MAIN TYPES OF NORMS FOR EDUCATIONAL AND PSYCHOLOGICAL TESTS

Type of Norm	Type of Comparison	Type of Group
Age norms	Individual matched to group whose performance he equals.	Successive age groups.
Grade norms	Same as above.	Successive grade groups.
Percentile norms	Percent of group surpassed by individual.	Single age or grade group to which individual belongs.
Standard score norms	Number of standard deviations individual falls above or below average of group.	Same as above.

Age Norms

For any trait that shows a progressive change with age, we can prepare a set of age norms. The norm for any age, in this sense, is the average value of the trait for persons of that particular age. Let us take the example of height. If we get a representative sample of 8-year-old girls, measure the height of each, and get the average of those measures, we determine the norm for height for that age group. Note that in this case the norm is nothing more than the average value. It is not the ideal value. Nor is it the value to be expected of each person in the group. It is the average value, no more and no less. It will pay to remember this in thinking about age and grade norms.

The average height can be determined in the same way for 9-year-olds, 10-year-olds, and each other age group in turn. The values will fall on some such curve as that shown in Fig. 7.1. Points for the curve will ordinarily be computed only for full-year groups, but the curve is to be considered continuous. That is, we can estimate points in between the year groups by referring to the continuous curve. Thus, in Fig. 7.1 a height of 60 inches corresponds to (or is average for) the age 12, while 50 inches corresponds to about 7 years and 8 months.

We can refer any height measurement to this scale and find for what age it would be average. Each girl's height can be interpreted as being the average height for a girl of a particular age. Thus, the girl who has a height of 60 inches can be described as being as tall as the average girl of 12 years. If we also know how old the girl actually is, we can judge whether she is tall, average, or short for her age. Thus, if Mary is 55 inches tall and is only 8 years old, we know that she is tall for her age. Her height is average for a 10-year-old.

The age framework is a relatively simple and familiar one. "He is as big as a 12-year-old" is a common way of describing a youngster. For a trait that shows continuous and relatively steady growth over a period of years, the age framework is a convenient one. Its familiarity and convenience are its major advantages. Age norms have a number of disadvantages, and these we must now consider in more detail.

The big issue in using age norms is whether we can reasonably think of a year's growth as representing a standard and uniform unit. Is the growth from age 5 to age 6 equal to the growth from age 10 to age 11, and similarly for each age on our scale? As we push up the age scale, we soon reach a point where we see that the year's growth unit is clearly inappropriate. There comes a point, some time in the teens or early 20's, when growth in almost any trait that we can measure slows down and finally stops. In Fig. 7.1 the slowdown

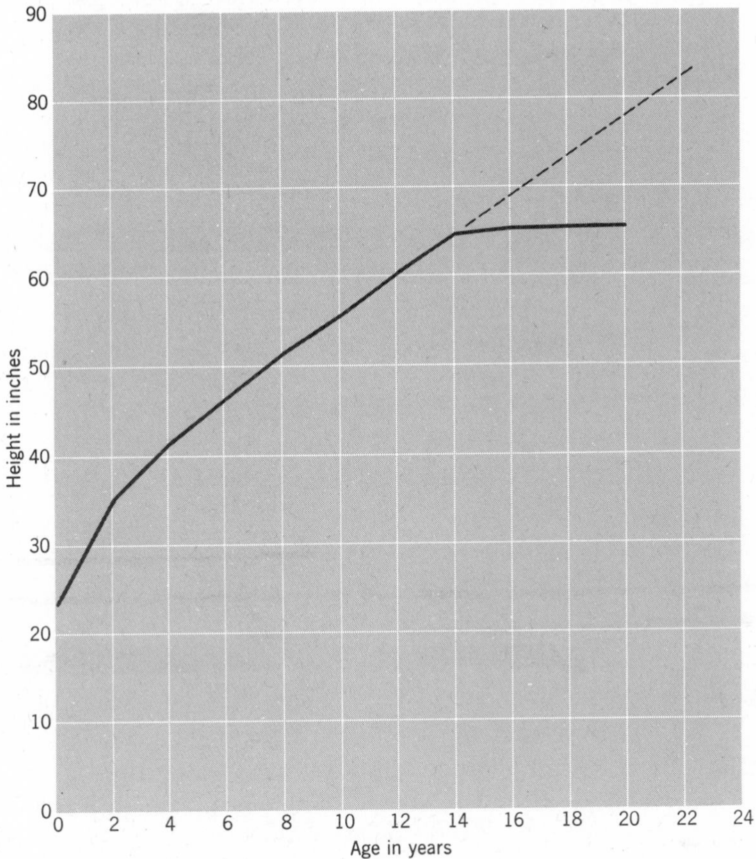

Fig. 7.1 Girls' age norms for height. (Adapted from Boynton, 1936.)

takes place quite abruptly after age 14. A year's growth after 14 seems clearly to be much less than a year's growth earlier on the scale. After about 14 or 15, the concept of height-age ceases to have any meaning. The same problem of a flattening growth curve is found, varying only in the age at which it occurs and in abruptness, for any trait that we can measure. The failure of the unit "one year's growth" to have uniform meaning is most apparent as one considers the extremes of age, but there is no guarantee that this unit has uniform meaning even in the intermediate range.

The problem introduced by the flattening growth curve is most apparent when we consider the individual who falls far above the average. What age equivalent shall we assign to a girl who is 5 feet 10 (70 inches) tall? The average woman *never* gets that tall at any age. If we are to assign any age value, we must invent some hypothetical extension of our growth curve such as the lightly dotted line in Fig. 7.1. This line assumes that growth after 14 continues at about the same rate that was typical up to age 14. On this extrapolated curve, the height of 5 feet 10 is assigned a height-age of about 16 years, 6 months. But this is a completely artificial and arbitrary age equivalent. It does *not* correspond to the average height of 16½-year-olds. It does not correspond to average height at *any* age. It merely signifies "taller than average."

This same type of artificial age equivalent must be used for ability or achievement tests to express the performance of bright pupils in their teens. Mental growth curves also show a leveling off similar to that illustrated in Fig. 7.1. After the age of 14 or 15, increases become smaller and gradually disappear. The increase from age 15 to 18 may be no more than that from age 11 to 12, and after 18 there may be little or no further rise. Thus, when we report a mental age of 18 or 20 on a test such as the Stanford-Binet, we do *not* mean that this individual is performing like an average 18-year-old or 20-year-old. These age-equivalents represent an arbitrary extension of the score-to-age conversion, like that shown by the dotted line of Fig. 7.1. Such arbitrary and artificial values are required if we are to have some way of representing the performance of the upper half of our teenage and adult population.

It is also true that growth curves are not entirely comparable for different functions. From test to test, rate of growth and time of reaching a maximum differ substantially. How shall we compare age scores on a vocabulary test and a maze-tracing test, for example, if the first continues to rise up to and into the twenties, while the second reaches a maximum in the early teens? For a 10-year-old to have reached the 12-year-old level may represent appreciably different degrees of superiority for different traits.

Two years' acceleration may also have quite different meaning, depending on the age level at which it occurs. A 5-year-old who is as tall as the 7-year norm is much more outstanding than the 10-year-old who reaches the 12-year norm. This fact has led to the development of the intelligence quotient and other types of quotients (which we shall consider presently) to allow for differences in age of the examinees. But the basic difficulty of inequality of the age unit at different points in the age scale still remains.

Of course, age norms are primarily appropriate for traits that depend on general normal growth. A trait showing no continuous improvement over an age range (such as acuity of vision) cannot possibly be expressed in terms of a scale of age units. One that depends primarily upon specific educational experiences, such as facility in arithmetical operations, seems to be more reasonably related to the educational framework of school grades than to the biological framework of years of growth.

Finally, though it does not directly concern the consumer of tests, it is worth noting that from the viewpoint of the test producer age norms present some serious practical problems. It is often difficult to get together a truly representative sample of individuals of a given age. Thus, if one wanted a cross section of 12-year-olds one would have to look for some of them in the elementary school and some in the junior high school. They would have to be assembled from quite a range of school grades. Then as one moves toward the older ages the sample one needs to reach is widely scattered—some in school, some at college, some in the military establishment, and some in the world of work. To reach a truly representative sample of 18-year-olds, for example, is a very forbidding task. This is one more reason why the usual age norms for tests become suspect as one moves up into the teens.

In summary, age norms, which are based on the performance of the average person at each age level, provide a readily comprehended framework for interpreting the performance of a particular individual. However, the equality of the age units is open to serious question. As one goes up to adolescence and adulthood, age ceases to have any meaning as a unit in terms of which to express level of performance. Age norms are most appropriate for the elementary-school years and for abilities that grow as a part of the general development of the individual. Physical and physiological characteristics such as height, weight, and dentition, and psychological traits such as general intelligence appear to be ones for which this type of norm is most acceptable.

A table of age and grade norms for the Lorge-Thorndike Intelligence Test, Multilevel Verbal Form 1, Level A is shown in Table 7.3 on page 218. This level of the test is designed for use in the fourth grade with pupils who are about nine years old.

Grade Norms

Grade norms have many of the characteristics of age norms, differing only in that the reference groups are grade groups instead of age groups. That is, a test is given to representative groups in each of a series of school grades, and the average score is determined for each grade. Scores lying between the norm for two successive grades are assigned fractional credits by interpolation. The standard terminology assigns the value 5.0 to average performance at the beginning of the fifth grade, 5.5 to average performance at the middle of the grade, and so forth.

Table 7.3 shows grade equivalents as well as age equivalents for the Lorge-Thorndike Intelligence Test. Thus, the table shows that a child who gets a raw score of 65 is performing at a level that would be average for a youngster of 9 years, 11 months, or of a youngster in the sixth month (tenth) of the

TABLE 7.3 AGE AND GRADE EQUIVALENTS FOR LORGE-THORNDIKE INTELLIGENCE TEST, MULTILEVEL VERBAL FORM 1, LEVEL A

Raw Score	Equiv. Age	Equiv. Grade	Raw Score	Equiv. Age	Equiv. Grade	Raw Score	Equiv. Age	Equiv. Grade	Raw Score	Equiv. Age	Equiv. Grade
1	6-1	—	26	7-11	2.6	51	9-1	3.8	76	10-8	5.5
2	6-2	—	27	7-11	2.7	52	9-2	3.9	77	10-10	5.6
3	6-4	—	28	8-0	2.7	53	9-2	3.9	78	10-11	5.7
4	6-5	—	29	8-0	2.8	54	9-3	4.0	79	11-0	5.8
5	6-6	—	30	8-1	2.8	55	9-4	4.0	80	11-2	5.9
6	6-7	—	31	8-1	2.9	56	9-4	4.1	81	11-3	6.0
7	6-8	—	32	8-2	2.9	57	9-5	4.1	82	11-5	6.1
8	6-9	—	33	8-3	3.0	58	9-6	4.2	83	11-6	6.2
9	6-10	—	34	8-3	3.0	59	9-6	4.2	84	11-7	6.3
10	6-11	—	35	8-4	3.1	60	9-7	4.3	85	11-9	6.5
11	7-0	—	36	8-4	3.1	61	9-8	4.4	86	11-11	6.6
12	7-1	—	37	8-5	3.2	62	9-9	4.4	87	12-0	6.8
13	7-2	—	38	8-5	3.2	63	9-9	4.5	88	12-2	6.9
14	7-3	—	39	8-6	3.3	64	9-10	4.6	89	12-4	7.1
15	7-3	—	40	8-6	3.3	65	9-11	4.6	90	12-6	7.2
16	7-4	—	41	8-7	3.3	66	10-0	4.7	91	12-7	7.3
17	7-5	—	42	8-7	3.4	67	10-0	4.8	92	12-9	7.4
18	7-6	—	43	8-8	3.4	68	10-1	4.8	93	12-10	7.5
19	7-7	—	44	8-8	3.5	69	10-2	4.9	94	13-0	7.7
20	7-7	2.2	45	8-9	3.5	70	10-3	5.0	95	13-2	7.9
21	7-8	2.2	46	8-10	3.6	71	10-3	5.1	96	13-4	8.0
22	7-8	2.3	47	8-10	3.6	72	10-4	5.1	97	13-6	8.2
23	7-9	2.4	48	8-11	3.7	73	10-5	5.2	98	13-8	8.3
24	7-9	2.4	49	9-0	3.7	74	10-6	5.3	99	13-11	8.5
25	7-10	2.5	50	9-0	3.8	75	10-7	5.4	100	14-2	8.7

Reproduced by permission of Houghton Mifflin Co.

fourth grade.* If the test had been given to a fourth grade in early October (corresponding to grade 4.1), we would conclude that this child was performing at a level a little above the national average. If it also turned out that he had just had his ninth birthday, we would say that he was almost a year accelerated in his intellectual development.

Grade norms have somewhat the same limitations as age norms. In particular, there is no guarantee that growth of one grade is the same amount of growth at all grade levels. The equality of units is even more suspect in the case of grade norms, because educational gains depend upon the content and emphasis

* Since the school year is about 10 months long, a month is conventionally treated as one-tenth of a school year.

in school instruction. The use of grade units to express growth only makes sense for those subject areas in which instruction is continuous through the school program. Since instruction in most of the basic skill subjects tapers off during high school, grade norms above the eighth or ninth have little direct meaning. In most cases, these are extrapolated values similar to those for the upper ages of age norms. Of course, grade norms for most high-school subjects would be essentially meaningless, since these are taught in only one or two grades.

The slowing down of gains at the upper grade levels makes it very difficult to express the performance of a very able child in terms of the grade framework. Many a superior child in the seventh or eighth grade can only be designated 11+ in terms of grade norms for standard school subjects. That is, his performance surpasses that of the average child in the highest grade for which norms are meaningful.

A further caution must be introduced with respect to the interpretation of grade norms. Consider a bright and educationally advanced child in the third grade. Suppose we find that on a standardized arithmetic test he gets a score for which the grade equivalent is 5.9. This does *not* mean that our child has a mastery of the arithmetic taught in the fifth grade. He got a *score* as high as that gotten by the average child at the end of the fifth grade, but this higher score was almost certainly obtained in part by superior mastery of third-grade work. The average child falls well short of a perfect score on the topics that have been taught at his grade level. Thus, the able child can get a number of additional points of score (and consequently a higher grade equivalent) merely by complete mastery of this material. This is worth remembering. The fact that our child has a grade equivalent of 5.9 need not mean that the child is ready to move ahead into sixth grade work. It is only the reflection of a score and does not tell in what way that score was attained.

Grade norms are relatively easy to determine, since they are based on the administrative groups already established in the school organization. In the directly academic areas of achievement, the concept of grade level is perhaps a more meaningful one than age level. It is in relation to his grade placement that a child's performance in these areas is likely to be interpreted and acted upon. Outside of the school setting, grade norms have little meaning.

To summarize, grade norms, which relate the performance of an individual to that of the average child at each grade level, are useful primarily in providing a framework for interpreting the academic accomplishment of children in the elementary school. For this purpose they are relatively convenient and meaningful, even though we cannot place great confidence in the equality of grade units. They have little value for other types of groups or of measures.

Percentile Norms

We have just seen that in the case of age and grade norms we give meaning to an individual's score by determining the age or grade group in which he would be just average. But it will often make more sense to compare him to his own age or grade group—to a group of which he may legitimately be considered a member. This is the type of comparison we make when we use percentile norms.

We saw in Chapter 5 how we could compute for any set of scores the median, quartiles, and any percentile. For each score value, we can compute the percent of cases, p, falling below that score. Any person getting that score then surpasses p percent of the group on which the percentile values were computed. We will say that he falls at the pth percentile, or has a percentile rank of p.

Table 7.4 shows percentile norms of boys in the first semester of the ninth grade tested on each of the subtests (and one combination of two subtests) of the *Differential Aptitude Test Battery, Form L.* Look at the column headed Verb. Reas. (*Verbal Reasoning*). The entries in this column are raw scores. Thus, a

TABLE 7.4 PERCENTILE NORMS FOR *Differential Aptitude Tests.*

FORM L GRADE 9F   **FALL (First Semester) PERCENTILE NORMS**

BOYS	Raw Scores									N=2400+
Percentile	Verb. Reas.	Num. Abil.	VR+NA	Abst. Reas.	Clerical S and A*	Mech. Reas.	Space Rela.	LU-I: Spell.	LU-II: Gram.	**Percentile**
99	44-50	38-40	77-90	44-50	75-100	61-68	54-60	93-100	48-60	99
97	42-43	36-37	73-76	43	67-74	60	51-53	89-92	45-47	97
95	39-41	34-35	68-72	42	62-66	58-59	48-50	85-88	41-44	95
90	36-38	32-33	64-67	41	59-61	56-57	44-47	81-84	37-40	90
85	34-35	30-31	61-63	39-40	56-58	54-55	41-43	77-80	35-36	85
80	32-33	28-29	58-60	38	54-55	53	38-40	74-76	33-34	80
75	30-31	26-27	54-57	37	53	51-52	36-37	72-73	31-32	75
70	28-29	25	51-53	36	51-52	50	34-35	69-71	30	70
65	26-27	24	49-50	35	50	49	32-33	67-68	28-29	65
60	24-25	23	47-48	33-34	48-49	48	30-31	64-66	27	60
55	22-23	22	44-46	32	46-47	47	28-29	62-63	26	55
50	21	20-21	41-43	31	45	45-46	26-27	60-61	25	50
45	20	19	38-40	30	44	44	24-25	58-59	23-24	45
40	18-19	18	36-37	28-29	43	43	22-23	56-57	21-22	40
35	17	17	34-35	26-27	42	42	20-21	54-55	20	35
30	15-16	15-16	32-33	24-25	40-41	40-41	19	52-53	19	30
25	14	14	29-31	22-23	38-39	38-39	17-18	50-51	18	25
20	13	13	27-28	19-21	36-37	36-37	15-16	47-49	15-17	20
15	11-12	12	25-26	14-18	34-35	33-35	13-14	44-46	13-14	15
10	9-10	10-11	22-24	11-13	31-33	30-32	12	41-43	11-12	10
5	8	8-9	18-21	8-10	25-30	27-29	11	36-40	9-10	5
3	6-7	6-7	15-17	5-7	17-24	23-26	10	30-35	7-8	3
1	0-5	0-5	0-14	0-4	0-16	0-22	0-9	0-29	0-6	1
Mean	22.4	20.9	43.3	29.3	45.6	44.8	27.9	61.3	25.2	**Mean**
SD	9.9	8.0	16.6	10.6	11.9	9.5	11.7	15.2	9.6	**SD**

score of 30 or 31 corresponds to the 75th percentile on this test. On the *Abstract Reasoning Test* (Abst. Reas.), a score of 31 corresponds to the 50th percentile. This score represents the same degree of excellence as a score of 21 on the *Verbal Reasoning Test.*

Note that not every percentile is given in Table 7.4. For most of the range, the percentiles are tabled in steps of 5, and sometimes several score points are listed opposite a given percentile value. If more detailed tables were given, these scores would correspond to different percentiles. However, no score is precisely accurate (see Chapter 6), so locating an individual to the nearest five percentiles is as close as is usually justified and certainly close enough for all practical decisions.

Percentile norms are very widely adaptable and applicable. They can be used wherever an appropriate normative group can be obtained to serve as a yardstick. They are appropriate for young or old, for educational or industrial situations. To surpass 90 percent of the reference comparison group signifies a comparable degree of excellence whether the function being measured is how rapidly one can solve simultaneous equations or how far one can spit. Percentile norms are widely used. Were it not for the two points that we must now consider, they would provide a framework very nearly ideal for interpreting test scores.

The first problem that faces us in the case of percentile norms is that of the norming group. On what type of group should the norms be based? Clearly, we will need different norm groups for different ages and grades in our population. A 9-year-old must be evaluated in terms of 9-year-old norms; a sixth grader, in terms of sixth-grade norms; an applicant for a job as stock clerk, in terms of stock-clerk-applicant norms. The appropriate norm group is in every case the group to which the individual belongs and in terms of which his status is to be evaluated. It makes no sense to evaluate the performance of a medical school applicant on a biology test by comparing his score with norms based on high-school seniors.

If we are to use percentile norms, then, we must have multiple sets of norms. We must have norms appropriate for each distinct type of group or situation with which our test is to be used. This is recognized by the better test publishers, who provide norms not only for different age or grade groups but also for special types of educational or occupational populations. However, there are limits to the number of distinct groups for which a test publisher can produce norms.

Published percentile norms will often need to be supplemented by the test user, who can build up norm groups particularly suited to his individual needs. Thus, a given school system will often find it valuable to develop local percentile norms for its own pupils. This will permit interpretation of individual scores in terms of the local group, a comparison that may be more significant for local problems than comparison with the national norms. Again, an employer who uses a test with a particular category of job applicants may well find it useful to accumulate norms for this particular group of people. Evaluating a new applicant will be much facilitated by these strictly local norms.

The second problem in relation to percentile norms is more serious. Again, we are faced by the problem of equality of units. Can we think of 5 percentile points as representing the same amount throughout the percentile scale? Is the difference between the 50th and 55th percentile equivalent to the difference between the 90th and 95th? To answer this, we must notice the way in which test scores for a group of individuals usually pile up. We saw one histogram of scores in Chapter 5 (p. 139). This picture is fairly representative of the way the scores fall in many cases. There is a piling up of cases around the middle scores and a tailing off at either end. The ideal model of this type of score distribution, which is called the *normal curve*, was also considered in Chapter 5 (pp. 151–153) and is shown in Fig. 7.2. The exact normal curve is an idealized mathematical model, but many types of tests and measures distribute themselves in a manner that approximates a normal curve. You will notice the piling up of most of the cases in the middle, the tailing off at both ends, and the symmetrical pattern.

In Fig. 7.2, four score points have been marked. These are, in order, the 50th, 55th, 90th, and 95th percentiles. Note that near the median the 5 percent of cases (the 5 percent lying between the 50th and 55th percentile) fall in a tall narrow pile. Toward the tail of the distribution the 5 percent of cases (the 5 percent between the 90th and 95th percentile) make a relatively broad low bar. Five percent of the cases spread out over a considerably wider range of scores in the second case than in the first. The same number of percentile points corresponds to about three times as many score points when we are around the

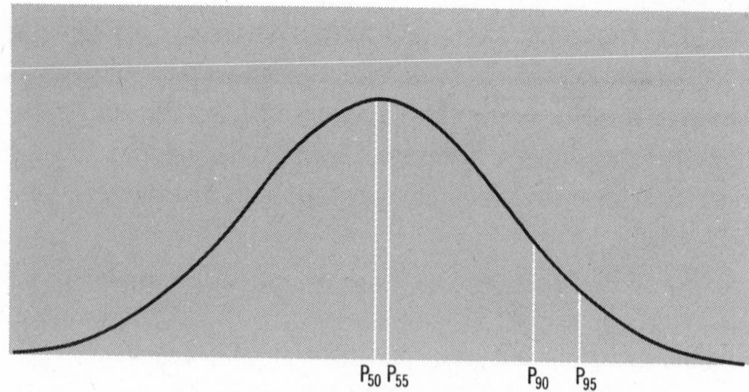

Fig. 7.2 Normal curve, showing selected percentile points.

90th to 95th percentile as when we are near the median. The further out on the tail we go, the more extreme the situation becomes.

Thus, percentile units are typically and systematically unequal. The difference between being first or second in a group of 100 is many times as great as the difference between being 50th and 51st. Equal percentile differences do not represent equal differences in amount. Any interpretation of percentile ranks must take into account the fact that such a scale has been pulled out at both ends and squeezed in the middle. Mary, who falls at the 50th percentile in arithmetic and the 55th in reading, shows a trifling difference in these two abilities, whereas Alice, with percentiles of 90 and 95, shows a marked difference.

PERCENTILE BANDS. Any measurement provides only an estimate of the true level of ability of an individual. This matter is discussed more fully in the section of Chapter 6 dealing with reliability. Bearing in mind the error of measurement characterizing a test score, some publishers have prepared norms tables in the form of *percentile bands.* For each raw score the manual reports, instead of a specific percentile corresponding to that score, a range of percentile values within which the true ability of the examinee may be presumed to lie. A section of such a table for the *STEP Reading Test* is shown in Table 7.5 on page 224. The table would be read as follows: A fifth-grade pupil with a raw score of 55 may be presumed to have ability falling somewhere in the range from the 77th to the 91st percentile of the reference group.

The objective in using percentile bands is to keep the test user from attaching unwarranted precision to a test score, and to encourage awareness of the variability of pupil performance from day to day and from one form to another of a test. The band that is usually reported extends one standard error of measurement on either side of the obtained score, so if we were to interpret the percentile band fully we should say something like: "There are about two chances in three that this examinee's true level of ability falls within these percentile limits." Thinking in terms of a band rather than a point helps in seeing which differences between subject areas for a single pupil, or between pupils in a given subject, are large enough so that we can have some confidence in their reality and feel a need to pay some attention to them.

To conclude, percentile norms provide a basis for interpreting the score of an individual in terms of his standing in some particular group. If the percentile is to be meaningful, the group must be one with which it is reasonable and appropriate to compare him. We will usually need a number of tables of percentile norms based on different groups, if we are to use a test with different ages, grades, or occupations. As long as percentiles for appropriate groups are supplied, this type of norm is widely applicable. But interpretation of percentile values is

TABLE 7.5 PERCENTILE BANDS CORRESPONDING TO RAW SCORES ON *STEP Reading Test* 4B (FALL TESTING)

Raw Score	Percentile Band		
	Grade 4	Grade 5	Grade 6
62	99.5–100	96–99.2	92–99.3
61	99.2–99.9	95–99.1	88–98
60	98–99.7	93–98	84–96
59	97–99.6	90–97	81–93
58	96–99.5	88–96	77–92
57	95–99.2	86–95	74–88
56	94–99	82–94	72–87
55	92–97	77–91	66–83
54	91–96	74–89	64–79
53	88–95	70–87	58–76
.	.	.	.
.	.	.	.
.	.	.	.
34–36	56–67	30–47	24–39
32–33	50–61	25–43	21–35
29–31	46–56	22–39	19–30
27–28	43–50	19–35	16–27
25–26	34–48	16–30	13–24
23–24	25–46	12–25	10–21
21–22	19–43	9–22	8–19
19–20	14–37	6–19	6–16
17–18	6–31	2–16	2–13
–16	0–25	0–12	0–10

Adapted from the *Manual for interpreting scores of the STEP Reading Test,* p. 23.

made more difficult by the fact that we have a systematically "rubber" scale whose units are small in the middle range and large at the extremes.

Standard Scores

Because the units of a score system based on percentiles are so clearly not equal, we are led to look for some other unit that does have the same meaning throughout its whole range of values. *Standard-score* scales have been developed to serve this purpose.

In Chapter 5, we became acquainted with the standard deviation as a measure of the spread or scatter of a group of scores. The standard deviation was a type of average of the deviations of scores away from the mean—the root-mean-squared deviation. Scores may be expressed in standard deviations away from the mean. Thus, in Table 7.4, the mean *Numerical Ability* score is 20.9 and the standard deviation is 8.0, so a person who got a score of 25 falls

$$\frac{25 - 20.9}{8.0} = 0.51$$

standard deviation units above the mean. A score of 15 would be 0.73 standard deviation units *below* the mean. In standard deviation units, we would call these scores +0.51 and −0.73 respectively.

Suppose we have given the *Differential Aptitude Test* to the pupils in a class and two pupils got the following scores on *Numerical Ability* and *Spelling:*

	Num. Abil.	*Spelling*
Henry	25	75
Joe	30	70
Mean	20.9	61.3
S.D.	8.0	15.2

Let us see how we can use standard scores to compare performance of an individual on the two tests, or performance on a test of the two individuals.

On *Numerical Ability* Henry is 4.1 points above the mean or 4.1/8.0 = 0.51 standard deviations above the mean. On *Spelling* he is 13.7 points or 13.7/15.2 = 0.90 standard deviations above the mean. Henry is about $\frac{4}{10}$ of a standard deviation better in spelling than in arithmetic. For Joe the corresponding calculations give

$$\text{Numerical} \quad \frac{30 - 20.9}{8.0} = 1.38 \qquad \text{Spelling} \quad \frac{70 - 61.3}{15.2} = 0.57$$

Thus, Henry did about as well on *Numerical Ability* as Joe did on *Spelling,* while Joe's *Numerical Ability* score turned out to be somewhat better than Henry's *Spelling.*

Each pupil's level of excellence is expressed as so many standard deviation units above or below the mean of the comparison group. This is a standard unit of measure having essentially the same meaning from one test to another. For aid in interpreting the degree of excellence represented by a standard score, see Table 5.6 (p. 152).

The type of score in standard deviation units that we have just presented is satisfactory except for two matters of convenience: (1) it requires us to use plus and minus signs which may be miscopied or overlooked, and (2) it gets us involved with decimal points which may be misplaced. We can get rid of the need to use decimal points by multiplying every standard deviation score by some constant, such as 10. We can get rid of minus signs by adding to every score a convenient constant amount such as 50. Thus, for Henry's scores on *Numerical Ability* and *Spelling* we have:

	Num. Abil.	*Spelling*
Mean of distribution of scores	20.9	61.3
Standard deviation of distribution	8.0	15.2
Henry's raw score	25	75
Henry's score in standard deviation units	+0.51	+0.90
Standard deviation score × 10	+5	+9
Plus a constant amount (50)	55	59

A table of standard scores for *Numerical Ability* based on this conversion, in which the mean is set equal to 50 and the standard deviation to 10, is shown in Table 7.6.

The standard scores in Table 7.6 are based on a simple equation that changes the size of the units and the location of group mean. In symbolic form the equation is

$$Z = 10\left(\frac{X - \bar{X}}{\text{S.D.}}\right) + 50$$

where **Z** is the standard score,
X is the raw score,
$\bar{\mathbf{X}}$ is the mean of the raw scores, and
S.D. is the standard deviation of raw scores.

TABLE 7.6 STANDARD SCORE EQUIVALENTS FOR NUMERICAL ABILITY TEST, NINTH GRADE—BOYS. (STANDARD SCORE MEAN = 50, *SD* = 10)

Raw Score	Standard Score	Raw Score	Standard Score	Raw Score	Standard Score	Raw Score	Standard Score
49	85	37	70	24	54	12	39
48	84	36	69	23	53	11	38
47	83	35	68	22	52	10	37
46	82	34	67	21	50	9	35
45	80	33	65	20	49	8	34
44	79	32	64	19	48	7	33
43	78	31	63	18	47	6	32
42	77	30	62	17	45	5	30
41	75	29	60	16	44	4	29
40	74	28	59	15	43	3	28
39	73	27	58	14	42	2	27
38	72	26	57	13	40	1	25
		25	55			0	24

The scale of scores is stretched out or squeezed together (depending on whether the original standard deviation is smaller or larger than 10), but the stretching or squeezing is uniform all along the scale of scores. Since the above equation is the equation of a straight line, this type of transformation of scores is called a *linear conversion.*

Frequently, standard-score scales are developed via the percentiles corresponding to the raw scores, making the assumption that the trait that is being measured has a normal distribution. This is called an *area conversion* of scores. Thus in the *Numerical Ability Test* it is found that 35 percent of ninth-grade boys fall below a score of 17. If one goes to a table of the normal curve, one finds that the baseline value in a normal curve below which 35 percent of cases fall is -0.39 standard deviations. Consequently, we would assign to a raw score of 17 a standard score of -0.39. Expressing this result on a scale in which the standard deviation is to be 10 and the mean 50, we have

$$T = 10(-0.39) + 50 = -4 + 50 = 46.$$

The designation *T*-score and the symbol *T* have often been used to identify this particular type of normalized standard-score scale.

Normalized standard scores make sense whenever it seems likely that the group is a complete one that has not been curtailed by systematic elimination at the upper or lower ends. Furthermore, they make sense whenever it seems likely that the raw score does not represent a scale of equal units. Many test makers systematically plan to include in their tests many items of medium difficulty and few easy or hard items. The effect of this is to produce tests that spread out and make fine discriminations among the middle 80 or 90 percent of pupils, while making coarser discriminations at the extremes. That is, the raw score units in the middle range correspond to smaller true increments in the ability being measured than do raw score units at the extremes. The true distribution of ability is pulled out into a flat-topped distribution of scores. The operation of normalizing the distribution reverses this process.

We could have used values other than 50 and 10 in setting up our conversion into convenient standard scores. The Army has used a standard-score scale with mean of 100 and standard deviation of 20 for reporting its test results. The College Entrance Examination Board has long used a scale with mean of 500 and standard deviation of 100. The Navy has used the 50 and 10 system.

Originally used in the Air Force, *stanine* scores have had some popularity in recent years. These are single-digit standard scores in which the mean is 5 and the standard deviation 2. The relationships among a number of the different standard-score scales, and the relationship of each to percentiles and to the nor-

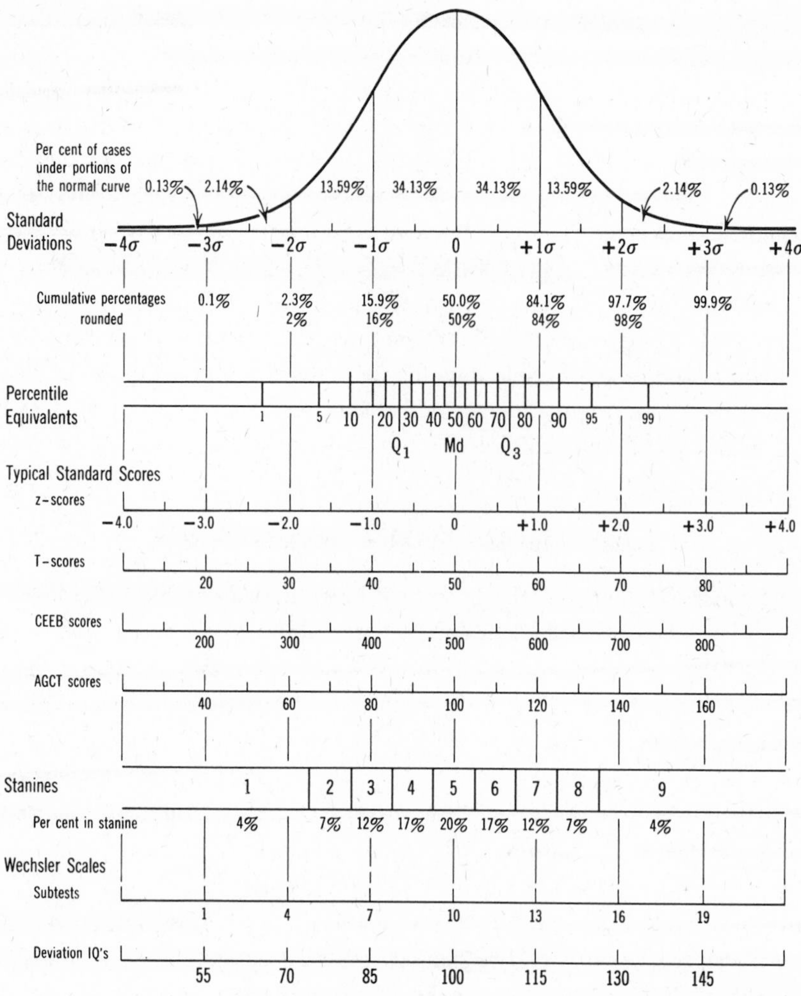

Fig. 7.3 Various types of standard score scales in relation to percentiles and the normal curve. (Reproduced by permission of the Psychological Corporation.)

mal curve are shown in Fig. 7.3. The model of the normal curve is shown, and beneath it are a scale of percentiles and several of the common standard score scales. This figure illustrates the equivalence of scores in the different systems. Thus, a stanine score of 7 corresponds to an Army standard score of 120, a Navy standard score of 60, a College Board standard score of 600, a percentile rank of 84. The particular choice of score scale is arbitrary and a matter of convenience. It is too bad that all testing agencies have not been able to agree upon a common score unit. However, the important thing is that the same score scale and comparable norming groups be used for all tests in a given organization, so that results from different tests may be directly comparable.

In summary, standard scores, like percentiles, base the interpretation of the individual's score on his performance in relation to a particular reference group. They differ from percentiles in that they are expressed in presumably equal units. The basic unit is the standard deviation of the reference group, and the individual's score is expressed as the number of standard deviation units above or below the mean of the group. Standard scores may be based on either a linear or an area (normalizing) conversion. Different numerical standard-score scales have been used by different testing agencies.

INTERCHANGEABILITY OF DIFFERENT TYPES OF NORMS

Whichever type of norm is used, a table of norms will be prepared by the test publisher. This will show the different possible raw scores on the test, together with the corresponding score equivalents in the system of norms being used. Many publishers provide tables giving more than one type of score equivalent. An example is given in Table 7.7 on page 230. Here we see the norms for the *Comprehension Test* of the *Gates-MacGinitie Reading Tests, Primary B.* Four types of norms are shown. The percentiles are based on a group tested early in the second grade. The standard-score scale assigns a mean of 50 and a standard deviation of 10 to an early second-grade group. Thus, a boy with a score of 21 can be characterized as:

1. Having a grade equivalent of 2.6.
2. Falling at the 79th percentile in the second-grade group.
3. Receiving a standard score of 58.
4. Receiving a stanine of 7.

From Table 7.7, it is easy to see that the different systems of norms are different ways of expressing the same thing. We can translate from one to the other, moving back and forth. Thus, a child who falls at the 66th percentile in the second-grade group has a grade equivalent of 2.3. A grade equivalent of 2.3 corresponds to a standard score of 54. The different systems of interpretation support one another for different purposes.

However, the different norm systems are not entirely consistent as we shift from one type of test to another. This is due to the fact that some functions mature more rapidly from one year to the next, relative to the spread of scores at a given age or grade level.

TABLE 7.7 NORMS FOR GATES-MACGINITIE READING TEST—PRIMARY B

Comprehension Norms—Primary B				
Grade Level 2.1 (Oct.)				
Raw Score	Standard Score	Percentile	Grade Score	Stanine
1	—	—	—	1
2	30	2	—	1
3	32	4	—	1
4	34	5	—	2
5	35	7	1.2	2
6	38	12	1.3	3
7	39	14	1.4	3
8	41	18	1.4	3
9	44	27	1.5	4
10	46	34	1.6	4
11	47	38	1.6	4
12	49	46	1.7	5
13	50	50	1.8	5
14	51	54	1.9	5
15	52	58	2.1	5
16	53	62	2.2	6
17	54	66	2.3	6
18	55	69	2.4	6
19	56	73	2.5	6
20	57	76	2.5	6
21	58	79	2.6	7
22	58	79	2.7	7
23	59	82	2.8	7
24	60	84	3.1	7
25	61	86	3.4	7
26	62	88	3.6	7
27	63	90	3.7	8
28	64	92	4.0	8
29	65	93	4.3	8
30	66	95	4.5	8
31	68	96	4.7	9
32	70	98	4.9	9
33	72	99	5.1	9
34	75	99	5.4	9

This can be seen most dramatically by comparing reading comprehension and arithmetic computation. The phenomenon is illustrated by the pairs of scores shown in Table 7.8, based on the Stanford Achievement Test Battery. It is assumed that the three boys were tested at the end of 2 months in the fifth grade. John received scores on both tests that were just average. His grade equivalent was 5.2 and he was close to the 50th percentile for pupils tested after 2 months in the fifth grade. Henry shows superior performance, but how does he compare in the two subjects? From one point of view, he does equally well in both; he is just one full year ahead of his grade placement. But in terms of percentiles he is much better in arithmetic than in reading, that is, 89th percentile as compared with 74th percentile. Will, on the other hand, falls at just the same percentile for both reading and arithmetic. In his case, his grade equivalent for reading is 7.3 and for arithmetic is 6.3.

TABLE 7.8 COMPARISON OF GRADE EQUIVALENTS AND PERCENTILES

	Paragraph Meaning			Arithmetic Computation		
	John	Henry	Will	John	Henry	Will
Raw score	28	36	46	14	20	21
Grade equivalent	5.2	6.2	7.3	5.2	6.2	6.3
Grade 5.2 percentile	52	74	90	56	89	90

The discrepancies that appear in the above example are due to differences in the variability of performance and rate of growth of reading and arithmetic. Reading shows a *wide* spread within a single grade group, relative to the change from grade to grade. Some fifth graders read better than the average eighth or ninth grader, so a grade equivalent of 8 or 9 is not unheard of for fifth graders. In fact a grade equivalent of 8.0 corresponds to the 95th percentile for pupils at grade 5.2. By contrast, a fifth grader almost never does as well in arithmetic as an eighth or ninth grader—in part because he has not encountered or been taught many of the topics that will be presented in the fifth, sixth, seventh, and eighth grades. Thus, fifth graders are more homogeneous with respect to arithmetic skills, or looked at another way, arithmetic shows more rapid gains from fifth to eighth grade than does reading.

This point must always be borne in mind, especially in comparing grade equivalents for different subjects. A bright child will often appear most advanced in reading and language, least so in arithmetic and spelling—when the results are reported in grade equivalents. This difference may result, in whole or in part, simply from the differences in the growth functions for the subjects, and need not mean a genuinely uneven pattern of progress for the child.

QUOTIENTS

In the early days of mental testing, after age norms had been used for a few years, the need was felt to convert the age score into an index that would express rate of progress. The 8-year-old who had an age equivalent of 10½ years was obviously better than average, but how much better? Some index was needed to take account of chronological age (actual time lived) as well as the age equivalent on the test (score level reached).

The expedient was hit upon of dividing test age by chronological age to yield a quotient. This procedure was applied most extensively with tests of intelligence where the age equivalent on the test was called a mental age and the corresponding quotient was an *intelligence quotient.*

The formula for computing the intelligence quotient in this way is given below and is illustrated for the 8-year-old who reaches the 10½-year level on the test.

$$IQ = \frac{100MA}{CA}$$

$$= \frac{100(10.5)}{8} = 131$$

How does an intelligence quotient come to have meaning? In the first place, it is obvious by the way in which the quotient was established that 100 should be average at every age group, since the average 10-year-old, for example, should fall exactly at the 10-year level on any test if the age equivalents were properly established. But how outstandingly good is 125? How poor is 80? Such questions as these can only be answered by becoming acquainted with the distribution of quotients that a particular test yields.

The intelligence quotient was originally developed in connection with the individual intelligence test of the type represented by the *Stanford-Binet* (see Chapter 10). The circumstance that made intelligence quotients from such a test as the *Stanford-Binet* relatively interpretable was that the mean and standard deviation remained relatively uniform from age to age. For this reason, an IQ of 125 signified about the same status, relative to his own age group, whether obtained for a 5-year-old or a 15-year-old. This situation would not necessarily be true and was not perfectly true even for this test, but in many instances quotients were found to maintain the same average and spread of values in different age groups sufficiently closely so that a common interpretation was appropriate at all age levels.

To all intents and purposes, such quotients represented a type of standard score. The 1937 revision of the *Stanford-Binet*, produced a standard score with a mean of approximately 100 and standard deviation of approximately 16 in a general sample of American children. This relationship of quotients to standard scores is explicitly recognized in most recent intelligence tests. For these tests, tables of IQ equivalents have been set up at each age level, and have been built so as to give the same mean and standard deviation for all age groups. As a matter of fact, the most recent edition of the *Stanford-Binet*, brought out in 1960, also uses standard scores designed so that the mean is 100 and the standard deviation 16 at each age level, rather than the MA/CA ratio that was the basis for the IQ in earlier editions.

The notion of the intelligence quotient or IQ is deeply imbedded in the history of the testing movement, and, in fact, in twentieth-century American culture. The expression "IQ test" is a part of our common speech. We are probably stuck with the term. But in the future IQ's will in most cases really be standard scores. And this is how we should think of them and use them.

In a number of recent tests of intelligence, the converted scores that are reported are, in fact, normalized standard scores, based on the type of normalizing area transformation that is discussed on page 227. These are usually referred to as Deviation Intelligence Quotients (DIQ's), since they are basically standard scores expressed as a deviation above or below a mean of 100.

Unfortunately the score scale for reporting IQ's does not have *exactly* the same meaning from test to test. The Wechsler test series (see Chapter 10) is based on a mean of 100 and standard deviation of 15, while the Binet and most group tests are based on a mean of 100 and a standard deviation of 16. Furthermore, tests are normed at different points in time and using different sampling procedures. This also leads to differences in the norms, and consequently in the distribution of IQ's they yield for any given school or community.

PROFILES

The various types of norms we have been considering provide a means of expressing scores on quite different tests in common units in such a way that they can be directly compared. There is no direct way of comparing a score of thirty words correctly spelled with one of twenty arithmetic problems solved. But if both scores are expressed in terms of the grade level to which they correspond or in terms of the percent of some defined common group that gets scores below that point, then they may be compared. The set of different test scores for an individual, expressed in a common unit of measure, constitute his *score profile.* The separate scores may be presented for comparison in tabular form by listing the converted score values. A record form showing the converted scores is given in Fig. 7.4. The comparison of different subareas of performance is made pictorially clearer by a graphic profile. Two ways of plotting profiles are shown in Figs. 7.5 and 7.6 on pages 235 and 236.

Figures 7.4 and 7.5 show a class record form and an individual profile chart for the *Iowa Tests of Basic Skills.* The class record illustrates the form in which data are reported back to schools by one of the large-scale computerized test-scoring organizations. The upper left-hand scores reported here are grade equivalents, and since the tests were given after the pupils had spent two months in the seventh grade, the norm for the country as a whole would be 7.2. The scores in the lower right of each box are percentile ranks for autumn testing in the seventh grade.

CLASS RECORD SHEET — **Iowa Tests of Basic Skills**

Grade 7 Semester (1st or 2nd) 1st School Building Shepard Date 11/ 6 /66 Form B

City, or District Woodford County Erie State N.Y. Teacher Mr. Peters

Names of Pupils	SEX	AGE		TEST V	TEST R	TEST L LANGUAGE SKILLS					TEST W WORK-STUDY SKILLS				TEST A ARITHMETIC SKILLS			
	(Write B or G)	Age in Years at Last Birthday	Months Since Last Birthday	Vocabulary	Reading Comprehension	Spelling	Capitalization	Punctuation	Usage	TOTAL TEST L	Map Reading	Reading Graphs and Tables	Knowledge and Use of Reference Materials	TOTAL TEST W	Arithmetic Concepts	Arithmetic Problem Solving	TOTAL TEST A	COMPOSITE V, R, L, W, A
				V	R	L-1	L-2	L-3	L-4	L	W-1	W-2	W-3	W	A-1	A-2	A	C
Anthony G.	M	12	8	66 39	64 36	75 57	95 84	37 7	78 60	71 51	58 26	68 43	60 29	62 33	77 63	83 80	80 73	69 46
Grant O.	M	12	4	92 89	101 97	80 65	90 78	87 76	88 76	86 77	105 98	98 94	102 98	102 98	102 98	88 88	95 95	95 91
Glenna O.	F	13	2	71 49	68 44	76 58	102 93	81 66	67 44	82 70	75 57	81 71	81 69	79 69	79 67	67 40	73 57	75 58
Janet G.	F	13	8	58 25	60 29	53 22	47 13	44 13	58 31	50 15	69 46	57 25	40 3	55 18	48 6	59 25	54 13	55 20
Gustav J.	M	12	10	78 65	76 61	80 65	105 96	104 96	78 60	92 87	90 87	51 17	67 42	69 48	79 67	77 66	78 69	78 66
Robert C.	M	13	3	56 22	63 34	69 47	55 24	44 13	54 29	55 23	72 52	73 54	60 29	68 46	68 42	63 32	66 39	62 33

Fig. 7.4 Class record sheet for *Iowa Test of Basic Skills.* (Reproduced by permission of Houghton Mifflin Co.)

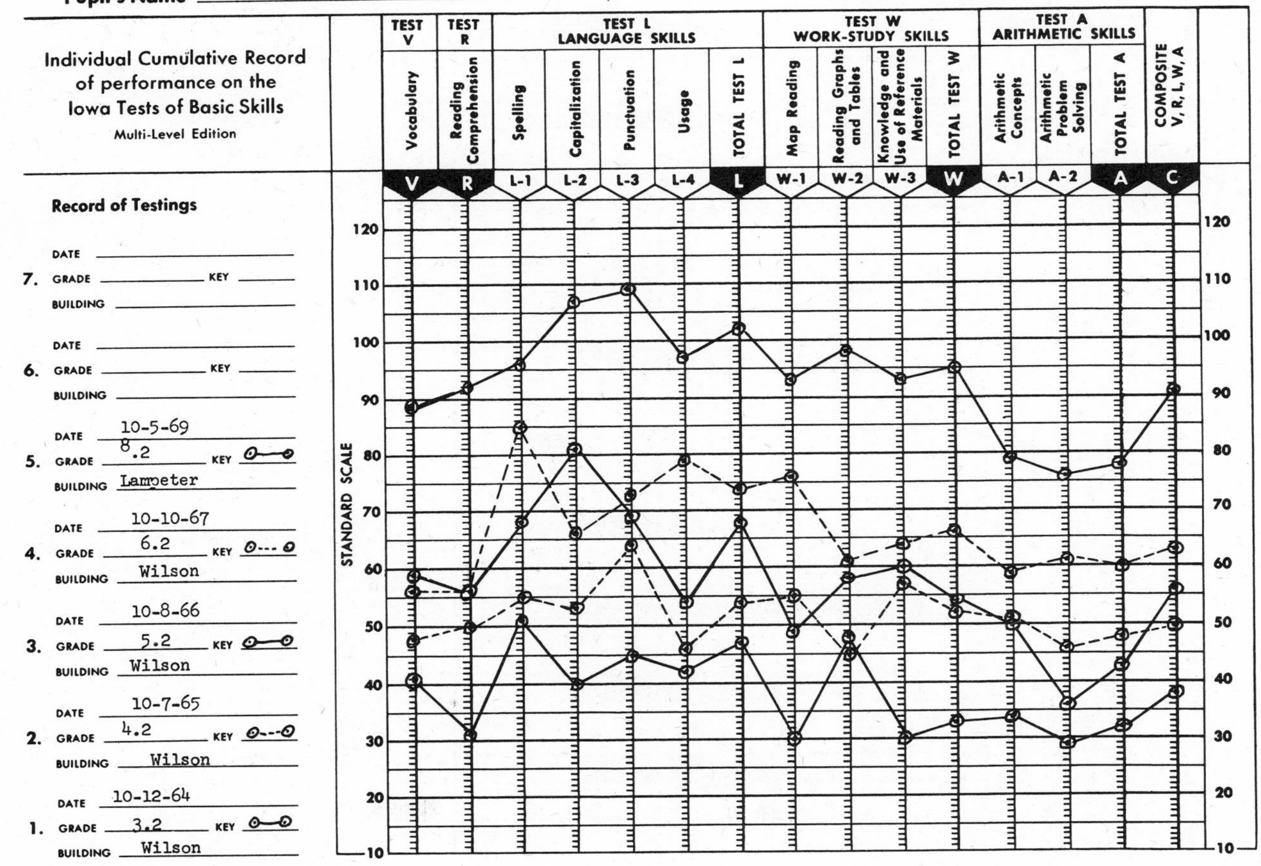

Fig. 7.5 Pupil profile chart for *Iowa Test of Basic Skills.* (Reproduced by permission of Houghton Mifflin Co.)

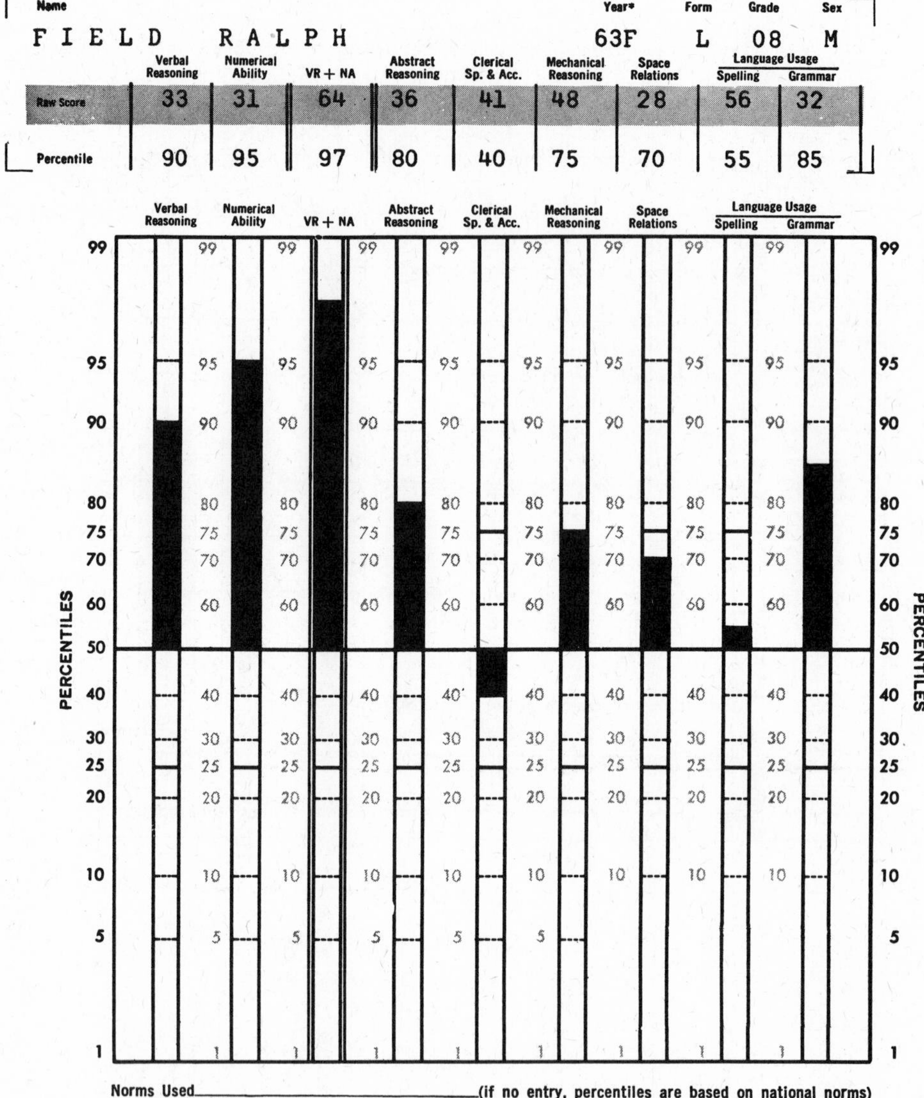

Fig. 7.6 Pupil profile chart of *Differential Aptitude Tests.* (Reproduced by permission of the Psychological Corporation.)

Figure 7.5 shows data for five testings of a boy in grades 3.2, 4.2, 5.2, 6.2, and 8.2. The so-called "standard scale" referred to towards the left is actually a scale of grade equivalents. Thus, this pupil had a vocabulary grade equivalent of 4.1 when he was tested in the third grade. In the fourth grade, his grade equivalent was 4.8, and in the fifth grade it was 5.9.

The results show him to have been generally above the national average in his vocabulary score, though he fell below it at the sixth-grade testing. Again, an examination of his profile for the eighth-grade test indicates that he was strongest in language skills and weakest in arithmetic. Some of the hazards of paying a great deal of attention to small ups and downs of a profile can be seen in a comparison of performance on successive testings. Thus, spelling appears as the highest peak in the profile for third grade testing, but is just average a year later; graph and table reading is next to highest in grade 3, but shows an actual drop between grades 3 and 4 and is the lowest point in the grade 4 profile. There are a number of other inconsistencies from one testing to the following one. It is possible that some of these shifts are meaningful, but many of them stem from nothing more than the error of measurement in subtests that are rather short and not very reliable.

Figure 7.6 shows a type of profile chart for the component tests of the *Differential Aptitude Test Battery*. This battery undertakes to appraise different aspects of ability important in a high-school guidance program. Note that in this case the different tests are represented by separate bars, rather than points connected by a line. The scale used in this case is a percentile scale, but in plotting percentile values appropriate adjustments have been made for the inequality of percentile units. That is, percentile points have been spaced in the same way as they are in a normal curve, being more widely spaced at the upper and lower extremes than in the middle range. This percentile scale corresponds to the percentile scale that is shown in Figure 7.3 (p. 228). By this process, the percentile values for an individual are plotted on an equal unit scale. A given linear distance can reasonably be thought of as representing the same amount of ability whether it lies high, low, or near the middle of the scale. By the same token, the same distance can be considered equivalent from one test to another.

Note that in Fig. 7.6 the bars have been plotted up and down from the 50th percentile. For this type of norm, the average of the group constitutes the anchor point of the scale, and individual scores can be referred to this base level. This type of figure brings out the individual's strengths and weaknesses very dramatically.

The profile chart makes a very effective way of representing the scores for an individual. In interpreting profiles, however, several cautions must be borne in mind. In the first place, procedures for plotting profiles assume that the norms for the several tests are comparable. Age, grade, or percentile scores must be based upon equivalent groups for all the tests. The best guarantee of equivalence is, of course, a common population used for all tests. This is the situation that commonly prevails for the different subtests of a test battery. Norms for all are established at the same time on the basis of testing a common group. The guarantee of comparability of the norms for the different component tests is one of the most attractive features of an integrated battery. If separately developed tests are plotted together, we can usually only hope that the groups on which norms were established were comparable and that the profile is an unbiased picture of relative achievement in the different fields. Where it is necessary to use tests from several different sources, one solution is to develop local norms on a common population and to plot individual profiles in terms of those local norms.

A second problem is that of deciding how to interpret the ups and downs of a profile. Not all the differences that appear in a profile are meaningful, either in a statistical or a practical sense. We must decide which of the differences deserve some attention on our part and which should be ignored. This problem arises because no test score is completely exact. The problems of reliability and of the error of measurement in a test score were considered in Chapter 6. Reporting scores in percentile bands, as discussed on pp. 223–224, is one way of dealing with this problem. If the percentile band, rather than a specific percentile, were plotted in Fig. 7.6, one could see by inspection which bands overlapped and which were clearly separate. An alternate procedure is to calculate the approximate vertical distance on the standard-score scale of the profile chart that corresponds to the standard error of measurement, and then use a ruler to help judge which differences are large enough to merit attention. (For Fig. 7.6 this vertical distance is approximately one-half inch.) Of course, there is no magic size at which a score difference suddenly becomes worthy of attention, and any rule of thumb is at best a rough guide. But differences must be big enough so that (a) one can be reasonably sure that they will persist, and (b) they are big enough to make a difference, before one starts to interpret them and base actions on them.

Organizing the separate test scores of an individual into a graphic profile is, then, a very effective way of dramatizing the high and low points in a score pattern. Such a profile may be plotted whenever scores from several different tests are expressed in the same units. However, a profile must be interpreted with a good deal of caution, because even unreliable differences may look quite impressive.

USING NORMS

We have seen that norms provide a basis for interpreting the scores of an individual. Converting the score for any test taken singly into age or grade equivalent, percentile or standard score, permits an interpretation of the level at which the individual is functioning on that particular test. Bringing together the set of scores for an individual in a common unit of measure, and perhaps exhibiting these scores in a profile, brings out the relative level of performance of the individual in different areas.

The average performance for a class, a grade group in a school, or the children in a grade throughout a school system may be similarly reported. We then see the average level of performance within the group on some single function or the relative performance of the group in each of several areas. Norms provide a frame within which the picture may be viewed and bring all parts of the picture into a common frame. Now what does the picture mean, and what should we do about it?

Obviously we cannot, in a few pages, provide a ready-made interpretation for each set of scores that may be obtained in a practical testing situation. However, we can lay out a few general guiding lines and principles that may help to forestall some unwise interpretations of test results.

The most general point that we must make is that test results, presented in terms of the types of converted scores that have been explained in this chapter, are a *description of what is,* rather than a *prescription of what should be.* They make it possible to compare an individual or a class with other individuals and classes with respect to one or more aspects of accomplishment or personality, but they do not in any absolute sense tell us whether the individual or the group is doing "well" or "badly." They do not provide this information for several reasons that we shall now consider.

1. *Converted scores give relative rather than absolute information.* They tell whether a pupil has as high achievement as other pupils or whether a class scores as high as other classes. But they do not tell us whether the basic concepts of numbers are being mastered or whether pupils read well enough to comprehend the instructions for filling out an income tax return. Furthermore, they give us little guidance as to how much improvement we might expect from *all* pupils if our educational system operated throughout at 100 percent efficiency.

It must be remembered that by the very nature of relative scores, there will be as many below average as above. When "the norm" means the average of a reference group, it is a statistical necessity that about half the group will be, to a greater or lesser degree, below average—unless all individual differences are to be eliminated. There has been an enormous amount of foolishness—both in single schools and in state-wide legislation—about bringing all pupils "up to the grade norm." Conceivably, this might be done temporarily if we had a sudden and enormous improvement in educational effectiveness—but then the next time new norms were established for the test, it would take a higher absolute level of performance to "read at the sixth-grade level," for example, so we would be back again with half the pupils falling at or below the average.

2. *Output must be evaluated in relation to input.* Test results typically give a picture of output—of the individual or group as it exists at the present time, after a period of exposure to educational effort. But what of the input? Where did the group start?

The notion of input is a complex and rather subtle one. Our conception of input should include not only earlier status on the particular ability being measured; not only individual potential for learning, so far as we are able to appraise this; but also the familial circumstances and environmental supports that make it easier for some children to learn than for others. Parental aspirations for the child, parental skills at tuition and guidance of learning, parental discipline and control, linguistic patterns and cultural resources in the home are part of the input just as truly as are the biological characteristics of the young organism. Furthermore, peer group and community attitudes are an additional real, though possibly modifiable, part of the input so far as the prospects for learning for a given child are concerned.

We still do not know too well how to measure input. Some of the overly simplified approaches to the problem will be discussed in Chapter 10, when we consider the use of "expectancy tables" to view a child's achievement in the light of his performance on an aptitude test. For the present, we must be content to recognize that the adequate appraisal of input is no simple matter, and that, correspondingly, the appraisals of output as "satisfactory" or "unsatisfactory" is something we do with only modest confidence.

3. *Output must be evaluated in relation to objectives.* The design, content, and norms for published standardized tests are based on the authors' perception of common national curricular objectives. The topics included, their relative emphasis, and the levels at which they are introduced reflect that general national pattern. To the extent, then, that a given school system deviates in its objectives and curricular emphases, from the national pattern as interpreted by the test maker, its output at a given grade level can be expected to deviate from the national norms. If computational skills receive little emphasis, it is reasonable that computational facility will be underdeveloped. If map reading has been delayed beyond the grade level at which it is introduced into the test, it is

reasonable that relative standing on that part of the test will suffer. Unevenness of local profile, in relation to national norms, should always lead one to inquire whether the low spots represent failures of the local program or a reflection of a considered deviation of emphasis from what is typical in schools more generally.

If these considerations are borne in mind, and the test interpreter also maintains a healthy respect for the standard error of measurement when he is concerned with results for a single individual, test results, as they are reported to teacher, principal, superintendent or school board, will be interpreted and used with increased wisdom and restraint.

SUMMARY STATEMENT

A raw score, taken by itself, has no meaning. It gets meaning only by comparison with some reference group or groups. The comparison may be with:

1. A series of age groups (age norms).
2. A series of grade groups (grade norms).
3. A single group, indicating what percent of that group the score surpassed (percentile norms).
4. A single group, indicating standard deviations above or below the group mean (standard scores).

Each alternative has certain advantages and certain limitations, which we have considered.

To get an index of brightness from age norms, quotients such as the intelligence quotient were devised. These become meaningful and usable when they have approximately the same standard deviation for all age groups. In that case, they are essentially standard scores and should be thought of as such.

If the norms available for a number of different tests are of the same kind and are based on comparable groups, all the tests can be expressed in comparable terms. They can then be shown pictorially in the form of a profile. Profiles emphasize score differences within the individual. When profiles are used, care must be taken not to overinterpret minor ups and downs of the profile.

Norms represent a descriptive framework for interpreting the score of an individual, a class group, or some large aggregation. However, before a judgment can be made as to whether an individual or group is doing well or poorly, allowance must be made for ability level, cultural background, and curricular emphases. The norm is merely an average, not a strait jacket into which all can be forced to fit.

QUESTIONS AND EXERCISES

1. A pupil in the seventh grade received a raw score of 13 on the *Metropolitan Reading Test, Intermediate Level.* What additional information would be needed to interpret this score?

2. Why do standardized tests designed for use with high-school students almost never use age or grade norms?

3. What limitations would national norms have for use by a county school system in rural West Virginia? What might the local school system do about it?

4. What assumption or assumptions lie back of the development of age norms? Grade norms? Normalized standard scores?

5. In Fig. 7.3, p. 228, why are the standard scores evenly spaced whereas the percentile scores are unevenly spaced?

6. You are a guidance counselor and have given Form L of the *Differential Aptitude Battery* to a ninth grade in October. Using Table 7.4, prepare a summary report and interpretation for a boy with the following scores:

Verbal Reasoning	18	Mechanical Reasoning	54
Numerical Ability	23	Clerical Speed and Acc.	45
Abstract Reasoning	31	Spelling	48
Spatial Relations	39	Sentences	22

7. School A gives a battery of achievement tests each May in each grade from the third through the sixth. The median grade level in each subject in each teacher's class is reported to the superintendent. Should they be reported? If so, what else should be included in the report? In what ways might a superintendent use the results to advantage? What uses should he avoid?

8. Miss B prides herself that each year she has gotten at least 90 percent of her fifth-grade group "up to the norm" in each subject. How desirable is this as an educational objective? What limitations or dangers do you see in it?

9. School C operates on a policy of assigning transfer students to a grade on the basis of their average grade standing on an achievement battery. Thus, a boy with a grade score of 6.4 on the battery as a whole would be assigned to the sixth grade, no matter what his age or his grade in his previous school. What values do you see in this plan? What limitations?

10. The superintendent of schools in city D noted that school E fell consistently about a half grade below national norms on an achievement battery. He was distressed because this was the lowest of any school in his city. How justified is his dissatisfaction? What more do you need to know to answer this?

11. The board of education in city F noted that the second and third grades in their community fell substantially below national norms in arithmetic, though coming up to the norms in other subjects. They propose to study this further. What additional information do they need?

12. Look at the manual for some test, and study the information that is given about the norms.

a. How adequate is the norming population? Is adequate information given about this?
b. Figure out the chance score (i.e., the score to be expected from blind guessing) for each test, and note its grade equivalent. What limitations does this suggest on use of the test?
c. What limitations are there on the usefulness of the test at the upper end of its range?
d. How many raw score points correspond to one full year on a grade equivalent scale?

REFERENCES

Boynton, B. The physical growth of girls. *University of Iowa Studies in Child Welfare,* 1936, **12,** No. 4.

SUGGESTED ADDITIONAL READING

Anastasi, A. *Testing problems in perspective.* Washington, D.C.: American Council on Education, 1966. Pp. 241–280.

Bennett, G. K., Seashore, H. G., & Wesman, A. G. *Differential Aptitude Tests manual.* New York: Psychological Corp., 1959. Chapters 4, 5.

Doppelt, J. E. How accurate is a test score? *Test Service Bulletin No. 50.* New York: Psychological Corp., 1956.

Ebel, R. L. Content, standard test scores. *Educational and Psychological Measurement,* 1962, **22** (1), 15–26.

Wesman, A. G. Expectancy tables—a way of interpreting test validity. *Test Service Bulletin No. 38.* New York: Psychological Corp., 1949. Pp. 1–5.

Womer, F. B. *Test norms: Their use and interpretation.* Washington, D.C.: National Association of Secondary School Principals, 1965.

CHAPTER 8

Where to Find Information about Specific Tests

THE NATURE OF THE PROBLEM

THE production of educational and psychological tests has been going on for only half a century, but during that time literally thousands of different tests have been produced. A comprehensive bibliography extending to about 1945 contained entries for 5,294 different tests. Buros (1961) produced a bibliography of tests for English-speaking examinees that were available in 1961 from commercial publishers, and the list contained 2,126 entries. Some of these have since become unavailable, but new ones have appeared to take their places, and the number of currently available tests is almost certainly still above 2,000, not counting those instruments that appear only in the research literature.

Not only is the total number of tests great. So also is the variety. Tests vary widely in testing procedures, in content, and in group for which designed. There are paper-and-pencil tests, individual performance tests, rating scales, self-rating procedures, observational procedures, and projective techniques. There are measures of attitude, of interest, of temperament, of personal adjustment, of intellect, of special aptitudes, and of all aspects of school achievement. There are tests designed for infants, for preschool children, for school children and adolescents, and for adults.

No one book can hope to introduce a student to even a representative sampling of tests of all types, covering all sorts of content for all age levels. The following chapters will introduce some of the most important and most widely known tests, discussing them as examples of many others. But this book cannot give a complete treatment of any particular age group or subject area, and there are so many special situations in which a reader may be interested or for which he may need a test that the tests discussed here may include not even one that fits his particular need.

Since it is impossible to list and evaluate all or even most of the tests that might be of concern to an audience with varied interests, we shall approach the problem at a different level. We shall try to guide the reader to sources in which he can find the available tests listed, and in some cases evaluated, and we will try to guide the reader in evaluating the tests he locates. The present chapter discusses resource materials for finding tests and for finding out about them. Chapter 6 has given an orientation in the factors to be considered in evaluating the suitability of a particular test for a particular purpose.

The knowledge of where to go to find out about tests of a particular type and how to evaluate one when found is probably more important than predigested information about a particular test. Tests change and the purposes of the test user change. It is impossible to anticipate what type test will be required for some future need. The important thing is to know how to go about finding the tests available for that need when it arises and how to evaluate their relative merits.

There are several different types of questions about a test or an area of measurement for which one may seek answers. Some of the types of questions are:

1. What tests have been developed that might serve my present need or purpose?
2. What are the *new* tests in my field of interest?
3. What is test A, of which I have heard, like? For what groups and purposes was it designed? Who made it? How long does it take and how much does it cost? What skills are needed to give and use it?
4. What do specialists in the field of measurement have to say about test A? How do they evaluate it, in comparison with competing techniques?
5. What basic factual material do we have on test A? What are its statistical attributes? What are its relationships to other measures?
6. What research has been done studying or using test A?

Let us see what materials are available to us as we try to answer questions such as these. These resources include (1) text and reference books in special areas of testing, (2) the *Mental Measurements Yearbooks,* (3) test reviews in professional journals, (4) publishers' test catalogues, (5) each test itself together with its accompanying manual, (6) articles in professional journals reviewing a broad field of testing, and (7) educational and psychological abstract and index series. These will be considered in turn, the most useful items will be identified, and the information to be obtained from each type of source will be indicated.

TEXT AND REFERENCE BOOKS IN SPECIAL AREAS

There are a number of text and reference books covering more specialized areas of testing. When the scope is limited to include only elementary-school tests, tests for diagnosis of individual maladjustment, or tests for vocational placement, it becomes possible to cover the field in more detail. A book dealing with tests of a particular type provides a good general introduction to the materials of the field. Such a book usually acquaints the reader with a representative selection of established tests in the area—those which the author considers worthy of mention. In addition, some evaluation of each test is usually given, indicating the purposes for which it may well be used, and what the writer considers to be its strengths, weaknesses, and distinctive characteristics. The book will usually also contain some discussion of the problems of testing in the field it covers, apart from discussion of specific tests.

It is not possible to list all the books that might prove useful to some reader. However, a brief list is included in the suggested readings at the end of the chapter. Criteria for including titles, where several alternatives existed, were recency and judged quality of treatment. In addition, an attempt has been made to cover a wide range of specialized interests.

One limitation of books, such as those listed, becomes apparent from an examination of the publication dates. At the time that these were selected (1968), each was judged to be the most recent good book in its field and yet some were already a number of years old. When one adds to this the time that has elapsed in the preparation and printing of the book, it is easy to see that a book reviewing a field cannot be relied upon for current materials. The typical textbook gives information about well-established and accepted tests, but recently published devices or techniques that are still in the experimental stages are not likely to be represented. There is a lag of several years between production of a device and the reporting of it in books reviewing an area of testing.

Another feature of most books surveying a field, which may be in some cases an advantage and in others a disadvantage, is that they are selective. They must be. The author cannot discuss everything, so he must pick the items he wishes to present. He selects for discussion the tests he considers valuable. Insofar as his judgment is sound, he does a real service to the novice in the field, who is thus led directly to the more important and valuable material. However, this means that the reader cannot expect to use a textbook as a source to lead him to all the tests in an area and permit him to compare them. For a full listing of the tests of any particular type he will have to look elsewhere.

THE MENTAL MEASUREMENTS YEARBOOKS

Probably the most useful single reference source for the person needing to make choices and plan programs in the field of testing is the series of *Mental Measurements Yearbooks* prepared by Buros (1938, 1941, 1949, 1953, 1959, 1965). Six *Yearbooks* have now been published, and when the sixth one appeared in 1965, the author was already making plans for the next volume in the series.

The *Yearbooks* undertake to provide a listing and one or more frank and critical reviews of each new standardized test that is published. A large panel of reviewers has cooperated in the preparation of these volumes, each reviewer evaluating two or three tests in an area in which he is presumed to be competent. The tests of more general interest are appraised by two and sometimes even more reviewers. The reviews are fairly full, pointing out strengths and weaknesses of a test, comparing it with others in the field, and indicating the purposes for which the reviewer considers it useful. A review does, of course, represent the opinion of a specific individual. It expresses his biases as well as his wisdom, and should be read with a recognition of human fallibility. However, the reviewer is a disinterested outsider who presumably does not stand to gain either from the test's success or its failure.

In addition to reviews of tests, the *Yearbooks* also include the factual items about each test that a potential user is likely to need—such items as author, publisher, publication date, cost, time to administer, grades for which suitable, and number of forms available. Finally, for each test the *Yearbooks* give a cumulative bibliography of books and articles that have appeared dealing with that particular test. These bibliographies are quite extensive, amounting in the case of one test to 3,030 titles.

The *Yearbooks* have two other features that add to their value to the test user. One is a section on books and monographs related to measurement problems.

This section undertakes to list all the significant books on measurement for the period covered and in addition gives excerpts from the reviews of these books that have appeared in psychological and educational journals. The bibliography and reviews provide a guide to, and evaluation of, publications in the field.

Also valuable is a very complete index and directory section. This includes (1) a directory and index of the publishers of the tests and of the books on measurement reviewed in the volume, (2) a directory and index of the periodicals that have included reviews of tests or books on testing, (3) an index of titles of books and tests, (4) an index of names occurring in any connection, and (5) a classified index of tests organized by content or type. These indices make it possible to locate any test or type of test, to locate the complete original of any excerpted test review, and to get in touch with the publisher of any test.

When a question arises about a test or a type of test, the *Mental Measurements Yearbooks* are the volumes for which one reaches almost automatically. They are a "must" for any individual or any office that must answer frequent questions about tests or testing.

A valuable supplement to the *Mental Measurements Yearbooks* is *Tests in Print,* which lists all commercially available tests using the English language. The date of this listing was 1961, but an updating of the list is provided in the classified index of tests in the *Sixth Mental Measurements Yearbook.* This index provides a list of tests known to be available in 1964.

The *Yearbooks* are not too convenient to use if one wishes to cover early as well as current tests in a particular area. At the present writing, there are six of them, published in 1938, 1941, 1949, 1953, 1959, and 1965. To cover the tests in any field, the reader must search all six volumes. A new test is ordinarily reviewed in the first *Yearbook* that came out after it was published, and reviews may sometimes also appear in subsequent volumes. Space limitations did not permit review in the 1938 *Yearbook* of all the older tests that were thought to merit review, and reviews of some of these first appeared in later volumes. Even the set of volumes taken together does not undertake to be *exhaustive* in its coverage of tests of a given type. However, if he brings together the material in the complete series, the reader will probably find an appraisal of any test that he is likely to consider using, published up to the time that planning for the last *Yearbook* was completed. The first two *Yearbooks* cover tests up to about 1939; the third covers the period from 1940 through 1947; the fourth deals with material from 1948 through 1951; the fifth brings us up to 1958, and the sixth to 1964.

JOURNAL TEST REVIEWS

We still face the problem of getting information on the *latest* tests and testing developments. One way of keeping up with important new tests is through reviews in professional journals. At different times in their history, different educational and psychological journals have included test reviews. The most useful journal in 1968 is probably the *Journal of Educational Measurement,* though the *Journal of Counseling Psychology* also occasionally includes reviews. These sources should keep the test user up to date on the most significant new educational and psychological tests within a year or so of their appearance.

TEST PUBLISHERS

The most current information on what tests are available is probably to be obtained from the test publishers themselves, either through correspondence or through their catalogues. There are many publishers, too many to list here, so that gathering information from all of them would be quite an undertaking. However, the number who publish *extensively* in the testing field is a good deal more limited. A number of the most important publishers are listed in Appendix V together with their addresses and some indication of the types of material and the services they supply.

The limitations of a test publisher as an entirely unbiased source of information on the *values and limitations* of his own publications are, of course, obvious. Reversing Marc Antony, we may say he comes to praise his tests, not to bury them. However, as a source of information about, rather than evaluation of his tests, he can be very helpful. In Chapter 6 we have considered how the potential user may go about appraising a new test for himself in the light of the information he can get from the test producer and from other sources.

TEST AND MANUAL

The individual who is seriously considering using a particular test will certainly need to examine the test itself and the manual the publisher has prepared to go with it. Each publisher's catalogue will indicate the price for which a specimen set of each test may be obtained. The specimen set contains a copy of the test itself, the instructions for administering and scoring, and part or all of the supplementary materials available to the user to help in interpreting the test.

The amount of supplementary materials included in a specimen set varies from one publisher to another. The potential user can legitimately expect the publisher to include in a specimen set materials that will provide all the information he needs in order to arrive at a decision as to the suitability of the test for his purposes. He should be skeptical of any test for which the information supplied him is incomplete. The individual who wishes to examine a number of different tests without buying specimen sets of each may be able to find a test file in the library or the guidance department of his local university.

To obtain specimen sets of tests, the applicant must ordinarily present some sort of credentials. A letter on the official letterhead of his school or institution will often suffice. A note from the university where he is studying may serve the function. The limitations that publishers place upon the distribution of their materials depend upon the nature of the materials. They will often refuse to distribute tests that require special skills to administer and interpret unless the applicant can give evidence that he has the training and skills that qualify him to use those materials.

A detailed examination of the test itself will provide the potential user with a basis for judging how well the content of the test and the form of test exercises correspond to the objectives and functions he wishes to measure. The accompanying material, which we have collectively called the test manual, is a very important part of any test. It varies enormously in quality and comprehensiveness from one test to another. In some of the better current tests, his collateral material becomes almost a book. It provides a great variety of important information to help in using and interpreting the test. We have indicated in Chapter 6 (pp. 202–204) the types of information a test user has a right to expect to find in the test manual. A manual that provides all this information becomes a very important source for information about the test.

Manuals differ greatly not only in comprehensiveness but also in impartiality and integrity. Probably no test manual is entirely free of a promotional element. However, sometimes the manual becomes to a very large extent a promotional device focused on increasing the sales of the test. The potential user must always be aware of this aspect of the manual and must endeavor to discount appropriately claims made for the test. There often appears to be an inverse relationship between the grandeur of the claims that are made and the evidence on which they are based. The reader will do well to keep his attention focused on the evidence presented in the manual, to view claims in the light of this evidence, and to be extremely suspicious of the test whose manual makes sweeping claims but presents very little data.

JOURNAL REVIEW ARTICLES

It is sometimes useful to refer to summary articles covering recent developments in tests and testing. The most regular of these in recent years has been the triennial summary in the *Review of Educational Research.* This journal undertakes to summarize research in a number of different sectors of education. Its publication schedule is arranged so that a given area is treated every 3 years. Material on tests and measurements was reviewed in the February, 1968, issue, which was devoted to educational and psychological testing. Similar reviews appeared in 1965, 1962, and every third year back to 1932. Because of the volume of material to be covered, these reviews are very condensed, but they do introduce the reader to new tests and testing research and provide him with a bibliography of original references to which he can go for a fuller report on any topic in which he is interested.

Since 1950, the *Annual Review of Psychology* has provided a yearly review and bibliography on selected psychological topics. Chapter headings such as "Individual Differences" and "Theory and Techniques of Assessment" suggest sources for material of possible interest to the psychological tester.

An annotated bibliography on reading has appeared in recent years in the *Journal of Educational Research.* This deals with reading tests—as well as with other reading problems.

An additional journal source that may be of interest to a test user who is especially concerned with predictive validities of different tests is a section entitled Validity Studies Section, that appears in alternate issues of *Educational and Psychological Measurement.* A somewhat similar section has also appeared in *Personnel Psychology* under the heading of Validity Information Exchange.

ABSTRACTS AND INDICES

Two final sources that must be brought to the attention of the serious student are the *Psychological Abstracts* and the *Education Index.* These are basic bibliographic sources in the fields of psychology and education respectively. Each undertakes to provide a complete listing of current publications in its respective field. The field for the *Psychological Abstracts* is rather more narrowly defined, being restricted to scientific and technical publications in psychology. Each publication is represented not merely by title but also by an abstract indicating the nature of the report and the major findings. An annual subject index and author index aid in locating desired material. In addition, the "Table of Contents" at the beginning of each issue will suggest headings under which relevant tests and research concerning tests will be listed.

The *Education Index* covers a considerably wider range of material, since it deals with the whole broad area of education and includes popular and professional materials as well as those of a more technical and scientific nature. It gives references only, providing no information about the nature and content of the item. Material is topically organized, and the user who looks under such topics as ability tests, educational measurement, mental tests, or personality tests will find most of the material relating to measurement in education.

The joint use of the *Psychological Abstracts* and the *Education Index,* supplemented by the other sources discussed previously, should enable the student who wishes to dig to the roots of a measurement problem to locate the bulk of the work that has been done on that problem.

SUMMARY STATEMENT

At the beginning of this chapter a number of questions were suggested to which a test user might wish answers. The important sources of information about tests and testing have now been discussed. By way of summary, we may try to relate the sources to the questions. An attempt has been made to do this in Fig. 8.1. At the top of this chart are listed various questions one might raise about a test, type of test, or testing problem. On the side are listed the most important types of source material referred to in this chapter. In each cell is a symbol to represent the extent to which the source should help in answering the question. The symbol ** is used to designate one of the sources that would probably be *most* helpful and to which one would turn first. Sources marked * are ones that would also be expected to contribute to the needed answer. Sources marked ? are ones that might perhaps provide some useful information. Where there is *no* entry at all, the source is not likely to be helpful in that connection. A critical study of this table, with analysis of the reasons for the various entries, should leave the reader well prepared to go out and get for himself the information he needs in order to select a test or as background for a specific testing problem.

Sources	To Find Out, in Any Field					
	What tests there are	What *new* tests there are	What test X is like	What specialists think of test X	What facts we have about test X	What research has been done on or with testing problem Y
Texts in special areas of measurement	*		*	?	*	*
Mental Measurements Yearbooks	**	?	*	**	*	**
Reviews in current professional journals		**	*	*		
Publishers' catalogues	*	**	*			
Test blank and manual			**		**	*
Review articles in *Review of Educ. Research,* etc.		*		?	?	*
Tests in Print	**					
Psychological Abstracts		*			*	**
Education Index		*				*

Key: **—Most helpful. *—Somewhat helpful. ?—Possibly helpful.

Fig. 8.1 Appraisal of sources of information about tests and testing.

QUESTIONS AND EXERCISES

1. Using the sources indicated in the text, prepare as complete a list as you can of currently available standardized tests for a specific grade and purpose (i.e., tests in first-year Spanish, reading readiness tests, tests in American history for the twelfth grade, etc.).

2. Using the *Mental Measurements Yearbooks,* find out what reviewers think of a particular test that you are interested in.

3. Using the *Sixth Mental Measurements Yearbook,* find out what reviewers have to say about one of the following titles that interests you:

Berdie, R. F. and others. *Testing in Guidance and Counseling.*
Dressel, P. L. and associates. *Evaluation in Higher Education.*
Lado, R. *Language Testing: The Construction and Use of Foreign Language Tests.*

Levine, E. S. *The Psychology of Deafness: Techniques of Appraisal for Rehabilitation.*

Miner, J. B. *Intelligence in the United States—With Conclusions for Manpower Utilization in Education and Employment.*

Shuey, A. M. *The Testing of Negro Intelligence.*

Osgood, C. E., Suci, G. J., and Tannenbaum, P. H. *The Measurement of Meaning.*

4. To what sources would you go to try to answer each of the following questions? To which would you go first? What would you expect to get from each?

a. What test should I use to study the progress of two class groups in beginning French?
b. What kinds of norms are available for the *Stanford Achievement Tests*?
c. Is the *Rorschach Test* of any value as a predictor of academic success in college?
d. Has a new revision of the *Wechsler Adult Intelligence Scale* been published yet?
e. What intelligence tests have been developed for use with the blind?
f. What are the significant differences between the *Metropolitan Achievement Tests* and the *Comprehensive Tests of Basic Skills*?
g. How much does the *Otis-Lennon Mental Ability Test* cost?
h. What do testing people think of the *Brainard Occupational Preference Inventory*?

5. Look at two or three publishers' catalogues. Compare the announcements of tests of the same type. How adequate is the information that is provided? How objective is the presentation of the tests' values and limitations?

REFERENCES

Buros, O. K., Educational, psychological, and personality tests of 1933, 1934, and 1935, *Rutgers Univ. Bull.*, Vol. 13, No. 1, Studies in Education, No. 9, New Brunswick, New Jersey, School of Educ., Rutgers University, 1936.

Buros, O. K., Educational, psychological, and personality tests of 1936, *Rutgers Univ. Bull.*, Vol. 14, No. 2A, Studies in Education, No. 11, New Brunswick, New Jersey, School of Educ., Rutgers University, 1937.

Buros, O. K., *The 1938 mental measurements yearbook,* New Brunswick, New Jersey: Rutgers University Press, 1938.

Buros, O. K., *The 1940 mental measurements yearbook,* Highland Park, New Jersey: *The Mental Measurements Yearbook,* 1941.

Buros, O. K., *The third mental measurements yearbook,* New Brunswick, New Jersey: Rutgers University Press, 1949.

Buros, O. K., *The fourth mental measurements yearbook,* Highland Park, New Jersey: Gryphon Press, 1953.

Buros, O. K., *The fifth mental measurements yearbook,* Highland Park, New Jersey: Gryphon Press, 1959.

Buros, O. K., *Tests in print.* Highland Park, New Jersey: Gryphon Press, 1961.

Buros, O. K., *The sixth mental measurements yearbook.* Highland Park, New Jersey: Gryphon Press, 1965.

SUGGESTED ADDITIONAL READING

Allen, R. M. & Allen, S. P. *Intellectual evaluation of the mentally retarded child.* Beverly Hills, California: Western Psychological Services, 1967.

Allen, R. M. & Jefferson, T. W. *Psychological evaluation of the cerebral palsied person: Intellectual, personality, and vocational applications.* Springfield, Illinois: Charles C. Thomas, 1962.

Bauman, M. K. *Tests used in the psychological evaluation of blind and visually handicapped persons.* Washington, D.C.: Association of Workers for the Blind, 1968.

Berg, Harry D. (Ed.) *Evaluation in social studies,* Thirty-Fifth Yearbook of the National Council for the Social Studies. Washington, D.C.: National Council for the Social Studies, 1965.

Della-Piana, G. M. *Reading diagnosis and prescription: An introduction.* New York: Holt, Rinehart and Winston, Inc., 1968.

Fleishman, E. A. *The structure and measurement of physical fitness.* Englewood Cliffs, New Jersey: Prentice-Hall, 1964.

Gronlund, N. E. (Ed.) Selecting standardized tests. *Readings in measurement and evaluation.* New York: Macmillan, 1968. Pp. 215–250.

Hardaway, M. *Testing and evaluation in business education.* (3rd ed.) Cincinnati, Ohio: Southwestern Publishing Co., 1966.

Latchaw, M. & Brown, C. *The evaluation process in health education, physical education and recreation.* Englewood Cliffs, New Jersey: Prentice-Hall, 1962.

Lehman, P. R. *Tests and measurements in music.* Englewood Cliffs, New Jersey: Prentice-Hall, 1968.

Levine, E. S. *The psychology of deafness: Techniques of appraisal for rehabilitation.* New York: Columbia University Press, 1960.

Mathews, D. K. *Measurement in physical education.* (3rd ed.) Philadelphia, Pennsylvania: Saunders, 1968.

The National Council of Teachers of Mathematics. *Evaluation in mathematics,* Twenty-Sixth Yearbook. Washington, D.C.: The National Council of Teachers of Mathematics, 1961.

CHAPTER 9

Standardized Achievement Tests

oooooooooooooooooooooooooooooooooooooooooooooooooooooooooooooooooooooooooooooooooooooooooooooooo

WE turn our attention now to consideration of specific kinds of tests and procedures that have been used to appraise different attributes of individuals. In Chapters 9, 10, and 11 we shall discuss published tests of ability, and in Chapters 12 through 15 we shall discuss procedures for appraising personality. The distinctions between the concepts of ability and personality have been discussed in Chapter 2, pp. 24–25.

Ability tests are conventionally divided into *aptitude tests* and *achievement tests.* In this chapter we shall be considering achievement tests, while aptitude tests will be discussed in the following two chapters.

The difference between achievement tests and aptitude tests is not a clear-cut one. Examination of samples of the two kinds of tests sometimes reveals a high degree of overlap in content. On both types, one is likely to find arithmetic reasoning and vocabulary subtests, and group tests of both kinds usually require some skill in reading. Both achievement tests and aptitude tests have been used to predict future performance, although, generally, when we use an achievement test we are interested in determining what a person *has* learned to do *after* he has been exposed to a specific kind of instruction. The procedures used to define the content of an achievement test are also somewhat different from those used to construct aptitude tests. In the construction of an achievement test, efforts are made to determine the knowledge and skills that are commonly taught at different grade levels and the test items are constructed to appraise these. The procedures used to construct a standardized test of achievement are very similar to those discussed in Chapters 3 and 4 for teacher-made tests, and, indeed, the modern standardized achievement test is a direct outgrowth of classroom tests.

The specifications for content of an aptitude test, by contrast, are usually based on analysis of the demands of some type of job or jobs together with some theory or construct about human traits. Test tasks tend to be based on common, often out-of-school experiences, unrelated to any specific curriculum or course of study.

In 1845, Horace Mann introduced a uniform written examination in the Boston public schools to take the place of oral examinations of students by visiting school committeemen. Mann's purposes in introducing the uniform written examination were to free examinations from interference by the examiner, to insure that all students answered the same questions, to require all students to answer a large number of questions, and to administer the test under uniform conditions. These characteristics of Horace Mann's uniform written examination are applicable to today's standardized achievement tests.

The word "standardized" in a test title means only that all students answer the same questions and a large number of questions under uniform directions and uniform time limits, and that there is a uniform or standard reference group to the performance of which a student's performance can be compared. The term "standardized" does *not* mean that the test measures what should or could be taught at a particular grade level, or that the test provides "standards of achievement" that students should or could reach at a particular grade level. All that a standardized test does is describe *present* performance on a uniform set of tasks administered, presumably, under uniform conditions, either for an individual student or the students in a grade in a school system. The description is basically in relative terms, that is, in relation to the performance of a sample carefully chosen to represent the country as a whole or to represent some more delimited norm group. But a somewhat more absolute interpretation can be arrived at by examining the specific tasks that pupils are and are not able to handle.

STANDARDIZED VERSUS TEACHER-MADE TESTS

As we have indicated in the previous discussion, standardized achievement tests do not represent anything new and strange in the measurement of academic achievement. They are made up of the same types of items and cover many of the same areas of knowledge as teacher-made tests. In what ways, then, do they differ from teacher-made tests? What are the advantages and limitations of each? For what purposes should each be used?

First, let us look at the ways in which the commercially distributed standardized tests differ from teacher-made tests. The major differences between the two types of tests are summarized below.

Standardized Achievement Test	*Teacher-made Test*
1. Based on content and objectives common to many schools throughout the country.	1. Based on content and objectives specific to teacher's own class or school.
2. Deals with large segments of knowledge or skill, usually with only a few items appraising any one skill or topic.	2. May deal either with a specific limited topic or skill or with larger segments of knowledge and skill.
3. Developed with the help of professional writers, reviewers, and editors of test items.	3. Developed usually by one teacher with little or no outside help.
4. Uses items that have been tried out, analyzed, and revised before becoming part of the test.	4. Uses items that have rarely been tried out, analyzed, or revised before becoming part of the test.
5. Has high reliability typically.	5. Has moderate or low reliability typically.
6. Provides norms for various groups that are broadly representative of performance throughout the country.	6. Limited usually to the class or a single school as a reference group.

There are two aspects of the construction of standardized tests that should be mentioned because they basically affect the usefulness of standardized tests. First, if the tests are to be based on the content and objectives common to many schools throughout the country, the test makers must identify the universe of common content and objectives to be sampled. To do this, they must systematically survey a representative sample of textbooks used in the schools, courses of study or curriculum guides, reports of committees of professional societies, and opinions of experts in the field. The adequacy of the test depends, to a large extent, upon how well this step is carried out. If it is done well, many schools will find that the content and skills appraised by the test are, for the most part, included within their own objectives. If it is not done well, the correspondence between a school's objectives and those of the test is likely to be poor.

If a universe of common content and objectives cannot be identified in an area, then either a nationally standardized test in the area cannot be constructed or, if constructed, is likely to be unsatisfactory. For example, the social studies curriculum in certain grades of many elementary schools is focused on knowledge of the local community or state; thus, there is little content that is common throughout the elementary schools of the country. The same situation holds for science in the elementary schools where there has been little in common, either in content or objectives, from one school system to another. As a result, there are very few standardized achievement tests for the elementary grades in social studies or science and those that are available for the upper elementary grades tend to be limited to recall of a miscellaneous collection of specific facts.

Second, the time required to construct a standardized test is relatively long. As we mentioned previously, the first step in constructing a standardized achievement test is development of the plan and specifications for the test. Then, items have to be written, reviewed, edited, and tried out on groups similar to those for whom the test is intended. Next, item analysis must be done. On the basis of the results of the item analysis, the items for the final form of the test are selected, or items may be revised and new items written and tried out again. When all of the items for the final form of the test are ready, the tests have to be printed, schools recruited that will yield a representative national sample of students, and the tests administered to the sample of students. Tests must then be scored, raw scores tabulated, and norms developed. Additional data need to be gathered and analyses carried out to permit determination of reliability and correlations with other measures. Manuals for administering the test and interpreting the results must be prepared. All of these steps in the construction of an achievement test take time. The lapse of time between starting the analysis to establish the plan for the test and final publication of the test for use in the schools can be as much as 3 to 5 years.

The investment of money and effort in the construction of a sound standardized achievement test and the amount of time required result in a test that is fixed for a period of years in terms of broad, common objectives. The test is based on existing curricula and objectives. If the analysis of these curricula and objectives is perceptively done, a test will be based on emerging curricular trends and will follow the leaders in the field. However, no test is likely to deviate far from what *is being* taught; it does not represent what could or should be taught. It is not a very flexible tool. It cannot be adapted to suddenly emerging needs, to local emphases, or to particular limited units of study. The distinctive features of the standardized test represent important advantages for some purposes and disadvantages for others.

A standardized test is valuable particularly in two kinds of situations: (1) those in which comparisons need to be made, and (2) those in which there are large numbers of people about whom decisions need to be made, but for whom the decision maker has no common or comparable data. There are a number of situations in education where comparisons need to be made. These include the comparison of an individual's achievement level in different subject matter areas, the comparison of an individual's level of achievement with his potentiality for achievement, or the comparison of groups or classes taught by different methods. Marks given by different teachers based on different types of evidence and using different and personal standards of evaluation provide no basis for comparisons extending beyond a single class and subject area. The common set of tasks, the norms, and the high reliability of the standardized tests make such comparisons possible.

The second kind of situation can be illustrated by a junior high school that receives students from five different elementary schools. The administrators of the junior high school are faced with the problem of assigning students to classroom groups and the teachers are faced with the problem of determining the achievement status of individual students in order to plan effective learning activities. All of the students entering the school will have marks of some kind from previous teachers, but marks assigned by teachers are difficult to interpret. One rarely knows anything about the nature or sources of the data that entered into the assigning of marks. One teacher may have relied almost entirely on competence as demonstrated on tests, while another may have placed heavy emphasis on conscientiousness and neatness in completing assigned homework. Teachers within a school and between schools vary markedly in their philosophy of marking and in the assigning of grades. One teacher's "A" may be another teacher's "C." In this kind of a situation, one needs some uniform data on all students that will help to "calibrate" and give some common meaning to judgments made by the previous teachers. A standardized test can provide such uniform data. It should be emphasized here that in this situation, both standardized test results and data from previous teachers should be used to arrive at the final decision on placing students in classrooms and planning instructional activities.

In light of the differences between standardized tests and teacher-made tests and the special values of the standardized test, we propose that chief reliance should be placed on standardized tests when the results of testing are to be used to:

1. Compare achievement with potentiality for an individual or a group.
2. Compare level of achievement in different skills or in different subject areas for an individual or a group.
3. Compare achievement between different schools and classes.
4. Study pupil growth over a period of time.

Chief reliance should be placed on teacher-made tests when the results are to be used to:

1. Determine how well students have mastered a limited unit of instruction.
2. Determine the extent to which distinctive local objectives have been achieved.
3. Provide a basis for assigning marks.

We recommend that both standardized tests and teacher-made tests be used, as well as any other method of appraisal that yields relevant information, when results are to be used to:

1. Diagnose individual learning disabilities.
2. Assign students to classrooms or learning groups.
3. Counsel students on educational and vocational choices.
4. Select students for special programs.

From the above discussion, we see that standardized and teacher-made tests both have important functions to perform in education. To a large extent, they are different functions. The two types of evaluation supplement one another; they are not competitors.

Standardized tests of achievement have been developed for practically every subject in the school curriculum. It would be impossible to give even a brief treatment of all subject areas in the pages that can be allotted to achievement tests in this book. Rather than listing and briefly describing a large number of existing tests, we have decided to orient the discussion around the problems and issues that arise in choosing and using standardized achievement tests and to use specific tests to illustrate these problems and issues. A number of specific tests of all types are listed with brief annotations in Appendix IV.

SELECTING A STANDARDIZED ACHIEVEMENT TEST

Before we can proceed intelligently with either the preparation of a test in an area or the choice of one from among those already existing, we must answer two questions.

1. Are we primarily interested in obtaining information on the general status of an individual or group of individuals in a skill or subject matter area, or are we primarily interested in diagnosing specific strengths and weaknesses of an individual within that skill or subject matter area?
2. What are the skills and understandings that we want to evaluate?

The answer to the first question will direct attention to the type of test (survey or diagnostic) that should be examined and to specific technical aspects of the test that should be considered such as correlation among subtests and reliability of subtests. The answer to the second question provides the framework for judging the validity of a test.

A test does not have validity in the abstract; its degree of validity is in relation to a particular situation and a particular purpose. The statement implies that the selection of a test for use in a particular school should be based on that school's objectives of instruction in the field in question. An analysis of objectives helps to identify the strengths and weaknesses of a given test in an area and also should make clear the limitations of any standardized test as the sole bias for evaluating a pupil, a teacher, or a program.

To illustrate the process of analyzing objectives and selecting a standardized achievement test, let us use the area of reading. The list of reading objectives for grades 1 through 8, shown in Table 9.1, was derived by combining material from a recent text on the teaching of reading (Harris, 1962) and the curriculum guide for a state-wide program in developmental reading (Miller, 1963).

The Committee on Evaluation (or whatever its title might be) of a school system could use sources such as these, if their own school system did not have an already formulated statement of reading objectives.

The curriculum guide illustrated problems that are likely to face any school when it undertakes to analyze and define, in terms of student behaviors, the objectives of an area of instruction. The guide was organized in three columns, (1) goals, (2) teaching suggestions, and (3) materials. The column headed "goals" contained many phrases in terms of activities of the teacher, together with some objectives stated in terms of student behavior. The second column contained a mixture of activities that the teacher would carry out and objectives stated in terms of the student. To arrive at the set of objectives in Table 9.1, the teachers' activities were analyzed to determine their purpose in terms of student development, and the goals and objectives oriented in terms of the teacher were recast in terms of the behavior expected of the student.

The outline of objectives provided in Table 9.1 is a little imposing! It brings out the complexity of the learning that is involved in any segment of the school curriculum. Of course, the list was planned to include all of the objectives for grades 1 through 8, and it is understood that the emphasis on achieving each objective changes as one goes from grade to grade. Thus, in the first three grades, major emphasis is on the objectives of developmental reading, particularly the mechanics of reading, and on developing interest in reading and favorable attitudes toward it. In the upper elementary grades, the emphasis shifts to reading comprehension abilities, functional reading abilities, and development of reading interests and attitudes. It is important to keep the change in emphasis across grades in mind as one examines tests for particular grades.

TABLE 9.1 OBJECTIVES OF READING IN A SCHOOL SYSTEM, GRADES 1 THROUGH 8

I Developmental Reading Abilities

A. The Mechanics of Reading
   1. Has good eye-movement habits
   2. Has adequate sight vocabulary
   3. Has skill in identifying words through the use of
      (a) Context, either verbal or pictorial
      (b) Phonetic analysis
      (c) Structural analysis, that is, compound words, root words, prefixes, suffixes, constructions, syllabication
   4. Has skill in reading orally
      (a) Uses appropriate phrasing
      (b) Pronounces words accurately
      (c) Uses punctuation as guide to expression, phrasing, and emphasis
      (d) Uses rhythm and emphasis appropriate to selection

B. Reading Comprehension Abilities
   1. Has rich, extensive vocabulary
      (a) Matches words and definitions
      (b) Recognizes antonyms
      (c) Recognizes synonyms
      (d) Identifies appropriate meaning of multimeaning words
   2. Comprehends and interprets phrases, sentences, and paragraphs
      (a) Answers questions on important facts and details
      (b) Answers questions on stated sequence or relationships
      (c) Answers questions on implied ideas or relationships
      (d) Identifies main idea of passage or selection
      (e) Follows directions
      (f) Predicts outcomes or draws conclusions
      (g) Makes reasonable inferences or generalizations
      (h) Makes comparisons
      (i) Identifies author's purpose
      (j) Identifies mood or tone
      (k) Identifies writer's view point, attitude or feeling
      (l) Recognizes literary devices and forms
      (m) Judges accuracy or authenticity of content
      (n) Relates feeling and characters to own experience
   3. Adjusts reading rate to purpose of reading and kind of material

C. Uses Organizing Skills That Aid in Remembering What Is Read Such As:
   1. Classifying information
   2. Analyzing related items in sequence
      (a) Chronologically
      (b) In order of importance
   3. Summarizing material
   4. Preparing outlines
   5. Taking notes
   6. Formulating meaningful questions

D. Remembers What Is Read
   1. Reports what has been read
   2. Answers specific factual questions
   3. Identifies sequence and relationships

II Functional Reading Abilities

A. Knows How to Locate Information
   1. Knows how to alphabetize
   2. Knows how to use guide words
   3. Knows how to use pronouncing key and diacritical marks
   4. Knows how to use table of contents, index, glossary, appendix, preface
   5. Knows how to use encyclopedia and other reference works

B. Functional Comprehension Skills
   1. Knows specialized vocabulary
   2. Applies reading skills to textbook materials
   3. Develops specialized reading skills
      (a) Interprets maps
      (b) Interprets graphs and tables
      (c) Interprets diagrams

III Recreational Reading Habits

A. Shows Interest in Reading
   1. Enjoys reading as a leisure time activity
   2. Selects appropriate reading materials for himself
   3. Reads a variety of materials
   4. Plays games involving reading or words

B. Has Desirable Attitudes Toward Reading
   1. Notices and reacts to various kinds of reading materials in the environment such as bulletin boards, posters, signs, labels, etc.
   2. Explores new areas of reading independently
   3. Approaches reading with a definite purpose in mind
   4. Uses reading as a means of exploring and enriching life
   5. Uses reading to improve his own character and to develop his own personality

Suppose that a school has analyzed its objectives in the field of reading and has produced (or accepted) a list such as the one that appears in Table 9.1. What are the next steps in selecting an appropriate reading test for use? First, a comprehensive list of available tests should be made using current copies of test publishers' catalogues. If copies of Buros' *Mental Measurements Yearbooks* are available, reviews of the available tests should be consulted and the tests that the reviewers uniformly judge to be poor tests should be eliminated from consideration. Specimen copies of the remaining tests should be obtained for examination. Each of the tests should be carefully examined to determine which of the school's objectives in reading can be appraised by using that test. Table 9.2 on pages 266 and 267 shows one way of organizing such an analysis. Ideally, one should do such an analysis for each level of the test of each publisher; however, to save space in the illustration, we have combined the different levels and have shown the objectives covered by all levels of the test.

The table has the names of the tests that have been examined in the left-hand column. The next column indicates the grades for which a level of the test is available. For example, for the grade range from 1 to 8 the *California Reading Test* has four levels, Lower Primary for grades 1 and 2, Upper Primary for grades 2 through 4, Elementary for grades 4 through 6, and Junior High for grades 7 through 9. The other columns in the table represent the major categories of objectives from Table 9.1. The entries in each of the columns under a major objective, are the number or letter and number of a specific objective falling in the major category. Thus in the category of mechanics of reading (IA) the *California Reading Test* has been judged to have items that test for sight vocabulary (2) and skill in identifying words through the use of context (3a). If one or more of the objectives of reading in Table 9.1 are measured in a subtest of a battery other than the reading subtest, this has been indicated by enclosing the number of the objective in parentheses. For example, the *Iowa Tests of Basic Skills* has items measuring all of the objectives under location of information (IIA1 through 5), but these items appear in the Work Study Skills subtest, so this has been indicated by the parentheses. It should be mentioned that the classification of items by the skill being measured is a subjective procedure. The classification in Table 9.2 represents our judgments; another person classifying the same items might arrive at a somewhat different result.

The first seven tests in the table are group survey tests of reading, and all except the *Gates-MacGinitie Reading Tests* are parts of achievement batteries. The primary use of the group survey tests of reading is to appraise the general status or level of an individual or group. Tests 8 and 9 are group diagnostic tests and 10 and 11 are individual diagnostic tests. The purpose of these kinds of tests is to appraise intra-individual differences in order to provide cues as to why a student is having difficulty in reading.

What does an analysis such as that in Table 9.2 reveal? First, it shows that the objectives related to interests in reading (IIIA), attitudes toward reading (IIIB), and the use of organizing skills that help in remembering what is read (IIC) are not appraised by any of the tests. If these are to be evaluated by a school system, some other technique will have to be developed. Second, it shows that only the individually administered *Diagnostic Reading Scales* provides for assessing whether a student adjusts his rate of reading according to purpose and difficulty of material (IB3), and only this test and the *SRA Reading Record* appraise memory for what is read (IID1,2). In other words, measurement of these two skills is seldom included in reading tests. Third, the analysis points up the difference in focus between the individual diagnostic tests and the survey tests. The diagnostic tests concentrate on the objectives of the mechanics of reading (IA) whereas the survey tests tend to concentrate on vocabulary (IB1) and comprehension skills (IB2), although several do provide some appraisal of sight vocabulary (IA2) and word analysis skills (IA3a,b). Fourth, the table shows the differences among the survey tests both in the range of reading skills appraised and the placement of the items appraising the skills in the test battery. For example, the *California Reading Test* includes the work-study type of reading skills (IIA and IIB) in the reading score, but the other tests that provide for the appraisal of these skills place them either in the work-study skills score (*Iowa* and *SRA*), the language skills score (*Metropolitan* and *Stanford Achievement Test*), or social studies test score (*Metropolitan, Stanford,* and *STEP*).

All of the tests except the *Gates-McKillop Reading Diagnostic Test* provide for some measure of reading comprehension. However, the range of comprehension skills appraised by each test varies enormously. The *Spache* test measures only recall of specific items of factual information and the *SRA Reading Record* measures only identification of the main idea of a passage. Most of the survey tests have items that tap the abilities to recognize stated facts (IB2a), to understand implied facts and relationships (IB2c), to follow directions (IB2e), to discern the purpose or main idea of the selection (IB2d), and to draw conclusions (IB2f) or make simple inferences (IB2g). Only two of the survey tests, *Iowa Tests of Basic Skills* and *STEP,* appraise evaluation of what is read (IB2h through m).

Table 9.2 shows whether a particular reading test has at least one item appraising a specific reading skill; it does not show how adequately each is measured nor does it show the type of stimulus material used. Thus, for example, both the *California Reading Test* and the *Iowa Tests of Basic Skills* appraise the

TABLE 9.2 ANALYSIS OF READING TESTS ACCORDING TO COVERAGE OF OBJECTIVES FOR DEVELOPMENTAL READING, GRADES 1–8

		Category of Objectives									
Test	Grade	IA	IB1	IB2	IB3	IIA	IIB	IIC	IID	IIIA	IIIB
1. *California Reading Test* (Survey Achievement Battery)	1-2, 2-4, 4-6, 7-9	2; 3a	b,c	a,b,c, d,e,f		1; 2; 4	1; 3b, c				
2. *Gates-MacGinitie Reading Tests* (Survey)	1,2,3, 2-3, 4-6, 7-9	2	c	a,b,c, d,f,g							
3. *Iowa Tests of Basic Skills in Reading* (Survey Achievement Battery)	3,4, 5,6, 7,8	3a	c,d	a,b,c, d,e,f, g,h,i, j,k,l		(1) (2) (3) (4) (5)	(3a) (3b) (3c)				
4. *Metropolitan Achievement Test–Reading* (Survey Achievement Battery)	1,2, 3-4, 5-6, 7-9	2,3a	a,c, d	a,b,c, d,g		(1) (2) (3) (4) (5)	(3a) (3b) (3c)				
5. SRA *Achievement Series–Reading* (Survey Achievement Battery)	1-2, 2-4, 4-9	2; 3a 3b	a,c, d	a,b,c, d,e,f, g		(4) (5)	(3b)				
6. *Sequential Tests of Educational Progress* (*STEP*) *Reading* (Survey Achievement Battery)	4-6, 7-9	(3a)		a,b,c, d,e,f, g,h,i,j, k,l, (m)			(3a) (3b) (3c)				

7. *Stanford Achievement Tests–Reading* (Survey Achievement Battery)	1-2, 2-3, 4-5, 5-7, 7-9	2, (3b)	a, (b) c	a,c,g		(2) (3)	(1) (3a) (3b) (3c)	
8. SRA *Reading Record* (Group diagnostic)	6-9	3a	c	d		4	1; 3a, b,c	1,2
9. *Stanford Diagnostic Reading Test* (Group diagnostic)	2-4 4-8	3b,c	a	a,c,g				
10. *Gates-McKillop Reading Diagnostic Test* (Individual)	May be used at any grade level	1; 2; 3a,b, c; 4a, b,c,d	a					
11. *Spache Diagnostic Reading Scales* (Individual)	May be used at any grade level	1; 2; 3a,b, c; 4a, b,c,d		a	3			2

Note. Objectives in parentheses are measured by tests other than reading in the battery ability to read graphs and tables (IIB3b), but, at the fifth grade level, the *California* uses only five items based on a single bar graph to appraise this skill, whereas in a separate subtest the *Iowa* uses 25 items based on six different graphs or tables of different kinds. Since the reliability of the appraisal of a particular skill depends, in part, upon the number of items calling for the use of the skill, judgments as to the extent to which a fifth-grade student has learned to read graphs can be made with much more confidence on the basis of the score from the *Iowa* than from the *California*. The point being made here is that in selecting an achievement test for use, one should give consideration to the adequacy of the appraisal of each skill as well as to the variety of skills appraised.

Another consideration in selecting an achievement test is the nature of the content covered by the test. In a reading test, the content is the stimulus material used to appraise the reading skills. An examination of the stimulus material used on the tests listed in Table 9.2 makes it apparent that there is considerable variation both in length and kind of content. The *Gates-MacGinitie* tests, at all levels, use very short passages of two or three sentences to measure comprehension skills. The two *Stanford* tests base comprehension largely on short passages, twenty to fifty words, that contain blanks to be filled in from the answer choices provided. The other tests use stimulus materials that vary in length from a single sentence to passages containing 200 to 350 words, often including a series of questions on a single passage. All of the tests use stories, social studies, and science for stimulus material but only the *Iowa* and *STEP* use poetry, plays, and letters and only the *SRA Reading Record* uses advertisements, labels, and a page from a telephone directory.

Having assembled the kind of information that is summarized in Table 9.2 and commented upon in the previous paragraphs, the Committee on Evaluation must now move to a decision. The central consideration in that decision is which of the tests that they have examined and analyzed provides the best match to the objectives of *their* school system and the best basis for making the decisions that must be made in their school.

In this discussion, we have been trying to emphasize four main points that apply not only to reading but to any segment of the school program. The points are these:

1. The teaching of reading, or of any segment of the school program, is a complex undertaking directed toward the achievement of a variety of different objectives.
2. A specific existing test will provide an appraisal of only certain objectives.
3. Some of the objectives are not likely to be appraised by any existing test procedure.

4. The selection of the most suitable achievement test for use in a particular school requires (1) that the school's objectives in an area be clearly formulated and (2) that available tests be analyzed in detail to determine in which one the content conforms most closely to the school's objectives and which one has adequate reliability for the purpose for which it is to be used.

DIAGNOSTIC TESTING

A survey achievement test undertakes to provide a general, overall appraisal of status in some area of knowledge or skill. A diagnostic test undertakes to provide a detailed picture of strengths and weaknesses in an area. Furthermore, it is anticipated that this detailed analysis will suggest causes for deficiencies and provide a guide for remedial procedures. A survey reading test tells us that Johnny, who is starting the fourth grade, performs on our test of reading paragraphs at a level typical of the usual child beginning the second grade. A series of diagnostic tests indicates that Johnny has a fair sight vocabulary of common words, but no skills for working out unfamiliar words, that he is unable to blend sounds to form words, that he does not recognize the sounds that correspond to letter combinations, and that he makes frequent reversal errors. These findings, together with others, provide the basis for planning remedial teaching of word analysis and phonic skills that are specifically directed toward Johnny's deficiencies. Development of diagnostic tests involves two steps (1) analysis of the complex performance—be it reading, multiplying fractions, or using a microscope—into its component subskills, and (2) developing tests for the component skills, free, as far as possible, from any other source of difficulty.

It has become fashionable in recent years to call many tests "diagnostic tests." In a sense, any test that yields more than a single overall score is diagnostic. Even if there are only two part scores, say, one for word knowledge and one for paragraph comprehension, the test makes it possible for us to say that Johnny showed better ability in word knowledge than he did in reading connected prose. This is certainly *one* diagnostic clue. Diagnosis is, after all, a matter of degree. We may probe and analyze with varying degrees of thoroughness and detail. We must ask, concerning any test purporting to be diagnostic: How complete and how adequate are the diagnostic cues that this test provides? It is easy to overstate the value of the diagnostic information provided by a particular test.

Usually, the user of a diagnostic test is concerned with those pupils who are seriously deficient in some skill such as reading or arithmetic. Though one might be concerned with the specific strengths of the strong, usually one is concerned with the specific weaknesses of the weak. With this focus of concern, the desirable psychometric properties of a diagnostic test are quite different from those we seek in a survey test. We do not care whether the test will make differentiations among the top eighty or even ninety percent of pupils. If half or three quarters of the class get perfect scores on a subtest, this need not trouble us. The crucial question is: Does deficiency in this skill constitute a critical gap in the repertory of skills that a pupil needs in order to develop competence in a subject area?

As a consequence, the norms need to be especially complete for the lower range of percentiles so that one can express accurately the degree of a deficit. Again, the precision of measurement needs to be as high as possible over the range of scores representing the bottom ten or fifteen percent of a typical group. The conventional reliability coefficient is rather inadequate to express this particular aspect of precision of measurement, and it would be reasonable to expect the publisher of a diagnostic test to report the standard error of measurement at several low score levels. Unfortunately, almost no publishers do this.

Since all the subtests of a diagnostic test battery are related to some one general area of skill, such as reading, it is natural that the subtests show sizable intercorrelations. The pupil who is deficient in one is likely to be deficient in others. Thus, for many pupils the variations from test to test will be too small to be interpreted with confidence, and hypotheses as to the nature of a pupil's disability must be considered quite tentative. Only occasionally will a pupil show a pattern of deficits so uneven that one can point with confidence to a particular source of the more general deficiency in achievement.

Finally, it should be pointed out that the psychometric attributes desired in a survey and in a diagnostic test are so contradictory that a test that serves well for one purpose will almost certainly be poor for the other. The survey test should provide tasks of varying, but mostly moderate difficulty to produce a spread of scores for the whole range of pupils, while a diagnostic test should be easy for most pupils and should spread out the few at the bottom for whom a specific subskill constitutes a special difficulty. A well-designed diagnostic test could be completely inadequate to measure the abilities of the top half or three quarters of an ordinary school class. Conversely, a survey test will provide only a very general and rough appraisal of the deficiency of the poor performer.

Most of the published diagnostic tests presently available are designed to investigate sources of reading difficulty. Let us use these to illustrate specifically the problems and issues in diagnostic testing. From the preceding discussion, one would expect a diagnostic test of reading for the elementary grades to concentrate on those component skills of reading illustrated by the objectives under mechanics of reading (IA1,2, and 3) in the list of objectives given in Table 9.1,

p. 263, with secondary emphasis on extent of vocabulary (IBI) and elementary comprehension skills (IB2a,b,c,d). A good diagnostic test of reading should also provide opportunity to observe the process of reading so that one can determine the efficiency of eye-movement patterns and effectiveness in using word-attack skills to decode the meaning of written material. It should also provide a large enough number of items of each type so that the degree of deficit in each component skill will be reliably determined. And finally, the diagnostic test should provide norms on adequate and appropriate normative groups to make possible comparisons of performance on the different parts. How well the existing diagnostic tests meet these criteria can best be shown by looking at two of the tests in Table 9.2, pp. 266–267, the *Stanford Diagnostic Reading Test* and the *Gates-McKillop Reading Diagnostic Test.*

The *Stanford Diagnostic Reading Test* Level I is a group test designed for use from the middle of grade 2(2.5) to the middle of grade 4(4.5). It has the following subtests.

Test 1: Reading Comprehension. Twenty-five reading passages containing blanks to be filled in from the choices provided at the end of the passage. Sixteen of the 25 passages have between 10 and 20 words.

Test 2: Vocabulary. The examinee chooses one word from among three that best completes the sentence that the examiner reads.

Test 3: Auditory Discrimination. Examinee listens to two words read by examiner and indicates whether they have the same beginning, same middle, or same ending sound.

Test 4: Syllabication. Examinee selects from among three choices the first syllable of the stimulus word (*Example:* Maybe ☐ Ma ☐ Mayb ☐ May).

Test 5: Beginning and Ending Sounds. Pictures are presented as stimuli and the examinee chooses from among four choices, the letter or letters with which the name of the pictured object begins or ends.

Test 6: Blending. Three groups of letters representing sounds are presented and examinee has to mark one of each group to correspond to the word that examiner says.

Test 7: Sound Discrimination. Examinee chooses from among three words the one that contains the same sound as the underlined part of the stimulus word.

How adequate is the *Stanford* test as a diagnostic test of reading? Examination of the subtests in relation to Table 9.2, shows that the subtests measure a relatively limited number of reading skills with emphasis on certain skills in phonics. The test can reveal whether the student can deal adequately with certain aspects of phonics in isolation, but it will not reveal how effectively he uses these skills in the actual process of reading. The manual for the test states that the test scores at the low end of the distribution are more reliable than those at the upper end but no data are provided to support the statement. The section in the test manual on interpretation of results recommends looking at differences between scores on subtests. But how many of these are, in fact, both sufficiently reliable and sufficiently different to be usefully diagnostic for an individual student?

Table 9.3, which shows the intercorrelations and reliabilities for each of the subtests for a sample of third graders, brings out the dilemma of a diagnostic test. Since the subtests all involve reading, it is not surprising that the intercorrelations are high, and, in fact, they average 0.61. Fortunately, the subtest reliabilities are also quite high, only subtest 4 falling below 0.87. Thus, each subtest does measure something over and beyond the ability that is common to them all. However, if we apply the formula for the reliability of a difference score that we encountered on p. 197, we come up with a number of values that are somewhat disquieting. Thus, tests 5, 6, and 7, all concerned with matching

TABLE 9.3 INTERCORRELATIONS AND RELIABILITIES FOR *Stanford Diagnostic Reading Test* FOR GRADE 3 *

Test	1	2	3	4	5	6	7
1. Reading comprehension		.64	.65	.63	.72	.71	.68
2. Vocabulary			.59	.30	.49	.50	.54
3. Auditory discrimination				.52	.61	.60	.61
4. Syllabication					.61	.63	.58
5. Beginning and ending sounds						.81	.78
6. Blending							.76
7. Sound discrimination							
Reliability (split-half)	.95	.88	.96	.79	.87	.94	.94

* People who read about tests and testing will frequently have occasion to study tables of correlations like Table 9.3. In the table, the column at the left lists the different variables and numbers them in order. The numbers (but not the names) are repeated across the top of the table. Look at the row labeled "1 Reading comprehension." The numbers that appear in this row are the correlations of "reading comprehension" with each of the other variables. The first figure, .64, is the correlation between "reading comprehension" and variable 2, "vocabulary." This means that there is a fairly strong tendency for high reading comprehension scores to go with high vocabulary scores. The next figure, .65, is the correlation of "reading comprehension" with "auditory discrimination," and the other entries are to be read in the same way. The correlation between any two variables will be found in the row and column whose numbers correspond to those variables. In the table, the reliability coefficients for the variables are shown in the last row.

of sounds show intercorrelations averaging almost .80. For these tests, the reliability of the difference scores are as follows: 5 versus 6, 0.50; 5 versus 7, 0.57; 6 versus 7, 0.75. Clearly, any judgment that a pupil was having more difficulty with sound blending than with identifying beginning and ending sounds would have to be a very tentative one, and the cases where these two scores differed by a large enough amount to make the judgment with confidence would be few indeed. By contrast, the reliability of the difference between the vocabulary test and the blending test is estimated to be 0.82, so that there would be many more individuals for whom these quite different-seeming components of reading would, in fact, yield significantly different scores.

The point that we make is that, due to the basic community of function measured and to the generality of human achievements, most pupils will show fairly small differences on the subtests of a diagnostic battery, and these will be not only small, but unreliable. The cues from examining a subtest profile must be considered tentative leads. Only in rare cases will specific deficiencies, in relation to average performance, be so pronounced and so dramatic that they can be seized upon with confidence.

To some extent, a "group diagnostic test" is a contradiction in terms. Diagnosis is inherently individual, and is appropriate for the individual who is having difficulty. A test that is pitched at a difficulty level suitable for identifying special difficulties of those in, perhaps, the bottom quarter of a grade group is not a good test for assessing achievement in the total group, or even for separating the bottom quarter from the top three quarters. Thus class-wide or system-wide use of a diagnostic test should generally be considered an inefficient procedure. A diagnostic test should be designed to discriminate accurately areas of specific deficiency, and not to appraise relative competence throughout the full range of ability. Examination of the distribution of scores of the *Stanford Diagnostic Reading Test I* suggests that the test may be too difficult to serve as an effective diagnostic test in the third grade, since most pupils will be encountering a good deal of difficulty with all the subtests, and will be too easy to serve as a general measure of achievement in the fourth grade, where the upper half of the class will show relatively little spread of scores.

The *Gates-McKillop Reading Diagnostic Test* is individually administered and can be used for students in grade 2 and above. There are 17 subtests, but not all subtests need to be given to all examinees. Although the tests need not be given in any definite order, they are arranged in the test booklet so that the broader, more comprehensive reading abilities are tested before the more specific and detailed ones. The basic tests are as follows:

I *Oral Reading:* Seven paragraphs of increasing difficulty are presented for the student to read orally. The words used provide many opportunities for the student both to make errors and to apply word attack skills. The more difficult passages are hard enough to extend even fairly able elementary school pupils.

II *Words: Flash Presentation:* Words of increasing difficulty are exposed to view for one-half second and the examinee must identify the word.

III *Words: Untimed Presentation:* Examinee reads words of increasing difficulty and complexity. The examiner keeps a record of the methods of word attack used.

IV *Phrases: Flash Presentation:* Examinee must read phrases of two to four words after one-half second of exposure.

V *Knowledge of Word Parts:* Word Attack

- V-1 *Recognizing and Blending Common Word Parts:* Examinee is required to read a list of nonsense words that are made up of common word sounds.
- V-2 *Giving Letter Sounds:* Examinee gives the sounds of the letters of the alphabet.
- V-3 *Naming Capital Letters*
- V-4 *Naming Lowercase Letters*

VI *Recognizing the Visual Form of Sounds*

- VI-1 *Nonsense Words:* Examinee identifies the written form of the nonsense word pronounced by the examiner.
- VI-2 *Initial Letters:* Examinee identifies the written form of the first letter of a word pronounced by the examiner.
- VI-3 *Final Letters:* Examinee identifies last letter of a word pronounced by the examiner.
- VI-4 *Vowels:* Examinee identifies the vowel used in the middle of a nonsense word.

VII *Auditory Blending:* Examinee pronounces a word that the examiner has given in parts, for example, ch – ump.

In addition to the basic tests, there are four supplementary tests: spelling, oral vocabulary, syllabication, and auditory discrimination.

The manual provides a standard code for recording errors and hesitations made by the student in reading passages, words, and letters. Checklists are provided in the *Pupil Record Booklet* for recording the quality of oral reading, and persistence and versatility in working with difficult material. Grade and age norms are provided for each test, but the sample used for the norms is not described. The manual presents no data on reliability or intercorrelation of the tests. It does present tables for classifying scores as very low, low, or normal progress either in relation to actual grade placement or in relation to the grade score obtained on the oral reading passages. Thus, the psychometric data presented for each of the subtests are really quite limited. We can hope that the pupil's performance is accurately appraised by each of the little subtests, but we really can't be sure since the relevant data are not provided.

Many of the subtests of the *Gates-McKillop* are clearly, and intentionally quite easy for the normal reader. Thus, the approximate grade equivalent at which an average pupil gets at least 90 percent of the items on some of the subtests right is shown below.

Naming Capital Letters	2.0
Naming Lowercase Letters	2.2
Giving Letter Sounds	4.0
Recognizing Initial Letters	3.5
Recognizing Final Letters	3.7
Recognizing Vowels	5.0

Thus, on these tests any substantial number of items wrong represents a sign of trouble, even for pupils in the middle elementary school.

For diagnosis, a test such as the *Gates-McKillop* yields much more valuable information than a group test because it provides opportunity to observe the process of reading, that is, the student's behavior while he is reading. The tasks included in the test require the student to deal with both the complex task of reading connected prose and the simpler components of reading. In a sense, the test presents a systematic plan for investigating probable sources of difficulty in reading. If the classroom teacher follows the advice given in the manual to study the student's answers, the nature of his errors, and the patterns of his responses, rather than to focus on numerical scores, then the teacher should be able to gain some cues as to where to start remedial instruction.

Diagnostic testing in any field must go beyond the immediate field of skill or knowledge and seek information on all background factors that contribute to success or difficulty in the particular area. To understand the child with reading difficulty, we need information on his vision, his hearing, his general intellectual level, his interests, and his emotional adjustment. A thorough diagnostic study will include tests of visual acuity, muscular balance and fusion, hearing, intelligence (nonverbal or individual), and interview or questionnaire information about factors in the student's background and present life that may be relevant. Diagnostic study becomes essentially a directed, comprehensive case history of an individual; directed in that it is focused on the academic problem, but comprehensive in that it covers all potentially significant features of both the skill area and the individual's personal life.

ACHIEVEMENT TESTING IN THE SCHOOLS

In the previous sections we have pointed out some of the basic characteristics of standardized achievement tests and some of the differences between and functions of survey and diagnostic achievement tests. We have also pointed out that the selection of a standardized achievement test for use should be based on the objectives of a particular school and the uses that the school wants to make of the results. Goslin (1967) has pointed out that the most frequently reported use of test results in both the elementary and secondary schools is to diagnose learning difficulties. However, the other important uses of test results at the two levels of education differ markedly. At the secondary level, the emphasis on test use is on guiding the individual in vocational and educational choices, whereas in the elementary school the emphasis is on grouping children for instruction and for individualizing instruction. The differences in test use at the two levels are quite understandable when they are related to the nature of school population and the objectives and curriculum at each level.

The elementary school is faced with the task of taking a large number of students about whom relatively little is known in the beginning and organizing effective instruction for them. It is also dealing with children at a time when they are undergoing rapid changes in all areas of growth, both academic and physical. The elementary school is responsible during grades 1 through 6 for developing the basic skills of learning, that is, reading, language, work study-skills, and mathematics. For all children of elementary school age, there is a common core of objectives directed toward this end.

By the end of grade six, a considerable amount of relevant information on students has been accumulated, particularly in the area of the basic skills. Emphasis in the curriculum changes from the development of these skills to more specialized content areas. Choices among subjects and curricula are more widely available to all children. The ultimate goals both of the individual student and the various curricula and programs become differentiated; thus, there are fewer objectives common to all students at the secondary level.

The differences between the elementary and secondary schools on all these factors lead to a different set of problems in selecting appropriate tests. We will discuss these in the following sections.

Testing in the Elementary School

The basic information needed by the elementary school in order to organize and individualize instruction is an appraisal of the level of competence of the student in each of the basic skill areas. The appraisal instrument, to be maximally useful, should provide the basis for judging intra-individual differences as well as interindividual differences. The type of instrument that appears to be most suitable as a source for this information is the survey achievement test battery. Goslin (1967), in a survey of 714 elementary schools, reported that 85 percent of the schools used a survey achievement battery in one or more grades.

The batteries represent "package" achievement testing programs ready-made for the school's use. The typical battery covers the core knowledge and skill segments of the curriculum and may have as few as four or as many as ten or eleven component tests. A large number of achievement batteries is available, but only about six are widely used in elementary schools. Space does not permit a detailed description of these batteries, but the interested reader can refer to Section D of Appendix IV and to the Buros' *Mental Measurements Yearbooks* for descriptions and evaluations of them.

While the batteries have many similarities in general organization, they differ in many details. All of them provide for appraisal of reading comprehension, language skills, and mathematics, and most provide for appraising vocabulary. However, even in these areas, they differ in the way each is appraised, the specific skills measured in each area, and the manner of reporting of scores for different skills. Some of the differences among the batteries have already been discussed in relation to the problem of selecting a test (see pp. 264–268). Even when the different batteries have subtests bearing the same label, these subtests do not necessarily measure identical skills or give the same relative emphasis to the skills. The batteries also differ with respect to the inclusion of subtests on subject matter content. The *Iowa Tests of Basic Skills* and the *California Achievement Tests* are limited to the basic skills at all levels, whereas the *Stanford Achievement Test,* the *Metropolitan Achievement Test,* and the *SRA Achievement Series* add subtests on science and social studies beginning at the fourth-grade level. The *STEP* tests have separate tests on science and social studies, but these are essentially tests of reading and study skills rather than of subject matter.

The chief virtues of the single battery of tests, as compared with a program made up of separate tests chosen from a variety of different sources, are those of unity and of convenience. A test battery is unified in two important respects. First, it is based upon a unified and integrated plan. The parts have been selected and the content of each planned with an eye to the whole. Within the limits of the professional skill and understanding of the team of authors, the product is a unified whole in which the parts fit together to cover the range of objectives that they deem important and feasible to appraise with a standardized test. Because of the differences in the objectives appraised by a particular subtest or in the placement of items in different subtests, a school that tries to assemble its own battery from single tests or from subtests drawn from different batteries may end up with a set of tests that provides duplicate measures of certain skills and no measure of other skills.

A battery is unified in one other important respect. It has a unified set of norms. The norms for all the subtests are based on the same sample of students and expressed in the same form. This makes direct comparisons of scores among the different subtests possible. We do not have to ask whether our reading test was tried out on the same type of group as our arithmetic test, or how the grade equivalent scores of our spelling test compare with the precentile equivalents of our language usage measure. When tests are assembled from different sources, these problems can be matters of real concern. The lack of equivalence of norms on different tests arises primarily from differences on three points: (1) the representativeness of the normative sample; (2) the time in the school year at which the test was standardized; and (3) the year in which the test was standardized. On the first point, although none of the batteries commonly used in elementary schools today base their norms on volunteer samples or "samples of convenience," publishers of the different batteries have varied in the effort expended and techniques used to obtain normative samples that are representative in terms of geographical area, socioeconomic status, school size, and community size. On the second point, a number of recently published achievement tests provide norms for the beginning, middle, and end of the school year. However, only one of these is determined by actual test data for students in a particular grade; the others are obtained by interpolation, usually assuming growth at a uniform rate through the school year. The process of interpolation is not likely to lead to identical norms, particularly if the actual testing was carried out at different points in the school year for different tests. Finally, the influence of the year in which the test was standardized can best be illustrated by an example from the *Technical Supplement* for the *Stanford Achievement Test,* comparing the grade equivalent scores on the 1953 and the 1964 batteries. A sixth-grade student whose score earned him a grade equivalent of 9.0 on the word meaning subtest of the 1953 battery would receive a grade equivalent score of only 8.0 for that same score using the norms for the 1964 battery on the same test. On this test, and some others of the battery, there appears to have been a substantial nationwide improvement in performance in the course of a decade, so that old and new norms are not equivalent. Of course, it would be possible for a school system to assemble its own battery and develop local norms for the different subtests to make comparisons possible, but this would limit interpretations to the school system as a reference group.

The "package" testing program based on a standard battery has certain limitations. Some sections of a battery may fit a particular local curriculum better than others. Some subtests of one battery may fit modern curricular objectives, whereas another battery may seem better in another area. Some publishers have tried to introduce some flexibility into the batteries by making them available for sale as separate tests (*STEP, Stanford,* and *Metropolitan*) or as partial batteries (*Stanford* and *Metropolitan*). With these batteries, it would be possible to omit one or more of the tests. The discrepancy between a test and the set of local objectives may lie in the fact that the test covers only some of the objectives in a subject area and not all of them; it may lie in the fact that much of what the test measures falls outside the objectives of that school. The first situation is quite common; the second relatively rare. This is well illustrated by the tests of quantitative skills that appear in all school batteries. These tests have been a source of concern to teachers in many schools. The elementary school mathematics programs have been in a turmoil over the past ten years. Some schools have "traditional" mathematics programs and some have "modern" mathematics programs which vary considerably. Almost all of the elementary school batteries test for basic quantitative concepts and for problem solving and some (*Stanford Achievement Test, Metropolitan Achievement Test,* the *California Achievement Test,* and the *SRA Achievement Series*) test for computational skills. All of these represent objectives of all mathematics programs; so that most of what is in the current tests is relevant, even though the school may want to supplement the test with other kinds of appraisals developed locally. It is only when a subtest includes material that is unrelated to or inconsistent with a school's objectives that it becomes important to replace that subtest in the school's testing program. The analysis of a battery of tests to determine how well the content and skills being appraised match those of the school is facilitated by the complete analyses of the content and skills covered by the tests that are presented in some of the manuals (*Iowa Tests of Basic Skills* and *STEP*).

Testing in the Secondary School

As one moves from grade 6 to grade 7 and higher, there is a shift in educational emphasis from development of competency in the basic skills of learning to development of competency in more specialized subject matter areas. More choices among particular courses are available and students and parents need help in making decisions. Objectives of the school for different students and objectives that students have for themselves become more differentiated. All of these factors must be considered in the selection and use of standardized achievement tests in the secondary schools. They indicate that a single uniform program of achievement testing, particularly in grades 9 and above, is likely not to be too satisfactory.

There is probably greatest uniformity among secondary schools in the United States in their college preparatory or "academic" courses and it is for these courses that some of the best standardized achievement tests have been constructed. The *Cooperative Achievement Tests* are good illustrations of this kind of test. Tests are available in the major academic areas: English, foreign language, mathematics, social studies, and science. The *Cooperative English* tests, designed for use in grade 9 and above, provide measures of reading comprehension and of both effectiveness and mechanics of English expression. The *Modern Language Association Cooperative Foreign Language Tests* are a series of tests that provide for appraisal of listening, speaking, reading, and writing in five languages: French, German, Italian, Russian, and Spanish. There are two levels of difficulty of each, suitable respectively for the first and second years of language study in secondary school or college and the third and fourth years of language study. The series of mathematics, social studies, and science tests have separate tests corresponding to the segments of the typical program of studies in secondary schools in grades 7 through 12. Some of the tests within the series provide for the kinds of advanced placement courses, such as calculus, found in many secondary schools. The authors of the *Cooperative* test series have been very conscious of the many innovative and forward-looking curricula that have been developing in secondary education, and have attempted to base the tests in part on the content and objectives introduced in these curricula. Norms for tests on a definite segment of subject matter are based on a sample of students who have taken the course appropriate to the test. Tests such as these must be administered near the end of the course, so use of the results is limited to determining relative final status of students and to providing some data on which the teacher may judge the effectiveness of his teaching.

In secondary schools where most of the students take a college preparatory curriculum, tests such as those described in the previous paragraph can serve most of the needs of the school for achievement testing. However, in schools where large numbers of students take programs other than college preparatory, it becomes somewhat more difficult to find suitable achievement tests. All of the skills batteries designed for testing in the elementary school have levels that can be used through grade 8 or 9 and several (*Metropolitan Achievement Test*, *Stanford Achievement Test*, *STEP*, and the *California Achievement Test*) also have high school level batteries. Most of these batteries continue the emphasis on the basic skills from the lower levels, although the *Metropolitan* and *Stanford* also have social studies and science subtests.

There are batteries of tests that have been designed specifically for use in grades 9 through 12. Two of the most widely used high school batteries are the *Tests of Academic Progress* and the *Iowa Tests of Educational Development.* The *Tests of Academic Progress* include six subtests: social studies, composition, science, reading, mathematics, and literature. The literature subtest is a reading comprehension test based on different kinds of literary forms with some emphasis in the items on the interpretation of literary devices and use of literary background. The composition test is a multiple-choice test that includes items appraising spelling, grammar, effectiveness of expression, and mechanics. The social studies, science, and mathematics tests sample from the various courses in the area that are commonly taught in the secondary school.

The *Iowa Tests of Educational Development* (*ITED*) go beyond the fields of content knowledge and undertake to appraise abilities to locate, read, and understand materials in the different subject areas, thus attempting to test ability to obtain and use knowledge as well as the amount of knowledge already obtained. Both of these batteries are well constructed and have excellent manuals, but both share the same weaknesses. Both have attempted to construct tests that could be used for any group of students in any curriculum in any secondary school in the United States. As a result, schools may find that although the tests do appraise some of the common objectives for all students, they do not relate directly to any specific course in the school. The second problem can best be illustrated by reference to the *ITED*. In this battery, the intercorrelations among the nine tests range from .57 to .78 with a median intercorrelation of .70, indicating that there is not much differentiation in the abilities being appraised by the separate subtests. The manual of the *ITED* reports correlations between the composite score and intelligence test scores for various groups that range from a low of .57 to a high of .85 with a median correlation of about .74. This correlation is almost as high as the correlation of the separate subtests with the composite score. Thus, there is little difference either between what is measured by the different parts or between the total and a general measure of scholastic aptitude.

From the preceding discussion, we can see that achievement testing at the secondary school level presents problems that are quite different from those at the elementary school level. There are many achievement tests and batteries available for use in grades 7 through 12, and a listing of these will be found in Appendix IV. Selection of an appropriate achievement test should be based on a careful analysis of the school's objectives in each curriculum or program and an explicit statement of the purposes for which the test results are to be used. The two batteries of tests mentioned in the previous paragraph and the series of *Cooperative Tests* present excellent content analysis of each subtest that should help in determining how suitable these tests are for use in a particular school.

USING THE RESULTS OF SURVEY ACHIEVEMENT TESTS

Since survey achievement tests are the most widely used type of standardized test, consideration should be given to the ways in which the results of the testing are or could be used and to the soundness of each. Various things are done with the results from achievement testing, some useful, some relatively futile, and some positively harmful. In some schools, tests are merely given, scored, incorporated in some type of summarizing report, and filed away. This is one form of futility. Unless some constructive use is made of test results, the school would be better off to save the money and time that are invested in testing. We assume in what follows that some further actions will be taken.

First steps toward the effective use of test results should be taken long before the tests are administered or the tests are scored. In our discussion on selecting tests for use, we emphasized the need to analyze the school's own instructional objectives and to state specifically the purposes for which the results are to be used. If one person, or a small group, does this analysis and makes the final selection of achievement tests, every effort should be made to make sure that *all* classroom teachers, counselors and other specialists, administrators, and others who will receive the results of the tests are briefed on the rationale underlying the choices and thoroughly understand what content and skills are and are not being appraised by the tests. This type of understanding is basic to constructive use of the test results.

In order that the results of achievement tests may be interpreted accurately and the results used constructively, each person in the school who receives the results should have a good understanding of the type of converted score used in reporting the results. He needs to know the advantages, disadvantages, and idiosyncracies of the normative scale. He needs to know what kinds of interpretations can and cannot be made. These issues have been discussed in Chapter 7. The test user should also understand the standard error of measurement (see Chapter 6) and the problems of interpreting profiles (Chapter 7). To improve the quality of test use and interpretation, schools frequently need to provide in-service instruction for teachers and other school personnel oriented around the technical aspects of tests and testing.

Let us turn our attention to an examination of uses of test results.

Diagnosis of Learning Difficulties

According to Goslin (1967), about 69 percent of the secondary schools and 79 percent of the elementary schools reported using standardized test results for diagnostic purposes. There are two ways in which a survey test can contribute to individual diagnosis. On the one hand, scores on a test can be used to identify individual students for more intensive study. On a battery of tests, one can look for gross irregularities in performance on different subtests or for scores that deviate markedly from a pupil's grade placement. However, scores are only cues or red flags indicating that something may be wrong. The cues need to be followed up with other procedures to obtain leads as to probable causes of the low scores.

The second way that a teacher can use a survey test to get cues about an individual is by inspecting that individual's set of answers. For example, let's assume that two sixth-grade students have been given the reading comprehension test of the *Iowa Tests of Basic Skills* in October (that is, at grade 6.1) and both have obtained grade equivalent scores of 4.2. An examination of the answer sheets for each one showed that the first student had answered only 20 questions, but had gotten all of them correct whereas the second student had answered all 76 items of the test and gotten only 20 correct. Inspection of the items that the second student got correct showed that 15 out of the 20 required him to recognize facts or details specifically stated in the passage. We might tentatively conclude that the first student was a slow reader who needed help in the mechanics of reading, while the second pupil's problem lay more in the aspects of comprehension and inference. These hypotheses would provide the basis for planning remedial activities. Examination of the pattern of responses on a survey test can provide much better cues for diagnostic follow-up than do the test scores alone.

Identifying Underachievers

Identifying underachievement is really a special kind of diagnosis, but here one is usually interested in discrepancies between actual achievement and predicted achievement, rather than in low scores in relation to grade placement. The concept of underachievement is a tricky one and the term is used rather loosely in the school situation. Since the identification of underachievers requires the use of a predictor, usually an intelligence test, the problems and issues related to it will be discussed in Chapter 10.

Appraising Gains or Growth in Achievement

Teachers and other personnel in the schools attach great importance, at least verbally, to growth or gain after a period of instruction as an indicator of achievement. A measure of growth involves the difference between two scores at two different points in time, and, thus, the problems of low reliability associated with difference scores arise. The measurement of gain generally involves the use of two highly correlated tests typically given about a year apart. The reliability of gain scores is often too low to permit meaningful statements about individuals, but is usually adequate for comparison of groups. The reader is referred to the discussion of the reliability of difference scores and general issues of reliability in Chapter 6 for an explanation of this point.

Another difficulty in the use of gain scores is variation in the opportunity for gain at different score levels. Individuals who score near the top of the test on the initial administration have approached the "ceiling" of the test and have a relatively small opportunity to increase their score on the second administration. Individuals at the top of the distribution also must get more difficult items correct in order to increase their score. On the other hand, students who score low on the first administration of the test have a much greater opportunity to increase their score and can do so by getting more of the less difficult items on the test correct. In other words, gain scores do not represent equal increments of ability all along the line.

In the elementary school, the use of grade equivalent norms to compare gains over different years and across different tests in a battery of tests causes some difficulty because of the differences in within-grade variability of scores on different tests and on the same test as one goes from grade 1 through grade 6. We have discussed the problem of comparability of grade equivalent norms on different tests in Chapter 7. A similar problem arises in another context. In testing students from minority groups, the term "cumulative deficit" has been frequently used to indicate that minority group children earn grade equivalent scores on achievement tests that deviate by increasing amounts from their grade placement as they move from grade 1 through grade 6. But just as children in general vary more in height or weight as they grow from birth to maturity, so also they vary more in reading ability. Part of this increased difference between slum children and middle-class children can be attributed to the increased variability of the scores for the total group as one goes from grade 1 through grade 6. For example, suppose a student had taken the Paragraph Meaning test of the *Stanford Achievement Test* for the first time in October of grade 2 (grade placement 2.1) and had then taken it again in October of each successive year, that is, 3.1, 4.1, etc. Let us suppose that on these successive testings the student earned the following grade equivalent scores on the test: 1.7, 2.5, 3.0, 3.9, and 4.7. The discrepancies between the student's actual grade placement and the grade equivalent score earned each year would then be 0.4, 0.6, 1.1, 1.2, and 1.4; but inspection of the norms tables for the test shows that each of the grade equivalent scores that he earned falls at the 20th percentile of the normative group for the corresponding grade. In other words, his position relative to his own grade group has not changed over the years; he is no better and no worse in relation to the normative sample in grade 6 than he was in grade 2.

Counseling Parents and Students

The word "counseling" here is used broadly. It can mean the type of counseling given at entrance to senior high school on choices of courses, or simply talking with a student at the elementary school level about his strengths and weaknesses. In counseling a student or a parent, the counselor should use all relevant information about that student. Cumulative data on a student's performance on survey tests of achievement can provide relevant information. Counseling in this context should be focused on immediate decisions and actions and should avoid premature shutting off of more remote choices, as by advising a parent that his fifth-grade child is "not college material."

Grouping Students for Instruction

Every school system that has more than one class at each grade level is faced with the task of assigning children to classroom groups. The assignment can be done at random, but if any attempt is made to form classroom groups that have certain characteristics, then the results of a survey achievement battery can help to group the children. Grouping should not be done on the basis of scores on a survey achievement test alone; all relevant information should be used to help place the students. If one wants to group children for instruction so that within a class the range of achievement levels in some subject area is reduced, then the grouping should be done on data most relevant to that subject area. In many elementary schools, grouping of children is based on a reading score alone or on the average score for the total battery. When children are assigned to classroom groups on the basis of reading scores, the range of reading levels can certainly be reduced, but this does not guarantee that the range of achievement levels will be reduced in mathematics, for example. Grouping on the basis of average total score on a battery is not wholly satisfactory because the average score obscures the differences among the subtests. For example, two students at the beginning of the fifth grade could have identical average total scores of 5.2 on a battery of tests, but one student could have obtained this score by being extremely low on half of the tests and extremely high on the other half, whereas the other student could have obtained this average by obtaining average scores on all of the tests. Since the only purpose of grouping is to be able to make better adaptations of instructional procedures and materials for the individuals in the group, one can do this best on the basis of information about each area of achievement, and the adaptation can be most incisive if one forms separate groups for each subject area.

Planning Instructional Activities

Every fall, each teacher in most schools faces a new group of students. Within the limits set by the course of study, he must plan a program of activities for the group as a whole and must adapt that program as best he can to each of the students in the group. He must decide where to pick up the various skill subjects, how much time to devote to review of materials presumably taught in the previous year, and how fast to move ahead. He must plan appropriate enrichment experiences and materials for independent work. He must also plan for remedial work for some students.

To do these things, he needs to get to know the pupils in the group as quickly, thoroughly, and accurately as possible. Standardized achievement tests can provide comparable data on all the students in the class. The scores will provide a guide as to whether the group is superior, average, or slow in each of the skill or subject matter areas and will also indicate the range of achievement levels that the teacher must deal with in the classroom. They may indicate group areas of relative strength and weakness. They will call attention to subgroups of students who will need different kinds of instruction and materials.

The teacher will obtain much more information about the needs of the students if he examines item analysis data for his class. Item analysis data can be obtained as a part of the scoring services provided for a number of standardized tests and many school systems buy the service. Item analysis data provide more specific information on strengths and weaknesses than does the score alone. For example, a fourth-grade teacher who sees that the average score on knowledge and use of reference materials for his beginning fourth-grade class is low can conclude that his class may need work in this general area, but the score gives him no clues as to just where to start working. However, if the item analysis data show that the majority of class correctly answered the items on alphabetizing, table of contents, and use of the index, but a relatively small proportion correctly answered the items on the use of the dictionary and encyclopedia, then he has more specific cues and can start working on the indicated weaknesses.

Evaluating the Curriculum of a School or School System

As part of a total appraisal of the effectiveness of its program, a school system may well wish to include measures of progress in basic skills. An achievement battery provides a convenient tool for doing this. The results will show how well the particular school or school system has progressed on the several components of the battery in relation to the norming groups. However, in interpreting this progress, three cautions must be borne in mind.

1. The evaluation is only partial, not complete. The battery can give information only on the range of skills that it covers, and these skills represent only a fraction of the objectives of the modern school. Because they are so conveniently measurable, they may become overvalued. This is an insidious danger. The school system must seek to supplement standardized achievement tests with broader and more informal appraisals of other objectives if it is to obtain a well-rounded evaluation of its program.

2. Local emphases may differ from those that characterized the national sample. The particular school system may have placed heavier emphasis upon reading or may have delayed the introduction of formal instruction in arithmetic. Insofar as local emphasis and effort are atypical, local accomplishment may be expected to be atypical. Evaluation of achievement in the single school or school system must take account of distinctive local emphases.

3. Evaluation of pupil performance in a school must take account of the characteristics of the pupil population. Schools, communities, and even regions differ in the economic and cultural level of the population served. Associated with these differences are differences in average level of ability as measured by intelligence tests. The expectancy for achievement must be tempered to take these factors into account. This may be approximated by developing regional norms or norms for schools of a particular type.*

* Care must be exercised in the interpretation of performance for a school building or school system. Norms developed for individual pupils cannot automatically be applied to a group. Thus, a school building in which the reading percentile of the median pupil falls at the 70th percentile of the national norms should not be thought of as a "70th percentile building." Building averages, and to even a greater extent systemwide averages, are much less variable than single pupils. Thus, on the *Iowa Test of Basic Skills Composite Score* (1964) a level of achievement corresponding to the 70th percentile for individuals in the fifth grade would correspond to the 99th percentile for a school as a whole.

Evaluating the Teacher

Goslin (1967) reported that approximately 42 percent of secondary school administrators and 4 percent of elementary school administrators consider standardized achievement test results to be important in judging the effectiveness of the teacher. Where this practice exists, the effectiveness of the teacher is judged by the performance his class shows on standardized tests given at the end of the year. The difference between the elementary schools and the secondary schools in percentages endorsing this use of test results in Goslin's survey might be due to the fact that most achievement tests in the secondary schools are given at the end of the year, whereas a large proportion of the elementary schools test in the autumn. Autumn testing tends to eliminate the evaluation practice because the students in any given class are likely to have had several different teachers the preceding year, and it is laborious to assemble the results for any one teacher.

The use of test results to evaluate the effectiveness of a teacher seems questionable at best, and quite possibly vicious. It fails to take account of a number of important considerations. First, the achievement of a class group is a function of their whole previous educational history, not merely of the year just past. Except in a brand new subject, it is unreasonable to hold the teacher who has taught a group for a single year solely responsible for their present status. Second, achievement depends on aptitude and on out-of-school cultural experiences, as well as on schooling. Unless the evaluator is prepared to make an appropriate adjustment for the intellectual and socioeconomic level of a particular class—and class groups can differ widely in these respects—no reasonable base-line can be provided for evaluating what the teacher has accomplished. Third, the skills measured by an achievement battery represent only a fraction of the objectives of a modern school. Comparison of teachers with respect to this partial criterion neglects much of their work and may provide a very unfair evaluation of relative worth of two teachers whose strengths lie in different directions. Fourth, placing a premium upon easily testable skills when evaluating the teacher is almost inevitably going to lead the teacher to overvalue those skills in his teaching. As he is judged, so will he judge. Skills will tend to become the one central theme of his teaching, at the expense of all the other outcomes the school is trying to achieve. He will, with varying degrees of directness, teach for the tests. Finally, one may mention the demoralizing effect upon teachers of a mechanical, external evaluation that is subject to all the technical limitations discussed above.

SUMMARY STATEMENT

The typical standardized achievement test is superficially similar to an objective test made by the classroom teacher. However, it is based on large segments of knowledge or skill common to the programs of many schools, and it provides norms. These features mean that it is appropriately used in making broad comparisons—between schools or classes, between areas of achievement, or between achievement and aptitude.

Just as an analysis of the objectives to be measured was indicated as the first step in thoughtful construction of a classroom test, so an analysis of objectives is a prerequisite for evaluating a published test. The test can only be evaluated in terms of its congruence with the objectives that the teacher or school is trying to achieve.

Most widely used standardized tests are survey tests, giving a general appraisal of level of accomplishment in a broad area. If the teacher is to work constructively with the pupil, such survey results need to be supplemented by more specific and diagnostic information. Some published diagnostic tests exist, and these can be supplemented by informal teacher appraisals. However, the reliability of difference scores and, consequently, of differential diagnoses is often low. Diagnostic clues should be considered quite tentative.

Standardized achievement test batteries are very popular for elementary school use. In these, the advantage of unity in plan and standardization must be weighed against the inflexibility of a single total battery. The published batteries are similar in general design, though they differ in (1) content subjects included, (2) emphasis on work-study skills, (3) balance of emphasis among different areas, and (4) specific pattern of items in each field.

At the secondary school level, one is less likely to find a battery that is suitable for appraising the objectives of all programs or for use with all students. Since programs are more differentiated at this level and since the goals of the students are less similar, standardized testing needs to be more differentiated. Subject matter content tests become more important particularly for the college preparatory group, and measurement of basic skill becomes less important.

When used with discretion and proper reservations, standardized achievement tests can serve a useful purpose as one type of evidence (1) to diagnose learning difficulties, (2) to appraise gains in achievement of groups, (3) to counsel parents and students, (4) to group students for instruction, (5) to plan instructional activities, and (6) to evaluate the curriculum. Standardized test results should rarely, if ever, be used as a basis for evaluating the effectiveness of individual teachers.

QUESTIONS AND EXERCISES

1. What are some common misconceptions about standardized tests? To what misuses of the test results would these be likely to lead?

2. For which of the following purposes would a standardized test be useful? For which should a teacher expect to make his own test? Why?

   a. To determine which pupils have mastered the addition and subtraction of fractions.
   b. To determine which pupils in a class are below expectation in arithmetic computation.
   c. To determine the subjects in which each pupil in a class is strongest and weakest.
   d. To determine for a class which punctuation and capitalization skills need further teaching.
   e. To form subgroups in a class for the teaching of reading.

3. Get a curriculum guide covering the content and objectives of a subject that you are teaching or plan to teach. Examine a standardized achievement test for that subject. Which of the objectives in the curriculum guide are adequately measured by the test? Which ones are not? How adequately is the content covered by the test?

4. Make a critical comparison of two achievement test batteries for the same grade. How do they differ? What are the advantages of each from your point of view?

5. Suppose you are teaching mathematics in the first year of junior high school. List the steps you would take to diagnose the weaknesses of the pupils.

6. The manual of test W states that it can be used for diagnostic purposes. What should you look for to determine whether it has any real value as a diagnostic aid?

7. Why should we be specially concerned about the reliability of the scores resulting from a set of diagnostic tests? What implications does this have for using and interpreting such tests?

8. A senior high school, which draws from three feeder junior highs, has a special accelerated program in mathematics. What are the advantages and disadvantages of selecting students for this program on the basis of a standardized achievement test in mathematics given at the end of the 9th grade?

9. The *Iowa Tests of Basic Skills* presents norms (*a*) for pupils in the country as a whole, (*b*) for pupils in major geographical regions, (*c*) for pupils in large cities, (*d*) for pupils by IQ level, and (*e*) for building averages. How might different ones of these be used by a school principal in St. Louis, Missouri?

10. The town of M gives the *Stanford Achievement Tests* to pupils in grades 4 and 6 and records on the cumulative record card only the grade equivalent for the whole test. What are the disadvantages of this type of record?

11. You have given a standardized achievement battery in October to your 4th grade class. How might you, as teacher, use the results?

12. Using a centralized scoring service, a school buys item analysis data that show the percent of pupils answering each item correctly for each grade and each classroom in the school. How could the school as a whole use these results? How could individual teachers use them?

13. In high school H, where pupils are assigned to English sections on a presumably random basis, the principal finds that there are marked discrepancies in the distribution of grades awarded by different teachers. How could results from a standardized test help the principal in dealing with this problem?

14. Miss Carson, a 6th grade teacher, says: "I am not as much interested in a pupil's level of performance as I am in the growth that he shows while he is in my class." From a measurement point of view, what problems does this point of view raise?

15. The school system of Centreville is proposing to introduce a revised mathematics curriculum on an experimental basis in selected elementary schools. They wish to evaluate the effectiveness of the program before introducing it throughout the system. How adequate would a standardized achievement test in elementary school mathematics be for this evaluation? What problems would arise? How might these be dealt with?

REFERENCES

Goslin, D. A. *Teachers and testing.* New York: Russell Sage Foundation, 1967. Chapter 2.

Harris, A. J. *Effective teaching and reading.* New York: Albert McKay, 1962.

Miller, H. *The Montana program for developmental reading, grades 1–8.* Helena, Montana: State Superintendent of Public Instruction, 1963.

Lindquist, E. F. & Hieronymus, A. N. *Iowa Tests of Basic Skills: Manual for administrators, supervisors, and counselors.* Boston: Houghton Mifflin, 1964.

SUGGESTED ADDITIONAL READING

Chauncey, H. & Dobbin, J. E. *Testing: Its place in education today.* New York: Harper & Row, 1963. Chapters 3, 5, 6. Pp. 37–53, 66–107.

Durost, W. N. *Manual for interpreting Metropolitan Achievement Tests.* New York: Harcourt, Brace & World, 1962.

Ebel, R. L. Standardized achievement tests: Uses and limitations. In C. I. Chase and H. G. Ludlow (Eds.), *Readings in educational and psychological measurement.* Boston: Houghton Mifflin, 1966. Pp. 217–223.

Educational Testing Service. *Cooperative Sequential Tests of Educational Progress: teacher's guide.* Princeton, New Jersey: Educational Testing Service, 1959.

Educational Testing Service. *Cooperative Sequential Tests of educational progress: Technical report.* Princeton, New Jersey: Educational Testing Service, 1957.

Educational Testing Service. *Handbook for Cooperative Mathematics Tests.* Princeton, New Jersey: Educational Testing Service, 1964.

Lavin, D. E. *The prediction of academic performance: a theoretical analysis and review of research.* New York: Russell Sage Foundation, 1965.

Lindquist, E. F. & Hieronymus, A. N. *Iowa Tests of Basic Skills: Manual for administrators, supervisors, and counselors.* Boston: Houghton Mifflin, 1964.

Scannell, D. P. *Tests of academic progress: Teacher's manual.* Boston: Houghton Mifflin, 1964.

CHAPTER 10

Standardized Tests of Intelligence or Scholastic Aptitude

ACHIEVEMENT AND APTITUDE

In the previous chapter, we were interested in tests as measures of the end result of school instruction. In this chapter and the next, we shall be interested in tests as predictors of some future performance by the individual. However, whether our interest centers on outcomes of past learning or on potential for the future, all we can test is *present performance.*

Present performances are tied with varying degrees of closeness to organized school instruction. Thus, the American youth who can decipher the meaning of "Arma virumque cano," or of

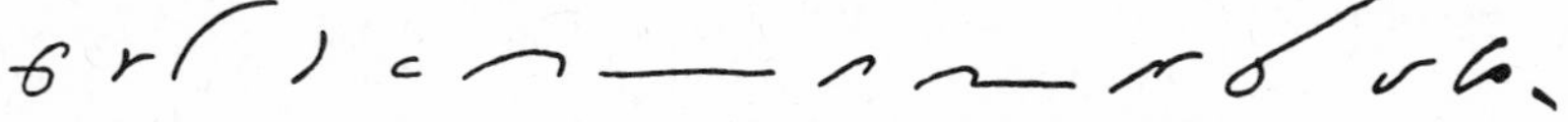

almost certainly learned these in school, in Latin class in the one case and in shorthand class in the other, and these tasks serve only as indicators of progress resulting from systematic instruction. Other performances depend jointly on school and out-of-school experiences—understanding words, working out quantitative problems, following the train of thought in a complex prose passage. These are taught in school, but perfected also in the day-by-day experiences of life.

Still others relate to what is taught in school only very remotely—such as tasks involving problem solving with spatial, pictorial, and other nonverbal materials, and, of course, all the performances that are mastered before the child gets to school.

It should be emphasized that *any* performance depends to some degree upon life experiences—if not upon school experiences. Any verbal test requires that a person must have learned to speak the language; any pictorial test calls for an acquaintance with the objects that are portrayed; any test of whatever sort requires that the person must have learned to put forth effort and do his best in test situations. By the same token, *any* performance depends to some extent on the genetic potential of the person—his genetic potential as a human being, and his specific genes as an individual. Thus, the aptitude tests that we discuss in these two chapters differ from achievement tests discussed in Chapter 9 only in being *less* dependent upon specific segments of *school* instruction and in being used to make inferences about the future, rather than to draw conclusions referring to the past. They cannot claim to be pure measures of innate potential for learning.

GROUP INTELLIGENCE TESTS

Most of the intelligence testing carried on in this country is done with group tests that can be given to a whole class at one time. We will describe one series of group tests, to illustrate some of the characteristics of instruments of this type. A listing of other widely used series, with their key characteristics, will be found in Appendix IV.

The *Lorge-Thorndike* series of intelligence tests is made up of three parts: nonreading tests for use in the primary grades, verbal tests for grades 4 through 13, and nonverbal tests for grades 4 through 13. Each test is made up of several subtests within which the items are of the same type and progress from easy to difficult. As we shall see, each is available in several levels for pupils with different degrees of intellectual maturity.

The primary test (Cognitive Ability Test) has four subtests: oral vocabulary, relational concepts, multimental, and quantitative concepts. The material in the test booklet is entirely pictorial, and sample items are shown in Fig. 10.1. The tasks are presented to the pupil orally. For the four items in the illustration, the oral directions are substantially as follows:

> *Oral Vocabulary:* "Fill in the oval under the picture that shows the rat . . . the rat."

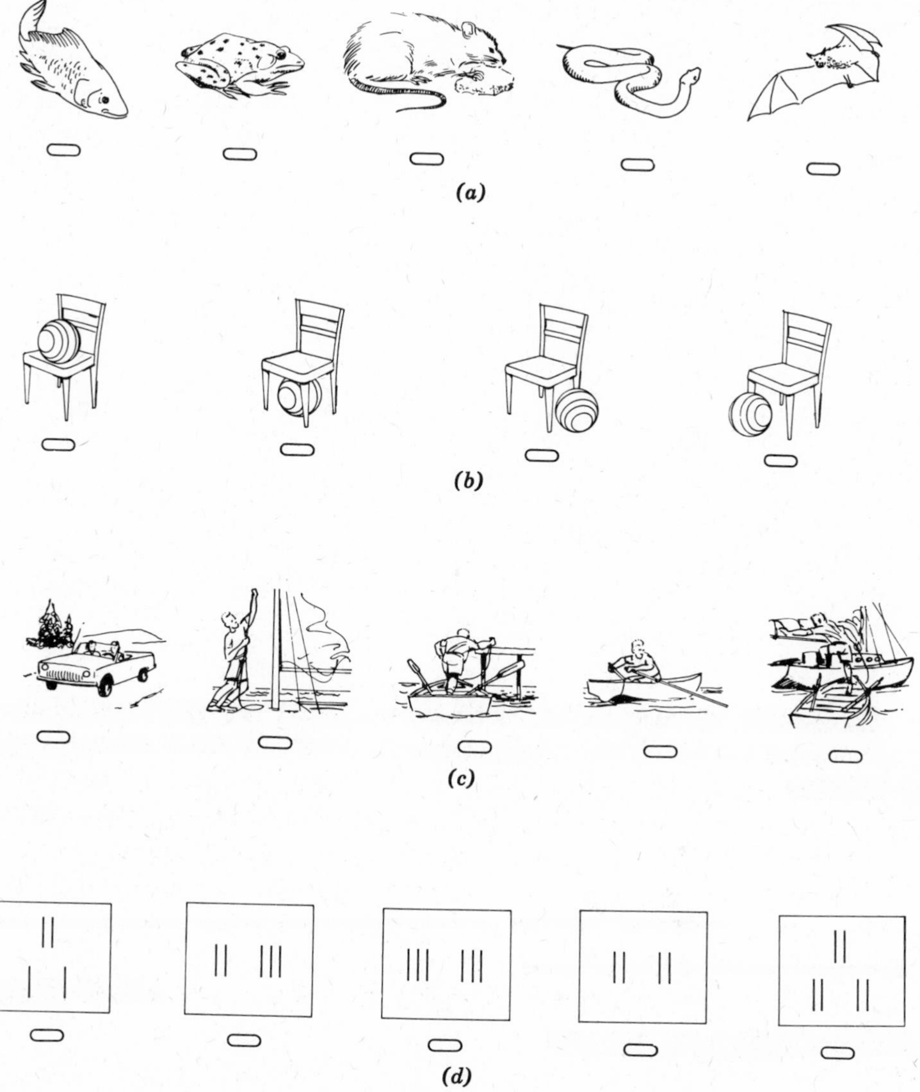

Fig. 10.1 Sample *Cognitive Ability Test* items. (*a*) Oral vocabulary; (*b*) Relational concepts; (*c*) Multimental; (*d*) Quantitative concepts. (Reproduced by permission of Houghton Mifflin Co.)

Relational Concepts: "Fill in the oval that shows the ball is on the chair . . . the ball is on the chair."

Multimental: "Look at the row of pictures. One does not belong with the others. One is different. Fill in the oval under the one that does not belong with the others.

Quantitative Concepts: "Find the box that has two sets of two sticks in it . . . two sets of two sticks. Fill the oval under that box.

VOCABULARY

Appropriate A. liable B. cunning C. charm D. suitable E. similar

SENTENCE COMPLETION

For a civilization so proficient in the practice of science, we are astonishingly ________ in our understanding of it.
A. thorough B. backward C. advanced D. unproductive E. confused

ARITHMETIC REASONING

A 12 ft. x 15 ft. rug is how many times as large as a 6 ft. x 9 ft. rug?
A. 2 B. 2½ C. 3⅓ D. 1⅔ E. none of these

VERBAL CLASSIFICATION

Cotton Wool Silk A. dress B. sew C. fibre D. linen E. cloth

VERBAL ANALOGY

Forest is to **tree** as **garden** is to
A. rake B. gladiolus C. blossom D. flower E. fruit

Fig. 10.2 Sample *Lorge-Thorndike* verbal test items. (Reproduced by permission of Houghton Mifflin Co.)

The verbal test includes five subtests designated respectively vocabulary, sentence completion, arithmetical reasoning, verbal classification, and verbal analogies. An example of each type of item is shown in Fig. 10.2. The correct answer has been underlined for each item. In order to provide tasks that are suitable for children as low as the fourth grade and as high as the beginning of college (which means difficult enough for most adults), this test has been produced in a "multilevel" format. The items in each subtest range from easy 4th grade to difficult 13th grade. However, pupils of a given age or grade take only part of the tasks, starting and stopping at different places. There are eight overlapping levels of the test. Thus for the vocabulary test the normal testing pattern would be:

Grade	*Level Taken*	*Begins at Item*	*Ends at Item*
4	A	1	25
5	B	6	30
6	C	11	35
7	D	16	40
8	E	21	45
9	F	26	50
10–11	G	31	55
12–13	H	36	60

Each pupil is tested with 25 vocabulary items, and these can be picked to be the most appropriate for his group's ability level. The total test is made up of 100 items divided among the five types shown in Fig. 10.2.

In order to have a measure that does not depend upon verbal, and especially upon reading ability, a nonverbal series is also provided. Samples of the three item types—figure analogies, number series, and figure classification—are shown in Fig. 10.3. In each type of item, the examinee must determine the relationship among the drawings or numbers that make up the stem of the item, and then find the choice that fits or completes the relationship. The nonverbal test is also prepared in the multilevel format, permitting the examiner to select the range of difficulty most appropriate for the group.

The verbal and nonverbal tests have a substantial correlation—as they should if they are both to be conceived as measures of intellectual performance. However, the correlation of about .70 in a grade group is lower than the reliabilities of the two tests, which are roughly .90, by a large enough margin so that they are seen to be measuring somewhat different functions. Generally, the nonverbal type of test is a somewhat poorer predictor of school performance than the verbal measure, and this is hardly surprising in view of the heavily verbal nature of much of what is taught in school. However, one suspects that for certain pupils who have encountered difficulties in learning to read or for certain groups with a meager background in English, the nonverbal measure provides a more accurate picture of academic potential.

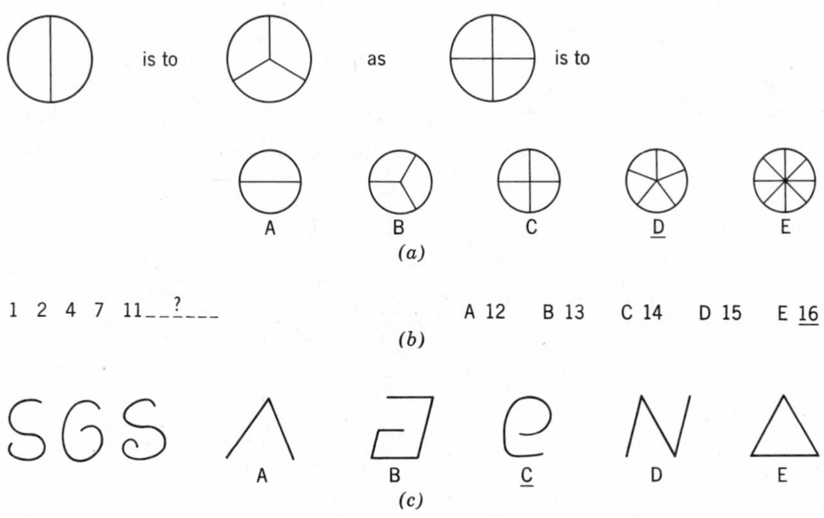

Fig. 10.3 Sample *Lorge-Thorndike* nonverbal test items. (*a*) Figure analogies; (*b*) Number series; (*c*) Figure classification. (Reproduced by permission of Houghton Mifflin Co.)

The *Lorge-Thorndike* tests, and a number of others, follow a pattern of several separately-timed subtests. We have also already mentioned the graduated multi-level format. A few tests mix all types of items together in what is called an omnibus arrangement (*Henman-Nelson, Otis-Lennon*). Many tests are published in 3 or 4 distinct levels, each of which is designed to be used in a range of several grades, and must, therefore, contain items easy enough for the slower pupils in the lowest grade and hard enough for the brighter pupils in the highest grade.

Tests for children in the primary grades usually call for the responses to be marked in the test booklet itself. In the upper elementary grades, separate answer sheets are often used, though consumable test booklets where the answer is marked in the booklet are also used to some extent. Most tests for older groups use separate answer sheets. Electronic optical scanning devices have now been developed to the point that it is possible to score by machine even the primary level tests where the pupil has marked his response in the test booklet.

A number of group tests of intelligence are listed and briefly characterized in Appendix IV, Section A. We will next turn our attention to two widely used individual tests—tests that must be given to one examinee at a time in a face-to-face interview type of setting.

THE REVISED *STANFORD-BINET* TESTS OF INTELLIGENCE

The individual test that over the years has had the widest use with school-age children is the *Stanford-Binet,* brought out by Lewis M. Terman in 1916 as an adaptation of the earlier work of Binet and Simon in France. A revised version of the test was published in 1937 by Terman and Merrill, and this has been somewhat further revised in 1960 (Terman and Merrill, 1960). The current revision, which uses the best items from the two forms of the test brought out in 1937, is known as *Form L-M*. It provides a set of tests for each of twenty levels of ability, starting with tests suitable for the average 2-year-old and going up to four levels suitable for differentiating the abilities of average and superior adults. To illustrate the content of the test, we have picked four levels at different points on the scale and listed the tests of each level with brief descriptions.

Two-and-a-Half-Year Level

1. *Identifying Objects by Use.* (Card with 6 small objects attached.)
   "Show me the one that we drink out of." etc.
   Three out of 6 for credit at this level.
2. *Identifying Parts of Body.* (Large paper doll.)
   "Show me the dolly's hair." etc.
   Six out of 6 parts for credit at this level.*
3. *Naming Objects.* (Five small objects.)
   "What is this?" (Chair, automobile, etc.)
   Five out of 5 for credit.
4. *Picture Vocabulary.* (Eighteen small cards with pictures of common objects.)
   "What's this? What do you call it?"
   Eight out of 18 for credit at this level.*
5. *Repeating Two Digits.*
   "Listen; say 2." "Now, say 4, 7." etc.
   One out of 3 for credit.
6. *Obeying Simple Commands.* (Four common objects on table.)
   "Give me the dog." "Put the button in the box."
   Two out of 3 correct for credit.

Six-Year Level

1. *Vocabulary.* (Graded list of 45 words.)
   "When I say a word, you tell me what it means. What is an orange?" etc.
   Six words correct to receive credit at this level. Words like tap, gown.*
2. *Differences.*
   "What is the difference between a bird and a dog?" "Wood and glass?"
   Two out of 3 correct for credit.
3. *Mutilated Pictures.* (Five cards of objects with part missing.)
   "What is gone in this picture?" or "What part is gone?"
   Four out of 5 for credit.
4. *Number Concepts.* (Twelve 1-inch cubes.)
   "Give me 3 blocks. Put them here."
   Four out of 5 different numbers correct.
5. *Opposite Analogies.*
   "A table is made of wood; a window of ______."
   Three out of 4 correct for credit.

* Scored also at one or more other levels.

6. *Maze Tracing.* (Mazes, with start and finish points marked.)
   "The little boy wants to go to school the shortest way without getting off the sidewalk. Show me the shortest way."
   Two right out of 3 for credit.

Twelve-Year Level

1. *Vocabulary.* (Same as 6-year level.)
   Fifteen words correct for credit at this level. Words like juggler and brunette.
2. *Verbal Absurdities.* (Five statements.)
   "Bill Jones' feet are so big that he has to pull his trousers on over his head. What is foolish about that?"
   Four out of 5 right for credit at this level.
3. *Picture Absurdities.*
   Picture showing person's shadow going wrong way. "What is foolish about that picture?"
4. *Repeating 5 Digits Reversed.*
   "I am going to say some numbers, and I want you to say them backwards."
   One out of 3 correct for credit.
5. *Abstract Words.*
   "What do we mean by pity?"
   Three out of 4 for credit at this level.
6. *Sentence Completion.* (Four sentences with missing words.)
   "Write the missing word in each blank. Put just one word in each."
   Three out of 4 required for credit at this level.

Superior Adult—Level II

1. *Vocabulary.* (Same as 6-year level.)
   Twenty-six words for credit at this level. Words like mosaic, flaunt.
2. *Finding Reasons.* (Two parts.)
   "Give three reasons why a man who commits a serious crime should be punished."
   Both parts right for credit.
3. *Proverbs.* (Pearls before swine, etc.)
   "Here is a proverb and you are supposed to tell what it means."
   One out of 2 correct for credit.
4. *Ingenuity.*
   A 5-pint can and a 3-pint can to get exactly 2 pints of water.
   Three out of 3 problems correct for credit.

5. *Essential Differences.*
   "What is the principal difference between work and play?"
   Three out of 3 correct for credit.
6. *Repeating Thought of Passage.*
   Short paragraph on the value of life.
   Four out of 7 essential ideas must be reproduced for credit.

The above examples illustrate the variety of material included in the test. Note that the specific tests vary from one level to another. Many of the tests at the lower age levels are quite concrete, dealing with little objects and pictures. At the upper levels, the tests tend to be more abstract and quite heavily verbal. The various tests include tasks calling for display of past learnings, perception of relations, judgment, interpretation, sustained attention, immediate memory, and other cognitive processes.

The tasks were selected so as to be of appropriate difficulty for the average child of the age level to which they were assigned. In testing a child, the examiner begins at a level where the child is likely to succeed, but only with some effort. If the child fails these and appears discouraged, the examiner will drop back to an easier level. Otherwise, he will move ahead level by level until he reaches a level at which the child fails all tests. When the upper limit has been established, the examiner will be sure to go back and establish the level at which the child can do all the tasks. Often, a few quite easy tests will be given at the end to build up the child's morale.

The child is credited with the basal age at which he passes all tasks plus a credit for tasks passed at more advanced levels. Each task passed at a given level credits the child with the same number of months of mental age. Thus, where there are 6 tests at each year age level, passing a single test gives a credit of 2 months of mental age. For example, child A

Passed all tasks at 6-year level	=	6 yrs. basal age
Passed 3 of 6 tasks at 7-year level	=	6 mos. credit
Passed 1 of 6 tasks at 8-year level	=	2 mos. credit
Failed all tasks at 9-year level	=	0 credit
Resulting in a mental age of		6 yrs., 8 mos.

Level of achievement is expressed as a mental age, arrived at as indicated above. The mental age describes the level at which the child is performing. But this takes no account of the child's life age. Performance in relation to a group of children of his own age is expressed as an IQ. The IQ's for this latest revision of the *Stanford-Binet* are deviation IQ's, that is, they are essentially standard scores for which the mean is 100 and the standard deviation 16 at each age level. Insofar as the normative groups are adequate and comparable from one age to another, an IQ has the same meaning at one age as at any other. Tables for converting MA's to IQ's are provided from age 2-0 (2 years, no months) up to age 16-0. For individuals over 16 years of age the table is entered with a chronological age of 16-0. The standard scores are designed to have a mean of 100 and a standard deviation of 16.

THE *WECHSLER INTELLIGENCE SCALES*

The second major individual intelligence test is the *Wechsler Adult Intelligence Scale* (*WAIS*) (Wechsler, 1955). This test was originally developed for adults, and the materials and tasks were chosen with an eye to their appropriateness for adults. The pattern of organization of the test differs from that of the *Binet*. Whereas the *Binet,* developed for children, is organized in successive age levels, the *WAIS* is organized by subtests representing types of tasks. The titles of the subtests are given below. In each case, the subtest is illustrated by an item of roughly average difficulty. (The illustrative items are similar to those in the test, but are not actually included in it.)

Verbal Subscale

1. *General Information.*
   What day of the year is Independence Day?
2. *General Comprehension.*
   Why do people buy fire insurance?
3. *Arithmetic Reasoning.*
   If eggs cost 60 cents a dozen, what does one egg cost?
4. *Similarities.*
   In what way are *wool* and *cotton* alike?
5. *Digit Span.*
   Listen carefully, and when I am through, say the numbers right after me.

   7–3–4–1–8–6

   Now I am going to say some more numbers, but I want you to say them backward.

   3–8–4–1–6

6. *Vocabulary.*
   Tell me the meaning of *corrupt.*

Performance Subscale

7. *Digit-Symbol Substitution.*

Code

△	○	▱	×	8
1	2	3	4	5

Test

△	8	×	○	△	▱	8	×	△	8

etc.

8. *Picture Completion.*

I am going to show you a picture with an important part missing. Tell me what is missing.

1968

S	M	T	W	T	F	S
		1	2	3	4	5
6	7	8	9	10	11	12
13	14	15	16	17	18	19
20	21	22	23	24	25	26
27	28	29	30	31		

9. *Block Design.*

Using the four blocks, make one just like this.

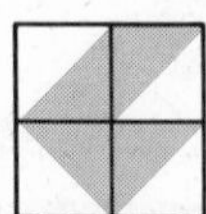

10. *Picture Arrangement.*

The pictures below tell a story. Put them in the right order to tell the story.

11. *Object Assembly.*

If these pieces are put together correctly, they will make something. Go ahead and put them together as quickly as you can.

Each subtest of the *WAIS* yields a separate score, which is then converted into a standard score for that subtest. The subtest standard scores are combined in three different groupings to yield total scores, and from these total scores, three different types of IQ's may be read from norm tables. The three IQ's are (1) a verbal IQ from subtests 1 through 6, (2) a performance IQ from subtests 7 through 11, and (3) a total IQ from all the subtests put together. The separate verbal and performance IQ's may have diagnostic significance in the case of certain individuals with verbal, academic, or cultural handicaps. The IQ on the *WAIS* is also a standard score, but set to make the mean of the normative sample 100 and the standard deviation 15.

As we have indicated, the original *Wechsler Intelligence Scale* was designed for adults. It was suitable for use with adolescents and with adults of all ages.

Subsequently, however, the material has been extended downward to make tests for children. The same general pattern of subtests has been used, although the tasks change their character somewhat as one gets down to the younger age levels. In fact, one may question whether the parallelism between the nature of the subtests for 4-year-olds and for adults is real or only superficial. Two lower levels of the test are now available, the *Wechsler Intelligence Scale for Children* (*WISC*) (Wechsler, 1949), is recommended for ages from 7 to 15, while the *Wechsler Preschool and Primary Scale* (*WPPSI*) (Wechsler, 1967), is designed for use with children from 4 to 6½.

The features that distinguish the *WAIS* from the 1960 edition of the *Stanford-Binet* are:

1. Original test items specifically designed for adults.
2. Organization by subtests rather than by age levels.
3. Provision for separate verbal and nonverbal IQ's.

All these features seem like sound adaptations in a test for adults. Most psychometricians would probably agree now in preferring the *WAIS* as a measure for adolescents and adults, though its relation to academic success is perhaps not as clearly established as is the *Binet's*. (As a matter of fact, at these ages a printed group test would usually seem more appropriate for academic prediction.)

With the addition of the *WISC* and the *WPPSI*, the Wechsler series can now be used with children as young as 4 years of age. The *WPPSI* is quite new and untried by the profession. Therefore, for children up to the age of 6 or 7, the *Stanford-Binet* must still be considered the standard instrument. For children from 7 to 15, a decision between the two tests is not an easy one. The *Binet* is reported to be somewhat more difficult and time-consuming to give. The usual *Binet* procedure of carrying the examinee through to the point where he encounters a long series of failures is judged to be a seriously upsetting matter for some emotionally tense children. The separate verbal and performance IQ's of the *WISC* should be quite useful in some cases in understanding children whose verbal development is either very accelerated or retarded. It has diagnostic value for some children with special educational disabilities. However, the *Binet* is probably a somewhat more reliable measure. (No directly comparable data are available.) The test items entering into the *Binet* have had the benefit of trial in earlier forms, with opportunity to revise and select on the basis of that experience. The ultimate basis for choice will be the validity of the inferences that can be made from each in the situations in which they are actually used. Prediction of academic success can apparently be made about equally well from either test. It seems likely that the two tests are about equally useful for children with mental ages of 7 or above.

ABBREVIATED INDIVIDUAL TESTS

A major problem in using individual intelligence tests is that they are distressingly costly in time of trained examiners. This has led to various attempts to provide abbreviated adaptations of the *Binet* or *Wechsler,* as well as to produce other shorter and simpler individual tests. Abbreviations of the *Binet* or *Wechsler* that omit either certain subtests (Doppelt, 1950) or a fraction of the test items (Mogul and Satz, 1963) correlate quite well with the complete test, but are less reliable as would be expected with a shortened test.

Of all the subtests in the *Binet* and *Wechsler,* the one that has consistently shown the highest correlation with total score has been the vocabulary test. This has led several test makers to produce picture-vocabulary tests as abbreviated test devices. The Full-Range Vocabulary Test (Ammons and Ammons, 1948) uses a set of 16 plates, each with four pictures on it. A word is spoken, and the examinee indicates which of the four pictures it refers to. The plates are reused with words of increasing difficulty, so that a total of 80 words can be tested. The same general procedure is used with the Peabody Picture Vocabulary Test (Dunn, 1959) except that a different set of pictures is used for each of the words tested. Thus, the materials required are kept very simple, and a quick estimate of ability is obtained. The score is, of course, highly dependent upon a limited verbal type of ability, but the procedure functions fairly efficiently within that limitation.

NONLANGUAGE AND PERFORMANCE TESTS

Most of the widely used intelligence tests depend, to some degree, on language and include tasks presented in verbal terms. This is natural, since the bulk of our learning and thinking makes use of language. For the usual person and in relation to the usual type of academic learnings, aptitude for learning can be tested more efficiently by tasks that involve language than by those that do not. However, for some groups or situations this is not so. The most obvious example is that of groups who do not speak the language or speak it only slightly. When an individual has limited command of English, results from a verbal test in English are in large measure meaningless. Children who have had little opportunity to attend school may suffer a special handicap on a test that relies upon materials close to school learnings. For groups of this sort, tests have been developed that do not require language. In some of these, only the test tasks are nonlanguage in character; in others the instructions can be given by pantomime and no language need be used at any point during the testing.

We have already seen one nonverbal test in the nonverbal form of the *Lorge-Thorndike*. Another test that is entirely nonverbal in content and that has norms both for verbal and pantomime presentation of instructions is the *Chicago Nonverbal Examination* (Brown, 1940). The test is made of 10 subtests. The nature of the task in each subtest is described and illustrated below.

Test 1: Digit-Symbol. "Write under each drawing the number that is beneath that drawing in the first row."

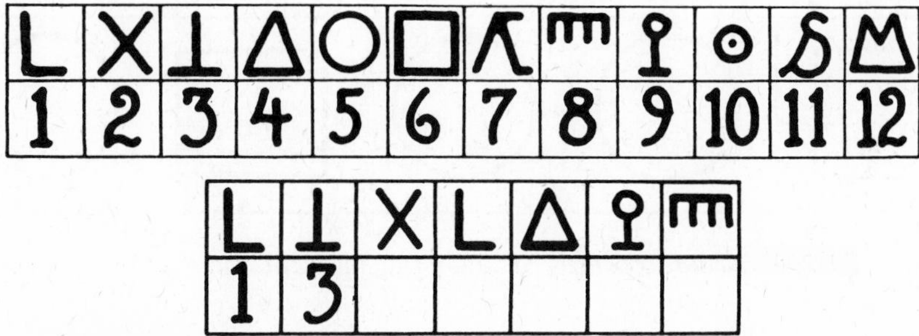

Test 2: Multimental. "Draw a cross through the one thing . . . in each row that is different from all the others."

Test 3: Block-Counting. "Count the number of blocks it takes to make each pile."

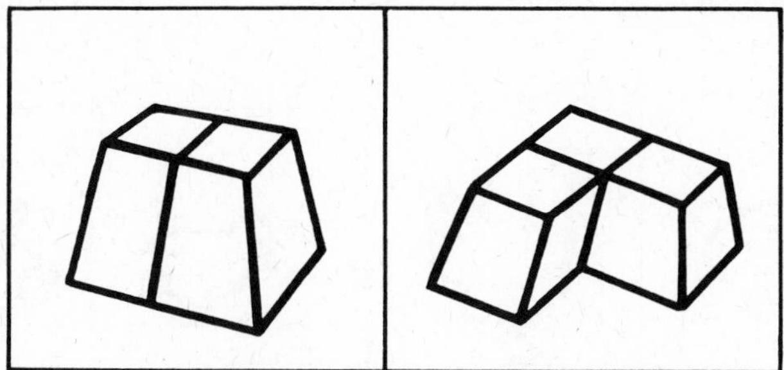

Reproduced by permission of Roberta W. Brown

Test 4: Paper Form Board. "Put a mark on two drawings . . . which go together to make the drawing on the left."

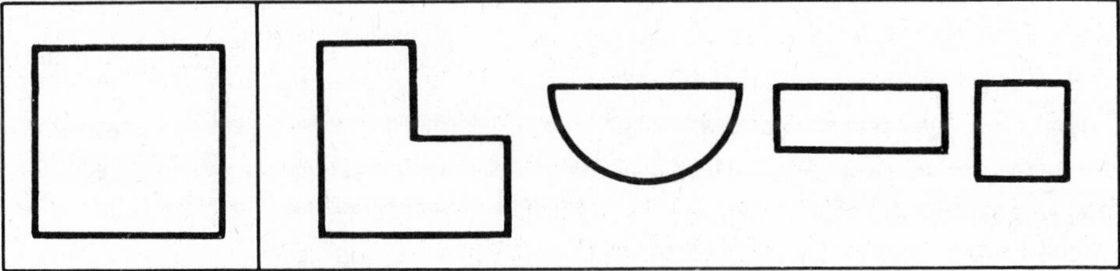

Test 5: Form Perception. "Put a mark on one drawing . . . that is just like the first drawing on the left."

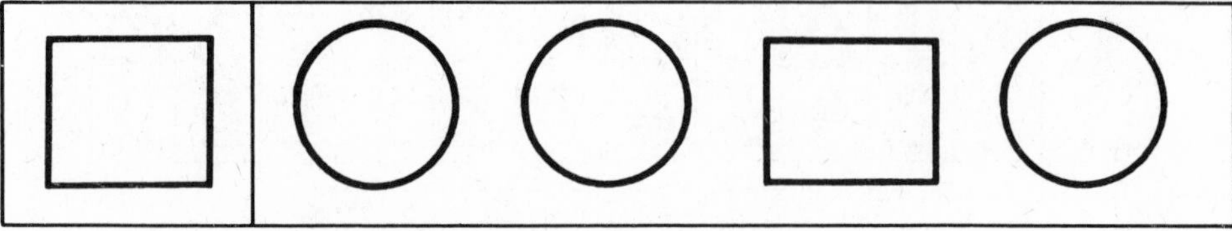

Test 6: Picture Arrangement. "Arrange the parts of the picture so that they will make a real picture."

Test 7: Story Sequence. "Number the pictures in the order in which they appear in the story."

Test 8: Absurdities. "Put a cross on the thing that is wrong in each picture."

Test 9: Part-Whole. "Put a mark on one thing . . . that goes with the thing on the left."

Test 10: Digit-Symbol. (See test #1.)

When the administration is with pantomime directions, scores tend to run a little lower and to be somewhat more variable. This suggests that, for some children at least, it is harder to get the idea of what they are to do from pantomime than from verbal directions.

Nonlanguage tests show fairly substantial correlations with the more widely used verbal measures. For the *Lorge-Thorndike,* the correlation is about .65 to .70, and for the *Chicago* about .60 to .65, indicating that a common underlying ability can account for a good deal of what is measured by both verbal and nonverbal tests. However, the correlation is enough below the reliabilities of the separate tests so that we know that each is in part unique in what it is measuring. With usual groups, the nonlanguage test may be expected to be somewhat less effective as a predictor of school achievement. The value of the nonlanguage test is for atypical individuals or groups, that is, the deaf, the foreign born, or the individual with a special reading or language disability. Used together with a verbal test, a nonlanguage measure may provide useful diagnostic cues as to the nature of pupil difficulties in learning.

Individual tests are also available that do not require the use of language. We have already described the *Wechsler Adult Intelligence Scale* and referred to the performance IQ provided by this test. The performance IQ is based upon five subtests that do not require the subject to use language once he has been instructed as to the nature of his task. A performance test that is widely used with children, as a supplement to the *Binet* when a verbal handicap is suspected, or for groups with which the *Binet* would not be appropriate is the *Arthur Point Scale* (Arthur, 1943).

The current form of the *Arthur Point Scale* (Form II) is made up of the following five subtests:

1. *Knox Cubes:* The examiner taps four cubes in a specified sequence, and the subject must reproduce the sequence.
2. *Seguin Form Board:* Ten geometric figures are to be placed into the corresponding holes in the board as rapidly as possible.
3. *Healy Picture Completion:* A large picture is displayed with uniform size square cutouts, and subject must choose, from a set of square blocks, the one portraying an object that best fits into each hole.
4. *Porteus Mazes:* Simple pencil mazes are to be traced without retracing and without crossing the boundary lines.
5. *Arthur Stencil Design:* Material is a set of colored cards, and a set of cutouts of various designs and colors. Subject must select the appropriate card and cutouts and assemble them in the proper order, so as to match a master design that is shown him.

A point score is allowed the subject for his performance on each subtest of the *Arthur Scale*. The score depends in some subtests upon the speed with which the task was completed, in others upon the correctness of the solution or the number of graded tasks solved. The point credits for the subtests are summed to give a total point score, and this is converted to a mental age equivalent. An IQ is computed by dividing mental age by chronological age. The IQ's appear to have about the same distribution as for the *Revised Binet*.

There have been a number of other attempts to evaluate intellectual ability through performance tasks, ideally ones that would be usable in different countries and different cultures. One of the most widely known is the *Draw-a-Man Test,* developed by Goodenough in the 1920's and revised and extended by Harris in 1963 (Harris, 1963). The child is asked to draw first a man and then a woman, being instructed "Make a picture of a man. Make the very best picture that you can; take your time and work very carefully . . . Be sure to make the whole man, not just his head and shoulders." A scoring scheme has been provided that allocates points for completeness and maturity of representation. Thus, 5 points can be earned for eyes: (1) eyes present, (2) brow or lashes, (3) detail of pupil, (4) vertical-horizontal proportion, and (5) direction of glance. Reliability of the resulting score is fairly modest; correlation between the man and the woman drawing is only about 0.75. Correlation with *Stanford-Binet* IQ averages about .50, so the drawing provides only a very rough estimate of this standard individual type of test.

The individual performance test must generally receive the same evaluation as group nonlanguage tests. For an English-speaking person with normal environmental opportunities and without specialized language or reading handicap, it represents a less efficient way of appraising mental development than the more widely used verbal test. However, as a way of checking on whether there *is* a specialized language handicap it represents a valuable supplemental tool. It makes it possible to check upon individuals who appear retarded on the verbal type of test to see whether the retardation is general or whether it is a localized deficiency in the language area. A performance test such as the *Arthur Point Scale,* which can be given with pantomime instructions, is also useful in testing deaf children, non-English-speaking children, and other types of special groups.

INFANT AND PRESCHOOL TESTS

The first intelligence tests were made for school-age children. However, it was not long before the theoretical interests of child psychologists and the practical needs of child-care and placement agencies stimulated the attempt to develop procedures for appraising intelligence in preschool children and even in infants. Any appraisal procedures with young children obviously had to be individually administered. Also, they had to be based upon behavior that was spontaneously exhibited by or could be elicited from children of the age being studied. Infant tests, therefore, had to take on a very different character from later appraisals. Arnold Gesell (1940) pioneered in designing tests based on observation of the child's postural, perceptual, manipulative, and social responses. Does he sit up? Stand up? Walk? Will he turn to look at a light? Notice a face? Can he pick up a block? A spoon? A little pellet? By what type of a grasping motion? How does he react to strange adults? To another infant?

Observations of large numbers of infants showed a typical developmental sequence in the different aspects of the child's development. Performance B followed A, and was followed by C. Norms have been established representing the average age at which a particular behavior manifests itself. The child may be assigned a developmental age, based upon the behavior he shows. Retests after a short interval show the child to be fairly consistent in his level of performance. If he is advanced at one testing, he will tend to be advanced at the other. The developmental schedules provide a moderately reliable picture of the individual *at that point in time.*

TABLE 10.1 CORRELATION OF INTELLIGENCE TESTS DURING FIRST YEAR OF LIFE WITH LATER MEASURES *

(Correlations based on pooling of successive tests)

Age at Later Test	Age at Initial Test			
	1, 2, 3 Mos.	4, 5, 6 Mos.	7, 8, 9 Mos.	10, 11, 12 Mos.
4, 5, 6 mos.	.57			
7, 8, 9 mos.	.42	.72		
10, 11, 12 mos.	.28	.52	.81	
13, 14, 15 mos.	.10	.50	.67	.81
18, 21, 24 mos.	−.04	.23	.39	.60
27, 30, 36 mos.	−.09	.10	.22	.45
42, 48, 54 mos.	−.21	−.16	.02	.27
5, 6, 7 yrs.	−.13	−.07	.02	.20
8, 9, 10 yrs.	−.03	−.06	.07	.19
11, 12, 13 yrs.	.02	−.08	.16	.30
14, 15, 16 yrs.	−.01	−.04	.01	.23
17, 18 yrs.	.05	−.01	.20	.41

* Tests used were: 1–15 months, *California First-Year Mental Scale;* 18 months–5 years, *California Preschool Scale;* 6 years and older, *Stanford-Binet* (Bayley, 1949).

What significance does acceleration or retardation in development during the first year or so of life have for predicting later intelligence? The answer for normal children in normal home environments is shown in Table 10.1, which gives, for one rather typical study, the correlation of infant tests given at the ages of 1 to 12 months, with intelligence tests at various later ages. The picture seems quite clear. For these normal infants, without any particular pathology, the infant tests give a fairly good prediction of developmental status a few months later, but their value as predictors drops rapidly as the time interval increases. The infant tests provide essentially *no* prediction of intellectual status at school age.

When there is some sort of neuropathology, however, the situation may be rather different. In one longitudinal study of infants seen in a hospital, usually because some pathology of the central nervous system was suspected (Knobloch and Passamanick, 1967), the correlation between *Gesell Developmental Quotient* at an age of 16 to 52 weeks and *Stanford-Binet* IQ at 6 to 10 years of age was 0.70. However, the sample of 135 included 40 cases that were judged to have some type of pathological condition and these had an average IQ on retesting of

55. Thus, schedules for the systematic observation of infants seem to have some value in identifying children who will later be classified as mentally defective, but no value on the positive end for forecasting degrees of intellectual talent.

There have been a number of different tests prepared primarily for use with preschool children, that is, the age range from about 18 months to 5 years. As a matter of fact, as we have seen, the *Stanford-Binet Intelligence Scale* has tests going down to the 2-year level and may be considered a preschool test. It would compare very favorably with the other tests available for this age level, though it is somewhat more verbal than many of the others. A good many of the preschool tests have tended to get away from the verbal material that appears so heavily in group tests for older children and also in the *Stanford-Binet.*

One test for preschool children that has received wide use is the *Merrill-Palmer Scale* (Stutsman, 1931). This is most suitable for children from 2 to 4, though it can be used with children slightly older and slightly younger. The test is made up of 38 little subtests, of which only 4 call for verbal response by the child. A number of the tasks call for gross motor coordination (standing on one foot) or finer eye-hand coordination (building block tower, cutting with scissors). Form and object perception and motor control combine in a number of form-boards in which cutouts must be fitted into the appropriate hole. The tasks make use of a variety of materials interesting to the child, blocks, pictures, scissors, balls, etc., so that cooperation can usually be obtained, a real problem with children at these ages.

The *Merrill-Palmer Scale* has fairly satisfactory reliability, especially above about 30 months. Correlations with retests 6 months later have been reported (Ebert and Simmons, 1943) as follows for different age groups:

24 months	.63
30 months	.76
36 months	.78
42 months	.80

The correlation with school-age *Binet* is about .40 for a *Merrill-Palmer* test at age 2; about .45 to .50 for one at age 4.

The *Minnesota Preschool Scale* (Goodenough, 1940) is another example of a test designed for preschool groups. The 26 tests in this scale tend to be more like those of the *Binet*. Six tests taken at random from one form of the *Scale* are described briefly. They are:

Test 2: Pointing Out Objects in Pictures. Card with man, chair, apple, house, and flower on it. Child is asked to point to each in turn.

Test 5: Imitative Drawing. Experimenter makes vertical stroke; then a cross. Child is asked to imitate each in turn.

Test 8: Imitation. A set of 4 cubes, on which experimenter taps in specified sequence. Child instructed to imitate the sequence of taps.

Test 14: Colors. Cards colored red, blue, pink, white, and brown. Child is asked to name the color.

Test 20: Paper Folding. Examiner folds paper with three consecutive folds. Child is asked to copy exactly.

Test 24: Giving Word Opposites. Child is asked to give words meaning opposite of cold, bad, thick, dry, dark, and sick.

Test materials are quite simple. Copying, imitating, and responding to simple verbal relations enter into a number of the tests.

This test appears to be somewhat more reliable than the *Merrill-Palmer.* Correlation between two forms of the test given within a few days of each other was found to be .89. Below 3 years, this test did not correlate very well with later *Binets,* but the *Minnesota* given between 3 and 4 gave a correlation with *Binets* at school age of about .60. However, IQ's on the *Minnesota Preschool Scale* have quite a different spread from those for the *Binet* so a preschool IQ on this test is not readily equated to later *Binet* performance (Goodenough and Maurer, 1942).

CULTURE-FREE AND CULTURE-FAIR TESTS

Many workers in the field of aptitude testing have been distressed by the fact that test performance depends upon the experiences the person has had. Every test maker has recognized this to a degree and has tried to base test items upon experiences that would be common to the group for whom the test was planned. But some have perhaps taken too narrow a view of the group for whom the experiences should be common. Certainly the test that incorporates pictures of the usual American house, automobile, or football is not suitable for an Australian Bushman who has seen none of these objects. The typical American test assumes the common core of an American culture. Some critics have gone further and asserted that the typical test is based upon an urban middle-class American culture. Both in its highly verbal content and its emphasis upon speed, competition, and doing one's best, it is said to be centered in the middle-class culture and values.

Several attempts have been made to develop tests that are "culture free," or if not that at least "culture fair." These are closely related to the nonverbal and performance tests described in the previous section, because a culture-free test is almost necessarily nonverbal. It must not only be nonverbal but must also be free of the content of any particular culture.

One attempt to develop such a test is the *Cattell Culture Fair Intelligence Test.* The *Cattell Test* is based on the premise that general intelligence is a matter of seeing relationships in the things with which we have to deal, that the ability to see relationships can be tested with simple diagrammatic or pictorial material, and that for a test to be usable in different cultures the pictures should be of forms or objects which are fairly universal, that is, not peculiar to any cultural group. Items illustrating the different types of tasks are shown in Fig. 10.4 on page 316. The evidence that the test is in fact useful for widely different cultures is largely lacking, but the tasks constitute one further interesting nonverbal group test that may prove usable, particularly in research studies.

One test that was developed in Great Britain and has been used in many countries is the *Progressive Matrices Test* (Raven, 1956). The type of item is similar to the last two samples in Fig. 10.4. Two types of progression or relationship are established, one in the horizontal and one in the vertical direction. The examinee is required to pick the choice that correctly fills the missing entry in the lower right-hand corner of the matrix.

An attempt to develop a test that imposes no penalty on different classes in American society was found in an instrument called the *Davis-Eells Games.* This test series involved no written language but did require quite long oral directions. Types of items included:

1. *Best ways,* in which three pictures are shown in the test booklet, and the examinee is orally instructed to mark the one that is the best way to carry a pile of packages, get over a fence, etc.
2. *Analogies,* in which the analogies are presented in pictures and are of the type, "Glove is to hand as sock is to: arm, leg, foot."
3. *Probabilities,* in which a picture is shown and the examinee must select the one of three orally presented choices that indicates what probably led up to or is represented in the picture.
4. *"Money,"* a task based on complex directions for following certain rules for combining coins to make specified sums.

This test was designed to avoid the cultural biases, particularly socioeconomic biases within the American culture, thought to characterize previously existing tests. However, studies of the test in recent years have failed to confirm that it did so. IQ's from the *Davis-Eells Games* were found to have about as high a correlation with indices of socioeconomic status as those for any other test. We

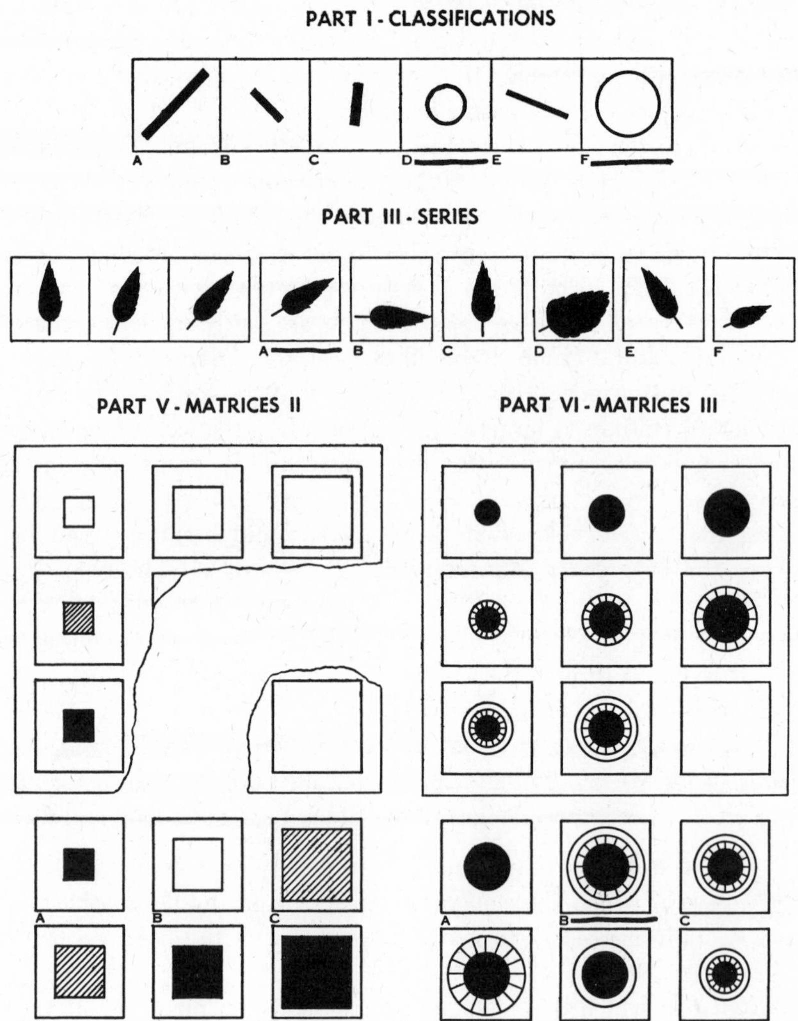

Fig. 10.4 Sample items from *Cattell Culture Fair Intelligence Test.* (Copyright 1944, Institute for Personality and Ability Testing, 1602 Coronado Drive, Champaign, Ill. Reproduced by permission.)

must conclude that either there basically *is* a relationship between mental ability and socioeconomic status, or that the *Davis-Eells Games* has failed to eliminate the bias which its authors believed to characterize other tests. Since this type of test is laborious to give and relatively unreliable, it has little to recommend it on other grounds. We must conclude that it does not appear very useful as a measurement tool at the present time.

GROUP VERSUS INDIVIDUAL TESTS AS MEASURES OF INTELLIGENCE

We have seen that intelligence tests fall into two main patterns, group tests and individual tests. The types of tasks presented to the examinee are a good deal alike in both patterns. However, the two procedures have certain significant differences. These may be summarized as follows:

Group Tests	*Individual Tests*
Problems presented in printed booklet. Read by examinee. Personal contact with examiner a minimum.	Problems presented orally by examiner in face-to-face situation.
Tasks presented and test timed as a unit, or separate time limits for each subtest.	Problems presented one at a time, usually without indication of time limits.
Individual usually responds by selecting one of a limited set of response options printed in the test booklet.	Individual usually responds freely, giving whatever response seems appropriate to him.

These differences in procedure have several important implications for the conduct of testing and for the results that may be obtained from such testing. In the first place, when test tasks are presented orally to the subject and he does not have to read them for himself, his performance is much less dependent upon his reading skills. The child who has lagged behind in acquiring these skills is not penalized for this specific failure.

The effect of reading disability upon intelligence test performance is shown clearly in a study (Neville, 1965) comparing individual *WISC* scores and *Lorge-Thorndike Verbal* test scores for good, mediocre, and poor readers in a fifth-grade class. Reading groups were defined by scores on the reading section of the *Metropolitan Achievement Test* at the end of the fourth grade. Intelligence tests were given during the fifth grade to 18 pupils in each reading group. IQ's on the tests were as follows:

	Lorge-Thorndike Verbal	*WISC* Verbal	*WISC* Performance	*WISC* Total
Good readers	113	110	106	109
Mediocre readers	95	96	96	96
Poor readers	82	89	94	90

The verbal group test shows a good deal more relationship to the reading test than does either part score or the total score on the individual test. The difference between good and poor readers is 31 IQ points in the one case, and from 12 to 21 in the other.

The results reported above are probably somewhat extreme, because reading ability was defined by a test involving a test of word knowledge as well as of connected reading, and word knowledge is also directly measured in the *Lorge-Thorndike* test. Furthermore, the study was carried out with elementary-school children, for whom the actual mechanics of reading still present some problems. One may anticipate that less difference would be found for high-school or college students. Furthermore, some current group tests are either partly or wholly nonlanguage in their content and would be relatively independent of reading skills. However, this study points out very clearly the caution with which a group test IQ must be interpreted for a person who departs markedly from the average in his reading skills. A low group test IQ for a poor reader cannot be taken at face value. It should always be checked with a test that does not involve reading.

The presentation of problems one at a time by an examiner is also a factor of some significance in determining what the test is likely to yield. Especially with younger children, maintaining continuity of attention and effort on a group test may be a problem, and variations in this respect are certainly a significant factor in test score. When each problem is separately presented by the examiner, this serves to reestablish the child's orientation to the task and to maintain his effort. What is equally important, the examiner is in a position to observe lapses of interest and effort and to take some account of them in interpreting the results.

The individual intelligence test is essentially a well-standardized interview situation. The tasks to be presented to the examinee are specifically formulated, and detailed standards are provided for evaluating his responses. However, the face-to-face relationship of an interview prevails. This offers the alert examiner a wealth of opportunities for observing the examinee and noting poor motivation, distractibility, signs of anxiety and upset, and other cues that will help in interpreting the actual test performance. At the same time, the demands upon the examiner are considerably heavier. If valid testing is to result, the tasks must be presented in a standard way, interest and cooperative effort must be maintained, and a uniform standard must be applied in evaluating responses.

The free-response item in the individual test fits into the interview setting of the individual test and reinforces both its strengths and its limitations. Potentially, the free response of the examinee can tell us more about him than the mere record of which option he has chosen from a set of five. There is more of the quality of his own behavior available to us. We can see just how he goes about defining a word, whether by class and differentia (that is, an orange is a round, orange-colored, citrus fruit) or by use (an orange is to eat). We can note the speed and sureness of his attack on a problem task. But we must also depend on the examiner to interpret and evaluate the responses, and at this point subjectivity is likely to creep into the examining. Careful attention must be paid to the standard samples provided in the test manual, and experience under supervision is indicated before an examiner can expect to give and score an individual intelligence test in a way that will yield results comparable to those of other examiners.

In general, the limitations of group tests are most acute and the advantages of individual tests most pronounced with young children. Printed group tests cannot be used successfully with children below school age. They cannot read and have difficulty in manipulating a pencil, following instructions, or maintaining sustained attention for the period that is required for taking a test. These same factors continue to present fairly serious problems for testing in the primary grades. However, the factor of cost makes individual testing impractical for most large-scale users of tests, so that with older individuals the overwhelming majority of the intelligence tests used are paper-and-pencil group tests.

RELIABILITY AND STABILITY OF MEASURES OF INTELLIGENCE

We have already presented some evidence on the reliability of measures of intelligence in connection with our discussion of infant and preschool tests. The reliability of those early measures is found to be quite modest, with values often falling between .60 and .80. For tests at school age, reliabilities are more promising. Considering the group tests first, we find that when correlations between two forms of the same test are reported for an age group or a grade group they usually fall between .80 and .90. A few are higher. Unfortunately, the authors of some tests report only odd-even reliabilities, and it is difficult to estimate how much these are inflated. (See discussion on pp. 184–186.) Comparisons of different tests are made difficult by variations in the procedure used for estimating reliability and in the type of group for which results are reported.

The correlations reported by the authors (Terman and Merrill, 1960) between Form L and Form M of the *Stanford-Binet Intelligence Scale* ranged from .85 to .95 for different age groups. For ages from 2 to 6, the median value was .88, whereas for ages above 6 the median was .93. Since Form L-M was prepared by selecting the better items from both Form L and Form M, one may anticipate that the reliability of the new form is at least as high as these values.

The reliability reported in the manual for the *Wechsler Adult Intelligence Scale* is .96 for the verbal IQ, .93 for the performance IQ, and .97 for the full scale IQ. These are split-half reliabilities, and consequently should be discounted somewhat in relation to the reliability reported for the *Binet*. Split-half reliabilities for the *Wechsler Intelligence Scale for Children* are reported to be .92 at age 7½, .95 at age 10½, and .94 at age 13½.

Though the variations in procedure for estimating reliability and in type of group tested make it difficult to arrive at an unequivocal answer, it does seem that the individual intelligence tests yield a somewhat more reliable measure than do the commonly used group tests. This is probably in part a reflection of the somewhat longer actual testing time, in part a result of more uniform motivation and effort when working under the eye of the examiner.

The reliabilities of intelligence tests are reasonably satisfactory, and they are among the most dependable psychological measuring instruments. However, the chance errors in an IQ are still enough to require that we be quite tentative in our interpretation. Thus, Table 10.2 shows the spread of IQ's that could have been expected on Form M of the *Binet* if that form had been given to a group of pupils all of whom had received exactly the same IQ on Form L. Note that the IQ's spread over a range of more than 25 points, and that less than a third of the cases fall in the center 5-point interval. And it must be remembered that these figures are for the *Stanford-Binet,* one of our most reliable tests. Thus, an IQ of 100 must not be thought of as meaning "exactly 100," but rather "probably between 95 and 105, *very* probably between 90 and 110, almost certainly between 85 and 115."

TABLE 10.2 EXPECTED DISTRIBUTION OF *Stanford-Binet* FORM M IQ'S FOR CASES ALL WITH FORM L IQ'S OF 100

IQ	*f*
113+	3
108–112	9
103–107	23
98–102	30
93–97	23
88–92	9
87 and below	3

Stability Over a Period of Years

In addition to knowing the precision with which an intelligence test appraises an individual's abilities at a particular time, we would like to know how consistently the individual maintains his position in his group from one year to the next or over a considerable span of years. How confidently can we predict what scholastic aptitude an individual will show when he is of college age from his performance on a test at age 2? Age 6? Age 10? Evidence on this point is presented in Figs. 10.5 below and 10.6 on page 322.

Figure 10.5 shows the findings from one extensive study using individual tests. The final test is the *Stanford-Binet* in every case. The initial test is the *California Preschool Scale* up through 5 years and the *Stanford-Binet* after that age. Note that for the early tests the prediction is rather poor and drops as the interval is increased. A test at age 2 correlates only .37 with one at age 6 and .21 with one at age 14 or 15. As we go up the age range, however, the correlations are higher and the drop is less. A test given at age 8 or 9 correlates .88 with one at age 10 and still correlates .86 with one at age 14 or 15. For normal children

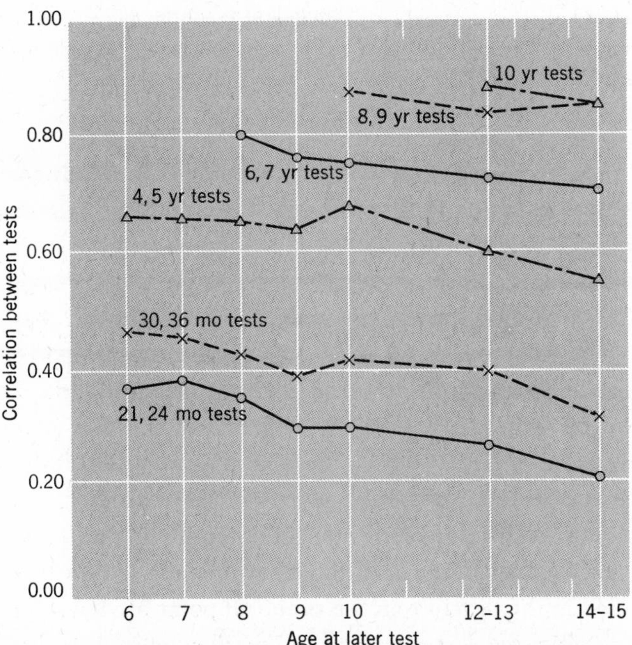

Fig. 10.5 Effect of age at initial testing and test-retest interval on prediction of later *Stanford-Binet* IQ from earlier test. (Adapted from Honzik, McFarlane, and Allen, 1948.)

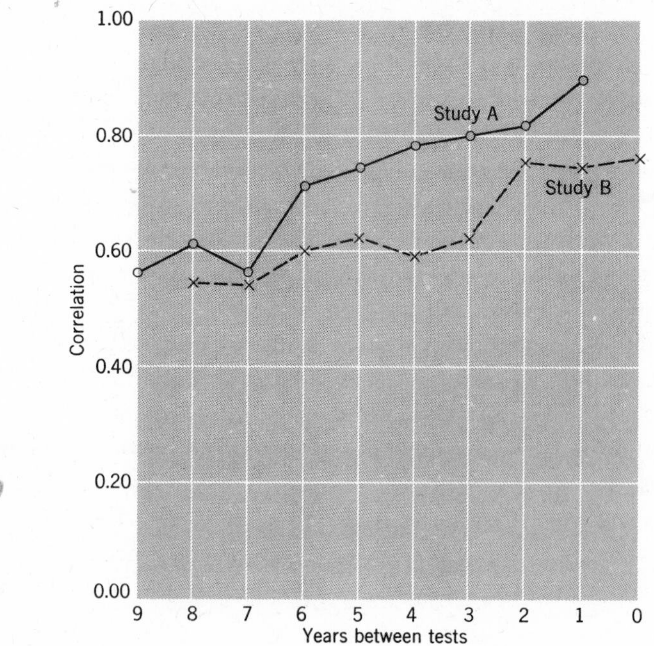

Fig. 10.6 Effect of test-retest interval on prediction of group intelligence at end of high school from earlier group tests. (Study A adapted from J. E. Anderson, 1939; Study B adapted from R. L. Thorndike, 1947.)

in a typical environment, a *Stanford-Binet* at age 8 or 9 appears to provide almost as accurate a forecast of ability near the end of high school as would the same test given several years later.

Two sets of data on stability of group-test performance over time are presented in Fig. 10.6. The two follow the same general pattern, though they differ a good deal in detail. As we increase the time interval, the correlation coefficients tend to drop more or less steadily. The earlier tests at around grade 3 or 4 correlate perhaps .50 to .60 with the end-of-high-school test, but for a test in grade 9 or 10 the correlation is .70 to .80. In these studies of group tests, the tests that were used differed at the different ages. For this reason, it is not clear how much the lower correlation over the longer intervals is due to growth changes in the subjects over a span of years and how much it is due to changes in the material included in the tests. From the practical point of view, Fig. 10.6 suggests that a group intelligence test needs to be supplemented by new testing every 3 or 4 years if pupil records are to provide an accurate indication of current ability level.

During the years of maturity, stability of intelligence test performance is marked even over long intervals. Owens (1954), retesting Iowa State University students some 30 years later when they were about 50 years old, found a correlation of .77 with their scores as college freshmen. In another 25-year longitudinal study (Bradway and Thompson, 1962), correlations were obtained as shown below.

	1941 Binet	*1956 Binet*	*1956 WAIS*
Preschool *Binet* (1931)	.65	.59	.64
Adolescent *Binet* (1941)		.85	.80
Adult *Binet* (1956)			.83

Several factors probably combine to produce the lack of stability over time in early intelligence tests. First, factors of maintenance of attention and effort are quite different in the young child than they are at a later date. Second, the types of performances that serve as marks of intelligence change in nature as one goes from infancy through childhood to adulthood, becoming more and more verbal, abstract, and symbolic. Finally, the amount of intellectual growth that has already occurred becomes larger and larger, in relation to that which is still to take place. Thus, the correlation between an intelligence test given to 15-year-olds and one given to the same group 10 or 20 years later is high because almost all of the complete intellectual growth has taken place by age 15 (Bloom, 1964).

THE PRACTICAL IMPORTANCE OF INDIVIDUAL DIFFERENCES IN MEASURES OF INTELLIGENCE

To what extent are the individual differences that are brought out by tests of intelligence of importance in the practical affairs of life? Do they enable us to predict to a useful degree how an individual will perform in school, on a job, or in other life adjustments?

Intelligence and School Success

First, let us consider academic success. From the many hundreds of investigations of intelligence test scores in relation to academic success, a number of conclusions can safely be drawn. These may be summarized as follows:

1. *The correlation of intelligence test score with school marks is substantial.* Viewing all the hundreds of correlation coefficients that have been reported, a

figure of .50 to .60 might be taken as fairly representative. Though this constitutes a very definite relationship, it is only necessary to turn back to Fig. 5.7 and the discussion of correlation on p. 155 to realize that there are still many marked discrepancies between intelligence test score and what a particular youngster does in school.

2. *Higher correlations have been found in elementary schools than in high schools and in high schools than in colleges.* Past studies have indicated a drop in correlation from perhaps .70 in elementary school to .60 in high school and .50 in college. The drop in correlation is probably to be explained by the decreased range of intellectual ability in the college groups. A relatively small percentage from the lower half of a school population have gone on to college, and specific colleges draw from an even more restricted ability range. Although more and more young people are going to college, the clientele of specific colleges continues to be fairly homogeneous in ability.

3. *Previous school achievement has given correlations with later school success as high as or higher than intelligence test score.* In predicting college marks, for example, high-school record has usually shown correlations at least as high as those resulting from a scholastic aptitude test at entrance.

4. *Intelligence test and achievement combined give still better prediction.* By pooling information on previous school achievement and intelligence test score, the correlation with later school achievement can be raised above that yielded by either factor alone. The two types of information supplement one another. School marks provide evidence on motivation and on study skills and habits of work, as well as on basic ability; the uniform, objective aptitude test compensates for the variability in standards of achievement from school to school.

5. *Intelligence tests correlate higher with standardized measures of achievement than with school marks.* Correlations between an intelligence test and total score on an achievement battery in the .70's or even .80's are not unusual. Thus, for representative samples of over 2,500 in each grade, the *Lorge-Thorndike Intelligence Test* gave correlations with the *Iowa Tests of Basic Skills* in different grades as follows:

	L-T Verbal	*L-T Nonverbal*
Iowa—Vocabulary	.71–.82	.56–.65
Reading	.68–.82	.53–.69
Language	.73–.79	.61–.67
Study Skills	.72–.81	.62–.78
Arithmetic	.66–.75	.61–.71
Composite	.79–.88	.65–.77

6. *The degree to which intelligence tests are related to academic success depends upon the subject matter.* As one would expect, the more academic

subjects, which depend more completely upon the same kinds of verbal and numerical symbols as those that bulk so large in intelligence tests, show the higher correlations. Thus, one summary of studies in secondary and higher education (St. John, 1930) reports an average correlation of .46 with natural science grades and .38 with English grades and foreign language grades but only .28 with shop work and .22 with grades in domestic science.

The fact that intelligence tests correlate with academic achievement and school progress is unquestioned. From the very way in which the tests were assembled it could hardly be otherwise. How these facts should be capitalized upon in educational planning and individual guidance is a more troublesome matter. We will return to it later in the chapter.

Intelligence in Relation to Occupational Level

We turn our attention now to out-of-school accomplishments and consider how intelligence test scores relate to achievement in the world of work. There are two types of questions that we may raise: (1) How do workers in different kinds of jobs compare in measured intelligence? (2) Within a given kind of job, to what extent is intelligence related to job success?

In relation to the first question, we have a good deal of evidence stemming from the testing of recruits carried out during World War II. Data for a selection of representative jobs are shown in Table 10.3 on page 326. This table shows the 10th, 25th, 50th, 75th, and 90th percentiles on *Army General Classification Test* standard score (based on standardization with an average value of 100 and a standard deviation of 20). A marked gradient is noticed from such occupations as accountant, teacher, and lawyer to such occupations as barber, miner, and lumberjack. The gradient follows fairly closely the educational requirements or average educational background for each occupation. In general, one may say that occupations select out individuals jointly on the basis of educational level and of intelligence. Whether intelligence enters as a significant factor excepting as it relates to educational level is more difficult to determine. In any event, the net result is appreciable difference between different occupational groups in performance on intelligence tests.

While noticing the differences between groups, one must not forget the substantial score range within each group. Individuals differing widely in abstract intelligence function together in the same occupation. Thus, the upper 10 percent of meat cutters did as well on the *AGCT* as the average lawyer. The bottom 10 percent of lawyers showed no more intellectual ability than the upper 10 percent of miners. In spite of group differences in average score, there are still wide *individual* differences *within* groups.

TABLE 10.3 *AGCT* STANDARD SCORES OF OCCUPATIONAL GROUPS IN WORLD WAR II

	Percentile				
Occupational Groups	10	25	50	75	90
Accountant	114	121	129	136	143
Teacher	110	117	124	132	140
Lawyer	112	118	124	132	141
Bookkeeper, general	108	114	122	129	138
Chief clerk	107	114	122	131	141
Draftsman	99	109	120	127	137
Postal clerk	100	109	119	126	136
Clerk, general	97	108	117	125	133
Radio repairman	97	108	117	125	136
Salesman	94	107	115	125	133
Store manager	91	104	115	124	133
Tool maker	92	101	112	123	129
Stock clerk	85	99	110	120	127
Machinist	86	99	110	120	127
Policeman	86	96	109	118	128
Electrician	83	96	109	118	124
Meat cutter	80	94	108	117	126
Sheet metal worker	82	95	107	117	126
Machine operator	77	89	103	114	123
Automobile mechanic	75	89	102	114	122
Carpenter, general	73	86	101	113	123
Baker	69	83	99	113	123
Truck driver, heavy	71	83	98	111	120
Cook	67	79	96	111	120
Laborer	65	76	93	108	119
Barber	66	79	93	109	120
Miner	67	75	87	103	119
Farm worker	61	70	86	103	115
Lumberjack	60	70	85	100	116

Adapted from N. Stewart, 1947.

Intelligence and Job Success

What can we say about the relationship of intelligence test score to success within particular jobs? A summary of the findings reported in a number of different studies is presented in Table 10.4.

TABLE 10.4 VALIDITY OF INTELLIGENCE TESTS AS PREDICTORS OF TRAINING AND PROFICIENCY CRITERIA

	Training	Proficiency
Executives and administrators		.30
Foremen		.25
Clerks	.48	.30
Sales clerks		−.10
Salesmen		.33
Protective service	.53	.25
Personal service	.50	.07
Vehicle operators	.18	.14
Trades and crafts	.41	.18
Industrial workers	.38	.19

Adapted from E. E. Ghiselli, 1966.

When the criterion being predicted is success in a training program, the average correlations tend to run from .40 to .50 (with the one exception of the .18 for vehicle operators), and these values are not greatly different from the values obtained for success in school. When the criterion is one of job proficiency, the correlations are uniformly lower, ranging from −.10 for sales clerks to .33 for salesmen, and averaging about .20 over all occupations. In part, the lower correlations may be due to limitations in the *criterion* of job success. Whether success is measured by supervisors' ratings, as is usually the case, or by some index of production on the job, the indicator is likely to be unreliable and biased by a number of considerations that have nothing to do with the real efficiency of the worker. Insofar as this is true, no test given to the individual can be expected to predict the criterion.

All in all, we may conclude that (1) intelligence is related to occupational group membership and (2) though the relationship of intelligence test score to job success is usually positive, it is likely to be quite low. Prediction of on-the-job achievement appears a good deal less accurate than prediction of school achievement.

INTELLIGENCE TESTING AND THE CULTURALLY DEPRIVED

We have pointed out repeatedly that tests designed to measure intelligence are necessarily samples of present behavior, and that present behavior is a function not only of innate potential, but also of the life experiences of the individual. Makers of tests try to base them upon the experiences that are common to all children growing up in our society. But no experiences are universally or equally experienced by all. And some key experiences that are taken for granted in a middle-class culture may be meager or absent in most ghetto homes.

There is abundant evidence that intelligence test performance is influenced by general cultural background. Recruits in the United States Army showed a gain equivalent to almost one full standard deviation between World Wars I and II (Tuddenham, 1948). Tennessee mountain children showed IQ's in 1940 averaging 10 points higher than found for children in the same area in 1930 (Wheeler, 1942). Even since World War II, restandardizations of ability tests have found a rising trend in general population norms. These changes are associated with a complex of social changes, including longer years of schooling for children and for their parents, greater accessibility and mobility of people—especially those in the rural areas, the development and almost universal availability first of radio and then of television, and perhaps improvement in the materials and procedures of education.

The shifts that have just been described are upward shifts, reflecting extended and enriched experiences. But there are still groups in the United States, in the urban ghettos and in the rural backwaters, who do not fully share in the cultural enrichment of our times. Rather, they suffer a deprivation both in material things and in conditions that support intellectual growth and development in children. Some of the deficits that have been mentioned in the impoverished environment of the poor, and most acutely in the environment of the Negro poor are:

1. Generally restricted language patterns by those with whom he comes in contact.
2. Primarily restrictive and erratic discipline.
3. Absence of stable relationships with a supportive adult.
4. Attitudes of alienation from and powerlessness toward the social and educational "Establishment."
5. Lack of the toys, books, games, and other stimulus materials found in more favored homes.

Studies repeatedly show lower test performance for children from lower socioeconomic groups, and especially for the Negro poor, in the United States. There seems little question that a substantial part of this deficit is to be accounted for by environmental deficits of the types we have mentioned. Whether all of the difference is to be attributed to the conditions of life is probably unanswerable in any definitive way. The deficiency is not peculiarly or even primarily in verbal measures. Thus, Lesser, Fifer, and Clark (Lesser et al, 1965) studied test performance on several types of ability measures for middle-class and lower-class children from Jewish, Negro, Puerto Rican, and Chinese families. The results are shown in Fig. 10.7. It can be seen that the Negro child performed relatively *better* on verbal tests than on any other type. Also, the difference in level between middle-class and lower-class children showed up in all four ethnic groups and on all types of tests.

Whatever the original patterns of causation, by the time the child comes to school, and even more completely by the time he is a candidate for admission to a program of higher education or a job, the differences are there. The issue then becomes: What do any test results signify, in the case of persons from a deprived group, so far as potential for future achievement is concerned? Are the relationships between measures of present ability and future outcomes as high for pupils from limited backgrounds as for the generality of pupils? For a given score, how should the prognosis be modified, if at all, by knowledge that

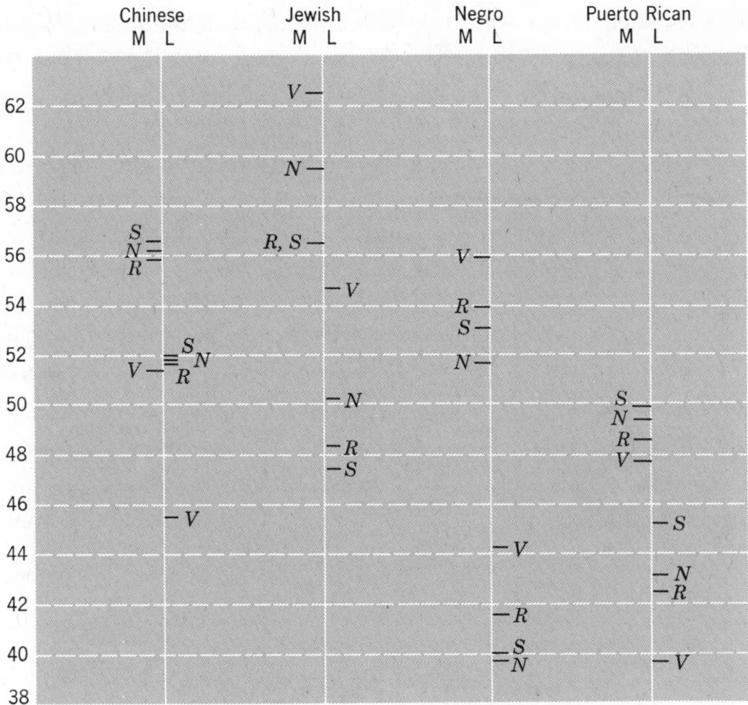

Fig. 10.7 Relative achievement of middle-class and lower-class children of different ethnic groups. *Key:* *N*, number; *R*, reasoning; *S*, spatial; and *V*, verbal. (Adapted from Lesser, Fifer, and Clark, 1965.)

the score was earned by a pupil from a meager environment? Since his score may have been held down by his environmental limitations, should we predict a higher school or job performance for him than for his more favored classmate who matches him in initial score? Should we predict essentially the same outcome for both? Or does experience indicate that the child from the more limited background will lapse back to a lower final level?

These questions are easier to ask than they are to answer. This is so, in part, because the answer may vary a good deal depending upon the age at which the initial measure was obtained. The answer will also depend very markedly upon what happens to the person in the interval between initial testing and the final assessment of outcomes. Because public policy has discouraged keeping separate records by race and socioeconomic level, there is less information than we might like on the predictive accuracy of aptitude test measures for Negro pupils and for general groups of pupils from low socioeconomic families. Studies of the prediction of academic achievement in predominantly Negro colleges (Stanley and Porter, 1967) yield correlations of much the same size as those found in other institutions. Again, when studied in integrated college settings, a given level of aptitude test score seems to predict about the same level of achievement for black and for white students (Cleary, 1968). Readiness tests, given to entering first-grade children, have been found to predict end-of-year achievement about equally well for Negroes, Mexicans, and Orientals as for Caucasian children (Mitchell, 1967). When no intervention is made to ameliorate conditions under which ghetto children grow up, the prognosis seems to be less favorable for a ghetto child than it is for a middle-class child starting at the same test level. There is some tendency (Coleman, 1967) for the lower socioeconomic Negro child to drop further down in the distribution of his age-mates the older he gets. Programs to break into the cycle of impoverishment and low ability have been numerous in recent years. These tend, in almost all cases, to emphasize *early* intervention, accepting the proposition that effective intervention must take place early in the life-history of the individual, while initial language and thought patterns are being established. Under these circumstances, it appears to have been possible to produce appreciable positive shifts in the mental growth curves, though it is still not clear how permanent the gains have been.

EXPECTED ACHIEVEMENT

One of the problems faced by any teacher or guidance worker is to know what level of achievement can reasonably be expected of any given child, and as a corollary of this, whether the child is doing as well as could reasonably be expected. The literature on underachievement would fill a good-sized library, and much of it is nonsense. At the very crudest level, we could set the same standard of expectancy for all children of a given age—and, in a sense, this is what the schools do when they admit all children to school at age six and expect all pupils to learn to read in the first grade. No tempering of expectation is introduced based upon other facts that are known about the child—his home background or his performance on a test of academic aptitude. Any child who falls below the average of all children is thought of as an underachiever, and educational effort and public concern are focused on bringing all children up to average—"up to the norm." This conception of what is to be expected is illustrated in diagram *A* of Fig. 10.8 on page 332.

But we now know that all 6-year-olds or all 10-year-olds are *not* the same—with respect to either native endowment or life experiences. The differences show up on our measures of academic aptitude as well as on any other measures that we can apply to children. How shall we take these differences into account in setting expectations and in conceiving of underachievement? One possibility is to expect each child to achieve in school at a level exactly matching his performance on measures of scholastic aptitude. The child who falls at the 99th percentile in aptitude is then expected to fall at the 99th percentile on achievement, the one at the 75th to be also at the 75th, and the one at the very bottom in aptitude to be at the very bottom in achievement. Any discrepancy through which achievement falls below aptitude is conceived as underachievement. This conception is shown in diagram *B* of Fig. 10.8.

But this conception is just as faulty as the conception that the same standard should be set for all. This second conception implies a +1.00 correlation between measures of aptitude and of achievement, and we simply do not find such a correlation. Nor should we. Putting aside for the moment errors of measurement, which are very real in both aptitude and achievement appraisals, the two involve somewhat different things. Especially as we consider marks by teachers, these reflect interest, effort, ability to understand what the teacher wants and skill at pleasing him, as well as capability in some special segment of academic content. So the correlation of aptitude with achievement is positive but not perfect, and the pupils at the very top in measured aptitude will be above average, but not necessarily at the very top in achievement. The realistic situation is displayed in diagram *C* of Fig. 10.8. A child at a given aptitude score level must be viewed in relation to the *average achievement of all pupils at his aptitude level.* He should be considered an underachiever if he falls seriously below that average performance.

A number of test publishers who offer both a measure of scholastic aptitude

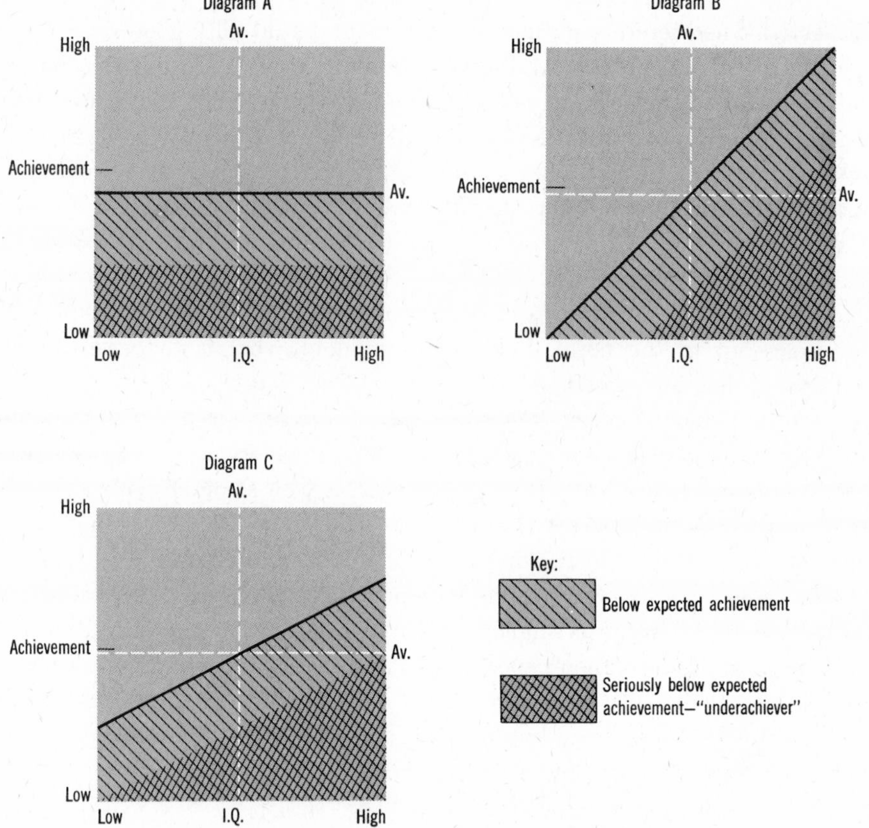

Fig. 10.8 Three conceptions of expected achievement.

and a measure of academic achievement provide some type of joint norms table indicating the level of achievement to be expected for a person who has performed at a particular level on the aptitude test. The tables are often provided separately by school grade or by chronological age. These tables are designed to help the teacher or guidance counselor judge whether the pupil is "doing as well as should be expected" in the light of his performance on the aptitude test.

The basic data from which tables of expected achievement are prepared are two-dimensional scatter-plots of achievement versus aptitude of the sort that we first encountered in Chapter 5. Taking a slice from such a plot, we can find the *average* achievement for a given level on the aptitude test, and this average value is certainly our best estimate of the expected value. However, very few children will fall exactly at the average value, and the question that we then have to face is whether the person falls far enough above or below the average of pupils at his aptitude test level for it to be a matter of interest or concern to us. A few publishers have produced actual percentile tables of achievement-for-aptitude-level. A fraction of such a table, based on the *Lorge-Thorndike Intelligence Test* and the *Iowa Test of Basic Skills,* is shown in Table 10.5 on pages 334–335.

The presentation of the information in Table 10.5 is a little difficult to follow at first exposure. Let us try to make clear how the table is to be read. There are four sections of the table shown. Each section applies to the pupils in a given Deviation IQ range on the *Lorge-Thorndike*—the first to those with DIQ's below 70, the second to those in the range 70–79, the third 80–89, and the fourth 90–99. The complete table in the *ITBS Manual* included additional sections for 100–109, 110–119, 120–129, and 130 and over.

Within a given section, the column on the extreme left shows the grade equivalent (GE), but without a decimal point. That is, the entry 45 should be read 4.5, or fifth month of the fourth grade. Each of the other columns refers to one of the subtests or tests of the *ITBS,* that is, Vocabulary, Reading, etc. The entries in each of these columns are percentiles.

Knowing a child's DIQ, we select the proper section of the table that corresponds to that IQ. Within the section, we select the column corresponding to a certain subtest, and the row corresponding to the pupil's grade equivalent (GE) on that subtest. Thus, if fifth grader Peter had obtained an IQ of 95 and a reading grade equivalent of 4.5, the table shows that his achievement is at the 40th percentile within his IQ group.

A full table like Table 10.5 is certainly the best way of making data on expected achievement available to test users. One sees directly not only whether a pupil is above or below what would have been predicted from knowledge of his aptitude test score but also how extreme his deviation is from the group average. A child who falls at the 40th percentile of his IQ group is hardly in any real sense an "underachiever," while one who falls at the 5th percentile would appear to be. However, these discrepancy scores are somewhat tricky creatures at best, and are to be approached with a good deal of circumspection.

First, no "aptitude" tests are pure measures of native potential. They are measures of what have sometimes been called "developed abilities." And those abilities are influenced by many of the same factors that influence academic achievement. A stimulating and supportive home environment, good language skills, interest in reading, application to school learning will all have some effect on aptitude measures, just as they will on academic achievement. Thus, when we set a low expectancy for achievement on the basis of low "aptitude" we may be saying in part "because this child has not achieved, he cannot be expected to achieve," and we may be perpetuating in our expectations the child's past failure to learn.

TABLE 10.5 PERCENTILE DISTRIBUTION OF *ITBS* GRADE EQUIVALENTS BY *Lorge-Thorndike* IQ.

GRADE 5: VERBAL

IQ LEVEL: BELOW 70

GE	Voc.	Rdg.	Test L: Language					Test W: Work Study				Test A: Arith.			Comp.
	V	R	L-1	L-2	L-3	L-4	L	W-1	W-2	W-3	W	A-1	A-2	A	C
56	99	99	99	99	99	99	99	99	99	99	99	99	99	99	99
55	99	99	99	99	99	99	99	99	98	99	99	99	98	99	99
54	99	99	99	99	98	99	99	98	98	99	99	99	97	99	99
53	99	99	99	99	98	99	99	97	97	99	99	99	96	99	99
52	99	99	99	99	97	98	99	96	96	99	99	98	95	99	99
51	99	99	98	99	97	97	99	95	94	98	99	97	94	99	99
50	99	98	98	99	96	97	99	94	93	97	98	96	93	99	99
49	98	97	97	98	96	96	99	93	91	96	97	95	92	98	99
48	97	96	96	97	95	95	99	91	90	95	96	93	90	97	99
47	97	95	95	96	94	95	99	90	88	93	95	92	88	96	99
46	96	94	94	95	93	94	99	88	86	91	93	90	86	94	98
45	95	92	92	94	92	92	98	85	83	89	91	88	84	93	97
44	93	90	90	93	90	91	97	83	81	86	89	86	81	91	96
43	92	88	89	91	88	90	96	80	78	84	87	83	78	88	94
42	90	85	87	90	87	88	94	77	76	80	84	80	74	86	93
41	89	82	84	88	84	87	93	73	73	76	80	75	70	82	91
40	86	78	82	86	81	85	91	69	70	72	74	71	66	77	88
39	84	74	79	84	78	83	89	65	66	67	68	66	62	71	86
38	81	70	76	80	74	81	86	61	62	63	61	60	57	65	81
37	78	65	73	76	70	78	84	57	58	58	54	55	53	58	75
36	75	60	69	71	66	75	80	52	53	54	46	50	49	51	67
35	71	55	66	66	62	72	75	48	48	48	38	44	44	44	56
34	67	49	62	62	58	69	69	44	44	44	32	39	39	36	46
33	62	44	58	57	53	64	61	40	39	38	26	34	34	30	36
32	58	40	55	52	49	60	53	36	35	33	22	30	30	24	28
31	54	36	52	46	45	56	45	32	31	28	17	26	26	19	22
30	48	31	48	40	40	51	37	27	26	22	13	21	22	14	16
29	43	27	44	35	36	46	29	23	22	18	10	17	18	10	12
28	38	23	40	29	32	42	22	19	18	14	07	13	15	08	09
27	33	18	36	24	27	37	16	15	14	10	05	10	13	05	07
26	28	15	32	19	23	32	11	12	12	08	04	08	11	04	05
25	23	11	28	15	19	28	08	09	09	06	03	06	09	03	03
24	18	08	24	12	16	23	05	06	07	04	02	04	07	02	02
23	13	06	20	10	12	19	03	05	05	03	01	03	05	01	01
22	09	05	16	08	09	15	02	03	04	02	01	02	04	01	01
21	06	04	12	06	07	11	01	02	03	01	01	01	03	01	01
20	04	03	09	04	05	08	01	01	02	01	01	01	02	01	01
19	02	02	06	03	03	05	01	01	01	01	01	01	01	01	01
18	01	01	04	02	02	03	01	01	01	01	01	01	01	01	01
17	01	01	02	01	01	02	01	01	01	01	01	01	01	01	01
16	01	01	01	01	01	01	01	01	01	01	01	01	01	01	01

IQ LEVEL: 70-79

GE	Voc.	Rdg.	Test L: Language					Test W: Work Study				Test A: Arith.			Comp.
	V	R	L-1	L-2	L-3	L-4	L	W-1	W-2	W-3	W	A-1	A-2	A	C
64	99	99	99	99	99	99	99	99	99	99	99	99	99	99	99
63	99	99	99	99	98	99	99	99	99	99	99	99	99	99	99
62	99	99	99	99	98	99	99	99	99	99	99	99	99	99	99
61	99	99	99	99	98	99	99	99	99	99	99	99	99	99	99
60	99	99	99	98	97	99	99	98	99	99	99	99	99	99	99
59	99	99	99	98	97	99	99	98	98	99	99	99	98	99	99
58	99	99	98	97	96	99	99	97	97	99	99	99	98	99	99
57	99	99	98	97	96	98	99	97	96	99	99	99	97	99	99
56	99	99	97	96	95	98	99	96	95	98	99	98	96	99	99
55	98	98	97	95	94	97	99	95	94	98	98	97	94	98	99
54	98	98	96	95	93	97	98	94	92	97	98	96	93	98	99
53	97	97	96	94	92	96	98	93	90	96	97	95	91	97	99
52	97	97	95	93	91	96	97	91	89	94	96	94	89	96	99
51	96	96	94	92	89	95	96	89	87	93	95	92	87	95	98
50	95	95	92	90	88	94	95	87	85	91	93	90	84	93	98
49	94	94	90	89	86	93	94	84	82	89	92	88	82	90	97
48	93	92	89	88	84	92	94	82	80	86	90	86	79	88	96
47	92	91	87	86	82	90	92	80	78	83	88	84	76	85	95
46	91	89	85	85	80	88	90	77	76	80	86	81	73	82	94
45	89	86	82	83	78	86	89	74	73	76	83	78	70	78	92
44	88	84	79	80	76	84	86	71	70	72	80	74	66	73	90
43	86	80	77	78	74	81	84	68	67	69	76	71	62	69	88
42	83	76	74	75	70	78	81	64	64	64	72	67	58	64	86
41	80	72	71	72	68	75	79	61	61	61	68	63	54	59	83
40	76	67	68	68	65	72	76	58	58	56	62	58	50	54	78
39	72	63	64	64	61	69	71	55	54	52	55	54	47	49	73
38	68	58	61	60	57	65	66	52	50	48	48	48	43	44	65
37	63	53	57	55	53	62	62	48	47	45	40	44	39	39	55
36	58	48	54	51	49	58	57	44	43	41	34	39	35	33	46
35	54	43	50	46	45	54	51	40	39	37	28	34	31	28	37
34	50	38	46	41	40	50	45	36	35	33	22	29	27	23	28
33	46	34	43	36	36	46	40	32	31	28	18	24	24	18	21
32	41	29	39	32	32	42	34	28	27	23	14	19	20	14	15
31	37	25	35	28	28	38	29	25	23	19	10	14	17	10	10
30	33	20	32	24	24	34	24	21	18	14	08	11	14	08	07
29	28	17	28	20	21	31	18	17	14	10	06	07	12	06	06
28	24	14	24	16	18	28	13	13	11	07	05	05	10	04	04
27	20	12	21	13	15	24	08	09	09	05	04	04	08	03	03
26	16	09	17	10	12	20	05	06	07	04	03	03	06	02	02
25	12	08	14	08	10	17	03	05	05	03	02	02	05	01	01
24	10	06	12	06	08	14	02	03	04	02	01	02	03	01	01
23	07	05	09	05	06	11	01	02	03	01	01	01	02	01	01
22	05	04	07	04	04	08	01	01	02	01	01	01	01	01	01
21	03	03	05	03	03	05	01	01	01	01	01	01	01	01	01
20	02	02	04	02	02	03	01	01	01	01	01	01	01	01	01
19	01	01	02	01	01	02	01	01	01	01	01	01	01	01	01
18	01	01	01	01	01	01	01	01	01	01	01	01	01	01	01

IQ LEVEL: 80-89

GE	Voc.	Rdg.	Test L: Language					Test W: Work Study				Test A: Arith.			Comp.
	V	R	L-1	L-2	L-3	L-4	L	W-1	W-2	W-3	W	A-1	A-2	A	C
69	99	99	99	99	99	99	99	99	99	99	99	99	99	99	99
68	99	99	99	98	98	99	99	99	99	99	99	99	99	99	99
67	99	99	99	98	98	99	99	99	99	99	99	99	99	99	99
66	99	99	98	97	97	99	99	99	99	99	99	99	99	99	99
65	99	99	98	96	97	99	99	99	99	99	99	99	99	99	99
64	99	99	97	96	96	99	99	99	99	99	99	99	99	99	99
63	99	99	97	95	96	99	99	99	99	99	99	99	98	99	99
62	99	99	96	94	95	98	99	98	98	99	99	99	98	99	99
61	99	99	96	94	94	98	99	98	98	99	99	99	97	99	99
60	99	98	95	93	94	97	98	97	96	98	99	98	96	99	99
59	98	98	94	92	93	96	98	96	95	98	99	98	95	98	99
58	98	97	94	92	92	95	97	95	94	97	99	97	94	97	99
57	97	97	93	91	91	95	96	93	92	96	98	96	93	97	99
56	97	96	92	90	90	94	95	92	90	95	97	94	92	96	99
55	96	95	90	88	89	93	94	90	88	93	96	93	90	94	98
54	95	94	89	87	87	91	92	88	86	92	94	92	87	93	98
53	94	93	88	86	86	90	91	85	84	90	93	90	85	91	97
52	92	91	86	84	84	89	90	82	82	87	91	88	82	89	96
51	90	89	84	82	82	87	88	79	80	85	89	85	79	87	94
50	88	86	80	80	80	85	86	76	78	82	86	83	76	85	92
49	86	84	78	78	77	83	84	72	75	78	84	80	73	81	90
48	84	80	75	74	74	80	82	69	72	74	80	76	70	77	88
47	81	77	72	71	71	77	79	65	69	69	76	72	66	72	86
46	79	73	68	68	68	74	76	62	66	64	72	68	62	67	82
45	76	69	64	64	64	71	72	58	63	60	67	63	58	61	79
44	72	65	60	61	60	68	68	54	59	55	61	58	54	56	74
43	69	61	56	58	56	64	64	50	56	50	55	54	50	51	68
42	65	57	53	54	52	60	60	46	53	46	49	48	46	46	61
41	61	53	50	50	48	57	56	43	50	42	44	44	42	41	54
40	58	49	46	46	45	54	52	40	46	38	37	39	38	36	46
39	54	45	42	42	41	50	48	37	42	34	31	34	34	31	39
38	50	41	38	39	37	46	44	34	38	31	26	29	30	26	33
37	46	37	35	34	34	43	38	31	34	28	21	24	26	22	27
36	42	33	32	30	30	40	33	28	30	24	16	19	22	18	20
35	38	29	29	26	27	36	27	24	26	21	12	15	19	14	15
34	35	24	26	22	24	33	22	22	23	18	10	13	16	10	10
33	31	20	23	18	22	30	18	18	20	15	07	10	14	08	06
32	28	17	20	15	19	28	14	15	16	12	06	08	11	06	04
31	24	14	18	13	16	25	10	13	13	10	04	06	10	04	03
30	20	11	16	10	14	22	08	10	10	08	03	04	08	02	02
29	17	09	14	08	12	19	06	08	08	06	02	03	06	01	01
28	14	07	12	07	10	16	04	06	06	04	01	02	05	01	01
27	11	05	10	05	08	14	02	04	04	02	01	01	04	01	01
26	09	04	09	04	07	11	01	02	03	01	01	01	03	01	01
25	06	03	07	03	05	09	01	01	02	01	01	01	02	01	01
24	04	02	06	02	04	07	01	01	02	01	01	01	01	01	01
23	03	01	04	01	03	05	01	01	01	01	01	01	01	01	01
22	02	01	03	01	02	03	01	01	01	01	01	01	01	01	01
21	01	01	02	01	01	02	01	01	01	01	01	01	01	01	01
20	01	01	01	01	01	01	01	01	01	01	01	01	01	01	01

IQ LEVEL: 90-99

GE	Voc.	Rdg.	Test L: Language					Test W: Work Study				Test A: Arith.			Comp.
	V	R	L-1	L-2	L-3	L-4	L	W-1	W-2	W-3	W	A-1	A-2	A	C
76	99	99	99	99	99	99	99	99	99	99	99	99	99	99	99
75	99	99	99	98	99	99	99	99	99	99	99	99	99	99	99
74	99	99	99	97	98	98	99	99	99	99	99	99	99	99	99
73	99	99	98	97	98	98	99	99	99	99	99	99	99	99	99
72	99	99	98	96	97	98	99	99	99	99	99	99	99	99	99
71	99	99	97	95	96	97	99	99	99	99	99	99	99	99	99
70	99	99	97	95	96	96	99	98	98	99	99	99	99	99	99
69	99	99	96	94	95	96	99	98	98	99	99	99	99	99	99
68	99	99	95	93	94	95	98	97	97	99	99	99	99	99	99
67	99	99	94	92	93	94	98	97	97	99	99	99	98	99	99
66	98	98	93	91	92	93	97	96	96	98	99	99	98	99	99
65	98	98	92	89	90	92	97	95	95	97	98	98	97	99	99
64	98	97	91	88	89	91	96	94	94	96	98	97	96	99	99
63	97	96	90	86	87	90	94	92	93	94	97	96	95	98	99
62	96	95	88	85	86	88	93	91	92	93	96	95	94	97	99
61	95	94	86	83	84	87	92	89	90	92	94	94	92	96	98
60	94	93	85	81	83	85	90	88	87	90	93	92	90	94	97
59	92	91	83	80	81	83	87	85	85	88	91	90	88	92	96
58	90	89	80	78	78	81	85	83	82	85	89	88	84	90	95
57	88	88	78	76	76	79	82	80	79	83	87	85	81	87	93
56	86	85	75	73	73	76	79	77	76	80	84	82	76	84	90
55	83	83	72	70	70	73	76	74	73	76	81	78	72	80	88
54	79	79	69	67	67	70	73	70	70	72	78	75	68	76	84
53	76	74	65	64	64	68	70	66	67	68	74	71	64	72	80
52	72	69	62	61	61	65	67	62	64	64	69	67	60	68	75
51	68	65	59	58	58	62	63	59	61	59	65	62	56	64	70
50	64	60	55	55	54	59	59	55	58	53	60	58	52	58	64
49	60	56	52	52	50	57	54	50	55	49	54	54	48	54	58
48	56	52	49	48	47	54	51	46	52	44	49	49	44	50	52
47	52	48	46	45	44	51	47	42	49	40	44	45	42	46	47
46	48	44	43	42	40	49	43	39	46	36	38	41	38	41	41
45	44	40	40	38	36	46	39	35	42	33	33	37	35	37	35
44	41	36	36	36	33	43	35	32	39	30	28	33	32	32	29
43	38	32	33	33	30	40	32	29	35	26	24	29	29	28	24
42	34	27	30	30	28	38	28	27	32	23	20	25	26	24	18
41	30	24	28	27	25	35	24	23	29	20	16	21	23	19	14
40	26	20	25	24	22	33	20	20	26	17	12	18	20	15	11
39	23	17	22	21	20	30	17	18	23	15	10	14	17	12	08
38	20	15	19	18	18	28	14	16	20	13	08	11	15	09	06
37	17	13	16	15	16	26	11	13	17	11	06	09	12	07	04
36	15	11	14	12	14	23	09	12	15	09	04	07	10	05	03
35	13	10	12	10	13	21	07	10	13	07	03	06	08	03	02
34	11	08	11	08	11	18	05	08	11	06	02	04	07	02	01
33	10	07	09	07	10	16	04	07	09	05	01	03	06	01	01
32	08	06	07	06	09	14	03	05	07	04	01	02	05	01	01
31	07	05	07	05	07	12	02	04	06	03	01	02	04	01	01
30	06	04	05	04	06	10	01	03	05	02	01	01	03	01	01
29	05	03	04	03	05	08	01	02	04	01	01	01	02	01	01
28	04	02	03	02	04	07	01	01	03	01	01	01	02	01	01
27	03	02	03	01	03	05	01	01	02	01	01	01	01	01	01
26	02	01	02	01	03	04	01	01	01	01	01	01	01	01	01
25	02	01	02	01	02	03	01	01	01	01	01	01	01	01	01
24	01	01	01	01	01	02	01	01	01	01	01	01	01	01	01
23	01	01	01	01	01	01	01	01	01	01	01	01	01	01	01

Second, just because of the substantial correlation between measures of scholastic aptitude and of academic achievement, the discrepancies between them are appraised at a pretty low level of reliability. Thus, the percentile values reported in Table 10.5 are much less dependable than percentiles that would be reported for a complete grade group or age group. The reliability of these difference scores range from about .50 to .70 for different sections of the achievement test, whereas the reliabilities of the aptitude and achievement tests taken separately are around .90. So, it is only as the individual shows a rather extreme deviation, in percentile terms, from the average value of his IQ group that we can say with confidence that his performance falls above or below expectation.

USING INTELLIGENCE TEST RESULTS IN SCHOOLS

There are, in general, three types of settings in which standardized tests are used in schools, and intelligence tests should be considered in relation to each of these. Standardized tests may enter into administrative policy as a basis for administrative decisions on such matters as class grouping, promotion, eligibility for certain classes and curricula, and the like. Standardized tests may be used by the classroom teacher as aids to understanding the individual pupils with whom he must deal and in making adaptations and adjustments to their individual needs. Tests may be used by the guidance staff of the school in planning the most effective use of special resources for diagnostic and remedial teaching, in helping the pupil and his family arrive at sound and realistic educational and vocational plans, and in helping understand personal adjustment crises when they arise. We may consider intelligence tests in each of these contexts.

Intelligence Tests and the School Administration

Intelligence tests are likely to enter into the actions of the school administration either (1) through a policy of using test results as one basis for forming the group for a classroom or (2) through regulations specifying score levels that permit or require some special action, e.g., assignment to a slow-learning class, eligibility to take algebra, eligibility for a special school, etc. What is an appropriate attitude toward administrative actions of these sorts?

GROUPING BY INTELLECTUAL ABILITY. The policy of forming class groups, at least in part on the basis of the intellectual level of the pupils, remains a common one. In a survey of 714 public elementary schools, carried out about 1963, Goslin (1967) found that about 30 percent reported using individual intelligence tests and about 40 percent group intelligence tests as one basis for grouping students.*

However, the procedure remains a controversial one. In part, this is due to the varied and somewhat contradictory results obtained in studies of the effects of ability grouping (Goldberg et al, 1966). In part, it is due to the variety of specific practices subsumed under the same label of "ability grouping" or "homogeneous grouping." In part it is based upon the different initial biases of those discussing the problem.

It is probably impossible to make any single general evaluation of ability grouping that would apply to all instances of the practice. It can be pointed out that grouping together pupils of like mental ages is only a *first step* to permit adapting class program and procedures to the abilities of the pupils in the class. What is most important is the adaptations that are actually made in materials and procedures after the grouping has been carried out—and also what attitudes exist or can be developed in the community toward the grouping and the adjustments that accompany it. It should also be noted that groups formed on the basis of intelligence test scores will still be quite heterogeneous with respect to academic skills. The correlations of intelligence and achievement, and of different aspects of achievement are low enough so that forming groups on any one measure will still leave quite a range of performance on any of the others. In a departmentalized program, as in high school, effective grouping in separate subject areas can be based on a combination of an intelligence test and a measure of achievement in the subject area. Though a general evaluation of achievement can be combined with intelligence test score for elementary school pupils, it is not possible to get a group homogeneous for all subject areas.

Many of both the gains and hazards of ability grouping have been claimed to lie in relatively intangible areas of interest, attitude, and adjustment. Evaluations in these areas have generally been quite inadequate. Thus, it is still largely a matter of opinion whether the bright child develops better work habits and leadership traits or feelings of snobbishness and superiority from being in a special class group.

Ability grouping for the bulk of pupils is one issue, and special classes for the relatively extreme deviate is a somewhat different one.

How about the highest and lowest 2 or 3 or 5 percent in intelligence? Here we must recognize that special administrative provisions are possible only in a community of some size. Unless there are perhaps 500 children per grade in the school system, there will not be enough extreme deviates to fill a class group. The problem of the extreme deviate becomes most acute in the case of the low

* These percents overlap somewhat, so the total using some type of intelligence test is at least 40 but less than 70.

deviate, because of the obvious problems that the slow learners have in adapting to the activities and tempo of a regular classroom. Special class groups have not been a universal panacea, but they do permit adaptation of the type of class activities and the rate of progress to the interests and abilities of the slower learners.

The very bright child is usually a less conspicuous problem in the regular class. He gets the regular work done. His boredom is less apparent. Furthermore, the alert teacher can often provide supplementary activities which will keep him profitably occupied. However, there is evidence (Justman, 1953) that children of high ability who are placed in special groups can master the regular school curriculum more rapidly than they would in regular classes, or engage in a wide range of enrichment activities without falling behind children in regular schools. Furthermore, there is no real evidence that membership in special class groups results in undesirable personality attributes in these children. In view of the importance of individuals of high ability for our society and in view of the long period of training that most of them must undergo to take a role in the professional groups of our society, special provisions to accelerate or enrich their early training would seem to be a sound social provision where such provisions are administratively feasible.

INTELLIGENCE TEST SCORE AS AN ADMINISTRATIVE PREREQUISITE. Intelligence test results enter into administrative actions when a certain level of intelligence is specified as a prerequisite for some action in relation to a pupil. Generally speaking, the relationship of intelligence test score to educational progress or success is low enough and the variety of factors involved is great enough so that rigid administrative standards on intelligence seem rather questionable. Intelligence is often a factor that should receive consideration, together with other factors, in arriving at a decision with respect to any individual. But room for flexibility of action is needed, in the light of all relevant factors. An administration should formulate general policy with respect to the use of intelligence tests for admitting pupils to special groups, but the policy should be one which permits actions on individual cases to be taken in the light of a variety of relevant factors.

Intelligence Tests and the Classroom Teacher

The classroom teacher will want to use intelligence test results as an aid to understanding each pupil in the class and to providing the school experiences that will be most helpful to that pupil. The child's level as measured by an intelligence test provides one of the best clues available to the teacher as to the child's potentialities for learning the abstract symbolic aspects of the school curriculum. The test results provide a guide as to what can reasonably be expected of each pupil: whether the pupil should be expected to move along as rapidly as the rest of the class, whether the pupil's achievement is falling enough behind expectation to suggest the need for special diagnostic or remedial procedures, or whether the pupil's abilities are enough ahead of those of the bulk of the class so that the teacher should try to provide special activities and opportunities for enriching the regular program.

There are certain cautions that need to be observed when the classroom teacher makes use of intelligence test scores for his pupils. An enumeration of the pitfalls may help the reader to avoid them.

1. The general intelligence test, especially the group test, is a measure of ability to work with symbols, abstract ideas, and their relationships. This is one quite limited type of ability. The test does not encompass ability to work with things or people, or perhaps the ability to solve many types of concrete and practical problems. The child who is low on an intelligence test will probably have trouble with the academic aspects of the conventional school curriculum. However, he may have a good level of skill or ability in the many non-abstract aspects of living—mechanical, social, artistic, musical. The teacher should seek these strengths, capitalize upon them, and build upon them. *Above all, the teacher must recognize that intelligence test score is not a measure of personal worth and must avoid rejecting the child whose aptitude for academic pursuits is low.*

2. The verbal group intelligence test that is ordinarily used for school-wide testing is sufficiently dependent upon reading and arithmetical skills that a low test score must be interpreted cautiously for a poor reader or low achiever in arithmetical skills. If possible, individuals of this sort should be tested also with an individual test or a nonverbal group test to determine whether the low performance is due to limited ability, or whether it is a reflection of limited reading and number skills.

3. Intelligence test results for a child whose social and cultural background differs radically from that of the rest of the group should be interpreted with caution. The possibility of some degree of environmental deprivation should be borne in mind.

4. If it is known or suspected that a child was emotionally disturbed at the time of testing, results should be considered quite tentative. Motivation and effort are needed for sound test results.

5. The standard error of measurement should always be very real to the test interpreter. An IQ of 90 should always signify to the teacher "IQ somewhere between 80 and 100."

Intelligence Tests and the Guidance Staff

Intelligence tests have their most obvious function in the educational program as sources of information important to persons responsible for counseling and helping the child with problems of personal and social adjustment, making provisions for special educational activities for him, helping him to decide on appropriate educational objectives, and working with him to formulate vocational plans. In plans and decisions of all these types, it is important to have a clear picture of the pupil's intellectual abilities as one aspect of the total picture of the pupil as an individual.

In educational guidance information about scholastic aptitude is especially important. This information should receive very serious consideration in deciding what is an appropriate educational objective for the pupil; that is, whether to plan for college and if so the kind of college to plan for, or what type of high school curriculum to select. In vocational counseling, more specialized ability measures, of the kinds we shall consider in the next chapter, are desirable as a supplement to the general intelligence test, but these specialized tests are not so important for educational planning. For understanding a child who is having problems in school, whether with his school work or his personal adjustments, an estimate of his intellectual level is essential. As we have indicated elsewhere, individual tests and nonlanguage tests are highly desirable supplements to the usual group test when any reading or language handicap is suspected.

The specific situations and circumstances under which intelligence tests may be used in guidance are so many and varied that they cannot each be discussed here. Some further consideration is given to tests in the guidance program in Chapter 18.

SUMMARY STATEMENT

Tests of ability include tests of achievement and of aptitude. Though aptitude tests usually depend less directly upon specific teaching than do achievement tests, it must be recognized that any test performance is in some degree a function of the individual's background of experience. Aptitude tests are distinguished at least in part by their function—to predict future accomplishments.

Among the most thoroughly explored and widely used aptitude tests are tests of intelligence. As these have been developed, they tend to emphasize abstract intelligence, the ability to deal with ideas and symbols, and may even be thought of as scholastic aptitude tests.

The two main patterns of tests have been group tests and individual tests. Group tests, resembling the short-answer achievement test in format, are much more economical to use and are satisfactory for many purposes when the examinees are normal groups of school age or older. However, the individual tests have a number of advantages and are useful particularly with (1) young children, (2) emotionally disturbed cases, and (3) cases with special educational disabilities.

Special tests have been developed for infant and preschool groups, for groups with educational and language handicaps, and for groups from varied cultures and social classes. These may be of practical value in special cases, though they serve more often as research tools.

Intelligence test results for school-age children are about as reliable as any of our psychological measurement tools. The widely used individual tests such as the *Stanford-Binet Intelligence Scale* and the *Wechsler Intelligence Scales* are probably somewhat more reliable than the typical group test, though the differences are not large. In spite of the high reliability, appreciable differences may be expected between one testing and another.

When intelligence test scores are studied in relation to achievement in the world, the most clear-cut relationships are with academic achievement. However, it is also true that there are substantial differences in test performance between persons in different types of jobs. Furthermore, success in at least some types of jobs has been found to be related to the abstract intelligence measured by our tests.

Group differences in intelligence (that is, sex, race, age differences) must be interpreted quite tentatively, in view of the differences in background for these different groups. However, *individual* differences in intelligence are important facts, which we need to use wisely in helping individuals in their adjustment to the world of the school and of work.

QUESTIONS AND EXERCISES

1. It has been proposed that all intelligence tests should really be called scholastic aptitude tests. What are the merits and the limitations of this proposal?

2. Why is it better to depend upon a good intelligence test for an estimate of a pupil's intelligence than upon ratings by teachers?

3. In each of the following situations would you elect to use a group intelligence test or an individual intelligence test? Why?

   a. You are studying a boy with a serious speech impediment.
   b. You are selecting students for a school of nursing.

c. You are preparing to counsel a high-school senior on his educational and vocational plans.
d. You are making a study of the Mexican children in a school system in Arizona.
e. You are working with a group of delinquents in a state institution.

4. In which of the following situations would you routinely first give the *Arthur Point Scale* rather than the *Stanford-Binet?* Why did you decide as you did?

a. For testing Puerto Rican children entering school in New York City.
b. For selecting children for a special class of gifted children.
c. For evaluating intelligence in a school for the deaf.
d. For studying children who have reading problems.

5. What are the implications for child placement agencies of the data on infant tests presented on p. 312?

6. Why do two different intelligence tests given to the same pupil quite frequently give two different IQ's.

7. Are the usual group intelligence tests more useful for guidance for professional occupations or for skilled occupations? Why?

8. A news article reported that a young woman who had been committed to a mental hospital with an IQ of 62 had been able to raise her IQ to 118 during the 3 years she had spent there. What is misleading about this news statement? What factors could account for the difference between the two IQ's?

9. In what respects are intelligence tests better than high-school grades as predictors of college success? In what respects are they less good?

10. Why do intelligence tests show higher correlations with standardized achievement tests than they do with school grades?

11. Comment on the statement: "College admissions officers should discount scholastic aptitude test scores of applicants who come from low socio-economic groups."

12. You are a fourth-grade teacher. You have given a group intelligence test to your class and gotten IQ's from it. What additional information would you want to have on the pupils? What sorts of specific action and plans might grow out of the test results?

13. An eighth grader has received the following IQ's on the *Lorge-Thorndike Intelligence Test, Verbal:* Grade 4–98, Grade 6–106, Grade 8–104. What would be the best figure to represent his "true" scholastic aptitude?

14. A school in a prosperous community gave *Stanford-Binet* intelligence tests to all entering kindergartners and all first graders who had not been tested in kindergarten within the first week or two of school. How desirable and useful a procedure is this? Why?

15. A school system wanted to set up procedures to identify pupils to receive remedial instruction in reading. These were to be those pupils whose reading was falling seriously behind their potential for learning to read. What would be a sound procedure for accomplishing this?

REFERENCES

Ammons, R. B. & H. S. *Full-Range Picture Vocabulary Test.* Missoula, Montana: Psychological Test Specialists, 1948.

Anderson, J. E. The limitations of infant and preschool tests in the measurement of intelligence. *Journal of Psychology,* 1939, **8,** 351–379.

Arthur, G. *A point scale of performance tests.* (2nd ed.) New York: Commonwealth Fund, 1943.

Bayley, N. Consistency and variability in the growth of intelligence from birth to eighteen years. *Journal of Genetic Psychology,* 1949, **75,** 165–196.

Bloom, B. S. *Stability and change in human characteristics.* New York: Wiley, 1964.

Bradway, K. P. & Thompson, C. W. Intelligence at adulthood: A twenty-five year follow-up. *Journal of Educational Psychology,* 1962, **53,** 1–14.

Brown, A. W. The development and standardization of the Chicago Non-verbal Examination. *Journal of Applied Psychology,* 1940, **24,** 36–47, 122–129.

Cleary, T. A. Test bias: Validity of the Scholastic Aptitude Test for Negro and white students. *College Entrance Examination Board Research Bulletin,* June 1966.

Coleman, J. S. et al. *Equality of educational opportunity.* Washington, D.C.: United States Government Printing Office, 1966.

Doppelt, J. Estimating full-scale score on the Wechsler Adult Intelligence Scale from scores on four sub-tests. *Journal of Consulting Psychology,* 1956, **20,** 63–66.

Dunn, L. M. *Peabody Picture Vocabulary Test.* Minneapolis, Minn.: American Guidance Services, Inc., 1959.

Ebert, E. & Simmons, K. The Brush Foundation study of child growth and development. I: Psychometric tests. *Monograph of the Society for Research in Child Development,* 1943, **8,** No. 2.

Gesell, A. et. al. *The first five years of life: A guide to the study of the pre-school child.* New York: Harper, 1940.

Ghiselli, E. E. *The validity of occupational aptitude tests.* New York: Wiley, 1966.

Goldberg, M. L., Passow, H. & Justman, J. *The effects of ability grouping.* New York: Teachers College Press, 1966.

Goslin, D. A. *Teachers and testing.* New York: Russell Sage Foundation, 1967.

Goodenough, F. L. & Maurer, K. M. The mental growth of children from two to fourteen years: A study of the predictive value of the Minnesota Preschool Scales, *University of Minnesota Institute of Child Welfare Monograph,* 1942, No. 19.

Goodenough, F. L., Maurer, K. M., & Van Wagenen, M. J. *Minnesota Preschool Scales: Manual of instructions.* Minneapolis, Minnesota: Educational Test Bureau, 1940.

Harris, D. B. *Children's drawings as measures of intellectual maturity.* New York: Harcourt, Brace & World, 1963.

Honzik, M. P., McFarlane, J. W. & Allen, L. The stability of mental test performance between two and eighteen years. *Journal of Experimental Education,* 1948, **17,** 309–324.

Justman, J. A comparison of the functioning of intellectually gifted children enrolled in special progress classes in the junior high school. Unpublished doctoral dissertation, Columbia University, 1953.

Knobloch, H. & Passamanick, B. Prediction from the assessment of neuromotor and intellectual status in infancy. In J. Zubin and G. A. Jervis (Eds.), *Psychopathology of mental development.* New York: Grune & Stratton, 1967.

Lesser, G. S., Fifer, G., & Clark, D. H. Mental abilities of children from different social-class and cultural groups. *Monographs of the Society for Research in Child Development,* 1965, **30,** No. 4.

Mitchell, B. C. Predictive validity of the Metropolitan Readiness Tests and Murphy-Durrell Reading Readiness Tests for white and Negro students. *Educational and Psychological Measurement,* 1967, **27,** 1047–1054.

Mogul, S. & Satz, P. Abbreviation of the WAIS for clinical use: An attempt at validation. *Journal of Clinical Psychology,* 1963, **19,** 298–300.

Neville, D. The relationship between reading skills and intelligence test scores. *The Reading Teacher,* 1965, **18,** 257–262.

Owens, W. A., Jr. The retest consistency of Army Alpha after 30 years. *Journal of Applied Psychology,* 1954, **38,** 154.

Raven, J. C. *Progressive Matrices.* London: H. K. Lewis, 1956 (U.S. Distributor, Psychological Corp.)

St. John, C. W. Educational achievement in relation to intelligence as shown by teachers' marks, promotions and scores in standard tests in certain elementary grades. *Harvard University Studies in Education,* 1930, 15.

Stanley, J. C. & Porter, A. C. Correlation of scholastic aptitude test score with college grades for Negroes versus whites. *Journal of Educational Measurement,* 1967, **4,** 199–218.

Stewart, N. A.G.C.T. scores of army personnel grouped by occupations. *Occupations,* 1947, **26,** 5–41.

Stutsman, R. *Mental measurement of pre-school children, with a guide for the administration of the Merrill-Palmer Scale of mental tests.* Yonkers, New York: World Book, 1931.

Terman, L. M. & Merrill, M. A. *Stanford-Binet Intelligence Scale, manual for the third revision, form L-M.* Boston: Houghton Mifflin, 1960.

Thorndike, R. L. The prediction of intelligence at college entrance from earlier tests. *Journal of Educational Psychology,* 1947, **38,** 129–148.

Tuddenham, R. D. Soldier intelligence in World Wars I and II. *American Psychologist,* 1948, **3,** 54–56.

Wechsler, D. *Wechsler Adult Intelligence Scale.* New York: Psychological Corporation, 1955.

Wechsler, D. *Wechsler Intelligence Scale for Children: Manual.* New York: Psychological Corp., 1949.

Wechsler, D. *Wechsler Preschool and Primary Scale of Intelligence.* New York: Psychological Corporation, 1967.

Wheeler, L. R. A comparative study of the intelligence of east Tennessee mountain children, *Journal of Educational Psychology,* 1942, **33,** 321–334.

SUGGESTED ADDITIONAL READING

Anastasi, A. Culture fair testing. In N. E. Gronlund (Ed.), *Readings in measurement and evaluation.* New York: Macmillan, 1968. Pp. 280–286.

Bayley, N. A new look at the curve of intelligence. In A. Anastasi (Ed.), *Testing problems in perspective.* Washington, D.C.: American Council on Education, 1966. Pp. 384–399.

Bloom, B. S. *Stability and change in human characteristics.* New York: John Wiley & Sons, 1964.

Brim, O. G., Jr. American attitudes toward intelligence tests. In J. T. Flynn and H. Garber (Eds.), *Assessing behavior: Readings in educational and psychological measurement.* Reading, Massachusetts: Addison-Wesley, 1967. Pp. 160–170.

Lavin, D. E. *The prediction of academic performance, a theoretical analysis and review of research.* New York: Russell Sage Foundation, 1965.

McNemar, Q. Lost: Our intelligence. Why? In C. I. Chase and H. G. Ludlow (Eds.), *Readings in educational and psychological measurement.* Boston: Houghton Mifflin, 1966. Pp. 180–197.

Miner, J. B. *Intelligence in the United States.* New York: Springer, 1957.

Shuey, A. M. *The testing of Negro intelligence.* (2nd ed.) New York: Social Science Press, 1966.

Stott, L. H. & Ball, R. S. Infant and preschool mental tests: Review and evaluation. *Monographs of the Society for Research in Child Development,* 1965, **30,** No. 3.

Thorndike, R. L. *The concepts of over- and under-achievement.* New York: Teachers College Press, 1963.

CHAPTER 11

The Measurement of Special Aptitudes

THE tests that we reviewed in Chapter 10 were tests of general mental ability. In many cases they resulted in a single score that represented an overall appraisal of the individual's ability to deal with abstract ideas and relationships. However, we found that a number of them did produce two or more scores of a more specialized nature that were designed to provide more specific and analytical information about the individual, for example, the verbal and performance IQ's of the *Wechsler* scales. The concern for specific information on more restricted segments of the ability domain has led to the development of test batteries and single tests to measure specialized aptitudes. It is these tests that we shall consider in the present chapter. We will direct our attention first to batteries and tests designed for vocational guidance and vocational selection. Then we will consider specialized tests for prognosis and prediction in special school subjects and in special types of schools. Finally, we will take a brief look at tests in the specialized fields of art and music, and at efforts to appraise "creativity."

VOCATIONAL APTITUDE BATTERIES AND TESTS

One of the first practical matters with which psychologists were concerned was guiding young people into the types of work in which they would be happy and successful and selecting for an employer those men who would be efficient and satisfied in the jobs that he was trying to fill. As psychologists began to study jobs, it seemed apparent that different ones required different special abilities as well as different levels of general mental ability. The automotive mechanic required a good deal of mechanical knowledge, but little verbal fluency, while the lawyer needed verbal comprehension but not mechanical skill. The bookkeeper needed good ability with numbers, while the watchmaker needed fine coordination in his finger movements. The ability requirements of jobs appeared to differ along a number of specialized dimensions.

At the same time, research demonstrated that human abilities are to some degree specialized. This has been shown in studies of the correlations between different tests. Consider the correlations shown in Table 11.1 between six tests of a battery used for classification of men in the U.S. Air Force (DuBois, 1947). Note that the correlations between the first two tests are relatively high. These are both tests that are quite verbal in nature and they appear to define a factor of ability to deal with verbal relationships. Tests 3 and 4 are both numerical tests and are substantially correlated. Tests 5 and 6, which correlate substantially with each other, both involve speed of visual perception.

There has been a large volume of research on the organization and structure of human abilities during the last 50 years. Much of it has employed a technique known as *factor analysis* to try to tease out the underlying mental factors. Factor analysis starts with a table of correlations such as we have shown in Table 11.1, but ordinarily with a much larger table including a much larger number of test variables. By computational procedures that we shall not go into in any detail here (for an introduction to factor analysis, see Guilford, 1954), the factor analyst attempts to identify a small number of underlying factors that can account for the complete set of relationships among the test variables. Each test has a "loading" on each of the factors, corresponding to the correlation of the test with the factor, and the analyst tries to arrive at a pattern of factor loadings that is simple

TABLE 11.1 INTERCORRELATIONS OF SELECTED AIR FORCE APTITUDE TESTS

	1	2	3	4	5	6
1. Reading Comprehension	. . .	**.50**	.05	.23	.13	.11
2. Navigator Information	**.50**	. . .	.16	.25	.17	.15
3. Numerical Operations	.05	.16	. . .	**.44**	.27	.11
4. Dial and Table Reading	.23	.25	**.44**	. . .	.39	.23
5. Speed of Identification	.13	.17	.27	.39	. . .	**.43**
6. Spatial Orientation	.11	.15	.11	.23	**.43**	. . .

and psychologically meaningful. The correlations in Table 11.1 can be quite well represented by the following set of loadings on three factors:

	Factor		
	I	II	III
Reading Comprehension	.72	.04	.04
Navigator Information	.70	.14	.08
Numerical Operations	.08	.71	.00
Dial and Table Reading	.28	.57	.30
Speed of Identification	.13	.37	.58
Spatial Orientation	.13	.02	.63

We can see that Reading Comprehension and Navigator Information have substantial loadings on the first factor and only on the first factor, which can perhaps be identified as a verbal factor. Numerical Operations has an appreciable loading only on factor II, which we can call a number factor. Dial and Table Reading has its largest loading on factor II (number), but this is a complex test calling, in some measure, for all three of the factors. The last two tests, which are primarily speeded perceptual tests, have their largest loadings on factor III, which we will therefore call a perceptual factor. However, Speed of Identification also has an appreciable loading on factor II, and since this test has nothing to do with numbers, this loading suggests that our interpretation of factor II as a number factor may need to be modified to include the aspect of speed. The interpretation of factors is something that must be provided by the investigator, from his understanding of the nature of the tests that do and do not show loadings on a given factor.

Research has indicated that one can distinguish quite a number of special ability factors, such as verbal comprehension, word fluency, numerical fluency, perceptual speed, mechanical knowledge, spatial visualizing, and inductive and deductive reasoning. It is also true that most of these abilities are to some degree related to each other. The tests of general intelligence discussed in the last chapter reflect a pooling of several of these separate factors, together with accentuation of their common core.

The data on essentially cognitive or intellectual abilities lend themselves to several alternate interpretations, depending upon how one chooses to think of the core of overlap among different tests, portrayed visually in Fig. 11.1.

One interpretation that has been put forth most vigorously by English psychologists (Vernon, 1960) pictures individual differences in intellectual abilities as resembling, essentially, a branching tree, with the main trunk being a general intellectual ability, two main branches representing school-related as opposed to

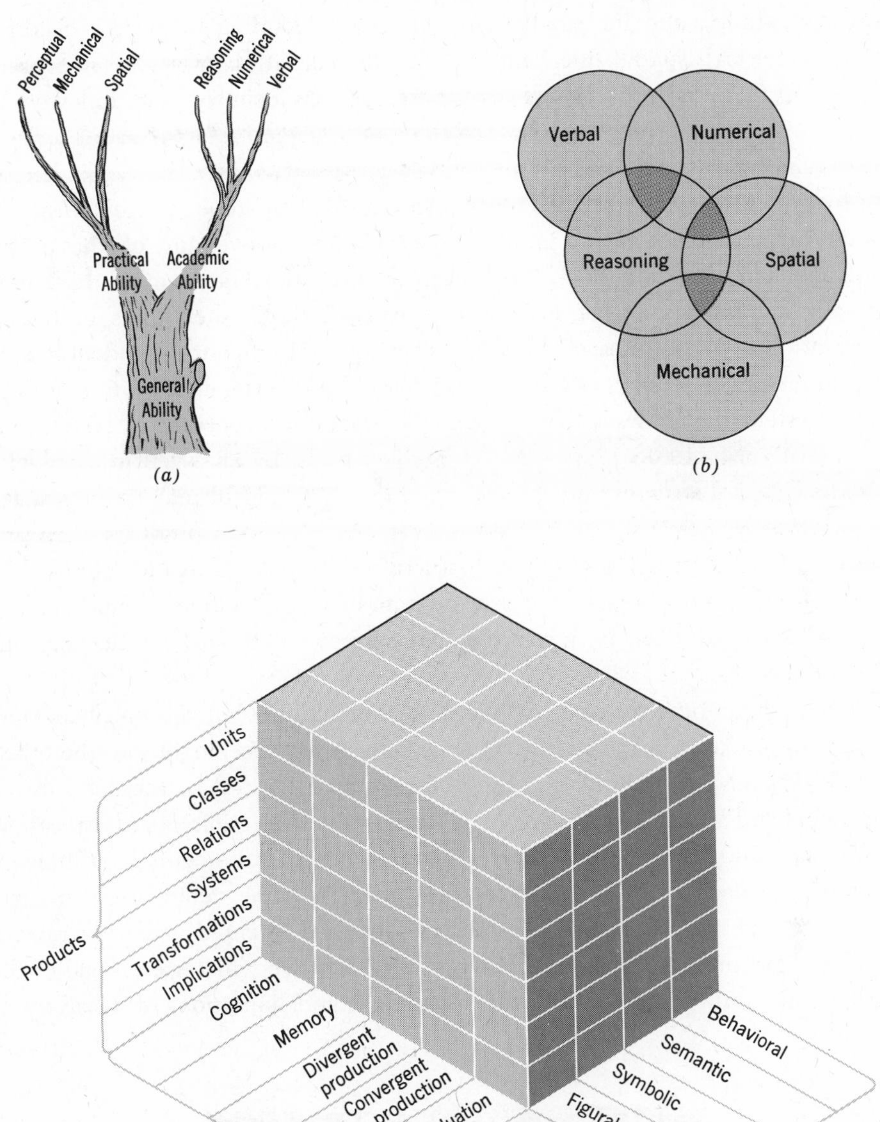

Fig. 11.1 Ways of conceiving cognitive abilities. (*a*) Hierarchical structure; (*b*) Multiple factor structure; (*c*) Guilford's three-way structure.

"practical" ability, and the smaller branches corresponding to more specialized verbal, numerical, spatial, mechanical, and other abilities. A second interpretation, set forth initially by Thurstone (1938) in this country, and followed by many of his disciples, pictures a limited number of separate factors, each appearing in some types of test and life performance, with each measure dependent on only two or three of the set of factors. No one of Thurstone's factors was considered to be really general in nature, or to rank above any of the others. Thurstone had originally identified seven factors, but the number had been gradually increased as other investigators worked with other kinds of test. A review of ability test research in 1951 (French, 1951) tentatively identified 59 different factors of all sorts as having been found by investigators up to that date.

In a systematic analysis that carried the notion of specialized factors still further, Guilford (1967) proposed that intellect could be analyzed in terms of a three-dimensional structure on the basis of (1) what kind of material was acted on, (2) what actions were carried out with it, and (3) what products were produced. Guilford proposed a $4 \times 5 \times 6$ structure that resulted in 120 cells, and he has carried on a monumental research program of test development and analysis to see whether tests can be generated that correspond to each of the logically identifiable cells.

Through theoretical research on the nature of abilities on the one hand and the applied research on the validity of specific tests for specific jobs on the other, psychologists have been guided in the design of aptitude test batteries for use in educational and vocational guidance and in personnel selection and classification. Since about 1940, these batteries have come to occupy quite central positions in the testing scene, so we will need to study them in some detail. First, we will examine two of the most widely used batteries, one oriented primarily toward school use and the other toward industrial use. Then we will review some of the evidence on validity and consider the advantages and limitations of a battery of this sort.

The Differential Aptitude Test Battery

This battery was originally brought out by the Psychological Corporation in 1947, as a guidance battery for use at the secondary school level, and a revised form that is more efficient to administer was produced in 1963. In the design of the battery, some attention was paid to having separate tests with low intercorrelations, but the main focus was on getting measures that would be meaningful to high school counselors. So we find that, with the exception of the test of clerical speed and accuracy, intercorrelations are about .50. However, since the reliabilities of the parts are about .90, it is clear that each measures an ability somewhat distinct from those measured by the others. The eight subtests are briefly described and illustrated below.

1. *Verbal Reasoning.* Items are of the double-analogy type, that is, ? is to A as B is to ? Five pairs of words are provided to complete the analogy.

Example

_______ is to water as eat is to _______.

A. Continue . . . drive
B. Foot . . . enemy
C. Drink . . . food
D. Girl . . . industry
E. Drink . . . enemy

2. *Numerical Ability.* Consists of numerical problems emphasizing comprehension rather than simple computational facility.

Example

$$\frac{1}{4} \div \frac{1}{8} =$$

A 1/32
B 1/8
C 1/2
D 2
E none of these

3. *Abstract Reasoning.* A series of problem figures establishes a relationship or sequence, and the examinee must pick the choice that continues the series.

Example

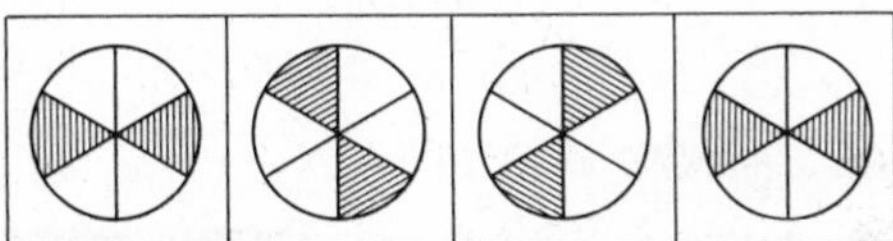

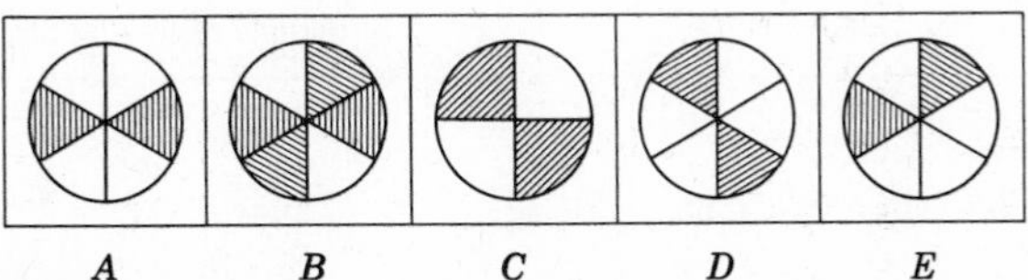

4. *Space Relations.* A diagram of a flat figure is shown. The examinee must visualize and indicate which solid figure could be produced by folding the flat figure as shown on p. 352.

Example

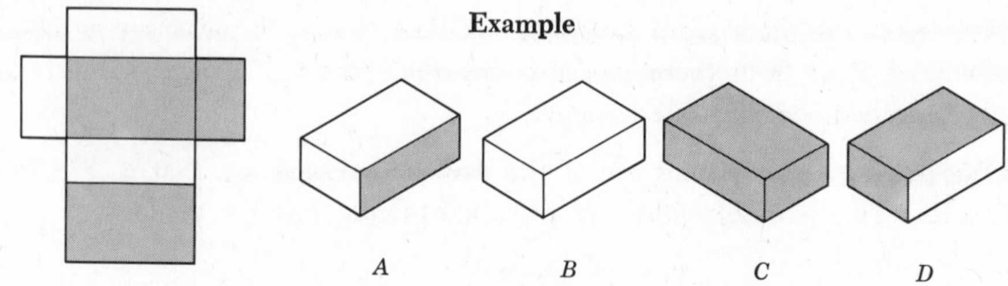

5. *Mechanical Reasoning.* A diagram of a mechanical device or situation is shown, and the examinee must indicate which choice is true of the situation.

Example

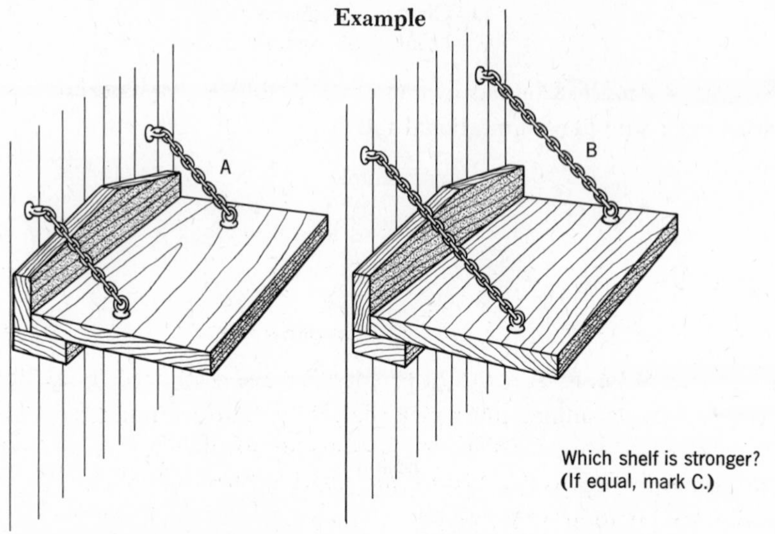

6. *Clerical Speed and Accuracy.* Each item is made up of a number of combinations of symbols, one of which is underlined. The examinee must mark the same combination on his answer sheet.

Example

Test Items

V.	AB	AC	AD	AE	AF
W.	aA	aB	BA	Ba	Bb
X.	A7	7A	B7	7B	AB
Y.	Aa	Ba	bA	BA	bB
Z.	3A	3B	33	B3	BB

Sample of Answer Sheet

V	AC	AE	AF	AB ▮	AD
W	BA	Ba	Bb ▮	aA	aB
X	7B ▮	B7	AB	7A	A7
Y	Aa	bA ▮	bB	Ba	BA
Z	BB	3B	B3	3A	33 ▮

7. *Language Usage: Spelling.* A list of words is given, some of which are misspelled. The examinee must indicate for each word whether it is correctly or incorrectly spelled.

Examples

	Right	Wrong
definate	⁞	⁞

8. *Language Usage: Sentences.* A sentence is given, divided by marks into four subsections. The examinee must indicate which section—A, B, C, or D—contains an error; if there is no error, he marks E.

Example

1. Ain't we /	going to /	the office /	next week?	⁞	⁞	⁞	⁞	⁞
A	B	C	D	A	B	C	D	E
2. I went /	to a ball /	game with /	Jimmy.	⁞	⁞	⁞	⁞	⁞
A	B	C	D	A	B	C	D	E

The tests of the *DAT* are essentially power tests, with the exception of the *Clerical Speed and Accuracy Test,* and time limits are in most cases 30 minutes. Total testing time for the battery is about 5 to 5½ hours, and it requires at least two separate testing sessions. Percentile norms are available for each grade from the eighth through the twelfth. Norms are provided for each of the subtests, and also for the combination of V and A, which may be used as a general appraisal of scholastic aptitude. An illustration of the profile form on which results may be plotted is shown on p. 236.

The General Aptitude Test Battery (GATB)

The *General Aptitude Test Battery* was produced by the Bureau of Employment Security, U.S. Department of Labor, in the early 1940's. It was based upon previous work in which experimental test batteries had been prepared for each of a number of different jobs. Analysis of the more than 50 different tests that had been prepared for specific jobs indicated that there was a great deal of overlapping among certain ones of them, and that only about 10 different ability factors were measured by the complete set of tests. The *GATB* was developed to provide measures of these different factors. In its most recent form it includes 12 tests and gives scores for 9 different factors. One is a factor of general mental ability (G), resulting from scores on three tests (*Vocabulary, Arithmetic Reason-*

ing, and *Three-Dimensional Space*) that are also scored for more specialized factors. The other factors, and the tests that contribute to each are described below.

1. *Verbal Aptitude.* Score is based on one test, Number 4, *Vocabulary.* This test requires the subject to identify the pair of words in a set of four that are *either* synonyms or antonyms.

Examples

a. cautious	b. friendly	c. hostile	d. remote
a. hasten	b. deprive	c. expedite	d. disprove

2. *Numerical Ability.* The appraisal of this aptitude is based upon two tests. The first of these, Number 2, *Computation,* involves speed and accuracy in simple computations with whole numbers.

Examples

Subtract (−)	256 83	Multiply (×)	37 8

The second test entering into the *Numerical Ability* score, Number 6, *Arithmetic Reasoning,* involves verbally stated quantitative problems.

Example

John works for $1.20 an hour. How much is his pay for a 35-hour week?

3. *Spatial Aptitude.* One test, Number 3, *Three-Dimensional Space,* enters into appraisal of this aptitude. The examinee must indicate which of four 3-dimensional figures can be produced by folding a flat sheet of specified shape, with creases at indicated points.

Example

Example of Spatial Aptitude

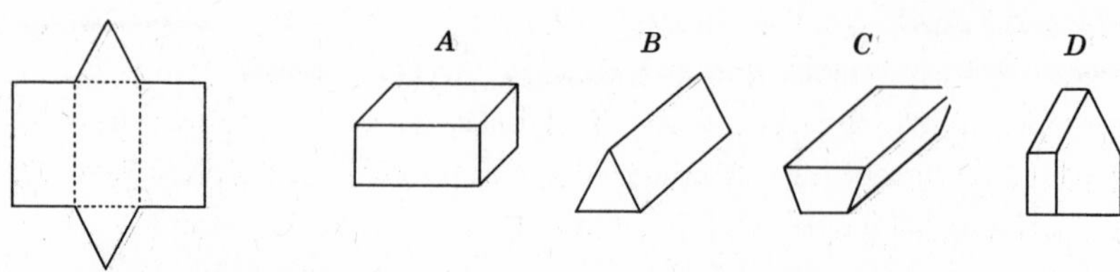

4. *Form Perception.* This aptitude involves rapid and accurate perception of visual forms and patterns. It is appraised in the *GATB* by two tests, Number 5, *Tool Matching,* and Number 7, *Form Matching,* which differ in the type of visual

stimulus provided. Each requires the examinee to find from among a set of answer choices the one that is identical with the stimulus form.

Examples

Example of Tool Matching

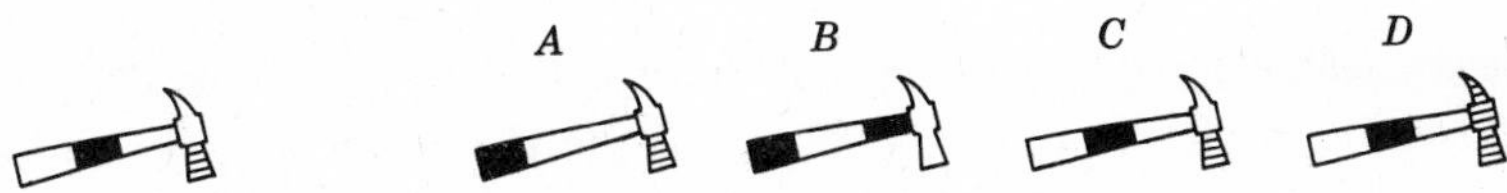

Example of Form Matching

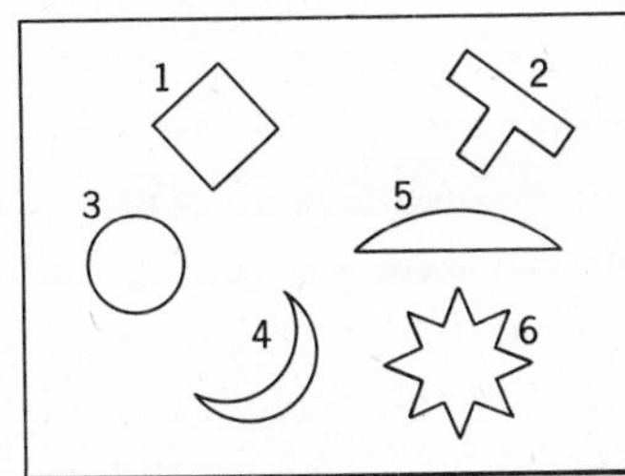

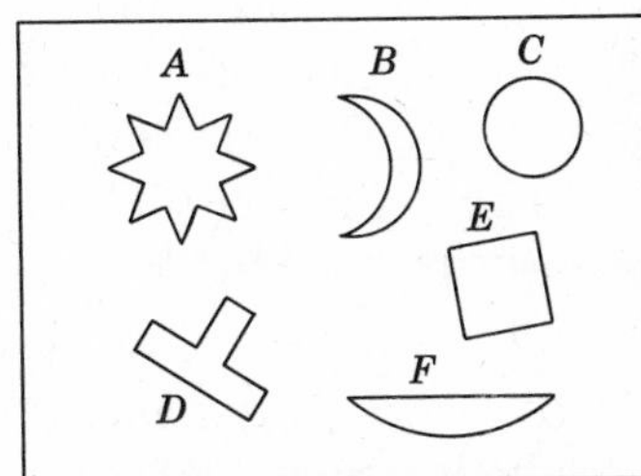

5. *Clerical Perception.* This aptitude also involves rapid and accurate perception, but in this case the stimulus material is linguistic instead of purely spatial. The test, Number 1, *Name Comparison,* presents pairs of names and requires the examinee to indicate whether the two members of the pair are identical, or whether they differ in some detail.

Examples

John Goldstein & Co.—John Goldston & Co.
Pewee Mfg. Co.—Pewee Mfg. Co.

6. *Motor Coordination.* This factor has to do with speed of simple but fairly precise motor response. It is evaluated by one test, Number 8, *Mark Making.* The task of the examinee is to make three pencil marks within each of a series of boxes on the answer sheet to yield a simple design. The result appears approximately as follows:

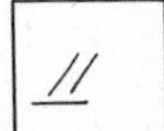  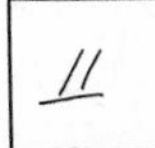 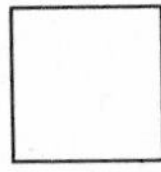

etc.

Score is the number of boxes correctly filled in a 60-second test period.

7. *Manual Dexterity.* This factor involves speed and accuracy of fairly gross hand movements. It is evaluated by two pegboard tests, Number 9, *Place,* and

Number 10, *Turn*. In the first of these, the examinee uses both hands to move a series of pegs from one set of holes in a pegboard to another. In the second test, the examinee uses his preferred hand to pick a peg up from the board, rotate it through 180°, and reinsert the other end of the peg in the hole. Three trials are given for each of these tests, and score is the total number of pegs moved or turned.

8. *Finger Dexterity.* This factor represents a finer type of dexterity than that covered by the previous factor, calling for more precise finger manipulations. Two tests, Number 11, *Assemble,* and Number 12, *Disassemble,* use the same piece of equipment. This is a board with 50 holes in each of two sections. Each hole in one section is occupied by a small rivet. A stack of washers is piled on a spindle. During *Assemble,* the examinee picks up a rivet with one hand, a washer with the other, puts the washer on the rivet, and places the assembly in the corresponding hole in the unoccupied part of the board. He assembles as many rivets and washers as he can in 90 seconds. During *Disassemble,* he removes the assembly, returns the washer to its stack, and returns the rivet to its original place. Score is the number of items assembled or disassembled as the case may be. The apparatus tests are all arranged so that at the completion of testing the equipment has been returned to its original condition, and is ready for the testing of another person.

A comparison of the *GATB* and the *DAT* brings out that the *DAT* has tests of mechanical comprehension and language which the *GATB* lacks, while the *GATB* includes form perception and several types of motor tests that are missing in the *DAT*. Thus the *GATB* is more work oriented and less school oriented in its total coverage. Inclusion of the several types of motor tests results in somewhat

TABLE 11.2 INTERCORRELATIONS OF *GATB* APTITUDE SCORES FOR 100 HIGH-SCHOOL SENIORS *

	G	V	N	S	P	Q	K	F	M
G–Intelligence									
V–Verbal	73								
N–Numerical	74	42							
S–Spatial	70	40	34						
P–Form Percept.	43	34	42	48					
Q–Clerical Percept.	35	29	42	26	66				
K–Motor Coord.	–04	13	06	–03	29	29			
F–Finger Dext.	–05	–03	–03	01	27	20	37		
M–Manual Dext.	–06	06	01	–03	23	16	49	46	

* Decimal points have been omitted.

lower correlations, on the average, for the *GATB*, though the "intellectual" tests correlate about as highly as those of the *DAT*. The correlations among the different aptitude scores of the *GATB* are shown in Table 11.2 for a group of 100 high school seniors. Excluding the correlations with G, which involves the same tests appearing in V, N, and S, the correlations range from −.06 to .66. The three motor factors show fairly marked correlations, but they are practically unrelated to the remaining tests. The perceptual and intellectual tests also show quite a bit of relationship to one another, and this is most marked between the two types of perceptual tests.

There are quite substantial correlations between the corresponding factors of the *DAT* and the *GATB*. Representative values from one study (U.S. Employment Service, 1967) are as follows:

Verbal	.74
Numerical	.61
Space	.65
Clerical	.57

However, the correlations are low enough so that it is clear that the tests cannot be considered identical. One important difference is the fact that the *DAT* tests are in most cases purely power tests, while the *GATB* tests are quite highly speeded.

Other Aptitude Batteries

A number of other aptitude batteries have been produced, mostly since 1950. There is generally less information available on these than on the *DAT* or the *GATB*, so their usefulness is less fully established. The batteries are briefly described in Appendix IV.*

There are also a good many single aptitude tests. Many of these are much like the tests that have been described as components of the *DAT* or *GATB*. The batteries have, of course, usually adapted ideas from the most effective single tests and incorporated measures that have been successful in previous use. Thus, the *Bennett Mechanical Comprehension Test* was the predecessor and model for the *DAT Mechanical Reasoning Test*. The *Minnesota Vocational Test for Clerical Workers* provided the model for the *Clerical Perception* factor in the *GATB*. The various early mechanical aptitude and clerical tests have been re-

* Fuller reports on each of seven different batteries, together with an evaluation by one outside expert, appeared in the *Personnel and Guidance Journal* from September 1956 through September 1957, and have been brought out as a separate monograph entitled *The Use of Multifactor Tests in Guidance*.

viewed by Bennett and Cruickshank (1942, 1948), and, of course, more recent tests will be found reviewed in the *Mental Measurements Yearbooks*.

Validity of Aptitude Batteries

Now we must inquire into the usefulness of aptitude batteries such as the *DAT* and the *GATB*. We must inquire to what extent such a battery can provide us information that permits us to make better, more varied, and more differentiated predictions than those that are possible from a test of general mental ability or scholastic aptitude. The types of predictions with which we are most likely to be concerned are predictions of success in specific school subjects or major fields, predictions of success in specific jobs for which the individual is an applicant, and predictions of success in general fields of the world of work.

DIFFERENTIAL PREDICTION OF ACADEMIC SUCCESS. We have seen that scholastic aptitude tests have fairly good overall validity for predicting academic success. One thing that we might hope is that an aptitude battery would tell us in *which* subject areas a student is *most* likely to be successful. Will Walter do better in English or in mathematics, in science or in French, in mechanical drawing or in history? A battery can do this to the extent that different tests in the battery are valid for different subjects. To what extent is this the case?

The manual for the *DAT* provides extensive data on the correlations of each of the subtests with achievement in a number of school subjects. Some of these results are summarized in Table 11.3. This table shows the median value of the correlations, and also ranks the eight subtests, and the combination of verbal and numerical, with respect to their correlations with each subject.

The first thing that we notice is that certain subtests are among the highest for almost all subjects. Thus, *Verbal Reasoning* and *Numerical Ability* are each among the better predictors for all subjects. Recognizing this, the authors of the *DAT* provided a single score combining these two subtests. We see from the table that *VR* + *NA* is as good a predictor or better than *any* of the subtests for *all* subjects, including typing and industrial arts. To a considerable extent, the abilities that underlie academic ability are general abilities, and a common scholastic test will give about as good a prediction of any of them as we can get.

At the same time, Table 11.3 does show a little indication of differential validity. *Spelling* and *Grammar* are somewhat more useful as predictors of English grades than of grades in industrial arts, and conversely *Abstract Reasoning* and *Space Relations* are somewhat more useful for industrial arts than they are for English. But this is the sharpest distinction that appears in the table. Even in this case, the validity of the test battery as a predictor of *difference* in achieve-

TABLE 11.3 MEDIAN CORRELATION OF *Differential Aptitude Test* SCORES WITH SCHOOL GRADES IN DIFFERENT SUBJECTS

Test	English	Mathematics	Science	Social Studies, History	Languages	Typing	Industrial Arts
Verbal Reasoning (*VR*)	.52(2.5) *	.40(4)	.50(2)	.49(3)	.46(4)	.38(4)	.32(4)
Numerical Ability (*NA*)	.50(4)	.52(1.5)	.48(3)	.49(3)	.41(5)	.43(2)	.32(4)
VR + *NA*	.57(1)	.52(1.5)	.56(1)	.55(1)	.54(1)	.44(1)	.36(1)
Abstract Reasoning (*AR*)	.42(6)	.41(3)	.40(5)	.37(6)	.25(6)	.34(6)	.35(2)
Clerical Speed and Accuracy (*CSA*)	.28(8)	.20(9)	.24(9)	.26(8)	.16(9)	.30(7)	.24(8)
Mechanical Reasoning (*MR*)	.22(9)	.24(8)	.28(8)	.22(9)	.17(8)	.26(8)	.27(7)
Space Relations (*SR*)	.30(7)	.30(6.5)	.34(7)	.30(7)	.20(7)	.24(9)	.32(4)
Spelling (*Spell.*)	.46(5)	.30(6.5)	.38(6)	.42(5)	.48(3)	.36(5)	.19(9)
Grammar (*Gram.*)	.52(2.5)	.39(5)	.46(4)	.49(3)	.50(2)	.40(3)	.30(6)

* Number in parentheses shows rank of that test for that subject.

ment between English and industrial arts appears to be no more than .20 or .25. Thus, we are able, primarily, to predict general level of educational achievement; differential prediction of performance in one area rather than another must be made only very tentatively at best.

PREDICTION OF SPECIFIC JOB SUCCESS. We may next ask how successful a battery of aptitude tests will be in predicting the success of workers in a specific job. Will tests have validity high enough to make them useful either to a State Employment Service or to an employer in selecting workers for employment? Will different tests predict success in different jobs? The manual for the *GATB* provides an impressive array of data on the differences between workers in different jobs and on correlations of the tests with success either in training programs or on the job. The data often fall short of being ideal because the validation is concurrent (rather than predictive); because the data are for workers already employed rather than job applicants; because the samples are small; because the sample is often limited to workers in a single plant or company; and because there is no independent cross-validation.* However, the accumulation of data is quite impressive, and provides the best pool of data that we have in which a common battery was validated against criteria of success in a wide range of different jobs.

We have selected from the total array of jobs 23 in which the number of cases was at least 100 and in which correlations of test scores with a job criterion were available. The evidence is presented in Tables 11.4 and 11.5 and, for four of the jobs, in Fig. 11.1. Table 11.4 shows average standard scores (using a norm system in which the mean is 100 and the standard deviation is 20) for each occupational group. Group differences are clearly quite marked, both in level and in pattern. Thus, computer programmers are highest in the factor scores representing *G* (general intelligence) and *N* (numerical) and on these two scales they fall more than 1.5 standard deviations above the population mean. By way of contrast, electronics assemblers fall well below the population average in *N*, and are highest in motor coordination and manual dexterity, where they fall half a standard deviation above the general population average. To bring out the patterning, the highest mean score for each occupation has been shown in the table in boldface type.

Table 11.5 on page 362 shows validity coefficients for each factor against a job-success criterion for each occupation. The criterion was, in most cases, some type of rating by a supervisor. The first nine columns of the table show validity coefficients for single factor scores, including all coefficients that differed significantly from

* Especially in exploratory studies in which a battery of tests is being tried out, it is important to verify validities discovered in an initial study by checking the same tests with a new independent sample, a process to which the term cross-validation has been applied.

Table 11.4 Mean *GATB* factor scores for specific occupations

Occup. Code	Title	General Intell.	Verbal	Numer.	Space	Form Percept.	Clerical Percept.	Motor Coord.	Finger Dext.	Manual Dext.
		Factor								
020	Computer programmer	**132**	125	131	122	120	128	117	109	113
078	Medical technologist	126	127	122	117	126	**130**	122	114	117
079	Dental assistant	104	105	102	107	116	**117**	114	112	114
	Surgical technician	97	102	93	97	107	**108**	**108**	106	107
193	Air traffic control specialist	**118**	114	115	113	109	111	112	101	106
195	Case worker	116	**120**	112	105	102	119	115	99	98
202	Stenographer, typist	106	104	106	108	**119**	113	114	105	103
208	Typesetter-perforator operator	110	113	106	104	107	**120**	114	102	101
212	Teller, bank	111	111	110	107	115	**120**	114	107	101
213	Tabulating machine operator	111	109	112	106	110	**116**	112	106	107
219	Clerk, general office	108	109	111	101	114	**123**	117	. . .	. . .
241	Claim adjuster	**116**	109	**116**	114	108	111	107	97	107
276	Salesman, construction machinery	**113**	109	107	111	100	104	102	96	98
317	Food service worker	82	85	80	91	85	91	91	87	**97**
319	Fountain girl	95	98	95	95	101	**104**	**104**	99	102
355	Nurse aid	89	95	85	91	91	**100**	**100**	86	94
	Psychiatric aid	95	**97**	90	95	88	94	96	91	91
375	Patrolman	112	110	106	112	108	106	112	101	**117**
529	Asparagus sorter	96	99	91	**96**	97	99	101	97	**108**
601	Tool-and-die maker	109	100	105	**119**	111	101	104	106	**115**
690	Fancy stitcher (shoes)	93	93	91	94	96	99	**101**	95	**101**
712	Dental-laboratory technician	96	96	91	102	98	96	99	98	**108**
726	Electronics assembler	95	100	89	100	104	105	111	108	**113**

TABLE 11.5 VALIDITY OF *GATB* FACTOR SCORES AND OCCUPATIONAL APTITUDE PATTERNS FOR SPECIFIC OCCUPATIONS

		Factor										
Occup. Code	Title	General Intell.	Verbal	Numer.	Space	Form Per-cept.	Cler-ical Per-cept.	Motor Coord.	Finger Dext.	Man-ual Dext.	Occupational Aptitude Pattern	
020	Computer programmer	36		40	24					28	#1	28
078	Medical technologist		22				22					
079	Dental assistant	57	32	40	51	28	22		21			
	Surgical technician	34	28	24	32	20	22					
193	Air traffic control specialist		21	27		19				19	#3	23
195	Case worker			22							#3	27
202	Stenographer, typist	39	37	41		20	42	30	18	18	#36	18
208	Typesetter-perforator operator	30	21	31			25	17			#36	25
212	Teller, bank								45			
213	Tabulating machine operator	34	22	36	20		15				#9	21
219	Clerk, general office	26	22	23			15				#13	16
241	Claim adjuster	20	20	32			26	31			#6	24
276	Salesman, construction machinery	32	19	29	23			22				
317	Food service worker							22	26	35		
319	Fountain girl								21	28	#32	19
355	Nurse aid	23	15	25		18		21				
	Psychiatric aid	31	25	29	23	23	24	19	19	22		
375	Patrolman					20						
529	Asparagus sorter					19		23	17	18	#34	20
601	Tool-and-die maker	60	30	48	50	40	36			16		
690	Fancy stitcher (shoes)	28	19	30	29	50	45	53	49	46	#31	47
712	Dental-laboratory technician	32	21	20	32			22	21	24	#28	43
726	Electronics assembler	23		19	22	20			28	29	#16	17

Decimal points of correlation coefficients omitted.

zero. Thus, it is possible to see which tests gave a prediction for which jobs and how good the predictions were. In every instance, at least one of the nine factors correlated with job success at a level significantly different from zero, though many of the correlations are small. Most are in the 20's, though a few go up to the 40's and 50's. There is clearly a fair amount of differential patterning of the validity coefficients. Thus, the spatial factor has correlations of .50 with success as a dental assistant and as a tool-and-die maker, but is not significantly related to success in 13 of the 23 jobs. Manual dexterity is a significant factor for fancy stitchers and food service workers, but not for 12 of the jobs. There are 8 of the jobs in which the General Intelligence factor fails to show a significant correlation, and so on down the line.

The last column in Table 11.5 shows the validity of Occupational Aptitude Patterns for the 13 of the 23 occupations for which this information is reported. In their original use of the *GATB* for screening individuals for a specific job, the U.S. Employment Service staff established minimum qualifying scores on the two, three, or four aptitude factors that appeared to be most effective in differentiating successful workers in the job from those who either were unsuccessful in it or did not enter it. Thus, for computer programmer, the qualifying scores were: *G*–115, *V*–105, *N*–110, and *S*–105. In order to develop a more manageable counseling and screening procedure the Employment Service undertook to group occupations into families in which, either on the basis of validity data or of an analysis of the job, the aptitude requirements were judged to be similar. A total of 36 families were set up, each with its unique pattern of cutting scores. Thus, Occupational Pattern #1, which includes engineers of all types, physicians, and urban planners, as well as computer programmers, has cutting scores set at: *G*–125, *N*–115, and *S*–115. Pattern #36, which includes a wide range of stenographers, stenotypists, and typists has cutting scores set at: *G*–105, *Q* (clerical perception)–100, and *K* (motor coordination)–90.

The relationships between qualifying on the aptitude pattern and being judged successful on the job, shown in this last column, are positive and statistically significant in each case, but none of them are large. The whole array of 196 validity coefficients for jobs for which the validity of the classification into "accepted" and "rejected" is made on the basis of the proposed occupational aptitude pattern is as follows:

Validity	*No. of Coefficients*
.60 +	9
.50–.59	23
.40–.49	42
.30–.39	62
.20–.29	51
.10–.19	9

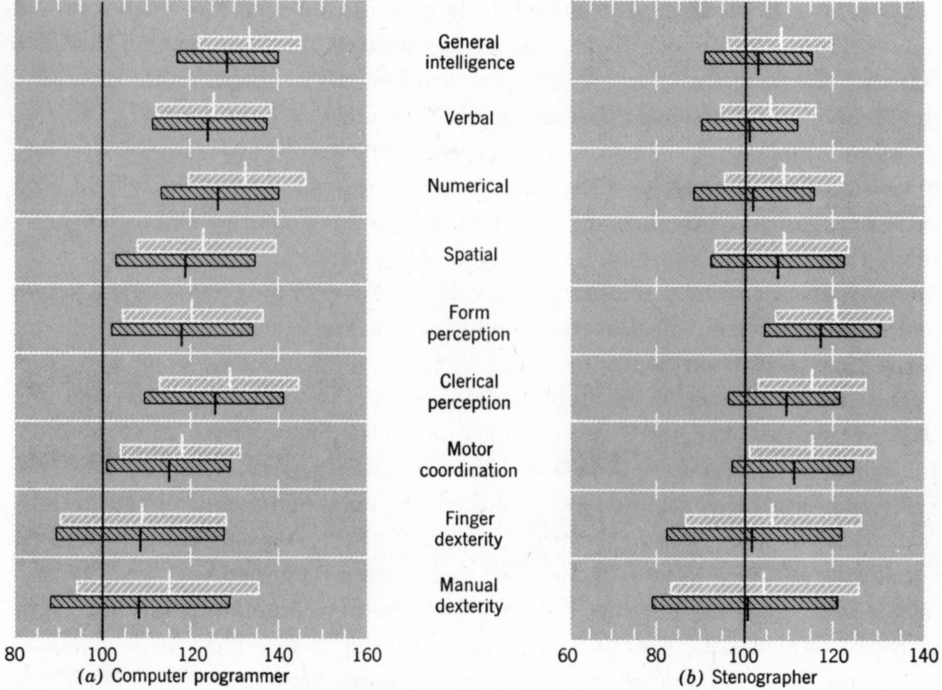

Fig. 11.2 **Ability profiles for four occupations.**

The median of these 196 coefficients is .36. To show what this level of validity would mean in the case of a job in which ⅓ of those tested were rated as unacceptable on the basis of the tests and ⅓ of the employees were rated as unsatisfactory by their supervisor, the following example is provided:

	Rated on Job	
Rated on Tests	Unacceptable	Acceptable
Acceptable	15	52
Unacceptable	18	15

Thus, with the definitions of acceptable and unacceptable provided in the example, 78 percent of those passed by the tests turned out to be acceptable on the job as compared with 45 percent of those failed on the test. This appears to be a representative picture of the effectiveness of a test battery for prediction of job performance.

In Fig. 11.2, we have taken four jobs and assembled all the evidence relative to the effectiveness of the test battery for differentiating degree of success in each job. Each of the four charts shows the evidence relating to one job. The nine rows in the chart show the data for the nine factor scores of the *GATB*

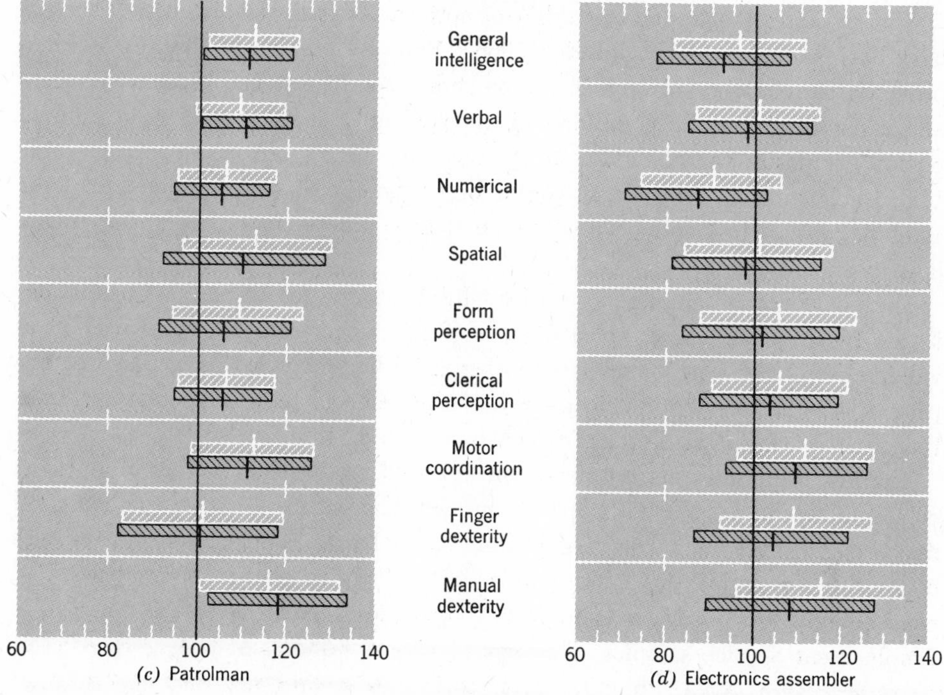

(c) Patrolman

(d) Electronics assembler

battery. For each row there are two bars, the upper one representing scores of workers judged successful and the lower bar the scores of workers judged unsuccessful. The bar includes a range from plus one standard deviation to minus one standard deviation, and the long mark in the middle represents the mean of the group. Thus, looking at the group of computer programmers, one sees that they are superior on all the measures, but that the superiority is greatest, on the average, in general intelligence and in numerical ability. On these tests, not only is the average high, but the groups are relatively homogeneous (that is, the bars are short). Furthermore, on these two factors there is a relatively large difference between the workers judged successful and those judged unsuccessful. Stenographers differ less from the general average and in their case the various lines of evidence point to the perceptual measures as especially important. Patrolmen are most outstanding in manual dexterity but most homogeneous in general intelligence. Electronics assemblers show a peak on manual dexterity, and this differentiates the better from the poorer workers, but the long bars indicate that the group is quite heterogeneous.

A comparison of the four charts will provide a reasonable picture of the degree to which different abilities describe different occupations and predict success in them.

A large number of separate studies of aptitude tests in relation to job success have been summarized by Ghiselli (1966). Where a number of different sources provided correlations between scores on some type of test and success in a general category of job, he combined all the available data to produce a kind of pooled composite validity index. Selections from his report are shown in Table 11.6. Each entry is an average, often of a number of correlations. For some combinations of test and occupation no data could be found, so these entries have been left blank.

The pooled correlations reported by Ghiselli rarely go above .30. Correlations in the twenties are fairly typical. For a given category of job, the variation in validity from one type of test to another is rather modest. Thus, these results present a rather less optimistic picture of the value of tests of special aptitudes than that portrayed in the *GATB* results in Table 11.5.

The less promising picture may stem in part from the blurring resulting from combining quite a span both of jobs and of tests within a single coefficient. It may be, however, that the larger numbers of cases represented in Ghiselli's composite correlations are more stable, less subject to chance fluctuations, and consequently less likely to yield large correlations than the rather small U.S. Employment Service samples. The true picture of validity of tests as predictors of success at a given job in a given company, and of the distinctiveness of different abilities as predictors for different types of jobs probably lies somewhere between the pictures presented in these two tables.

TABLE 11.6 AVERAGE VALIDITY OF DIFFERENT SORTS OF TESTS FOR BROAD CATEGORIES OF JOBS (ADAPTED FROM GHISELLI, 1966)

	Intellectual Abilities	Spatial, Mech. Abilities	Perceptual Accuracy	Motor Abilities
Executives, administrators	.29	.18	.24	. . .
Foremen	.24	.23	.14	. . .
Clerical occupations	.27	.20	.27	.15
Sales clerks	−.10	. . .*	−.05	. . .
Salesmen	.31	.07	.21	. . .
Protective service	.23	.16	.17	.19
Personal service	.03	. . .	−.10	−.05
Vehicle operators	.14	.20	.36	.30
Trades and crafts	.19	.23	.22	.19
Industrial occupations	.16	.16	.18	.17

* Three dots indicate that data are unavailable, or are based on less than 100 cases.

FORECASTING SUCCESS IN THE WORLD OF WORK. For the school or college guidance counselor, special aptitude tests are useful insofar as they permit him to forecast some years in advance the general field of work for which a student will be able to complete training and in which he will be successful. The counselor cannot know what *specific* company the student will work for, or what exact job position he will fill. He deals in relatively long range forecasts over relatively broad categories. What evidence can be offered on the long-range forecasting effectiveness of aptitude test results?

Probably the most extensive study bearing on this problem is one in which approximately 10,000 men, who had originally been given an extensive battery of aptitude tests in the Air Force during World War II, were followed up some 13 years after the time of testing (Thorndike and Hagen, 1959). Test results were related to entry into and persistence in an occupation and to reported income and other indicators of success in that occupation. Even in a group of 10,000 men, samples in many occupations were small. However, it was possible to assemble samples large enough to merit analysis for about 125 occupational groupings.

The results on prediction of occupational *success* contrast rather sharply with those reported in the previous section. There was *no* convincing evidence of *any* relationship of test scores to success within an occupation for those men who had entered a specific occupation. Correlations were generally small, about as often negative as positive, and the total set of correlations could quite possibly have arisen as a result of chance deviations from a true correlation of zero. It appeared that when the men might enter an occupation such as law anywhere in the country, in many different kinds of settings both public and private, the test battery was quite unable to predict who would achieve the largest income, report the most satisfaction, or perceive himself as most successful in his field. It is important for the counselor to realize that such predictions are probably not possible for him. However, differences *between* occupations were still found in this long-range study, and were comparable in size and degree of specialization to those shown in Table 11.4. Thus, early test scores are related to occupational membership a number of years later, even though there is no good evidence that they are predictive, over a long time span, of occupational success.

A good deal more substantial study, but one that is still incomplete is the so-called "Project Talent" (Flanagan and Cooley, 1966), in which a 5 percent sample of American high school students (close to 500,000 in all) was tested with a comprehensive battery of ability, interest, and temperament measures. The groups are being followed up one year and five years after high school, and it is planned that they will be followed up again after 10 and 20 years. Some of the data from the one-year follow-up are displayed in Fig. 11.3. Examinees

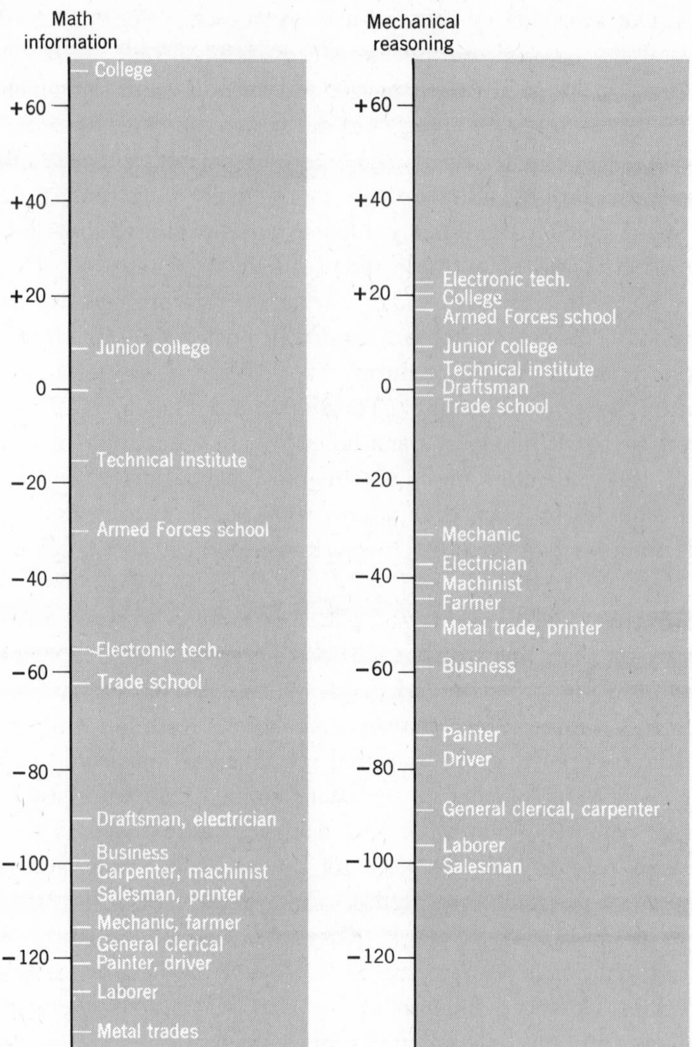

Fig. 11.3 Mean test scores of educational and occupational groups.

were grouped according to the type of training program or occupation in which they were engaged. Average score was determined for each of the tests in the battery. Scores are expressed as deviations from the group mean, where the group mean is set at zero and the standard deviation at 100. The figure shows the constrasting results for a test of mathematics information and one of mechanical reasoning. The mathematics test shows a gradient from four-year college through other types of training program down to the different worker groups. On the mechanical test, college students still score near the top, but certain worker groups join them, while salesmen end up as "low man." Of course, these results represent only quite immediate outcomes, and it will be some time before one sees what the long-range relationships are. It is one of the ironies of personnel research that by that time our testing procedures or the structure of the world of work, or both, may have gone through fairly drastic restructuring, so that the applicability to 1980 of the then available results may be called in question.

PROGNOSTIC TESTS

One group of aptitude tests is made up of tests designed to predict readiness to learn or probable degree of success in some specific subject or segment of education. These are called prognostic tests. A group of tests in this category that have been widely heralded and have received considerable use are the "reading readiness" tests. These tests are designed to be used with children, usually shortly after their entry into the first grade, to give the school as accurate an indication as possible of the child's ability to progress in reading. They provide information the teacher can use in assembling working groups within the class, in deciding upon the amount and type of prereading activities to provide, and in judging how soon to start a formal reading program. In some communities where kindergarten attendance is quite general, tests at the end of kindergarten are looked to as one basis for organizing first-grade groups for the following year. The sorts of tasks that appear in these tests may be seen from Table 11.7 on page 370.

The reader who compares the tasks in Table 11.7 with the sample intelligence test items shown on pp. 294–304 will be aware of a substantial degree of similarity. In both, knowledge of word meanings appears. Both deal with recognition of sameness and differences, with analysis and classification. However, the reading readiness tests tend to emphasize more exclusively the materials of reading, letters and words. They include the components or early stages of the reading task. The basic question now becomes: Does the special slant which is given in the reading readiness test result in increased validity? Is the special test an improvement over a measure of general or academic aptitude? This is the question that must be raised for any type of prognostic test or special aptitude test.

The general trend of the evidence does seem to support the higher validity of the readiness tests specifically designed to forecast progress in learning to

TABLE 11.7 TYPES OF TASKS INCLUDED IN REPRESENTATIVE READING READINESS TESTS

Type of Test Task	*Gates-MacGinitie*	*Harrison-Stroud*	*Lee-Clark*	*Metro-politan*	*Murphy-Durrell*
Recognition of words	*	*			
Recognition of letters	*			*	*
Discrimination of sounds	*	*			*
Blending of sounds	*				
Comprehension of verbal material—words, sentences, directions	*	*	*	*	
Visual form discrimination or matching	*	*	*	*	
Copying symbols	*			*	
Number concepts				*	
Learning words in standard lesson					*

read, though incisive comparative studies are hard to find. The correlation of reading readiness tests with reading measures at the end of the first grade are typically about .60 to .65, and the subtests that have the highest validity have fairly consistently been those involving quite directly component reading skills, that is, recognizing or discriminating the visual form of letters or words. These correlations are probably somewhat higher than a generalized aptitude test would give for this specific criterion—reading performance at the end of grade 1.

Prognostic tests have been developed for various other subjects and levels, and the last few years have witnessed some renewal of interest in these tests. Carroll and Sapon (1958) and Pimsleur (1966) have each brought out a battery of foreign language prognosis tests and the *Symonds Foreign Language Prognosis Test* has been restandardized. The older Orleans prognostic tests for algebra, geometry and foreign languages continue to be available. The authors of all these tests offer evidence to show that the specialized tests provide a better prediction of achievement in the special subject area than is possible from a general measure of scholastic aptitude. However, one may still question whether, within the areas of academic achievement, special prognostic tests can improve the predictions based upon a combination of measures of general intelligence and previous academic achievement in related areas enough to justify their use. The demonstration that they can has not been sufficiently impressive to result in widespread adoption of the tests.

Special prognostic tests seem likely to be more useful as predictors of success in rather special types of academic tasks that have had no counterparts at earlier levels of school experience. Thus, the *Turse Shorthand Aptitude Test,* for which a correlation of .67 with later achievement in shorthand has been reported, may be useful as a supplement to other information about the pupil in evaluating probable success in shorthand training. The *ERC Stenographic Aptitude Test* and the *Bennett Stenographic Aptitude Tests* have given comparable results. These tests include such tasks as spelling, transcribing symbols, dictation under speed pressure, and word discrimination.

PROFESSIONAL-SCHOOL APTITUDE BATTERIES

One other group of aptitude tests, so-called, are the tests that have been developed to select individuals for particular types of professional training. Many types of professional schools, sometimes individually but more often operating through their professional organizations, have instituted testing programs for the selection of their students. Testing programs are in operation for selecting students for engineering, law, medicine, dentistry, veterinary medicine, nursing, and accounting, to mention a few.

The tests used in these professional-school batteries tend to be tests of reading, quantitative reasoning, and apprehending abstract relationships, with the balance and emphasis shifted somewhat to conform to the academic emphasis of the particular training program. They are largely minor variations upon the same theme—a relatively high-level measure of scholastic aptitude and achievement. The different professional aptitude tests would correlate very substantially with one another or with a measure of general intelligence, and, indeed, it should be expected that they would because the abilities required to succeed in training for the different professions have much in common. The similarities outweigh the differences. The common core is adapted to the professional field, as by giving more emphasis to quantitative materials for engineering and more to verbal materials for law. It is supplemented in some cases by rather highly specialized tests, for example, a test of chalk-carving for dentistry. These variations are superimposed upon the basic theme of scholastic aptitude and achievement.

MEASUREMENT OF MUSICAL APTITUDE

When we come to such fields as music and art, the need for special measures of aptitude becomes quite apparent. Grades in these subjects are usually among those least well predicted by general measures of scholastic aptitude. Furthermore, the specialized nature of outstanding talent in these fields has long been recognized. Our problem is to determine what the components of this talent are and devise ways of appraising them.

In musical ability one large component is executive or motor, the ability to master the patterns of action required for playing an instrument. Aptitude measures have largely avoided this domain, perhaps because of its specificity to a particular instrument. Most measurement has been directed toward the perceptive and interpretive aspects of music.

Hearing music involves in the first place various types of sensory discrimination —discrimination of pitch, of loudness, of temporal relations. It involves in the second place perceiving the more complex musical relations in the material, interval relationships, the pattern of a melody, the composition of a chord, the relationship of a harmony to a melody. Third, it involves esthetic judgments about the suitability and pleasingness of a melody or harmony, a rhythmic pattern, or a pattern of dynamics.

The most thoroughly investigated musical aptitude test battery, the *Seashore Measures of Musical Talents,* is directed primarily toward measuring simple sensory discriminations, though with some attention to perceiving slightly more musical material. The tests have analyzed music down so far that very little music remains. Thus, there are the following subtests:

1. *Discrimination of Pitch:* judging which of two tones is higher.
2. *Discrimination of Loudness:* judging which of two sounds is louder.
3. *Discrimination of Time Interval:* judging which of two intervals is longer.
4. *Judgment of Rhythm:* judging whether two rhythms are the same or different.
5. *Judgment of Timbre:* judging which of two tone qualities is more pleasing.
6. *Tonal Memory:* judging whether two melodies are the same or different.

The items are on phonograph records, with a series of items of each type. Within each type, the judgments become progressively more difficult.

The analytic approach to musical aptitude is evident in the above list of subtests. Critics have contended that the analysis has removed the tests a great way from any genuinely musical material and that fine discriminations of pitch, time, and intensity are really not called for in the activities of the musician. Validity studies of the *Seashore* tests have been somewhat conflicting, yielding appreciable correlations with measures of musical success in some instances and very low correlations in others. The value of the analytic test is still a matter of doubt and controversy.

A recently developed test that is based on more complex and more genuinely musical material is the *Gordon Musical Aptitude Profile* (Gordon, 1965). This test, recorded on tape, consists of tests of musical perception, in which the examinee must judge whether an "answer" phrase is the same as or different from the "question" phrase. There are four such subtests in which the comparison is to be based, respectively, on (1) melody, (2) harmony, (3) tempo, and (4) meter. These are followed by three subtests in which the examinee must judge which of two musical selections is better. In the first, or phrasing test, two renditions differ in musical expression; in the second, or balance test, the two renditions have different endings; in the third test, designated style, the two renditions differ in tempo.

The test appears to have been developed with a good deal of psychometric sophistication and thoroughness. Reliability is quite acceptable—in the .70's for the seven separate subscores, the .80's for the three main sections, and .90 to .95 for the composite score based on all of the parts. The test is quite new (published in 1965) so that available validity data are largely those supplied by the author in the test manual, but these seem generally promising and, in certain instances, quite dramatic. Thus, seven correlations with music teachers' estimates of the musical talent of members of their choral or instrumental group were reported as ranging from .64 to .97!

In an exemplary longitudinal study, Gordon (1967) followed up groups of students over a three-year period. Tests were given in the fourth or fifth grade, and were put away and not made available to either music teachers or evaluators of the pupils' performance. Complete classes were tested, composed of pupils who had had no previous formal musical training. For the three years of the follow-up, they received one period a week of instrumental instruction. Each pupil was tested with a standard set of performance tests for his instrument—"etudes" that were tape recorded and judged without knowledge of who was performing. In addition, teacher ratings were obtained, and an achievement test on music reading and notation was given.

Correlations of total test score with the three criterion measures at the end of one, two and three years were:

	1 Year	*2 Year*	*3 Year*
Performance Test	.53	.69	.68
Achievement Test	.61	.61	.71
Teacher Rating	.37	.39	.35

The test clearly provides a good prediction of later musical performance, one that appears to get better the longer the period of musical training that is covered. It is worth noting that objective and unbiased performance measures were more predictable than were the ratings by teachers.

The test appears to be a significant addition to the procedures available for assessing musical promise.

TESTS OF ARTISTIC APTITUDE

Several types of tests are available relating to aptitude for art. In the first place, there have been tests of esthetic judgment. That field is now fairly well dominated by the *Meier Art Judgment Test.* Each item consists of a pair of pictures of art objects. One is an acknowledged masterpiece. The other is that same masterpiece systematically distorted in some specified way. The examinee must choose the better picture in each pair, the test blank indicating the respect in which the two specimens differ.

A test of the judgmental aspect of art ability is the *Graves Design Judgment Test.* This differs from the *Meier Test* in that all the items consist of abstract and nonrepresentational material. The members of a pair differ in some single aspect of design, that is, balance, symmetry, variety. Judgment of design is presumably divorced from any particular object or content.

In an attempt to get at the productive, as distinct from the purely judgmental, aspect of art, several tests (*Horn, Knauber, Lewerenz*) require the subject to produce drawings, based on certain limiting "givens." Thus, in the *Horn Art Aptitude Inventory,* a pattern of lines and dots is provided, and from this material the examinee must produce a sketch. The type of item is indicated in Fig. 11.4. The products must be evaluated by subjective rating, according to standards given by the authors, but they present some evidence that this can be done rather reliably even by nonartists.

The *Lewerenz Tests in Fundamental Abilities of Visual Art* use dot patterns to elicit drawings, whereas the *Knauber Art Ability Tests* use various assigned drawing tasks. Both these last two tests also present problems in shading, perspective, and composition.

Art tests have been rather generally successful in differentiating art students or art teachers from other groups. However, it has been argued that they accomplish this because they are in large measure achievement tests rather than aptitude measures. There has been relatively little study of these tests as aptitude measures with untrained individuals. Studies of art students have indicated that test performance is reasonably predictive of later art-school success. Thus, Horn and Smith (1945) found a correlation of .66 between score on the Horn test at the beginning of the year and average faculty rating of success in a special high-

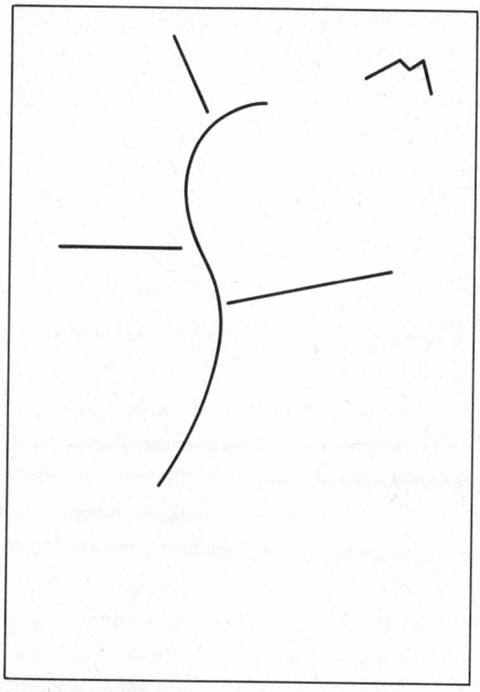

Fig. 11.4 Example of type of item used in *Horn Art Aptitude Inventory.*

school art class at the end of the year. Barrett (1949) correlated four art tests with grades in a ninth-grade art course and with ratings of pupils' art products, with the following results:

	Course Grade	*Ratings of Product*
McAdory Art Test	.10	.13
Meier Art Judgment Test	.37	.35
Knauber Art Ability Test	.33	.71
Lewerenz Fundamental Art Abilities Test	.40	.76

Thus the last two tests, requiring production of drawings by the examinee, had about the same correlation with grades as did the *Meier Art Judgment Test* but much higher correlations with appraisals of student products.

We can see from the above that the test tasks that require art students to do the sorts of tasks they will be taught to do in art class predict their later achievement. How far down to untrained pupils this can be pushed remains to be determined.

Since the keying of art tests of all types depends upon a pooling of judgments, obtaining a high score requires conformity to the accepted esthetic standards. There is real question as to the applicability of these tests (or the tests of musical aptitude) in a distinctly different culture. There is also the possibility, though it is a fairly unlikely one, that a highly talented but unconventional person will be penalized on the tests.

APPRAISING CREATIVITY

Consideration of tests in the fields of music and art leads one rather naturally to the topic of creativity. One criticism that has been directed at ability tests of the usual type is that they focus on what may be called *convergent thinking*. In convergent thinking, the examinee is called upon to zero in on *the* right answer to a problem for which an answer has already been determined. He is asked to define a word, solve an arithmetical problem, find the next number to continue a series, or identify the one thing that doesn't belong in a set. Often, he chooses the right answer from among the four or five choices that are supplied to him. The critics point out, however, that much of life's activity involves *divergent thinking*, the generating of novel responses to situations, responses that are original, unusual, varied, and hopefully effective in handling the largely unstructured problem that the person is called upon to solve.

In recent years a number of investigators have attempted to develop tests of divergent thinking and perhaps of creativity. Guilford included divergent thinking as one of the five operations upon intellectual materials in his *Structure of Intellect* (see p. 350), and he and his students have undertaken to produce a number of tests that exemplify this function. Typically, the tests call upon the examinee to generate multiple responses to a problem, for example, different uses for a wire coat hanger. The responses are scored in terms of fluency (number of responses), flexibility (number of different categories of responses), and originality (number of rare responses given by few other respondents). Torrance (1966) has produced tests oriented more toward young children and toward graphic or pictorial, as well as verbal response. Thus, in one test the subject is presented with a page of plain circles, and his task is to make each circle into a picture, producing as many pictures and as varied a set as he can.

If "divergent thinking" or "creativity" are to be useful constructs for educational and psychological measurement, the tests of them must (1) be relatively uncorrelated with the tests of convergent thinking that make up conventional aptitude batteries, and (2) show some coherence in the sense that different tests of "creativity" correlate with each other. In addition, they should (3) have some significant correlates in the world of practical events. The tests have had only modest success on any of these counts. Correlations with conventional tests of convergent thinking are not high, but they are quite generally positive and appreciable. Correlations of different "creativity" measures have been modest at best and the notion of a generalized trait of creativity receives only limited support. The extent to which the creativity tests are predictive of achievement either in or out of school is still a matter of controversy, some investigators reporting substantial relationships and others failing to find any. Thus, the tests must still be thought of as research tools, rather than as instruments that are of proven value for use either in schools or in industry.

SUMMARY STATEMENT

Though general intelligence tests bear some relationship to success in many fields, efficient vocational guidance or personnel classification calls for tests more specifically directed at the abilities called for by each kind of job. Analytical studies of human abilities support the genuineness and importance of these special abilities. Numerous tests of special abilities have appeared, and more recently tests of this sort have been organized into comprehensive aptitude batteries for use in vocational guidance or personnel classification.

Special tests to evaluate readiness to undertake particular educational tasks have also been developed. The most widely used of these are reading readiness tests. Other types of prognostic tests have been less widely used, perhaps because their function is reasonably well served by measures of scholastic aptitude and academic achievement. Professional school aptitude batteries appear to be variations upon the basic theme of scholastic aptitude tests.

The fields of music and art have produced a number of ability tests. However, highly analytic tests have not been very clearly successful. More complex tests involve an unknown admixture of previous training. These show reasonably good validity and may provide an improved and at least relatively objective way of appraising status and, hence, promise in the field.

Tests of "divergent thinking" and "creativity" are currently attracting a good deal of attention, but their usefulness as psychometric tools is still uncertain.

QUESTIONS AND EXERCISES

1. A number of aptitude test batteries have been developed for use at the secondary-school level, but almost none for the elementary school. Why is this? Is it a reasonable state of affairs?

2. What are the advantages in using a battery such as the *Differential Aptitude Tests* instead of tests selected from a number of different sources? What are the limitations?

3. Step by step, what would need to be done to set up a program for selecting students for a dental school?

4. How could a high-school counselor use the data of Table 11.3? What are the limitations on the usefulness of this material?

5. How might the counselor use the data of Tables 11.4 and 11.5? What are their limitations?

6. How sound is the statement: "The best measure of aptitude in any field is a measure of achievement in that field to date."? What are its limitations?

7. What are the differences between a reading readiness test and an intelligence test? What are the advantages of using the readiness test rather than an intelligence test for first-grade pupils?

8. To what extent are tests like the *Horn Art Test* measures of aptitude? To what extent are they measures of achievement?

9. In what ways could a follow-up study of graduates of a high school help in improving the school guidance program?

10. Why have aptitude test batteries shown up better in discriminating *between* jobs than in predicting success *within* a single job category?

11. What special problems arise in attempting to measure an attribute such as "creativity"? What procedures seem to have promise for overcoming these problems?

12. Have the students in a class write down all the uses they can think of for *old newspapers*. Try to set up a scoring system for the results to appraise (1) fluency, (2) flexibility, and (3) creativity. What problems did you encounter in the data-gathering and analysis?

13. What do psychologists hope to accomplish by *factor analysis*? What problems do they encounter when they use these procedures?

REFERENCES

Barrett, H. O. An examination of certain standardized art tests to determine their relation to classroom achievement and to intelligence. *Journal of Educational Research*, 1949, **42**, 398–400.

Bennett, G. K. & Cruickshank, R. M. *A summary of clerical tests.* New York: Psychological Corp., 1948.

Bennett, G. K. & Cruickshank, R. M. *A summary of manual and mechanical ability tests.* New York: Psychological Corp., 1942.

Carroll, J. B. & Sapon, S. M. *Modern Language Aptitude Test.* New York: Psychological Corp., 1958.

DuBois, P. (Ed.) *The classification program,* Army Air Forces Aviation Psychology Program Report No. 2. Washington, D.C.: United States Government Printing Office, 1947.

Flanagan, J. C. & Cooley, W. W. *Project Talent: One-year follow-up studies.* Pittsburgh, Pennsylvania: University of Pittsburgh School of Education, 1966.

French, J. W. The description of aptitude and achievement tests in terms of rotated factors. *Psychometric Monographs,* 1951, No. 5.

Ghiselli, E. E. *The validity of occupational aptitude tests.* New York: John Wiley, 1966.

Gordon, E. *Musical Aptitude Profile.* Boston, Massachusetts: Houghton Mifflin, 1965.

Gordon, E. *A three-year longitudinal predictive validity study of the Musical Aptitude Profile.* Iowa City, Iowa: University of Iowa Press, 1967.

Guilford, J. P. *Psychometric methods.* New York: McGraw-Hill, 1954.

Guilford, J. P. *The nature of human intelligence.* New York: McGraw-Hill, 1967.

Horn, C. A. & Smith, L. F. The Horn Art Aptitude Inventory. *Journal of Applied Psychology,* 1945, **29**, 350–355.

Pimsleur, P. *Pimsleur Language Aptitude Battery.* New York: Harcourt, Brace & World, 1966.

Thorndike, R. L. & Hagen, E. P. *10,000 Careers.* New York: John Wiley, 1959.

Thurstone, L. L. Primary mental abilities. *Psychometric Monographs,* 1938, No. 1.

Torrance, E. P. *Torrance Tests of Creative Thinking.* Princeton, New Jersey: Personnel Press, 1966.

United States Employment Service. *Manual for the General Aptitude Test Battery, Section III: Development.* Washington, D.C.: United States Department of Labor, 1967.

Vernon, P. E. *The structure of human abilities.* (Rev. ed.) London: Methuen, 1960.

SUGGESTED ADDITIONAL READING

Carroll, J. B. Factors of verbal achievement. In A. Anastasi (Ed.), *Testing problems in perspective.* Washington, D.C.: American Council on Education, 1966. Pp. 406–413.

Crutchfield, R. D. Creative thinking in children: Its teaching and testing. In *Intelligence: Perspectives 1965.* The Terman-Otis Memorial Lectures. New York: Harcourt, Brace & World, 1966. Pp. 33–64.

Eysenck, H. J. Uses and limitations of factor analysis in psychological research. In A. Anastasi (Ed.), *Testing problems in perspective.* Washington, D.C.: American Council on Education, 1966. Pp. 355–359.

French, J. W. The logic of and assumptions underlying differential testing. In A. Anastasi (Ed.), *Testing problems in perspective.* Washington, D.C.: American Council on Education, 1966. Pp. 321–330.

Ilg, F. L. & Ames, L. B. *School readiness: Behavior tests used at the Gesell Institute.* New York: Harper & Row, 1964.

Guilford, J. P. Potentiality for creativity and its measurement. In A. Anastasi (Ed.), *Testing problems in perspective.* Washington, D.C.: American Council on Education, 1966. Pp. 429–435.

Guilford, J. P. Three faces of intellect. In N. E. Gronlund (Ed.), *Readings in measurement and evaluation.* New York: MacMillan, 1968. Pp. 262–279.

Humphreys, L. G. The nature and organization of human abilities. In N. E. Gronlund (Ed.), *Readings in measurement and evaluation.* New York: Macmillan, 1968. Pp. 253–261.

Super, D. E. & Crites, J. O. *Appraising vocational fitness by means of psychological tests.* New York: Harper & Row, 1962. Chapters 8–15.

Super, D. E. *The use of multifactor tests in guidance.* Washington, D.C.: American Personnel and Guidance Association, 1958.

Thorndike, R. L. Some methodological issues in the study of creativity. In A. Anastasi (Ed.), *Testing problems in perspective.* Washington, D.C.: American Council on Education, 1966. Pp. 436–448.

CHAPTER 12

Questionnaires and Inventories for Self-Appraisal

THE last three chapters have been devoted to measures of ability: what the individual *can* do under test conditions and motivation to do his best. We shall move on now to measurement of other aspects of personality—to the appraisal of what he *will* do under the natural circumstances of life. Both in our discussions of personality and in our efforts to develop instruments of appraisal, we must recognize that the person is a unified whole. Any aspects or traits that we may separate out are separated out for our convenience. They do not exist as separate entities. They are only aspects of or ways of looking at the unitary person. However, it is inevitable that we do pick the person to pieces to study and understand him. We cannot look at everything at once.

In Chapter 2 we identified the following five segments of personality.

Temperament refers to the individual's characteristic mood, activity level, excitability, and focus of concern. It includes such dimensions as cheerful-gloomy, energetic-lethargic, excited-calm, introverted-extroverted, and dominant-submissive.

Character relates to those traits to which definite social value is attached. They are the "Boy Scout" traits of honesty, kindliness, cooperation, industry, and such.

Adjustment is a term that we shall use to indicate how well the individual has been able to make peace with himself and the world about him. Insofar as the individual can comfortably accept himself and his world, insofar as his ways of life do not get him into trouble in his social group, he will be considered well adjusted.

Interests refer to tendencies to seek out and participate in certain activities.

Attitudes relate to tendencies to favor or reject particular groups of individuals, sets of ideas, or social institutions.

METHODS OF STUDYING PERSONALITY

Most of the evaluation techniques we shall consider in this and the following chapters have to do with one or more of the aspects of personality identified above. To what sources may we go for evidence on these aspects when we wish to study an individual? First, we can see what the individual has to say about himself. Second, we can find out what others say about him. Third, we can see what he actually does, how he behaves in the real world of things or people. Fourth, we can observe how he reacts to the world of fantasy and make-believe.

What the Individual Says About Himself

One obvious source for information about a person is that person himself. No one else has as intimate and continuous a view of Johnny as Johnny has of himself. He is aware of hopes and aspirations, worries and concerns that may be well hidden from the outsider. To get at the individual's view of himself we may interview him, probing those areas that seem sensitive or significant. Another approach is to incorporate the questions that might be asked in a face-to-face interview into a uniform questionnaire or personality inventory. The choices the individual makes in responding to the set of questions are scored in various ways to provide a picture of him as he describes himself. These procedures will be elaborated in this chapter, and their strengths and weaknesses pointed out.

Appraisal Through the Opinion of Others

For some purposes, we may be interested in how a person is perceived by his fellow beings. Is he seen as a friendly fellow worker? A fair teacher? An industrious pupil? A convincing salesman? A generally desirable employee? The opinion of others may be the significant fact in certain settings. It is also a very convenient way of getting a summary appraisal of a fellow man. For these reasons, rating procedures have been widely used. We shall consider their values and limitations in the next chapter.

Measures of Behavior

It can be argued that for practical purposes an individual's personality is what he does, rather than what he says or what is said about him. The problem is to develop procedures for appraising genuine behavior, not distorted for the purpose of making a good impression. Some attempts have been made to do this with objective tests, and we shall consider these briefly in Chapter 14. Of more importance and current interest are procedures for observing the individual and for recording or evaluating his responses as they are seen by an observer.

The World of Imagination and Fantasy

What an individual will tell about himself in response to questions is limited by his willingness to reveal himself, his understanding of himself, and his understanding of the language in which the questions are presented. For this reason, indirect methods have been sought to avoid these limitations and permit him to "open up" more fully. One indirect avenue is that of fantasy, imagination, and make-believe. We may study what the person sees in ink blots, what stories he tells about an ambiguous picture, what play scenes he acts out with dolls, what he does with paints and modeling clay. These materials and others have been used to elicit imaginative productions that psychologists have studied as a source of understanding of children and adults. The individual is allowed to express himself through play materials or to project his own interpretations into ambiguous stimuli, and thus to reveal himself to us. These are expressive and projective techniques for personality appraisal. We shall undertake to describe and evaluate them in Chapter 15.

INTERVIEW

If we wish to find out about a person, one way to do so is to ask him questions and to evaluate his answers. This inquiry may be, to some degree, structured, controlled, and standardized with respect to the questions asked only, with respect to both the questions and the possible answers, or with respect to neither questions nor answers. If we think of questions and answers as representing two dimensions that may extend from very fluid to very structured and controlled, we can represent several forms of questioning as shown in Fig. 12.1 on p. 384.

Falling at the structured, controlled end of the continuum with respect to

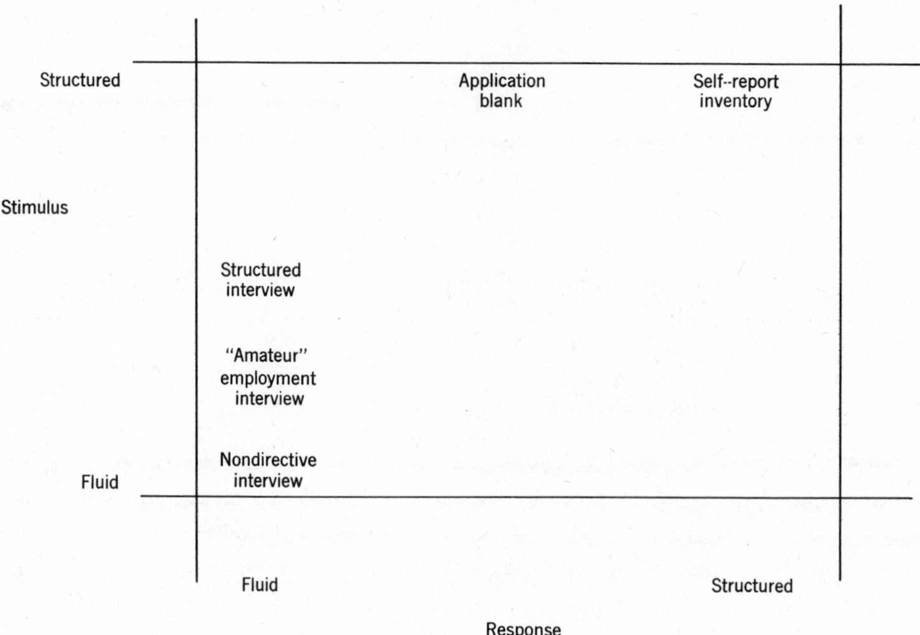

Fig. 12.1 Relationships among self-descriptive techniques.

both question and response are the many self-report inventories of which we shall speak later in the chapter. These present each person with a uniform set of questions in predetermined order, and provide him with a limited set of categories or options from among which he must make his choice.

The typical application blank is equally structured so far as the questions are concerned, but provides more flexibility on the response side. The responses are often (though not always) constructed by the respondent, providing opportunity for a response that is uniquely descriptive of him.

At the other extreme, that is, the open and unstructured end on both question and response, is the nondirective, therapeutic interview and, often, the untrained employment interview. It is impossible to tell in advance, or from one case to the next either what questions will be asked or what form the responses will take. This is, for the interview, both a strength and a weakness. It is a strength in that it makes it possible to adapt the questioning to the individual case, following up in depth those lines of inquiry that seem most relevant and productive. It is a weakness in that it makes it very unlikely that the same evidence will be obtained for all interviewees. In the extreme case, there may be large gaps in the interview coverage, and highly relevant material may be missed because the appropriate questions were not asked. This variation in what is covered certainly accounts, in part, for the discouragingly low consistency that emerges in the impressions that different interviewers get when they interview the same person.

The problem for the interview is to maintain the virtues of flexibility while at the same time achieving a reasonable degree of uniformity. One approach to this has been to develop various patterns of structured interview, in which a specified set of topics is systematically covered, but not always in the same order or in the same detail. This approach is intermediate in degree of structure and control in the stimulus (question) dimension, and pretty open and fluid in the response dimension. Through training and through an interview record form, interviewers are led to cover systematically a set of topics that have been identified as relevant and to record the relevant information provided on each, and in this way the lapses and biases of the single interviewer are minimized.

The popularity of the interview is *not* based primarily upon its demonstrated validity as a device for appraising people. In fact, evidence for the validity of the impressions or conclusions derived from interviews is spotty and rather contradictory. Interview procedures are basically subjective, variable and heavily dependent upon the skill of the interviewer. It has repeatedly been demonstrated that different interviewers interviewing the same person come up with quite varied impressions of him. The variability arises in part from variation in the questions asked and the lines of inquiry intensively pursued. It arises in part from differences in interpretation and evaluation of the responses the individual makes. The typical interview is not a precise or efficient psychometric technique. Furthermore, individual interviews place very heavy demands upon the time of interviewing personnel, demands which may be prohibitive in a number of situations. To economize on interviewer time, then, and to provide an inquiry that is uniform in presentation and procedure for evaluation, the printed questionnaire has been developed. The self-report questionnaire or inventory is essentially this: a standard set of questions about some aspect or aspects of the individual's life history, feelings, preferences, or actions, presented in a standard way and scored with a standard scoring key.

The alternate approaches to interrogating the individual have opposite advantages. One trades off the objectivity, reliability, comparability from person to person, and economy provided by the multiple-choice inventory for the flexibility and adaptability to the individual case provided by the interview. A potential user must decide in each situation what compromise of these values is most suited to his needs.

THE BIOGRAPHICAL DATA BLANK

An obvious and important use of the questionnaire is as a means of eliciting factual information about the individual's past history. Place and date of birth, amount and type of education and degree of success with it, nature and duration of previous jobs, hobbies, special skills, and a host of other biographical facts can be determined most economically through a blank filled out by the individual himself. It is the economy and efficiency of this approach that makes it particularly appealing. Though his reports may be inaccurate in some respects, the individual himself is probably the richest single repository for the factual information we would like to have about him.

The problems in using questionnaires to elicit facts are primarily problems of communication. When questions are preformulated and appear in printed form and answers are written down, misunderstanding may occur either in the respondent's interpretation of the question or in the using agency's interpretation of his response. If there is no personal interaction, these misunderstandings cannot be cleared up with an oral question or a further probing into the area of uncertainty. It is important, therefore, that a fact-finding questionnaire be very carefully worded and that it be tried out in preliminary form with small groups to make sure that the ambiguities have been cleared out of it.

An interview to supplement the questionnaire may be desirable in order to permit clarification of any of the responses to questionnaire items that are puzzling to the user or to get fuller information on some points. As a matter of fact, one appropriate use of self-report inventories of all types is to provide a jumping-off place for an interview, the questionnaire providing leads that may be followed up in the interview.

Sometimes the factual information on an application blank has been used to determine whether the applicant meets certain specified minimum requirements for a job, that is, is 21 years of age, has a valid driver's license, etc. Sometimes it is used as part of the raw material available to a personnel officer, director of admissions, or scholarship committee on the basis of which a clinical decision is made as to the individual's desirability as an employee or a student. Increasingly, in recent years, biographical data blanks have been analyzed item by item and empirical keys have been developed to predict some criterion of job or life performance.

Thus, a study (McGrath, 1960) of the application blanks and purchase contracts of samples of new car buyers identified 24 items that discriminated between those who completed payments for their cars and those who had the cars repossessed. When the scoring key developed on one sample of cases was applied to a new second sample, score correlated approximately 0.50 with completion of payments in the new sample. Empirically scored biographical data blanks were first successfully used on a large scale in the selection of airplane pilots and navigators during World War II. Other situations to which empirical weighting of the items in an application blank or a biographical inventory have recently been applied with promising results are in the prediction of creativity in adolescents (Schaefer and Anastasi, 1968) and in scientists (Buel et al, 1966), of job turnover in unskilled (Scott and Johnson, 1967) and clerical (Buel, 1964) employees, and of sales, research, and general engineering interest (Chaney and Owens, 1964). Thus, the procedure appears to have promise in quite a range of practical situations. Determination of the proper scoring weights is a fairly major research undertaking (England, 1961), but once a scoring system has been developed the scoring of individual blanks proceeds rapidly. If the number of applicants justifies doing so, it is even possible to prepare biographical data blanks in multiple-choice form with separate answer sheets and to score these by machine as one would any standard test.

INTEREST INVENTORIES

One aspect of the individual's makeup that we would like to study, both to understand him as a person and to help in such immediately practical problems as educational and vocational guidance, is the domain of interests and aversions, preferences for activities and surroundings. Of course, in the matter of vocational interests, the simplest procedure would seem to be to ask the individual how much he would like to be an engineer, for example. However, this doesn't work out very well in practice. In the first place, people differ in the readiness with which they exhibit enthusiasm. "Like very much" for person A may signify no more enthusiasm than "like" for person B. In the second place, people differ substantially in the nature and completeness of their understanding of what a particular job means in terms of activities and conditions of work. "Engineer" to one person may signify primarily out-of-doors work; to another it may carry a flavor of the laboratory or drafting board; to still another it may signify vaguely a high-prestige, science-oriented job. These varied and incomplete meanings cause a response to the single question, "How much would you like to be an engineer?" to be a rather unsatisfactory indicator of the degree to which the individual has interests really suitable for the profession of engineering. It is for these reasons that psychometricians have undertaken to broaden the base of information and to ask a whole array of questions about the individual's likes and dislikes, rather than simply to ask directly about preference for particular jobs.

The Strong Vocational Interest Blank

One of the best known instruments for appraising interests is the *Strong Vocational Interest Blank for Men.* Originally published by E. K. Strong in 1927, it has been extensively revised in a 1966 edition, brought out by a group of his disciples. The 1966 version of the inventory is made up of 399 items, mostly dealing with liking for or preference between occupations, school subjects, amusements, activities, types of people. For the major part of the test, examinees respond by marking L, I, or D (Like, Indifferent, Dislike), but on some items they choose between competing activities. A response is called for to each item. About 60 different scoring keys are available for the blank. Most of the keys are for specific occupations, largely at the professional level, such as accountant, advertising man, Air Force officer, or architect, but there are also keys with a more general reference designated Academic Achievement, Masculinity-Femininity, Occupational Introversion-Extroversion, Occupational Level, and Specialization Level.

The scoring key for each occupation was developed by comparison of a group of men who were successfully engaged in that occupation with a reference group of men-in-general. Thus, the percent of men in occupation A choosing the L, I, and D options to item 1 is compared with the percent of men in general choosing these same options. If enough more men in occupation A choose a particular option, that option receives a plus score for occupation A. If the percent is smaller for occupation A, the option receives a minus score.

Table 12.1 shows the scoring key for ten items in the blank for four different occupational keys. Note the weights for the different items. Note that some or all of the options for a given item may receive a zero weight.

An individual's score is obtained by summing up the plus and minus credits corresponding to the responses he has chosen. Since the responses scored are different for each occupation, a separate scoring key is required, and a separate score is obtained for the examinee for each scale. Thus, a series of scores is obtained showing how closely the responses given by an examinee correspond to those typically given by each specific occupational group. Raw scores are translated into a standard score scale in which 50 represents the mean for men in the specific occupation. A scale of letter grades is also provided, in which A represents close resemblance to the particular occupational group, B+, B, and B− lesser degrees of resemblance, and C+ or C interest patterns quite different from those of that occupational group.

TABLE 12.1 SCORING WEIGHT FOR SAMPLE ITEMS AND KEYS OF THE *Strong-Vocational Interest Blank for Men*

	Scoring Key											
	Engineer			Social Worker			Farmer			Mortician		
Item	L	I	D	L	I	D	L	I	D	L	I	D
Actor	−1	0	+1	+1	0	−1	0	0	0	0	0	0
Advertiser	−1	0	+1	0	0	0	−1	0	+1	0	0	0
Artist	0	0	0	0	0	0	−1	0	+1	0	0	0
Astronomer	0	0	0	0	0	0	0	0	0	−1	0	+1
Athletic director	−1	+1	+1	0	0	0	0	0	0	0	0	0
Auctioneer	−1	−1	+1	0	0	0	0	0	0	0	0	0
Author of novel	−1	0	+1	+1	−1	−1	−1	0	+1	−1	0	+1
Author of technical book	+1	0	−1	0	0	0	−1	0	+1	−1	0	+1
Airplane pilot	0	0	0	0	0	0	+1	0	−1	0	0	0
Buyer of merchandise	0	0	0	0	0	0	0	0	0	+1	−1	−1

Table 12.2 on page 390 shows the standard scores and letter ratings on the occupational scales of the original form of the blank for one college freshman. This young man shows interest patterns resembling closely (A) those of chemists, farmers, and mathematics and science teachers. His interests are also quite like (B+) those of physicians, dentists, engineers, and carpenters. His interests are very *unlike* (C−) those of YMCA secretaries, city school superintendents, ministers, and life insurance salesmen.

Strong also developed a *Vocational Interest Blank for Women* that closely followed the pattern of the blank for men, and this has also been revised. The women's blank was not developed as fully as the blank for men, and seems to have been less successful in differentiating specific occupational groups. This may be because vocational interests are less central in the lives of many women, being confounded by general "homemaker" interests, with the result that interest profiles in women tend to be less clear-cut and meaningful.

With some 60 different scoring keys, hand-scoring of the *Strong* would be a very imposing enterprise. However, the development of optical scanners and computer programs has reduced the task to manageable proportions. There are a number of agencies that provide a scoring service. Cost depends upon the amount of scoring, but the publishers estimate complete costs for booklet and scoring at 90¢ for a single individual and perhaps half this much when a considerable volume of testing and scoring is involved.

There are two points about the construction of the *Strong Blank* to which we

TABLE 12.2 SCORES ON *Strong Vocational Interest Blank* FOR A COLLEGE FRESHMAN

	Occupation	Standard Score	Letter Rating
I.	Artist	26	C+
	Psychologist	22	C
	Architect	29	C+
	Physician	42	B+
	Dentist	41	B+
II.	Mathematician	26	C+
	Engineer	44	B+
	Chemist	52	A
III.	Production manager	39	B
IV.	Farmer	59	A
	Carpenter	44	B+
	Math and science teacher	48	A
V.	YMCA physical director	34	B−
	Personnel manager	21	C
	YMCA secretary	Low *	C−
	Social-science teacher	17	C
	City school superintendent	Low *	C−
	Minister	Low *	C−
VI.	Musician	25	C+
VII.	CPA	16	C
VIII.	Accountant	25	C+
	Office worker	25	C+
	Purchasing agent	28	C+
	Banker	22	C
IX.	Sales manager	19	C
	Real estate salesman	17	C
	Life-insurance salesman	Low *	C−
X.	Advertising man	19	C
	Lawyer	20	C
	Author-journalist	24	C

* "Low" designates a standard score of 15 or lower.

wish to call especial attention at this time. In the first place, the person taking the test responds by choosing one of a set of response categories for each item (L, I, D). A particularly effusive individual *could* choose all L's, and a particularly jaundiced one *could* choose all D's. There is a certain amount of freedom to impose one's own standards upon the task. Secondly, the keys are externally determined. That is, they are defined by the responses of a particular job group and not by any internal logic. We wish now to contrast the *Strong Blank* with the *Kuder Preference Record,* which is different with respect to both of these features.

The Kuder Preference Record (Vocational)

The *Kuder Preference Record (Vocational)* is made up of triads, or sets of three options. Typical sets might read:

> Go for a long hike in the woods.
> Go to a symphony concert.
> Go to an exhibit of new inventions.
>
> Fix a broken clock.
> Keep a set of accounts.
> Paint a picture.

In each set the individual is required to mark the one he would like to do *most* and the one he would like to do *least.*

Scoring keys were established on the basis of the *internal* relationships of the items. Thus, a study of the responses to the items showed that a number of items dealing with mechanical activities tended to hang together. If a person chose one he was likely to choose others, and if he rejected one he was likely to reject the others. Moreover, items in this group showed relatively little relationship to the remaining items. The items grouped together in a distinct cluster. From the nature of the items it was evident that this cluster related to mechanical interest. Those items having a substantial correlation with this cluster were included in a scoring key that gave a score for mechanical interest.

In the same way, other clusters were identified and built up in which the items went together but were largely independent of items not in the cluster. Scoring keys were developed for these. The *Preference Record* now yields scores for the following interest clusters: outdoor, mechanical, computational, scientific, persuasive, artistic, literary, musical, social service, and clerical. Raw scores are converted into percentiles, separate norms being supplied for male and female high-school students and for male and female adults.

TABLE 12.3 *Kuder Preference Record* SCORES OF A COLLEGE FRESHMAN *

Interest Area	Raw Score	Percentile Equivalent
Outdoor	71	95
Mechanical	58	87
Computational	17	16
Scientific	60	93
Persuasive	25	07
Artistic	30	68
Literary	23	78
Musical	12	45
Social service	36	46
Clerical	19	01

* Scores for same individual shown in Table 12.2.

In Table 12.3, the *Kuder* scores are given for the same college freshman whose *Strong* scores were shown in Table 12.2. On the *Kuder*, this young man stands highest on outdoor, scientific, and mechanical interest. He is very low on clerical and persuasive interests. These findings can be studied in relation to his interest in specific occupations, as shown in Table 12.2. The two sets of results are obviously consistent and support one another.

Comparison of Strong and Kuder Inventories

The interest inventories that we have discussed have illustrated a number of variations in the patterning of self-descriptive instruments. Let us look a little more closely and critically at these contrasting patterns for organizing the choices that the individual is to make.

BASIS FOR SELECTING ITEMS TO BE INCLUDED IN KEY. We saw in the *Strong Vocational Interest Blank* that the items to be weighted in a key were selected and the weights determined by the actual relationship between response to the item and membership in a job group. The key was established *empirically* by the relationship between test response and a life criterion outside the testing situation. By contrast, in the original form of the *Kuder*, the items were selected with the intent of getting a cluster that was statistically and psychologically homogeneous, that is, all concerned with mechanical activities, all relating to scientific activities, etc.

The score that comes from a homogeneous cluster of items permits a clearer and more immediate psychological interpretation. When the items are all chosen because of their relationship to one another, there is a common theme tying them together. We can describe the person in terms of such constructs as "mechanical interest," "scientific interest," or "clerical interest." However, the job-related key has its advantages too. Its relationship to a particular life criterion is clearer and more direct, so that if a counselee is concerned with a specific career choice for which a key is available, the job-oriented key is directly relevant. We might summarize by saying that the homogeneous key appears to have clearer validity as a description of the individual (construct validity), while the job-oriented key has more obvious predictive validity for satisfaction in a specific job.

FORCED-CHOICE VERSUS CATEGORICAL RESPONSE. In the *Kuder Preference Record,* we saw an item format in which each item forced a choice between three alternatives. Essentially, the individual is required to rank the options from most to least preferred. Under these circumstances, each person must make the same number of selections and the same number of rejections as any other person. Thus, individual differences in enthusiasm or in tendency to be affirmative rather than negative are ruled out. And, for every time the examinee chooses one interest area, he must reject some other. He cannot be positive toward everything. So each person's record must show both areas of acceptance and areas of rejection.

Other self-descriptive instruments, such as the *Strong Vocational Interest Blank,* do not have this feature. There, on most of the sections of the test, it is possible for the examinee to mark L and express a liking for every activity. Such behavior might accurately represent a wide range of enthusiasms on the part of the examinee, but it might also represent certain habits of responding to questionnaires—what test makers have come to speak of as "response sets." A number of such tendencies have been identified in questionnaire responses—a tendency to be defensive and respond with socially desirable responses, a tendency to be acquiescent and agree with any statement, a tendency to be conservative and avoid any extreme ratings of self (or others). When we speak of a "response set," we are thinking of a rather superficial habit or trick of responding that isn't in any true sense descriptive of the person. It is, in large part, to escape the influence of such "response sets" that the forced-choice format for questionnaire items has been developed.

IPSATIVE VERSUS NORMATIVE SCORES. When items are arranged in a forced-choice format and every respondent must make as many rejections as he does selections, in a sense each person's score must add up to zero. (That is, we are thinking of an affirmative choice as counting as plus one, and a rejection as counting as minus one.) For every scale of the instrument that yields a plus score, there must somewhere be a minus score, and the plusses and minuses must balance. The pattern of choices and rejections becomes, then, a pattern of relative preference, and the base line is the individual himself. Scores that are expressed in relation to the individual as a base line have been designated *ipsative* scores. A profile of ipsative scores describes the peaks and valleys of an individual's profile, using only the individual himself as a reference point.

By contrast, *normative* scores describe the individual by external reference to a group of persons, identifying his standing in such a group. The scores that we have become familiar with for ability tests—IQ's, grade equivalents, etc.—are all normative scores. And the standard scores and letter ratings for the *Strong Vocational Interest Blank* are also normative scores referring to criterion groups in different occupations. But the *Kuder Preference Record* percentiles are basically ipsative. Because a choice of one interest area means a rejection of some other, any person's Kuder profile will show about as many values above the 50th percentile as below. The record will show his interest in any one area relative to *his* interest in other areas.

Ipsative scores are somewhat tricky things to interpret. The thing to remember is that by forcing the number of a person's selections and rejections, we have sacrificed the possibility of getting a measure of the individual in relation to any external bench mark, and we have abandoned the hope of discovering any differences in overall level between individuals. Each individual is forced to the same base line. However, by forcing the individual to make choices between alternatives, we have maximized the sensitivity of our procedure for identifying differences *within* the individual—the peaks and valley of his individual interest or temperamental profile.

Reliability and Validity of Inventoried Interests

The *Strong Vocational Interest Blank* is one of the most thoroughly investigated psychometric tools we have, and, though the history of the *Kuder Preference Record* is shorter, it too has been intensively studied. Both instruments yield scores that are reasonably reliable for individuals in their teens or over. Thus, for 285 Stanford University seniors Strong (1943) reports odd-even reliabilities for the separate occupational scales ranging from .73 to .94, with an average value of .88. A number of reliability studies with the *Kuder*, based on analysis of a single testing, give values averaging about .90. The reliability of the scores extracted from these interest inventories compares favorably with that of scores on ability tests.

For the *Strong* (Mallinson and Crumrine, 1952; Strong, 1943, 1951, 1952), there is evidence that interests show a good deal of stability over time, at least in adolescents and adults. Data on the average correlation at different ages and over different periods may be summarized as follows:

	Upper Elementary School	*High School*	*College Freshmen*	*College Seniors*
1 or 2 years	.55	.65	.80	. . .
3 to 5 years	.30	. . .	.75	.75
6 to 10 years	. . .	.50	.55	.70

The stability is low in the elementary school, but for persons of college age stability compares favorably with that for intelligence tests.

In appraising the validity of an interest inventory as a *description* of how the individual feels about activities and events in the world about him, the main issue is the truthfulness of his responses. There isn't really any higher court of appeal for determining a person's likes and preferences than the individual's own statement.

A number of studies have indicated that inventories such as the *Strong can* be faked (Garry, 1953; Longstaff, 1948). If a group of examinees is told to try to respond the way that life insurance salesmen would, they are generally rather successful in making themselves appear like life insurance salesmen. However, this is no indication that the blank *will* be faked, even when used as an employment device.

When the inventory is used for counseling and to help the respondent, as is most often the case, there is probably little reason to anticipate intentional faking. The individual may be expected to report his likes and dislikes as he knows them. His self-knowledge is perhaps imperfect, so his reports may be inaccurate in some respects. Thus, he may say that he would like to attend symphony concerts because he feels that that is the thing to say, but his actions may belie his statement; he may in fact avoid concerts whenever they come his way. This lack of self-insight is a real problem. But it is probably mitigated somewhat, in the inventory approach to interests, where isolated points of poor insight will have only minor effects upon a final score.

The validity of interest inventories as predictors of later behavior is another matter. Scoring keys for the *Strong* were established by comparing men who were already in the occupation with men-in-general. *Kuder* occupational interest profiles have also been prepared by determining the average level in each of the interest areas for individuals already working in the occupation. But the common interest patterns of individuals in a field of work may have grown out of their work. The men may have come to exhibit certain common patterns from the very nature of their work experience. The crucial evidence on predictive validity would come from testing a group *before* they entered the world of work and determining whether those who later entered and continued in a particular occupation had distinctive interest patterns *before* they entered the occupation. This is an expensive operation, expensive in the time that must elapse before men can become settled in their occupation and expensive in the dissipation of cases among literally hundreds of occupations.

Strong (1951) had been able to follow some groups who were tested as college undergraduates and obtained some evidence on the extent to which students with interests characteristic of a particular occupation tended to enter that occupation and to persist in it. For the typical individual, the occupation in which he was actually working 10 years later ranked second or third for him among all the scales of the *Strong*. Considering group averages, those who remained in an occupation received higher interest scores for that occupation than for any other occupation and higher than those who switched to some other occupation.

Berdie (1965) located the twelfth grade *SVIB* records of students who had completed specialized professional programs at the University of Minnesota. Percents showing high interest (A or B+) on each of four scales are shown below in relation to the professional training completed.

	Completed Training in			
High Interest on Scale for	*Medicine*	*Law*	*Accounting*	*Mechanical Engineering*
Physician	49	2	6	21
Lawyer	18	50	18	2
Accountant	5	19	43	6
Engineer	33	0	15	73

Although the relationship falls well short of perfection, it is clear and striking and the discrimination among the groups is quite sharp.

McCully (1954) followed up a group of men who had been given the *Kuder* as a part of Veterans Administration counseling at the end of World War II. They were located several years later, and their occupation determined. Table 12.4 shows the average standard scores on each of the ten *Kuder* interest areas for those occupational groups that were large enough to justify study. The results show clear-cut and fairly substantial differences in pattern of interest for different occupations. Thus, evidence with respect to both the *Strong* and the *Kuder* indicates that they have a certain amount of validity as predictors of occupational choice.

TABLE 12.4 MEAN *Kuder* STANDARD SCORES OF DIFFERENT OCCUPATIONAL GROUPS *

	Mechanical	Computational	Scientific	Persuasive	Artistic	Literary	Musical	Social Service	Clerical
Accounting and related	**−78**	**152**	−32	37	**−82**	19	2	−14	**118**
Engineering and related	**56**	45	**82**	−16	7	1	−21	−46	−41
Managerial work	−28	44	−18	**56**	−27	19	−15	−2	42
Clerical—computing and recording	−27	**67**	−9	9	−50	4	3	−14	**68**
General clerical work	−19	−3	−31	−9	−14	22	3	17	30
Sales—higher	**−65**	−14	−40	**111**	**−54**	38	17	18	30
Sales—lower	−19	−12	−25	**79**	−32	10	6	15	16
General farming	22	−25	−16	−37	−4	−49	−42	12	−10
Mechanical repairing	**81**	−21	3	−40	28	−28	−30	−40	−29
Electrical repairing	**66**	−3	27	−35	5	−41	−13	−19	−29
Bench crafts (fine)	**63**	−5	12	−24	38	−23	−20	−33	−2

* Based on a mean of 0 and a standard deviation of 100 for the reference group of 2,797 employed veterans.

Interest and Ability

It is important not to confuse measures of interest and ability. Interest measures tell us nothing directly about ability and, generally speaking, the relationships between interests and abilities are quite low. A representative set of correlations is shown in Table 12.5 on page 398. Correlations of .20 or more are shown in boldface type. There are only six correlations as great as .20 and only one over .30. Highest correlation is between verbal ability and literary interest, next is between spatial ability and artistic interest, and third is between numerical ability and computational interest. The correlations all make sense, but they are also all quite modest in size. Interest measures and ability measures deal with two quite distinct aspects of fitness for a field of study or work. Each provides information that supplements the other. Interest is not a substitute for ability, and, conversely, ability to learn the skills of a job is no guarantee of success or satisfaction in the job.

Table 12.5 Correlation of aptitude and interest factors

Kuder Interest Scale	General Aptitude Test Battery Factor								
	General Intell.	Verbal	Numer-ical	Spatial	Form Percept.	Clerical Percept.	Motor Coord.	Finger Dext.	Manual Dext.
Outdoor	01	−07	−04	11	−04	**−20**	−19	−04	−04
Mechanical	−02	−06	−04	19	−02	−12	−11	08	06
Computational	14	06	**25**	12	10	15	07	03	12
Scientific	16	10	10	12	04	−02	−03	10	04
Persuasive	−12	−07	01	−16	−11	06	07	−08	02
Artistic	10	07	−10	**26**	07	−04	04	12	04
Literary	14	**32**	04	00	02	06	05	−07	00
Musical	−02	06	−08	04	−05	04	07	00	**−11**
Social service	−10	−09	04	**−20**	06	04	−01	−04	−04
Clerical	**−24**	−14	06	−18	−02	08	00	−02	00

Adapted from the Manual of the General Aptitude Test Battery.

Standardized interest inventories have been developed primarily for their contribution to vocational counseling and job placement. With this purpose in mind, they are directed at groups of high-school age or older. The *Kuder,* with its relatively general interest areas, has been used satisfactorily at about the ninth grade and above. The *Strong,* focusing on specific occupations and with a particular emphasis upon occupations at the professional level, is suitable primarily for senior high school pupils with definite plans to go to college and for college groups. As in almost all inventories, these instruments involve a good deal of reading. Their use with individuals who fall below eighth or ninth grade reading level would probably present serious problems. An inventory that was designed specifically for counseling with respect to skilled and semiskilled occupations is the *Minnesota Vocational Interest Inventory.* The items were chosen to be promising as differentiators between different trades.

Following the empirical keying procedure of the *Strong,* scoring keys were developed for 21 specific occupations such as baker, carpenter, and electrician. However, at the same time, nine homogeneous scales were set up in terms of the statistical and psychological coherence of groups of items, more in the *Kuder* tradition. The authors offer the homogeneous scales not as something that will be directly helpful in occupational counseling, but as an aid to understanding the nature of the interests of persons in a given occupation. Thus, the finding that the Truck Driver scale shows positive correlations with homogeneous scales designated Mechanical, Electronics and Outdoors and negative correlations with Health Service, Office Work, and Sales Office may help to give a clearer picture of the typical truck driver.

Several other interest inventories are listed and briefly described in Appendix IV.

TEMPERAMENT AND ADJUSTMENT INVENTORIES

Self-report inventories have been extensively developed in the areas of temperament and personal adjustment. In these areas we again encounter instruments developed to yield scores for internally consistent clusters of behaviors, as did the *Kuder Preference Record,* and instruments built with keys based on reference to some external criterion, as was the *Strong Vocational Interest Blank.*

The basic material of all temperament and adjustment questionnaires is much the same. They draw from an extensive catalogue of statements about actions and feelings. To these the individual responds by indicating whether each is or is not characteristic of him. In many cases, a "?" or "uncertain" category is provided for the person who does not wish to endorse an unequivocal "Yes" or "No" answer. In the case of adjustment questionnaires, questions are culled from case studies, writings on various types of adjustment problems, suggestions of psychiatrists, and similar sources. For the normal dimensions of temperament, a review of psychological and literary treatments of personality differences and a systematic scrutiny of previous questionnaires, together with the personal insights of the investigator, provide the raw material for assembling items.

There are a large number of temperament and adjustment inventories. We shall describe three in some detail, illustrating distinctively different patterns. These are the *Guilford-Zimmerman Temperament Survey*, the *Minnesota Multiphasic Personality Inventory* (*MMPI*), and the *Thorndike Dimensions of Temperament* (*TDOT*). Then we shall undertake a more general evaluation of the validity of inventories in this area and of the conditions under which we may expect them to be of value.

The Guilford-Zimmerman Temperament Survey

The *Guilford-Zimmerman Temperament Survey* is the most recent development in a series of instruments on which Guilford has worked, each of which has attempted to identify and measure a number of internally coherent dimensions of personality that are clearly distinct from one another. Guilford has started with a pool of items and studied the intercorrelations among them, using the methods of factor analysis to which we referred on p. 347. He has identified distinct personality factors or foci, and tried to build up clusters of items to measure each. The objective is to get separate scales that are internally coherent and that are relatively independent of other scales. Thus, if a factor of "sociability" is identified, one attempts to get a cluster of items focusing on "sociability" that correlate substantially with each other, so that the person who subscribed to one item is likely also to subscribe to others. This cluster should be quite independent of other clusters relating to "dominance," "impulsiveness," and so forth, so that the correlations between the different clusters are quite low. This is the same basic approach as the one we saw in the *Kuder Preference Record*.

The *Guilford-Zimmerman* inventory provides scores appraising the clusters named and characterized below. Each cluster is characterized both by descriptive phrases and by two illustrative items.

GENERAL ACTIVITY. A high score indicates rapid pace of activities; energy, vitality; keeping in motion; production, efficiency, liking for speed; hurrying; quickness of action; enthusiasm, liveliness.

Sample Items

You start to work on a new project with a great deal of enthusiasm. (+)
You are the kind of person who is "on the go" all of the time. (+)

RESTRAINT. A high score indicates serious-mindedness; deliberateness; persistent effort; self-control; *not* being happy-go-lucky or carefree; *not* seeking excitement.

Sample Items

You like to play practical jokes upon others. (−)
You sometimes find yourself "crossing bridges before you come to them." (+)

ASCENDANCE. A high score indicates habits of leadership; a tendency to take the initiative in speaking with others; liking for speaking in public; liking for persuading others; liking for being conspicuous; tendency to bluff; tendency to be self-defensive.

Sample Items

You can think of a good excuse when you need one. (+)
You avoid arguing over a price with a clerk or salesman. (−)

SOCIABILITY. A high score indicates one who has many friends and acquaintances; who seeks social contacts; who likes social activities; who likes the limelight; who enters into conversations; who is *not* shy.

Sample Items

You would dislike very much to work alone in some isolated place. (+)
Shyness keeps you from being as popular as you should be. (−)

EMOTIONAL STABILITY. A person with a high score shows evenness of moods, interests, etc.; optimism, cheerfulness; composure; feelings of being in good health; *freedom from* feelings of guilt, worry, or loneliness; *freedom from* day dreaming; *freedom from* perseveration of ideas and moods.

Sample Items

You sometimes feel "just miserable" for no good reason at all. (−)
You seldom give your past mistakes a second thought. (+)

OBJECTIVITY. The high scorer is defined as *free from* the following: egoism, self-centeredness; suspiciousness, fancying hostility; ideas of reference; a tendency to get into trouble; a tendency to be thin-skinned.

Sample Items

You nearly always receive all the credit that is coming to you for things you do. (+)
There are times when it seems everyone is against you. (−)

FRIENDLINESS. High scores signify respect for others; acceptance of domination; toleration of hostile action; *freedom from* hostility, resentment, or desire to dominate.

Sample Items

When you resent the actions of anyone, you promptly tell him so. (−)
You would like to tell certain people a thing or two. (−)

THOUGHTFULNESS. The high-scoring person is characterized as reflective, meditative; observing of his own behavior and that of others; interested in thinking; philosophically inclined; mentally poised.

Sample Items

You are frequently "lost in thought." (+)
You find it very interesting to watch people to see what they will do. (+)

PERSONAL RELATIONS. High scores signify tolerance of people; faith in social institutions; *freedom from* self-pity or suspicion of others.

Sample Items

There are far too many useless laws that hamper an individual's personal freedom. (−)
Nearly all people try to do the right thing when given a chance. (+)

MASCULINITY. The high-scoring person is interested in masculine activities; not easily disgusted; hardboiled; inhibited in emotional expression; resistant to fear; unconcerned about vermin; little interested in clothes, style, or romance.

Sample Items

You can look at snakes without shuddering. (+)
The sight of ragged or soiled fingernails is repulsive to you. (−)

Since each of these clusters can be thought of as a dimension having two ends, just as we have north and south, east and west, there is an opposite end of each dimension that can be characterized as just the reverse of the description given above. Items marked (−) characterize this opposite end. Of course, most people do not score at either extreme on these dimensions. Here, as elsewhere, a continuous range of variation with most people occupying an intermediate position is the characteristic pattern. Most people are neither outstandingly active nor conspicuously lethargic, neither clearly ascendant nor clearly submissive. People can rarely be well described by clear-cut personality *types.* They are described as showing different *traits* in varying *degrees.*

Choosing the names for the clusters presented above was a bit of a problem, because the clusters do not correspond exactly to the language labels we bring with us. Each cluster is defined by the items that went into it and that were

TABLE 12.6 INTERCORRELATIONS AND RELIABILITIES OF THE TEN SCALES OF THE *Guilford-Zimmerman Temperament Survey*

	Scale	Intercorrelations									Reliability *
		2	3	4	5	6	7	8	9	10	
1	General activity	−.16	.34	.35	.34	.14	−.17	.24	−.03	.30	.79
2	Restraint		−.08	−.21	.08	.05	.25	.42	.14	−.01	.80
3	Ascendance			.61	.35	.41	−.25	−.19	−.04	.29	.82
4	Sociability				.23	.36	−.06	.04	.18	.21	.87
5	Emotional stability					.69	.37	−.13	.34	.37	.84
6	Objectivity						.34	−.04	.43	.32	.75
7	Friendliness							−.03	.50	.26	.75
8	Thoughtfulness								.22	−12	.80
9	Personal relations									.35	.80
10	Masculinity										.85

Reproduced by permission of the Sheridan Supply Company.
* Kuder-Richardson formula, based on 912 college students.

grouped together because they actually went together in the responses of people taking the inventory. The titles are approximate. Each cluster can be understood more exactly only by a close study of the items of which it is composed.

Table 12.6 shows the reliabilities of the separate scores, and the intercorrelations of the scores. The reliabilities cluster about .80 and are adequate, though not strikingly high. The attempt, in developing this inventory, was to identify a number of relatively independent aspects of personality. This means that the correlations of the different scores should be low. They tend to be. However, certain of the scores show rather substantial correlations. Attention may be directed to Ascendance and Sociability, Emotional Stability and Objectivity, Friendliness and Personal Relations, and Restraint and Thoughtfulness. These pairs of scores are far from independent, and the information provided by the scores is overlapping. In a sense, the inventory is only partially efficient because of the duplication in the different scores. It is as if we were in part saying the same thing over again. In most cases, however, each score provides information about a new and distinctive aspect of the individual.

The *Guilford-Zimmerman Inventory* has several characteristics that it may be well to summarize at this time.

1. It is based upon the responses of normal everyday people, not of the overtly maladjusted or the institutionalized.

2. Its scales are set up by internal analysis, by study of the "going together" of groups of items.

3. Responses are taken at face value. Their significance is assumed to be given by their obvious content.

4. The respondent may endorse as many or as few of the items as he wishes; his choices are not forced or constrained.

The Minnesota Multiphasic Personality Inventory

By contrast, let us consider the *Minnesota Multiphasic Personality Inventory*, which differs radically with respect to the first three characteristics from the *Guilford-Zimmerman Temperament Survey*. The *Minnesota Multiphasic Personality Inventory* was originally developed as a tool for studying individuals suspected of exhibiting some degree of psychopathology. With this objective, a pool of items was assembled from statements appearing in books on psychiatry and abnormal psychology and from case-study records. The attempt was to make the array of statements about symptoms, actions, and attitudes comprehensive, including all that seemed at all promising as indicators of personality malfunctioning. The items were tried out on a group of "normals" and on a number of hospitalized groups selected as representing specific patterns of maladjustment. The process of developing scoring keys was basically the same as that for the *Strong Vocational Interest Blank;* that is, the items in a given key were those that differentiated a particular pathological group from the group of "normal" control cases. Nine clinical scales were developed in this way, and, supplemented by a social introversion scale, these nine provide the basic score profile for the test.

The scale labels, and the types of groups upon which they were originally based are presented briefly below.

Hypochondriasis (*Hs*). Individuals showing excessive worry about health, often accompanied by reports of obscure pains and disorders.

Depression (*D*). Individuals suffering from chronic depression, feelings of uselessness and inability to face the future.

Hysteria (*Hy*). Individuals who have reacted to personal problems by developing physical symptoms such as paralysis, cramps, gastric complaints, or cardiac symptoms.

Psychopathic Deviate (*Pd*). Persons showing lack of deep emotional response, irresponsibility, and disregard of social pressures and the regard of others.

Paranoia (*Pa*). Persons tending to be excessively suspicious and sensitive, with feelings of being picked on or persecuted.

Psychasthenia (*Pt*). Patients troubled with excessive fears (phobias) and compulsive tendencies to dwell on certain ideas or perform certain acts.

Schizophrenia (*Sc*). Patients characterized by bizarre and unusual thought or behavior, and a subjective life tending to be divorced from the world of reality.

Hypomania (*Ma*). Persons tending to be physically and mentally overactive, with rapid shift in ideas or actions.

Masculinity-Feminity (*Mf*). Persons tending to identify with the opposite sex, rather than their own.

The flavor of the items in the *MMPI* is best conveyed by quoting a sample of them, and the first 10 items in the full set of 555 are quoted below. After each item are listed the code designations of the scales for which the item is keyed. The symbols (+) and (−) tell whether it is the "Yes" or the "No" response that adds into that key.

1. I like mechanics magazines. *Mf*(−)
2. I have a good appetite. *Hs*(−), *D*(−), *Hy*(−)
3. I wake up fresh and rested most mornings. *Hs*(−), *Hy*(−), *Pt*(−)
4. I think I would like the work of a librarian. *Mf*(+)
5. I am easily awakened by noise. *D*(+)
6. I like to read newspaper articles on crime. *Hy*(−)
7. My hands and feet are usually warm enough. *Hs*(−), *Hy*(−)
8. My daily life is full of things that keep me interested. *D*(−), *Hy*(−), *Pd*(−), *Pt*(−), *Sc*(−)
9. I am about as able to work as I ever was. *Hs*(−), *D*(−), *Hy*(−)
10. There seems to be a lump in my throat much of the time. *Hy*(+), *Pt*(+) *

The *MMPI* was originally developed in the psychiatric hospital, but use of the instrument has spread far beyond those limits. It has been widely used as a screening device for personality problems in colleges, military and governmental groups, and as a research tool in literally hundreds of studies in all sorts of settings.† This widespread use of an instrument and a set of scales with a basically psychopathological orientation raises serious questions of both a methodological and an ethical nature. We will consider first a number of problems of measurement methodology, and then the ethical issues that arise in the use of an instrument of this type.

HETEROGENEITY OF SCORING KEYS. The empirical procedure, in which items were placed in a particular scoring key if they were responded to differentially by the modest-sized hospitalized clinical group, led to a rather mixed array of items in a number of the scoring keys. Some refer to fairly obvious clinical symptoms, while others, which have been labeled "subtle" items, appear to have nothing to do with the particular pattern of pathology. These

† This is one of the half-dozen most widely studied psychometric devices, and up to the time of the *6th Mental Measurements Yearbook,* no less than 1,394 theses, articles, and books had appeared using or studying it.

two subgroups of items are not only different in apparent nature, but also unrelated (even slightly negatively related) statistically. Thus, the items making up a score lack coherence. It seems likely that much of the variation in score among a group such as college students is produced by variations in responding to the "subtle" items, since few of them are likely to ascribe to themselves the more obvious symptoms of pathology. So the scores may represent some quite different aspect of personality in normal groups than is suggested by the pathological criterion groups on which the keys were originally established.

OVERLAPPING OF SCALES. The instrument exhibits a converse characteristic (which tends to be true of the *Strong Vocational Interest Blank* and other empirically keyed instruments, as well) of overlapping among the different scales. Different scales show positive correlations which run as high as .80 (*Sc* versus *Pt*). The correlations arise, in part, because some of the same items are keyed for several scales; in part, because items of similar flavor are keyed in different scales; and, in part, from certain response sets that we shall examine presently. As a result, it appears that a large part of what is being measured by the nine regular scales could be accounted for by two or at most three underlying common factors. The complete score profile appears to be a redundant and, perhaps, inefficient way of describing the personality differences that the scales do, in fact, assess.

RESPONSE SETS. Associated with their obvious pathological reference, many of the items of the *MMPI* have a very low level of desirability as a form of behavior to attribute to oneself. Judges assessing the items are reasonably consistent in rating the different items for social desirability, and these social desirability ratings have a number of interesting correlates. First, social desirability has a very substantial correlation, .86 in one study, with the probability of endorsing the item. The "better" something is generally perceived to be, the more likely people are to say it is true of them. Second, the tendency to mark socially desirable items is itself a reliable individual characteristic. A group of items selected and keyed to yield a social desirability score provides a score that is as stable and dependable as any of the other scores produced by the instrument. Third, this social desirability score shows very substantial correlations (mostly negative) with many of the other scores on the *MMPI*. In part, the instrument is measuring the individual's tendency to be self-defensive or self-derogatory.

The authors of the test have recognized this problem, and have devised several scales to try to identify either conscious or unconscious distortion of results. There are four such verification or correction scales:

"?" The number of items on which the individual refuses to mark either "Yes" or "No," seen as an indication of defensiveness and withdrawal from the test task.

"L" The number of obviously "good" but extremely improbable behaviors that the examinee claims, seen as an indication of rather naïve defensiveness and overclaiming.

"F" The number of very rare and unusual responses that the individual makes, seen as a sign that the respondent may not have understood and followed the directions.

"K" The tendency to choose responses given by clinically identified abnormals who had shown normal profiles on the test, seen as an indicator of subtle defensiveness and tendency to describe oneself in a good, a "socially desirable" light.

However, the problem is far from completely solved. It remains a problem in part because it is hard to tell how much of "social desirability" responding represents a relatively superficial response set on the part of the individual, how much represents a more deep-seated defensiveness on his part, and how much represents a completely genuine high level of self-regard.

A corollary response set that has been of some concern on the *MMPI* is one of acquiescence or "yes-saying." The structure of the instrument is such that most of the items are so phrased that a "Yes" answer means endorsing some symptom or behavior as characteristic of oneself. Thus, any element of suggestibility, of readiness to agree, would lead to endorsing many symptoms. And, to the extent that the symptoms are preponderantly unfavorable ones, acquiescence would lead to elevated scores on a number of the clinical scales.

THE ISSUE OF INVASION OF PRIVACY. Whenever an individual is called upon to provide information about himself the issues of invasion of privacy and even of self-incrimination are potential problems. The problem becomes important in proportion as the information sought is private, personal, and possibly derogatory in nature, as is true of a psychopathology-oriented inventory such as the *MMPI*.

If the self-reported information is being used only in the individual's behalf and is freely and willingly given, as would be typical of information provided in the context of counseling or therapy, then the problem of invasion of privacy is minimal. Ethical behavior on the part of the person gathering the information, whether by interview or by questionnaire, requires only that the confidentiality of the information be maintained, and that it be used only for the purpose for which it was obtained. When information is gathered for research purposes, a similar guarantee of confidentiality is ethically required, but in addition "informed consent" seems a reasonable requirement. That is, the individual should voluntarily agree to provide the information, knowing what kind of information he is being called upon to supply and, in general terms, how it will be used.

The most serious questions of invasion of privacy arise when the individual is asked to supply information that may, in fact, be used against him, as in a selection or an employment situation. How much right does a school or college, an industrial employer, or an agency of local or federal government have to require the individual to provide information about himself that may be used to screen him out of training, employment, or a role in national affairs? Of course, the rights of the individual are not absolute; the claims of society and its institutions must also receive consideration. Under some circumstances, as with highly sensitive positions central to the national security, the concerns of society may be paramount. Again, a university has some responsibility to invest its resources in students who are likely to provide to society a return (though not necessarily an economic return) on the investment. Even an industrial concern has responsibilities to its stockholders, its other employees, and its customers to function efficiently and produce products or services of good quality. Thus, one is faced with a weighing of competing values: how serious is the intrusion upon the individual on the one hand, and how crucial is the information to a genuine and important social gain on the other? These questions have been raised more thoughtfully and insistently in recent years.

In contrast with the *Guilford-Zimmerman*, we note that the *MMPI:*

1. Is based upon the distinctive responses of selected groups of persons—in this case, groups each presenting a particular psychopathology.
2. Has scales that are defined by these abnormal groups.
3. Is not concerned with the apparent meaning of an item, but only with whether it functions—whether it serves to differentiate between the abnormal and the control group.

It thus follows the general pattern of the *Strong Vocational Interest Blank.* In common with the *Guilford-Zimmerman,*

4. It permits any number of items to be endorsed, leaving the respondent free of constraint in this regard.

Let us look now at an inventory that makes use of the forced-choice pattern of response.

The Thorndike Dimensions of Temperament

This inventory was designed to assess ten bipolar normal dimensions of temperament that have a good deal in common with those included in the *Guilford-Zimmerman Temperament Survey.* The polarities have been labeled

Social versus solitary
Ascendant versus withdrawing

Cheerful versus gloomy
Placid versus irritable
Accepting versus critical
Tough-minded versus tender-minded
Reflective versus practical
Impulsive versus planful
Active versus lethargic
Responsible versus casual

However, the form of presenting the items is somewhat distinctive.

The basic format consists of 20 sets of 10 items each. In a given set, there is one item relating to each of the above 10 polarities. Items were selected in terms of their intercorrelations—high with their own scale and as low as possible with the other nine scales. The items put together in a set have been rather closely matched on popularity, that is, the frequency with which they are chosen by people as being descriptive of them, and consequently may be presumed to be fairly well matched on social desirability. The examinee is instructed to select the three items in each set that are *most* descriptive of him and the three that are *least* descriptive. The remaining four may be presumed to be intermediate. The examinee gets a high "sociable" score if he chooses the items expressed in the sociable direction ("I like noisy parties") as most characteristic of him and items stated in the solitary direction ("Sometimes I just have to get away from people") as least characteristic.

Note that the instrument uses a forced-choice format and that the choices are among items matched for popularity. This is intended to minimize the role of any response sets of social desirability or acquiescence.* The sets of 10 items require the examinee to balance each dimension against all other nine each time he makes a choice, so that each set of choices provides the maximum amount of information. The instrument is not fully ipsative (that is, the 10 scores do not have to add up to the same total for every one), because half the items are stated in terms of one end and half in terms of the other end of the polarity, but the combination of forced-choice form of the item sets and of initially selecting items with low relationships to scales other than their own produces a set of scores with relatively low intercorrelations (of the 45 scale intercorrelations, only 2 for men and 4 for women are as high as .30). Scores show good correlations with self-ratings and modest correlations with ratings by associates. Some groups, such as salesmen, show very distinctive profiles. Other aspects of validity remain, for the most part, still to be investigated.

* However, individuals instructed to "fake good" *do* still show consistent tendencies to raise or lower specific points in their profile.

Evaluation of Temperament and Adjustment Inventories

How well can we hope to describe temperamental characteristics and personal adjustment through the individual's responses to a series of questions? Perhaps we can clarify the issue by asking what a person must do to fill out an inventory adequately. Completing one of these inventories usually requires that the respondent be (a) able to read and understand the item, (b) able to stand back and view his own behavior and decide whether the statement is or is not true of him, and (c) willing to give frank and honest answers. Each of these points raises certain issues about the validity of self-report instruments.

One problem in inventories of all types is that of reading load. This problem is partly one of sheer amount of reading. Especially in those inventories that try to appraise a number of different traits, it is usually necessary to have several hundred items to provide enough scope and reliability. The slow reader may have trouble getting through so much verbiage, or may give up and start responding without really reading through the item. The problem is partly one of level of reading, that is, of the complexity of structure and abstractness of ideas involved. If the vocabulary or concepts are beyond the respondent's comprehension, he may again give up the attempt really to understand and may respond in a superficial or random fashion. (The F scale of the *MMPI* was designed to protect against this hazard.) Thus, inventories are of questionable value for those of low literacy, be they adults or children.

Related to, but somewhat different from the problem of *reading* the items in an inventory is the problem of *interpreting* them. Thus, suppose the question is phrased, "Do you often like to do things by yourself?" The reader may be able to decode this statement perfectly competently, but still have trouble deciding (1) how frequently this type of event has to occur to be "often," (2) what kinds of "things" are referred to—that is, studying, going walking, going out to dinner, and (3) whether liking implies an active seeking out or a passive acceptance of solitary activity. Variation in interpretation could produce quite a variation of response, and interpretation problems of this sort can arise for highly literate persons as well as for poor readers.

A second problem is that of self-insight. Inventories require the individual to conceptualize and classify his own behavior—to decide whether certain descriptions or classifications of behavior are true of him. This implies a certain ability to stand back from himself and view himself objectively that may be difficult to achieve. In fact, the person whose adjustment is most unsatisfactory may be the one who is least able to achieve this objectivity and to face his own deficiencies. Studies have shown repeatedly that those who are rated low by their associates on some desirable trait tend to grossly overrate themselves. Thus, the ill-tempered girl is likely not to recognize her own irascibility; the overbearing boy may be unaware of his boorishness.

When inventories are built according to the pattern of the *Strong VIB* or the *MMPI,* such a lack of self-insight may not be of crucial importance. For these inventories, the keying of an item is based not on its obvious content but on the empirical fact that it did distinguish between criterion groups. If Henry has marked that he would like to be author of a technical book, he has behaved in the way engineers typically behave. The question of whether engineers on the one hand or Henry on the other *really* want to write technical books is not central to our interpretation. The point is that they have both reacted to the question in the same way, so we give Henry a credit on the engineer key of the *Strong.* On the other hand, where items and scores are interpreted on the basis of their manifest content and taken at face value, as is true of the *Guilford-Zimmerman* inventory or the *Kuder Preference Record,* non-insightful responses will lead to an untrue picture of the person who makes them.

A third problem is the willingness of the respondent to reveal the way he perceives or feels about himself. For personality inventories, frank and honest response by the examinee is essential for a valid picture. In most cases, the general significance of the items is reasonably apparent to the reader. Moderately sophisticated examinees (that is, college upperclassmen) usually find it possible to "fake good" or "fake bad" on self-descriptive inventories (Yonge and Heist, 1965), though they seem to be less able to simulate a particular pattern of strength or weakness. Even when the subject cannot fake successfully, if he tries to do so he will certainly give a distorted picture of himself. Inventory scores will only be useful when most respondents are answering in the way that they consider to represent themselves. The importance of providing protection against distortion is sufficiently great so that control scores to detect it have been introduced into the *MMPI* and certain other inventories.

This means that personality or adjustment inventories cannot be used, or can be used only with caution, when the examinee feels threatened by the test or feels that it may be used against him. Inventories have not generally proved useful in an employment situation, perhaps for this reason. If an inventory is given to elementary school pupils (and perhaps in high school and college) in the typical school setting, in which a test is something to do your best on and the teacher is often someone to get the best of, one is inclined to doubt whether many of the pupils will be willing to reveal personal shortcomings that they may be aware of. Generally speaking, in any practical situation we should consider an adjustment inventory to be no more than a preliminary screening device that will locate a group of individuals who *may* be having problems of adjustment or *may* be in conflict with their environment. Final evaluation should always await a more personal and intensive study of the individual. Furthermore, a good score on an adjustment inventory is not a guarantee of good adjustment; it may characterize a person who is protective, defensive, or unable to face and to acknowledge very real problems.

Personality inventories are a product of the middle-class American culture. The extent to which items have equivalent meaning for other national cultures, or even for the lower socioeconomic level in America, has not been fully explored. Some additional caution is necessary in interpreting results for members of other cultural groups.

EVIDENCES OF VALIDITY. Those inventories that have been developed as measures of adjustment usually show a moderate level of *concurrent* validity. That is, they differentiate between groups established on other grounds as differing in adjustment. Thus, the *MMPI* was set up to distinguish between diagnosed pathological groups and normals and continues to do so in new groups. Other inventories have been tested by their ability to differentiate less extreme groups and have stood up fairly well under the test.

When it comes to *predictive* validity, the results are less encouraging. In civilian studies (Ellis, 1946, 1953; Ghiselli and Barthol, 1953; Super, 1942) inventory scores have generally failed to predict anything much about the future success of the individual either in school, on the job, or in his personal living. Military experience (Ellis and Conrad, 1948) with these instruments has been somewhat more promising. There have been a number of studies showing substantial relationship between scores based on inventories and the subsequent judgment resulting from a psychiatric interview. Relationships to subsequent discharge from the service have also been sufficiently good to indicate that an inventory could serve a useful function as a device to screen for careful interview those who appeared to be potential misfits.

THE PRACTICAL USE OF TEMPERAMENT AND ADJUSTMENT INVENTORIES. We must now ask what use should be made of temperament and adjustment inventories in and out of school. In the light of the factors that can distort scores and the limited validity these instruments have shown as predictors, we must conclude that they should be used very sparingly. Our feeling is that an adjustment inventory should be used only as an adjunct to more intensive psychological services. If facilities are available to permit intensive study of some of the group by psychologically trained personnel, an inventory may serve as a means of identifying persons likely to profit from working with a counselor. However, there is little that a classroom teacher can do to dig behind and test the meaning of an inventory score. Accepted uncritically, the score may prove very misleading. We believe that little useful purpose is served by giving an adjustment inventory and making the results available to the teacher, especially the teacher of an elementary-school child.

The multidimensional temperament inventories are still too new for us to have much evidence on the social or practical validities of the different scales. Their use for vocational guidance or personnel selection can hardly be recommended at the present time. It *may* be that persons having certain patterns of temperamental characteristics should be guided towards or away from certain types of jobs. This seems plausible to many people. However, our information about the personality patterns in specific occupations is too limited, and the range of variation within occupations is probably too wide to make much practical use of such personality appraisals at the present time.

ATTITUDE QUESTIONNAIRES

One further type of self-report instrument deserves brief mention. This is the attitude questionnaire, designed to appraise an individual's favorableness towards some group, proposed action, social institution, or social concept. Questionnaires can be grouped into two main types, surveys and scales.

The attitude survey is well illustrated by the Gallup and similar polls. Such a poll contains a number of questions dealing with different aspects of some topic of concern to the inquirer, each question offering two or more possible answers. Thus a survey exploring college students' attitudes towards the United Nations might probe a number of aspects of UN functioning by questions such as:

How successful has the UN been in maintaining peace?
_____ (1) Very successful.
_____ (2) Somewhat successful.
_____ (3) Unsuccessful.
_____ (4) No opinion.

Should large and small countries have an equal vote in UN decisions?
_____ (1) All should have an equal vote.
_____ (2) Large nations should have a greater voice.
_____ (3) Undecided.

Responses to the single questions in such a survey can be tallied and frequencies determined for different kinds of groups. However, the items are not meant to be combined into a single score, since they deal with quite different and specific aspects of a social problem or social institution.

A survey provides only the most rudimentary sort of "measurement," dividing respondents into three or four distinct categories on the basis of their response to a given question.

In contrast to attitude *surveys* are attitude *scales,* which attempt to express an individual's attitude with respect to a problem or issue on a single dimension of favorableness-unfavorableness, and to quantify that attitude in a single score. There are two main patterns for attitude scales:

1. *Scaled statements.* In this form, statements are scaled in terms of their degree of favorableness on the basis of extensive preliminary work. Thus, if we were preparing this type of attitude scale toward the United Nations, we would start with a large pool of items. They might include the following:

The UN is a strong influence for peace.
The UN is a waste of time and effort.
The UN does about as much harm as good.
The UN is the most important force for good in the world today.

A corps of judges would be assembled and each judge asked to sort these statements into a set of piles, each pile representing a different degree of favorableness toward the UN. The judge does *not* indicate his agreement or disagreement with the statement; he gives his interpretation of its meaning and significance. Each statement receives a scale value based on the average of these judgments and an ambiguity index based upon the spread of the ratings. (The more the judgments spread out, the more ambiguous the statement is.) From the pool of items tried out, about twenty are chosen that are spaced out over the range of scale values and are relatively unambiguous. These constitute the attitude scale.

When this type of attitude scale is administered, the respondent marks all the statements with which he agrees. His score is the average of the scale values of the statements he endorses.

2. *Summed score.* In the other common format, the basic statements are much the same, except that neutral statements are avoided. Each statement is unequivocally either favorable or unfavorable. The respondent reacts to each statement on a five-point scale, ranging from strong agreement to strong disagreement. Thus, a section of a questionnaire in this format might read:

The UN is a strong influence for peace.	Strongly agree	Agree	Uncertain	Disagree	Strongly disagree
The UN will only make trouble.	Strongly agree	Agree	Uncertain	Disagree	Strongly disagree

The questionnaire can be scored quite simply by giving five points for strong endorsement of a favorable statement, four points for agreement, three points for uncertainty, and so forth. The scoring is reversed for the unfavorable statements. Items not correlating well with the total score on the scale can be weeded out to make the scale more efficient and more reliable. An individual's raw score is the sum of his scores for the separate items. The raw score can, of course, be converted into a percentile or standard score if this seems desirable.

Both forms of attitude scale usually have satisfactory reliabilities, typically in the .80's. The two types of scales yield scores that intercorrelate very highly, and for most practical purposes there does not seem to be a great deal of choice between them. The greater simplicity of preparation of a summed-score type of inventory will commend it to most persons who wish to use an attitude scale as an aspect of some type of educational evaluation or research project. In either case, the scale will yield only a single general favorableness–unfavorableness score for an attitude area. A number of the potentially useful attitude instruments have recently been assembled in book form, where they are readily accessible to the potential user (Shaw and Wright, 1967; Miller, 1964).

The big qualification about attitude scales is that they operate purely on a verbal level. The individual doesn't *do* anything to back up his stated attitude. The scales deal with verbalized attitudes rather than actions. Of course, an attitude scale is obviously fakeable. If we recognize that it represents the verbalized attitude that the individual is willing to express to us and work within that limitation, an attitude scale appears to be a useful research tool or tool for experimental evaluation of educational objectives lying outside the domain of knowledges and skills.

SUMMARY AND EVALUATION

In this chapter we have considered self-report inventories as instruments for studying personality. An inventory of this sort is essentially a standard set of interview questions presented in written form.

The individual's report about himself has one outstanding advantage. It provides an "inside" view, based on all the individual's experience with and knowledge about himself. However, self-reports are limited by the individual's limited

1. Ability to read the questions with understanding.
2. Self-insight and self-understanding.
3. Willingness to reveal himself frankly.

One type of questionnaire that has proven valuable in selection and placement is the biographical data blank, in which the individual provides factual information about his past history. A scoring key developed for the particular job has been found to have useful validity in several different instances.

Interest inventories provide satisfactorily reliable descriptions of interest patterns. These patterns persist with a good deal of stability, at least after late adolescence, and appear to be significant factors for vocational planning.

The validity of adjustment and temperament inventories is more open to question. Inventories of all types can be distorted to some extent if the individual is motivated to distort his responses. Thus, the integrity of the responses depends upon the motivation of the person examined. This depends, in turn, upon the setting in which and purposes for which the inventory is used. In school, industrial, or military use of adjustment inventories, one suspects that the motivations may often favor distorted responses. In any event, inventories of this type have not generally shown high validity. They should be used only with a good deal of circumspection.

Attitude questionnaires have been developed to score the intensity of favorable or unfavorable reaction to some group, institution, or issue. Though these represent only verbal expressions of attitude, they are useful research tools.

QUESTIONS AND EXERCISES

1. How satisfactory is the method that was used in validating the *Strong Vocational Interest Blank*? What limitations do the procedures have? In what ways should they be checked?

2. What are the relative advantages of the *Strong Vocational Interest Blank* and the *Kuder Preference Record*? Under what circumstances would you choose to use one and under what circumstances the other?

3. What is the relationship between measures of interest and measures of ability? What does this suggest as to the ways in which the two types of tests should be used?

4. Most civilian studies have failed to find interest or adjustment inventories very useful in personnel selection. What are the reasons for this?

5. Compare the advantages and disadvantages, for personnel selection or academic admissions, of the information obtained from

   a. An interview.
   b. A personal history form.
   c. A self-descriptive inventory.

6. What is meant by the term "response set"? What are some potentially important response sets? How might they influence the interpretation of results on personality inventories?

7. How serious a problem is invasion of privacy with personality measures? What uses of such measures are acceptable? What controls on their use should be introduced? How and by whom?

8. What conditions must be met if a self-report inventory is to be filled out accurately and give meaningful results?

9. How much trust can we place in adjustment inventories given in school to elementary-school children? What factors limit their value?

10. What important differences do you notice between the *Guilford-Zimmerman Temperament Survey* and the *Minnesota Multiphasic Personality Inventory*? For what purposes would each be more suitable?

11. What purposes are served by the control scales (*L, K, F, ?*) on the *Minnesota Multiphasic Personality Inventory*? What would be the comparable issues in personality rating scales? How might one adapt the ideas of control scales to ratings by other persons?

12. What factors limit the usefulness of paper-and-pencil attitude scales? What other methods might a teacher use to evaluate attitudes?

13. Prepare the rough draft for a brief attitude scale to measure teachers' attitudes towards objective tests.

14. With what kinds of groups can adjustment inventories be used most satisfactorily?

REFERENCES

Berdie, R. F. Strong Vocational Interest scores of high school seniors and their later occupational entry. *Journal of Applied Psychology,* 1965, **49,** 188–193.

Buel, W. D. Voluntary female clerical turnover: The concurrent and predictive validity of a weighted application blank. *Journal of Applied Psychology,* 1964, **48,** 180–182.

Buel, W. D., Albright, L. E., & Glennon, J. R. A note on the generality and cross-validity of personal history for identifying creative research scientists. *Journal of Applied Psychology,* 1966, **50,** 217–219.

Chaney, F. B. & Owens, W. A. Life history antecedents of sales research and general engineering interests. *Journal of Applied Psychology,* 1964, **48,** 101–105.

Ellis, A. Recent research with personality inventories. *Journal of Consulting Psychology,* 1953, **17,** 45–49.

Ellis, A. & Conrad, H. S. The validity of personality inventories in military practice. *Psychological Bulletin,* 1948, **45,** 385–426.

Ellis, A. The validity of personality questionnaires. *Psychological Bulletin,* 1946, **43,** 385–440.

England, G. W. *Development and use of weighted application blanks.* Dubuque, Iowa: William C. Brown, 1961.

Garry, R. Individual differences in ability to fake vocational interests. *Journal of Applied Psychology,* 1953, **37,** 33–37.

Ghiselli, E. E. & Barthol, R. P. The validity of personality inventories in the selection of employees. *Journal of Applied Psychology,* 1953, **37,** 18–20.

Longstaff, H. P. Fakability of the Strong Interest Blank and the Kuder Preference Record. *Journal of Applied Psychology,* 1948, **32,** 360–369.

Maier, N. R. F. & Thurber, J. A. Accuracy of judgments of deception when an interview is watched, heard and read. *Personnel Psychology,* 1968, **21,** 23–30.

Mallinson, G. G. & Crumrine, W. M. An investigation of the stability of interests of high school students. *Journal of Educational Research,* 1952, **45,** 369–383.

Mayfield, E. C. The selection interview—a re-evaluation of published research. *Personnel Psychology,* 1964, **17,** 239–260.

McCully, C. H. The validity of the Kuder Preference Record. Ed.D. dissertation, George Washington University, 1954.

McGrath, J. J. Improving credit evaluation with a weighted application blank. *Journal of Applied Psychology,* 1960, **44,** 325–328.

Miller, D. C. *Handbook of research design and social measurement.* New York: David McKay, 1964.

Schaefer, C. E. & Anastasi, A. A. Biographical Inventory for identifying creativity in adolescent boys. *Journal of Applied Psychology,* 1968, **52,** 42–48.

Scott, R. D. & Johnson, R. W. Use of the weighted application blank in selecting unskilled employees. *Journal of Applied Psychology,* 1967, **51,** 393–395.

Shaw, M. E. & Wright, J. M. *Scales for the measurement of attitudes.* New York: McGraw-Hill, 1967.

Strong, E. K. Interest scores while in college of occupations engaged in twenty years later. *Educational and Psychological Measurement,* 1951, **11,** 335–348.

Strong, E. K. Nineteen-year follow-up of engineer interests. *Journal of Applied Psychology,* 1952, **36,** 65–74.

Strong, E. K. Permanence of interest scores over twenty-two years. *Journal of Applied Psychology,* 1951, **35,** 89–91.

Strong, E. K. *Vocational interests of men and women.* Stanford, California: Stanford University Press, 1943.

Super, D. E. The Bernreuter Personality Inventory: A review of research. *Psychological Bulletin,* 1942, **39,** 94–125.

Yonge, G. D. & Heist, P. A. The influence of suggested content on faking a personality test. *American Educational Research Journal,* 1965, **2,** 137–144.

SUGGESTED ADDITIONAL READING

Bass, B. M. & Berg, I. A. (Eds.) *Objective approaches to personality assessment.* New York: Van Nostrand, 1959. Chapters 1, 3, 5, 6.

Edwards, A. L. *The social desirability variable in personality assessment and research.* New York: Dryden Press, 1957.

Edwards, A. L. *Techniques of attitude scale construction.* New York: Appleton-Century-Crofts, 1957.

Guilford, J. P. *Personality.* New York: McGraw-Hill, 1959. Chapters 8–9.

Kleinmuntz, B. *Personality measurement.* Homewood, Illinois: Dorsey Press, 1967. Chapters 1, 2, 3, 6, 7, 8.

Kuder, F. G. *Kuder Preference Record Occupational, Form D, research handbook.* (2nd ed.) Chicago: Science Research Associates, 1957.

Layton, W. L. (Ed.) *The Strong Vocational Interest Blank: Research and uses.* Minneapolis, Minnesota: University of Minnesota Press, 1960.

Pittell, S. M. & Mendelsohn, G. A. Measurements of moral values: a review and critique. *Psychological Bulletin,* 1965, **63**, 129–156.

Richardson, S. A., Dohrenwend, B. S., & Klein, D. *Interviewing: Its forms and functions.* New York: Basic Books, Inc., 1965.

Ulrich, L. & Trumbo, D. The selection interview since 1949. *Psychological Bulletin,* 1965, **63**, 100–116.

Vernon, P. E. *Personality assessment: A critical survey.* New York: John Wiley, 1964. Part III and Chapter 16.

CHAPTER 13

The Individual as Others See Him

IN the last chapter we considered the information about personality that could be gotten from inventories in which the individual describes himself. A second main way in which an individual's personality shows itself is through the impression he makes upon others. The second person serves as a reagent reacting to the first personality. How well does A like B? Does A consider B a pleasing person to have around? An effective worker? A good job risk? Does A consider B to be conscientious? Trustworthy? Emotionally stable? Questions of this sort are continually being asked of every teacher, supervisor, former employer, minister, or even friend. We must now inquire how fruitful it is to raise such questions and what precautions must be observed if the questions are to receive useful answers.

We shall first give brief consideration to the unstructured letter of recommendation. Then we shall examine rating scales and rating procedures. Finally, we shall consider some special forms of rating: nominating techniques and forced-choice rating procedures.

LETTERS OF RECOMMENDATION

The most fluid form for getting an impression of one person through the eyes of a second person is to invite the second person to talk or write to you about him. Such a communication could be obtained in any setting, but occurs most commonly when person A is a candidate for something: admission to a school, a scholarship or fellowship, a job, membership in a club, or a security clearance. He then furnishes the institution, placement agency, or employer the names of people who know him well or know him in a particular capacity, and that agency obtains statements about A from B and C, who know him.

How useful and how informative is the material that is included in free, unstructured communications describing another person? Actually, in spite of the vast numbers of recommendations written every year, very little of a solid and factual nature is known about their adequacy or the effectiveness with which they discharge their function. Opinion as to their value varies widely, but factual studies of the reliability and validity of the information that is gotten from a letter of recommendation or of the extent to which recommendations influence the action taken with respect to an applicant are fragmentary in the extreme.

One analysis (Siskind, 1966) of 67 letters written for 33 internship applicants found 958 statements to be distributed as follows:

1. Positive statements	838	(87%)
2. "Don't know" statements about a characteristic	17	(2%)
3. Statements referring to natural shortcomings, the result of inexperience or youth	44	(5%)
4. Other statements indicative of shortcomings	59	(6%)

Siskind suggests that the letter writers "want to see angels" among their students or that they "only want to write about angels." In any event, it is easy to see that the vast preponderance of positive statements makes the discriminating use of such reference letters difficult.

Readers *do* use such letters, and there is evidence (Harrington, 1943) that they are able to agree fairly well in judging how positive a letter is, and that there is a moderate degree of consistency ($r = .40$) between letters written about a given person. One clue as to how this occurs comes from a study (Peres and Garcia, 1962) of adjectives used in a series of letters written in support of applicants for engineering jobs. Of 170 different adjectives extracted from the letters, almost all were positive in tone, but when these were applied as ratings to "best" and "worst" present employees, they differed enormously in the degree to which they differentiated these groups. Thus, the applicant could be called "congenial," "helpful," and "open" or he could be called "ingenious," "informed," and "productive." The first three were applied about equally often to the best and poorest workers, while the last three were highly differentiating as between these two groups. Apparently, the validity of the inferences drawn from a letter of reference depends to a considerable extent upon the degree to which the recipient has learned to "read between the lines," weighting the nice things that are said by an appropriate "discrimination factor" that identifies whether it is the job-relevant or the tangential virtues that are mentioned.

The extent to which a letter of recommendation provides a *valid* appraisal of an individual and the extent to which it is accurately diagnostic of outstanding points, strengths or weaknesses, is almost completely unknown. However, we cannot be very sanguine. Most of the limitations that we shall presently discuss in connection with more structured rating scales apply with at least equal force to uncontrolled letters. In addition, each respondent is free to go off in whatever direction his fancy dictates, so that there is no core of content common to the different letters about a single person or to the letters dealing with different persons. One letter may deal with A's social charm; a second, with B's integrity; and a third, with C's originality.

Although, as we have just seen, a user of recommendations does develop an internal weighting schema for comments of different kinds, such a schema is probably neither very precise, very stable, nor very uniform from reader to reader. Add to this the facts that (1) the applicant usually is more or less free to select the persons who will write about him and may be expected to pick those who will support him and that (2) recommenders differ profoundly in their propensity for using superlatives, and the prospect is not a very rosy one.

Further research studies of the validity of free descriptions of one person by his fellows are urgently needed. In the meantime, recommendations will continue to be written—and perhaps to be used. We must turn our attention to more structured evaluation procedures.

RATING SCALES

Undoubtedly, it was, in part, the extreme subjectivity of the unstructured statement, the lack of a common core of content or standard of reference from person to person, and the extraordinary difficulty of quantifying the materials that gave impetus to the development of rating scales. Rating procedures attempt to overcome just these deficiencies. They attempt to get appraisals on a common set of attributes for all raters and ratees and to have these expressed on a common quantitative scale.

We all have had experience with ratings, either in making them or in having them made about us or, more probably, in both capacities. Rating scales appear in a large proportion of school report cards, more clearly in the nonacademic part. Thus, we often find a section phrased somewhat as follows:

	1st Period	*2nd Period*	*3rd Period*	*4th Period*
Effort	______	______	______	______
Conduct	______	______	______	______
Citizenship	______	______	______	______
Cooperation	______	______	______	______
Adjustment	______	______	______	______

H = superior S = satisfactory U = unsatisfactory

Many civil service agencies and industrial firms send rating forms out to persons listed as references by job applicants, asking for evaluations of the individual's "initiative," "originality," "enthusiasm," or "ability to get along with people." These same companies or agencies often require supervisors to give merit ratings of their employees, rating them as "superior," "excellent," "very good," "good," "satisfactory" or "unsatisfactory" on a variety of traits or in overall usefulness. Colleges, medical schools, fellowship programs, and still other agencies call for ratings as a part of their selection procedure. Beyond these practical operating uses, ratings have been involved in a great many research projects. All in all, vast numbers of ratings are called for and given, often reluctantly, in our country week by week and month by month. Rating other people is a large-scale operation.

Often ratings are retrospective, summarizing the impressions developed by the rater over an extended period of contact with the ratee. Sometimes they are concurrent, arising out of an interview or a period of observation. Almost universally, a rating involves an evaluative summary of past or present experiences in which the "internal computer" of the rater processes the input data in complex and unspecified ways to arrive at the final judgment. By contrast, in systematic observational procedures (to be considered in the next chapter) the observer tries to function only as an accurate recorder, leaving the synthesis and interpretation of the observations as a separate process.

The most common pattern of rating procedure presents the rater with a set of trait names, perhaps somewhat further defined, and a range of numbers, adjectives, or descriptions that are to represent levels or degrees of possession of the traits. He is called upon to rate one or more persons on the trait or traits by assigning him or them the number, letter, adjective, or description that is judged to fit best. Two illustrations are given of rating scales, drawn from a program for evaluation of management personnel.* The first is one of a series of trait ratings. This part of the evaluation instrument calls for ratings of the following traits: job know-how, judgment, leadership, ability to plan and organize, communication ability, initiative, dependability, and human relations. For the trait of

* These have been made available through the courtesy of the Personnel Department of Mack Trucks, Inc.

leadership, the rater is instructed as shown below. The actual rating scale follows these instructions.

LEADERSHIP

Consider his ability to inspire confidence. How much respect does he command as an individual, not merely because of his position? Do people look to him for decisions? Is he afraid to "stick his neck out" for what he believes? Does he have teamwork?

Completely lacking. Definitely a follower with equals. Does not try to convince others that his way is best. ☐	Tries to lead with some success, but has never achieved a strong position. Is passive in directing his subordinates. ☐	Good leader. People wait to hear what he has to say. Respected by colleagues. People call for his opinion. ☐	Exceptional leader. Able to take over and pull things into shape. People seem to enjoy going along on his side. Is respected by subordinates and colleagues. ☐

An over-all summary rating is also called for, and this takes the form shown below.

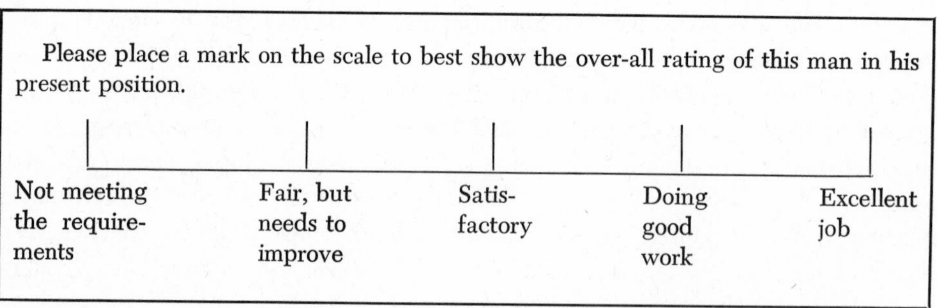

Please place a mark on the scale to best show the over-all rating of this man in his present position.

Not meeting the requirements	Fair, but needs to improve	Satisfactory	Doing good work	Excellent job

These are only illustrations of a wide range of rating instruments. We shall turn presently to some of the major variations in rating patterns. Right now, however, let us consider some of the problems that arise when we try to get a group of judges to make these appraisals.

PROBLEMS IN OBTAINING SOUND RATINGS

The problems in obtaining valid appraisals of an individual through ratings are of two main sorts. First, there are the factors that limit the rater's *willingness* to rate honestly and conscientiously, in accordance with the instructions given to him. Second, there are the factors that limit his *ability* to rate consistently and correctly, even with the best of intentions. We shall need to consider each of these in turn.

Factors Affecting the Rater's Willingness to Rate Conscientiously

When ratings are collected, it is commonly assumed that each rater is trying his best to follow the instructions that have been given him, and that any shortcomings in his ratings are due entirely to human fallibility and ineptitude. However, this is not necessarily true. There are at least two sets of circumstances that may impair the integrity of a set of ratings: (1) The rater may be unwilling to take the trouble that is called for by the appraisal procedure; and (2) the rater may identify with the person rated to such an extent that he is unwilling to make a rating that will hurt him. Each of these merits some elaboration.

UNWILLINGNESS TO TAKE THE NECESSARY PAINS. At best, ratings are a bother. Careful and thoughtful ratings are even more of a bother. In some rating procedures the attempt is made to get away from subjective impressions and superficial reaction by introducing elaborate procedures and precautions into the rating enterprise. Thus, in one attempt to improve efficiency rating procedures for Air Force officers (Preston, 1948) an elaborate form was introduced that was to serve as a combined observational record and rating form. Fifty-four specific critical behaviors were described relating to officer efficiency. Scales were prepared describing degrees of excellence in each type of behavior. The accompanying instructions called upon raters to observe their ratees for a period before the official ratings were to be given and to tally on the rating form instances that had been observed of desirable and undesirable acts within each of the behavior categories described on the scale. After a year or two of use this form was discarded, in part at least because of its complexity and because raters were not willing to devote the time and thought that would have been required to maintain the preliminary observational records on which the ratings were to be based.

In a lesser degree, one suspects that perfunctoriness in carrying out the operation of rating is a factor contributing to lowered effectiveness in many rating programs. Particularly if the number of pupils or employees to be rated is large, the task of preparing periodic ratings can become a decidedly onerous one. Unless raters are really "sold" on the importance of the ratings, the judgments are likely to be hurried and superficial ones, given more with an eye on finishing the task than with a concern for making accurate and analytical judgments.

IDENTIFICATION WITH THE PERSONS BEING RATED. Ratings are often called for by some rather remote and impersonal agency. The Civil Service Commission, the Military Personnel Division of a remote Headquarters, the personnel director of a large company, or the central administrative staff of a school system are all pretty far away from the first line supervisor, the squadron commander, or the classroom teacher. The rater is often closer to the persons being rated, the workers in his office, the junior officers in his outfit, the pupils in his class, than to the agency that requires the ratings to be made. One of the first principles of supervision or leadership is that the good leader looks out for the needs and welfare of his followers or subordinates. Morale in an organization depends upon the conviction that the leader of the organization will take care of the members of the group. When ratings come along, "taking care of" becomes a matter of seeing to it that one's own men fare as well as—or a little better than—those in competing groups.

All this boils down to the fact that in some situations the rater is more interested in providing a "break" for the people whom he is rating and in seeing that they get at least as good treatment as other groups than he is in providing accurate information for the using agency. This situation is aggravated in many governmental and official agencies by a policy of having the ratings public and requiring that the rater discuss with the person being rated any unfavorable material in the ratings. A further aggravation is produced by setting up administrative rulings in which a minimum rating is specified as required for promotion or pay increase. No wonder, then, that ratings tend to climb or to pile up at a single scale point. Thus, in certain governmental agencies during World War II the typical rating, accounting for a very large proportion of the ratings given, was "excellent." "Very good" became an expression of marked dissatisfaction, while a rating of "satisfactory" was reserved for someone you would get rid of at the first opportunity.

It is important to realize that a rater cannot always be depended upon to work wholeheartedly at giving valid ratings for the benefit of the using agency, that making ratings is usually a nuisance to him, and that he is often more committed to his own subordinates than to an outside agency. A rating program must be continuously "sold" and policed if it is to remain effective. And there are limits to the extent to which even an active campaign can overcome a rater's natural inertia and his interest in his own little group.

Factors Affecting the Rater's Ability to Rate Accurately

Even when a group of raters are presumably well motivated and doing their best to provide valid judgments, there are still a number of factors that operate to limit the validity of those judgments. These center around the lack of opportunity to observe, the covertness of the attribute, ambiguity of the quality to be observed, lack of a uniform standard of reference, and specific rater biases and idiosyncrasies.

OPPORTUNITY TO OBSERVE THE PERSON RATED. One factor that must always be borne in mind as a consideration limiting the accuracy of rating procedures is limited opportunity on the part of the rater to observe the person being rated. Thus, the high-school teacher teaching four or five different class groups of 30 pupils each and seeing many pupils only in a class setting may be called upon to make judgments as to the "initiative" or "flexibility" of these pupils. The college instructor who has taught a class of 100 pupils will receive rating forms from an employment agency or from the college administration asking for similar judgments. The truth of the matter is that effective contact with the person to be rated has probably been too limited to provide any adequate basis for the judgment that is being requested. True, the ratee has been physically in the presence of the rater for a good many hours, possibly several hundred, but these have been very busy hours, concerned primarily with other things than observing and forming judgments about pupil A. Pupil A has had to compete with pupils B, C, D, and on to Z and also with the primary concern with teaching rather than judging.

In a civil service or industrial setting much the same thing is true. The primary concern is with getting the job done, and although in theory the supervisor has had a good deal of time to observe each worker, in practice he has been busy with other things. We may be able to "sell" supervisors on the idea of devoting more of their energy to observing and evaluating the persons working for them, but there are very real limits to the amount of effort that can be withdrawn from a supervisor's other functions to be applied to this one.

We face not only the issue of general opportunity to observe, but also that of specific opportunity to observe a particular aspect of the individual's personality. Any person sees another only in certain limited contexts, in which only certain aspects of his behavior are displayed. The teacher sees a child primarily in the classroom, the foreman sees a workman primarily on the production line, and so forth.

We might question whether a teacher in a thoroughly conventional classroom has seen a child under circumstances which might be expected to bring out much "initiative" or "originality." The college instructor who has taught largely through lectures is hardly well situated to rate a student's "presence" or "ability to work with individuals." The supervisor of a clerk doing routine work is poorly situated to appraise "judgment." Whenever ratings are proposed, either for research purposes or as a basis for administrative actions, we should ask with respect to each trait being rated: Has the rater had a chance to observe these people in enough situations of the sort in which they could be expected to show variations in this trait so that his ratings can be expected to be meaningful? If the answer is "No," we would be well advised to abandon the ratings.

In this connection, it is worth while to point out that persons in different roles may see quite different aspects of the person to be rated. Her pupils see a teacher from quite a different vantage point than does the principal. Classmates in Officer Candidate School have a different view of the other potential officers than does the drill instructor. In getting ratings of some aspect of an individual, it is always appropriate to ask who has the best chance to see the relevant behavior displayed. It would normally be to this source that we should go for our ratings.

COVERTNESS OF TRAIT BEING RATED. If a trait is to be appraised by an outsider, someone other than the person being rated, it must show on the outside. It must be something that has its impact on the outside world. Such characteristics as appearing at ease at social gatherings, having a pleasant speaking voice, and participating actively in group projects are characteristics that are essentially social. They appear in interaction with other persons and are directly observable. They are *overt* aspects of the person being appraised. By contrast, attributes such as "feeling of insecurity," "self-sufficiency," "tension," or "loneliness" are inner personal qualities. They are private aspects of personality and can only be crudely inferred from what the person does. They are *covert* aspects of the individual.

An attribute that is largely covert can be judged by the outsider only with great difficulty. Little of inner conflict or tension shows on the surface, and where it does show it is often in masquerade. Thus, a child's deep insecurity may express itself as aggression against other pupils in one child, or as withdrawal into an inner world in another. The insecurity is not a simple dimension of overt behavior. It is an underlying dynamic factor that may break out in different ways in different persons or even in the same person at different times. Only a thorough knowledge of the individual, combined with a good deal of psychological insight, makes it possible to infer from the overt behavior the nature of his underlying covert dynamics.

One can see, then, that rating procedures will be relatively unsatisfactory for the inner, covert aspects of the individual. Qualities that depend upon very thorough understanding of a person plus wise inferences from his behavior will be rated with low reliability and little validity. Ratings have most chance of being accurate for those qualities that show outwardly as a person interacts with other people, the overt aspects. Experience has shown that these can be rated more reliably, and one feels confident that they are rated more validly. The validity lies in part in the fact that these social aspects of behavior have their meaning and definition primarily in the effects of one person on another.

AMBIGUITY OF MEANING OF DIMENSION TO BE RATED. Many rating forms call for ratings of quite broad and abstract traits. Thus, in our illustration on p. 423 we included, among others, "citizenship" and "adjustment." These are neither more nor less vague and general than the attributes included in other rating schedules. But what do we mean by "citizenship" in an elementary-school pupil? By what actions is "good citizenship" shown? Does it mean not marking up the walls? Or not spitting on the floor? Or not pulling little girls' hair? Or bringing newspaper clippings to class? Or joining the Junior Red Cross? Or staying after school to help the teacher clean up the room? What *does* it mean? Probably no two raters would have just exactly the same things in mind when they rated a group of pupils on "citizenship."

Or consider "initiative," "personality," "supervisory ability," "mental flexibility," "executive influence," or "adaptability." These are all examples from rating scales in actual use. Though there is certainly some core of uniformity in the meaning that each of these terms will have for different raters, there is with equal certainty a good deal of variability in meaning from one rater to another. In proportion as a term becomes abstract, its meaning becomes variable from person to person, and such qualities as those listed above are conspicuously abstract.

The rating that a given child will receive for "citizenship" will, then, depend upon what "citizenship" means to the rater. If it means to rater A conforming to school regulations, he will rate certain children high. If to rater B it means taking an active role in school projects, the high ratings may go to quite different children. A first problem in getting consistent ratings is to achieve consistency from rater to rater in the meanings of the qualities being rated.

UNIFORM STANDARD OF REFERENCE. A great many rating schedules call for judgments of the persons being rated in some set of categories such as

Outstanding, above average, average, below average, unsatisfactory.
Superior, good, fair, poor.
Best, good, average, fair, poor.
Outstanding, superior, better than satisfactory, satisfactory, unsatisfactory.
Superior, excellent, very good, good, satisfactory, unsatisfactory.

But how good is "good"? Is a person who is "good" in "judgment" in the top tenth of the group with whom he is being compared? The top quarter? The top half? Or is he just *not* one of the bottom tenth? And what *is* the group with whom he is supposed to be compared? Is it all men of his age? All employees of the company? All men in his particular job? All men in his job with his length of experience? If the last, how is the rater supposed to know the level of judgment that is typical for men in a particular job with a particular level of experience?

The problem that all these questions are pointing up is that of forming a standard against which to appraise a given ratee. Variations in interpretation of terms and labels, variations in definition of the reference population, and variations in experience with the members of that background population all contribute to variability from rater to rater in their standards of rating. The phenomenon is a familiar one in academic grading practices. Practically every school that has studied the problem has found enormous variations among faculty members in the percent of A's, B's, and C's that they give. The same situation holds for any set of categories, numbers, letters, or adjectives, that may be used. Standards of interpretation are highly subjective and vary widely from one rater to another. One man's "outstanding" is another man's "satisfactory."

Raters differ not only in the level of ratings that they assign, but also in how much they spread out their ratings. Some raters are conservative, and rarely rate anyone very high or very low; others tend to go to extremes. This difference in variability of ratings serves also to reduce the comparability of ratings from one rater to another. These differences among raters appear not to be a chance matter but to be a reflection of the personal characteristics and value structure of the rater. Thus, in one study (Klores, 1966), it was found that supervisors who placed importance on a supervisor's personal relationships with subordinates gave higher and more uniform ratings than supervisors who placed importance on providing structure in the work situation.

SPECIFIC RATER IDIOSYNCRASIES. Not only do raters differ in general "toughness" or "softness." They also differ in a host of specific idiosyncrasies. The experiences of life have built up in each of us an assortment of likes and dislikes and an assortment of individualized interpretations of the characteristics of people. You may distrust anyone who does not look at you while he is talking to you. Your neighbor may consider any man a sissy who has a voice pitched higher than usual. Your boss may consider that a firm handshake is the guarantee of a strong character. Your golf partner may be convinced that blonds are flighty. These are rather definite reactions that may be explicit and clearly verbalized by the person in question. But there are myriad other more vague and less tangible biases that we carry with us and that influence our ratings. These biases help to form our impression of a person and color all aspects of our reaction to him. They enter into our ratings too. In some cases, our rating of one or two traits may be affected. But often the bias is one of general liking for or aversion to the person, and this generalized reaction colors all our specific ratings. Thus, the ratings reflect not only the general subjective rating standard of the rater, but also his specific biases with respect to the person being rated.

A different type of idiosyncrasy that is likely to influence overall judgments of effectiveness on a job (or in an educational program) is idiosyncrasy as to what types of behavior are desirable. Thus, Barrett (1966) found wide differences among supervisors of employees in closely similar jobs in the attributes that were considered important. Some raters considered "solving problems on one's own initiative" among the most important things a subordinate could do and some considered it among the least important. To the extent that such differences in values prevail, it is inevitable that supervisors will fail to agree on who are their more effective subordinates.

The Outcome of Factors Limiting Rating Effectiveness

What is the net result of these factors affecting the raters' willingness to rate conscientiously and ability to rate accurately? The effects show up in certain pervasive distortions of the ratings, in relatively low reliabilities, and in doubt as to the basic validity of rating procedures.

THE GENEROSITY ERROR. We have pointed out that the rater is often as much committed to the people he is rating as he is to the agency for which ratings are being prepared. Over and above this, there seems to be a widespread unwillingness on the part of raters, at least in the United States, to damn a fellow man with a low rating. The net result is that ratings tend quite generally to pile up at the high end of any scale. The unspoken philosophy of the rater seems to be "one man is as good as the next, if not a little better," so that "average" becomes in practice not the midpoint of a set of ratings but near the lower end of the group. It is a little like the commercial classification of olives, where the tiniest ones are called "medium," and they go from there through "large" and "extra large" to "jumbo" and "colossal."

If the generosity error operated uniformly for all raters, it would not be particularly disturbing. We would merely have to remember that ratings cannot be interpreted in terms of their verbal labels and that "average" means "low" and "very good" means "average." Makers of rating scales have countered this humane tendency with some success by having several steps on their scale on the plus side of average, so that there is room for differentiation without having to get disagreeable and call a person "average."

It is differences between raters in the degree of their "generosity error" that are more troublesome. To correct for such differences is a good deal more of a problem. We shall consider presently some special techniques that have been developed for that purpose.

THE HALO ERROR. Limitations in our experience with the person being rated, lack of opportunity to observe the specific qualities that are called for in the rating instrument, and the influence of personal biases that affect our general liking for the person all conspire to produce another type of error in our ratings. This is a tendency to rate in terms of overall general impression without differentiating specific aspects, of allowing our total reaction to the person to color our judgment of each specific trait. This is called "halo."

We can illustrate halo by a recent study (Blumberg, De Soto, and Kuethe, 1966) in which college students were asked to rate ten well-known personages (Joe Louis, Elizabeth Taylor, Einstein, etc.) on seven trait dimensions (witty, truthful, intelligent, genuine, emotionally stable, good-looking, and energetic). In spite of the diversity in the seven traits, some ratees tended to be rated high on all of them. About 10 percent of the variation was between different names, without regard to trait or who was doing the rating. This represented a universal perception of the person as "good" or "bad." Another 10 percent of the variation was general across traits, but was idiosyncratic to a particular rater. It constituted a personal generally positive or negative evaluation of a particular name. Thus, in total, about 20 percent of the variance represented halo.

In the usual rating situation, in which all of the traits to be rated are job-related or school-related, and in which the ratees are drawn from a common walk of life, we may anticipate that the role of halo would tend to be considerably greater.

Of course, some relationship among desirable traits is to be expected. We find correlation among different abilities when these are tested by objective tests and do not speak of the halo effect that produces a correlation between verbal and mechanical ability. Just how much of the relationship between the different qualities on which we get ratings is genuine and how much of it is spurious halo is very hard to determine. That some of the relationship is due to inability to free oneself from general biases seems clear, however, from examples such as the one we have just given.

RELIABILITY OF RATINGS. Studies have shown repeatedly that the between-raters reliability of conventional rating procedures is low. Symonds (1931) summarized a number of studies and concluded that the correlation between the ratings given by two independent raters for the conventional type of rating scale is about .55. There seems to be no good reason to change this conclusion after the lapse of years. When the two ratings are uncontaminated; that is, the raters have not talked over the persons to be rated, and where the usual type of numerical or graphic rating is used, the resulting appraisal shows only this very limited consistency from rater to rater.

If it is possible to pool the ratings of a number of independent raters who know the persons being rated about equally well, reliability of the appraisal can be substantially increased. Studies have shown (Remmers, et al, 1927) that pooling ratings functions in the same way as lengthening a test, and that the

Spearman-Brown formula (p. 192) can legitimately be applied in estimating the reliability of pooled independent ratings. Thus, if the reliability of one rater is represented by a correlation of .55, we have the following estimates for the reliability of pooled ratings:

2 raters	.71
3 raters	.79
5 raters	.86
10 raters	.92

Unfortunately, in many important practical situations it is impossible to get additional equally qualified raters. An elementary-school pupil has only one regular classroom teacher; a worker has only one immediate supervisor. Adding on other raters who have more limited acquaintance with the ratee may weaken rather than strengthen the ratings.

Reliability data on some of the newer types of rating devices to be discussed presently appear somewhat more promising. These data will be presented as the methods are discussed. One of the gains from basing ratings on specific tangible behaviors will be, it is hoped, that the objectivity, and hence the reliability, of the judgments will be increased.

VALIDITY OF RATINGS. All the limiting and distorting factors that we have been considering make us doubtful about the validity of ratings. Rater biases and rater unreliability operate to lower validity. However, it is usually very difficult to make any statistical test of the validity of ratings. The very fact that we have fallen back on ratings usually means that no better measure of the quality in question is available to us. There is usually nothing else against which we can test the ratings.

In one context, the validity of ratings is axiomatic. If we are interested in appraising how a person is reacted to by other people, that is, whether a child is well liked by his classmates or a foreman by his work crew, ratings *are* the reactions of these other persons and are directly relevant to the point at issue.

When ratings are being studied as predictors, statistical data can be obtained as to the accuracy with which they do in fact predict. This is something that must be determined in each setting and for each type of criterion that is being predicted. That ratings are in some cases the most valid available predictors is shown in studies of the ratings of aptitude for military service that have been given at the U.S. Military Academy (Personnel Research Section, 1953). These ratings by tactical officers and by fellow cadets correlated more highly with later ratings of performance as an officer than did any other aspect of the man's record at West Point. Correlations with ratings of effectiveness in combat in the war in Korea were about .50. This criterion is again a rating, but it is probably as close to the real "pay off" as we are likely to get in this situation. In other situations, of course, ratings may turn out to have no validity at all. Each type of situation must be studied for its own sake.

IMPROVING THE EFFECTIVENESS OF RATINGS

So far we have painted a rather gloomy picture of rating techniques as devices for appraising personality. It is certainly true that the hazards and pitfalls in rating procedures are many. But for all their limitations, there are and will continue to be a host of situations in which we will have to rely on the judgments of other people as a means of appraising our fellow men. The sincerity and integrity of a potential medical student, the social acceptability of a would-be salesman, the conscientiousness of a private secretary can probably only be evaluated through the judgment that someone makes of these qualities in the individuals in question. What can be done, then, to mitigate the defects of rating procedures? We shall consider first the design of the rating instrument and then the planning and conduct of the ratings.

Refinements in the Rating Instrument

The usual rating instrument has two main components: (1) a set of stimulus variables (the qualities to be rated) and (2) a pattern of response options (the ratings that can be given). In the simplest and most conventional rating forms, the stimulus variables consist of trait names and the response options consist of numerical or adjectival categories. Such a form was illustrated on p. 423. This type of format appears to encourage most of the shortcomings that we have been discussing in the preceding section. Consequently, many variations and refinements of format have been tried out in an attempt to overcome or at least minimize these shortcomings. The variations have manipulated the stimulus variables, the response options, or both. Some of the main variations are described below.

Refinements in Presenting the Stimulus Variables

Bare trait names represent unsatisfactory stimuli for a rater for two reasons. In the first place, as we pointed out on p. 429, the words mean different things to different people. The child who shows "initiative" to teacher A may show "insubordination" to teacher B, whereas teacher B's "good citizen" may seem to teacher A a "docile conformist." In the second place, the terms are quite abstract and far removed in many cases from the realm of observable behavior. Consider "adjustment," for example. We do not observe a child's adjustment. We observe a host of reactions to situations and people. Some of these reactions are perhaps symptomatic of poor adjustment. But the judgment about the child's adjustment is several steps removed from what we have a chance to observe.

Workers with ratings have striven to get greater uniformity of meaning in the traits to be rated, and they have attempted to base the ratings more closely upon observable behavior. These attempts have modified the stimulus aspect of rating instruments in three ways.

1. *Trait names have been defined.* "Social adjustment" is a rather nebulous label. It can be given somewhat more substance by elaborating on what the label is supposed to refer to, as:

> *Social Adjustment.* Interest in and skills of interacting with both children and adults in work and play situations. Willingness both to give and to take in interpersonal situations. Conformity to basic social norms of behavior.

The elaboration attaches a little more substance to a very intangible concept, and should provide for somewhat greater uniformity of meaning among a group of raters. However, we may doubt that a brief verbal definition will go very far toward overcoming the individual differences in meaning that different raters attach to the term and, consequently, to the rating task.

2. *Trait names have been replaced by several more limited and concrete descriptive phrases.* The abstract and inclusive term "social adjustment" might be broken down into several components each relating to a more limited aspect of behavior. Thus, we might have:

> Working with other children.
> Playing with other children.
> Interacting with teacher and other adults.
> Conforming to basic social norms and standards.

A judgment would now be called for with respect to each of the more restricted, and, hopefully, more tangible aspects of pupil behavior.

3. *Each trait name has been replaced with a subtantial number of descriptions of specific behaviors.* This carries the move toward concreteness and specificity one step farther. Thus the rubric "working with other children" might be replaced with something like:

> Takes an active part in group enterprises.
> Makes and defends suggestions.
> Accepts majority decisions.
> Does his share of the work.
> Helps others with their work.

A similar subdivision would be carried out for each of the three other major headings. These items are still more tangible and specific. There should be much less ambiguity as to what it is that is to be observed and reported on, though there is still an element of interpretation in deciding, for example, what level of involvement constitutes "taking an active part."

The replacement of one general term with many specific behaviors gives promise of achieving more uniformity of meaning from one rater to another. It may also bring the ratings in closer touch with actual observations that have been made of the behavior of the individual who is being appraised. Where the trait to be rated is one that the rater has really had no opportunity to observe, the attempt to replace the trait name with specific observable behaviors will often make this fact painfully apparent and will force the designer of the instrument to rethink the problem of relating his instrument to the observations that the rater has really had an opportunity to make.

The gains that a list of specific behaviors achieves in uniformity of meaning and concreteness of behavior judged are not without cost. The cost lies in the greatly increased length and complexity of the rating instrument. There are limits to the number of different judgments that can be asked of a rater. Furthermore, the lengthy, analytical report of behavior may be confusing to the person who tries to use and interpret it. The lengthy list of specific behaviors will probably prove most effective when (1) judgments are in very simple terms, such as simply present-absent and (2) there are provisions for organizing and summarizing the specific judgments into one or more *scores* for broad areas.

Refinements in Form of Response Categories

Expressing judgments about a ratee by selecting some one of a set of numbers, letters, or adjectives is still common on school report cards or in civil service and industrial merit rating systems. However, these procedures have little other than simplicity to commend them. As we saw on p. 429, the categories are arbitrary and undefined. No two raters interpret them in exactly the same way. A rating of "superior" may be given to 5 percent of employees by one supervisor and to 25 percent by another. One man's A is another man's B. Subjective standards reign supreme.

Various attempts have been made to manipulate the response options to try to achieve a more meaningful scale or greater uniformity from rater to rater.

1. *Percentage of group.* To try to produce greater uniformity from rater to rater and to produce greater discrimination among the ratings given by a particular rater, judgments are sometimes called for in terms of percentage of a

particular defined group. Thus, the professor rating an applicant for a fellowship is instructed to rate each candidate according to the following scale:

> Falls in the top 2 percent of students at his level of training.
> In top 10 percent, but not in top 2 percent.
> In top 25 percent, but not in top 10 percent.
> In top half, but not in top 25 percent.
> In lower half of students at his level of training.

Presumably, the specified percentages of a defined group provide a uniform standard of quality for different raters. However, the stratagem is usually only partially successful. Individual differences in generosity are not that easily suppressed.

2. *Graphic scale.* A second variation is more a matter of form than clarity of definition. Rating scales are often prepared so that judgments may be recorded as a check at some appropriate point on a line, instead of by choosing a number, letter, or adjective. For example:

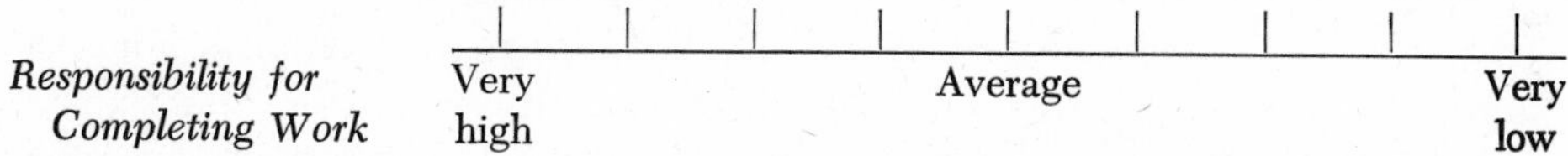
Responsibility for Completing Work
Very high
Average
Very low

The pattern often makes a fairly attractive page layout, is compact and economical of space, and seems somewhat less forbidding than a form which is all print. However, this particular variation does not seem to have much advantage other than attractiveness and convenience. One study (Blumberg et al, 1966) that compared various numerical and graphic formats for presenting the rating task, found format to be quite insignificant as a determinant of the ratings that were given.

3. *Behavioral statement.* We have seen that the stimuli may be in the form of relatively precise behavioral statements. Statements of this sort may also be used to present the choice alternatives. Thus, we may have an item of this type:

Participation in School Projects

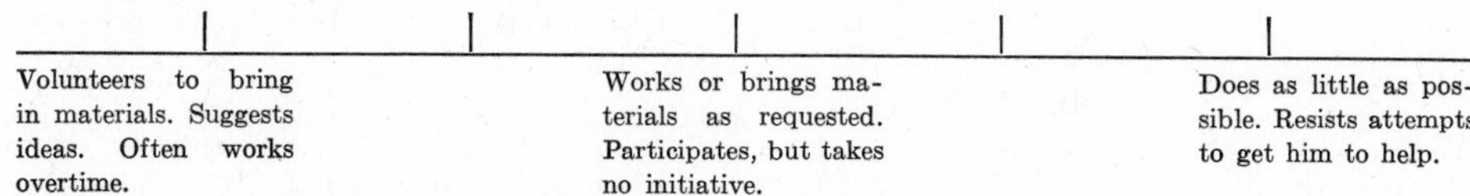
Volunteers to bring in materials. Suggests ideas. Often works overtime.
Works or brings materials as requested. Participates, but takes no initiative.
Does as little as possible. Resists attempts to get him to help.

In this case, three statements describing behavior are combined with a graphic scale, and are used to define three points on the scale. The descriptions may be expected to lend more concreteness and uniformity of meaning to the scale steps. However, these editorial provisions do not completely overcome rater idiosyncrasies, which continue to plague us.

4. *Man-to-man scales.* An early attempt to get more uniformity of meaning into the response scale, developed in World War I, used men instead of numbers,

adjectives, or descriptions to represent the scale points. The rater is asked to think of someone he has known well who was very high on the quality being rated. That person's name is then entered on the rating form to define the "very high" point on the scale. In the same way, the names of other persons known well by the rater are entered in spaces to define "high," "average," "low," and "very low." The five names then define levels for the trait. When a person is to be rated, the rater is instructed to compare him with the five persons defining the levels on the trait. The rater is to judge which man he most closely resembles on the trait in question. He is assigned the value corresponding to the step on the scale which that man occupies.

It was thought that the man-to-man feature would lend concreteness to the comparisions and overcome the tendency of some raters to be consistently generous. In cases in which all raters have a wide range of acquaintance, so that their scale persons may be expected to be fairly comparable, the procedure may make for more uniformity from rater to rater. But such scope of acquaintance and thoroughness of familiarity with suitable scale persons is likely to be somewhat unusual in the practical situations in which ratings must be made. Implicit comparison with other persons is involved in any rating enterprise, but explicit use of particular persons to define the steps on a rating scale has not been widely adopted.

5. *Present–absent.* When a large number of specific behavioral statements are used as the stimuli, the response that is called for is often a mere checking of those that apply to the individual in question. The person is then characterized by the statements that are checked as representing him. The rating scale becomes a behavior checklist. The set of items on p. 435 might constitute part of such a checklist.

If this type of appraisal procedure is to yield a score, the statements must be scaled or assigned score values in some way. The simplest way is merely to score them +1, −1, or 0, depending upon whether they are favorable, unfavorable, or neutral with respect to a particular attribute (that is, perseverance, integrity, reliability, etc.) or a particular criterion (that is, success in academic work, success on a job, responsiveness to therapy, etc.). An individual's score can then be the sum of the scores for the items checked for him.

If the additional elegance seems justified, more refined scaling procedures can be applied to the statements. Scale values can be based on their judged significance or the degree to which they had actually discriminated between successful and unsuccessful individuals. The score an individual receives is then based on an averaging of the scale values of the items that were checked as describing him. The reliability of such a checklist of scaled items has been found to be quite satisfactory in some instances. An early study (Richardson and Kuder, 1933) reported a correlation of .83 between total score given by two independent raters when rating salesmen. More recently (Ross et al, 1965) split half reliabilities from .72 to .95 and retest reliabilities from .77 to .93 were reported for scores on the four scales (aggressive, withdrawn, prosocial, and passive-aggressive) of the *Pittsburgh Adjustment Survey Scales* applied to elementary school boys.

Only limited use has been made of checklists as devices to yield scores on each individual, but they seem to present a promising pattern. They come the closest of any of the rating procedures to self-report inventories on the one hand and to ability tests on the other. A behavior checklist is in a sense a personality inventory that has been filled out by someone other than the person being described. The items can be selected and scored in much the same way.

One well-known behavior checklist that is more like an ability test is the *Vineland Social Maturity Scale* (Doll, 1953). This checklist is made up of items relating to self-help, self-direction, communication, socialization, and the like. Selected items from different levels of the scale are shown in Table 13.1. Norms were established for each item of the scale, representing the age at which the behavior

TABLE 13.1 ITEMS SELECTED FROM THE *Vineland Social Maturity Scale*

Item No.	Age Level (in years)	Item
1	0–1	"Crows," laughs
6	0–1	Reaches for nearby objects
11	0–1	Drinks from cup assisted
15	0–1	Stands alone
19	1–2	Marks with pencil or crayon
28	1–2	Eats with spoon
34	1–2	Talks in short sentences
37	2–3	Removes coat or dress
40	2–3	Dries own hands
44	2–3	Relates experiences
51	4–5	Cares for self at toilet
53	4–5	Goes about neighborhood unattended
68	7–8	Disavows literal Santa Claus
70	7–8	Combs or brushes hair
78	10–11	Writes occasional short letters
80	10–11	Does small remunerative work

appears on the average. The checklist is filled out by a rater who knows the child being appraised. Items the person does or can do are checked. A basal age is established for which all items are positive, and the person being rated is automatically given credit for all earlier items. Points are given for additional items passed. The table of norms gives developmental age equivalents for the point scores, and a developmental quotient may be computed that indicates the individual's rate of progress toward self-sufficiency and independence.

The checklist pattern has been used as a simple descriptive instrument, as in school reports to the home. The procedure is attractive in this setting because it can give information on specific aspects of pupil development. However, forms tend to become complicated and to confuse many parents, so this type of reporting has not been widely adopted.

6. *Frequency of occurrence, or typicality.* Instead of reacting in an all-or-none fashion to an item, as in the checklist, the rater can be given the choices that the behavior is "always," "usually," "sometimes," "seldom," or "never" characteristic of the ratee.* Or the ratee may be characterized as "very much like," "a good deal like," "somewhat like," "slightly like," or "not at all like" the behavior described in the statement. The terms indicating frequency or resemblance may vary; the ones given are only suggestive. An individual's score could now take account both of the significance of the statement and the point on the scale that was checked. That is, an important attribute could receive heavier credit than a minor one, and a check at the "always" step more credit than a check at "usually."

Indefinite designations of frequency or degree of the sort that are being suggested here will be differently interpreted by different raters, so the old problem of differences in rater standards is still with us. Moreover, when the number of specific behaviors being checked is substantial, a simple present-absent checking correlates quite highly with the more elaborate form.

7. *Ranking.* In those cases in which each rater knows a substantial number of ratees, he may be asked to place them in rank order with respect to each attribute being studied. Thus, a teacher may be asked to indicate the child who is most outstanding for contributing to the class projects and activities "over and beyond the call of duty," the one who is second, and so on. Usually, the ranker will be instructed to start at both ends and work in toward the middle, since the extreme cases are usually easier to discriminate than the large group of average ones in the middle. In order to ease the task of the ranker, tie ranks

* In formulating items to be responded to with the categories "always," "usually," etc., one must take care that no term expressing frequency is included in the statement of the item. Otherwise, one is faced with the syntactic atrocity of judging that Johnny "always" "usually accepts majority decisions."

may be permitted. If no tie ranks are permitted, the ranker may feel that the task is an unreasonable one, especially in a group of some size.

Ranking is an arduous task for the ranker, but it does achieve two important objectives. It forces the person doing the evaluation to make discriminations among those being evaluated. The ranker cannot place all or most of the persons being judged in a single category, as may happen with other reporting systems. Second, it washes out individual differences among raters in generosity or leniency. No matter how kindly the ranker may feel, he must put somebody last, and no matter how hardboiled he is, someone must come first. Individual differences in standards of judgment are eliminated from the final score.

If scores based on rankings by different judges are to be combined, there is one assumption that is introduced in rankings that may be about as troublesome as the individual differences in judging standards that have been eliminated. If we are to treat rankings by different judges as comparable scores, we must assume that the quality of the group ranked by each was the same. That is, we assume that being second in a group of twenty represents the same level on the trait being appraised, whichever group of twenty it happened to be. Usually we do not have any direct way of comparing the different subgroups, so about all we can do is assume that they are comparable. If the groups are fairly sizable and chosen more or less at random from the same sort of population, this may be a reasonable assumption. But with small groups or groups selected in different ways, the assumption of comparability may introduce substantial amounts of error into any scores based on ranks.

Ranks as such do not represent a very useful score scale. The meaning depends upon the size of the group: being third in a group of three is very different from being third in a group of thirty. Furthermore, steps of rank do not represent equal units of a trait. As we saw in our discussion of percentile norms (Chapter 7), in the usual bell-shaped distribution, one or two ranks at the extremes of a group represent much more of a difference than the same number of ranks near the middle of the group. For that reason, it is common practice to convert ranks into normalized standard scores in order to get a type of score that has uniform meaning without regard to the size of the group and uniform units throughout the score range. Special tables have been prepared to facilitate this conversion, and tables for groups of all sizes up to twenty-five may be found on pp. 90–92 of Symonds (1931).

The "Forced-Choice" Pattern

All the variations considered so far operated on the same basic pattern. The rater considered one attribute at a time and assigned the ratee to one of a set of categories or placed him relative to others on that particular attribute. We shall now consider a major departure from that pattern. The essence of the procedure we consider now is that the rater considers a *set* of attributes at one time and decides which one (or ones) most accurately represents the person being rated. Thus, an instrument developed for evaluating Air Force technical-school instructors (Highland and Berkshire, 1951) included sets of items such as the following:

a. Patient with slow learners.
b. Lectures with confidence.
c. Keeps interest and attention of class.
d. Acquaints classes with objective for each lesson.

The rater's assignment was to pick out the two items from the set that were *most descriptive* of the person being rated.

Note that all the statements in the above set are nice things to say about an instructor. As a matter of fact, they were carefully matched, on the basis of information from a preliminary investigation, to be just about equally nice to say about an instructor. But they differ a good deal, again based on preliminary investigations, in the extent to which they actually distinguish between persons who have been identified on other evidence as being good and poor instructors. The most discriminating statement is (a) and the least discriminating is (b). Thus, we could assign a score value of 2 to statement (a), 1 to (c) and (d), and 0 to (b). A person's score for the set would be the sum of the credits for the two items marked as most descriptive of him. His score for the whole instrument would be the sum of his scores for 25 or 30 such blocks of four statements. Such a score was found to have good split-half reliability (.85 to .90), so that this instrument provided a reliable score for the individual's desirability as an instructor in the eyes of a single rater. This does not, of course, tell anything about the agreement that would be found between different raters.

By casting the evaluation instrument into a forced-choice format, the maker hopes to accomplish three things:

1. He hopes to eliminate variation in rater standards of generosity or kindliness. Since the items in a set are all equally favorable things to say about a person, the kindly soul should have no particular tendency to choose one rather than another, and the true nature of the ratee should be the controlling factor.

2. He hopes to minimize the possibility of a rater intentionally biasing the score. In the ordinary rating scale, the rater is in pretty complete control of the situation. He can rate a man up or down as he pleases. In the forced-choice type of instrument, it is hoped that the rater will be unable to identify which are the significant choices and that therefore he will be unable to throw the score one way or the other at will. However, though there are some indications

that a forced-choice instrument is less fakeable than an ordinary rating scale, it is still far from tamper-proof in the hands of a determined rater.

3. He hopes to produce a better spread of scores and a more nearly normal distribution of ratings. By making all options equally attractive, one minimizes the effect of the generosity error, it is hoped, and gets a more symmetrical spread of scores. Again, there is indication that this result is achieved at least in part.

Forced-choice rating instruments are a relatively new development, dating from World War II, though the forced selection of one of a set of alternates had been used before that time in self-report inventories. The close similarity in the pattern of these forced-choice ratings to self-report instruments such as the *Kuder Preference Record* and the *Thorndike Dimensions of Temperament* should be apparent. Because of the relative novelty of the forced-choice pattern, evaluation of its usefulness in merit rating procedures and in personality appraisal is still incomplete. This format does appear to get away from some of the most troublesome limitations of conventional rating procedures. However, it has some limitations of its own. On the one hand, it has a tendency to create rater resistance, because of the difficulty of the judgments that the rater is called upon to make. Where the options are negative, that is, "Is this worker more stupid or more lazy?," the instrument has a good deal of the "Have you stopped beating your wife yet?" flavor. And even the judgment as to whether employee A is more intelligent or more industrious is not easy to make. There often seems to be no basis for comparing two quite different traits. On the other hand, the score that results from this type of instrument does not have any clear trait label or psychological interpretation, even if it is a relatively good predictor of some particular criterion. It gives us little help in building a descriptive picture and an understanding of the individual.

Developmental and exploratory work with forced-choice rating instruments continues. For example, a version produced in the Standard Oil Company of New Jersey as a Management Performance Report combines forced-choice with numerical rating. A set of four items would appear as follows:

	Fits poorly									Fits well
Follows work schedule closely	0	1	2	3	4	5	6	7	8	9
Has good work habits	0	1	2	3	4	5	6	7	8	9
Is a credit to his department	0	1	2	3	4	5	6	7	8	9
Makes decisions promptly	0	1	2	3	4	5	6	7	8	9

The numerical scale runs from a low of *0* to a high of *9*. The rater may use any part of the scale, with the one restriction that he may not use the same scale point for two statements. Thus, he can rate a man relatively low on all or relatively high on all. This takes some of the onus out of the forced ranking so far as the rater is concerned. In using the results, we may treat them either as conventional ratings, paying attention to the level checked, or as pure forced-choice rankings, ignoring the numerical values completely.

Refinements in the Rating Procedures

The best-designed instrument cannot give good results if used under unsatisfactory rating conditions. Raters cannot give information they do not have and cannot be made to give information they are unwilling to give. We must, therefore, try to pick raters who have had close contacts with the ratees and ask them for judgments on attributes they have had an opportunity to observe. We should give them some guidance and training in the type of judgments we expect them to make, and if possible they should have opportunity to observe the ratees *after* they have been educated in the use of the ratings. When there are several people who know the ratees equally well, ratings should be gathered from all of them and pooled. Every effort should be made to motivate the raters to do an honest and conscientious job. Let us consider these points further.

SELECTION OF RATERS. For most purposes, the ideal rater is the person who has had a great deal of opportunity to observe the person being rated in situations in which he would be likely to show the qualities on which ratings are desired. (Occasionally it may be desirable to get a rating of the impression which a person makes on brief contact or in a limited experimental situation.) It is also desirable that the rater take an impartial attitude toward the ratee. The desirability of these two qualities, thorough acquaintance and impartiality, is generally recognized in the abstract. However, the goals may be only partially realized in practice.

Administrative considerations usually dictate that the rating and evaluation function be assigned to the teacher in the school setting and to the supervisor in a work setting. The relationship here is in each case one of direct supervision. There is generally a continuing and fairly close personal relationship. But the relationship is a one-directional and partial one. The teacher or supervisor sees only one side of the pupil or worker, the side that is turned toward the "boss."

Those qualities that a boss has a good chance to see, primarily qualities of work performance, can probably be rated adequately by the teacher or supervisor. Thus, in one study (Judy, 1952) of airplane mechanics it was found that the ratings by a pair of supervisors on "job know-how" were as reliable as the pooled ratings by eight coworkers in a plane maintenance crew and that the supervisors' pooled rating correlated .53 with a written proficiency test, whereas the pooled rating for the coworkers correlated only .43. However, those qualities that show themselves primarily in relationships with peers or subordinates will probably be evaluated more soundly by those same peers and subordinates. The validity of the U.S. Military Academy peer ratings described on p. 433 is a case in point.

The lack of agreement between supervisor and pupil ratings of teachers is suggested in some of the following correlations from different studies:

Pupil's rating of excellence versus principal's rating (Cook and Leeds, 1947)	.39
Pupil's rating of excellence versus composite of 5 judges (Lins, 1946)	.28
Mean pupil rating of effectiveness versus administrator's rating (Brookover, 1940)	.08
Student versus administrator rating on general teacher effectiveness (Reed, 1953) School I	.40
School II	.50

A certain amount of overlap does exist, but the ratings appear also to have a good deal of uniqueness. The bird's eye and worm's eye views are not the same.

WHO SHOULD CHOOSE THE RATERS? The selection of persons to rate applicants for jobs or fellowships requires consideration from another point of view. In this setting, the applicant is usually asked to supply a certain number of references or to submit evaluation forms filled out by a certain number of individuals. The choice of the individuals is usually left up to him, and we may anticipate that he will select persons he believes will rate him favorably. It might be more satisfactory if the applicant were asked to supply the names and addresses of persons who stood in particular relationships to him and who should be able to supply relevant information, rather than leaving the applicant free to pick his own endorsers. Thus, a job applicant might be asked to give the names of his immediate supervisors in his most recent jobs; a fellowship applicant, to list the name of his major advisor and of any instructors with whom he had taken two or more courses. Thus, we are shifting the responsibility of determining who shall provide the ratings from the applicant to the using agency. Such a shift should reduce the amount of special pleading for the applicant.

SELECTION OF QUALITIES TO BE RATED. Two principles appear to apply in determining the types of information to be sought by rating procedures. First, it seems undesirable to use rating procedures to get information that can be provided satisfactorily by some more objective and reliable indicator. Score on a well-constructed intelligence test is a better indicator of intellectual ability than a supervisor's rating of intellect. When accurate production records exist, they are to be preferred to a supervisor's rating for productivity. Ratings are something to which we resort when we do not have any better indicator available.

Second, we should limit ratings to relatively overt qualities, ones that can be expressed in terms of actual observable behavior. We cannot expect the rater to look inside the ratee and tell us what goes on within. Furthermore, we must bear in mind the extent and nature of the contact between rater and person rated. For example, a set of ratings to be used after a single interview should be limited to the qualities that can be observed in an interview. The interviewee's neatness, composure, manner of speech, and fluency in answering questions are qualities that are observable in a single interview. His industry, integrity, initiative, and ingenuity are not, though these qualities might be appraised with some accuracy by the person who has worked with him for a time. Ratings should be of observable behavior—observable in the setting in which the man has been observed.

EDUCATIONAL PROGRAM FOR RATERS. Good ratings do not just happen, even with the proper raters and the proper instrument for recording the ratings. Raters must be "sold" on the importance of making good ratings and taught how to use the rating instrument. Pointing out the importance of "selling" a rating program is easier than telling how to do it. As we have indicated earlier, inertia on the one hand and identification with the ratee on the other are powerful competing motives. We cannot provide a course in direct selling at this point, but a job of selling needs to be done in almost any program for gathering ratings. Furthermore, the selling must continue if thoughtfulness and integrity of the appraisals are to be maintained.

It is desirable that raters have practice with the specific rating instrument. A training session, in which the instrument is used under supervision, is often desirable. The meanings of the attributes can be discussed, sample rating sheets can be prepared, and the resulting ratings reviewed. The prevailing generosity error can be noted, and raters cautioned to avoid it. Further practice can be given, in an attempt to generate a more symmetrical distribution of ratings. Training sessions will not eliminate all the shortcomings of ratings, but they should reduce somewhat the more common distortions considered earlier.

OBSERVATIONS MADE AS A BASIS FOR RATINGS. One objection to ratings is that they are usually made after the fact and are based on general unanalyzed impressions about the person rated. An attempt to get away from this dependence on general memory is sometimes made by introducing the rating program well in advance of the time at which the final ratings are to be called for. It is hoped that the raters will then be on the alert for and take specific note of behavior relating to the qualities that are to be rated. A record form can be developed in which critical areas of performance are identified, and space is provided for recording instances of desirable, as well as undesirable actions on the part of the ratee. A section from such a form, designed for use in evaluating student nurses (Fivars and Gosnell, 1966) is shown in Fig. 13.1 on pages 448–449. A final rating for each section would be based upon a review of the incidents, both positive and negative, that had been observed and recorded by the supervisor. However, recording of this type calls for a high level of commitment to, and cooperation in, the rating program. Where that level of involvement is achieved, advance notice and systematic recording may be expected to improve the rating process. Situations of this sort are probably rare, however.

POOLING OF RATINGS BY SEVERAL RATERS. One of the limitations of ratings is low reliability. If several people have had a reasonably good chance to observe the ratee, reliability can be improved by pooling their independent ratings (see pp. 432–433). Unfortunately, the number of persons well placed to observe a person in some particular setting, school, job, camp, etc., is usually limited. Often only one person has been in close contact with the ratee in a particular relationship. He has had only one homeroom teacher, only one foreman, only one tent counselor. Others have had some contact with him, but it may be so much less that their judgments add little to the judgment of the rater most intimately involved.

Note that we specified the pooling of *independent* ratings. If the ratings are independently made, the "error" components will be independent and will tend to cancel out. If, however, the judgments are combined through some sort of conference procedure, we cannot tell just what may happen. Errors may cancel out, wisdom may win, or the prejudices of the most dogmatic may prevail. Pooling independent judgments is the only sure way of balancing out individual errors and has been found in several studies (Personnel Research Section, 1952) to be more satisfactory than the conference type of procedure.

Nominating Techniques

If a teacher is to understand pupils, he must have some awareness of the values and standards that the group sets for its members—the peer culture—and of the role that each child plays in the group of his contemporaries—the peer group. The standards and values of his peers provide the sanctions and the rewards that are very influential in determining how a person will act and how content he will be in the group setting. The peer group can be quite a cohesive unit. In such a group any action by a teacher with respect to an individual child is often viewed not only as an action for or against him but also as an action for or against the group to which he belongs and which identifies with him. Thus, in order both to understand the individual and to understand how acts with respect to individuals affect the group climate, it is important to appraise the role of the individual in the group.

Studies have shown (Gronlund, 1959) that teachers do, in general, have a

Student's Name

____

Behaviors Needing Improvement

1. *Planning, organizing, and adapting nursing care*
   a. Failed to organize nursing care for maximum patient benefit.
   b. Failed to collect all equipment necessary for patient care.
   c. Took unwise shortcuts in giving nursing care.
   d. Failed to adapt procedure to situation.
   e. Used inadequate or improper substitute equipment.

Date	Item	What Happened

2. *Checking*
   a. Failed to check Kardex in administering medication, treatment.
   b. Did not check cards, labels, or names in medication procedure.
   c. Failed to see that laboratory orders were carried out.
   d. Did not question inconsistent medication, treatment, diet order.
   e. Failed to check requisition, equipment, or supplies.
   f. Neglected to check patient's condition.

Date	Item	What Happened

3. *Meeting the patient's adjustment and emotional needs*
   a. Refused request, was unkind, tactless, or indifferent.
   b. Did not provide recreational or diversional activity.
   c. Failed to recognize social service, spiritual, other needs.
   d. Did not explain or reassure patient about test, treatment, or policy; or misinformed patient.

Date	Item	What Happened

Fig. 13.1 Observational record form to serve as basis for rating. (After Fivars and Gosnell, 1966.) (Reproduced by permission of John C. Flanagan and of the Macmillan Company.)

Behaviors to Be Encouraged

1. *Planning, organizing, and adapting nursing care*
   A. Organized nursing care plan or equipment efficiently.
   B. Anticipated needs of others.
   C. Adapted nursing care plan to overcome difficulties.
   D. Adapted nursing care procedures to patient's needs
   E. Used adequate substitute equipment when necessary.
   F. Devised or suggested new technique for welfare of patient or for ward efficiency.

Date	Item	What Happened

2. *Checking*
   A. Checked Kardex frequently for new orders.
   B. Made special checks in medication procedure.
   C. Checked to see that laboratory orders were carried out.
   D. Noted inconsistency in medication, treatment, diet order.
   E. Checked equipment and supplies for shortage or defects.
   F. Made special checks on signs and condition of patient.

Date	Item	What Happened

3. *Meeting the patient's adjustment and emotional needs*
   A. Was reassuring, kind, and considerate to patient.
   B. Made arrangements for recreational or diversional therapy.
   C. Noted social service, home nursing, spiritual, other needs.
   D. Adapted explanation of teaching to patient's understanding.
   E. Effectively taught patient health principles or home care.

Date	Item	What Happened

Fig. 13.1 (*Continued*).

fairly good sense of which children are and which are not accepted by their peers. A correlation of about .60 between teacher ranking and the pooling of choices by members of the peer group appears to be fairly typical. But even a correlation of this size leaves room for marked discrepancies in perception of some individuals within a class. It is often difficult for a teacher to attribute to an active and, perhaps, troublesome child his true level of influence with his peers. So, to improve understanding of the social interplay in a classroom, of the reputation of each pupil among his peers, and the patterns of attraction and repulsion, peer ratings are often helpful.

A rating procedure that is very simple and quite effective for obtaining appraisals by peers is the *nominating technique.* We will consider this technique first as applied to social choices and rejections and then as applied more generally to trait ratings.

To improve their understanding of the social structure in a classroom, the patterns of friendship and leadership, teachers may use the simple expedient of asking pupils to name their choices of best friends or of work partners. For example, a teacher might say to a class: "For our unit on Mexico, we are going to need some committees of children who will work together on some part of the project. I would like to know which children you would like to have on a committee with you. Put your name on the top of the piece of paper I gave you. Then under it put the names of the children you would especially like to have on your committee."

We now have a series of nominations or choices for work partners. It is possible to show these choices pictorially by a diagram such as that shown in Fig. 13.2. This is called a *sociogram* and the procedure of constructing a sociogram is called *sociometry.*

From the sociogram shown in Fig. 13.2, we see that A and B are the most sought after members of the group: these are the "stars." Pupils J and O did not choose anyone and were not chosen by any other pupils: they are isolates. Pupils H and I chose each other, but were not chosen by any other pupils. Except for the mutual friendship between them, they too are isolates. Pupils P, Q, M, and N are fringers: they do not really belong to any of the groups but do make choices within the group.

Figure 13.2 shows the pattern of choices and attractions within the group. It would also be possible to have children indicate those class members whom they would definitely *not* want in their group. Calling for rejections presents some slight risks to individual and class morale but does permit a more complete picture of group structure.

The sociogram in Fig. 13.2 indicates that this is not a closely-knit group. The rather large number of isolates and fringers and the linkages across from one

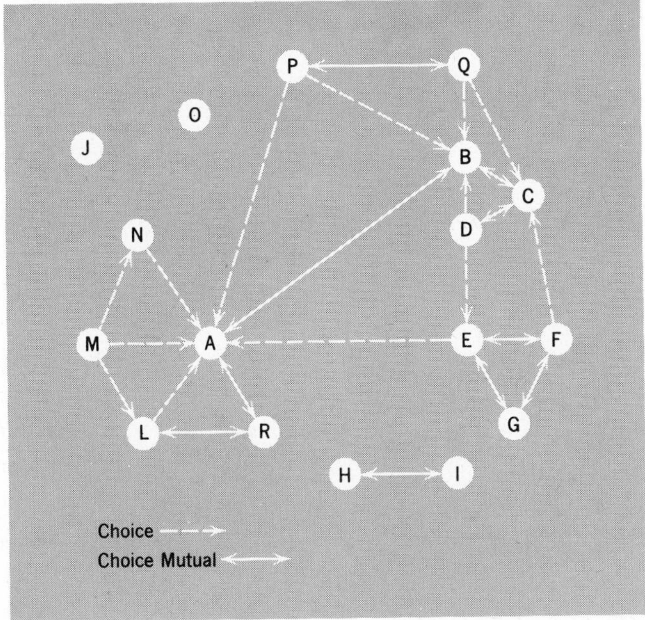

Fig. 13.2 Sociogram of fourth-grade class. *Key:* Choice →, Mutual choice ↔.

"clique" to the other suggest an unstable pattern which is in the process of changing and reforming. Thus, the sociogram might represent a class at the beginning of the school year, in which a residue of last year's friendships is mixed with new currents and in which pupils from other class groups and other schools are not yet integrated into the group. It is in such a setting as this that the teacher can be most effective in bringing isolates into the group or promoting new friendships.

After the teacher has determined which children are without friends or are relatively isolated in the group, he should try to find out why this is the case. Sometimes the explanation may be very simple. The child may be new to the group and have not yet had time to find his place in it. The normal opportunities to get acquainted, furthered by the teacher's efforts to bring out the new child's assets, may be all that is required. The child may be older or younger than the rest of the group, having friends in other classes or outside of school. The child may not live near any of the other children in the class. At other times, the reasons may be more subtle, and it may take a good deal of discreet sleuthing for the teacher to find out why Willie or Alice are not chosen by their classmates.

When the reasons are understood, the teacher can often help to remove them. Sometimes the simple process of coaching the child so that he develops competence in athletics may turn the trick. The teacher can arrange seats so that a child is placed near one for whom he expressed preference. Sometimes helping a child to develop everyday social graces or to improve his personal appearance is all that is needed to make him acceptable. If an isolate or fringer has special mechanical or artistic skills, giving him an opportunity to use these in class group activities may be effective.

In general, the teacher can help a child become integrated with and accepted by his peer group by (1) providing opportunity for developing friendly relations, (2) improving social skills, and (3) building up a sense of accomplishment or competence.

Sociometric choices describe the present flow of interaction among children rather than indicating any strong and permanent emotional structuring. However, the structuring of a class group affects the general emotional climate of the classroom. In a class where there are many isolates or children who are "fringers," that is, not completely accepted by a clique, the morale of the group tends to be low and group planning and coordinated group action is made more difficult. It is also true that the teacher in dealing with one child is quite frequently dealing with the clique to which the child belongs.

Sociograms frequently point up mistakes that a teacher makes in characterizing a child. Thus, when the teacher has judged a child and his position in his peer group by adult standards, sociometric devices point out these mistakes and give the teacher a framework for understanding behavior that taken by itself may seem unexplainable.

Sociograms have been used in various nonschool situations. In industry they have been used to form work groups and have been found to stimulate production. They have been used in institutions, especially those for juvenile offenders, to select house groups.

The sociogram by itself tells the teacher only what children are selected or rejected, not the reasons for selection and rejection. It is most useful when used in conjunction with good anecdotal records. For successful use, especially when rejections are asked for, there needs to be a friendly feeling between the teacher and the class. Furthermore, the teacher should actually use the nominations as far as possible in the way in which he has told the class he would use them.

The teacher should also remember that group structure is not static, especially in younger age groups. One sociogram made at the beginning of a school year will rarely provide an adequate picture of group structure through the year. Furthermore, neither choices nor rejections can be taken entirely at face value. When, as is sometimes the procedure, the number of choices is limited to "three best friends," failure to choose a particular pupil need not mean lack of friendly feeling for him. Choices may reflect the prestige of the person chosen and a desire to be associated with that prestige, rather than a link of friendship. The culture pattern in certain age groups dictates that rejections follow sex lines. Class and caste distinctions also introduce cultural factors influencing choice and rejection. A sociogram is at best a rough and tentative picture of the social currents and climate of the group.

A final word of caution should be sounded about attempting to use sociometric data to reconstruct a group or modify a child's role in it. We have offered some suggestions as to ways in which a teacher may try to help the relatively isolated child. However, any such manipulations call for a good deal of subtlety. Heavy-handed attempts by the teacher to manipulate the pupils in the group may only aggravate the ills he is trying to cure.

Other patterns for obtaining peer evaluations have been developed, and they have been used for other purposes beside the preparing of sociograms and the studying of social currents within the group. A slightly more complex form is the *Ohio Social Acceptance Scale,* in which each pupil reacts to each other pupil in the group, checking him under one of the following six categories: (1) My very, very best friends, (2) My other friends, (3) Not friends, but okay, (4) Don't know them, (5) Don't care for them, (6) Dislike them. From the pooled pupil responses, a score may be obtained for each child indicating the extent of his acceptance within the group. This or some other similar format provides a simple procedure for obtaining ratings by a group of peers, and their simplicity makes them usable even with elementary school children.

The *Syracuse Scales of Social Relations* (Gardner and Thompson, 1958) provide for an even more elaborate rating system, in which each pupil sets up his own personal man-to-man scale in relation to a person to "talk over your troubles with" and of a person to help you "make or do something." Each pupil in the class is then located by the pupil at some point on this scale. Results can be summarized in terms of average ratings given or received by a single pupil, or the class as a whole, and particular constellations of mutual attraction can be sought out.

Nominations may be used at any age level, and may be made with respect to any type of characteristic. For example, they have frequently been used in the armed services in Officer Candidate School, where each member of a unit may be asked to nominate a specified number of individuals in his unit who have shown the greatest evidence of "leadership" during the training course. He may also be asked to nominate those who have shown the *least* indication of leadership.

Taking all the nominations for the group as a whole, it is possible to arrive at a score for each individual, giving a plus for each favorable nomination and a minus for each unfavorable nomination.

A variation of the nominating procedure that has been used with school children has usually been referred to as the "Guess Who" technique or as "Casting Characters." In this procedure, the children are instructed somewhat as follows:

> Suppose we were going to put on a class play. The characters in the play are described below. For each character, you are to put down the names of one or more children in the class who would be good for that part because he or she is just like that anyway.
>
> "This person is always cheerful and happy—never grouchy or cross.
> "This person is always butting in and telling other people how to do things. He cannot mind his own business.
> "This person is very quiet and doesn't get into games or do things with other children."

The number of characters can be extended as desired. Each "character" is a description in fairly concrete terms of a quality of behavior in which the investigator is interested. Descriptions of opposite ends of a scale can be included —that is, friendly versus unfriendly, dominating versus submissive, etc.—and can be treated as positive and negative nominations on a single scale. Each child receives a score for each "character," based on the number of nominations he receives.

The attractive feature of the nominating pattern is its simplicity, which makes it rather painless to administer and usable with young groups or groups with little sophistication or experience in rating. It is feasible because the large number of raters make it possible to use a simple count of nominations instead of a rating of the usual type. However, nominating procedures do sometimes generate resistance. Students in military training programs have been known to "rig" the choices so as not to injure the chances of fellow students, and parent groups have reacted sometimes violently when children were asked to make negative responses of rejection or separation from their classmates. It is important to be aware of these sensibilities in students and in a community.

SUMMARY AND EVALUATION

In spite of all their limitations, evaluations of persons through ratings will undoubtedly continue to be widely used for administrative evaluations in schools, civil service, and industry, as well as in educational and psychological research. We must recognize this fact and learn to live with it. Granting that we shall continue to use ratings of different aspects of personality, we should do so with full awareness of the limitations of our instruments, and we should do so in such a way that these limitations are minimized.

The limitations of rating procedures arise out of:

1. A humane unwillingness to make unfavorable judgments of our fellows, which is particularly pronounced when we identify to some extent with the person being rated (generosity error).
2. Wide individual differences among raters in "humaneness" or, in any event, in leniency or severity of rating (differences in rater standards).
3. A tendency to respond to other persons as a whole in terms of our general liking or aversion and difficulty in differentiating out specific aspects of the individual personality (halo error).
4. Limited contact between the rater and person being rated—limited both in amount and in type of situation in which seen.
5. Ambiguity in meaning of the attributes to be appraised.
6. The covert and unobservable nature of many of the inner aspects of personality dynamics.
7. Instability and unreliability of human judgment.

In view of these limitations it is suggested that ratings will provide a most accurate portrayal of the person being rated when:

1. Appraisal is limited to those qualities that appear overtly in interpersonal relations.
2. The qualities to be appraised are analyzed into concrete and relatively specific aspects of behavior, and judgments are made of these behaviors.
3. A rating form is developed that forces the rater to discriminate and/or that has controls for rater differences in judging standards.
4. Raters are used who have had the most opportunity to observe the individual in situations in which he would display the qualities to be rated.
5. Raters are "sold" on the value of the ratings and trained in the use of the rating instrument.
6. Independent ratings of several raters are pooled when there are several persons qualified to carry out ratings.

Evaluation procedures in which the significance of his ratings is somewhat concealed from the rater present an interesting possibility for civil service and industrial use. This is true particularly when controls on rater bias are introduced through "forced-choice" techniques or a correction score.

Peer-nominating techniques have interesting possibilities for use in schools and other group settings. They permit sociometric analyses of the interpersonal relations of pupils in a classroom or the workers in a shop. "Guess Who" nominations permit a simple type of rating in the early grades.

QUESTIONS AND EXERCISES

1. If you were writing to someone who had been given as a reference by an applicant for a job in your company or for admission to your school, what should you do in order to obtain the most useful evaluation of the applicant?

2. Make as complete a list as you can of the different ratings used in the school that you are attending or the school in which you teach. What type of a rating scale or form is used in each case?

3. In the light of such evidence or opinion as you can obtain, how effective are the ratings that you identified in the previous question? How adequate a spread of ratings is obtained? How consistently is the scale used by different users? What is your impression of the reliability of the ratings? Of their freedom from halo and other errors?

4. What factors influence a rater's willingness to rate conscientiously? How serious is this issue? What can be done about it?

5. Why would three *independent* ratings from separate raters ordinarily be preferable to a rating prepared by the three persons working together as a committee?

6. In the personnel office of a large company, employment interviewers are called upon to rate job applicants at the end of the interview. Which of the following characteristics would you expect to be rated reasonably reliably? Why?

   a. Initiative.
   b. Appearance.
   c. Work background.
   d. Dependability.
   e. Emotional balance.

7. In a small survey of the report cards used in a number of communities the following four traits were most frequently mentioned as found on the report cards: (a) courteous, (b) cooperative, (c) health habits, (d) works with others. How might these be broken down or revised so that the classroom teacher could evaluate them better?

8. Which of the following would influence your judgment of a person in an interview? In what way?

   a. A very firm grip in shaking hands.
   b. Wearing a "loud" necktie.
   c. Generally pausing for a moment before replying to a question.
   d. Playing with keys on a key ring.
   e. Having a spot on his vest.
   f. Looking at the floor all during the interview.

9. Compare the reactions of several class members or of several acquaintances on the items of question 8. How general are the reactions? What basis in fact is there for them?

10. What advantages do ratings by peers have over ratings by superiors? What disadvantages?

11. What are the advantages of ranking over rating on a rating scale? What are the disadvantages?

12. Suppose that a forced-choice rating scale had been developed for use in rating the teachers in a city school system in order to get an evaluation of their effectiveness. What advantages would this rating procedure have over other types of ratings? What problems would be likely to arise in using it?

13. Make up a "Guess Who" form that might be useful to a teacher in finding out about the pupils in his class. If a class group is available to you, try the form out and analyze the results. What precautions should be taken in using the results?

14. Using a class group taught by some class member or made available by the instructor, get each child's choices for other children to work on a committee with him. Plot the results in a sociogram. What do the results tell you about the class and the pupils in it? What limitations would this sociogram have for judging the status of an individual child among his classmates?

15. Suppose you have been placed in charge of a merit rating plan which is being introduced in some company. What steps would you take to try to get as good ratings as possible?

REFERENCES

Barrett, R. S. The influence of supervisor's requirements on ratings. *Personnel Psychology,* 1966, **19,** 375–388.

Blumberg, H. H., De Soto, C. B., & Kuethe, J. L. Evaluation of rating scale formats. *Personnel Psychology,* 1966, **19,** 243–260.

Brookover, W. B. Person-person interaction between teachers and pupils and teaching effectiveness. *Journal of Educational Research,* 1940, **34,** 272–287.

Cook, W. & Leeds, C. H. Measuring the teaching personality. *Educational and Psychological Measurement,* 1947, **7,** 399–410.

Doll, E. A. *Measurement of social competence.* Minneapolis, Minnesota: Educational Test Bureau, Educational Publishers, 1953.

Fivars, G. & Gosnell, D. *Nursing evaluation: The problem and the process.* New York: Macmillan, 1966. Chapter 9.

Gardner, E. F. & Thompson, G. G. *Syracuse Scales of Social Relations.* New York: Harcourt, Brace and World, 1958.

Gronlund, N. E. *Sociometry in the classroom.* New York: Harper, 1959. Pp. 164–166.

Harrington, W. Recommendation quality and placement success. *Psychological Monographs,* 1943, No. 252.

Highland, R. W. & Berkshire, J. R. *A methodological study of forced choice performance rating.* San Antonio, Texas: Human Resources Research Center, Lackland Air Force Base, May 1951. (Research Bulletin 51-9.)

Judy, C. J. A comparison of peer and supervisory rankings as criteria of aircraft maintenance proficiency. Ed.D. Project Report, Teachers College, Columbia University, 1952.

Klores, M. S. Rater bias in forced-distribution performance ratings. *Personnel Psychology,* 1966, **19,** 411–421.

Lins, L. J. The prediction of teaching efficiency. *Journal of Experimental Education,* 1946, **15,** 2–60.

Peres, S. H. & Garcia, J. R. Validity and dimensions of descriptive adjectives used in reference letters for engineering applicants. *Personnel Psychology,* 1962, **15,** 279–286.

Personnel Research Section, AGO. *Analysis of an Officer Efficiency Report (WD AGO Form 67-1) using multiple raters.* Washington, D.C.: Adjutant General's Office, 1952 (PRS Report 817).

Personnel Research Section, AGO. *A study of officer rating methodology, validity and reliability of ratings by single raters and multiple raters.* Washington, D.C.: Adjutant General's Office, 1952 (PRS Report 904).

Personnel Research Section, AGO. *Survey of the aptitude for service rating system at the U.S. Military Academy, West Point, New York.* Washington, D.C.: Adjutant General's Office, 1953.

Preston, H. O. *The development of a procedure for evaluating officers in the United States Air Force.* Pittsburgh, Pennsylvania: American Institute for Research, 1948.

Reed, H. J. An investigation of the relationship between teaching effectiveness and the teacher's attitude of acceptance. *Journal of Experimental Education,* 1953, **21,** 277–325.

Remmers, H. H., Shock, N. W., & Kelly, E. L. An empirical study of the validity of the Spearman Brown formula as applied to the Purdue Rating Scale. *Journal of Educational Psychology,* 1927, **18,** 187–195.

Richardson, M. W. & Kuder, G. F. Making a rating scale that measures. *Personnel Journal,* 1933, **12,** 36–40.

Ross, A. O., Lacey, H. M., & Parton, D. A. The development of a behavior checklist for boys. *Child Development,* 1965, **36,** 1013–1027.

Siskind, G. "Mine eyes have seen a host of angels." *American Psychologist,* 1966, **21,** 804–806.

Symonds, P. M. *Diagnosing personality and conduct.* New York: Century, 1931.

SUGGESTED ADDITIONAL READING

Kleinmuntz, B. *Personality measurement.* Homewood, Illinois: Dorsey Press, 1967. Chapter 5.

Vernon, P. E. *Personality assessment: A critical survey.* New York: John Wiley, 1964. Part I.

CHAPTER 14

Behavioral Measures of Personality

oooooooooooooooooooooooooooooooooooooooooooooooooooooooooooooooooooooooooooooooooooooooooooooooooooo

WE have tended to define personality as the typical quality of an individual's behavior. It would be natural, then, to get an actual sample of his behavior as the basis for appraising his personality. Two possibilities are available to us. We may set up especially designed "test" situations, in which the individual's behavior may be scored or rated. Or we may plan to observe his behavior as it occurs spontaneously in his natural environment. Each of these has received attention from psychologists and educators, and we shall consider each in turn.

BEHAVIOR TESTS

In personality testing we are concerned with the typical behavior of the individual—what he *will* do under the ordinary conditions of life, rather than what he *can* do if he is trying to do his best. Under these circumstances, it is obvious that any test must usually be indirect and disguised, so that the examinee does not know what is being appraised. This appears to be especially true in the field of character testing.

Traits of character relate to behaviors in which society sets up definitions of what is "good" and what is "bad." We can hardly expect a child to report his dishonesties, for example, or to show them in a test situation in which he knows his honesty is being observed and appraised. Furthermore, he has probably managed to conceal most of his transgressions from teacher, camp counselor, or other adult who might be asked to rate him. We are almost forced back upon a concealed test to elicit such socially disapproved behavior. We shall describe in some detail the honesty tests devised by May and Hartshorne for the Character Education Inquiry (Hartshorne and May, 1928) in part for their intrinsic interest and in part because they illustrate the virtues and many of the limitations of this type of measurement procedure.

May and Hartshorne developed a comprehensive series of tests of honesty. These included situations in which the individual had a chance to cheat, situations in which he had an opportunity to lie, and situations in which it was possible for him to steal. Some of the situations are described below.

Situation A: Cheating on a test by copying. A test is given dealing with some topic related to school work, word knowledge, for example. The papers are collected. The next day the papers are passed out, and each pupil is allowed to score his own paper when the answers are read aloud. As a matter of fact, however, the papers have been accurately scored before they are returned without any marks being made on the paper. The amount that the pupil copies in and scores his own paper above the correct score is used as an indication of cheating.

Situation B: Cheating on a test by adding on. A speeded arithmetic test is given, and at the end of 3 minutes pupils are told to stop work. However, for several minutes papers are left on their desks while the teacher or test administrator is busy doing something else. Later a second test is given after which the papers are immediately collected. When performance on the first testing surpasses performance on the second test by a specified amount, this is taken as evidence that the examinee added onto his work after the time limit was up and before the papers were collected.

Situation C: Cheating in a game—peeking. The game is illustrated in Fig. 14.1. The instruction is to shut one's eyes and then put a dot in each circle in turn. Norms are prepared, based upon children tested with their view blocked so that they cannot peek. A child who performs unduly well, as determined by the "peek-proof" norms, is assumed to have peeked and helped himself.

Situation D: Cheating in an athletic contest. As a part of a "field day," each child is given a hand dynamometer to squeeze as a test of strength of hand. Three "practice" squeezes are given, and the adult observer notes and later records the best performance on these. Then the pupil is told to make additional squeezes "for the record." While he makes the squeezes, the adult is obviously busy with another child and not watching him. The child records his own performance on a record blank. Since fatigue tends to set in on successive squeezes, it is unlikely that he will show improvement. If the performance he

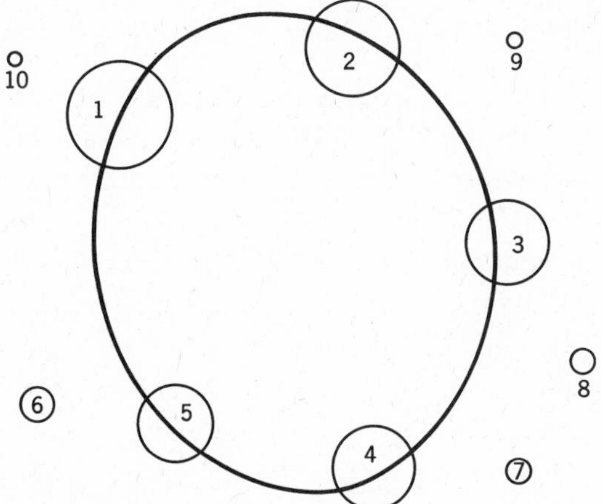

Fig. 14.1 Aiming test. (After Hartshorne and May, 1928.)

reports surpasses his practice squeezes by a specified amount, it is assumed that he has been unduly optimistic in recording his performance.

Situation E: Lying—self-glorification. In this test the child is asked a series of questions. Each question has to do with standards of behavior that are universally applauded but seldom achieved. Thus, one question reads "Do you always obey your parents cheerfully and promptly?" and another, "Do you always smile when things go wrong?" It is hard to know how many of a set of statements like this a child might truthfully endorse, but an attempt was made to determine this by having groups of graduate students think back to their childhood and respond as would have been true of them then. The child who marks an excessive number of items is deemed to be not angelic but untruthful.

Situation F: Stealing. A game is devised which uses a number of coins. These are in a box, and one box is passed out to each child. After the game is over, each child is told to put the coins back in the box and fasten it up. The boxes are collected. They have been unobtrusively coded, so it is possible to tell which child had which box. A check of the coins in the boxes makes it possible to determine which children have helped themselves to one or more of the coins.

As can be seen from the brief descriptions, the tests are quite involved and require rather extensive stage-managing. The details of the testing situation seem fairly critical, that is, how sure the child feels that he is free from observation, the manner in which the children are occupied when they are stopped in their work, and so forth. And it is crucial that the "security" of the test be maintained, for if the true purpose of the test were suspected, examinees could immediately conform to the approved social standard.

Evaluation of Behavior Tests of Honesty

How reliable and how valid are these situational tests of honesty? Reliability estimates are shown in Table 14.1. We can see that the reliabilities of single tests are rather modest, averaging about .50. In comparison with the aptitude and achievement tests we have been considering in the preceding chapters, these reliabilities are disappointing. The score of a pupil on any single test of the set used by May and Hartshorne would provide only the roughest indication of the typical behavior of that child. A single test would need to be extended by adding on several additional tests of the same sort if a satisfactorily stable and dependable measure were to be obtained. The single tests would appear to be useful primarily for the comparison of different groups of pupils.

When it comes to validity, we are put to it to find any outside standard against which to evaluate the tests. Teachers' ratings of pupils may be taken as one limited and imperfect criterion, and the classroom cheating tests showed a modest correlation with this criterion (average about .35). But before we look for outside criterion measures, we should perhaps ask how the different kinds of honesty tests correlate with each other.

Considering four different types of cheating tests carried out in the classroom situation, the authors found that on the average a test of one type correlated with a test of one of the other types only to the extent of .26. When some type of classroom cheating test was correlated with cheating in an athletic contest, the average correlation was found to be only .16, and with the stealing test the average correlation was .17. The lying test, also given in the classroom, averaged .23 with the other classroom tests and .06 with the two out-of-classroom tests.

Even though the reliabilities of the single tests are low, the correlations be-

TABLE 14.1 RELIABILITIES OF TESTS USED FOR MEASURING DECEPTION (From Hartshorne and May, 1928)

Type of Test	Reliability Coefficient
1. Copying from a key or answer sheet	.70
2. Adding onto one's score on a speeded test	.44
3. Peeping when one's eyes should be shut	.46
4. Faking a solution to a puzzle	.50
5. Faking a score in a physical ability test	.46
6. Lying to win approval	.84
7. Getting illicit help at home	.24

tween the different sorts of tests are a good deal lower. When the correlations involve different settings (that is, classroom versus gymnasium) or different types of behavior (that is, cheating versus stealing), the correlations drop still further. Many of them are not far from zero. Score on any one test depends only slightly upon a common factor running through all of the tests, and depends, to a considerable extent, on factors unique to that specific test situation.

What does this outcome signify?

From the practical point of view, it indicates that no one honesty test, and probably no battery of honesty tests, is going to permit us to make accurate predictions of behavior in a specific test or life situation. Our ability to identify the store clerk who will pilfer from the store or the citizen who will "chisel" on his income tax will be very meager, unless we can test him in closely similar situations. The specifics of the test situation on the one hand and the life situation on the other will water down any relationship.

From a theoretical point of view, it gives us a picture of behavior as dependent only to a modest degree upon generalized personality traits. The concept of trait is a useful one for organizing our description of a person. And there *is* an underlying coherence and continuity that gives meaning to his actions. But those actions are also situation-bound, and the specific habits of responding to specific situations are as important determiners as are broad underlying traits. This phenomenon is not peculiar to objective behavior tests; it also characterizes the items of self-report inventories. In fact, a single behavior test is in many ways like a single item on an inventory. Thus, in a sense, the test that provides the pupil an opportunity to revise his answer sheet as he scores it really asks a specific question in behavioral terms, to wit: Would you change the wrong answers if you scored your own paper? The series of tests collectively provide a multi-item behavior inventory. Collectively, they describe the underlying trend of the individual's behavior, but it is still true that his response to any one specific situation will be predictable only to a limited extent from his standing on the general trait, and will depend, to a substantial degree, on factors unique to the specific situation.

Other Types of Performance Tests

A number of psychologists have recently been exploring indirect performance measures as indicators of personality variables. Eysenck (1952) has developed a battery of performance measures to predict neuroticism. Some of the measures that have tended to discriminate between normal and neurotic groups are (1) the amount of body sway in response to a direct suggestion of falling, (2) the number of unusual responses on a multiple-choice free association test, (3) the speed of dark adaptation, (4) the number of food aversions, and (5) the length of time breath could be held. From a battery of eight or ten such specific tests Eysenck was able to get quite high reliability and fairly sharp discrimination between a normal and a neurotic group.

Witkin and others (1962) have developed a set of indirect performance tests to measure an attribute that they designate "field dependence." Field dependence is a way of perceiving in which the person is unduly influenced by and dependent upon the totality of the surrounding (typically visual) field. Three tests that correlate fairly substantially and that are used collectively to assess field dependence are:

1. *Tilting chair in a tilting room.* The subject is required to adjust the chair in which he sits to a vertical position when the tilted "room" gives visual cues that conflict with the postural cues from his own body.
2. *Rod and frame.* The subject is required to adjust a rod to a vertical orientation when the only visual reference is a frame that has been tilted at an angle to the normal vertical-horizontal orientation.
3. *Embedded figures.* The subject must find a simple figure that has been "hidden" in a more complex diagram.

This set of tests, primarily perceptual in nature, tends to bridge the gap between measures of ability and measures of personality. A number of tests of this sort have sometimes been spoken of as tests of "cognitive style." The tasks are cognitive in nature, but they are used for the insight that they give into personality characteristics. Thus, the person who is *independent* of the surrounding field on the three perceptual tests, is reported to be more self-sufficient in his social relationships, to have more elaborated defenses and controls to channel his impulses and direct his actions, to show problems of overcontrol, overintellectualization, and isolation when he presents a personality disturbance.

A possibly related area of personality functioning is that of aesthetic preference along a simplicity-complexity dimension. Barron (1953) has used a rather simple figure preference test in which the figures range from those that are neat, symmetrical, and geometrical to those that are complex, somewhat chaotic, and asymmetrical to elicit judgments of liking and disliking. Artists typically prefer figures of the second type. And persons from the general public who prefer the complex designs appear to show an array of personality attributes that differentiate them from the persons whose preferences are for the simple and balanced designs. As a research tool, the *Welsh Figure Preference Test* (Welsh, 1959) provides a pool of 400 figures that can be grouped and scored in various ways to provide cues as to personality variables. The most extensive effort to develop objective personality tests is a battery brought out by Cattell (1967) to appraise many of the personality factors that he had also identified in factor analytic studies of self-descriptive inventories and of ratings.

One feature that is common to many of the objective behavior tests is that they are indirect and "unobtrusive" measures. They are designed to make the examinee "task-oriented" rather than self-oriented. That is, the focus of his attention and effort is in getting an individual or group task completed quickly or effectively. By recording or observing some aspect of his performance that is only indirectly related to the assigned task, we hope to get information on his typical mode of functioning. The presumed advantage of this oblique approach is that we are able to bypass the defenses that an individual sets up against direct inspection of his personality. However, this advantage is gained only at considerable cost. The cost lies sometimes in the more involved, elaborate, and costly procedures for data collection. It lies sometimes in the lack of any obvious rationale for the test score, as when a measure of body sway is used as an indicator of neuroticism or when some category of response to an inkblot is interpreted as implying emotionality. When the significance of an item of behavior is not clearly implied by the nature of the act itself, as it is when hitting another child is counted as an aggressive act, it becomes crucial to validate and revalidate each indicator beyond the shadow of a doubt. It is the shakiness of this independent validation that leaves so many indirect assessment procedures so much in question at the present time.

These approaches are appealing, in that they presumably cannot be distorted by the subject to give a desired impression. However, the procedures are complex and time-consuming, and the predictive validity of the tests for socially important criteria is still largely undetermined. A large amount of research is needed before we will know whether objective testing to appraise personality can be useful.

SITUATIONAL TESTS AND ASSESSMENT PROGRAMS

During and since World War II a number of assessment programs have been set up for making a comprehensive appraisal of candidates for a particular type of training or assignment. Perhaps the most publicized of these was the program set up to screen personnel for the Office of Strategic Services during World War II. The program has been fully described (Assessment Staff, OSS, 1948), and some features of it will be worth considering here. Assessment programs have generally made use of a wide variety of techniques for evaluating the individual. They have included ability tests of several sorts, detailed interviews, and various types of fantasy and projective materials. However, one central element has been the situational test, in which the individual is placed in a more or less standardized task situation in which his behavior can be observed, his responses recorded, or various aspects of his reactions rated by observers.

Situational Tests in The OSS Assessment Program

For assessment by the OSS staff, each candidate was brought to an assessment center for a 3-day period of testing and evaluation. During this period he was continuously under observation and was subjected to a wide range of tests and stresses. In addition to ability tests of a number of kinds—tests of intelligence, mechanical ability, ability to observe and remember details—he was exposed to a number of "situational" tests. These consisted of staged situations, with fairly complete instructions and ground rules, presenting problems that the candidate was to solve, either individually or as a member of a group. The variety of situational tests used in the program was wide. Selected examples are described briefly in the following paragraphs.*

THE BROOK. Individuals worked in teams composed of five or six men. The group was brought to a stream about 8 feet wide. On the banks were a log, a rock, various boards, ropes, a pulley, and other items. They were instructed somewhat as follows:

> In this problem you have to use your imagination. Before you, you see a raging torrent so deep and so fast that it is quite impossible to rest anything upon the bottom of the stream. The banks are sheer, so it will be impossible for you to work except from the top of them.
>
> You are on a mission in the field, and having come to this stream you are faced with the task of transporting this delicate range-finder, skillfully camouflaged as a log, to the far bank, and of bringing that box of percussion caps, camouflaged as a rock, to this side. In carrying out this assignment, you may make use of any materials you find around here. When the job is done, all of you, as well as any material you have used, are to be back on this side.
>
> The limits within which you are to work are marked by the two white stakes on each bank (the stakes were approximately 15 feet apart), and you are not permitted to jump across the stream.

The behavior of each man in the group was observed, as the group went about solving the task, and each man was rated on such factors as energy and initiative, effective intelligence, social relations, leadership, and physical ability.

CONSTRUCTION. A single candidate was presented with the task of building a structure, using materials resembling oversized Tinker Toy. His task was de-

* For fuller descriptions and verbatim instructions, the reader is referred to Assessment Staff, OSS (1948).

scribed to him, and then he was told that the test was primarily one of leadership, since the work was to be done by two helpers whom he was to supervise. The "helpers" were called in, and the construction project began. However, the "helpers," who were carefully coached assistants, turned out to be sensitive, stupid, and obstructive, and their behavior ranged from "gold-bricking" to systematically heckling their supervisor. Again, the responses of the examinee to these frustrations were observed, and he was rated for emotional stability and leadership.

IMPROVISATIONS. This test was one of role-playing. Working in pairs, examinees were assigned roles in a dramatic situation and were told to enact the scene as they would handle it in real life. Thus, one situation was set as follows:

> A moved to a small city about 3 months ago and opened a business there. He has been doing quite well and one month ago sent in an application for membership in a club in the town. He has heard nothing in response to this application and goes to the home of B, a prominent member of the club, with whom he is pleasantly acquainted. (A is then sent out of the room and B is told that A has received several blackballs. A is then called back into the room.)

As before, aspects of each individual's personality, as they exhibited themselves in the role-playing situations, were rated by observers.

STRESS INTERVIEW. Candidates were instructed to assume that the following situation had occurred.

> A night watchman at 9:00 P.M. found you going through some papers in a file marked "SECRET" in a Government office in Washington. You are NOT an employee of the agency occupying the building in which the office is located. You had no identification papers whatsoever with you. The night watchman has brought you here for questioning.

The examinee was given 12 minutes to prepare a cover story to account for his presence in the compromising situation. Then he was subjected to an intensive and grueling interrogation, in which his statements were questioned, inconsistencies brought out, and every attempt made to trip him up and to make him feel foolish. He was rated on the quality of his story and his ability to maintain it and upon his evidence of emotional stability.

Further examples of situational tests might be cited, but these serve to show the essential characteristics of this type of approach to personality appraisal. The attempt is made to develop situations that approach realistic lifelike situations but still permit a reasonable amount of uniformity from person to person. The OSS staff considered desirable characteristics of situations to be that they (1) have a number of alternative solutions, (2) do not require highly specialized abilities, (3) reveal kinds of behavior that cannot be registered by mechanical means, (4) force the candidate to reveal dominant dispositions of his personality,

(5) involve interaction with other persons, and (6) require the coordination of numerous components of personality.

Leaderless Group Discussion

One procedure that provides a somewhat simplified version of the situational test, and consequently one that is more widely adaptable for practical use, is the "leaderless group discussion." This approach has been used when a number of individuals are to be appraised for some type of administrative or executive position, such as a school principalship. The candidates are assembled in small groups, a group of about six apparently working best. The group is assigned a topic to discuss or a problem to solve relevant to their background and the position for which they are candidates. They are allowed a substantial block of time—perhaps an hour—to carry on their discussion. During that time they are observed by a team of observers and a record is kept of the nature and extent of each man's contributions to the work of the group, or summary ratings are made of each group member on those traits and behaviors that can be exhibited in the group situation. A good deal of research has been done (Bass, 1954) on this type of group interaction as a personality appraisal device, and the results suggest that the behaviors shown in the limited test situation do have some validity as indicators of life behavior.

Situational Proficiency Tests

A type of appraisal related to those that we have been discussing, but still somewhat different in emphasis, is the situational proficiency test. Here, the emphasis is upon assessing competence on a set of tasks that simulate an actual job situation. Though the appraisal may be concerned partly with personal "style" of doing the work, it is also concerned with the adequacy with which the work is done. A type of procedure that has been used in various contexts is the "In-Basket Test." In this procedure the examinee, perhaps an elementary school principal (Hemphill, Griffiths, and Frederiksen, 1962), is given a description of the particular job that he is being called upon to fill, with a good deal of information and general background. Then he is faced with a task, one of which is described by Hemphill, et al as follows:

> The setting for In-basket A was Labor Day, the day preceding the first day of school. It was Marion Smith's first day on the job. A summer work commitment and the necessity of moving his family to a new community had precluded earlier attention to the many problems of the beginning of a school year. Marion Smith had managed a brief visit to his office on the preceding Friday, at which time he instructed his secretary, Ruth Platz, to get together those things that needed

his attention and to leave them on his desk. The materials in Packet A were the items she had assembled. Since it was a holiday, no one else was around, the switchboard was closed, and Marion Smith had to work on the contents of his in-basket without help. He had only 2 hours and 15 minutes to work, but, of course, wanted to get as much done as possible.

At the end of the period allotted to the principal for work on his in-basket material, he was asked to stop and complete a *Reasons-for-Action Form*, for which 45 minutes were allowed. (This form was completed out of role.) In completing the *Reasons-for-Action Form*, each principal indicated very briefly what he did in response to each item and why he did it. This information was needed to clarify (for later scoring) the nature of each course of action the principal had taken and the motives which prompted the action.*

Actually, this total assessment included three "in-baskets," together with a number of other procedures for gathering personality and ability data about the participants, and required a full week of testing.

Scoring of the mass of responses to this type of situational task is quite a formidable enterprise. In all, 68 scoring categories were used in this particular study. We will list only a few, together with the reliability associated with each.

Took usual course of action	.92
Number of subordinates involved individually	.84
Socially insensitive	.38
Discusses with superiors or outsiders	.58
Delays or postpones decision or temporizes	.81
Follows lead by subordinates	.77
Initiates a new structure	.78
Delegates completely	.31
Informality to subordinates	.92
Backs up teachers or staff officers	.06
Imposes controls: sets a deadline	.36

As can be seen, some categories of behavior can be evaluated with a good deal of consistency, while others are quite unstable. The translation of category scores such as these into a meaningful and valid description of a specific principal's competence in his job presents, of course, a whole series of further problems.

Evaluation of Situational Tests

Situational tests like the leaderless group discussion and those used in the OSS differ from the *May-Hartshorne* character tests in that, though they still deal with behavior in a somewhat disguised situation, they do not yield an actual record or product. Thus, in the *May-Hartshorne* stealing test, it was necessary only to count the coins left in the box to determine the examinee's score. The

* Reproduced by permission of the Teachers College Press.

tests were highly objective as far as the scoring was concerned. Situational tests are usually not objective. Though an attempt is made to present a relatively standard task situation, the evaluation of each examinee's behavior is through the observations and ratings by the staff of examiners.

The gain from this approach, which offsets the loss in objectivity, is a great increase in the range of behaviors that can be studied. Much that the individual does, especially in his relations with others, leaves no record once the behavior is past. An action showing aggression or resistance to domination, an integrating suggestion that promotes group harmony, assumption of the initiative, or lapsing into passive followership are actions that occur and are gone. We must observe them on the wing if we are to get them at all. This is what the situational test hopes to achieve—to provide the situations that will elicit behavior of this sort and to provide for its immediate observation and rating.

Situational tests appear to be adaptable to eliciting a variety of types of social and emotional behavior that have resisted measurement by any more objective form of test. However, they present a number of problems. A program involving a number of situational tests is costly. The tests are likely to be costly in the facilities and arrangements they require. They are almost certain to be costly in the time of professional personnel to supervise their administration and to evaluate the behavior exhibited in the test situation. The staging of the situations may call for a certain amount of dramatic skill on the part of the examiners, and there is a real problem in maintaining the uniformity of the situations from individual to individual and from group to group. Another problem is that of preventing leakage of information about the test tasks, so that the task is a novel one to each group as it is tested, and is approached by each group with the same background. In view of the practical difficulties involved, it is not surprising that the use of situational tests has been limited to rather elaborate assessment programs, arranged for evaluation of special types of personnel—undercover agents, clinical psychology trainees, or executives and administrators.

The actual value of situational tests and, in fact, of the whole elaborate assessment program remains somewhat of a question. Psychologists who have participated in the programs have been, in many cases, enthusiastic about the procedures. Whether the information that is elicited has real value in predicting important facts about the individual is another matter. In the OSS program, it was possible to obtain only a limited amount of evidence on the extent to which men who had gone through the assessment program turned out well in their job assignments. Ratings from overseas colleagues and evaluations by commanding officers were obtained in a fraction of the cases. Predictions of success did correlate significantly with success on the job. The evaluation that showed the highest correlation was rating for *effective intelligence*. The final rating for effective intelligence based on the complete 3-day program had a somewhat higher correlation with rated success on the job than did scores based on a brief objective test of verbal ability, but the difference was not great.

In another substantial program of situational testing designed for the selection of clinical psychology trainees (Kelly and Goldberg, 1959), there was no evidence that the addition of situational tests improved short-term prediction beyond what was possible from the individual's credential file, selected objective tests, and a brief autobiography. Furthermore, there was no evidence that any part of the assessment consistently gave a better than chance prediction of success 10 years later.

In summary, then, the situational type of test is an interesting additional tool for personality assessment. It seems to provide a direct opportunity to see the individual functioning in lifelike situations and thus to appraise a variety of aspects of leadership, cooperation, and social functioning. However, evidence for the value of the results as improving our prediction of the individual's success on the job is largely lacking. Because its practical value has not been demonstrated and because the techniques are costly in preparations required and in the time of testing personnel, situational testing must be considered a subject for research at the present time, rather than a proven tool for personnel evaluation.

SYSTEMATIC OBSERVATION

The situational test has introduced us to observation as a technique for studying the typical behavior of the individual. Observation in that instance was of what he did in specified test situations. We turn now to observation in the naturally occurring situations of everyday life. The situations of everyday life are probably less uniform from person to person than the test situations that we stage. Also, they are not loaded to bring forth the behaviors in which we are specially interested. However, the very naturalness of real life events and the fact that we do not have to stage special events just for testing purposes make observation of natural situations appealing to us.

Of course, we observe the people with whom we associate every day of our lives, noticing what they do and reacting to the ways in which they behave. Our impressions of pepole are continuously being formed and modified by our observations of them. But these observations are casual, unsystematic, and undirected. If we are asked to document with specific instances our judgment that John is a leader in his group or that Henry is undependable, we are usually put to it to provide more than one or two concrete observations of actual behavior to document our general impression. Observations must be organized, directed, and systematic if they are to yield dependable information about an individual.

We should perhaps pause to draw a distinction between the observational procedures that we discuss now and the rating procedures that we considered in Chapter 13. The basic distinction is this: when we are collecting observations, we want the observer to function as nearly as possible as an objective and mechanical recording instrument, whereas when we gather ratings we want the rater to synthesize and integrate the evidence that he has. The one function is purely that of providing an accurate record of the number of social contacts, suggestions, aggressive acts, or whatever the category of behavior may be in which we are interested. The *observer* serves merely as a somewhat more flexible and versatile camera or recording machine. In *rating*, by contrast, the human instrument must judge, weight, and interpret.

Systematic observational procedures have been most fully developed in connection with studies of young children. They seem particularly appropriate in this setting. On the one hand, the young child has not developed the covers and camouflages to conceal himself from public view as completely as has his older brother or sister, so there is more to be found out by watching him. On the other hand, he is less able to tell us about himself in words. So it has been in the study of infants and nursery-school children that observational procedures have had their fullest development.

Steps to Improve Observational Procedures

Many of the early studies of young children were accounts of the development of a particular child or of two or three children based on observations by a psychologist parent. These provided a general descriptive background for understanding the young child, but they were qualitative and lacking in precision. Careful research with the child or investigations to determine the effect of particular preschool environments or experiences require that we know not merely that he shows negativism and resistance, for example, but also how much or how often. The needs of measurement, as distinct from those of qualitative description, require observational procedures that will permit a statement of quantity, of amount. The procedures should be as objective and reliable as possible, with a minimum of dependence upon the whims and idiosyncrasies of the individual observer. To accomplish this, several precautions are typically undertaken. These are discussed below.

1. *Selecting the aspect of behavior to be observed.* One problem of the general observer of human behavior is that he does not know what he is looking for.

So much is happening in any situation involving one or more active human beings that some part of it must inevitably be missed. We cannot notice everything that happens, and we cannot record everything we notice, so in any program of systematic observation, we must first select certain aspects or categories of behavior to be observed. Thus, in a study of nursery-school pupils, we may be interested in aggressive behavior and may limit ourselves to instances of aggressiveness. In a research project to evaluate a school program, we may be interested in observing evidences of cooperation or of independently initiated activity and may restrict our observation to these.

2. *Defining the behaviors that fall within a category.* If we turn two observers loose without further ado to observe the occurrence of "aggressive acts" or "nervous behavior" in preschool children, we will find that there are many disagreements between them in the observations they make. The categories must be further specified. They must become more behavioral if we are to get good agreement between observers. What is an "aggressive act," a "nervous habit"? Do we wish to include name-calling in the first instance? Fidgeting in one's seat in the second? Just as we must analyze "ability to get and interpret data" into specific testable skills of using an index or making inferences from a bar chart, so must we translate "aggressive acts" into hitting, kicking, biting, pushing, grabbing, name-calling, and the like. An advance agreement on what is to be included, based upon prior studies of the domain in question, is a necessary condition of objective and reliable observation.

3. *Training observers.* Even with a carefully defined set of behaviors to be observed, disagreements arise between observers. Some of these are unavoidable due to fluctuations of attention or variation of scoring on close judgments. Others can, however, be eliminated by training. Practice sessions in which two or more observers make records of the same sample of behavior, compare notes, discuss discrepancies, and reconcile differences provide one means of increasing uniformity. Practice sessions watched and later criticized by an already trained observer represent another. Such procedures make for uniformity of interpretation and standard application of the observation categories.

4. *Quantifying observations.* If observations of some aspect of the child's behavior, his aggressive acts or his social contacts, for example, are to provide a measurement of the child, some form of quantification is required. The quantification usually takes the form of counting. The count may be of the number of times that a child shows a particular form of behavior during a period of observation. However, in this case one often has difficulty in deciding when one act ends and the next one begins. Johnny slaps Henry and then kicks him. Is this one aggressive act or two? If the actions flow over from one to the other, the decision may not be an easy one.

An expedient that has appeared to work well in a number of cases has been to break the period of observation up into quite short segments. These may be no more than a minute or even half a minute in length. Then the observation that is made is merely the occurrence or nonoccurrence of the particular category of behavior during each small segment of time. Thus, we might observe each child for ten 5-minute periods, each on a different day. The 5-minute periods might each be subdivided into ten ½-minute periods. For each of the ½-minute periods we would observe whether the particular child did or did not exhibit any of a set of defined aggressive behaviors. Each child would then receive a score, with a possible range from 0 to 100, indicating the number of periods in which he produced aggressive acts. Such scores, based on an adequate number of short samples of observed behavior, have been found to show quite satisfactory reliability. Thus, Olson (1929) found the reliability for twenty 5-minute observations of children's nervous habits to be .87 in one case and .82 in another.

5. *Developing procedures to facilitate recording.* An essential for accurate observational data is some procedure for immediate recording of what was observed. The errors and selectivity of memory enter in to bias the reporting of even outstanding and unusual events. In the case of the rather ordinary and highly repetitive events that are observed in watching a child in preschool, for example, an adequate account of what was observed is only possible if the observations are recorded immediately. There is so much to see and one event is so much like others that to rely upon memory to provide an accurate after-the-fact account of a child's behavior is fatal. This is certainly the case in any attempt at complete and systematic recording, though we shall find a place for selective observation and anecdotal recording of significant incidents of behavior some time after they have taken place.

Any program of systematic observation must, therefore, provide some technique for immediate and efficient recording of the events that are observed. There are many possibilities for facilitating recording of behavior observations. One that has been widely used has been to develop a systematic code for the categories of behavior that are of interest. Thus, preliminary observations will have served to define the range of aggressive acts that can be expected from 3- and 4-year-olds. Part of the code might be set up as follows: h = "hits," p = "pushes," g = "grabs materials away from," n = "calls a nasty name," and so forth. A record blank can be prepared, divided up to represent the time segments of the observations, and code entries can be made quickly while the child is observed almost without interruption.

If the observer is skilled in standard shorthand, of course, fuller notes of the observation can be taken. These can be transcribed and coded or scored later. In some cases, where a research project has liberal financial backing, more complete photographic or video-tape recordings of the observations may make possible a permanent record of the behaviors in a relatively complete form. These records can then be analyzed at a later date. Such resources are likely to be the exception, however, and in many cases it will be necessary to plan a simple and efficient code to provide an immediate and permanent record of what was observed. The important objectives here are to do away with dependence on memory, to get a record that will preserve as much as possible of the significant detail in the original behavior, and to develop a recording procedure that will interfere as little as possible with the process of observing the child.

ILLUSTRATIVE STUDIES USING DIRECT OBSERVATION

The ways in which direct observation has been used in studying aspects of the child's behavior and the impact of educational experiences upon him can best be indicated by selected illustrations. We have chosen three examples of quite different types of observational procedures and quite different problems to illustrate the applications of direct observation.

Personality Differences in Newborn Children

The study that we shall describe first (Birns, 1965) asked the rather simple question (but not necessarily one that is simple to answer): Are there consistent differences in children at or near the time of birth? We are limited in what we can observe in neonates, but responsiveness to stimulation seemed to be one observable trait. Arrangements were made, therefore, to stimulate babies with a soft tone, a loud tone, a cold disk, and a pacifier several times during the first 4 or 5 days of life. Each stimulus was presented 3 times at each of 4 different sessions, and 2 or 3 trained observers scored the intensity of the infant's response. The observers of the infant could report his responses as (a) inhibition or diminution of activity then underway, (b) no response, or (c) response rated on a 5-point scale from (1) "small eye, toe, or finger flicker; refers to movement of only one body part" to (5) "hard crying and any activity; major intense overall activation."

Two types of evidence were offered to support the proposition that there are consistent individual differences in responsiveness. First, responsiveness to the four different stimuli was compared, with the finding that the typical correlation of intensity from one to another stimulus was about .50. Second, responsiveness was compared across the four separate test sessions, and it was found that the typical correlation between separate sessions was about .40. These two findings were interpreted as supporting the position that consistent individual differences in an aspect of personality are already in existence within the first few days of life.

Personality Variables and "Identification"

The study we have just reported used observation in connection with the application of specific stimuli. A different pattern is illustrated in the next study (Sears et al, 1965), in which observation was carried on of children engaged in the normal activities of a preschool program. The observations provided one kind of data within a more extensive study of children's identification with their parents. Observations were focused on dependency, aggression, and adult role-taking.

The observation period for a given child was 10 minutes, and this period was divided into segments, each 30 seconds long. For each 30-second segment, the observer recorded the dominant behavior category from among a list of 29. The designations of some of these are as follows:

Giving facts and demonstrating knowledge	(Adult role)
Using real adult mannerisms	(Adult role)
Touching and holding others	(Dependency)
Positive attention seeking	(Dependency)
Direct physical aggression	(Antisocial aggression)
Tattling	(Prosocial aggression)

The schedule of observations was planned so that a child was observed at various times of day, on various days of the week, and by different members of the team of observers. The average number of 10-minute observation periods for any one child was 38. That is, the child was observed for a little more than 6 hours in total.

The score for a given child on a given behavior category was the proportion of time periods during which that behavior was coded as the dominant one. Categories were combined in various ways to give more comprehensive and stable scores. The reliability of certain of these combined scores for the total observation series is shown below, estimated in the one case from the correlation between observers and in the other from different segments of the series of observations.

	Between Observers	*Between Time Periods*
Total score–adult role	.77	.73
Total score–dependency	.74	.63
Total score–antisocial aggression	.85	.79
Total score–prosocial aggression	.74	.73

It can be seen that 6 hours of observation is none too much to provide dependable appraisals of these behaviors.

The sample studied consisted of only 40 children,* 20 boys and 20 girls, so that relationships reported must be considered quite tentative. From the extensive array of relationships reported among observational variables and of these with other types of measures, we shall pick out only a few illustrative items. In general, the aggressive behaviors were more coherently structured in the group as a whole than either dependency or adult role behaviors. That is, as a general trend, the child who was high on one type of aggressive behavior tended to be high on others. However, for boys, "tattling" did not seem to belong in the aggressive cluster, while for girls, "injury to objects" was unrelated to other aggressive actions. Only for girls did different types of adult role behaviors group together, and dependency behaviors appeared to have very little unity and cohesiveness for either sex. It appeared that active attention-getting, based on the individual's performance or product, was a very different type of behavior with very different significance in the life economy of the individual from the dependency exhibited in touching, holding, being near, or seeking reassurance from an adult. Generally speaking, hypothesized relationships between dependency and identification with adults were not confirmed by the results of the study.

Teacher Behaviors Influencing Pupil Attitudes and Achievement

A somewhat different application of techniques of direct observation is in the study of teacher inputs, of what goes on in a classroom, and its relationship to pupil outputs of knowledge or of attitude. Flanders (1965) studied verbal interaction in the classroom. Observers in the classroom recorded 6 hours of events in each class. A record was made about every 3 seconds, using the set of categories shown in Table 14.2 on page 478.

Flanders' interest centered primarily on the impact of the "indirect influence" forms of teacher talk as compared with the "direct influence" forms. Sixteen social studies and sixteen mathematics classes were observed, and the classes with the most "indirect" teachers were compared with those with the most "direct" teachers with respect to attitudes toward the teacher and achievement in a standard unit that was taught during the time that the observations were being made. The essential results are summarized in Fig. 14.2 on page 479, which shows the average achievement and attitude scores of each group, as well as the

* One of the practical problems of studies using observational procedures is that the time investment needed per child tends to be so great that samples studied are small, and results correspondingly undependable.

TABLE 14.2 CATEGORIES FOR INTERACTION ANALYSIS, 1959

Teacher Talk	Indirect Influence	1.* *Accepts Feeling.* Accepts and clarifies the tone of feeling of the students in an unthreatening manner. Feelings may be positive or negative. Predicting or recalling feelings are included.
		2.* *Praises or Encourages.* Praises or encourages student action or behavior. Jokes that release tension, but not at the expense of another individual, nodding head or saying "um hm?" or "go on" are included.
		3.* *Accepts or Uses Ideas of Student.* Clarifying, building, or developing ideas suggested by a student. As teacher brings more of his own ideas into play, shift to category 5.
		4.* *Asks Questions.* Asking a question about content or procedure with the intent that a student answer.
	Direct Influence	5.* *Lecturing.* Giving facts or opinions about content or procedure; expressing his own ideas, asking rhetorical questions.
		6.* *Giving Directions.* Directions, commands, or orders which students are expected to comply with.
		7.* *Criticizing or Justifying Authority.* Statements intended to change student behavior from unacceptable to acceptable pattern; bawling someone out; stating why the teacher is doing what he is doing; extreme self-reference.
Student Talk		8.* *Student Talk–Response.* Talk by students in response to teacher. Teacher initiates the contact or solicits student statement.
		9.* *Student Talk–Initiation.* Talk initiated by students. If "calling on" student is only to indicate who may talk next, observer must decide whether student wanted to talk.
Silence		10.* *Silence or Confusion.* Pauses, short periods of silence and periods of confusion in which communication cannot be understood by the observer.

* There is NO scale implied by these numbers. Each number is classificatory, designating a particular kind of communication event. To write these numbers down during observation is merely to identify and enumerate communication events, not to judge them.

range extending one standard deviation on either side of the mean. In this study, the classes of the more "indirect" teachers consistently showed up better on both the attitude and the achievement measures. Of course, it is not entirely clear whether using "indirect" measures is a cause or merely a symptom of good teaching, but there is at least a chance that the work of teachers can be improved by training them to make more use of the "indirect" categories of verbal interaction.

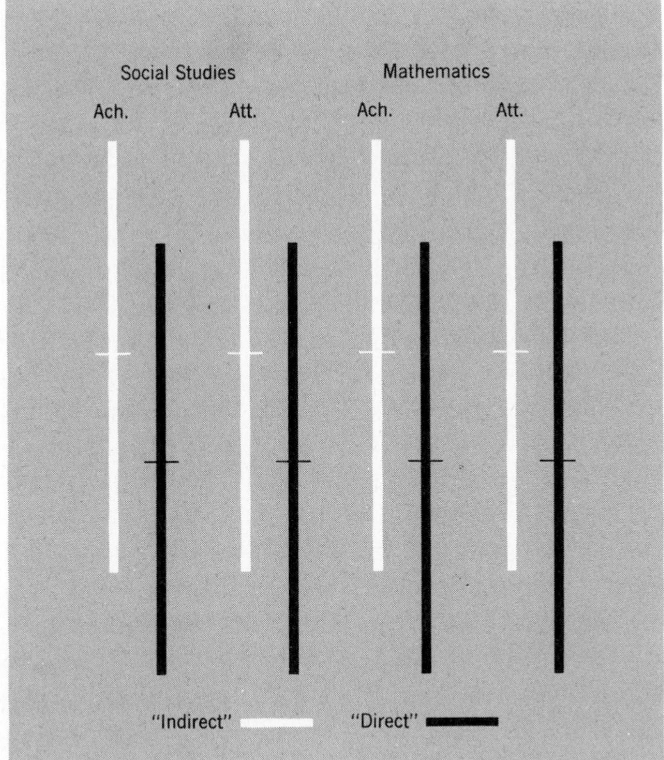

Fig. 14.2 Attitude and achievement of classes taught by "direct" and "indirect" teachers. (Adapted from Flanders, 1965.)

The three illustrations we have just sketched in have shown methods of direct observation used in rather different ways and applied to quite different problems. These examples are representative of many specific studies from among which the selection was made. They suggest the range of usefulness of this way of studying the individual person or groups of persons.

EVALUATION OF SYSTEMATIC OBSERVATION AS AN APPROACH TO PERSONALITY MEASUREMENT

We have described the nature of systematic observation, outlined some of the precautions necessary if the procedure is to be satisfactorily reliable and objective, and illustrated the application of the method to three quite different sorts of research studies. Now let us undertake an appraisal of the method, indicating some of its strengths and some of its limitations as a way of studying personality.

Advantages of Direct Observation

Procedures based on direct observation of the behavior of others have a number of features that make them attractive as personality evaluation devices. Some of the more significant points are considered below.

A RECORD OF ACTUAL BEHAVIOR. When we observe an individual, we get a record of what he actually *does*. We are not dealing with his rationalizations and protestations. If our observational procedures have been well planned and our observers carefully trained, our score is in large measure free from the biases and idiosyncrasies of the particular observer. Our record of the individual is not a reflection of what he thinks he is, or of what someone else thinks he is. His actions speak to us directly. If, as will be true in many cases, our concern is in what the person does or the way in which his behavior has been changed, then observation of his behavior is the most direct, and in many ways the most satisfying, way of getting the relevant information.

APPLICABLE IN A NATURAL SITUATION. One great advantage of observational techniques is that they can be applied to the naturally occurring situations of life. Observation is not restricted to a test situation, though we saw when we were describing situational tests that observation is often an important adjunct to a test situation. Observation can be carried out in the nursery school, in the classroom, in the cafeteria, on the playground, at camp, in the squadron day room, or anywhere individuals work or play in a public setting. There are, as we shall point out presently, practical difficulties and limitations that arise in stage-managing the observations. But in spite of these, direct observation is a widely applicable approach to studying individual personalities operating in a normal nontest setting.

USABLE WITH YOUNG CHILDREN AND OTHERS FOR WHOM VERBAL COMMUNICATION IS DIFFICULT. Observation is possible with small children, no matter how young. As a matter of fact, the younger the child, the easier it is to observe him. The infant is completely unselfconscious, and we can sit and watch what he does with no special procedures or precautions. With older children, it becomes necessary either to screen the observer from the subjects being observed or adapt them to him. The observer may be separated by a one-way vision screen so that he can see the child or children but they cannot see him. However, the requirement to provide such a physical setting seriously restricts the situations in which observation may be done. More often, and more simply, the observer may be present long enough and function sufficiently unobtrusively so that the subjects come to pay no attention to him, accepting him as a natural part of the surroundings.

The value of direct observation is greatest where its application is most feasible —with young children. Young children are quite limited in their ability to communicate through language. They do not have much experience or facility in analyzing or reporting their feelings or the reasons for their actions. They are often shy and resistant with strangers. For these groups especially, direct observation provides an important avenue of approach.

Limitations of Direct Observation

The factors we have just described contribute to the attractiveness of direct observation as a technique for studying individuals. However, it is by no means the answer to all our measurement problems. A number of factors seriously limit the usefulness of observational techniques. These range from very practical and down-to-earth considerations, which we shall consider first, to more fundamental theoretical issues.

COST OF MAKING THE OBSERVATIONS. Observation is costly primarily in the demands that it makes on the time of trained observers. In the illustrations we gave, each child or class was observed for a number of observation periods extending in some instances to several hours. When observations are to be made of a substantial number of individuals or class groups, the hours rapidly mount up. Systematic direct observation and recording of behavior is for this reason alone limited in its use to research projects, in which the necessary time commitments can be made. In routine school operations it is not practical to find the manpower required to make direct observations routinely of each pupil.

The cost of direct observation lies not merely in the observer time required in making the recordings. Any form of special setting or any form of mechanical recording represents an additional cost. Furthermore, when the original record is a running diary account, a motion picture, or a video tape of an individual's or a group's actions, analysis of the records is also likely to be time-consuming.

FITTING THE OBSERVER INTO THE SETTING. There is always a question of whether having an observer in any setting, watching and making notes of what goes on, will actually change what happens. In many of the situations one wishes to observe, it is not practical to have the observer invisible. One hopes, often with justification, that after an initial period of getting used to the observer all persons being observed will take him completely for granted and ignore him. However, this is easier in some situations than others. When the group is small, when it is necessary for the observer to follow its activities very closely, or when the group meets for too short a time to get used to being observed, the members may not be too successful in coming to think of the observer as a piece of the furniture.

ELIMINATING SUBJECTIVITY AND BIAS. When observational procedures are used, it is found necessary to use all possible precautions to keep the observer's interpretations and biases out of the observation. It is especially desirable that the observer not know too much about the study that is being done, not know what experimental treatment a specific child is receiving, and not know test scores or other facts about a child who is being observed. Our objective is to have the observer function purely as a recording instrument that is sensitive to, and makes a record of, certain categories of behavior. Most of the precautions we described on pp. 472–475 are directed toward that end. But at best we are only partially successful. The observer is always human. We may minimize his influence, but we cannot eliminate it. Especially when the phenomena we are studying are complex or involve an element of interpretation, we must beware of the role of the observer in the final result.

DETERMINING A MEANINGFUL AND PRODUCTIVE SET OF BEHAVIOR CATEGORIES TO OBSERVE. Any observation is selective. Only certain limited aspects of the individual's behavior can be observed and recorded. Furthermore, if observations are to be treated quantitatively they must be classified, grouped, and counted. Any system of classification is a somewhat arbitrary framework that we impose upon the infinitely varied events of life. It is not always easy to set up a framework that serves our purposes well. Thus, the reader may very well feel that the categories of behavior described on p. 478 do not cover well the range of teacher actions, or that the types of activities included under a given heading are inappropriate to that heading. Or we may have classified aggressive acts in terms of the overt behavior, hitting, pushing, or grabbing, whereas for our purposes it might have been better to classify by the precipitating event (if we could observe it): aggression in response to conflict over property, or as a reaction to verbal disparagement, or after thwarting of some activity in progress. In any event, scores based upon observations of behavior can be no more significant and meaningful than the categories we have devised for analyzing that behavior.

DETERMINING THE SIGNIFICANCE OF AN ISOLATED ITEM OF BEHAVIOR. Because of the need to achieve reliability and objectivity, the tendency has been to focus observation upon rather small and discrete acts, or at least to break the analysis of observational material up into small and discrete acts. There is a real danger that when this is done the meaning of the behavior, the true significance of the action, will be lost. Thus, we observe that 3-year-old A hugs 3-year-old B. Is this an act of affection? Or is it, as seems frequently the case at this age, an act of aggression? If the observation stands alone, we have no way of telling. Or suppose that A hits B. This is fairly clearly an aggressive act, but what does it signify in the life economy of A? Is it a healthful and adjustive reaction to earlier domination by B, a bursting of bonds that have shackled A? Or is it a displaced aggression built up by domination at home by a parent or older sibling? Or does it signify any one of a number of other things?

THE EXTERNAL CHARACTER OF OBSERVATION. What the illustration we have just given brings out is that observation is external. The "outsideness" is exaggerated when little bits of behavior are analyzed out of context. But the "outsideness" is a fundamental feature of any observational approach to studying behavior. We always face the problem of determining the meaning of the behavior and must recognize that what we have before us is only what the person does, not what it signifies.

INFORMAL OBSERVATION—THE ANECDOTAL RECORD

The systematic and continuous observations of pupil behavior that we have considered in the previous section are essentially research tools. They are too time-consuming to be practical and usually too specialized to be useful to classroom teachers trying to build up a better understanding of their pupils. However, every teacher is observing his pupils from day to day, and there is no reason why those observations should not be informally recorded as a guide to his own increased understanding or to that of others who will later deal with the pupils. Such reports of informal teacher observations of pupils have been called *anecdotal records*.

But why should the observations be *recorded?* Who should be observed? What should be recorded? How should the records be kept? What steps should be taken to organize and summarize them? What problems are commonly encountered in making and using anecdotal records? These are some of the points we shall need to consider.

Why Make a Record?

Of course teachers learn from observing pupils, but why record the separate observations? Why not trust to the teacher's memory to summarize in his own mind the observations he makes from day to day and allow him to report his evaluation of a pupil in a term-end descriptive statement or set of ratings?

The answer lies partly in the fallibility of human memory and the inadequacy of human beings as assemblers and combiners of facts about another person. We make many observations of other people, but we make *so* many that they all melt together in our memory, and only a rare few of the most striking experiences continue to retain their individuality. Even these become warped and distorted with the lapse of time. And the way the sharper memories are distorted, together with the flavor of the stew that is made of our blurred recollections of ordinary day-to-day experiences, depends as much on the rememberer as on the event. Our general reaction to a child, flavored by all our ingrained prejudices and warped by what we have heard about him or by our initial experiences with him, provides the framework into which our observations are fitted. All of the sources of difficulty with personality ratings that we discussed in the previous chapter bear witness to the fallibility of general impression and unguided memory. By contrast, a record of an event is one dependable datum that will remain unchanged from the time we made it until the time we want to refer to it. A set of such records provides stable evidence on which later appraisals can be based.

A further reason for not relying upon summary impressions of a child, as reported by the teacher at intervals, is that such reports have generally not proved too informative or useful. They are likely to be couched in general terms, often moralistic in tone, evaluating rather than describing, and telling more about the teacher's reactions to the child than about the child.

> Wilhelmina does not work nearly as hard as she should. She seems to be a bright child, and does well when she really tries. She can be very annoying at times.

What do we now really know about Wilhelmina? What chance do we have of understanding her or of working with her more effectively? We have a fairly good picture of a teacher's dissatisfaction, but know very little of a factual nature about the child.

Making a record of an observation of child behavior, a prompt record while the behavior is still fresh in the mind, can be a corrective for the limitations and distortions of memory. Such a record can come, with practice, to provide a relatively direct and objective report of actions, with the reactions of the observer kept down to a minimum.

> During art class Wilhelmina was very slow in starting work. She stopped her own work several times during the period to wander around the room and look at what other pupils were doing and tell them what was wrong with their pictures. Mary and Jane each told her to mind her own business and leave them alone.

This notation provides an item of factual information that can help us to know and understand Wilhelmina. It is a specific excerpt of behavior. Put together with a number of others, it may yield a factual and meaningful picture of the child.

Who Should Be Observed?

Anecdotal records may serve two rather different sorts of purpose. A first purpose may be to give teachers practice in studying children, with a view to deepening their understandings and increasing their sympathetic insights. If the records are serving as part of an in-service educational program in child study, it may be well to concentrate observations on two, or at most three or four, pupils. This will permit a completeness of observation and a fullness of reporting that would not otherwise be possible. The children will ordinarily be selected for observation in terms of the teacher's special interest in them. However, it would probably be unfortunate to focus exclusively or even primarily upon "problem" cases. There is much to be learned and much light to be cast on the child with special problems by studying the "normal" child, with his or her normal problems, quirks, and idiosyncrasies.

In schools in which anecdotal records have become a part of the basic cumulative record system, anecdotes should be reported for each child in the class group. In this case, it will naturally be necessary to be content with a much more limited sample of observations for any single child.

What Should Be Recorded?

This question divides into two. Which incidents should be made a matter of record? What should be included in the record of each?

ITEMS WORTHY OF RECORDING. Anecdotal records provide an informal and largely qualitative picture of certain aspects of an individual's behavior. There is no point in using them for aspects of his behavior that can be appraised by more objective and accurate methods. Intellectual ability, academic achievement, and creative skills are better shown by standardized tests on the one hand or by pupil products on the other. It is primarily aspects of social functioning or adjustment to personal problems that one hopes to illuminate by records of incidents of school behavior. The interactions of a child with the other children in the room, evidences of acceptance or rejection, aggression or withdrawal, events that throw light on the child's role in the group and his reaction to it are fit material for our pen. Indications of personal tensions and adaptations to them, habitual mood and temper, or special crises and adjustments are worth recording. We may ask in each case: What can this incident tell a reader who does not know the child—a guidance worker, a subsequent teacher—that he could not find out in some simpler, more objective way?

MATERIAL TO BE INCLUDED IN AN ANECDOTE. An anecdotal record should be an accurate factual report of an event in a child's life, reported with enough of the setting and enough detail so that it is a meaningful item of behavior. Such a report is far from easy to prepare. Experience with teachers who are starting to try to write anecdotes about their pupils indicates that there are three common deviations from the prescription we have given.

1. *The anecdote evaluates, instead of reporting.* It tells the teacher's reaction to the child. "John was a very difficult child today" is a report of how the teacher felt about John, not of what he did.

2. *The anecdote interprets, instead of reporting.* It gives the teacher's conclusions as to the reasons for behavior, instead of or as well as a report of what actually occurred. For example, we may see an item that reads: "Oscar simply cannot keep still in class now. He is growing so fast that he is restless all the time." The second sentence is pure interpretation, based upon extremely meager evidence, as far as we can tell. It tells us nothing about what happened. Explanations and interpretations are all very well in their place, if they are kept tentative and thought of only as hypotheses for further testing. But they should be clearly distinguished from description. The primary function of an anecdotal record is to describe a child's behavior.

3. *The anecdote describes in general terms, rather than being specific.* A report of this type would be the following: "Mary is not well accepted by the other children in the class. She usually stands on the sidelines at recess and does not take part in the games." This summarizing statement may be of some value in providing a picture of the child. However, it lacks the objectivity and concreteness that characterize the description of a single specific event. It incorporates more of selection and evaluation than we would like in our basic raw material.

A good anecdotal record has the following features:

1. It provides an accurate description of a specific event.
2. It describes the setting sufficiently to give the event meaning.
3. If it includes interpretation or evaluation by the recorder, this interpretation is separated from the description and its different status is clearly identified.
4. The event it describes is one that relates to the child's personal development or social interactions.
5. The event it describes is either representative of the typical behavior of the child or significant because it is strikingly different from his usual form of behavior. If it is unusual behavior for the child, that fact is noted.

The following three anecdotes are presented as conforming fairly well to the above specifications. Note that no attempt is made to phrase the anecdotes in full sentences. The emphasis is on ease of recording rather than on grammatical elegance. The reader may find it worthwhile to check them off point by point and see how he would like each changed to make it a more useful and meaningful piece of data about a child.

Class: 5A *Pupil:* Henry K. *Date:* 3/15/66

Class working as a group, Richard serving as chairman, discussing plans for class exhibit for local "Visit Your School Week." Henry's hand up and trying to talk almost continuously. Interrupted other children four or five times. Interruptions largely caustic or facetious comment. When Richard told him he was "out of order" because someone else was talking, he said, "Aw, nuts to you," and paid no more attention to the discussion.

(Typical of Henry's behavior a number of times lately. Aggressively seeking attention, then withdraws if rebuffed.)

Class: 8B *Pupil:* Peter Y. *Date:* 4/25/65

Peter drowsed off in social studies discussion period after lunch today. Faraway look; then eyes closed. Came to with a start when spoken to. Seemed attentive for few minutes, then dropped off again. Sleepy throughout the period.

(Same sort of thing several times in past two weeks. Is something preventing him from getting enough sleep? What is it?)

Class: 6B *Pupil:* Betsy R. *Date:* 10/6/65

Coming into class after morning recess Betsy slapped Sue, reason unknown. While getting seated, had a row with Jane about ownership of a pencil. Later in morning, pinched Ellen. Two or three other squabbles before lunch. Standing by herself after lunch, not playing with other girls.

(Very unusual for Betsy. Usually even tempered, well liked, and the center of the group.)

How Should Anecdotal Records Be Kept?

The exact mechanical format of anecdotal records is of secondary importance compared with the considerations of content. However, the usefulness of records will depend upon the ease with which the records for a particular pupil may be assembled, studied, and summarized. It is also important that the sheer mechanical burdens of keeping the records be kept to a minimum. One of the main practical problems in the use of anecdotal records has been the clerical burdens they impose.

The appropriate form for keeping records will depend upon the primary purpose for which they are being kept. If the records are serving to guide the teacher's study of two or three particular pupils, they may well be kept in the form of two or three separate logs or diaries. Successive entries should then be dated and entered in sequence in a notebook, on sheets of typewriter paper, or on file cards. When records are being made from time to time on all the pupils in a school, as a part of the regular cumulative record system of the school, a uniform method of recording that facilitates filing the records of each child in his individual file folder will be needed. The record form should be evaluated in terms of the total record system. If an individual file folder is used, an $8\frac{1}{2} \times 11$ sheet of paper will often prove suitable. The record form should provide space for identifying information (class, pupil, date, person making the record), the anecdote itself, and possibly for an evaluating comment.

What Should Be Done to Organize or Summarize Records?

Each original anecdotal record is an item of information about an individual. A series of records provides a whole set of such items. But for data to be useful they must be organized, summarized, and interpreted. The data in such an intelligence test as the *Binet* consist of a series of responses to specific items that are summarized in a mental age or IQ. Although the significant elements in a set of anecdotal records cannot be summarized as simply, some attempt at bringing the items together into an organized picture of the individual will usually be desirable.

At intervals, perhaps once a semester or possibly oftener if a child is being studied intensively, the anecdotes on an individual should be reviewed carefully. Recurring patterns should be noted. Any progressive changes should be brought out. A thumbnail sketch of the individual, as shown by the anecdotes, should be prepared. The attempt should be made to relate the anecdotal material to other facts that are known about the child: his health, intellectual ability, academic achievement, home surroundings, and family pattern. A tentative interpretation of the patterns may be attempted, if it is recognized that any interpretation is to be thought of as a set of very tentative hypotheses. In the summary, as in the records themselves, the descriptive summary and the interpretation of it should be kept clearly differentiated.

What Problems Arise in Making and Interpreting Anecdotal Records?

We have already indicated a number of the problems in making and using anecdotal records in the previous sections. These and some other issues will be considered in this section.

PROBLEMS ARISING OUT OF THE SELECTION OF ITEMS. The number of anecdotes that could be written about any individual is almost limitless. The written record must consist of a relatively small fraction of these, chosen by the observer as being significant or as typical of the child. The quality of the accumulated data depends upon the shrewdness and impartiality of this selection. Both the significance and the truthfulness of the picture will depend upon the ability of the observer to select items to record that are illuminating and truly representative. Bias by the observer can easily creep into both the selection and the recording of the items. For a child whom the teacher dislikes, it is easy to pick out and record only situations in which he appears in a bad light. If the teacher is unduly preoccupied with academic achievement or an orderly classroom, incidents relating to nonachievement or disorder may take a dominant role in the record. It is hard to know how much bias is introduced in a set of anecdotes by selectivity of this sort, but the problem is certainly a very real one.

PROBLEMS RELATING TO THE PHRASING OF THE ANECDOTE. Difficulties here center around the tendencies, which we have already considered, to include evaluation, interpretation, and generalities and to leave out the specific factual description. Problems of literary style are also occasionally a matter of concern. In this regard, the thing to remember is that anecdotes are valued not as literary gems but for the information they convey. Brevity and clarity, not literary elegance, are the objectives even to the point of writing in phrases rather than sentences.

PROBLEMS RELATING TO THE CLERICAL BURDEN. One of the most serious practical problems in any school program of anecdotal records is the sheer clerical burden of preparing, filing, and summarizing the records. These problems have tended to limit the systematic use of anecdotal records to preschools, where classes are small and where personal-social development is quite central to the school's concern, and to private schools and a few public schools in which the resources are far above the national average. Bearing in mind the burdens that a program of anecdotal records places upon the staff, any school system should move into anecdotal recording cautiously. Recording should be tried first for a few pupils in each class and gradually expanded if it seems to be yielding useful information. Recording procedures should be kept as simple as possible. Literary style and elegance of format should be minimized.

PROBLEMS RELATING TO USE. Like any other evaluation procedure, anecdotal records are useful only if they are used. One must take care that the records do not become an end in themselves. The records must be accessible. They must be summarized periodically, so that the user can refer to a concise summary. School personnel should be encouraged and trained to use them.

One specific problem is a feeling on the part of some teachers that they do not wish to be biased by what a previous teacher has said about a child. When what the previous teacher has said is primarily an expression of his reactions to the child, with a strong admixture of personal prejudice, this unwillingness is understandable. When the anecdotes and the summary become factual and descriptive, there is no longer any reason to object to having the information. It is as important for the teacher to start the year with information about the status of a child's personal and social development as it is to be informed about his reading and number skills.

Pseudoanecdotal Records

There appear in the student files of many school systems what we might refer to as "pseudoanecdotal records." These consist of narrative and evaluative statements by teachers, in which they characterize the social relationships, work habits, or personal appearance of a child. These are not in any real sense anecdotal *records,* because they are not in any direct way based on *observations* of the child. They are summarizing subjective appraisals of the child, including whatever aspect of his impression the teacher saw fit to record. Though they may have some value, they should be recognized for what they are, and not confused with the type of record we have been discussing earlier.

Summary Evaluation of Anecdotal Records

An anecdotal record provides a medium for recording the observation of a significant item of pupil behavior. When teachers have developed skill in selecting incidents and in describing them objectively, when the mechanics of record-keeping and summarizng are kept within reasonable bounds, and when the records are available for use by those whose concern it is to understand the individual pupil, such records can be a significant aid to working with children.

SUMMARY STATEMENT

One approach to personality appraisal is the direct measurement or the observation of some aspect of behavior. We may attempt to elicit typical behavior by actual test situations, such as those represented by the honesty tests of May and Hartshorne. These have the advantage that they can be scored as directly and objectively as an ability test. However, the tests are complex to develop and stage, have rather modest reliability, yield results which seem to be rather specific to the particular test situation, and are not readily adaptable to many of the aspects of personality in which we are interested.

The situational test represents a compromise between a standard test and an observational procedure. A lifelike test situation is developed, into which the examinee is placed. Typically, it is a social situation involving some type of interaction with other individuals and structured to emphasize the facets of the personality in which the investigator is particularly interested. Group discussion or group problem-solving represents one promising type of situation. For evaluation of the examinee's behavior, however, reliance is placed on observation and ratings. This permits a good deal more freedom in planning the test situations, and many sorts of interpersonal behavior may be observed. In large measure, however, the predictive value of the observations that can be made in such settings remains to be demonstrated.

Behavior in naturally occurring situations has been studied by techniques of direct observation. Steps that have been taken to refine the everyday observations we make of people include (1) limitation of observations to a single aspect of behavior, (2) careful definition of the behaviors falling within this category, (3) training of observers, (4) quantification of observations, as by a procedure of taking many short samples, and (5) development of procedures for coding and recording the observations.

Direct observation has the advantages of (1) representing actual behavior, (2) being applicable to natural life situations, and (3) being usable with young children and others with whom verbal communication is difficult. However, observational procedures present a number of problems, including (1) cost, (2) difficulty of fitting the observer into the situation, (3) difficulty of eliminating observer bias, (4) difficulty of setting up meaningful and productive categories to observe, (5) difficulty in determining the meaning of isolated bits of behavior, and (6) the fact that an observer inevitably has an outside view of the person whom he observes.

Systematically scheduled observation is rarely practical for teachers, job supervisors, or other persons for whom personality appraisal is secondary to other aspects of their job. Such a person may use informal anecdotal records to accumulate factual information about a pupil or employee. Informal observations should be factual reports of significant items of behavior; they should avoid evaluation, interpretation, and vague generalities. Recording of observations should be kept as simple as possible and the record should be reviewed and interpreted periodically to give an organized picture of the person who has been observed.

QUESTIONS AND EXERCISES

1. In their studies of honesty, Hartshorne and May report quite low correlations between different behavior tests of honesty. If this is true for other qualities as well, what does it mean for our understanding of people?

2. What implications do the findings of May and Hartshorne have for the classroom teacher when it comes to writing descriptions or evaluations of students for permanent school records?

3. Try to plan a number of behavior tests for some trait other than honesty.

4. Plan a situational test for use in a school or industrial situation. What would you hope to get from this test that you could not get in other ways? What would be the difficulties of using such a test as you have proposed?

5. How could the class discussion that takes place in most classes serve as the basis for systematic observation? Make a plan for recording these observations.

6. In a research study, you propose to use systematic observations of school children as a method of studying their social adjustment. What problems would you encounter? What precautions would you need to take in interpreting the results?

7. What advantages do systematic observations or short sample observations have over the observations of everyday life? What limitations do these more specialized procedures have?

8. If you are working in a classroom, make anecdotal records on some one child over a 1-week period. Observe as well as you can the guides for making anecdotal records given on pp. 485–490. What difficulties did you encounter in making the records?

9. Criticize the following anecdotal records:

a. "Mary continues to be a nuisance in class. She is noisy and not only fails to do her own work but keeps other children from doing theirs. I don't know what I am going to do about it."

b. "John had a good deal of trouble with his arithmetic today. He didn't seem to be able to get the idea of reducing fractions to a common denominator. Out of several problems he was able to identify the lowest common denominator only once."

10. In some educational situations, such as the clinical part of the education of nurses, evaluation depends entirely on observations made by a supervisor. For such a situation, compare the advantages and disadvantages of (a) systematic, regularly scheduled observations and (b) a program of anecdotal records.

11. As a class group, assemble the experiences of a number of schools or school systems in using anecdotal records. How many use them currently? With what sorts of groups? What sorts of problems are they encountering? How many have tried them and abandoned them? For what reasons?

REFERENCES

Assessment Staff, U.S. Office of Strategic Services. *Assessment of men.* New York: Rinehart, 1948.

Barron, F. X. Complexity-simplicity as a personality dimension. *Journal of Abnormal and Social Psychology,* 1953, **48,** 163–172.

Bass, B. M. The leaderless group discussion. *Psychological Bulletin,* 1954, **51,** 465–492.

Birns, B. Individual differences in human neonates' responses to stimulation. *Child Development,* 1965, **36,** 249–256.

Cattell, R. B. and others. *Objective personality and motivation tests: A theoretical introduction and practical compendium.* Urbana, Illinois: University of Illinois Press, 1967.

Eysenck, H. J. *The scientific study of personality.* New York: Macmillan, 1952.

Flanders, N. A. Teacher influence, pupil attitudes, and achievement. *U.S. Office of Education Cooperative Research Monograph.* Washington, D.C.: U.S. Government Printing Office, 1965, No. 12.

Hartshorne, H. & May, M. A. *Studies in deceit.* New York: Macmillan, 1928.

Hemphill, J. K., Griffiths, D. E., & Frederiksen, N. *Administrative performance and personality: A study of the principal in a simulated elementary school.* New York: Teachers College Press, 1962.

Kelly, E. L. & Goldberg, L. R. Correlates of later performance and specialization in psychology. *Psychological Monographs,* 1959, **73,** No. 482.

Olson, W. C. The measurement of nervous habits in normal children. *University of Minnesota Institute of Child Welfare Monograph,* 1929, No. 3.

Sears, R. R., Rau, L., & Alpert, R. *Identification and child rearing.* Stanford, California: Stanford University Press, 1965.

Welsh, G. S. *Welsh Figure Preference Test.* Palo Alto, California: Consulting Psychologists Press, 1959.

Witkin, H. A., and others. *Psychological differentiation.* New York: John Wiley, 1962.

SUGGESTED ADDITIONAL READING

Allen, R. M. *Personality assessment procedures.* New York: Harper, 1958. Chapters 16, 17, 18.

Almy, M. *Ways of studying children.* New York: Bureau of Publications, Teachers College, Columbia University, 1959. Chapter 2.

Kleinmuntz, B. *Personality measurement.* Homewood, Illinois: Dorsey Press, 1967. Chapter 4.

Selltiz, C., Jahoda, M., Deutsch, M., & Cook, S. *Research methods in social relations.* New York: Holt, Rinehart & Winston, 1964. Chapter 6.

Stern, G. G., Stein, M. I., & Bloom, B. S. *Methods in personality assessment.* Glencoe, Illinois: The Free Press, 1956. Chapters 1, 2, 3.

Vernon, P. E. *Personality assessment: A critical survey.* New York: John Wiley, 1964. Chapter 15.

Webb, J., Campbell, D. T., Schwartz, R. D., & Sechrest, L. *Unobtrusive measures: Nonreactive research in the social sciences.* Chicago: Rand McNally & Company, 1966.

Willey, R. D. *Guidance in elementary education.* (Rev. ed.) New York: Harper, 1960. Chapter 3.

CHAPTER 15

Projective Tests

IN the last three chapters, we have considered the possibilities of studying a person through (1) what he tells us about himself, (2) the impression he makes on others, and (3) his observable actions. There is one further avenue of approach that we must now examine. We may be able to learn about the individual by seeing how he perceives and interprets the world. One way of doing this is to provide him with relatively indefinite and unstructured stimuli and observing how he structures them for us. The various techniques for doing this may be collectively identified as *expressive and projective techniques.*

Psychologists have long recognized that the perceiving of even quite definite stimuli—an accident, a scene staged before a class, the content of a picture—is dependent upon the individual perceiver. Examine Fig. 15.1. Does it show a dumbbell or a pair of glasses? Some people interpret the picture as one, some as

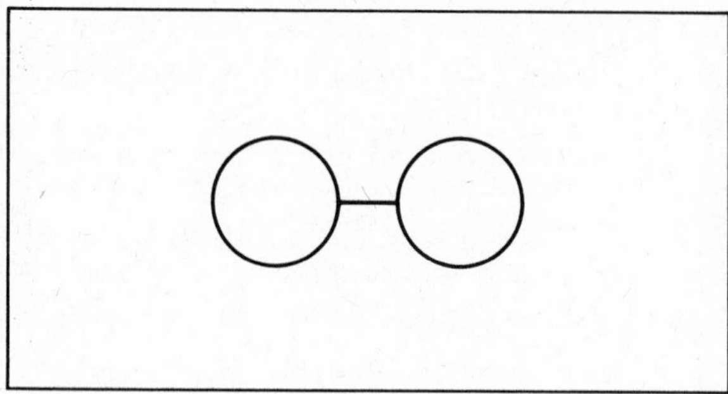

Fig. 15.1 Ambiguous picture.

the other. Their perception can be controlled to some extent by the set or expectation that we set up by formal instructions or by previous pictures. But it is determined, in part, by more permanent individual predispositions—the individual's background of experiences, interests, and concerns.

The vaguer the stimulus, the more opportunity there is for the individual to project himself into the report. Projective tests take advantage of this situation. They operate with quite unstructured materials: a vague and ambiguous picture, an inkblot, a word or two of a sentence, some modeling clay, or paper and finger paints. Furthermore, the instructions place relatively little restriction or constraint upon the respondent. Under these conditions, there is the greatest diversity of product produced. The basic assumption of projective methods is that under these circumstances the production depends in large measure upon basic personality factors in the person being tested and that an appropriate analysis of the productions can reveal that personality structure. The basic procedure common to projective techniques is:

1. To present the subject with a series of fluid, weakly structured stimuli.
2. To give instructions that emphasize freedom of response.
3. To analyze his productions for insight into his basic personality dynamics.

For at least some of the projective media, materials and procedures have been standardized and are widely used. In addition, there are numerous exploratory and unstandardized projective media. We shall describe in some detail the two that are probably most extensively used, mention briefly several others, and then try to apply to projective tests the same criteria of evaluation that we have used with other measurement procedures.

THE *RORSCHACH TEST*

The *Rorschach Test* (Rorschach, 1942) has been so widely publicized now that it is probably familiar in a general way to most readers of this book. The basic material is ten inkblots, nonsense patterns produced by putting blobs of ink on a piece of paper and folding the paper over so the two halves blot. But these are not just any old inkblots. They were selected by Hermann Rorschach, the original investigator, after trying out thousands of different blots with patients in mental institutions, because they appeared particularly effective in eliciting a richness of diagnostic material.

Sample inkblots, like those in the *Rorschach Test,* are shown in Fig. 15.2 on page 496. These blots are entirely black and white, as are five of the blots in the

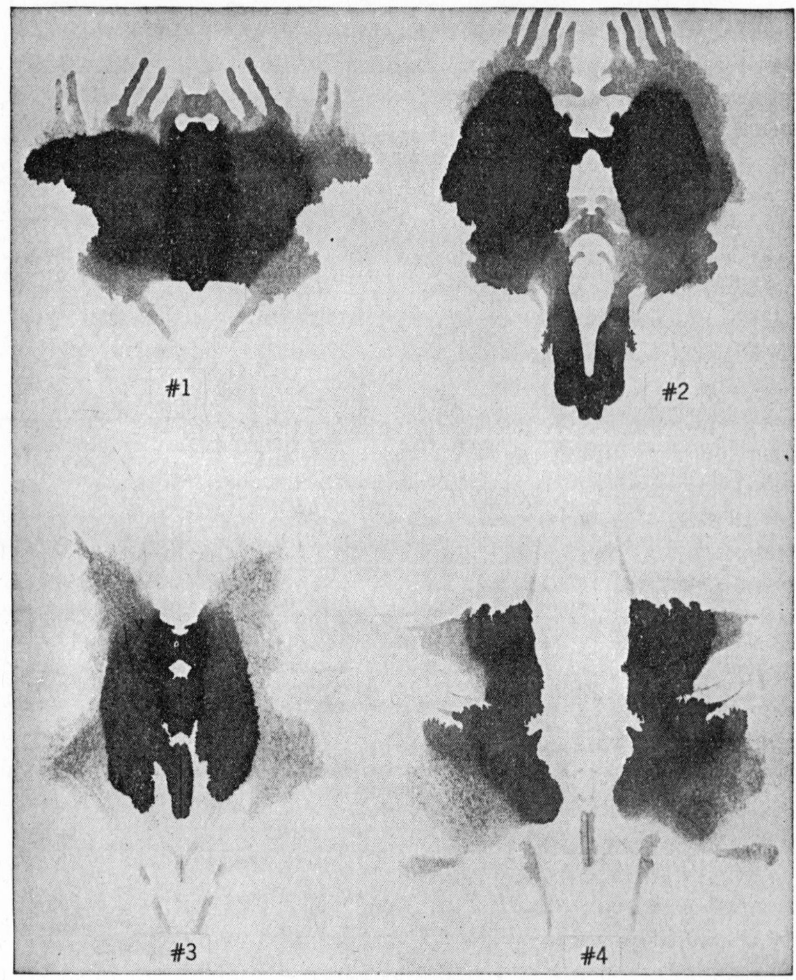

Fig. 15.2 Rorschach-type inkblots.

Rorschach series. Two *Rorschach* blots contain bright red blotches in addition to the black and white, while three are made up only of colored patches of various hues. The symmetrical blots are mounted in the center of white cards and may be turned and viewed from any angle. The cards are presented to the subject one at a time in a specified order. The order of presentation is considered important because the subject's reaction to the sudden appearance of color is thought to be a significant element in his reaction to the test materials.

The test is introduced to the subject in a rather ambiguous way—"People see all sorts of different things in these cards. I'd like you to tell me what you see." When the subject is seated, the examiner hands him card I with instructions: "Tell me what you see. What might this be?" The subject is allowed as much time as he wants for a given card and is permitted to give as many responses to it as he wishes. He is also allowed to turn the card around and look at it from any angle to find things in it. However, he is not instructed to look for many items and is not told that he may rotate the card. Instructions are kept to the barest minimum, this presumably making the performance depend more completely on the person being examined.

During the initial presentation, the examiner keeps a record of the time between presentation of each card and the initial response to it. He records each response as it is given and the position of the card when the response is seen. Notes are also made of any significant behavior by the subject during testing, that is, evidences of upset, rejection of a card, etc.

After the initial presentation of the cards, the examiner goes over them with the subject again, questioning him about his responses. The questioning helps the examiner to find out where each item was seen in the blot and what aspect of the blot (form, color, etc.) primarily determined what the subject saw. It gives an opportunity for further clarification of anything that may have been obscure in the subject's initial response. Notes are made as needed and become part of the raw test record.

Scoring a Rorschach Record

The raw *Rorschach* record contains a mass of diverse material, and procedures of analysis must be applied to bring some order out of the chaos of details. Several different scoring schemes for the *Rorschach* have been developed (Beck, 1944; Klopfer and Kelley, 1942; Klopfer, 1954). The scoring procedure described here is the one developed by Klopfer. Only the major features of the scoring procedure are discussed in this section.

Rorschach and his followers have identified a number of different categories of response which are thought to have diagnostic significance. In addition to the simple count of number of responses, three main aspects of each response are considered important. These are location, determinant, and content.

In general, location is scored by determining the area of the blot to which the response corresponded. The subject can use the whole blot (W) for his response, as when he calls blot 1 of Fig. 15.2 a "crab's shell." He may base his response on a large subdivision of the blot (D), as when he reports each half of blot 2 to be "an Indian's head." He may base his response on some small usual detail (d), as when the upper center part of blot 2 is seen as two witches talking.

The determinant refers to the characteristic of the blot that caused the subject to see it as he did. The principal determinants are the shape or form of the blot (F), color (C), movement (M) and shading (k). As a rule, the greatest number of responses in a record are elicited by the shape of the blot. A further coding may be assigned to form responses depending upon whether the form of the blot appears to fit the response well (F+) or quite poorly (F−). It is quite common to have a response based jointly on two determinants. Thus, a response may depend upon both the shape and color of the blot, or the shape and shading of the blot. Thus, a subject may see blot 3 as a reflection of a bear in the water. The response would be coded for both determinants, the dominant one being listed first (that is, if this response was made primarily because of the shape of the blot, it would be coded FK, F for form and K for the depth or vista response).

The content categories refer to what it is that is seen in the blot. Among the categories used are human beings, animals, parts of human beings, parts of animals, nature, and inanimate objects. Recurrent content themes are particularly noted, as are content elements that appear to tell a story.

In addition to the three aspects of analysis noted above, each response is also classified as a frequently occurring or popular response (P) or as a rarely given or original response (O). There are a number of additional categories which are noted in the analysis of the record, that is, use of white space, rare edge details, etc. It is not possible or desirable to try to indicate the complete scoring procedure here.

After the single responses have been coded, a summary tabulation is prepared for the record. The frequency of each category is determined, and a number of ratios between different categories are calculated. It is this quantitative summary, plus the qualitative notes on the subject's reactions, on which interpretation is primarily based. The single response has significance only as it becomes part of this total.

Interpreting the Rorschach Record

Rorschach specialists would agree that the heart of the *Rorschach* method is the final integrative synthesis of the material that results from scoring the test. This is also the most difficult part of the undertaking, calling as it does for the evaluation and synthesis of many separate cues. Writers about the *Rorschach* insist that adequate interpretations can be made only by persons who have both a broad psychological background and extensive experience with the instrument itself. Just how much training is required would probably be a matter of debate, but clearly the interpretation of a record is not something to be undertaken by the teacher, the usual guidance worker, or many psychologists without the required special training. Any abbreviated presentation of the manner of interpretation must necessarily represent an oversimplification and do the method some injustice.

The *Rorschach* record is considered by its exponents to provide information about the whole functioning personality. They consider it appropriate to ask and expect help on questions like the following: How does this person usually attack a problem? Does he characteristically first look at the problem as a whole and then break it down into component parts or does he build up the total solution from its main parts? Does he deal with the main features of a problem or does he bog down in details and never reach the main problem? Does he approach problems in a rigid, set manner, or is his approach flexible? What is his intellectual level and how effectively does he use his intelligence? Is he overly ambitious? How does he handle his emotions?

Factors that are considered to be associated with the intellectual level of the subject are clearness of perception of form, ability to organize the blot into forms using the whole of the blot, number of original responses, total number of responses, and variety of content.

The location of the response in the blot and the approach in responding to each blot are said to represent the individual's way of solving problems. Using the whole blot is associated with intellectual ambition, and a person who is striving beyond his ability is expected to produce poor whole responses (that is, to force a high level of organization even where it is not appropriate). Breaking the blot into small, unusual details is considered to be characteristic of compulsive people who insist that the response must exactly match the form of the blot. The common-sense approach is illustrated by the frequent use of D, or usual details. Exponents of the *Rorschach* consider it to be particularly effective in revealing how well the individual uses his intelligence. However, estimates of intelligence based on the *Rorschach* have shown only rather modest correlations with scores on the conventional intelligence test.

The subject's use of color, texture, and shading are thought to give evidence about his emotional life. Pure color or color naming responses are considered to indicate a lack of emotional control. When color is combined with form but the form predominates, it is taken to indicate that the individual has a lively emotional life but that he has control of his emotions. Texture and shading responses are usually interpreted as indications of anxiety, feelings of inadequacy, or depression. Vista or three-dimensional responses receive much the same interpretation.

The movement (M) responses are associated with the inner life of the individual. Rorschach expressed the belief that movement responses represent a strongly felt wish experience. Many interpreters feel that M is a correlate of the color (C) response and shows internalized emotion whereas the C response represents the externalized emotional reaction.

The content of the *Rorschach* responses provides cues for understanding other types of responses. In the different content of the responses, the subject reveals his different personal experiences. It is from the content or symbolism of the content that the analogy is made between a *Rorschach* record and a dream.

Adaptations of Inkblot Tests

A number of adaptations have been developed, stemming from the original *Rorschach Test.* Some of these use the same plates, but modify the administration. Thus, there are procedures for group administration using a projector, and procedures for multiple-choice response in which the examinee selects a certain number from a given set of options. Other sets of blots have been prepared designed to be a parallel form of the blots in the original *Rorschach* series. The most systematic and radical revision is the *Holtzman Inkblot Technique* (Holtzman et al, 1961), in which two alternate sets of 45 blots each have been prepared, involving a richness of color and complexity of design considerably beyond that in the original series. With the greater number of blots, it becomes possible to restrict the examinee to one response per blot, and still get scores of satisfactory reliability. This rules out individual differences in fluency of producing responses, a factor that complicated the interpretation of all the other scores on the original *Rorschach.* The *H.I.T.* has been the object of a good deal of research in the years since its appearance, and a number of interesting relationships have been reported. However, as is the case for so much of the research with projective instruments, the studies are in large part unreplicated, so that we must question how much confidence can be placed in the findings.

THE *THEMATIC APPERCEPTION TEST*

The *Thematic Apperception Test,* usually referred to as the *TAT,* was originally described by Murray and Morgan in 1935, as reported by Murray et al (1938). The basic material of the *TAT* is a set of 31 cards, one blank and the other 30 with pictures. Typically, the cards show one or two human figures (a few show more) pictured rather vaguely and ambiguously in different poses and actions. Some of the pictures are specifically for boys, some specifically for girls, some for males over 14, some for females over 14, and some for all groups. For a particular age and sex, there are 20 of the pictures that are supposed to be used, though in many cases the examiner limits himself to a smaller number of pictures that he considers particularly appropriate for his subject. A sample picture from Murray's *Thematic Apperception Test* is shown in Fig. 15.3. This particular picture is one used in the series for women.

The subject's basic task is to tell a story based on the picture. Before any of the pictures are shown to the subject, the examiner instructs him somewhat as follows: "I am going to show you some pictures. I want you to tell me a story about what is going on in each picture. What led up to it, and what will the outcome be?" The exact instructions may vary from time to time, but they always include the directions to produce a setting for the action in the picture and to indicate the outcome. The story told by the subject is recorded verbatim, either by the examiner or with a recording machine. There are no time limits and no limits on the length of the story. The example given below is a sample of the responses given to the picture in Fig. 15.3.

> This young girl wants to go out on her own and lead a good life, but this old woman wants to control her and make her do things as the old woman wants them done. Some of the things the old woman has told the girl were bad, but the girl had to do them anyway. She hates the old hag and gets tired of the control that the old woman has over her and kills the old hag. No one ever found out that the girl killed the woman so she is free to do what she wants.

Fig. 15.3 Sample picture from *Murray Thematic Apperception Test.*

Points that should probably be noted in the above story are submission to another, an unwillingness to assume responsibility for personal behavior, hostility, and a socially unacceptable method of solving the problem situation. It must be remembered that a single story is not especially significant in understanding the person. However, if these elements recurred in a number of stories, then the pattern would be considered to have much greater significance.

Scoring and Interpretation of the TAT

A number of different scoring schemes have been worked out for the *TAT* (Tompkins, 1947). Most of these are elaborate and time-consuming. One thing that all the scoring schemes have in common is that the *content* of the stories plays a central role in interpreting the record. This contrasts with the *Rorschach,* where the center of attention is not *what* the subject sees but *how* he sees it. Beyond this, there is little uniformity in procedure for analysis, the method of interpretation and aspects analyzed depending upon the original purpose of giving the test.

Originally Murray analyzed the stories according to needs and presses, the needs of the hero and the environmental forces (presses) to which he is exposed. Each story was analyzed; from the total set of stories each need and press received a weighted score; and the needs and presses were then arranged in rank order. At the same time, the relationships between the needs were investigated. Although this type of analysis appeared to yield a wealth of data, it is not generally followed today. Mastery of the need concept is difficult to achieve, and the analysis is quite laborious, requiring about 5 hours to interpret a set of twenty stories, on the average.

Most currently used scoring systems take account of the following:

1. The style of the story, including such factors as length of story, language used, originality, variation of content, and organizational qualities.
2. Recurring themes in the story: such themes as retribution, struggle and failure, parental domination, etc.
3. Relation of the outcome of the story to the rest of the plot.
4. Primary and secondary identification, the choice of hero for the story and person second in importance.
5. The handling of authority figures and sex relationships.

Whatever method of interpretation is used, it is recognized that the single response has significance only as an element in the total pattern. It is the recurring themes and features that are important for interpretation.

OTHER PROJECTIVE TECHNIQUES

During the last 35 years, a host of other projective procedures have been proposed and have been developed to a greater or lesser degree. A number of these bear a close resemblance to the *TAT*. The *Four-Picture Test* of Van Lennep requires the subject to use four vague water-color pictures involving persons in different grouping and relationships in composing a story. This is alleged to bring out the subject's attitude toward life. The *Schneidman Make a Picture Story Test* (*MAPS*) requires the subject to make his own picture and corresponding story from a set of 67 cardboard figures spread out before him. The examiner presents one of a set of standard backgrounds, and the subject selects whichever of the 67 figures he chooses, arranges them on the background and creates his story. Additional backgrounds may be presented if the examiner chooses to do so, eliciting further arrangements and additional stories. The more active participation by the subject is reported to result in longer and richer stories than those from the *TAT*, but the unstandardized nature of the task makes it difficult to arrive at any norms or any standard way of scoring the product.

Graphic and plastic art materials have also been used to provide the raw material for projective analyses. Children's painting and finger painting and various types of clay modeling have provided unstructured media into which the child could project himself. Doll play also has provided an opportunity for dramatic expression for young children. The child is provided a set of dolls representing the various members of a family constellation and is given the materials with which to construct a stage setting. He is encouraged to act out any type of story or scene that appeals to him. Acting out problem situations in the make-believe setting is used not only as a source of information about the child's problem, but also as a form of therapy through which the child is provided with an opportunity to express, and presumably eventually relieve, his anxieties and tensions.

Verbal materials have also been used to some extent as media to elicit the individual's projections. The classical form of verbal projective test is the word association test, in which stimulus words are read one after another and the subject responds to each with the first word he thinks of. Cues to problem areas are obtained from words to which the subject responds very slowly, words on which he blocks and makes no response, and words to which he responds with unusual associations. The word association procedure is not widely used at the present time because it does not appear to provide very rich insights into the person being studied.

Sentence completion is another form of verbal test that has received some attention. The subject is provided the beginnings for a number of sentences such as:

I wish that I ______________________________.
When Mary's mother left she ______________.
The trouble with people is that they ________________.

He is instructed to go through the list quickly, providing an end for each sentence. One published version, the *Rotter Incomplete Sentences Blank* (Rotter, 1950) provides a scoring guide for coding the responses as unhealthy, neutral, or positive and healthy responses, and some normative data are provided for college groups. Thus, the blank can be used as a screening device to locate individuals who appear to present adjustment problems. Other forms of sentence completion test have been analyzed in terms of the content of the responses in much the same way as the *TAT* and give indications of feelings, attitudes, and reactions to things and people rather than indicating underlying personality structure and dynamics. The ease with which it can be administered to a group makes it attractive, but the verbal production required limits its use to fairly literate individuals. The nature of the response that he is making is fairly apparent to the subject, and it is relatively easy for him not to reveal himself on the test if he does not choose to.

THE ESSENTIAL NATURE AND PRESUMED ADVANTAGES OF PROJECTIVE TESTS

We have seen something of the diversity of projective methods and of the wide range of materials and media they use. Now we must ask what the common core running through them is and determine what advantages they may claim over other methods of studying the individual. Four points will be noted.

First, the tasks presented to the individual are usually both somewhat novel and quite unstructured. The subject cannot depend upon established, conventional, and stereotyped patterns of response. Rather, he is thrown back upon himself and must delve within himself for the response. He must create it anew in the test situation.

Second, the nature of the appraisals being made is usually well disguised. The subject is ordinarily not aware of the true purpose of the test, and even if he does have a general idea of the nature of the appraisal he does not know what aspects of his response are significant or what significance they have. The test is usually given under a neutral guise as one of imagination or artistic ability so that the examinee is "task-centered" rather than "self-centered." The individual is not called upon to verbalize his anxieties or emotions or to reveal himself directly and consciously to the tester. What revelation occurs is largely indirect and outside the subject's awareness. Thus, inhibitions and conscious controls may be bypassed, and intentional distortion of the picture presented is difficult for any but the most sophisticated subject.

Third, most of the tests make little or no demand on literacy or academic skills. They are nonreading, largely independent of any particular language, and in some cases, such as finger-painting or working with clay, do not involve speech at all. This extends greatly their scope of applicability. They may be used with children, even quite young children below school age. They may be used with illiterates or non-English speaking persons. They may be used in different cultures.

Fourth, they undertake to provide a view of the total functioning individual. They do not slice off one piece or trait for analysis. They preserve, it is alleged, the unity and integration of the total personality. To the clinically oriented user this appears a great virtue. In practical work, one must deal with the whole person, not just his limited intelligence, or his lack of emotional control, or his strong identification with his father. There is an appeal to a test that aspires to appraise the individual as a total functioning unity. Whether this is, in fact, the best way to understand him is another matter. We may be seduced by the shibboleth of "the whole child" into vagueness and fuzziness that results in a poorer picture of the whole than if we had looked more analytically and carefully at one aspect at a time. In buying a house, there are considerations of basic construction, type of roof, size of rooms, quality and adequacy of heating plant, plumbing and electrical equipment, accessibility and quality of schools and shopping areas, character of the neighborhood, esthetic appeal of the structure, cost, and many others. A more rational choice of house could probably be made by identifying these components and considering them one at a time than by giving a global reaction to the proposition as a totality. In the same way, it is possible that the total individual may be appraised more accurately and a truer description of him prepared if we concentrate our information-gathering upon one aspect at a time. It is, in any event, a fundamental issue and one on which no agreement is currently available as to how analytical an approach should be to provide the best basis for viewing the whole.

EVALUATION OF PROJECTIVE METHODS

We must now attempt to evaluate projective methods in terms of the criteria which we set forth in Chapter 6, attempting to see how they meet our requirements of validity, reliability, and practicality. Most of our data and illustrations will refer to the *Rorschach*, since this test has been studied longer and much more intensively than the others. The general problems we encounter in attempting to evaluate this test apply pretty generally to all. However, information on many of the varied techniques is fragmentary in the extreme.

Validity of Projective Techniques

In the general discussion of validity in Chapter 6, we distinguished three broad aspects of validity. These we designated content validity, construct validity, and criterion-related validity. Let us examine the validity of projective techniques, and specifically of the *Rorschach* under these three general headings.

CONTENT VALIDITY. We said that a test such as a high school biology test has high validity when the knowledges and skills called for by the test match accurately the knowledges and skills that we have set up as the objectives of our instruction. The test then accurately represents what we are trying to teach. It has high content validity, because the obvious, manifest content of the test corresponds well with our most thoughtful analysis of what the pupil is expected to have learned.

This type of validity—validity exemplified by the direct matching up of test content with life behavior—has no application in the case of projective techniques. The essence of projective testing is that it deals with the inner, concealed aspects of personality dynamics, and that these are revealed only indirectly by the interpretation of subtle signs in the individual's interpretation of what he sees. Thus, we must exclude content validity as an approach to the evaluation of projective techniques. Their validity must be appraised in other ways.

CONSTRUCT VALIDITY. Projective techniques are alleged to provide a basis for describing inner personality dynamics. The prominence of various determinants in a *Rorschach* record, for example, is thought to have significance for understanding manner of attacking problems, level of anxiety and ways of dealing with it, control of tensions, creativity, or some of a host of other aspects of the dynamic interplay in the personality. The projective techniques are esteemed for what the responses are presumed to *signify*, so the primary focus of inquiry into the validity of the techniques will be upon their validity as assessments of psychological constructs.

We have used the word "technique" rather than "test" in the last few paragraphs to set the stage for a distinction we wish to make between the projective procedures and those that we might speak of as psychometric tests. An instrument such as the *Guilford-Zimmerman Temperament Survey* yields a set of scores. Each score is based on a separate set of items, and can be thought of as a measure of an hypothetical distinct trait. Validation consists of trying to obtain other evaluations of the trait, as by ratings, and correlating the test scores with them, or of trying to predict the reasonable life correlates of such a trait and seeing whether these correlates do in fact appear. The validation of each score is a separate enterprise, and there is little or no interaction between the scores.

By contrast, a projective technique such as the *Rorschach* yields a mass of response material that is initially quite unstructured. The twenty or thirty responses to the blots may be classified in a variety of ways—by location, by use of color, by content—and one may study not only the single responses and single aspects, but also various relations among them. There is almost no limit to the number of different scores and indices, of varying degrees of subtlety and complexity, that can be obtained from this sample of behavior. And by the same token, there is no limit to the number and variety of hypotheses that can be generated concerning the *significance* of these indices in relation to different constructs describing personality. These hypotheses may relate not merely to single indices, such as the percent of W, or whole card, responses, but to ratios, patterns, and interrelationships of indices of any degree of complexity.

Validation of the *Rorschach* is, then, not an all-or-none proposition, but a piecemeal undertaking of validating each of the interpretive hypotheses. If one is to have confidence in the significance of a *Rorschach* record, each of the hypotheses as to what signifies what must be individually validated. This is an imposing undertaking, and one that is fraught with many difficulties.

A first major difficulty is to translate the hypotheses, originally expressed in terms of inner personality dynamics, into hypotheses concerning behavior. Thus, Rorschach hypothesized that M (human movement) responses are an indication of "more individualized intelligence, more creative ability, more 'inner' life . . . and measured stable motility." How does one identify individuals with "more creative ability"? One possibility would seem to be to choose a group of professional artists; Roe (1946) studied such a group to see if they generally showed a large number of M responses. Her results were largely negative, but what does this mean? Is the test faulty? Is the hypothesis linking a tendency to perceive movement with "creative ability" in error? Or is status as an artist an inadequate indicator of "creative ability"? The *Rorschach* enthusiast would prefer the last alternative and assert that creative potential in the personality cannot be judged by socially accepted creative production.

By contrast, the interpretation of M as indicating "stable motility" has yielded some confirmatory results. Thus, Singer and Spohn (1954) found that high M subjects were less restless during an unoccupied period in a waiting room and were more able to slow down a voluntary motor activity such as writing. Furthermore, the results have been confirmed in replication—a somewhat unusual event in research with projective instruments.

The interpretation of negative results, such as those by Roe referred to above, as due only to faulty experimental design is not altogether satisfying to the hard-nosed critic, who senses in the *Rorschach* devotee a certain reluctance to abandon, or in some cases even to modify, hypotheses even in the light of negative evidence. On the other hand, our general understanding of personality dynamics is not far enough advanced to permit us to predict with certainty the behavioral outcomes that *should* result from certain personality structures, so that faulty translations from inner life to observable behavior are quite possible. Furthermore, difficulties in observing and appraising behavior, together with the impact of situational factors outside the individual, may attenuate and obscure even logically sound predictions. So, negative findings have not been as devastating as one might have anticipated and the tendency of *Rorschach* hypotheses to survive in spite of a good deal of negative evidence is not too surprising. Attempting to account for the continued esteem with which some practicing clinicians view the *Rorschach,* in spite of the rather low yield of supporting evidence, Shaffer (1959) suggests:

> First, we have an intense need for a subtle and comprehensive instrument to assess personality. As recent research in social psychology shows, motivation and belief are highly related. When one has a strong need, evidence of little objective merit may be perceived as conclusive. Second, the *Rorschach* is projective for the examiner as well as the examinee. One readily "reads into" the vague verbalizations of the *Rorschach* protocol all that one already knows and believes about the examinee. For each individual examiner, therefore, the *Rorschach* seems to confirm his other knowledge and he has an intuitive and personal sense of the validity of the instrument. Third, the *Rorschach* is not wholly without validity—it is sometimes "right." And evidence from the psychology of learning shows that a schedule of intermittent reinforcements may form as strong a habit, and one as resistant to extinction, as reinforcement on every occasion.*

In the balance of research results, it is always a problem to judge whether negative outcomes should be written off as faulty predictions from the underlying hypotheses or as results of inadequate experimental design; whether they should encourage one to make modifications and adaptations of theory to accommodate the new findings, or whether they should cause one to abandon the whole structure (and perhaps the methodology that supports it) and begin again.

* Reproduced by permission of Gryphon Press.

Among psychologists, one will find almost all shades of opinion represented with respect to the *Rorschach*, and similarly, to other projective tests. There are those who dismiss most of the negative findings in attempts to validate *Rorschach* hypotheses as due to experiments that were inadequate or inappropriately conceived to really test the hypotheses that they were designed to test. There are those who would respond to the negative results by doctoring up the hypotheses, so that a new one sprouts out hydra-like as soon as one is chopped off. There are those who would view the balance of confirmation and non-confirmation as indicating that projective materials are a rich source of behavior samples, but that the structure of interpretation of these behavior samples still includes much that is questionable, unverified, and perhaps unverifiable, and that they hardly merit the central role they have come to hold for many clinical psychologists. There are those who would feel that the personality theory associated with projective tests is so esoteric, so out of touch with the picture of personality drawn from other sources, and so inadequately supported by the voluminous research literature on these procedures that psychologists would be well advised to concentrate their efforts elsewhere.*

There is one thing on which all can agree—enthusiast and critic alike—and that is that interpretation of *Rorschach* and other projective records is no enterprise for a novice. The structure of hypotheses based upon the indices is sufficiently subtle and complex that none but the well-trained can hope to arrive at valid personality descriptions from these instruments. If they are used at all, the use should be limited to the well-trained specialist. The teacher and counselor will do well to concentrate on behavior in life situations and limit interpretations to the fairly direct and manifest significance of the behavior. Attempts to interpret behavior samples in depth can lead the novice far astray.

CRITERION-RELATED VALIDITY. A third type of validation of test devices is found in their ability to predict socially significant outcomes. Thus, a scholastic aptitude test is valued in proportion as it gives a good prediction of academic success. We may ask how effective projective tests have proven in predicting significant outcomes for individuals.

One type of outcome that we might reasonably expect to find predicted by an appraisal of personality structure and personality dynamics is the psychiatric classification in which a person falls. Though there may not be a one-to-one correspondence between personality structure and form of psychiatric disability, there should be enough of a correspondence so that a good measure of the one would give a good prediction of the other. What have been the findings in this regard?

* For several extended reviews, reflecting quite varied evaluations of the *Rorschach*, see the *Fifth Mental Measurements Yearbook*, pp. 273–289, and the *Sixth Mental Measurements Yearbook*, pp. 492–509.

In different studies, in which experienced *Rorschach* analysts attempted to make "blind diagnoses" merely from the records, the reported degree of success has varied from quite high to little if any better than chance. Thus, Benjamin and Ebaugh (1938) reported agreement in 85 percent of 46 cases in which blind diagnoses based on the *Rorschach* alone were checked against independent diagnoses by a psychiatrist. However, the 30 years since the study was carried out have failed to produce a replication, so the results must be considered suspect.

Perhaps more typical of recent findings are those reported by Little and Shneidman (1959) in a study involving only 12 patients, but 72 clinicians. The 12 hospitalized patients were all male Caucasian veterans with 10 to 12 years of education and fell in the age range from 22 to 33. Thus, gross differences in aspects other than personality differences were controlled. Three patients, who were in the hospital because of fractures or requiring surgery, were carefully screened to be sure they showed *no* psychiatric disorder; three were cases of psychosomatic complaints without further emotional involvement; three had been diagnosed as neurotics; and three as psychotics—all showing a schizophrenic reaction.

All subjects were administered, by an experienced tester, the *Rorschach, Thematic Apperception Test, Make a Picture Story Test,* and *Minnesota Multiphasic Personality Inventory.* Examinee responses to the first three were recorded on tape and transcribed verbatim. In addition, a different examiner obtained a comprehensive and detailed psychiatric case history on each individual through a series of interviews.

In all, 48 clinicians studied the test data, each one working with a single test with which he was well experienced and reacting to data for only four cases (one from each of the four groupings). Twenty-four psychiatrists studied and evaluated the case histories, each one reacting to two histories. Thus, there were four evaluations of each case via each medium of study.

Several types of judgments were called for, and we shall consider these briefly. The first question was: How would you label this person diagnostically? Below are shown the 20 designations for Subject #2 (a normal person suffering from multiple fractures).

Rorschach

1. Schizoid character-depressive trends
2. Compulsive character
3. Passive aggressive personality disorder
4. Conversion reaction

TAT

1. Psychoneurosis, mixed, homosexuality
2. Anxiety neurosis
3. Neurotic, obsessive-compulsive
4. Character neurosis

MAPS

1. Passive aggressive personality
2. Neurotic reactive depression
3. Neurotic (hysteric)
4. Anxiety reaction with compulsive features

MMPI

1. Normal
2. Hysterical character
3. Without personality disorder
4. Psychoneurosis, conversion hysteric reaction

Case History

1. Within normal range—no psychiatric disorder
2. No psychiatric disease
3. No psychiatric disorder present
4. No psychiatric illness

A second type of judgment called for a rating of degree of the examinee's maladjustment, on a scale from 0 (making a good or adequate adjustment) to 8 (is a custodial case; cannot survive without care). Individual #2, whose diagnoses we have seen above, received average ratings in the five media as follows:

Rorschach	3.5
TAT	2.8
MAPS	3.5
MMPI	3.0
Case history	1.0

Taking all 12 cases, and pooling the 3 cases of each type and the four ratings of each case, we come out with overall average ratings as follows:

	Rorschach	*TAT*	*MAPS*	*MMPI*	*Case History*
"Normals"	4.5	4.8	4.8	3.3	1.6
Psychosomatic	3.6	4.4	5.4	4.3	3.8
Neurotic	4.1	4.5	4.6	5.1	6.8
Psychotic	6.0	6.2	5.7	7.1	7.4

All procedures have some slight success in separating the psychotics from the other groups, but all four of the tests produce ratings near the middle of the scale ("making a marginal or precarious adjustment") about equally for individuals in all the other three categories. Perhaps maladjustment, like beauty, is in the eye of the beholder.

Finally, each judge was asked to carry out a Q-sort with a set of 76 statements, sorting these into ones that were relatively greatly or slightly characteristic of the person under study. Q-sorts based on different instruments were correlated. If we may take the Q-sort from the case history as a type of criterion measure, since it is based directly upon the material reported by the subject, we find the following average correlations with case history Q-sort for the different instruments and types of subjects:

	Rorschach	*TAT*	*MAPS*	*MMPI*	*All*
"Normals"	03	−20	−22	30	−03
Psychosomatic	19	17	20	18	18
Neurotic	25	17	20	33	24
Psychotic	20	23	35	29	27
All subjects	17	09	14	27	17

The low correlations are partly the result of low reliability, since even with case history materials, two independent sorters using the same evidence produce sorts that correlate only .52 on the average. But even allowing for this fact, the lack of relationship is impressive. Only the *MMPI* produces consistently positive results. Notable is the tendency for *negative* relationships for the "normal" cases. The test interpreters persist in seeing pathological behavior when, in the case record, none exists.

All in all, this study hardly leads us to place great confidence in the interpretations drawn from projective instruments.

In another well-planned study, Chambers and Hamlin (1957) sent to each of twenty well-qualified judges a set of 5 *Rorschach* protocols. Different specific protocols were sent to the different judges, but each judge's set of five included the same five diagnostic categories: involutional depression, anxiety neurosis, paranoid schizophrenia, syphilitic brain damage, and simple feeblemindedness. Each judge knew the categories represented in his set of records and had the fairly straightforward task of matching *Rorschach* record and diagnosis. Results were better than chance, but far from perfect. The imbecile was correctly matched by eighteen of the twenty judges—but one wonders whether they might not have done as well from the results of a 5-minute vocabulary test. The other four diagnoses were correctly matched in 51 percent of the instances, better than chance for the group but too low to indicate confidence in an individual diagnosis. Being right half the time, when one could be right, by chance, a quarter of the time does not represent a satisfying degree of predictive accuracy in decisions as important as clinical diagnoses. On the other hand, a study (Eysenck, 1952), in which two experienced *Rorschach* analysts tried to separate the records of 60 neurotic boys from those of a control group that matched the neurotic cases in age and intelligence yielded percentages of success of 63 and 48. Flipping a coin could have been expected to give 50 percent accuracy in this two-way classification.

As in so much of the research with projective procedures, sometimes they seem to work and sometimes not. It is hard to say why. Many factors vary from one study to another—skill of analysts, heterogeneity of groups compared, and sharpness and clarity of the criterion, among others. But the total impression is that though the test provides some cues to diagnostic groupings, these cues are far from clear and dependable.

Another social outcome that clinicians have been interested in predicting is improvement under various types of therapy, and projective techniques have been studied with this end in view. Results have been generally discouraging. One or another sign may appear promising in one study, but when checked in a new sample these rarely hold up.

College success was an outcome that was predicted quite effectively by Munroe (1945) in one study. A correlation of −.49 was found between number of signs of maladjustment devised from an inspection technique of scoring the *Rorschach* and Student Work Committee rating for academic standing at Sarah Lawrence College. However, Cronbach (1950) was unable to achieve any useful prediction with University of Chicago freshmen, and it may be noted that Munroe has not reported confirmation of her results with new groups.

A quite different social outcome, elimination from flying training because of emotional disturbance, was studied by Holtzman and Sells (1954). A number of clinical psychologists were each asked to examine a series of case records for aviation cadets, each of which included among other things a *Rorschach* protocol. Some were men who had successfully completed training, and some were men who had been eliminated for fear of flying or some other personal reason (that is, not for lack of skill). The clinicians were asked to study the records on each man and classify him into the success or failure group. It was found that, although the clinicians showed some agreement in the way in which they portrayed a given man, they could do essentially no better than chance in picking those who would crack up in the training program. Though the procedures appeared to have modest reliability, so far as personality description was concerned, this description had no validity as a predictor of flying success. These results are consistent with those from other attempts to use the *Rorschach* as a predictor during World War II.

In general, the conclusion on predictive validity at this time must apparently be that the *Rorschach*, and probably other projective tests, have some validity as predictors of psychiatric diagnoses, though just how much seems quite uncertain. For other practical criteria we must be more pessimistic. There appears to be no *verified* evidence that they have validity for any other practical outcome in the world of day-to-day living.

Reliability

Arriving at a satisfactory basis for appraising the reliability of projective methods has also proved to be a tricky business. Separate equivalent or near-equivalent forms of the tests have rarely been prepared. The devotees of the tests protest that it is not possible to divide the test into equivalent halves. Memory of a previous testing is likely to distort retesting over a short time. And the test enthusiast is likely to protest that the total personality is changing from day to day, so that test results cannot be expected to remain stable over a period of time. One senses a certain flight from reality in all of this, a well-formed mechanism of defense. The tough-minded psychometrician would like to know what magic there is about one set of inkblots or one set of pictures that makes them irreplaceable. Why should it be essentially more difficult to produce a parallel set of blots than a parallel set of intelligence test items? He would also contend that aspects of personality so fleeting that they cannot legitimately be appraised by a retest after some lapse of time are probably also so superficial that they are of no importance.

But real problems in evaluating the reliability of projective methods do remain. These center around the question of what it is whose reliability is being appraised. Is it the reliability of some relatively objective component score, or is it the reliability of some inference from the test materials, or is it the reliability of the total descriptive picture? Probably each of these is worth studying. The last, the reliability of the descriptive picture, does not fit into the usual statistics of reliability, and one must fall back on matching or similar techniques. Let us inquire into reliability at each of the several levels.

RELIABILITY OF SINGLE SCORE COMPONENTS. Evidence on the reliability of single score components is available chiefly for the *Rorschach*. A number of split-half and retest reliability studies are available. Values reported differ from study to study and for the different types of subscores. However, correlations are quite uniformly positive and, in many instances, quite substantial. One would conclude that the major score components show a within-test consistency that is comparable with that of other personality measures.

Perhaps the most satisfying evidence of reliability is correlation of two comparable or near-comparable forms. A separate set of blots, the *Behn-Rorschach,* was designed to parallel the original *Rorschach Test*. Correlations between the two were determined by Eichler (1951). For total number of responses the correlation was about .70. Separate scoring categories showed correlations of from .45 to .70. The values were not greatly different when a retest was given with the original *Rorschach*. The relationships were all significantly positive but lower than we have come to expect with other test materials, particularly tests that are to be used for detailed individual diagnosis. Comparable figures were obtained by Meadows (1952) for the main score components. However, Meadows found many of the rarer and subtler scores to give reliability coefficients ranging from .40 down to zero.

RELIABILITY OF PREDICTIVE INFERENCES. It is *possible* that the single components of a projective test record may be of rather modest reliability, and yet that consistent inferences may be drawn from the total record. If we work with a single sample of the subject's behavior and two or more interpreters, we are studying only the reliability of the interpretation. If we provide the independent interpreters records from different testings, then we are testing the reliability of the test-interpreter combination. Few studies of the reliability of inferences from projective tests have been made. One related study by Palmer (1951) had trained interpreters make judgments about the persons whose *Rorschach* records they studied on a checklist of different attributes. Palmer found very low correlations between judges for judgments of this sort based on the same set of records.

RELIABILITY OF PERSONALITY DESCRIPTIONS. How accurately does the total picture given by a projective test maintain itself from one testing to another, or from one interpretation to another? Such evidence as we have presented on the extent to which *Rorschach* records can be matched with case materials or with diagnostic categories is indirect evidence of reliability. There must be some stability in the basic *Rorschach* record if it can be dependably matched with anything else. What *level* of precision the descriptive picture achieves, however, is almost impossible to determine from this sort of evidence. Little direct evidence on the problem is available.

Practicality

Projective tests are viewed by their proponents as clinical techniques that can be expected to give valid results only in the hands of persons having both special training in the technique and a high level of general sophistication in dynamic psychology. Furthermore, the tests are generally time-consuming both to give and to score. It seems clear, therefore, that if any use is justified by the validity that they demonstrate it will be limited to mental hygiene clinics, mental institutions, private clinical practice, and similar settings in which adequate resources are available. They are not, and probably never will be, techniques to be widely applied in schools. The teacher and the school administrator are interested in these approaches only as consumers. They may have occasion to hear some projective test or the interpretation of a test discussed in connection with a particular child. Their need is to know something of what the clinician hopes to be able to do with the test and to have some sense of the level of confidence to be placed in the results. With respect to this last point, a substantial admixture of skepticism seems to be indicated. But clearly, these procedures are for specialists in special situations, and the story of the help that they can provide even then is far from encouraging.

SUMMARY STATEMENT

During the past 35 years, the invention, exploration, and development of projective tests of personality has been, for many psychologists, the most exciting adventure in personality evaluation. The tests have had many ardent supporters and many severe critics.

When projective techniques were newly developed innovations in psychological procedure, one could forgive the incompleteness of the evidence on which their claims for a place in the practical and theoretical repertoire of psychological assessment were based. But now, 35 years and 5,300 publications later, it seems that one should be able to set higher standards for demonstrated reliability and validity. Truly, the mountain has labored!

It is still possible that in the array of different projective procedures, used in different ways by different experts, there may reside some kind of value and truth. But as the research studies have accumulated, skepticism has also mounted. The probability that valid inferences can reliably be drawn from the samples of behavior that persons produce in response to inkblots or pictures has seemed to decline, and the range of those inferences to shrink. Certainly, the procedures have hardly justified the central role that was assigned to them by many clinical psychologists in the 1940's and 1950's.

Perhaps the group of tests calling for response to ambiguous stimulus materials should be thought of as just one segment of the totality of indirect performance measures of personality. Within this domain, some techniques of value may be found, but it appears that the yield will be modest in proportion to the amount of digging that will be required.

QUESTIONS AND EXERCISES

1. What is projection? Give several examples from your own experience or your observations.

2. What basis is there for expecting a projective test to work? Why should we be able to tell anything about a person from the types of responses that he gives to projective test materials?

3. Why has there been such a divergence of opinion between clinical psychologists and specialists in measurement as to the value of projective tests?

4. In what ways are the situational tests described in Chapter 14 similar to projective techniques? In what ways do they differ?

5. Write down all the different things you can see in the four ink blots in Fig. 15.2. If possible, get three or four other people to do the same thing. Try to make a rough scoring in terms of the determinants given on pp. 497–498. Do you find common responses? Whole responses and detail responses? Movement responses? How do the different records compare?

6. Is it possible or desirable for you to make a psychological interpretation of the material obtained under question 5? What factors limit the interpretability of this sort of material?

7. Collect several stories in response to the picture in Fig. 15.3. What aspects of these look as if they might tell you something about the person? What cautions would need to be observed in interpreting this kind of material?

8. Pictures such as those used in the *TAT* have frequently been used to measure attitudes. What are the advantages and disadvantages of this method?

9. In what ways is the play of children a projective technique?

10. Classroom teachers frequently make inferences about students' personalities from their compositions, paintings, and other expressive products. What justification is there for this? What are the hazards in this type of action?

11. Making a drawing of a person has been used both as a way of assessing intelligence and a way of appraising personality. Suggest how aspects of the drawing might be used for each purpose. How could the inferences be validated? What differences do you see in the validation process?

REFERENCES

Beck, S. J. *Rorschach's test: Volume I: Basic processes.* New York: Grune & Stratton, 1944.

Benjamin, J. D. & Ebaugh, F. G. The diagnostic validity of the Rorschach test. *American Journal of Psychiatry,* 1938, **94,** 1163–1178.

Chambers, G. S. & Hamlin, R. W. The validity of judgments based on "blind" Rorschach records. *Journal of Consulting Psychology,* 1957, **21,** 105–109.

Cronbach, L. J. Studies of the Group Rorschach in relation to success in the college of the University of Chicago. *Journal of Educational Psychology,* 1950, **41,** 65–82.

Eichler, R. M. A comparison of the Rorschach and Behn-Rorschach inkblot tests. *Journal of Consulting Psychology,* 1951, **15,** 185–189.

Eysenck, H. J. *The scientific study of personality.* New York: MacMillan, 1952. Pp. 162–163.

Holtzman, W. H. and others. *Inkblot perception and personality: Holtzman Inkblot technique.* Austin, Texas: University of Texas Press, 1961.

Holtzman, W. H. & Sells, S. B. Prediction of flying success by clinical analysis of test protocols. *Journal of Abnormal and Social Psychology,* 1954, **49,** 485–490.

Klopfer, B. & Kelley, D. M. *The Rorschach technique.* Yonkers, New York: World Book, 1942.

Klopfer, B. *Developments in the Rorschach technique.* Yonkers, New York: World Book, 1954.

Little, K. B. & Shneidman, E. S. Congruencies among interpretations of psychological test and anamnestic data. *Psychological Monographs,* 1959, **73,** No. 476.

Meadows, A. W. An investigation of the Rorschach and Behn tests. Cited in H. J. Eysenck, *The scientific study of personality.* New York: MacMillan, 1952.

Munroe, R. L. Prediction of the adjustment and academic performance of college students by a modification of the Rorschach method. *Applied Psychology Monographs,* 1945, No. 7.

Murray, H. A. and others. *Explorations in personality.* New York: Oxford University Press, 1938.

Palmer, J. O. A dual approach to Rorschach validation: A methodological study. *Psychological Monographs,* 1951, No. 325.

Roe, A. The personality of artists. *Educational and Psychological Measurement,* 1946, **6,** 401–408.

Rorschach, H. *Psychodiagnostics* (translation by P. Lemkau and B. Kronenburg). New York: Grune & Stratton, 1942.

Rotter, J. B. *The Rotter Incomplete Sentences Blank.* New York: Psychological Corporation, 1950.

Shaffer, L. F. Review of H. Rorschach, *Psychodiagnostik.* In O. K. Buros (Ed.), *Fifth mental measurements yearbook.* Highland Park, New Jersey: Gryphon Press, 1959. Pp. 285–289.

Singer, J. L. & Spohn, H. E. Some behavioral correlates of Rorschach's experience-type. *Journal of Consulting Psychology,* 1954, **18,** 1–9.

Tompkins, S. S. *The Thematic Apperception Test.* New York: Grune & Stratton, 1947.

SUGGESTED ADDITIONAL READING

Allen, R. M. *Personality assessment procedures.* New York: Harper, 1958. Chapters 8–14.

Harrison, R. Thematic apperceptive methods. In B. B. Wolman (Ed.), *Handbook of clinical psychology.* New York: McGraw-Hill, 1965. Pp. 562–620.

Holzberg, J. D. Projective techniques. In I. A. Berg and L. A. Pennington (Eds.), *An introduction to clinical psychology.* New York: Ronald Press, 1966. Pp. 106–153.

Kinslinger, H. J. Applications of projective techniques in personnel psychology since 1940. *Psychological Bulletin,* 1966, **66,** 134–139.

Kleinmuntz, B. *Personality measurement.* Homewood, Illinois: Dorsey Press, 1967. Chapters 9, 10.

Shneidman, E. S. Projective techniques. In B. B. Wolman (Ed.), *Handbook of clinical psychology.* New York: McGraw-Hill, 1965. Pp. 498–521.

Vernon, P. E. *Personality assessment: A critical survey.* New York: John Wiley, 1964. Part II.

CHAPTER 16

Planning a School Testing Program

ooooooooooooooooooooooooooooooooooooooooooooooooooooooooooooooooooooooooooooooooooooooooooooooooooooo

We want to give some standardized tests in our school. What would you recommend?

I am on a committee to revise the testing program for our schools. These are the tests we plan to use, and the grades in which we plan to use them. Will you criticize this plan?

Probably every teacher of tests and measurements faces requests like these each semester. What standardized tests should be used? When should they be used? What constitutes a sound testing program?

THE CART AND THE HORSE

The trouble is that there is really no answer to such questions. Or, rather, the only answer is another series of questions. Before asking "What tests should we give?" one asks "What information do we need that we do not have now? When do we need it? How will we use it?" There are many situations in which giving tests can be a rather futile enterprise. What profit is there in a reading readiness test if all members of a class study reading together from the same primer at the same rate and time? Why give a reading test in the tenth grade if there are no provisions for differentiated individual work or remedial instruction? A functioning testing program should grow out of explicitly stated needs for specific kinds of information and plans for the ways that the test results will be used. A testing program can be planned only in terms of the purposes it is to serve. Tests given with no particular use in mind *may* find a use, *may* create their own market, but it hardly seems likely.

The starting place is the school, its curriculum, its students, its staff, and the decisions that need to be made for, with, and by students. It cannot be expected that each single teacher will have seen in advance how test data can be used in forwarding his activities with his class. Learning to use test information represents one aspect of in-service growth. But a testing program unrelated to local needs, local resources, and local levels of sophistication is unlikely to function effectively. Planning that does not center around constructive use of the test results and provide for increasing the total staff's understanding of the tests that are used in the program is likely to be sterile. For tests are given to be used, not to be filed. More important than planning *what* tests are to be *given* is planning *how* the tests are to be *used.*

This is why planning a testing program in the abstract or in a vacuum is so unsatisfactory. Defining functions and purposes is the horse. Let us put him out in front, and the cart carrying a program of tests will follow after.

FUNCTIONS OF A TESTING PROGRAM

The phrase *testing program* as used in this chapter refers to an organized schoolwide or systemwide program for administering standardized tests. We are restricting the use of the term to those programs in which the local school authorities have full control over which standardized tests will be given, when they will be given, and to whom they will be given. The term, as we are using it, does not include the wide variety of teacher-made tests that are prepared for use within a single class or school, the specialized testing procedures that may be carried on to study individual students, nor the testing programs that are controlled by agencies other than local school authorities such as the College Entrance Examination Board (CEEB) or state education departments.

Although, in our use of the term *testing program,* we stress local control and local needs, many of the needs for the information that tests can supply and many of the functions to be served by a testing program are common from one school system to another. We have discussed ways of using the results of various kinds of standardized tests in previous chapters. The reader is referred to Chapter 9, pp. 282–288 for uses of the results of standardized achievement tests, to

TABLE 16.1 FUNCTIONS OF A TESTING PROGRAM

Classroom Functions	Guidance Functions	Administrative Functions
Diagnosing learning difficulties	Preparing evidence to guide discussions with parents about their children	Assigning students to classroom groups
Evaluating discrepancies between potential and achievement	Helping the student make immediate choices	Placing new students
Appraising gains or growth in achievement	Helping the student to set educational and vocational goals	Helping to determine eligibility for special groups
Grouping students for instruction within a class	Improving counselor, teacher, and parent understanding of problem cases	Evaluating curricula, curricular emphasis, and curricular experiments
Planning instructional activities for an individual		Improving public relations
Identifying students who need special diagnostic study and remedial instruction		Providing information for outside agencies
Determining reasonable achievement levels for each student		

Chapter 10, pp. 336–340 for uses of intelligence and prognostic tests, and to Chapter 12, pp. 410–413 for uses of temperament and adjustment inventories. Additional discussion of the use of standardized test results in counseling and in personnel selection will be found in Chapters 18 and 19.

In Table 16.1, we present a summary of the most justifiable uses of test results. This summary may serve as a checklist to guide a review of local needs and uses. However, the applicability of these functions must always be checked in the local setting. One must ask, "Can we, or do we wish to, use tests for this purpose in our schools?"

QUALITIES DESIRED IN A TESTING PROGRAM

What are the general characteristics of a good school testing program? We shall consider three briefly: relationship to use, integration, and continuity.

Relation to Use

We have indicated in Table 16.1 a number of functions for which standardized tests are used in some school systems. The first step in planning a testing program for your schools is to review these and possibly other functions and determine how tests will be used in your schools. The testing should then be planned in relation to these uses. Tests should be selected and the times at which they are given should be chosen so that the needed information will be available and as up to date as possible at whatever time it is needed.

Thus, suppose teachers in the first grade wish to use test results to help them form subgroups that will move into reading at different rates. Our need is then for a reading readiness test. If almost all pupils go to kindergarten, the test might be scheduled for the end of the kindergarten year, say, in May. But more likely we will want to give the test in the first grade early in the fall, about the beginning of October, as soon as the pupils have settled down in their new class.

Or again, suppose that a differentiated high-school program is available for the 3 years of senior high school, and that counselors and pupils work out plans for the high-school program during the spring of the ninth grade in the light of available information on pupil aptitudes and achievement. In this setting, a program of aptitude and achievement testing during the first semester of the ninth grade will provide relevant and current information. Here, as everywhere, the important thing is to provide *what* will be used *when* it will be used.

Integration

The testing program should be seen as a whole. Information that is needed in the sixth grade is not unrelated to the information that was obtained in the fifth grade or to information that will be useful in the seventh grade. Each item of information gathered should be obtained at such a time and in such a way that it will make the maximum contribution to the total. Several aspects of integration merit consideration.

In an integrated program, it will usually be desirable to use the same series of tests over the grade range for which the series is appropriate. Thus, if the *Metropolitan Achievement Tests* are being used to measure progress in basic skills, it will probably be desirable to use them in any grade from first up to sixth, and possibly to eighth or ninth, in which an achievement battery is being used. The advantages are that norms are based upon the same sampling of communities from grade to grade, and the tests conform to a common outline of content and format. Thus, scores from one grade to the next are more nearly comparable, so that a truer picture may be obtained of pupil growth.

Integration implies particularly integration between the several divisions of the school program. Tests in junior high school should be planned in relation to those already given in the elementary school, and those in senior high should take account of junior high testing. An intelligence test given in the sixth grade need not be followed by a similar test at the beginning of the seventh grade. If aptitude tests are given in the ninth grade, there is limited gain from a similar battery in the tenth.

Integration between divisions of the school implies continuity of school records. The records accumulated about a pupil in the elementary school should follow him, in whole or in part, when he goes on to the secondary school. It may be that the complete record, especially if it is a very full one, should not stay in the active record file. However, key information should carry over into the record system of the higher school, and the full record should be available for reference if need be.

Integration means, finally, timing testing so that insofar as possible multiple purposes can be served. An attempt to serve two masters is always a compromise. However, it sometimes represents a sound use of limited resources. Thus, an intelligence test fairly early in the sixth grade can serve adequately for sectioning and guidance in the seventh grade and still be available as a resource for studying problem cases and issues of promotability in grade six. A scholastic aptitude test in grade ten or eleven gives as good a prediction of college success as one taken in May of the senior year and is also available for counseling purposes during two or three years of high school.

Continuity

The potential values of a testing program increase as it is continued over a period of years. Advantages of continuity in the program are two-fold. On the one hand, data accumulate in the records of the individual pupil. There are available to contribute to an understanding of the youngster not merely the results of tests given during the present year but also the data from earlier testings one or more years ago in lower grades. Present status can be seen in perspective in relation to earlier records. Thus, we can see whether Jerry's academic problems in the sixth grade have developed recently or whether they represent merely the continuation of an early trend; we can determine whether the difficulty Mary is having with long division is new or whether it has its roots in early difficulties with arithmetic fundamentals.

Continuity also is of importance in permitting a school system to get to know the particular tests it is using. We have emphasized at various points that a good deal of caution must be exercised in applying national norms to a local setting. Continued local use of a test or test series permits the development of local standards of expectancy. This may take the form of an informal and implicit tempering of national norms in interpreting local performance. It may take the form of an actual set of local norms. Thus, a suburban community with a very high percentage of pupils going on to college may find that percentiles based on its own school population provide a more appropriate framework for judging the academic status of its pupils than do national age or grade norms.

Getting to know tests implies getting to know what they measure, as well as establishing local standards of expectancy. If teachers work with the tests and test results, they will come to know what the test covers, what cues for diagnosing group strengths and weaknesses can be drawn from it, and what its limitations are. Both types of familiarity are desirable when teachers are using test results to help them with their work. For this reason, a school system will ordinarily wish to continue to use the same tests over a period of years, changing them only when they become out of date or when a study of other available tests indicates that there are ones available that represent a definite improvement over those that have been used in past years.

SUGGESTED PRIORITIES IN A TESTING PROGRAM

At the beginning of the chapter we indicated an unwillingness to prescribe a particular pattern for a testing program. This unwillingness stemmed in part from the different functions which the program may serve in different schools. It stemmed also from the wide variation in financial and professional resources available in different school systems. However, there is a general core of uniformity, in spite of diversity, and the same types of tests are available to all schools. That being so, we shall offer some suggestions on the tests we consider likely to prove most generally useful in a program at the different levels.

A Program for the Elementary School

In the elementary school, our concern centers in helping the individual to master the tools of learning and communicating while he is learning to live and work in a group of his peers. At the same time, the individual is building up a background of experience, knowledge, and understanding. It is in this setting that tests must function. Though it is difficult to arrange choices in an ordered sequence, since tests relate to each other and function in teams, we have attempted to do so roughly.

In all subsequent discussion it is assumed that children have been adequately examined for vision and hearing and general health status. We have thought of these measures as part of the physical examination rather than as part of the school testing program. They are, of course, of fundamental importance in guaranteeing a profitable educational experience for each child. There is nothing more tragic than the so-called "stupid" child in the back row, who got nothing out of school because he could not hear what the teacher was saying or could not see what was written on the blackboard.

READING TESTS. We are disposed to give first place in our program of elementary-school testing to tests of reading ability. Reading has always been the key avenue for acquiring all types of organized knowledge. Though in the present-day world its supremacy is challenged somewhat by movies, radio, and television, learning from books will continue to be at the heart of education, especially at the higher levels. For this reason, aiding the school in making early identification of poor progress in reading and in keeping track of reading progress through the school years seems to be among the most useful services a testing program can perform.

If very meager resources permitted only a single reading test, we suspect that we would give it at the end of the second or beginning of the third grade, so that it might be available to identify individuals for special help for a year or so before they reached the greater variety of content and the more extensive demands upon independent reading during the later elementary grades. However, we would like to be able to give a reading test every year or two from the beginning of the second grade throughout the elementary school.

GROUP INTELLIGENCE TEST. To aid in interpreting reading test results and other aspects of academic achievement, to help in setting expectations for pupils, and to aid in understanding problem cases, we would like to have results from intelligence testing. When we are thinking in terms of a minimum program and are considering the practical realities of time and cost, we must settle for a group test. If it is to be used in conjunction with our early third-grade reading test, it must be a non-reading test of intelligence. But group tests given as early as the beginning of the third grade do not have too satisfactory reliability or stability over time. If we can afford only a single group intelligence test, we would probably do well to delay it until the fourth or fifth grade, when the results will be more dependable. If a test is to be given in the second or third grade, we would want to be able to include at least one more group intelligence test during the upper elementary grades, fourth, fifth or sixth, the choice of grade depending upon plans for testing in junior high school. We would not object to additional tests, given fairly adequate resources. These would serve primarily to increase the reliability of our appraisal. We would be glad to have both verbal and nonverbal measures of intellectual ability.

BASIC SKILLS BATTERY. Competing with the intelligence test for second place in our program would be a battery covering the basic skill subjects. This would, of course, include reading and could replace the separate reading test. If the battery could be given only once, we would probably choose to give it in grade three or four, where the results could be used by the school for planning individual programs of instruction for pupils or for fitting pupils into special programs of remedial instruction. However, we would like to be able to test children with such a battery every year, starting in the third grade or possibly the second. We have a certain bias in favor of carrying out this testing in the fall, so that the fresh results may be available for use by the teacher who has worked with the testing.

READING READINESS TEST. On the assumption that the teachers in our school have an individualized program of instruction in reading for the first grade, we would place a reading readiness test next upon our list. We might possibly move it higher. We would view this test as a partial guide to the first-grade teacher in organizing subgroups for reading instruction and as a basis for helping him to evaluate the progress of individual pupils.

The four types of tests we have listed so far are the ones commonly found in school testing programs. Other types of tests will be found much less frequently. Some are not used because of cost; some, because what they have to offer seems less important.

INDIVIDUAL INTELLIGENCE TESTS. For most students in the elementary school, adequate appraisal of general intellectual abilities can be obtained from group tests of intelligence. There are situations, though, in which an individual intelligence test could be very useful. Most of these situations are those in which one is working intensively with an individual who has severe learning disabilities or emotional problems. We tend to view the individual intelligence tests as being supplementary to the regular school testing program.

ACHIEVEMENT TESTS IN CONTENT SUBJECTS. Some of the achievement batteries for the upper elementary grades include tests dealing with content areas of science and social studies. Although each school must decide for itself whether these tests offer valid appraisals of its curriculum, we feel that the nature of their content is such that they have limited usefulness either for helping teachers in their work with students or for helping to evaluate the curriculum in the school. We do not recommend them as important features of an elementary school program.

OTHER TYPES OF MEASURES. Other types of tests may be required for studying individual children. These include the diagnostic tests used in the special study of children with disability in a particular subject. They also include the techniques of clinical testing used by the school psychologist in studying a problem case. However, these represent supplements of the testing program rather than a basic part of it.

We have not recommended paper-and-pencil personality inventories because of (1) serious doubts as to the validity of the information they provide for an elementary school child and the soundness of the interpretations and constructive use that school personnel can make of the results; and (2) the objections of parents to the kinds of questions that are asked in these inventories. This does not mean that personality development of the elementary school child is of no concern to the school. Rather, it means that understanding the child as a person must depend upon observations of each pupil by the teacher and other school personnel.

A Program for the Secondary School

In the secondary school, the student faces a number of educational choices and decisions. He has to make choices of particular subjects or between different curricula. At the same time, he must start thinking about future educational or vocational plans. The curriculum has, to a considerable extent, moved beyond the basic skills toward increased emphasis on specialized subject matter. These shifts in emphasis appear to call for a corresponding shift in the pattern of the school testing program.

In planning a testing program for the secondary school, one wants to be sure that the diverse needs of both the college-bound and noncollege-bound student are met. The secondary school testing program should take into consideration college entrance tests such as the *CEEB Preliminary Scholastic Aptitude Test* and *Scholastic Aptitude Test*, and the tests of the American College Testing Program that are taken by the college-bound students. However, one of the most common faults of secondary school testing programs is the failure to provide for adequate appraisal of the noncollege-bound student. These students need counseling as much as, if not more than, the college-bound student. The planning of instructional activities and curricula requires an understanding of their general and specific abilities as well as of their status and progress in basic skills. There is a real need for schools to gather data on the effectiveness of their programs for the noncollege-bound student. The order of priority that we propose is outlined below.

SCHOLASTIC APTITUDE TEST. When several distinct high school curricula are available, a student must decide upon the kind of curriculum that he will pursue in high school. A related decision is how many academic courses he will take at one time and the level of the courses that is most suitable for him. During his high school program, he must decide how far up the educational ladder he will seek to go. A scholastic aptitude test is of value, as a supplement to school grades, in arriving at these decisions. It is also of value in interpreting the student's progress in school and in setting reasonable levels of expected achievement for him.

By high school age, the abilities measured by a scholastic aptitude test have become fairly well stabilized. There is little systematic shift from one year to the next. Thus, a tenth-grade test will serve to estimate scholastic aptitude at the end of the twelfth grade as well as one given later. For this reason, if only a single test is to be given, it may be given early, so that it can be used throughout the school program. Both verbal and nonverbal group intelligence tests can be used to obtain a more complete description of the student's abilities.

READING TEST. Skill in reading is important for both college-bound and noncollege-bound students. However, there is relatively little to be gained by giving a reading test unless the school provides either a developmental or remedial reading program. When such resources are available, results of reading tests can be used to place individuals in the appropriate program. Since the constructive use of a reading test implies appropriate action, it is desirable that the testing be done early in the program of the school, preferably in the eighth or ninth grade.

TESTS OF SPECIAL APTITUDES. For counseling of students, it is desirable to have appraisals of specialized aptitudes as well as general scholastic aptitude. Tests of specialized aptitudes are usually not well adapted for use below the eighth grade. The particular time at which they are used will depend upon the guidance program of the school. Testing should be timed so that results will be available when the counselor and the student must work together to decide on the student's program in secondary school. Usually these kinds of decisions must be made either in the eighth or ninth grade.

At this level, an educationally oriented battery such as the *Differential Aptitude Test Battery* is especially appropriate. If such a battery is used, it can take the place of the general scholastic aptitude test since certain subtests can be combined to give a suitable estimate of scholastic aptitude. For the noncollege-bound student, a vocationally oriented aptitude test such as the *General Aptitude Test Battery* could be given in the eleventh or twelfth grade.

ACHIEVEMENT TESTS IN CONTENT AREAS. Standardized achievement tests in the content areas for secondary schools have value in helping students make decisions about their future educational plans and also in helping the school to evaluate various aspects of its curriculum. Such tests are particularly of value in the ninth or tenth grades. They have little value for individual guidance if they are given in the twelfth grade.

INTERESTS. Although interests of a student are of value in helping him to make vocational and educational decisions, we have placed interest inventories relatively low in priority in a secondary school testing program. One reason for doing so is that interests of students of secondary school age are relatively unstable. Especially for college-bound students, the types of decisions that build upon vocational interests can usually be deferred until after the end of the secondary school program, by which point interest patterns have become somewhat more stabilized. Another reason is that the type of interest inventory that is appropriate at the secondary school level usually provides somewhat scanty data on the validity of the scores. If an interest inventory is given at the time that pupils first begin to think about and discuss the world of work, as is done in the ninth grade of some schools, it should be one, such as the *Kuder Preference Record,* that evaluates in terms of general interest areas rather than providing ratings for specific jobs. Early testing with such an inventory could appropriately be supplemented by a second testing with a more job-oriented inventory, such as the *Strong Vocational Interest Blank* or the *Minnesota Vocational Interest Inventory* in the eleventh or twelfth grades, especially for boys who are not planning to go on to college and who will be entering the world of work.

PROGNOSTIC TESTS We place prognostic tests very low in priority in our secondary school testing program. By the time that the student enters secondary school, there are usually extensive data on his abilities and achievement that can be used to estimate his probability of success in such fields as algebra and foreign languages. We doubt that the use of a special prognostic test for a subject will increase the accuracy of prediction of success in the subject enough to justify the additional testing. We also think it is undesirable to base decisions on admitting students to courses on the results of a single test.

PERSONALITY AND ADJUSTMENT INVENTORIES. We have serious reservations about the practical value of paper-and-pencil techniques for assessing personality at this level also. We do not recommend giving these kinds of inventories routinely to all students. However, this does not exclude their use by well-trained counselors or school psychologists for studying individual students.

A Testing Program for the College

At the college level, the diversity in programs, characteristics of students, and goals of students becomes even greater than at the high school level. This diversity is reflected in the functions that standardized tests are expected to serve at the college level. The primary functions served by standardized tests at the college level are (1) admissions, (2) academic placement, and (3) guidance and counseling of the individual student. Except for testing for admissions and placement, the college testing program is likely to be highly individualized to serve the needs of the student who has requested counseling.

Much of the admissions testing for both two-year and four-year colleges is done by external testing agencies, either the College Entrance Examination Board (CEEB) or the American College Testing program (ACT). These tests will be discussed in the section on external testing programs.

The problem of placing students in appropriate courses or sections of courses after admission to college arises in four general situations: (1) placement in freshman courses; (2) advanced placement for those students who have taken college-level courses in secondary schools; (3) credit for and exemption from courses that a student has studied outside of the formal classroom structure; and (4) placement of students transferring from another college. For placement in freshman courses, colleges have used either the relevant achievement test of the CEEB or the college freshmen level of the standardized achievement tests discussed in Chapter 9, pp. 279–282. If the CEEB achievement tests are used, they are usually taken by the student while in high school. If other standardized tests are used, they are usually given to all freshmen as a part of the freshman testing program, often during a freshman orientation week.

Advanced placement for those students who have taken college level courses in secondary schools is usually accomplished through the use of *CEEB Advanced Placement Examinations.* These examinations are administered once each year in May, and the results are available for use before the student enters college. The *College Level Examination Program* of the CEEB was established to enable those who have reached the college level of education outside the classroom through correspondence study, television courses, on-the-job training, independent reading, or any other means to demonstrate their level of achievement and to use the test results for college credit or placement. The same test series has been used for admission, placement, and guidance of students who wish to transfer from one institution to another. There are two types of examinations in the program: (1) the *General Examinations* that appraise achievement in five basic areas of the liberal arts: English Composition, Humanities, Mathematics, Natural Sciences, and Social Sciences-History; and (2) the 16 *Subject Examinations* designed to appraise achievement in specific college courses.

The major function of standardized testing in colleges is for guidance of individual students. This guidance may be educational, vocational, or personal. At the college level, problems in these areas tend to be individual rather than common. Furthermore, these services are likely to be offered only when the student requests them, although the request may come as a result of outside pressure. This suggests that the tests used should be selected in light of the problems being presented by each student; therefore the emphasis is on a highly individualized rather than on a uniform testing program.

There are some colleges, particularly two-year colleges, that require no uniform examinations of all students for admission to the college. In these colleges, a uniform freshman testing program could provide data that would be useful in placing students and in counseling students. In many colleges, the number of students who have difficulty in maintaining satisfactory scholastic standing is great enough to justify gathering common data on all students so that they are available for counseling. The priorities that we suggest are oriented toward these common guidance needs.

SCHOLASTIC APTITUDE. Since a substantial number of college students have difficulty in maintaining satisfactory scholastic standing, evidence on scholastic aptitude is often needed as a basis for counseling with respect to academic difficulties. Separate appraisal of verbal and quantitative abilities may be of value in permitting a more diagnostic appraisal. The test should be given at the time of admission so that the results may be available for use throughout the college program.

A battery of special aptitude tests could be used in place of the scholastic aptitude test. However, there appears to be somewhat less need for special aptitude tests in a college population than at the secondary level. The decision to go on to college has already somewhat narrowed down the range of occupations for which the group is preparing; the tests of mechanical, spatial, and clerical abilities are of rather less significance for college students than for a high school group.

READING. A measure of reading ability contributes some further basis for understanding problems of academic failure. It has a special function if the college provides a reading clinic in which remedial instruction may be obtained. A reading test given at the time of college entrance and interpreted in conjunction with the scholastic aptitude test provides one basis for locating students who might advantageously receive such special help.

INTERESTS. With final vocational choices drawing close, early in college appears to be a time at which a vocational interest test can advantageously be given to all students. Thus, if a test of interest in specific vocations, such as the *Strong Vocational Interest Blank,* is given during the sophomore year, the results can be available for consideration at the time that choices of major field are made. Since interest patterns at that age remain quite stable, the scores will be suitable for special counseling throughout the remainder of the college course.

ADJUSTMENT. The typical adjustment inventory is better suited to college students than it is to less mature and less educated groups. Where extensive counseling services exist, such an inventory might be used to identify individuals for further study. However, we have serious reservations as to the value of such a procedure. Ordinarily, at the college level, counseling is initiated at the request of the client. We question how effective or useful collegewide screening and

TABLE 16.2 SUGGESTED TESTS FOR SCHOOL TESTING PROGRAM

Type of Testing	Educational Level		
	Elementary	Secondary	College
General intelligence or scholastic aptitude	**	**	**
Reading	**	**	**
Basic academic skills	**	?	
Reading readiness	**		
Individual intelligence	*	?	?
Achievement in content subjects	?	**	*
Personality inventory		?	?
Interest inventory		*	**
Special aptitude tests or battery		**	*
Prognostic tests for special subjects		?	

bringing in students for conferences is likely to be. Use of the scores by departmental advisers and others without special training is hardly to be recommended.

Summary of Suggested Programs

Let us emphasize again that any testing program needs to be formulated by personnel in the local situation who are aware of local conditions, local purposes, and local resources. The proposals that have been outlined in this section are, at most, rough general guides. The highlights of this discussion have been organized in tabular form in Table 16.2. The most highly recommended tests are marked with a double asterisk. Tests considered useful supplements in an extensive testing program or of value for certain special purposes receive a single asterisk. Procedures deemed of doubtful value are indicated by a question mark. Where no mark is made, it indicates that the type of test is considered inappropriate, impractical, or of little value at that level for a classwide or schoolwide testing program.

PLANNING A TESTING PROGRAM

We have been discussing the possible functions, the qualities desired, and some suggested priorities in a school testing program. In the last analysis, though, each school system must assume the responsibility of planning and carrying out its own program. An outsider who knows nothing about the particular school system cannot design a good program for use there nor can a school system obtain an effective program just by taking over a program from a neighboring school system.

Each school system must decide on who will have responsibility for planning and directing the school program. The first responsibility of the group or person responsible for the testing program is to determine how the test results are to be used in the local situation. Then they must decide what tests will be used, in what grades, and at what time of the school year. Last, they must set the broad policies for scoring the tests and reporting the results. In the following sections we will discuss considerations related to planning a testing program.

Participation in Planning

The potential users of test results are classroom teachers, guidance personnel, specialists such as school psychologists and remedial reading teachers, supervisors, and administrative personnel. All of these people are faced with making decisions. The time that the decision needs to be made and the information needed to make it will vary. Since the results of the testing program should serve all potential users, the program must, of necessity, represent compromises in the selection of tests and in the time of the school year in which they will be administered. To achieve continuity and integration of the program, representation from all levels of the school, kindergarten through grade 12, should participate in the planning as a group, although some of the work may be done in subgroups.

In selecting achievement tests, one must know the nature of the curricula and the objectives and emphasis on objectives at each level of education in the local system. In a school, the people who are or should be most familiar with the objectives and nature of the curriculum in each area are the classroom teachers, subject-matter specialists, and supervisors of instruction; therefore, representatives from these categories should have a major role in selecting achievement tests.

Counselors, school psychologists, remedial reading specialists, and other specialists have a relationship with students and parents that is somewhat different from the relationships that classroom teachers have. The types of problems and issues that they face are also somewhat different. In addition, they tend to have more background in testing than do classroom teachers and should be expected to have more psychometric sophistication. These people should also be represented on the planning committee both for the contribution they can make in the selection of tests and to make sure that they have the information they need at the time it is needed.

Principals of schools, superintendents, and assistant superintendents face quite different problems from the other two groups. The administrative personnel are more likely to be involved in reporting to parent and community groups on the effectiveness of programs and the school as a whole. They must initiate or support requests for revision of programs and for budgets to add new programs or more or new kinds of personnel. They also need to be represented in the planning of the testing program.

In the climate that exists in many communities in 1968, it might be advisable to involve representatives of parent or other community groups in the planning of a school testing program. Although the involvement of such groups does not have to be continuous, there should be some systematic procedure for bringing into the deliberation of the committee on the testing program the opinions and feelings of this group.

Centralized Direction

Although the planning of a testing program should involve many people, one person needs to be designated in a school system as having major and ultimate responsibility for coordinating and carrying out the program. The title that this person carries varies from one school system to another but, just for convenience, we shall call him the director of testing.

The duties of the director of testing may include (1) coordinating the activities of the planning committee; (2) maintaining an up-to-date file of specimen tests; (3) providing for periodic review of the testing program and the use of test results; (4) planning the budget for the testing program; (5) carrying out such administrative details as ordering, storing, and distributing tests, making out detailed schedules for testing, and collecting tests or answer sheets for scoring; (6) providing for the scoring of the tests either by a test-scoring agency or locally; (7) planning and supervising analysis and tabulations of test results; (8) reporting test results to school personnel, parent groups, and the board of education; and (9) providing for in-service education of school personnel in administering, interpreting, and using tests.

From the list of possible duties of the director of testing, two things are quite clear. One is that directing a school testing program effectively requires a lot of time. Therefore, the person filling the position should be assigned the duty as a recognized part of his position and have enough time allocated to discharge his functions. Responsibility for the school testing program should not be added on to a full load of other duties. The second thing that should be clear is that the person filling such a role should have an educational and experience background in testing and in statistics as well as having some administrative and leadership qualities.

Selecting Tests for the Program

We have indicated in the previous sections that the kinds of tests to be given in a school depend upon the kind of information that the school needs to make decisions. For some kinds of decisions, one will need the information given by an achievement test; for others, one will need general intelligence tests; and for still others, one will need specialized aptitude batteries. The initial decision, then, involves the kinds of test that are needed; but then the choice must be made of one test out of the many that are available in each category.

In Chapter 9, pp. 261–269, we discussed the procedures that should be followed in selecting a reading test for use in a particular school. These procedures apply to the selection of any achievement test. The two major points to be kept in mind are that (1) the test should fit the objectives and curricular emphasis of the school, and (2) the test should have the psychometric qualities that justify using the results in the way that the school intends to use them. In addition to Chapter 9, the reader is referred to Chapter 6 for a review of the qualities desired in a test. The selection of other types of tests such as intelligence tests and specialized aptitude tests should be made primarily on the basis of their psychometric qualities. Although members of the test selection committee might quite appropriately react to the format and attractiveness of a particular test of this kind, the most crucial questions are: What evidence do the test authors provide for the validity of the test for the kinds of uses and interpretations that we want to make of the test results? How good is this evidence? Is the reliability adequate for the kinds of interpretations and uses that we want to make? How adequate are the norms for our purposes? Judgments of the adequacy of the technical data presented require some sophistication in statistics and test theory. A well-qualified director of testing could provide this service.

After the tentative selection of all the tests to be used in the program has been made, the totality should be examined critically to determine how much new and different information one is getting from each of the tests. One of the most common faults of school testing programs is redundancy. That is, time and money are invested in two or more tests that really get the same information from the same students at the same point in time. For example, a plan for testing ninth-grade students in February using both the *Differential Aptitude Test* (*DAT*) and a general intelligence test is inefficient and redundant. The combined scores from the Verbal Reasoning test and the Numerical Ability test of the *DAT* yield about the same information as that obtained from the general intelligence test. Since much more information can be obtained from the *DAT* than from the general intelligence test, if time and funds permit giving the longer and more complete aptitude battery, the general intelligence test should be dropped. It is probable that some other kind of test, or a general ability test at some other point in the student's school career would add a greater amount of new and useful information. Thus one should look for gaps as well as duplication.

Frequency and Time of Testing

One of the decisions that need to be made in planning a testing program is how frequently the selected tests are to be given, in what grades, and at what time of the year. To some extent the time of year that a particular kind of test can be given is limited by the nature of the test. For example, if an achievement test in algebra is to be given to ninth-grade students, it only makes sense to give it after the students have completed the course of study. On the other hand, an achievement test covering the basic skills of learning can be administered at almost any time. In the previous section on priorities in a testing program, we have indicated our preferences for both grade placement of various kinds of tests and the time of the year for giving those tests. However, the decision should be made in terms of local uses to be made of the test results and the time that the information is needed.

When considering the grades in which the tests are to be given, the committee should also decide on the level of the test to be used and whether adjustments in level are to be made within a particular grade. For example, if an achievement test battery is planned for the beginning of the fifth grade, are all students in the fifth grade to be given the level of the test designed for that grade? If so, one can expect that students who are poor readers will answer very few questions and thus will be appraised inadequately. One would obtain a better appraisal of what such a student *can* do if we gave him a lower level test. If the testing situation permits, one might gain by grouping pupils for testing in accordance with their expected level of achievement, then test each such group with the level most appropriate for it, without regard for official grade labels. The problem becomes more acute when one has an ungraded organization in the school. In this kind of organization, one would want to determine the placement of the tests according to the instructional level of the student, not by the number of years he has been in school.

When planning for frequency of testing, overtesting should be avoided. Redundancy in testing is one form of overtesting. A second type of overtesting can be illustrated by elementary school testing programs that provide for administering an achievement battery in October and again in May in grades 2 through 6. It is difficult to justify such a heavy testing program. Certainly, the differences in scores obtained from tests given in May in one grade to those given the following October are likely to be meaningless, and the results from the May testing are obtained too late in the year to have much use for instructional or guidance purposes. A third type of overtesting is the administration of a general intelligence test in every year of the school program. In general, if the results of any test administered in the program are not used, then one is overtesting.

Test Scoring and Test Analysis

One aspect of the planning of a testing program is deciding how the tests are to be scored and what kinds of analyses are to be made. At the present time, many tests are published in consumable and in reusable editions. With the consumable edition, the student marks his answers on the test booklet, whereas with the reusable edition the student marks his answers on a separate answer sheet. If the tests are to be scored by outside agencies, either separate answer sheets or machine-scorable booklets must be used, otherwise scoring costs will be prohibitive.

As a rule, scoring by outside agencies is more accurate than scoring by classroom teachers. In addition, the basic scoring services offered by most agencies include class lists and averages and reports of building and system averages. For a small additional charge, one can also obtain a pressure sensitive label containing the scores for each student on all tests. The pressure sensitive label can be pressed on the student's cumulative record form to provide a permanent record. This not only saves clerical time but also is more accurate than transcription by a clerk. The scoring services offered by different test publishers vary somewhat; therefore, the publisher's catalogue for the tests selected for use should be consulted.

Many classroom teachers feel that children are penalized when they have to use answer sheets, particularly the densely packed answer sheets such as MRC and Digitek. Studies (Dizney et al, 1966; Hayward, 1967; Miller, 1965; Slater, 1964) reveal no consistent differences in scores on unspeeded tests for students in grades 4 through 9, using different kinds of answer sheets. One study (Clark, 1968) showed slight but statistically significant differences between marking on the test booklet and using a separate answer sheet for slow-learning students, age 11 through 16. It is important to determine whether separate answer sheets were used in normative testing for a test, because norms will be strictly applicable only if local procedures conform to those used in the normative testing.

Setting Policy on Reporting Results

When the results of the school testing program become available, one must have a policy on who will receive reports of the results and how these results will be reported. In elementary and secondary schools, no disagreements are likely to arise on making the results of standardized achievement tests available to all professional personnel in the school, but some disagreement does exist on whether classroom teachers should have free access to intelligence test results. Since the results of intelligence tests are useful in planning learning activities for students and for helping to diagnose student difficulties in learning, it seems illogical to withhold such information from the classroom teacher who has major responsibilities for these functions. The reason given in a number of schools that withhold intelligence test results from teachers is that they misuse the results. If this is indeed the case, then the constructive action would be to plan in-service activities to improve the teacher's competence in interpreting and using the results, rather than to withhold the information.

A more important issue in reporting test results is whether students and parents should receive information about their performance on standardized tests. A survey (Goslin, 1967) on school policy for reporting results of standardized achievement tests and intelligence tests to parents and students showed that policies varied according to type of test and level of school. At the elementary school level, 80 percent or more of the schools reported having a policy of interpreting the results of standardized achievement tests to parents and students, but only 15 to 20 percent of the schools in the survey made it a policy to report actual scores. On the other hand, almost two-thirds of the elementary schools stated that intelligence test results were never reported to students, although an interpretation of the results could be given to parents if they requested the information. At the secondary level, information on test results tended to be more frequently reported to both parents and students than in elementary school, but again the policy appeared to be to give information only when the parent and student requested it. Secondary schools, like elementary schools, appeared to be reluctant to give either parents or students information on results of intelligence or aptitude tests. The same survey showed that teachers and counselors did not think that students and parents should be given the results of standardized testing whereas nearly two-thirds of the students in the secondary schools in the survey and 61 percent of the parents of elementary school children thought that the schools should report the results of standardized tests to them routinely.

Our opinion is that everyone concerned with or about the student should routinely receive some type of information about his performance on all kinds of standardized tests. To us, the question is not whether everyone should receive information, but how to give the information in such a way that it can be understood and used constructively by all concerned. We shall consider ways of doing this in a later section. The planning committee should decide on the policy and make plans to see that the policy is implemented.

A third aspect of policy to be considered is whether the results of the testing program for the system as a whole are to be reported routinely to lay groups. There are various groups in any community who may be potential audiences; for example, Parent-Teacher Associations, the Board of Education, the general community that supports the schools by paying taxes, and groups with special interests. Decisions about reporting to these kinds of groups are usually made at a high administrative level, but since all school personnel have a vested interest in the picture of school accomplishments being presented to these groups and since they are also frequently called on to interpret or explain the reasons for the results, the making of policy regarding how and to whom such reports shall be made should be the responsibility of a group with widely based representation.

LOGISTICS OF SCHOOL TESTING PROGRAM

Carrying out a program of testing throughout a school system is a fairly complex undertaking. If the testing is to proceed smoothly, and if standard testing conditions are to be maintained, a certain amount of advance planning is needed. The necessary tests and accessory materials need to be ordered and distributed to separate schools and classes. Supplementary local instructions need to be prepared and distributed. Detailed schedules for testing need to be prepared and distributed. Testers and proctors must be trained. Detailed arrangements for scoring the tests or collecting the tests for scoring must be made. In-service education activities must be planned for teachers who need help in the interpretation and use of the results. Reports of the results need to be prepared and submitted to various groups. Some of the more important issues in carrying out a testing program are discussed in the sections that follow.

Scheduling of Tests

After the original decision has been reached as to what tests are to be given, in which grades they are to be given, and at what time of the year they are to be given, an exact testing schedule must be worked out. The schedule for testing should be made available at the beginning of the year to all classroom teachers and other school personnel so that other school activities will not be planned for the same time. Tests should probably not be scheduled immediately before or after a major school holiday such as Christmas. If testing is to be done in the fall, it probably should not be scheduled before the third or fourth week of the session especially in elementary school.

The schedule should permit regrouping of children for testing. We have mentioned previously that it is desirable to administer a level of a test that is at an appropriate difficulty level for the student. For example, in the fifth-grade classes in a school system, there may be students for whom a third-grade level of a test might be most appropriate or others for whom a sixth-grade level might be most appropriate. Out-of-grade testing is highly desirable in these situations and the schedule should provide for it. If the program requires testing of kindergarten or beginning first-grade students, the schedule should provide for dividing the total class into small groups of not more than ten to fifteen students to provide the best testing conditions.

The most fundamental concerns in scheduling are that tests be given under standard conditions and that these conditions permit each examinee to perform at his best level. Thus, any unit of time scheduled for testing should be long enough to permit administration of a complete test, including a realistic allowance for distributing and collecting papers and for giving instructions. The novice is likely not to realize how much time is required beyond the basic testing time. Testing schedules should not be made too tight.

When more than a single test is to be given, however, as in the case of standardized aptitude or achievement test batteries, it is undesirable to give too many of the tests in one day or at a single sitting. For younger children especially, a break should be provided between parts of the test, and the program of testing should be divided into several segments and spread over several days. A number of the manuals for test batteries suggest ways in which the total testing time can be divided advantageously for children at different age levels. The purpose of the spread-out schedule is, of course, to minimize loss of interest and effort especially on the part of young children and of children who find the tests somewhat difficult and frustrating.

Secondary to the above considerations are those of economy and administrative convenience. Economy is achieved by re-using the same test booklets several times. When tests with separate answer sheets are to be used in several classes, a fairly complex testing schedule may be necessary in order to permit this re-use. (This schedule should provide some time for screening out booklets that have been marked up by examinees.) Greater flexibility of scheduling will be possible if the tests are purchased as separates, rather than bound together in a single booklet, because one class can use one part of the battery while some other class is using another part.

In departmentalized schools with class periods of a fixed length, it is administratively convenient if a unit of testing fits into a single class period. Many test publishers have taken account of this in designing their tests. However, this type of convenience should not be permitted to distort or interrupt the administration of any test. Enough time should be provided to permit the completion of a test at a single sitting. If the program of testing is worth doing, it is worth the upsetting of administrative routines.

Planning for Testing of Absentees

Whenever tests are scheduled over several days, one runs into the problem of students who are absent from one or more of the testing sessions. Some provision should be made for testing these absentees at other times, so that the data on students will be as complete as possible.

Preparation of Students for Testing

Advanced preparation of students for testing has as its objectives (1) establishing optimum motivation and cooperation during testing and (2) assuring that students are familiar with the procedures for the test, so that they will not be handicapped by novel and unfamiliar procedures.

Optimum motivation is that which results in serious and sustained effort without undue anxiety and tension. Because of wide pupil differences, it is not possible to achieve this ideal with every examinee. However, some advance explanation of and discussion about the tests may help to achieve it. The attitude should be conveyed that the tests are genuinely important, but not a desperate "life-or-death" matter. Constructive uses of the test results for individual guidance and educational adaptation can well be stressed. The older the students, the more complete the advance briefing that can profitably be given to them.

Since tests are designed to measure aptitudes and achievements rather than the tricks and skills of test-taking, it is desirable that all examinees have an opportunity to get acquainted with the general character of the test items and the mechanics of testing in advance. Some of the large-scale testing agencies, such as the Educational Testing Service and the Educational Records Bureau, prepare for distribution to examinees leaflets that describe the tests and give sample items. A school system might find it profitable to prepare similar practice materials for its own testing program.

When separate answer sheets are to be used by students for the first time, it may help to give advance practice with the mechanics of the answer sheet. The teacher might provide a similar answer sheet to be used with one of his own tests, or with sample items prepared to resemble those of the test itself.*

Environment for Testing

The desirable environment for testing is one in which examinees are (1) physically comfortable and emotionally relaxed, (2) free from interruptions and distractions, (3) conveniently able to manipulate their test materials, and (4) sufficiently separated to minimize tendencies to copy from one another.

The conditions of lighting and ventilation for testing should be at least as good as those maintained for teaching in a normal classroom. Especially for young children, the familiar surroundings of their own classrooms are to be preferred to those of cafeterias or auditoriums, where crowding and lack of good conditions for writing and for handling test materials may also be problems.

Casual interruptions in the classroom can be minimized by a "Test in progress—Do not disturb" sign on the door. Arrangements should be made with the school administration to suspend fire drills, public address announcements and, insofar as possible, bells and other unrelated signals during a period when testing is being carried out in one or more classes. Other steps to minimize delays and distractions include (1) seeing either that each examinee has an extra pencil, or that spare pencils are readily available, (2) making sure that children (especially young ones) have had a chance to visit the toilet before testing starts, and (3) providing clear instructions as to what to do for those examinees who finish their work completely before the time limit is up.

To be able to manipulate test materials conveniently, the examinee should have a desk or table on which to write, and enough room so that he can spread both the test and the answer sheet out before him. Working in chairs, perhaps with a lap-board, in an auditorium or gymnasium is far from ideal, especially if tests are speeded so that delays in paper-handling can lower the score of the examinee.

The problem of proctoring an examination (and sometimes of maintaining order) is made a good deal easier if desks or seats are well separated.

Selection and Preparation of Test Administrators

The administration of most group tests is simple enough so that any teacher should be able to handle it satisfactorily after a little special preparation and practice. However, some schools may find it more convenient administratively to have this function discharged by special personnel from the guidance staff

* Special practice materials are available from some publishers of standardized tests.

or from the school psychologist's office. No matter who administers the tests, all prospective administrators should have some in-service training with the specific tests that are to be used. The training has the objectives of (1) making the examiners thoroughly familiar with the tests and test manual and (2) standardizing procedures with respect to certain recurring problems and questions that frequently arise.

One worthwhile familiarization experience for examiners is "giving the test" to each other, that is, by reading the directions aloud exactly as they are given in the manual, and raising questions with one another. Taking the tests, at least in part, is another way of anticipating problems that are likely to arise in giving them. A few of the issues that are likely to arise in assuring standard and optimum testing conditions are the following:

VERBATIM DIRECTIONS. The examiner must understand that the directions in the manual for giving the test must be read verbatim. The examiner should not paraphrase the directions, add anything to them, or leave anything out. Studies on the effects of altering directions of a test (Lamb, 1967; Yamamoto and Dizney, 1965) have shown that changes in directions have differential effects on student performance. Changes from the published directions violate the standard conditions of the test and may invalidate the norms.

ANSWERING QUESTIONS. The principle to guide the examiner in answering student questions is that the student should have a clear understanding of what he is supposed to do. He should not be confused by the mechanics of testing or at a loss as to what the nature of the test is. Therefore, before testing starts, the examiner should use his best efforts to make the procedures and the task clear. He can repeat or paraphrase instructions, go over the practice examples, and, possibly, even supplement them. He should encourage questions at this point, and make every effort to clear up any misunderstandings.

Once a specific test starts, questions should be discouraged. Obviously, no help may be given on specific items, and no cues should be provided as to whether a pupil's answer is right or wrong. Questions on general procedure can be dealt with by repeating or paraphrasing the directions, but when a child expresses perplexity on a specific item he must be stalled off with "I'm sorry. I can't answer that. Do the best you can. If you get stuck go on to the next item."

TIMING. If the test has sections with very short time limits, that is, one or two minutes, each examiner should be provided with a stopwatch. For other tests, a watch with a second hand will suffice. When using an ordinary watch, a written record should be made of the exact time that a subtest was started and of the time that it is to stop, so that timing will not be thrown off by memory lapses. A simple homemade form will facilitate such recording.

PROCTORING. The examiner should circulate around the room, especially when a new subtest is being started, to check on the work of the examinees. He should check to make sure that each student is working on the correct pages, and that he is marking his responses in the proper place if a separate answer sheet is being used. Individual children may need to be encouraged to keep working or to go back and check their work.

Centralized Administration

Some schools attempt to obtain uniformity in administration of tests through the use of closed circuit television or the school intercommunication system. Hopkins et al (1967) described an experiment in the use of closed circuit television for testing fifth and sixth grade classes. They found that for large classes (55–90 pupils) the television administration resulted in higher mean scores, but for the regular size classes (20–35 pupils) teacher administered tests yielded higher scores. The differences between the two modes of administration were only about 0.2 of a grade equivalent.

Although one does gain uniformity in administration through highly centralized procedures, the gain is obtained through loss of flexibility in dealing with emergency or special situations in the classroom. No opportunity is provided to give extra instruction to slow groups on the procedures for handling test materials. If highly centralized administration of tests is done in a school system, it becomes very important to give adequate preparation to the students before testing.

Scoring

Most schools buy test scoring services, but sometimes tests are scored by classroom teachers. If the scoring is done by classroom teachers, adequate controls should be set up to insure that it is done accurately. Errors are particularly likely to creep into such operations as subtracting a correction for errors, adding part scores to make a total score, and going from raw to converted scores. It is especially important to check these steps. Surveys have repeatedly indicated the inaccuracy of teachers in scoring tests. If at all possible, the school system will find it advantageous to buy scoring services since these will produce more accurate results and be less expensive in the long run.

Recording Results of Tests

Since one of the purposes of a school testing program is to build a cumulative picture of the student's development as he progresses through school, all test results for a student should be recorded on a permanent record card. The simplest and easiest way to keep a record of a student's performance on tests is to buy the test scoring services that provides a pressure sensitive label reporting his scores. With these labels, one needs only to provide space on the cumulative record card for pressing on the labels. The space should provide for keeping the results of tests of the same type together; that is, all achievement test labels in one section, all general intelligence test results in another section, and all specialized aptitude tests in another section. Samples of pressure sensitive labels are shown in Fig. 16.1 on page 546.

If the school does not purchase such a scoring service, then all of the information shown on the label should be entered on the permanent record card.

Checking on Discrepant Results

There are a number of ways that systematic errors can occur in test results. When administering a test, the examiner can make a mistake in timing and give either less or more time than the instructions allow. When using tests in the multilevel format, students can be given wrong answer sheets or started in the wrong place. If tests are scored locally, gross errors can be made in counting the number right or in using a correction formula for arriving at the score. The wrong table can be used for transforming raw scores to converted scores or the table can be read incorrectly. For these reasons, all test results should be examined carefully for consistency and reasonableness before they are used.

A test may be inconsistent with others given at the same time, as when a student who has consistently scored two or more years above his grade placement on all parts of an achievement battery obtains an IQ of 80 on a group intelligence test. Instead of blithely labeling him an "overachiever," one should make sure that there were no gross errors in administering, scoring, or recording the intelligence test result. A test may be inconsistent with results from an earlier test of the same type, as when a student who had gotten an IQ of 130 on an intelligence test in the fifth grade receives an IQ of 90 on the same test in the seventh grade. Results of a test can be inconsistent for a whole class as when one fifth-grade class shows a marked drop in reading test scores both in terms of their fourth-grade scores and in terms of other similar fifth grades in the system. Such a result for a whole class usually indicates some serious error in the administration of the test.

A list should be made of all cases showing seriously discrepant results and these should be carefully checked. The papers should be rescored to make sure that the scoring is accurate. Computations and reading of norm tables involved in obtaining converted scores should be verified. Transcription of these scores

THE LORGE-THORNDIKE INTELLIGENCE TESTS NAME OF PUPIL	SEX	GRADE	DATE OF BIRTH		AGE	
			MONTH	YEAR	YEARS	MONTHS
Schnauzer, Gustav	M	10	11	51	15	10

LORGE-THORNDIKE VERBAL						LORGE-THORNDIKE NON-VERBAL						TOTAL I.Q.
RAW SCORE	I.Q.	GRADE %-ILE	AGE EQUIV.		GRADE EQUIV.	RAW SCORE	I.Q.	GRADE %-ILE	AGE EQUIV.		GRADE EQUIV.	
			YRS.	MOS.					YRS.	MOS.		
065	121	91	18	06	121	53	124	94	18	06	124	123

THE IOWA TESTS OF BASIC SKILLS NAME OF PUPIL	GR	V VOCABULARY		R READING		L-1 SPELLING		L-2 CAPITAL-IZATION		L-3 PUNCTU-ATION		L-4 USAGE		L TOTAL LANGUAGE	
		GE	PR	GE	PR	GE	PR	GE	PR	GE	PR	GE	PR	GE	PR
	3	41		34		40		33		26		41		35	
Schnauzer, Gustav	S		62		41		57		39		18		58		43

THE IOWA TESTS OF BASIC SKILLS NAME OF PUPIL	GR	W-1 MAPS		W-2 GRAPHS		W-3 REFER-ENCES		W TOTAL WORK-STUDY		A-1 CONCEPTS		A-2 PROBLEMS		A TOTAL ARITHMETIC		C COMPOSITE	
		GE	PR	GE	PR	GE	PR	GE	PR	GE	PR	GE	PR	GE	PR	GE	PR
	3	40		27		30		32		39		32		36		36	
Schnauzer, Gustav	S		60		21		26		33		56		33		47		48

THE IOWA TESTS OF BASIC SKILLS

Fig. 16.1 Samples of pressure sensitive labels.

should be checked. If no error is found in any of these steps, it may be desirable to refer the student for retesting with another form of the suspect test before a permanent record is made of the result.

PRESENTING THE RESULTS OF TESTING TO THE PUBLIC

We believe that a school or school system will get the maximum return from its investment in a program of standardized tests if the results of testing are reported to all persons or groups of persons who need the information. In any community, there are a number of groups to whom test results could be reported. First, there are the individual students and their parents. Second, there are the staff in the schools who have responsibility for instruction, curriculum, administration, and pupil personnel services. Third, there are official lay bodies such as the Board of Education that have responsibility for setting overall policy both in educational and budgetary matters. Fourth, there are special interest groups such as Parent-Teacher Associations whose support the school system wants. Fifth, there is the general public whose taxes and votes support the schools. Test results are reported to these various groups in order to achieve different goals; the groups differ in sophistication with reference both to education and to educational testing; and they differ from each other in the kinds of information that they need. However, in spite of these differences and whatever the audience, the general purpose of the report should be to summarize, organize, and interpret the test results so that a meaningful picture of the school's or the individual's accomplishments will emerge.

Reporting the Results of a Program of Testing

Before one can plan effective procedures for reporting the results of a program to any group, one must be very clear just what it is that one wants to communicate. What are the specific questions that one is attempting to answer through the use of test data? An explicit statement of these questions can help to make clear the ways in which the test data need to be analyzed and reported.

The general question "How well do students in each grade of our schools perform in relation to the national normative sample?" requires only a tabulation of all scores within a grade on each test and the computation of some kind of average score. This average score can then be compared to the national norms for building or system averages. On the other hand, if one asks "How effective have our curricular efforts been for students of different intelligence levels and different socioeconomic levels?" one must first group the students in each grade by socioeconomic level and within socioeconomic levels by the level of performance on an intelligence test. Within each subgroup, achievement scores will be tabulated, and average scores computed. Finally, one will have to search out some normative data for similar subgroups of pupils, and display the data for one's own school in comparison with this reference group.

Most of the questions that are likely to be asked involve various types of comparisons. Some of the kinds of comparisons that may be of significance are:

1. Comparisons of local group performance with national norms or more specialized norms.
2. Comparisons of local group performance on achievement tests with the level of performance on intelligence tests.
3. Comparison of achievement in different subject matter areas.
4. Comparison of the effectiveness of the school program with students of different racial, socioeconomic, or ability characteristics.
5. Comparison of different schools in the system or of different class groups within a school.
6. Comparison of groups that were taught in different ways or that had different curricula.
7. Comparison of the same group of individuals at different grade levels.
8. Comparison of groups at different grade levels within a school or school system.

The kinds of analyses that can be done of test results are limited by the types of comparison data that are available for the test and by the number of students in the grade or system who have certain characteristics. For example, a director of testing might want to compare the average score of each grade in his school system to other schools of similar ability and socioeconomic level in the nation. To accomplish this, he would need national norms of building averages by average intelligence and socioeconomic level of the building. In 1968, there were no such norms for any achievement test. Or suppose that a particular school wants to look at its achievement test results for each grade separately by ability level, but has in each grade only 5 to 10 students who fall below an IQ of 100 on the intelligence test that it uses. A separate analysis based on a sample size of 5 to 10 is likely to be so unstable as to be meaningless, so the ability range over which this analysis would be possible in this school would be quite limited.

The results of a program of testing may be presented either as written reports or orally. Most school systems will find it advantageous to use both methods, preparing a written report for permanent reference and using oral reports for effective communication with most groups. Important results should be presented in both tabular and graphic form. For each class and school or subgroup that one is interested in, scores will need to be tallied separately for each significant subtest. The scores useful in answering most questions will ordinarily be converted scores; that is, grade scores, standard scores, or percentiles for a particular grade group. If scores are to be compared across subtests, percentiles or standard scores that have comparable meanings across tests should be used instead of grade scores. Average scores (mean or median) will need to be obtained for each group. However, the simple average provides limited information, so for a more complete picture of the results, some measure of variability such as the standard deviation or the semi-interquartile range should also be computed. When reporting to school personnel, one might compute the 10th, 25th, 75th, and 90th percentiles in addition to the median so as to provide a more complete picture of the performance of the group. All of these will have to be organized in both tabular and graphic form.

Good graphic representation can facilitate understanding of the test results but one must guard against distorting the data in graphs in such a way that they lead to incorrect interpretation. The most common form of distortion comes from showing only part of the vertical scale. By doing this, it is sometimes possible to expand a part of the scale so that quite small differences appear to be quite large. One should also try to keep graphs as simple as possible; putting too many different things on one graph only confuses the audience. Illustrations of graphs representing different kinds of test data are shown in Figs. 16.2 through 16.6.

Figure 16.2 shows the median level of achievement for grades 3 through 7 for the Centreville school system. This graph makes it particularly easy to compare grades on each subject area, but it also permits comparisons across subject areas for a single grade group. Such a graph would be suitable for showing any type of audience how the average performance in each grade of this school compares to national norms for building averages. It is particularly suitable for lay audiences. To construct a graph of this type that presents an accurate picture, one needs to have norms for building averages. We are displaying averages for our school, and they should be compared with averages from other schools. Figure 16.3 shows the median performance of the same seventh grade compared to general national norms for individuals and to national norms for individuals who scored at the same IQ level as the average for this seventh grade. Comparison of Figs. 16.2 and 16.3 on pages 550 and 551 with respect to the height of the bars on each test brings out the effect of using norms for individuals rather than for system averages. Although both graphs show that this seventh grade performs above average on all tests, only Fig. 16.2 accurately shows how far the typical per-

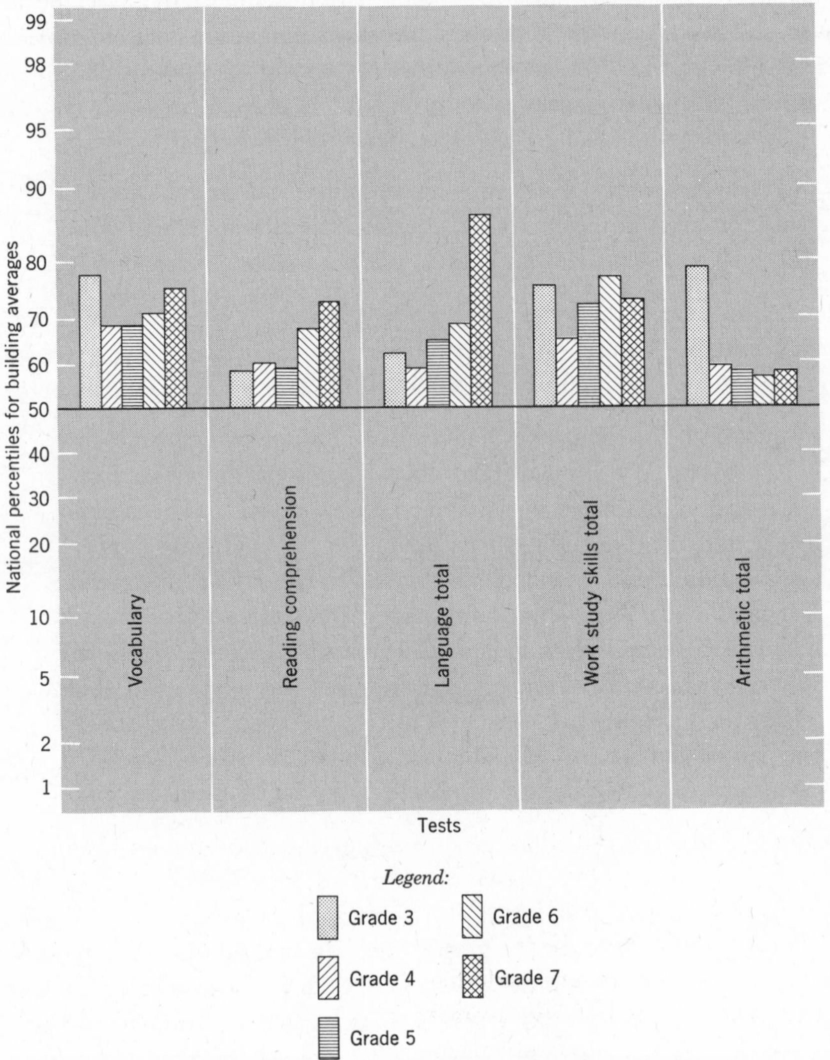

Fig. 16.2 Centreville median achievement by subject area and grade level in comparison to national norms for system averages (Iowa Tests of Basic Skills, given October 1968).

formance of this seventh grade surpasses the national norm for average scores of seventh-grade classes. Yet, since there are no norms for building averages by intelligence levels for the test used in this system, Fig. 16.3 has some value despite its limitations. First, it focuses attention on the fact that this seventh grade should be expected to perform above the national average. Second, it draws attention to the relatively poor performance of the group on arithmetic in relation to other seventh grade students with similar intelligence test scores.

Figure 16.4 on page 553 shows another way of comparing level of achievement and level of intelligence. In this school system, the *Stanford Achievement Tests* (1964) edition) and the *Otis Intelligence Test, Beta* were given to all seventh-grade classes. The graph shows the performance in reading comprehension by the middle half of those seventh graders who obtained scores at each stanine level

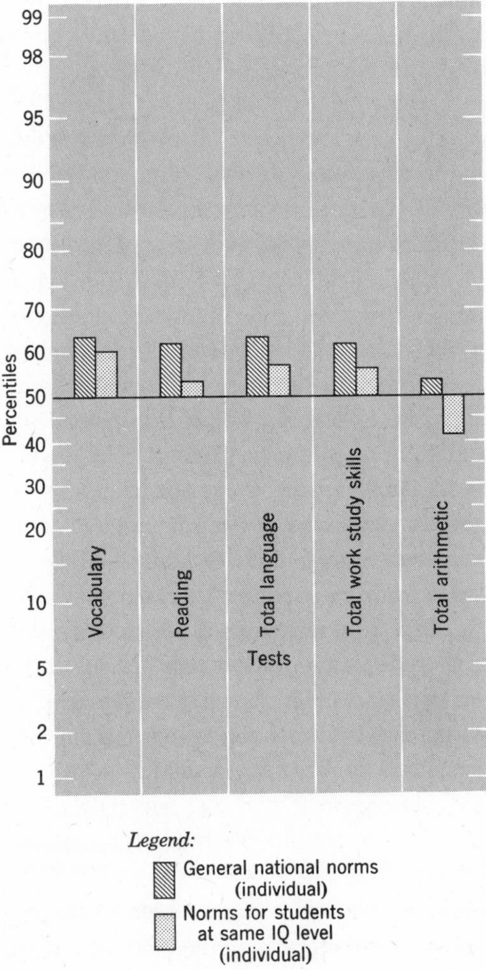

Fig. 16.3 Achievement of median seventh grade Centreville student in relation to general national norms and in relation to norms for students of same IQ level (Iowa Tests of Basic Skills, given October 1968)

on the intelligence test. This type of graph is particularly valuable for presentation to school personnel because it shows quite clearly that the reading program in the school was not as effective as it could be for students who fell at the sixth stanine or below on the intelligence test.

Figures 16.5 and 16.6 on pages 554 and 555 illustrate one way of presenting a picture of both typical performance and range of performance of a group. In these graphs, the bars representing achievement extend from the 10th percentile to the 90th percentile. The performance of the middle fifty percent is shown by the broad portion of the bar and the median is indicated by a horizontal line across the broad bar. The amount of detail in the graph makes it more suitable for school personnel than for most lay groups. Figure 16.5 permits comparisons among subtests for the seventh grade and Fig. 16.6 shows the performance of the same group of students in spelling from the second through the seventh grades.

It is perhaps worth emphasizing here that the test results brought out in any set of graphs and tables constitute only raw facts, not meaningful interpretations or conclusions. These interpretations must be supplied by the educator who is acquainted with the circumstances surrounding the test scores. Thus, if little emphasis is given to arithmetical computation in the school system for which seventh grade results are presented in Fig. 16.5, one would not expect high performance. If a school gives little emphasis to a particular skill in an early grade, but increases its emphasis on that skill in later grades, low achievement at an early grade should be expected; the school should present the analyses of the test data across grades, as was done in Fig. 16.6, to show whether the expected improvement in achievement does occur in the later grades. On the other hand, school teachers and administrators need to face frankly those situations where they have been less successful than they expected to be or wished they were. Many schools find it particularly difficult to make known results such as those shown in Fig. 16.5. The school from which these results were taken had a median stanine of 4 on the *Otis Intelligence Test*. Such a school may try to explain away the results on the basis that the average ability level of its seventh grade students is below that of the national normative sample. However, Fig. 16.4 shows that even when the level of ability is taken into account, the test results in reading are still poor on the whole, and similar analyses for arithmetic would probably show a similar picture. Some schools faced with such test results are tempted to bury the reports deep in a file so that they will never be seen or even to discontinue their standardized achievement testing program. Neither action is constructive; the problem of teaching the students to read is still there. Instead, the results should serve as a stimulus to determine why such results were obtained. The personnel in the school could seek answers to such questions as: Do we have a highly mobile student body? Are the quantity and quality of

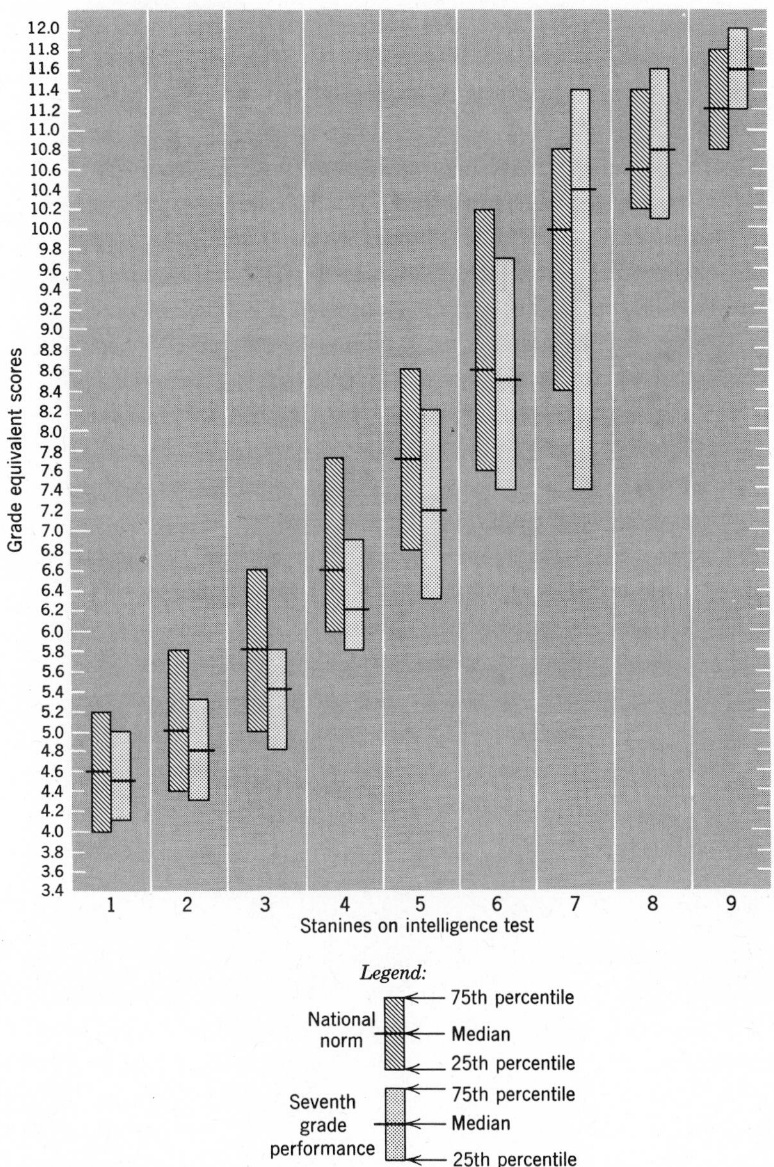

Fig. 16.4 Comparison of performance on Reading Achievement Test by level of performance on Intelligence Test for Easton seventh grade (Advanced Battery). (Stanford Achievement Tests, 1964 Edition, given October 1968.)

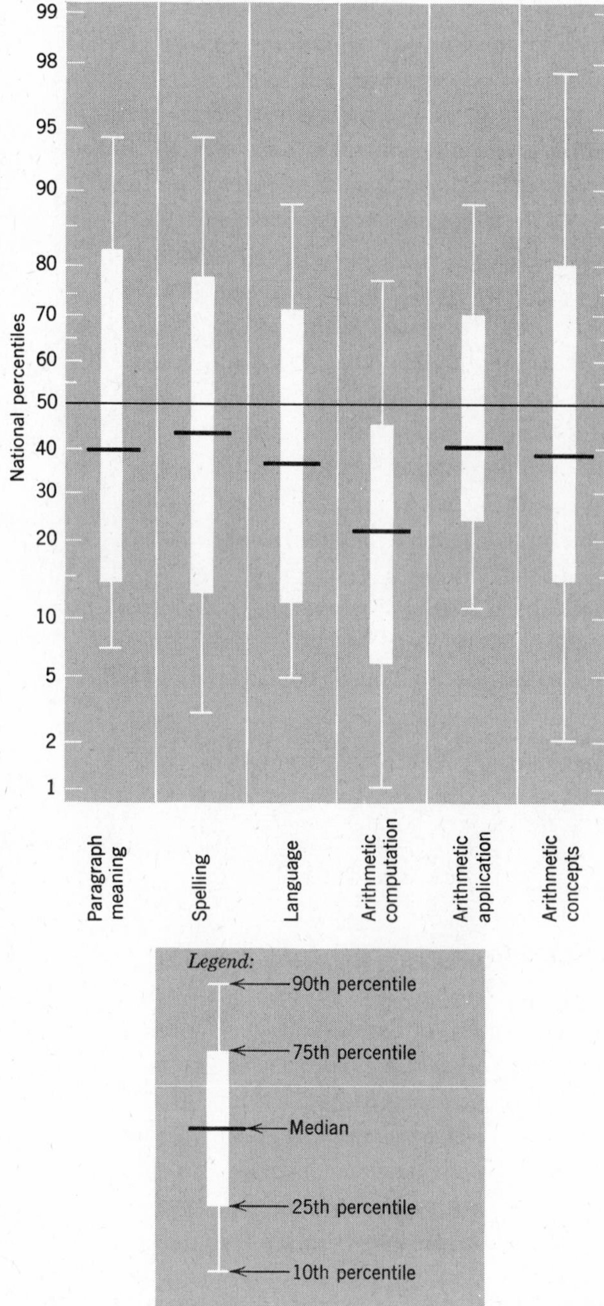

Fig. 16.5 Median achievement and range of achievement in Easton seventh grade in comparison with national norms (Stanford Achievement Tests, 1964 Edition, given in October 1968).

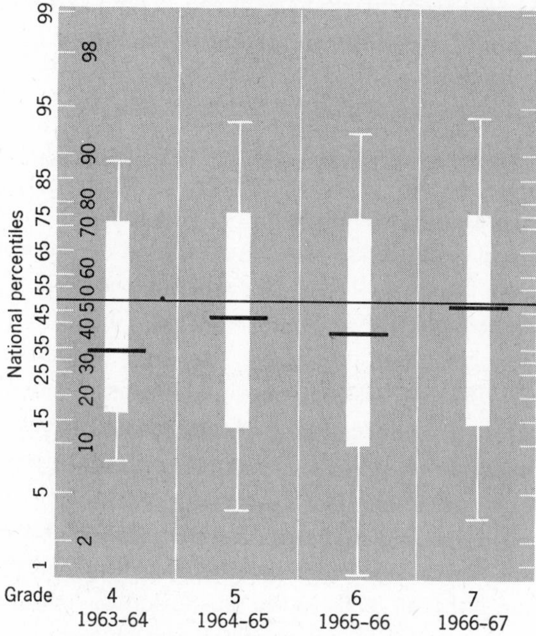

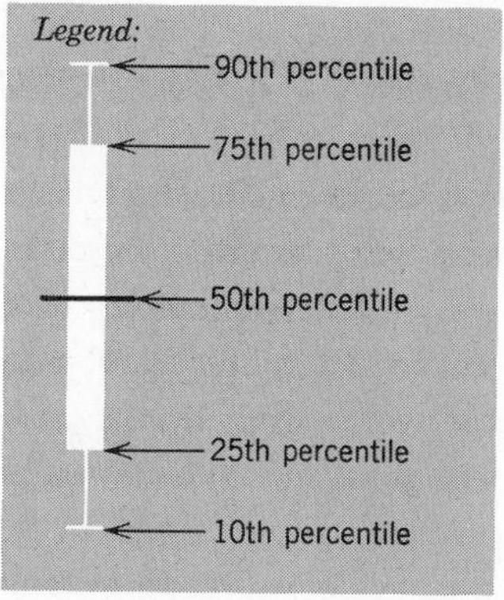

Fig. 16.6 Achievement of same students in grade 4 (1963–64) through grade 7 (1966–67)—spelling.

instructional materials for reading adequate for the kinds of students we have? Do the classroom teachers get enough help from supervisors and reading specialists? How much instructional time in reading does each child in each grade receive? Are class sizes too large for the teacher to provide for individual differences?

Item analysis data are particularly helpful to a school system in understanding the strengths and weaknesses of its program. These could be used to help the educator interpret the test results.

Reporting Test Results for the Individual

We have indicated in a previous section of the chapter that we believe that the individual student and his parents are entitled to information about the student's performance on any test that he takes in school. The problem, then, is to decide how the performance is to be reported. Should actual scores be reported or only an interpretation of scores?

The question can perhaps best be answered by asking two other questions. Given that no test has perfect accuracy, how precisely does it make sense to report scores? What information does the parent or pupil need in order to have an accurate picture of the situation or to reach a sound decision? The answer to the first question will lead to the conclusion that the accuracy of our measures permits reporting only in categories or bands, not in terms of precise scores. The answer to the second question leads to the conclusion that the student and parent need a sound *interpretation* of the score which can be better provided by school personnel than by the parent or student.

The counselor or teacher giving the interpretation must decide what frame of reference is to be used. One can use the individual as a frame of reference and interpret scores as being high, low, or intermediate in relation to the individual's other performances. Consider the following grade equivalent scores obtained by two girls on the *Iowa Tests of Basic Skills* in October of the seventh grade.

Test	*Nancy G.*	*Katrinka K.*
Vocabulary	4.6	8.5
Reading	4.6	8.5
Total Language	5.7	9.8
Total Work Study Skill	6.3	10.2
Total Arithmetic	5.6	9.6

If the individual student is used as the reference point, the interpretation for both students would be something like this: "Nancy (or Katrinka) performed best on the Work Study Skills and least well on the Vocabulary and Reading tests. Her performance on the Language tests and Arithmetic tests fell somewhere between the others." Such an interpretation gives the impression that the two girls had very similar performances on the battery of tests, whereas they were quite different. Nancy is a low achiever, and Katrinka is a high achiever. Although it is desirable to bring out the strengths and weaknesses in an individual's performance, the intraindividual interpretation can be too misleading to serve as the only basis for interpreting scores for an individual.

Other frames of reference that can be used for interpreting scores are national norms, local norms, norms by ability level, or norms for special groups. Which of these will be most appropriate depends upon the purpose that one is trying to achieve. In a single conference with a student or parent, one might need to use all of them. For example, to give a sound interpretation as to what the score means in terms of progress in the local school situation, local norms should be used. To show the student or parent how the student compares to the general population of his age or grade group, national norms should be used. To help the student or his parent set reasonable levels of expected achievement, norms by ability level should be used. In other words, the interpretation should be set in whatever frame of reference is needed for a particular pupil.

Interpretations of test scores are best given in face-to-face conferences with the student or parent. However, it is desirable to have on hand a record of performance that can be given to the student or parent to keep. Many test publishers provide a record form that has been designed to be given to students or sent home to parents. These record forms vary considerably. The best ones provide a simple description of the nature and purposes of the tests, an explanation of how to interpret the reported scores, and some kind of profile for recording the student's scores. Almost all of them provide for reporting exact scores, usually percentiles or stanines. The personnel in a school should examine the published reporting form for the test it uses to decide whether it wants to report test results in that way.

A school could design a report form for its own students. Such a form should provide for reporting the student's standing on all important subtests of the test battery used and should provide information on the nature and purpose of the tests. Since scores are not perfectly exact and parents and pupils may tend to overinterpret exact scores, it seems better to have a form that displays scores in rather broad categories. Figure 16.7 on page 558 shows a type of report form that a school system could construct for its own use. In this form, scores are grouped into five categories: High—95th percentile or higher, Above Average—76th percentile to 94th percentile, Average—25th percentile to 75th percentile, Below Average —6th to 24th percentile, and Low—5th percentile or lower. Any test that has percentile norms can be entered on such a form. The student's standing on each test can be shown in relation to general national percentile norms, local percentile norms, or percentile norms by intelligence test score. The use of the report form can be illustrated by taking the record of Roy Dawkins, a fourth-grade student in

Name: Dawkins, Roy | Grade: 4

School: Centreville Elementary | Date Tested: April 1968

Score Category	Vocab-ulary	Read-ing	Spell-ing	Capital-ization	Punc-tuation	Usage	Maps	Graphs	Refer-ences	Arith. Con-cepts	Arith. Prob-lems	L-T Intelli-gence Test
High (95th percentile or higher)												
Above Average (76th percentile to 94th percentile)			N L I	N				N				N
Average (25th percentile to 75th percentile)	N	N		L I	N L I	N L I	N		N	N	N	L
Below Average (6th percentile to 24th percentile)	L I	L I					L I	L I	L I	L I	L I	
Low (5th percentile or below)												

Fig. 16.7 Report of Performance on Iowa Tests of Basic Skills (ITBS) and Lorge-Thorndike Intelligence Tests (L-T).
Key: N, standing in relation to national norms for 4th grade students.
L, standing in relation to 4th grade students in Centreville School system.
I, standing in relation to 4th grade students in national sample with similar intelligence test scores.

TABLE 16.3 TEST RESULTS FOR ROY DAWKINS

Test	Grade Equivalent	General National Percentile	Local Percentile	National Percentile by Intelligence Level
Vocabulary	4.4	41	19	21
Reading	4.4	42	22	16
Spelling	6.4	82	76	84
Capitalization	5.8	71	49	65
Punctuation	5.0	56	33	38
Usage	5.0	55	52	34
Maps	4.0	28	08	16
Graphs	4.4	40	20	23
References	4.1	31	17	17
Arithmetic Concepts	4.1	31	19	14
Arithmetic Problems	4.2	34	20	20
Lorge-Thorndike Intelligence Test (IQ = 112)	5.2	78	55	

the Centreville Elementary School who was given the *Iowa Tests of Basic Skills* and the *Lorge-Thorndike Intelligence Test* in April, 1968. His performance on the tests is shown in Table 16.3 in terms of grade equivalent scores, general national percentiles, local percentiles, and national percentiles by intelligence level.

Roy's scores have been entered on the record form by using *N* to indicate national percentile norms, *L* to indicate local percentile norms, and *I* to indicate ability level percentile norms. Of course, only one type of norm could have been used or a separate form could be used for entering each type of norm. The use of all three on the same form is advantageous if one wants to emphasize the differences in Roy's standing in relation to the three reference groups. Before holding a conference with Roy or his parents, the teacher or counselor should assemble available data on Roy's performance in the classroom and, if possible, examine his answer sheet on the achievement tests so that he will have more specific information on Roy's strengths and weaknesses.

The oral report should include a short explanation of the tests. The student or parent should be permitted to look at the record as the teacher or counselor gives the interpretation. The interpretation might be something like the following:

> Roy's aptitude for school work is somewhat better than average among fourth graders in the country as a whole but it is just about average among the fourth-grade students in the Centreville schools. We would predict that he would most

probably be somewhat above average in achievement when compared to a national sample of fourth graders but only about average in achievement among Centreville fourth graders. Let's see how Roy's achievement meets our expectation.

In vocabulary and reading, Roy is just about average according to national norms but is somewhat below average in the Centreville fourth grade. His achievement on these tests indicate that he is likely to have some difficulty in keeping up with his school work for the rest of this school year and in the fifth grade. Roy is a slow reader and has difficulty in getting the main idea of a passage and answering questions that are not specifically answered in the reading material. We plan to work intensively with Roy on these skills for the rest of the year. You can help at home by using opportunities to encourage him to learn and use new words and to read during his free time.

In spelling, Roy is somewhat above average in relation to the national norm group, Centreville fourth graders, and his ability level. His spelling is one of his strong points. His scores on the capitalization, punctuation, and usage tests are about average for his ability level and among Centreville fourth graders.

Although Roy's scores on map reading and use of references are average according to national norms and his score on graphs is above average in terms of national norms, he is somewhat below average on all of these tests among our fourth graders and lower than we would expect him to be according to his ability level. Mastery of the skills measured by these tests is important in our mathematics, science, social studies, and language programs. If Roy is to achieve satisfactorily in these programs, he must gain better mastery of these skills. We plan to form some small groups of students like Roy and give them special work on these skills. From time to time, we will be giving Roy some special exercises on these skills to be done at home. You can help by seeing that Roy does these.

On the two arithmetic tests, Roy's scores were about average on national norms but below average for our fourth-grade students and for his ability level. Roy is having difficulty with fundamental operations and needs more practice on number facts. We will work with Roy on these skills. You might try to encourage Roy to practice arithmetic skills at home by using natural situations that involve money or measurement.

In the sample interpretation we have tried to illustrate three qualities that an interpretation should have:

1. It should be set in the frame of reference of the particular student. Test scores should be interpreted in terms of what is known about the student's aptitude and about his educational or vocational goals.

2. It should be directed toward positive and constructive action. It should emphasize the assets in a test profile or it should be oriented toward remedial action when achievement falls below what aptitude would lead one to expect.

3. It should be factual and dispassionate, rather than appearing to pass judgment on the individual. Test results should be reported truthfully and accurately.

The flavor should be one of working with the student and his parents to realize common goals rather than one of passing judgment on him.

EXTERNAL TESTING PROGRAMS

Up to this point, the discussion of testing programs has been limited to those over which the local school system has full control. In planning its own testing program, a school should take into consideration the external testing programs that are under the control of agencies outside the local system. There are three types of external testing programs that involve large numbers of students in the elementary and secondary schools: (1) college admissions and placement programs, (2) national scholarship testing programs, and (3) state-mandated testing programs. Each of these will be discussed briefly in the sections that follow.

College Admissions and Placement Programs

The oldest of the college admissions testing programs is the one conducted by the College Entrance Examination Board (CEEB). The Board began in 1900 to administer entrance tests for a limited number of "Ivy League" colleges. Early tests were essay in character, but an objective *Scholastic Aptitude Test* was introduced in 1926, and subsequently the achievement tests were gradually converted to objective format. The volume of College Board testing increased slowly at first, but then more and more rapidly as the number of schools requiring the tests increased and the percent of young people aspiring to go to college mounted.

The College Entrance Examination Board administers its tests at testing centers all over the world. Papers are centrally scored, and the results reported to the colleges the individual has designated, to his school, and to the individual himself. Generally, these tests are taken by the student during his senior year in high school. However, there were always some who took the tests as juniors and in 1959–1960 the College Board formalized the *Preliminary Scholastic Aptitude Test* for administration to college-bound juniors in secondary schools for use in guidance and for early admission to college. Further information about the tests in the series can be obtained from the publications of the College Board.

A second and newer program for college admissions, designed for smaller and less selective colleges than those for which the College Board program was tailored, is the American College Testing Program. The battery for this program consists of four tests of general skills in English, Mathematics, Social Studies and Science, respectively. Tests are administered at centers spread over the United States. Further information about the program can be obtained from the American College Testing Program, Iowa City, Iowa.

Certain of the states also run programs for admission to state-operated colleges in that state. These vary considerably from state to state. Information about them can usually be obtained either from the major state university or the state Department of Education.

Finally, there are various programs for admission to graduate schools or professional schools. The most widely used admission tests for graduate schools are the *Graduate Record Examination* administered by the Educational Testing Service and the *Miller Analogies Test* administered by the Psychological Corporation. Special tests are used by professional schools in such fields as law, medicine, dentistry, and accountancy. Information about the relevant tests can usually be obtained from the national association of the profession, from the admissions office of a professional school, or from one of the agencies mentioned above.

The Advanced Placement program of the CEEB has been described in the section on college testing programs. Descriptions of the Advanced Placement Program and the tests can be obtained from the publications of the Board.

Testing Programs for Scholarship Awards

Testing programs used in connection with scholarship awards represent one special development of some interest. The need for these programs arises from the fact that substantial scholarship funds come from sources outside of any particular university—from foundations, industry, and federal and state governments—so that some general appraisal of applicants is needed not related to the programs or policies of any single institution. The most ambitious testing program of this type is the one administered by the National Merit Scholarship Corporation. Identification of "semifinalists" has been based on a test that as of 1968 resembled closely the *Iowa Tests of Educational Development*. Since it has been the policy of the Corporation that awards be prorated by states, in proportion to the number of high-school seniors, the standard to qualify as a semifinalist has varied fairly widely from one state to another. (It has also been the policy that the cash value of the award vary depending upon the financial status of the family.)

Final award of scholarships has been based upon performance on College Entrance Examination Board tests, and upon such other factors as the evaluating panels chose to consider.

Other less extensive scholarship testing services have been developed and offered to the public by the College Board, the Educational Testing Service, and the Psychological Corporation.

State-Mandated Testing Programs

A number of states have mandated that certain tests be given in particular grades throughout the state. Some of the states use published standardized tests for the mandated program but other states, such as New York, use tests that are constructed by the State Education Department. The statewide programs have usually been instituted to serve two purposes: (1) quality control; that is, to help determine the effectiveness of the educational programs in local communities; and (2) to provide information that would help the state to allocate either special state funds or federal funds under state control to the local school systems.

The typical pattern found in state-mandated programs is to require testing in certain specified grades. Generally, the tests used focus on the basic skills, although some, like the *New York State Regents Examinations,* are designed to appraise achievement in college preparatory type courses in grades 9 through 12.

CONCERNS ABOUT EXTERNAL TESTING PROGRAMS

External testing programs of all kinds have caused educators considerable concern. Although each of the external programs has been designed to serve a valid educational purpose, one may ask whether these purposes do not at times conflict with other purposes of the schools where the tests are administered. Concern of the educators about external testing programs focuses on the effect that the tests have on the student who has to take them and on the educational program of the school.

Some educators feel that students in the secondary school are required to take too many external tests and that the time spent on these tests could be better spent on regular school work. However, most of the external tests for college admission and placement or for scholarship awards are administered outside of the regular school time, usually on Saturdays. Students are likely to take, at most, two or three during a year. Although scheduling the tests may be a nuisance for school administrators—and testing agencies must give some consideration to this—the burden on the time of the student can scarcely be considered serious.

Since college admissions tests loom as an important obstacle to secondary school students seeking admission to college, teachers, counselors, and others have expressed concern over the effects of anxiety on the test scores. A number of studies (S. B. Sarason et al, 1960; I. G. Sarason, 1961) have found statistically significant negative correlations between scores on test anxiety and scores on other tests. The negative correlations found in such studies do not, of course, indicate a direct causal relationship. One does not know just from the correlation whether high levels of anxiety caused the low test scores or whether previous low test scores caused the present high level of anxiety. French (1962) compared the performance of high school students on the CEEB *Scholastic Aptitude Test* under anxiety-arousing and relaxed conditions. He found that performance was essentially the same under the two conditions and that the concurrent validity of the test, as shown by correlation with high school grades, was just about the same under the two conditions.

A third concern, again related to college admissions testing, arises from pressure from students and parents for the school to set up programs for coaching students for the tests. The College Entrance Examination Board (1968) has sponsored or conducted a number of studies on the effects of coaching. The conclusion from the studies is that coaching is unlikely to produce appreciable gains on the test. This, however, will probably not prevent some schools and pupils from continuing to spend time trying to "beat the test."

A fourth concern stems from the feeling that college admissions testing programs are unfair or biased against minority groups. The studies that have considered this issue (Cleary, 1968; Munday, 1965; Stanley, 1967) show that the accuracy of prediction of college success using either the CEEB tests or ACT is about the same or higher for Negroes as for whites.

The fifth concern is that the external tests may pervert the educational program of the school, because the tests come to control the curriculum and the teachers focus on preparing for the tests. This problem is most likely to arise when the external tests are concerned with specific segments of the school curriculum, as is the case with the *New York State Regents Examinations.* Since the performance of student, teacher, and school are all judged to some extent by performance on the tests, they may assume a disproportionate importance. Anyone acquainted with secondary schools in New York State knows of classes that spend weeks, even months, in review of past Regents Examinations. One can certainly question whether this is the most rewarding investment of time for student and teacher.

Even when the test is less closely tied to the curriculum, the test may affect it through what the test does and does not emphasize. Thus, it has been argued that the relatively small role for actual writing in recent English tests of the

College Board has reinforced a tendency to reduce the number and variety of compositions called for in high school English courses, and has thus strengthened an undesirable trend. Certainly, it is important that external testing programs present desirable models, emphasizing the important goals of education and not distorting the pattern of the school program. When the testing programs deal with achievements of a nature sufficiently broad and basic so that they go beyond specific courses and course objectives, the danger of an unfavorable impact seems reduced.

In spite of the concerns that educators may have about the external testing programs, these programs are likely to be around for a long time. The schools should try to plan their own testing programs in such a way that they can maximize the potential usefulness of the external tests for their own students and for their own programs.

SUMMARY

Our central theme in this chapter has been that tests are given to be used and that uses are determined by local needs. An effective school testing program is related to local needs and helps build a continuous picture of the students' development from kindergarten through grade 12.

Table 16.1 summarizes the variety of functions that tests are often called upon to serve. Discussion of these functions may guide a local group in defining their purposes in testing. Planning for a school testing program and setting up policies related to it should be done by a committee that has representation from all levels of school personnel, but one person, the director of testing, should be assigned overall supervision for the program. Suggested priorities for a testing program for elementary and secondary schools and for colleges were given. These were summarized in Table 16.2.

Suggestions were given for carrying out the testing program so that standardized conditions are maintained. The importance of good cumulative records of test scores was stressed. The need to check scores for reasonableness was pointed out.

Effective use of test results requires setting up procedures for analyzing and interpreting the results to various interested publics. Group results need to be organized effectively in graphs and charts that reveal significant comparisons. Oral and written reports need to be given to school personnel and lay audiences.

The need to report the results of testing for an individual student to the student and his parent was stressed. Methods of reporting test results for an individual were discussed. Emphasis was placed on giving a sound interpretation of the score in terms of educational or vocational goals of the student rather than on reporting exact scores that are likely to be misused or misinterpreted.

Finally, external testing programs that impinge upon the school's own program were reviewed. The major external testing programs discussed were the CEEB and ACT examinations for college entrance, the National Merit Scholarship tests, and state-mandated programs. The concerns of educators over the external tests were discussed.

QUESTIONS AND EXERCISES

1. Suppose you have just started to work in a particular school system and you have been told that one of your major assignments during the first year is to revise the testing program now in use in the school system. What would be the first steps that you would take? Why would you take these steps?

2. "In school systems where programs are truly individualized for each child, a program of standardized achievement testing has no place." What is your reaction to this statement? On what do you base your response?

3. It has been suggested that if an elementary school uses a general achievement battery such as the Stanford Achievement Test or the Iowa Tests of Basic Skills each year, then any intelligence test it uses should be a nonverbal test. What are the arguments for this position? What are the arguments against it?

4. A school system wants to take parts of several achievement batteries to form an achievement battery that the teachers feel will be more suitable for the local curriculum. The system proposes to develop local norms and use only these for interpretation. What are the advantages and disadvantages of the proposal?

5. A secondary school, grades 9–12, in which approximately 70 percent of the graduates take no further education has a strong vocational program, jointly supported by the schools and local industries. In grades 11 and 12 there is a work-study program in which the students spend half the time in apprentice training and half in academic work. How should the testing program for this school differ from that in a suburban high school in which 80 percent of students go on to college?

6. A special liberal arts college is being set up to take students not eligible for regular college admission who have promise for completing a liberal arts program. The college will accept any student with promise over 18 years of age whether he has completed high school or not. Programs are to be set up to remedy deficiencies that students might have. Plan a testing program that would help the new college admit students and place them.

7. A school system gives a battery of achievement tests consisting of vocabulary, reading comprehension, spelling, English usage, and mathematical concepts and reasoning in October of each year in grades 2 through 6. It also gives a general intelligence test in grades 2, 4, and 6. How can the results of the testing be used in each of the following situations? How must the data from the testing be analyzed to serve each purpose? What would the limitations of test results be?

a. The students in the system are to be reassigned. Parents of children in school A object to sending their children to school B because they feel that the achievement level of their children will decrease.
b. The school system has appointed a committee to revise the elementary mathematics program.
c. One school in the system has had an ungraded organization for five years. School personnel want to keep it but the Board of Education wants to put the school under the graded organization because of costs.

8. A state Department of Education wants to start a statewide testing program in grades 2, 4, 6, 8, 10, and 12. The department needs data on reading, language, mathematics and general scholastic ability. The data are to be used to judge the effectiveness of educational efforts throughout the state and to allocate special funds. The following proposals have been made. What are the advantages and disadvantages of each of the proposals?

a. The state will construct tests of their own and norm them on the school population in the state.
b. A committee selected from various school districts in the state will select five published tests in each area. Local schools can then choose one of the five to use in their schools. Schools may test at any time between October 1 and December 31.
c. A committee selected from various school districts will select the best available published standardized test in each of the areas. All schools in the state must give the same test at the same time of the year.

9. Below are given data on Stanford Achievement Test, Arithmetic Problem Solving scores obtained by sixth grade students in the Paradise School System between 1964 and 1968. All tests were given during the first week in October.

Year	N	P_{10}	P_{25}	P_{50}	P_{75}	P_{90}
1964	273	4.2	5.4	6.4	8.0	11.3
1965	268	4.1	5.1	6.1	7.9	11.1
1966	277	3.1	4.4	5.9	7.4	9.5
1967	273	3.1	4.0	5.7	7.0	9.0
1968	275	3.0	3.8	5.2	7.0	9.0

Suggest several hypotheses to account for these results. What further information would you need to evaluate the reasonableness of the different hypotheses?

10. On p. 568 are shown the scores of Roger Tuthill, tested at the end of the 4th grade. Prepare a report to be used in conference with Roger's parents.

Grade 4—Tested May 1968

	National Norms			Local Norms	
	Grade Equivalent	Percentile Rank	Stanine	Percentile Rank	Stanine
Word knowledge	4.0	30	4	9	2
Word discrimination	4.9	55	5	25	3
Reading	4.2	35	4	28	3
Spelling	5.0	55	5	9	2
Language	5.5	67	6	18	3
Arithmetic computation	6.7	98	9	96	8
Arithmetic problem solving and concepts	7.8	98	9	99	9

11. In the previous question data were provided in terms of both local and national norms. What do the differences between the two tell about the nature of the local 4th grade group?

12. A school system gave the *Stanford Achievement Tests* to all pupils in the sixth grade in May. The *Otis-Lennon Mental Ability Test* had been given at about the same time. Grade equivalents for the 10th, 25th, 50th, 75th, and 90th percentiles for each test are shown below. Prepare a report to interpret these results to the Board of Education or a group of interested parents.

Stanford Achievement Tests

Grade 6—Tested March 1968

	P_{10}	P_{25}	P_{50}	P_{75}	P_{90}
Word meaning	3.3	4.2	5.0	5.7	6.8
Paragraph meaning	3.7	4.8	5.5	6.5	7.8
Spelling	3.6	4.4	5.4	6.8	7.9
Language	3.2	4.1	5.5	6.5	7.6
Arithmetic computation	3.9	5.0	5.7	6.5	7.3
Arithmetic concepts	4.0	4.7	5.5	6.4	7.5
Arithmetic application	3.7	4.5	5.5	6.6	7.6
Otis-Lennon Mental Ability Test IQ	81	91	98	112	120

REFERENCES

Clark, C. A. The use of separate answer sheets in testing slow-learning pupils. *Journal of Educational Measurement,* 1968, **5,** 61–64.

Cleary, T. A. Test bias: Prediction of grades of Negro and white students in integrated colleges. *Journal of Educational Measurement,* 1968, **5,** 115–124.

College Entrance Examination Board. *Effects of coaching on Scholastic Aptitude Test scores.* Princeton, New Jersey: College Entrance Examination Board, 1968.

Dizney, H. F., Merrifield, P. R., & Davis, O. L., Jr. Effects of answer-sheet format on arithmetic test scores. *Educational and Psychological Measurement,* 1966, **26,** 491–493.

French J. W. The effect of anxiety on verbal and mathematical examination scores. *Educational and Psychological Measurement,* 1962, **22,** 553–564.

Goslin, D. A. *Teachers and testing.* New York: Russell Sage Foundation, 1967. Pp. 25–33.

Hayward, P. A comparison of test performance on three answer-sheet formats. *Educational and Psychological Measurement,* 1967, **27,** 997–1004.

Hopkins, K. D., Lefever, D. W., & Hopkins, B. R. TV versus teacher administration of standardized tests: Comparability of scores. *Journal of Educational Measurement,* 1967, **4,** 35–40.

Lamb, G. S. Teacher verbal cues and pupil performance on a group reading test. *Journal of Educational Psychology,* 1967, **58,** 332–336.

Miller, I. A note on the evaluation of a new answer form. *Journal of Applied Psychology,* 1965, **49,** 199–201.

Munday, L. Predicting college grades in predominantly Negro colleges. *Journal of Educational Measurement,* 1965, **2,** 157–160.

Sarason, I. G. Test anxiety and the intellectual performance of college students. *Journal of Educational Psychology,* 1961, **52,** 201–206.

Sarason, S. B. et al. *Anxiety in elementary school children.* New York: Wiley, 1960.

Slater, R D. The equivalency of IBM mark-sense answer cards and IBM answer sheets when used as answer formats for a precisely-timed test of mental ability. *Journal of Educational Research,* 1964, **57,** 545–547.

Stanley, J. C. & Porter, A. C. Correlation of Scholastic Aptitude Test scores with college grades for Negroes versus whites. *Journal of Educational Measurement,* 1967, **4,** 199–218.

Yamamoto, K. & Dizney, H. F. Effects of three sets of test instructions on scores on an intelligence scale. *Educational and Psychological Measurement,* 1965, **25,** 87–94.

SUGGESTED ADDITIONAL READING

Bauerenfeind, R. H. *Building a school testing program.* Boston: Houghton Mifflin, 1963.

Bowles, F. *The refounding of the College Board, 1948–1963.* Princeton, New Jersey: College Entrance Examination Board, 1967.

Findley, W. G. Factors that affect test results. In N. E. Gronlund (Ed.), *Readings in measurement and evaluation.* New York: Macmillan, 1968. Pp. 150–158.

Findley, W. G. (Ed.) *The impact and improvement of school testing programs,* Sixty-second Yearbook of the National Society for the Study of Education. Chicago: University of Chicago Press, 1963.

McLaughlin, K. F. *Interpretation of test results.* Washington, D.C.: U.S. Government Printing Office, 1964.

Michigan State University Guidance Department. Designing and implementing a testing program. In D. A. Payne and R. F. McMorris (Eds.), *Educational and psychological measurement.* Waltham, Massachusetts: Blaisdell Publishing Company, 1967. Pp. 337–341.

Ricks, J. H., Jr. On telling parents about test results. *Test Service Bulletin No. 54.* New York: Psychological Corporation, 1959. Pp. 1–4.

Womer, F. B. Pros and cons of external testing programs. In D. A. Payne and R. F. McMorris (Eds.), *Educational and psychological measurement.* Waltham, Massachusetts: Blaisdell Publishing Company, 1967. Pp. 346–357.

CHAPTER 17

Marks and Marking

ONE educational activity closely related to the problems of measurement is that of evaluating student performance in some segment of schooling and recording and reporting that evaluation. Typically, the evaluation is summarized in some condensed and highly abstract symbol. A recent survey (NEA, 1967) of over 600 school systems indicated that a system of numerical or letter grades was used in about 80 percent of the systems, except at the first grade where the percent was 73 and in the kindergarten where it was 17. Use of these highly condensed symbols to convey the teacher's evaluation has frequently been criticized, for reasons that we shall consider presently, but the alternatives that have been offered to replace the conventional A, B, C, D, F and percentage systems have introduced problems of their own, and no fully satisfactory replacement for the course grade seems to be at hand. Especially in secondary school and college, it seems likely that marks will be with us for some time to come. Thus, it is important that we understand marks and marking both as cultural and as psychometric phenomena.

Marks and marking are very deeply imbedded in the educational culture. They become the basis, in whole or in part, for a wide range of actions and decisions within a given educational institution, between levels in the educational structure, and in the relations of the educational system to the outside world. Thus, eligibility for admission to certain programs or departments, for scholarship aid, for membership on athletic teams, even for continuing in school at the higher levels is determined in some measure by academic standing. Admission to college or graduate school is based, in part, on grades received at the previous academic level. The use of academic records as a basis for deferment of military service aroused a storm of controversy in academic circles, but the reporting of academic records to a potential employer as evidence that he may use in deciding whether to offer an individual a job has rarely been questioned. Thus, there are many points within the school at which marks interact with the administrative and instructional process. It is for this reason, in part at least, that marking systems are so durable and so resistant to change.

Like any other deeply ingrained aspect of a culture, marks and marking procedures are often taken for granted, with a minimum of rational analysis of their nature and their functions. As we examine them, our approach should be, in part, that of the cultural anthropologist, who looks at a set of odd but presumably meaningful behavior patterns and tries to understand the functions they serve and the manner in which they relate to the total culture of which they are a part. We should put aside our personal involvement, look at the phenomenon with the cold eye of the social scientist, try to identify the forces that shape and sustain present grading practices, and the pressures within the educational culture that make the practices at one and the same time both somewhat irrational and highly resistant to change.

FUNCTIONS SERVED BY MARKS

Marking and reporting practices are sustained partly by tradition, but partly by the real functions that they serve with a greater or lesser degree of adequacy. These functions relate to the needs of the student himself, to the needs of parents (or parent substitutes) in charge of the pupil and responsible for his upbringing, to the needs of the school in which the pupil is enrolled, to the needs of schools to which he may later be a candidate for admission, and to those of employers or others in adult society to whom the student may someday relate. Let us examine each of these categories of need to see how well marking and reporting practices serve them.

The student needs information about himself—to guide his present learning and his plans for his future. He needs immediate feedback to tell him what he knows and where his errors and deficiencies lie. Daily exercises, recitations, and quizzes provide this type of feedback. It is provided most completely and effectively in programmed instructional materials, in which the student receives immediate confirmation or correction of his responses. Periodic marks and report cards are too remote from his learning activities to provide this type of specific direction.

The student needs information defining what it is appropriate and important for him to learn. Again, what the teacher assigns as learning tasks and especially what she *corrects, grades, and returns to the pupil* defines for him what is considered important in school. Thus, White (1967) found that pupils in the elementary school tended to agree that spelling and arithmetic were the things that it was important to learn, because these were the papers that their teachers graded. But here again, it is testing and immediate feedback that are central, rather than a mark on a report card once in six or eight weeks.

The student needs information as to what sort of a person he is. Is he the sort of person who is good with words? With numbers? In science? In art? Is he the sort of person who should plan to go on to college? To major in chemistry? Course marks can and should play a part in building up this self-picture, though the variability of marking standards from school to school, department to department, and teacher to teacher presents many barriers to achieving a clear and accurate image. However, with all their technical limitations, marks remain one of the best predictors of later marks, and so are important in conveying information about likelihood of success in college generally, or in specific institutions or programs. Results for somewhat over 100,000 students followed up in a recent American College Testing Program study (Hoyt and Munday, 1966) showed the correlation with college freshman grades to be .58 for a composite of high school marks, .55 for a composite of standardized test scores, and .65 for the optimum combination of both types of information. So marks have a significant role to play in informing the individual (as well as the institution to which he may later apply) of his prospects for academic success.

Clearly, the pupil or the parent who looks at a report from the school and asks the question: What kind of learner am I? (is Johnny?) needs help in interpreting the marks that he receives. With the enormous variation that exists among schools and colleges, even a skilled counselor has his talents stretched to make a sound judgment of what any given record signifies in terms of any specific educational decision. But the marks showing on a report card constitute one important type of evidence to be interpreted to pupil or parent, and one of the standards for any marking and reporting system is that it be as interpretable as possible.

Parents have need for information about their child. They need information, at the simplest level, to reassure them that their child's school experience is proceeding satisfactorily or to alert them if problems are developing. The usual report card serves this need at least at a minimal level, but the amount of information that can be conveyed by a single symbol is so limited that many schools have felt a need to supplement the conventional report form in various ways. The 1966 NEA survey showed that about half the school systems scheduled conferences with parents of elementary school children—but the percent dropped to about a quarter in junior high and a fifth in senior high. In the primary grades, a third included narrative comments on the pupil in their reporting, a practice that occurred for about one fifth at grade 4 and only about a tenth in junior and senior high school.

Especially when a child is encountering educational difficulty, the conventional report card becomes a most inadequate communication medium. It can do little more than register the teacher's dissatisfaction with a pupil. It does not convey a diagnosis of the source of the difficulty or provide to either pupil or parent any suggestions for remedial action. Thus, at best but without any certainty that it will do so, it can cause the parent to seek out the teacher to find out more about the problem and what school and family can jointly do about it. This global and purely negative character of a low mark is its greatest weakness.

Parents need information to help them plan for their child's future. Their need here is one shared with the pupil himself, and the values and limitations of marks are those considered earlier. Again, parents need help in interpreting marks, together with standardized test data, in terms of the realistic expectancies that they present for future choices and actions. Most parents are poorly qualified to use either marks or standardized test scores for decision making, except as the implications of these data are interpreted to them.

Teacher evaluations, typically recorded as marks but sometimes amplified with narrative comments or anecdotal reports, serve a variety of functions within the economy of the school itself. Many of these functions are primarily administrative, though these may be quite central to the individual's educational future.

At the college level, probation and dismissal at one end and honors and distinction at the other stem from the pervasive Grade Point Average. In between, eligibility for admission to more advanced courses or for major study in a field may be based in considerable extent upon having "passed" or achieved a specified level in previous courses. In the culture of an educational system that is selective in its parts, if not in its entirety, these are administrative decisions that must be made, and if they are not made on the basis of teacher evaluations as recorded in course marks, they will be made in terms of special examinations or other procedures. There are also, of course, a host of nonacademic decisions in which marks play a role, such as eligibility to be a member of athletic teams—aspects of the culture that have a sometimes disturbing reality and importance.

It is these actions, so crucial to the individual student and so central to the functioning of the educational institution, that account for much of the irrationality of marking practices and of their resistance to rational change. An assortment of vested interests and personal convictions get bound up in grading systems and standards, and these can be as highly resistant to change as dietary habits that had their origins and rationale in an ancient prerefrigeration era. Thus, a science department that wishes to hold majoring in its field down to a limited number of the most promising students finds it convenient to grade severely in the introductory course so that most freshmen are discouraged from and few can qualify for advanced work in the department. An individual professor who fortifies his ego with the conviction that "standards must be maintained" can take satisfaction in the high rate of failure and the infrequency of A's in his classes—a trend that one of his colleagues might take to be evidence of poor teaching. Marking practices are expressions of individual and group value systems as much as they are dispassionate reports of student behavior. Should students in an "honors" section receive grades that reflect their achievement in relation to their total class, or in relation only to each other? And what about a "slow" or "minimum fundamentals" section? Should a student be penalized for handing in papers late, or get extra credit for doing optional work? Should students with the same level of scholastic aptitude get, on the average, the same grades irrespective of the subject or department involved? These are all questions of value that rarely get examined in detail and upon which members of a faculty seldom come to genuine agreement. As long as disagreement exists within the local educational culture on questions of value such as these, the technical efforts of the psychometrician to introduce a consistent rationale into grading practices will be futile.

Now that we have explored, in general terms, the role of marks in the educational culture, let us turn to some of the more specific and technical problems relating to the assignment of marks to pupils. We will organize the discussion around six main questions:

1. On what should a mark be based?
2. How should component data be weighted in arriving at a mark?
3. In how many categories or subdivisions should marks be reported?
4. What fraction of students should receive each mark?
5. In relation to what frame of reference should marks be formulated and how can they be related to that frame?
6. How can standards be equated from section to section, course to course, and department to department?

Note that many of these questions are phrased in terms of a "should," and that issues of value as well as fact arise in connection with each one of them. As we consider these questions in turn, we shall have to address ourselves first to the underlying issues of value and then to the problems of technique and implementation.

On What Should a Mark Be Based?

This question really breaks down into two parts: (1) What characteristics of a student should be represented in a mark, and (2) What types of evidence should be gathered to provide evidence on the designated characteristic or characteristics? The first question can be rephrased by asking: Should a mark represent as pure and accurate an appraisal of competence in a segment of the curriculum as can be devised, or should it be modified by factors other than that competence? Some of the potential modifiers are:

(a) Amount of work completed, as well as final level of competence reached. It is not unusual for teachers to permit students to raise their marks by doing additional amounts of work, with only limited attention to the quality of the work and almost entirely without regard to whether the additional work results in any higher level of competence on the part of the student. The mark then comes to signify conscientiousness and industry as well as, or perhaps even instead of competence.

(b) Mechanical aspects of work completed—neatness, legibility, correctness in the mechanics of written or oral expression. These are factors that the school welcomes and strives for in the work of its pupils, but one is impelled to ask how many of these factors should influence and how much they should influence a mark that reports competence in, say, history or biology.

(c) Aptitude, as this is indicated to the teacher by the results of scholastic aptitude tests or by the section to which the pupil is assigned. Should all pupils be judged in relation to a common standard, or should each be judged in relation to some indicator of potential to achieve?

Aside from personal convictions and a personal value system, it would seem that the only criterion that can be brought to bear on these questions is the criterion of use. For what purposes will a mark be used? In the light of these uses—such uses as we have discussed in the earlier sections of the chapter—what is the best foundation for a marking system? It seems to us that most purposes are best served by a mark that is as pure and unadulterated a measure of competence as can be devised, but others may see values in modulating competence by one or more other types of considerations. We would hope that the introduction of other factors is done as a result of deliberate examination of the issues, rather than as a casual and unanalyzed decision.

When the foundations for allocation of marks have been thought through by the instructor or by the teaching group, it is then essential to decide what types of tests, exercises, written reports, or other behaviors will provide evidence of the achievements that the mark is to represent. The choice of types of evidence can best be based upon the same type of analysis of the objectives of a course that was proposed in Chapter 3 as the basis for designing a well-balanced test. If the objectives have been clearly identified in behavioral terms, this statement will point to the types of evidence that will provide an indication of the extent to which those objectives have been achieved.

How Should Component Data Be Weighted?

A scrutiny of the list of objectives will usually suggest that certain class activities, certain assignments and exercises, certain reports and papers, and certain examinations are appropriate media for gathering evidence of the extent to which a student has achieved the course objectives. These separate indicators must be combined in some way if a single symbol is to be used to report a student's performance. How shall the weight for each component be determined?

In the last analysis, two factors determine the desirable effective weight for a given datum, that is, test, paper, recitation, etc. The first of these is the validity of the information that it provides. Validity in this context signifies the importance of the knowledge or skill that is reflected in the datum and the faithfulness with which it is reflected, uncontaminated by other irrelevant factors (such as verbal fluency or penmanship). Usually, the validity of a type of datum can only be assessed through judgment, possibly a pooled judgment of several instructors in an area. A second, but relatively minor consideration is reliability. The less reliable datum that incorporates a relatively large component of measurement error deserves a smaller weight, other things being equal, than the more reliable one. We may generally anticipate that reliability will be highest by a considerable margin for a carefully prepared objective test, intermediate for essay tests and for papers and essays, and lowest for the on-the-wing appraisal of oral contributions and participation in class. These trends should temper somewhat the weights that would otherwise be assigned on the basis of the judged validity of the datum.

Once an instructor has decided what weight he wishes each kind of data, that is, quizzes, papers, exams, etc., to receive, he will want to be sure that each does, in fact, receive that weight. Suppose that an instructor has given a 90-item objective exam for which the score is the number of items right, and a term paper that has been evaluated on a 5-point scale ranging from 5 = excellent to 1 = unsatisfactory, and that he has decided that in the final assessment of his students the exam should carry twice as much weight as the term paper. Suppose, further, that the two sets of scores have the following characteristics:

	Exam	*Paper*
Mean	63	3.2
Standard deviation	11	0.55

What must be done to these scores to produce the desired result?

Note the two standard deviations. That for the exam is 20 times as great as that for the paper. If we were simply to add the two scores for each individual, the exam would have 20 times as much effect as the paper in determining the individual's standing on the combined score. But we want its effect to be twice as great—so we must multiply the scores on the term paper by a factor of 10, making the mean 32 and the standard deviation 5.5 (see p. 226). The two standard deviations are then in the ratio of 2 to 1, and the effective weights are what we set out to produce. In summary, the effective weight of each component is determined by its standard deviation. To give variables the desired effective weights, we must multiply each variable by a factor that will adjust the standard deviations to the desired ratio. The desired multiplying constant C, can be found from the formula:

$$C_B = \frac{Wt_A \cdot SD_B}{Wt_B \cdot SD_A}$$

where Wt_A and Wt_B are the desired weights for two components;
SD_A and SD_B are the standard deviations of the components;
A is the component that is being used as an "anchor" variable; and
B is one of the variables whose weight is being adjusted to bring it into line with variable A.

How Many Categories Should Be Used?

Evaluations may be reported very crudely in only two categories such as "Pass" and "Fail," in three or four categories, in the widely used 5-letter A, B, C, D, F set of categories, in a 15-category system that attaches plusses and minuses to the above, or in a percentage system that nominally can take any one of a hundred values. How can we decide which is to be preferred? As usual, the issues are partly those of value and partly those of fact.

Arguments concerning the values involved tend to center around deemphasizing the competitive pressures and the presumably irrelevant goals represented by marks. It is maintained that this can best be accomplished by a very coarse grading system which, in effect, makes only a few gross discriminations. This gain is bought, of course, at the expense of most of the information that the marking system might possibly supply about the individual. We know only that he was judged passable in the course—or, in a 3-point system, we know for the great bulk of students that they were judged to be neither inadequate nor outstanding. Marks recede into the background except for the small group who fail, and perhaps for another small group who aspire to honors.

As the number of discriminations increases beyond a 2- or 3-category system, distinctions begin to be of importance for all students. If the number of categories is small, there are relatively few students who fall close to dividing lines between categories, and for these a very major gain or loss occurs depending on which way the decision goes. As the number of categories increases, the number of borderline decisions increases correspondingly, but each decision becomes less crucial in the total academic record of the student. There is a trade-off of increased frequency of potential error or unfairness in grading for decreased size of error.

The issue of fact that is relevant to the number of grading categories is the reliability of the evidence on which the decision is being made. Each component that enters into a final grade, as well as the grade itself, has an appreciable (if often unknown) standard error of measurement. If this error is large relative to the unit in which grades are reported, many of the discriminations that are reported will be without substance or meaning. Consider the following situation, which is artificial but is believed to be fairly realistic:

> A school reports grades in a "percentage" system. For a particular course, the grades have a mean of 85, a standard deviation of 7, a range from 53 to 98, and a reliability of .80.

Given the above data, we can determine that the standard error of measurement of this final grade is $7\sqrt{1 - .80} = 3.1$ percentage points. Harking back to our discussion of reliability in Chapter 6, we can recall that this means that about one third of our grades will differ from the person's hypothetical "true grade" by as much as 3 points and in 87 percent of cases the score assigned to a person will differ by at least one point from the one we would have assigned if we had known his true score! How useful is it to carry discriminations to this level of fineness if it means that 87 percent of the reported values are "wrong"? Even if the reliability of the final grade were 0.95, a value that is probably never reached in practice, there would still be 75 percent of "wrong" grades.

Suppose we grouped our data, and divided the score range into a smaller number of categories. How often would the reported grade be the "right" grade? Percent of correct assignments at four levels of reliability and three degrees of coarseness of grading are estimated below.

Categories	Reliability .60	.70	.80	.90
15 (A+ to F−)	27%	31%	37%	50%
5 (A to F)	70%	77%	85%	96%
3 (Honors, Pass, Fail)	91%	95%	98%	99.9%

The assumptions upon which the above table is based are complex, somewhat arbitrary, but still probably reasonably realistic. They would seem to suggest that trying to make discriminations into *more* than 15 categories is a fairly futile exercise, and that even this degree of fineness strains the precision of our judgments. Of course, being "wrong" by one or two categories on a finely divided scale is not a crucial matter, but trying to make discriminations far beyond the limits of our evidence seems a fairly fruitless enterprise.

How Many Should Get What Mark?

Over a perod of 50 years a great deal has been written, much of it nonsense, about the appropriate frequency distribution of the symbols that represent marks. Two primary principles need to be emphasized in this regard. First, the symbols that represent marks are basically an ordinal, not a cardinal system. No one would question that, in our conventional 5-letter system, A is better than B, B better than C, and so on down to F. But there is no such universal consensus that the 5 or 6 steps do or should represent *equal* steps of quality, so that an A is just as much better than a B as a D is better than an F. Second, the symbols are embedded in an educational culture in which the cultural role of the symbols is at least as important as their psychometric properties. The specification that a student must repeat a course if he is to receive credit for it is a sociocultural decision, not a psychometric one. The decision that a student shall be eligible to take further advanced courses in a department is a sociocultural one, not a psychometric one. It is these practical consequences that flow from a grade that determine its real meaning, and the exponents of the culture, not the statisticians, must decide to what proportion of a student group these consequences should accrue.

In most educational institutions, an uneasy equilibrium has been reached between the grading symbol system and the social consequences of particular grades. Percent of academic failure remains fairly stable from year to year; average grades within a department maintain themselves at a fairly stable level, though varying from department to department; new faculty members are informally initiated into the culture and maintain its general character, though superimposing their individual idiosyncrasies upon it. But the equilibrium is an intuitive, unexamined sort of thing. It is unresponsive to changing events, such as a systematic shift in the character of a student body, and often maladaptive in some of its characteristics. The cultural norms as to how grading symbols are used throughout a school or college are worthy of conscious scrutiny to make sure that the categories are, in fact, being used in ways that serve the purposes of the institution itself and the larger educational system of which it is a part.

One possible decision, after such a scrutiny, is that successive symbols should represent equal steps along an interval scale. How is one to achieve equal units for a composite of various types of information expressed in various units, which may or may not be equal? There may well be question as to whether this can be done in a way that will give much confidence in the outcome. However, one technique that has a certain reasonableness for courses that are taken by large and relatively unselected groups of students is to assume that competence is distributed in accordance with the normal curve. The range of the normal curve can then be divided into equal segments, and the percentage of cases falling in each segment determined from a table such as the table in Appendix III. One solution to this problem is shown below:

Symbol	*Range on Normal Curve*	*Percent of Cases*
A	+1.5 to +2.5 or higher	7%
B	+0.5 to +1.5	24%
C	−0.5 to +0.5	38%
D	−1.5 to −0.5	24%
F	−2.5 or below to −1.5	7%

Thus, if this system were applied to a freshman survey math course, 7 percent would be awarded A's, 24 percent B's, and so on.

Of course, the fact that it is possible to assign marks by such a system does not mean that it is sensible to do so. This can only be judged in terms of the impact that such a procedure will have upon the practical actions that flow from the allocation of marks. Is it socially desirable, in the context of the institution in question, that 7 percent fail freshman math? Would the purposes of the institution be better served if the percent were larger? Smaller? Only a wise examination of the purposes of the institution and the impact of the failure percentage upon those purposes can provide an answer.

In Relation to What Frame of Reference Should Marks Be Assigned?

There are three quite different reference frames within which marks may be assigned. We may label these

Performance in relation to perfection
Performance in relation to potential
Performance in relation to peers

Performance in relation to perfection implies degree of complete mastery. There may be some limited segments of curricular material for which it is possible to make a complete catalogue of that which exists to be learned. Common examples would be (a) the 100 multiplication "facts," (b) the symbols representing the chemical elements, (c) the names of the bones in the body. Where the number of items is finite and definable, it is possible to test the examinee with all or a representative sample of them, and report his performance as a percent of perfect performance.

However, the instances in which the concept of complete or perfect learning applies are few, often seem somewhat trivial, and may be illusory. Thus, the child who can answer the question "What does 4×5 equal?" may fail on the question "What will four 5-cent candy bars cost?" Does he "know" the multiplication combinations if he cannot apply them in a problem context? Thus, complete mastery as a frame of reference for the use of marking symbols is of quite limited utility.

One frame that has had a fair amount of support is that of using symbols to report performance in relation to some estimate of potential to perform. It is argued that the type of information that is useful—in part, to a school, but especially to a parent—is whether achievement measures up to what the individual's underlying talents make possible. We are dealing here with the issue of under- and overachievement discussed in Chapter 10. And we face many of the same technical problems that we faced at that time. How do we get a measure of "potential" that is independent of and uncontaminated by present achievement? Can teachers make the required judgment of achievement-in-relation-to-potential, divorcing it from simple achievement? The one study addressed specifically at this point (Halliwell, 1960) indicates pretty clearly that they cannot, and that those who received high ratings were the bright youngsters—not the "overachievers." In addition to a serious question of whether teachers *can* make the required judgments in a sufficiently reliable and valid manner, there is also the question, in relation to a number of the contexts in which marks are used, of whether this really is the desired information to be conveyed by a marking symbol. Where decisions relate to more advanced courses to be taken or recommendation for further education or for a job, what one may wish to know is not whether Joe does the best he can, but what he can, in fact, do.

The third reference frame, performance in relation to peers, undertakes to express individual performance in relation to some reference group. This is the type of referent that is used in standardized test norms, as described in Chapter 7, where the peer group is some very far-flung national sample. Such a reference group has been used, at least to a limited extent, to calibrate grading practices nationwide in Swedish schools, but usually the reference group for school marks is conceived in much more limited terms. It may be the total student body of the institution or some unit of it, the total group taking some course, the total group in a particular instructor's section, or the shadowy and ill-defined total group of previous students that shape an instructor's impressions of what is good, or average, or poor performance. Problems in the use of a peer group as a reference frame involve first the value judgment of what peer group provides the most appropriate reference frame and then the technical problems of anchoring the marks that are awarded to that frame.

Arguments for using a very inclusive reference frame, for example, the total freshman class in a college or all the sixth graders in a school system, center on matters of fairness and equity. An individual of a given level of ability, it is argued, should have an equal chance of getting a particular mark no matter what particular teacher, class group, or subject area is involved. However, this conception of equity to the individual comes into conflict with other values in the educational system. For the student, an issue is that of providing for each individual an opportunity for success at his own level. This would imply evaluating the individual in terms of progress from his previous level of competence, and is closely related to the idea of achievement in relation to potential. For the institution and for society, it can be argued that needed levels of particular talents (specifically, cognitive and intellectual talents) vary as between different fields and occupations, and that the reference group should be those in a specific field, such as physics or vocational agriculture, rather than the total body of students.

The simplest reference frame is one that does not go beyond the single instructor. Marks could then be assigned either in relation to a specific class group or in relation to the more general but more vague inner standard held by the instructor. If the specific class is used to provide the reference frame, there is always the possibility that the students in one class may be in some way unrepresentative, so that each student may receive either an unfair penalty or an unwarranted bonus because of the nature of that reference group. If the "inner standard" is used, one is troubled by its subjectivity and its variability from instructor to instructor and possibly from time to time for a given instructor.

Which evil is the lesser depends primarily on the size and randomness of the group in the course. If the class is very small, that is, 10 or 15, there would seem to be little question that the "inner standard" needs to be called on to check the representativeness of that class. As the group gets larger, and especially as it is known that no special selective factors have been operating to send a particular type of student into it, one gradually gets more and more faith in the probabilities operating in successive samples from a common population, and is prepared to assign marks on a predetermined basis treating the total group as a uniform reference frame. The shift from "inner standard" to "class reference group" is a matter of degree. With intermediate size classes of 25 to 40 pupils, one might be inclined to temper any standard allocation of grades somewhat to take account of one's impression of the caliber of the group, in relation to others taught previously or concurrently, while in large lecture courses of 100 or more, one might reasonably feel that the uniformity of successive groups was well beyond the stability of one's own subjective judgment.

Equating Standards

Whatever general group is selected to provide the reference frame, some technique is needed to anchor a specific group to that frame. There must be some item or items of information available for the complete reference group (or a fair and representative sample of it). Where the reference group is all the students in all the sections of a course, and the course has been so taught that it includes a core of common content and objectives, an examination on that common core provides a reasonable anchoring device. For more wide-ranging groups one may use grade-point averages in previous courses or a common scholastic aptitude test as a rough and only partly satisfactory anchor.

Let us work through an illustration to show how an anchoring test might be used. Suppose that a college has three sections of a general psychology course, taught at different hours by different instructors, but using a common text and syllabus. The instructors, working together, have assembled a common final examination that they agree is equally suitable for each of their sections. A few items may be more appropriate for one section, but these are balanced by a few more appropriate for each of the others. The exam is given to all sections and the results are shown in Table 17.1.

It is the college grading policy that in unselective introductory courses, the allocation of grades will ordinarily be approximately 15% A's, 25% B's, 40% C's, 15% D's, and 5% F's, and the instructors agree that they know of nothing peculiar about this year's introductory psychology course that would require a change in this policy. Working from the distribution of total scores for the total class, we have 15% of 150 = 22, so the top 22 students, approximately, should represent A's. These are students with scores of 75 or over.* The next 25% $\times$ 150 = 38 students, representing B's are those with scores of 65–74. Continuing on down, we get the complete picture shown in Table 17.2.

This table specifies the *number* of each grade to be awarded within each section, but does not specify *which individuals* are to receive which grade. This

* The frequency distribution was designed so the letter breaks come out at even class-intervals, which would not ordinarily be the case with real data.

TABLE 17.1 SCORES IN THREE SECTIONS OF COURSE

Score	Section I	Section II	Section III	Total Group
85–9	1	2	1	4
80–4	2	4	1	7
75–9	3	7	1	11
70–4	5	9	6	20
65–9	6	6	6	18
60–4	6	7	19	32
55–9	4	5	19	28
50–4	5	4	3	12
45–9	2	2	2	6
40–4	4	0	0	4
35–9	0	3	2	5
30–4	2	1	0	3
N	40	50	60	150

would presumably be based on each student's complete record, giving only the desired weight in the total to the common anchor test. Thus, a pupil in section I who earned only a B on the common test might be one of those eventually awarded an A because of the excellence of the rest of his record. In practice, it might be agreed that each instructor would be permitted to make minor deviations from his allocated frequencies where near ties occurred, or where other evidence suggested a somewhat different shape of the distribution of performance in his group.

As set forth, the example illustrated a strict equi-percentile conversion from the anchoring test to the final mark. That is, the percent of each grade awarded corresponds, step-by-step, with the percent in that category on the common test. This is not unreasonable when the anchor test clearly and directly represents

TABLE 17.2 GRADE DISTRIBUTION IN THREE SECTIONS

			Section I		Section II		Section III	
Grade	Score	Total	No.	%	No.	%	No.	%
A	75–89	22	6	15	13	26	3	5
B	65–74	38	11	28	15	30	12	20
C	55–64	60	10	25	12	24	38	63
D	40–54	22	11	28	6	12	5	8
F	Below 40	8	2	5	4	8	2	3

the common elements in the objectives of the specific course. When anchoring is based on some more indirect indicator of competence, such as general grade-point average or a measure of scholastic aptitude, it may seem reasonable to temper the variation among groups based on this indirect indicator, letting each group regress somewhat closer to the general average. Thus, in our illustration, section II would be allocated more than 15% of A's, but less than 26%; section III less than 15%, but more than 5%. The less directly relevant the anchor measure, the more tempering that would be appropriate—so that general grade-point average might be given essentially no weight in determining what would be an appropriate number of A's, B's, and C's in, for example, a course in piano playing.

Statistical methods of controlling standards within sections of a course, or even between courses, work reasonably well for large courses with a common curriculum, and for fairly general student groups. They run into difficulties when groups are small or specialized. Under these circumstances, any rigid adherence to certain percentages of particular grades seems unwarranted. Sampling variations in the character of the group from one semester to another will be too large, and variations in the nature of students enrolling for different courses too marked. Under these circumstances, the reference group tends to become the somewhat ill-defined one that a single instructor carries around imbedded somewhere in his cortex of "the typical English 212 student," against which he rates his present class. Clearly, this is a highly subjective, unstable, and individualistic reference frame. However, it is the one that *does* control grading standards in a very large part of contemporary education, and it will certainly continue to do so. Where a course is quite specialized or where the student group is one that has quite distinctive characteristics, it may be inevitable that this be so.

SUMMARY STATEMENT

Marks and marking systems are deeply embedded in the educational culture and serve, though limpingly, a number of legitimate educational ends. For this reason, they are likely to survive for some time to come. Among the purposes served with at least a minimal level of success are (1) informing parents about how their child is perceived by the school, (2) helping to form the individual's picture of himself as a learner and to set his goals for further levels of learning, (3) regulating the flow into specific programs and activities within an educational institution, and (4) monitoring admission to later educational institutions and the world of work.

Like any deeply ingrained aspect of a culture, grading and marking practices involve motivations that are only partly accessible to examination at the conscious level, and are correspondingly resistant to change. Before practices can be made psychometrically more sound, their bases must be brought out and subjected to conscious, even self-conscious scrutiny. Since many, perhaps most, of the issues relating to the assignment of marks are issues of value, an examination of marking practices must address itself first and foremost to a clarification of these values. A few suggestions are offered of psychometric procedures for attaining specific values of equivalence and comparability, if it is decided that these are values worth seeking.

QUESTIONS AND EXERCISES

1. It has been proposed that while the A, B, C, D, F system of grading is relative, a percentage system represents an absolute appraisal. What are the arguments for and against this point of view? Are there any systems of appraisal that are based on an absolute standard? Identify one, and give the evidence to support your position.

2. In what ways is the marking system in a school similar to a rating procedure? In what ways does it differ? What factors that limit the effectiveness of ratings also limit the effectiveness of a marking system? How could the suggestions for improving ratings given in Chapter 13 be used to improve marking procedures in a school?

3. How is the general level of ability of the class that a student is in likely to affect the marks he will get? How ought it to affect them?

4. What should be the role of student self-appraisal in evaluating educational progress? What are the limits of such appraisal?

5. Try to get copies of the report cards used in one or more school systems. Examine them, and compare them with the cards obtained by other class members. What similarities and differences do you note? What shortcomings do you feel they have?

6. Talk to a school principal or superintendent and find out what changes have been made in reporting practices while he was in the school system. Why were they made? How satisfied is he with the result? What provisions are made for parent-teacher conferences? How satisfactorily have these worked out? What problems have arisen? How well does the present system of marking and reporting serve the functions listed on pp. 572–575?

7. What problems arise when one tries to have marks on a report card take account of aptitude and effort?

8. Comment on the proposition: "A course grade is most useful when it measures as accurately as possible the pupil's mastery of the direct objectives of the course and is not messed up with any other factors."

9. For a course that you teach or plan to teach, list the types of evidence you would plan to consider in arriving at a course grade. Indicate the weight to be given to each. Why have you allocated the weights in this way?

10. You have decided to give equal weight, in a biology course, to (a) a series of quizzes, (b) a final exam, and (c) laboratory grades. A study of the score distributions shows that the quiz SD equals 10, the exam SD equals 15, and the laboratory SD equals 5. How must you weight the raw scores in order to give the desired weight to the three components of the final grade?

11. When is it appropriate to "mark on a curve"? When not? When it is, how should the fraction to get each grade be determined?

12. What steps would you propose to take to reduce differences between instructors in grading standards?

13. In college Y there are ten sections of freshmen English. What steps could be taken to assure uniform grading standards, so that a student is not penalized by being in a particular section?

14. It has been proposed that "schools should abandon marks and report only 'Pass' and 'Fail' for students." What would be the gains from such a procedure? What would be the losses? How would the functions now served (admittedly imperfectly) by marks be discharged? How adequate would these alternate procedures be?

15. A school principal remarked to his Board of Education: "We have higher standards than Mason High. Our passing mark is 70, and theirs is only 65." What assumptions is he making in this statement? How defensible are they?

16. It has been suggested that marks must be approached as a cultural rather than a psychometric phenomenon. What merit is there in this point of view? What are some of its implications?

REFERENCES

Halliwell, J. W. The relationship of certain factors to marking practices in individualized reporting programs. *Journal of Educational Research,* 1960, **54,** 76–78.

Hoyt, D. P. & Munday, L. Academic description and prediction in junior colleges. *American College Testing Program Research Reports 1966 No. 10.* Iowa City, Iowa: American College Testing Program, 1966.

National Education Association. Reports to parents. *NEA Research Bulletin,* 1967, **45,** 51–53.

White, M. A. & Boehm, A. Child's world of learning: Written workload of pupils. *Psychology in the Schools,* 1967, **6,** 70–73.

SUGGESTED ADDITIONAL READING

Ebel, R. L. *Measuring educational achievement.* Englewood Cliffs, New Jersey: Prentice-Hall, 1965. Chapter 13.

Harris, C. W. (Ed.) *Encyclopedia of educational research.* (3rd ed.) New York: Macmillan, 1960. Pp. 783–789.

Palmer, O. Seven classic ways of grading dishonestly. In D. A. Payne and R. F. McMorris (Eds.), *Educational and psychological measurement.* Waltham, Massachusetts: Blaisdell Publishing Company, 1967. Pp. 299–302.

Smith, E. R. et al. *Appraising and recording student progress.* New York: Harper, 1942. Chapters 9–11.

Wood, D. A. *Test construction: Development and interpretation of achievement tests.* Columbus, Ohio: Charles E. Merrill, 1960. Pp. 67–77.

Wrinkle, W. L. *Improving marking and reporting practices in elementary and secondary schools.* New York: Rinehart, 1947.

CHAPTER 18

Measurement in Educational and Vocational Guidance

Mr. Wilson, guidance counselor at Center High School in one of the more enterprising small cities in Georgia, has a conference scheduled with Walter Kay, a tenth-grade pupil. This is the first conference. From the regular school testing program, Mr. Wilson has the following aptitude and interest test percentiles for Walter:

Differential Aptitude Tests		*Kuder Preference Record, Vocational*	
Verbal Reasoning	80	*Outdoor*	57
Numerical Ability	75	*Mechanical*	12
VR + NA	80	*Computational*	86
Abstract Reasoning	65	*Scientific*	98
Space Relations	80	*Persuasive*	18
Mechanical Reasoning	80	*Artistic*	38
Clerical Speed and Accuracy	50	*Literary*	86
Language Usage: Spelling	70	*Musical*	73
Language Usage: Sentences	75	*Social Service*	61
		Clerical	22

Walter's course grades for the previous year gave him an academic average of 84 (or B), and placed him about 60th in a class of 200. Walter's father is a fairly successful local business man. Walter has indicated on a questionnaire that he wants to become a doctor.

What significance do these test results have for Walter's expressed vocational goal? Do they imply greater suitability of other vocational goals? How are the results and their significance to be conveyed to Walter? These are not easy questions to answer, but suitable answers to them are at the heart of counseling. We must examine them in some detail.

THE SIGNIFICANCE OF TESTS FOR A VOCATIONAL GOAL

To judge the suitability of Walter's vocational goal in the light of his test scores, one thing we need to know is what the chances are that someone with Walter's score pattern who starts out for that goal will in fact be able to reach it. This is a large order. Let us break it down, to see what is implied in it. The analysis will suggest on the one hand why the long-range forecast is such a formidable enterprise, and on the other the immediate issues with which the counselor needs to be concerned. In Walter's case we need to be able to estimate

1. The probability that he would be accepted as a student by a college.
2. The probability that he would complete a premedical program successfully, if accepted.
3. The probability that he would be accepted by a medical school if he completed premedical training.
4. The probability that he would be graduated from medical school, if accepted.
5. The probability that he would achieve minimum standards of success and satisfaction as a doctor, if he were graduated from medical school.

What sort of judgment can be made with respect to the probability that Walter will successfully get over each of these hurdles?

The first hurdle is getting into college. Since colleges are likely to pay primary attention to high-school achievement and to measures of scholastic aptitude, we should examine the evidence we have on these points. Walter stands high in the second quarter of the class (70th percentile) in ninth-grade marks in his school. (Our present information does not tell us what level of achievement this would represent in terms of broader norms.) A pooling of the Verbal and Numerical scores on the *DAT* comes close to representing scholastic aptitude and provides a fairly good predictor of academic achievement. Norms for tenth-grade boys place Walter at the 80th percentile on the composite of these two tests. The aptitude tests and school achievement are in rather close agreement, and we can feel fairly secure in the picture of ability level that is provided us.

Tests Interpreted in Terms of Expectancy

Now what about college? Walter has stated that he wants to go to the University of Georgia. What are the chances that he would be admitted?

The College Entrance Examination Board puts out a *Manual of Freshman Class Profiles* (CEEB, 1965) and the 1965–67 edition of this book shows the following characteristics for the group of freshmen enrolled in 1964 at the University of Georgia:

	SAT–Verbal	*SAT–Math*
90th percentile	578	613
75th percentile	516	562
50th percentile	450	502
25th percentile	390	450
10th percentile	348	403

The average high school grade for admitted men was reported to be a B–.

Walter's school marks, as of the ninth grade, appear up to or a bit better than the average of admitted men. We must now try to translate his tenth-grade *DAT* scores into estimates of *SAT* scores in the twelfth grade. Fortunately, the *DAT* manual (Bennett et al, 1966) provides a formula (p. 5–48) that permits us to make this forecast, though with a fairly sizable standard error of estimate. Entering Walter's scores into the prediction equation, we arrive at estimates as follows:

SAT–Verbal	485
SAT–Math	570

Walter appears to fall comfortably above the average of admitted freshmen at the University of Georgia in 1964. Unless standards for admission rise rapidly between that date and the time when he actually makes his application (and the average *SAT Verbal* score *did* rise about 50 points between 1957 and 1964), his prospects of being admitted seem very good.

If Walter changed his goal to some other college, we would probably have to adjust the forecast. The selectivity of collegiate institutions varies widely. Thus, at Yale, the 10th percentile on *SAT Verbal* was reported to be 578, so that Walter's score would place him far below most of those who were accepted, and his chance of being admitted would seem almost nil. In contrast, there are other colleges in Georgia in which Walter's scores would place him close to the 90th percentile of the entering freshman class. The variation in admission standards of American colleges is almost unbelievable. The *Manual of Freshman Class Profiles* includes colleges with average *SAT Verbal* scores as high as 725 and as low as 375 (a range of 3½ standard deviations), and this includes only those institutions that used the College Board tests. The many junior colleges and community colleges are hardly represented. Thus, the problem that is almost the typical one both for counselor and student is not *whether* to plan for college, but rather *which* college or type of college to plan for.

Walter's second hurdle is doing satisfactory work in the premedical program. We have concluded that Walter could reasonably expect to get into the University of Georgia, but how well is he likely to do after he has been admitted? The state of Georgia provides us more information than most other places, because a continuing study has been made of success in the different Georgia colleges in relation to *SAT* scores and high-school average (Regents of the University System of Georgia, 1967). A prediction equation has been prepared for each college, making the most effective combination of *SAT* scores and high-school grades to predict freshman grade-point average (GPA) at that college. In 1965–66, the equation for University of Georgia males was:

$$.0020V + .0015M + .575H - .97$$

where H is high-school average expressed on a scale on which A is 4.0, B is 3.0, etc. Entering Walter's estimated V and M scores and ninth grade H into the equation, we have:

$$(.0020)(485) + (.0015)(570) + (.575)(2.9) - .97$$

which comes out to equal 2.53. That is, our best estimate is that Walter will get grades midway between B and C. He is about equally likely to do better than this, or to do worse. But again, our estimate has attached to it a sizable standard error, and must be recognized as quite tentative.

No separate data are available for *completing* college, but our hunch would be that if no untoward personal or financial problems arose to interfere, Walter should be able to cope with work at the level set by that university. Presumably the premedical program, with its science courses, is more demanding than many of the other undergraduate programs, so that Walter would find it more difficult to shine there than elsewhere, but it rather looks as though he should be able to do at least passing work.

Predicting beyond entry into, and initial success in college, Mr. Wilson's path becomes a good deal more thorny. Walter's long-range prospects depend so much upon how successful he is in the intermediate steps that we should perhaps not even try to project our estimates beyond the freshman year of college. But let us make the attempt. Let us forecast that his undergraduate grade-point average will be about a C+. This seems reasonable in the light of the expectancy for freshman grades and the somewhat more rigorous demands of a premedical program.

The third hurdle Walter faces is getting into medical school. What is now our best projection of Walter's prospects for entry into and success in medical school? The prospects for acceptance in medical school will depend, among other things, on Walter's undergraduate grades and his performance on the *Medical College Admissions Test.* We have made an estimate of his probable grades at the University of Georgia. Can we now get some estimates of *MCAT* score?

Predicting performance on a set of tests that are still 6 to 8 years in the future is obviously a risky enterprise. However, we do have some data tying the *Medical College Admissions Test* to other tests and to general population norms (Gee, 1959). A score corresponding to the 80th percentile of the high-school population appears to be the equivalent of roughly 435 on the *MCAT* (whose scores are expressed once again as standard scores with mean of 500, S.D. of 100). If Walter holds his own through high school and college, this is a reasonable prediction for him, but with a sizable margin for error in the forecast.

Given this *MCAT* score and a C+ college record, can Walter hope to get into medical school? The answer varies from year to year depending on the supply-demand situation. In 1968 it appears to be "perhaps." In 1966 about one third of applicants at the *MCAT* score level of 435 were admitted. In another 10 years the answer may have changed. The answer also depends to a very great extent on *which* school. Many medical schools admit almost no one with scores this low; there are a few for whom it has been close to average for the entering class. So we would have to conclude that medical school admission is a *possibility* for Walter if his intermediate educational progress comes at least up to our predictions, and if he shows good judgment in choosing the medical schools to which to apply.

The fourth hurdle is completing medical school successfully. The proportion of students admitted to medical school who are subsequently eliminated is rather small—about 10 percent—and a good part of the elimination is for reasons other than academic. Even at Walter's predicted *MCAT* level the nationwide elimination rate is only 15 to 18 percent. So perhaps we should not try to predict this rather faraway event. If Walter is accepted by a school, he certainly has a good fighting chance of graduating from it.

The fifth hurdle is establishing himself as a successful doctor. Given that Walter has graduated from medical school, what are his prospects? At this point, we had better frankly admit that we don't know. Success is a tricky thing even to define, much less to predict. And there is no evidence that grades and tests available at age 15 give us any basis for forecasting it. About all we can say, from information now available to us, is that if Walter gets his M.D. his chances of making a living in medicine are as good as the next man's. If he fails to do so, the causes probably lie outside the domain covered by our tests—or by any tests that we could give to a 15-year-old.

We have tried to show in the illustration of Walter Kay the kind of thinking a counselor must go through, either explicitly as we have done or implicitly and intuitively as is perhaps more typical, in order to arrive at a judgment as to the reasonableness of a career plan. We have tried to show the complexity, and in some spots the fragility of the chain of reasoning that is involved. The information available to permit a counselor to carry through this type of reasoning is much less than it should be. We need (1) better norming procedures and conversion tables, so that performance on one test at one grade level can be more readily translated into level of performance on some other test at some other grade level, (2) more and better expectancy tables to permit us to forecast later achievement from earlier indicators of ability, and (3) better ways of organizing this information for and making it available to those who will have to use it. However, even if data were much more extensive and much better organized than at present, our forecasts would still need to be quite tentative.

The need for tentativeness is shown by the standard error of estimate attached to the prediction of grades at the University of Georgia by the best prediction equation. This standard error is approximately ¾ of a letter grade. Thus, though we arrived at 2.5 as our best prediction for Walter's GPA, even if we had 12th grade marks and *SAT* scores on which to base this estimate there would still be about one choice in six that he would manage to get an average above 3.25 (that is, a high B average) and one in six that he would fall below 1.75 (that is, a low C). The range of possible outcomes is quite great.

Any predictions that try to jump two or three stages in the educational or vocational ladder are even more hazardous, since the more remote step depends so much upon the intermediate steps. This is especially true when the prediction jumps from the sheltered academic halls to the harsh world of work. School achievement and job achievement do not correspond at all closely. Prediction of job success, as we indicated more fully in Chapter 11, is a risky undertaking at very best. It would seem wise, therefore, to focus on the immediate step to be taken, and to leave future decisions somewhat fluid. Granting that present decisions must be made with an eye to future choices, we must recognize that those choices *are* in the future. They cannot be made definitely now. Choices should be made as the choice points arise, and while they should be made with an awareness of their implications for the future, a maximum of flexibility should be retained for redirecting future action.

In Walter's case, the counselor could clearly endorse a college preparatory program in school. He could support Walter's particular choice of a college as a reasonable and realistic one, and could lead Walter to expect that he would be able to handle work at that college without undue difficulty. The definitive choice of a premedical program is one that Walter does not have to make for 2 or 3 years, and application to medical school is still further in the future. Decisions on these problems could be left for the future, with the recognition that his goal is a somewhat demanding one and that whether it will look realistic when the time comes will depend upon what Walter has achieved in the interim.

Interest Measures in Relation to Vocational Goals

So far we have paid no attention to the interest scores. This is partly because they relate less directly to success in the academic training that is prerequisite for Walter's objective; correlations of interest scores with academic achievement in general or in specific areas are generally rather low. In part we have avoided bringing interest into the picture because the manner in which interest patterns are related to job success and job satisfaction is far from clear. As we indicated in Chapter 13, most of the information on interest patterns of particular occupational groups is based on persons already in the occupation. Furthermore, it is not clear how close to the typical member of an occupation a person needs to be in order to be happy or successful in the occupation. In many fields, such as engineering, there are wide variations in *specific jobs* within the occupation. Some may involve much social contact work and some little; some may involve primarily outdoor work and some indoor, and so on. Thus, there may be a place for individuals with quite different interest patterns within a single occupation. Closeness of correspondence with the typical may be pointed out to the counselee, but we would hesitate to counsel avoidance of an occupation solely because his interest pattern departs from what is typical of that occupation.

In Walter's case, we may compare his percentiles on the *Kuder* with the average percentiles for physicians and surgeons as a group. The comparison is shown on the following page.

Clearly, there are some appreciable discrepancies—discrepancies of 50 percentile points or more. However, on the interest dimension that is highest for physicians (scientific), Walter gets an extremely high percentile—actually 19 percentile points above the physician mean. Walter's high computational interest appears unusual for a physician, but other than that the two patterns appear fairly congruent. If we rank the ten interest areas in order, for Walter and for the physician group, we find that the correlation is about +0.6, confirming our impression that the two patterns are a good deal alike.

	Walter	Physicians and Surgeons
Outdoor	57	60
Mechanical	12	37
Computational	86	32
Scientific	98	79
Persuasive	18	26
Literary	38	62
Artistic	86	61
Musical	73	58
Social Service	61	60
Clerical	22	27

We have now done about as much as we can in terms of the evidence before us to assess the realism and suitability of Walter's expressed goal. Our best judgment would indicate that the next steps toward the goal are entirely feasible ones for Walter, though the final goal appears somewhat demanding for him. His interest pattern is generally congruent with the goal that he has expressed. At this point, obviously, we need to get better acquainted with Walter as a person. (Often, this getting acquainted would have preceded testing, but it is assumed that in this instance the test data were gathered as part of a routine group testing program.) This getting acquainted will depend in part upon the other types of information about Walter that are already a matter of record; in part upon conference with Walter.

STABILITY OF OCCUPATIONAL CHOICE

One very serious question that arises in counseling at any level is whether an occupational choice is stable or is likely to change. A subsidiary question, acknowledging that some changes are likely, is whether test data give any basis for judging whether a change is likely, and, if so, in what direction the change is likely to take place.

One substantial body of data bearing on this question comes from Project Talent (Flanagan and Cooley, 1966). Project Talent was (and is) a massive study in which a 5 percent sample of U.S. high-school students (almost a half million) were given two days of testing, including measures of different abilities, different areas of interest, and different aspects of temperament. In addition, a wide variety of biographical items was recorded for each student. The students

TABLE 18.1 PERCENT OF OCCUPATIONAL CHOICES REMAINING THE SAME ONE YEAR AFTER HIGH SCHOOL

	Grade of Initial Choice			
Occupation	9th	10th	11th	12th
Physical scientist	10	14	25	28
Physician	24	40	35	59
Teacher	24	28	40	49
Salesman	5	12	10	22
Barber	6	12	22	21
Writer	6	9	10	46
Farmer	20	22	34	44

were followed up a year and 5 years after completing high school, and, as the project continues, there are plans to do follow-ups after 10 and 20 years.

The one-year follow-ups give an initial picture of the stability of occupational choices. Results for a few occupations are shown in Table 18.1. The picture is clearly one of a vast amount of change over the period from grade 9 to the year after high school and, even over an interval of a single year from the 12th grade, the shifts are frequent enough to be a matter of serious concern.

Of course, career plan changes may be minor in nature, as when a shift is made from civil engineer to mechanical engineer. They may be major, as when a shift is made from mechanic to lawyer. Some indication of amount of shifting among six broad categories is shown for 9th grade males in Table 18.2. In all, 58 percent of the group moved from their original category to some other.

One question we may ask is which of these groups are most alike and which

TABLE 18.2 FREQUENCY OF CHANGES AMONG SIX OCCUPATIONAL GROUPS FROM GRADE 9 TO POST-HIGH SCHOOL YEAR

	Post-High School Plans						
Grade 9 Plans	1	2	3	4	5	6	Grade 9 Totals
1. Physical science	**965**	291	378	545	121	79	2,379
2. Biological-medical	106	**377**	173	213	29	37	935
3. Humanities	49	47	**261**	120	36	19	532
4. Business (with college)	57	50	140	**440**	24	39	750
5. Technical	94	28	67	97	**316**	128	730
6. Business (no college)	36	27	72	178	93	**125**	531
Post-high school totals	1,307	820	1,091	1,593	619	427	5,857

most different. With an extensive battery of tests, expressing similarity and difference between a number of occupational groups becomes a pretty involved matter, because there are so many specifics with respect to which resemblance may be examined. But often much of what a test battery is measuring that actually differentiates among a number of groups can be reduced to a small number of dimensions, rather like the "factors" that we spoke of on pp. 347–350. Thus two ability dimensions could account for most of the differences among the six occupational groups, from the talent data as shown in Fig. 18.2. One dimension is from high academic achievement, as represented by English expression, mathematics, reading comprehension, and the like, to low academic achievement. Not surprisingly, this dimension sharply separates the college-bound from the noncollege-bound groups. The second dimension differentiates those who are *relatively* strongest in tests of mechanical and visualizing abilities from those who are relatively strongest in information about sports and literature. This dimension tends to separate the physical science and technician groups at one extreme from the college business and humanities occupations at the other—perhaps a "thing-oriented" versus a "person-oriented" dimension.

Figure 18.1 shows only the center of each group—its arithmetic mean in both

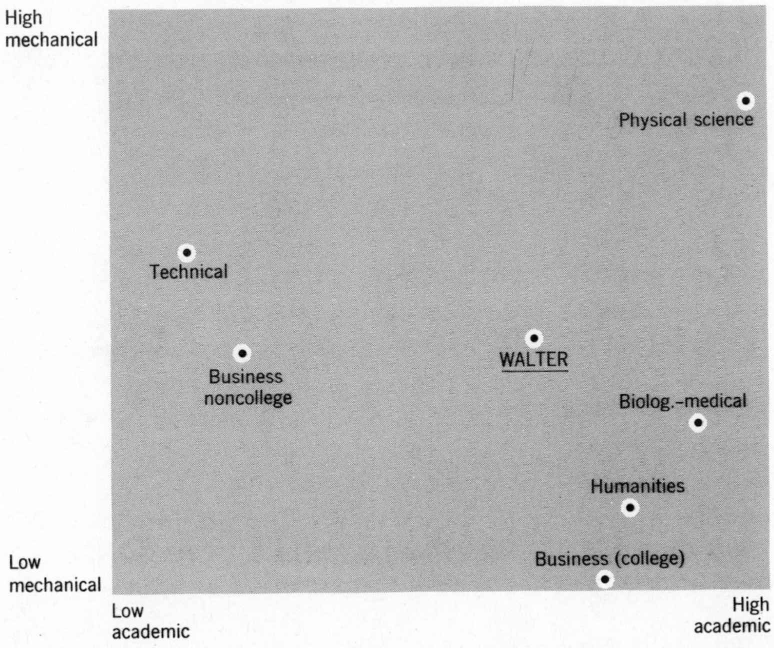

Fig. 18.1 Location of centroids of occupational groups in two-dimensional ability space.

dimensions. But just as it is possible to show through a histogram (and especially with a function such as the normal curve) the frequency at any point along a one-dimensional score scale, so it is also possible to calculate the frequency with which members of any occupational group occur at any point in this two-dimensional space (or in the same way, for a space of three or more dimensions). The calculations would be very laborious by hand, but present no great problem to a computer. Thus, if we were to find that Walter's *DAT* scores should be interpreted as locating him at the point labeled "Walter" in Fig. 18.1, we could compute the relative probability that a person falling at that point would be a member of each of the six occupational groupings. The table might look something like this:

Physical science	21
Biological-medical	14
Humanities	19
Business (with college)	28
Technical	10
Business (no college)	8

The probabilities shown above are probabilities based only on the frequencies and the characteristics of young men in the six occupational groupings as of one year out of high school. They take no account of the fact that Walter had

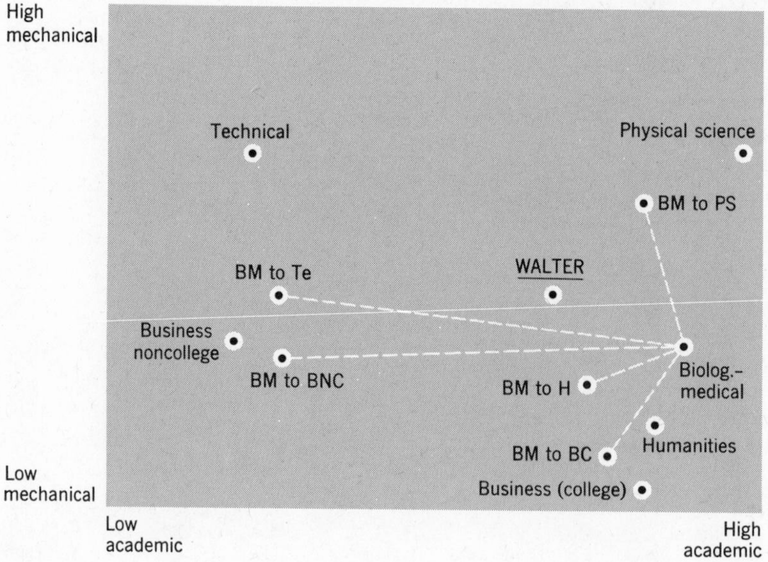

Fig. 18.2 Location of six major groups and change groups from biological-medical in two-dimensional ability space.

actually chosen in the ninth grade an occupation in the group designated biological-medical. What can we do differently, knowing that fact? We can extend our analysis, using the extensive Talent data, to look at those who in the ninth grade chose a biological-medical occupation, and who may be, one year out of college, in any of the six occupational groups. Figure 18.2 adds this information to that shown in Fig. 18.1. The new points that are connected to B-M with dotted lines represent the centroids of groups who *started out* choosing biological-medical occupations, but who moved away to one of the five other groupings. One can see that they differ considerably from those who have remained in the biological-medical grouping, and that they have moved toward the group that started and stayed in the occupational category to which they now belong. We could now compare Walter with the six groups, all of whom started out in biological-medical, estimating the probability that he will stay put or make each one of the possible changes. The results might look something like this:

Physical science	11
Biological-medical	41
Humanities	19
Business (with college)	23
Technical	3
Business (no college)	4

In our illustration, Walter falls more or less in the middle of the different occupational centroids, and so the probabilities for him are determined more by the general rate of change out of Biological-Medical and into the other categories, than by his special resemblance to any one occupational group. By contrast, for a person whose scores placed him in the extreme upper right-hand corner of Fig. 18.2, probability of shifting to physical science would be considerably greater than it was in Walter's case, and probability of shifting to business considerably less. Given this type of information, we would have another angle from which to approach the realism of Walter's choice. Entirely apart from the issue (which we considered earlier) of whether he has the ability to complete medical training, we have an estimate of whether he will still hold this vocational goal five years from now.

Data and techniques are just becoming available for the type of discriminant analysis that we have just been describing. It is likely to be some years before it will be practical to assess probabilities in the manner that we have illustrated in this section. But with the proliferation of computers and the gradual accumulation of data about occupations and occupational choices, something not far from this may be typical in the counseling process of the 70's and 80's.

COMMUNICATING TEST RESULTS

It would be rather generally accepted in present-day counseling that the important goals of the counseling process are that the counselee shall understand himself, accept himself, and arrive at a program of action to which he himself is committed in the light of the evidence. If these objectives are to be achieved, the general implications of the test results must be communicated to the client. There are two keys to this statement. One is "communicated to the client"; the other is "general implications." Let us consider each of these a little further.

The Meaning of Communication

What we communicate to someone else must be distinguished from what we say to him. A teacher may say to a child, "You're a dumb bunny." What she communicates is very likely: "I don't like you." The message sent and the message received are quite different in this case and in many others. Our problem, in working with a client, is not simply one of stating in an accurate and objective manner what the tests show. It is one of having the client comprehend and accept a particular picture of himself, one that may be quite a bit different from the picture he has held heretofore.

Really communicating with a client, really getting him to accept the implications of test results and incorporate them into his picture of himself, is far from easy. This is true particularly when the change in his self-picture involves adopting a less flattering view of himself. Communicating with parents who have made firm commitments for their child's future, and who may be satisfying their own needs vicariously through their child, is often even more difficult.

There have been a number of attempts to study experimentally different ways of presenting test data. However, the findings do not point out some one procedure as particularly effective. We can at best suggest a few guiding principles.

1. Change in the self-picture should be thought of as a gradual and continuing process. Presentation of test implications may be more effective if it is a continuing process, influencing all the counselor's contacts with the client, rather than a single dramatic event.

2. Test results gain meaning and significance in relation to other life experiences. The attempt should be made to relate the test findings to other experiences in and out of school. Where test results and other experiences, that is, of academic or work success, are congruent, they serve to reinforce and give

meaning to each other. Thus, in our instance, Walter's aptitude measures and school standing are in essential agreement, and each reinforces the other as an appraisal of aptitude for college work. Where test results and other types of evidence are at variance, a search with the counselee for the reasons for the discrepancy may provide a deeper basis for self-understanding.

3. The individual should take an active role in relating the test results to himself and his plans. We have succeeded in communicating only what the client himself sees. One way of assuring and testing that communication is to have him participate in interpreting the findings. This does not mean that he can be expected to work out the technical significance of a test score. This is a job for the counselor. Rather, once the technical interpretation has been made he should participate in relating the results to his own problems or plans.

The Objectives of Communication

In our communication, what we wish to convey to the client are the *general implications* of the test results. It is usually neither necessary nor particularly desirable to report to the client his exact scores or exact standing on tests. Reporting exact values may have several undesirable effects. The report is likely to convey an impression of precision not at all justified by the basic data. To tell a child's parents that his IQ is 117 or to tell an adolescent that he falls at the 78th percentile on a test conveys an atmosphere of exactness and finality quite inappropriate for our educational and psychological measuring instruments. It ignores the standard error of the score. As we have emphasized repeatedly, any test score must be thought of as identifying a fairly broad range within which the individual's true ability lies. This concept is very difficult to convey to parent or child if an exact score value is reported.

The concept of range can best be incorporated in the manner in which the test results are presented and interpreted to the client. Thus, an IQ of 107 (or one of 96) for an elementary-school child in a typical school might be reported as "about like most children in ability to do school work." An IQ of 120 in this context could be reported as "can be expected to learn school work somewhat more easily than most." One of 85 might be expressed as "will probably have more difficulty than many children in doing school tasks." These phrasings are only suggestive. The point is that our report is expressed (1) in broad and rather general terms, (2) in terms of its practical implications, and (3) somewhat tentatively.

When working with tests for which the norms are given in percentiles, we have to be particularly careful about our interpretations. This is due to the unequal units of the percentile scale. The large middle range of percentile values does not represent any very great spread in level of performance on most tests, and we must be careful not to overinterpret percentile differences occurring in this range. Anything from the 25th to the 75th percentile should probably be thought of as "about average," and reported as such. Thus, in describing Walter's test results to him, we might say, "Your aptitude test scores show abilities on these tests somewhat better than the average boy in the tenth grade. You did about as well on one test as on another, though there is a suggestion that your clerical speed is a little below the other abilities. Your scores on tests related to college were a bit above the average of the total group who enter the University of Georgia, but well below the average for such colleges as Harvard and Princeton. You'll have to see how you do in high school and college before you can tell much about the chances of getting into medical school. Your areas of highest interest were scientific, computational, and literary." This is probably as much of an interpretation as this set of test data warrants, though other aspects of the tests might merit further discussion in relation to specific educational or vocational plans.

Related to the problem of conveying a false impression of exactness is that of overemphasizing and overvaluing the test results in the client's mind. This danger is seen perhaps most dramatically in the case of an IQ reported to a parent. In some degree most parents live vicariously through their children. Some compete through their children. They know enough about an IQ to recognize it as a mark of status. You can get ahead of Mrs. Jones next door by having a brighter child in much the same way that you can by having a more expensive car or a new fur coat. Conversely, a low IQ may be a basis for self-reproach or for rejecting a child. These are unworthy, even vicious, uses of test results. They are fostered by meager understanding of tests and by personal involvement. This type of misuse of test results is another reason why the counselor usually prefers to report test findings only in general terms.

TESTS IN THE IDENTIFICATION OF VOCATIONAL OBJECTIVES

In the case of Walter, as we have just been describing it, we had to deal with a boy who had expressed a definite educational and vocational goal. Our initial problem was to try to assess the prospects that his goal could be achieved. Clarification of Walter's plans and objectives would have to include communicating to him an estimate of the plausibility of his expressed objective. But suppose that a counselee comes in who expresses no definite objective, or suppose Walter wishes to consider other possible objectives. What then? Let us organize our consideration of this situation around another case.

Consider this second case, that of Henry White, who is a classmate of Walter's. Henry's father works as a railroad conductor. Henry has stated that he does not know what he wants to do when he grows up. His test percentiles are as follows:

Differential Aptitude Tests		*Kuder Preference Record, Vocational*	
Verbal Reasoning	25	*Outdoor*	16
Numerical Ability	55	*Mechanical*	17
VR + NA	35	*Computational*	97
Abstract Reasoning	40	*Scientific*	77
Space Relations	55	*Persuasive*	46
Mechanical Reasoning	60	*Artistic*	58
Clerical Speed and Accuracy	40	*Literary*	45
Language Usage: Spelling	20	*Musical*	47
Language Usage: Sentences	30	*Social Service*	46
		Clerical	76

In academic work, Henry is about 135th in the class of 200.

This case presents us with quite a different situation from the one we faced with Walter Kay. There our problem initially was to appraise the appropriateness of a stated objective. In Henry's case, no objective is expressed. Our problem is to see whether certain areas of educational or vocational activity appear particularly indicated by the test evidence and, if so, to help Henry get better acquainted with these possibilities.

Henry, who is below average both on the intellectual aspects of the aptitude battery and in scholarship, does not seem a strong candidate for college education. He may not aspire to any formal education beyond high school. However, with the ever-increasing proportion of high-school graduates continuing with some type of post-high school program, the possibility of Henry's continuing after the 12th grade should certainly be considered. However, in Henry's case, the type of institution would need to be chosen with care. The estimate of 12th grade *SAT* scores from his 10th grade *DAT* record yields values of

Verbal	308
Math	451

Scores that low are found in Georgia colleges, but not many of them. Thus, any education planned beyond high school should probably be in a type of institution and a type of program making rather modest intellectual demands.

Positive guidance of Henry in relation to immediate educational choices would depend to a considerable extent upon sharpening up his thinking about vocational objectives. What can we say about Henry's vocational prospects? What type of vocational objective is suitable for him in the light of his test scores? What steps should a counselor take to help Henry set up suitable and more definite vocational goals? When these steps have been taken, the resulting plan may provide guides as to the high-school program that would be desirable, for example, clerical, vocational, prebusiness, general, or possibly college preparatory.

Limitations of Aptitude Measures for Identifying Suitable Vocational Goals

If we limit ourselves for the moment to the *DAT* subtests, we must admit that they provide only limited help in establishing a vocational goal for Henry and that what they provide is largely negative. If we exclude collegiate education, we exclude those jobs that depend upon college or professional education. We do not need to consider law, medicine, engineering, architecture, or similar professional occupations. The low verbal, spelling, and sentences scores may also steer us away from some noncollegiate jobs with a heavy linguistic loading, for example, stenographer. However, that still leaves us perhaps 90 percent of the world of work to choose from. Should Henry think of becoming a mechanic? A farmer? A salesman? A conductor like his father? Any of these and many others appear quite possible in the light of his aptitude profile.

Why can we offer no more specific positive guidance on the basis of Henry's abilities? Basically, four considerations enter in.

1. *Profile not sharply differentiated.* In Henry's case there isn't too much difference in his different abilities. His scores on this testing range from the 20th percentile (*Spelling*) to the 60th (*Mechanical*), but in this middle percentile range the error of measurement is such that his relative standing on any pair of tests could quite possibly be reversed if he were retested with another form of the tests. Even assuming that the obtained scores are approximately correct, most of the differences are not large enough to have great practical significance. We may feel that the lower scores on the tests of verbal comprehension and language usage have some significance for vocational planning, but beyond this there is not much to say.

Many people will show test profiles of this general type. Their abilities are all at about the same level. Their test scores provide a general indication of level of ability but limited cues as to specific strengths and weaknesses. With no special strengths or weaknesses, they appear about equally likely to succeed in many different types of jobs.

2. *Lack of unique relationship of ability profile to job success.* Even when a person is distinctively higher on one or two abilities than on others, this need not mean that there are one or two specific jobs in which he will be uniquely successful. The boy whose specially high point is mechanical comprehension may do well as an automotive mechanic, but he may also do well as a telpehone repairman or as a farmer. The person high on numerical ability may be successful as a bookkeeper or as a surveyor. For the typical individual there are at least several superficially rather different jobs for which his ability pattern is equally suitable and many others for which his talents are adequate. In terms of their aptitude requirements, jobs come in sizable families, and one family merges gradually into the next. Fitness for different jobs is a matter of degree, and any person is about equally well suited to a number of jobs. Positive guidance can, therefore, be only in terms of broad segments of the world of work. There is no one job for which each person is best fitted.

3. *Lack of knowledge of the ability requirements of jobs.* Over and above the limitations arising out of overlap in the true ability requirements of jobs, there are limitations stemming from our own ignorance. Our knowledge of what abilities are required by what jobs is still quite limited. We are not in a position to state with confidence what abilities a high-school student should display if he is to become a successful plumber, shoe salesman, truck driver, or service-station operator. We do not know what people who have been successful and contented in these jobs were like when they entered the world of work or what they are like now. We do not know what types of people have tried to work in these fields and failed. We have a good deal of information about the abilities that are required to succeed in advanced training but only scattered information about what is required to succeed in a job.

A fair part of the information that does exist is not readily available in published form. Part of it has been done for specific private companies and has not been made public, either through specific policy or because of pressure of other activities. Part of it has been gathered by such government agencies as the U.S. Employment Service, and serves primarily the functions of the gathering agency.

4. *Techniques to measure certain abilities are inadequate.* We have developed sound and practical tools of measurement for only part of the range of human abilities. One most impressive gap lies in the area of social skills and techniques. Abilities to understand and react sagaciously to problems involving other people appear to be important in many sales, contact, and managerial jobs. We have no tests of demonstrated validity in this area. Skill in practical problem solving, not solving puzzles of a verbal and academic sort, is a related area in which we do not measure very well. Other important gaps also exist. Our inability to make

sound and distinctive suggestions about job possibilities stems in part from our inability to appraise important distinguishing aptitudes.

Role of Interest Measures in Identifying Vocational Objectives

So far we have not discussed the use of the interest inventory results in Henry's case. When the problem is to explore areas of work and focalize vocational objectives, the interest measures may be of as much or more value than ability measures. They should not be interpreted rigidly or taken as Gospel truth, but they do provide a starting point for discussion. Thus, the counselor could explore with Henry his apparent interest in computational and clerical types of activities. If the test scores were supported in discussions, the next step might be to provide Henry with a chance to become acquainted with possible clerical types of work in his community, either through reading or hearing about the jobs or through vacation or part-time employment.

Summarizing, in view of all the above it appears clear that guidance with relation to vocational plans will in most instances have to be couched in rather general terms. Guidance with regard to general educational level will be quite possible. Some indications of broad areas and types of jobs will often be appropriate. Beyond this, there is much free space within which interest, local opportunity, exploratory tryout, and individual idiosyncrasy may freely operate.

RESOURCES FOR JUDGING THE EDUCATIONAL AND VOCATIONAL SIGNIFICANCE OF TEST SCORES

Before he can provide constructive guidance to a client's thinking about educational or vocational plans, a counselor must have a clear picture in his own mind of the educational and vocational implications of the counselee's test scores. He must have an estimate of the probability of realizing a stated objective or a picture of objectives that are appropriate. To what sources may the counselor turn to build up his skills of evaluating test patterns in a sound and realistic manner? Where can he find help in translating a set of test scores into a prediction of probable success?

Ready-made tables showing the chances for success in any given job at different test score levels are largely nonexistent at the present time. Perhaps they never can exist. For now, the counselor must be content with much more modest aids. We will consider a few of these.

Revised Minnesota Occupational Rating Scales

This little monograph (Paterson et al, 1953) provides ratings of some 400 occupations with respect to the minimum level of (1) academic ability, (2) mechanical ability, (3) social intelligence, (4) clerical ability, (5) musical ability, (6) artistic ability, and (7) physical agility required to succeed in the occupation. Ratings are given in four levels, which are generally to be interpreted as follows:

A: above the 90th percentile of the adult population
B: 76th to 90th " " " " "
C: 26th to 75th " " " " "
D: 1st to 25th " " " " "

The exception is the scales for musical and artistic ability, in which A is defined as the 97th percentile or higher, B as the 90th to 96th percentile, and C as the 26th to 90th percentile. The ratings are frankly a synthesis of judgments and these judgments were made a good many years ago. However, they were the judgments of highly trained individuals whose professional careers had centered around the study of jobs and the requirements of jobs.

We might consider our two illustrative cases to see what guidance the scales can give us. First, considering Walter with his aspiration to be a doctor, we have the following picture:

	Physicians	Walter
Academic	A	B−
Mechanical	B	B−
Social	B	?
Clerical	C	C
Musical	D	?
Artistic	D	?
Physical	B	?

On the basis of this judgmental standard, we would have to question more seriously whether Walter has the academic aptitude to become a doctor. We would need information from other sources about Walter's social ability and physical agility to judge whether these also represent points of discrepancy.

Let us now suppose that Henry is considering trying to get a clerical job with the railroad that employs his father. He hopes that he might work as a ticket agent or possibly as station agent in a small town. The evidence appears in the following table:

	Station Agent	Henry
Academic	C	C
Mechanical	C	C
Social	C	?
Clerical	B	C
Musical	D	?
Artistic	C	?
Physical	C	?

We would have to judge whether the discrepancy between the evidence we have on Henry's clerical skill and the demands of the job is a sufficient basis for discouraging this particular goal. Further evidence should be sought on Henry's clerical skills.

Test Manuals

Some test manuals provide information on the scores of particular occupational groups. The report may include no more than the median score for specific groups. We saw such figures for the *General Aptitude Test Battery* in Table 11.4. Sometimes rather complete norms may be provided for individuals in particular occupations. Thus, the *Minnesota Vocational Test for Clerical Workers* provides percentile norms for the following groups of workers in the clerical field:

Women: Office machine operators.
Stenographers and typists.
General clerical workers.
Routine clerical workers.

Men: Bank tellers.
Accountants and bookkeepers.
General clerical workers.
Routine clerical workers.
Shipping and stock clerks.

On the average, members of these occupational groups score substantially higher on this test than do workers in general. A score set at perhaps the 10th percentile of persons employed in one of these occupations might constitute a warning level in the guidance of aspiring students.

A test manual that provides extensive standards on the occupational requirements of jobs is the manual for the *General Aptitude Test Battery* (*GATB*) of the U.S. Employment Service. This manual identifies thirty-six "occupational aptitude patterns" and proposes minimum aptitude standards for each. Thus, pattern 1 is defined by minimum scores of 125* on *G* (general intelligence), 115 on *N* (numerical ability), and 115 on *S* (spatial ability). Assigned to this pattern are a great variety of engineering jobs, as well as physician and surgeon, computer programmer, and urban planner. Thirty-five other patterns are given, requiring different aptitude combinations and different minimum levels, and many specific jobs are assigned to each.

For many of the jobs, the evidence upon which the determination of minimum scores and the assignment of jobs to patterns is based is rather limited, and the evidence is open to some criticism on technical grounds. However, the *GATB* data available in the records at the U.S. Employment Service represent one of the major pools of data on the relation of tests to job success. The manuals for this test will repay careful examination by the counselor.

Data on Army General Classification Test

Information on the level of general intellectual ability of individuals in different occupations is provided by World War II *Army General Classification Test* data. The data for selected occupations are shown in Table 10.3. A much more complete table, covering many more occupations, may be found in the original journal article (Stewart, 1947). This table shows the general intellectual level of young men who had entered different occupations. However, it gives no indication of requirements for more specialized abilities.

Follow-Up Studies

A few follow-up studies of men tested with an interest test or an aptitude test battery have been carried out on a scale large enough to give some picture of the sort of men that work in different occupations. Table 12.4 shows the picture for a group of veterans tested with the *Kuder Preference Record*. Data are available for some 10,000 Air Force veterans of World War II who were tested in 1943 and located in 1955–56, describing the test profile for about 125 occupational groupings (Thorndike and Hagen 1959). Eventually, one may hope that follow-up data from the half million students tested in Project Talent, referred to earlier in the chapter, will further enrich the picture of different occupations. The characteristics of the people who *have* gotten into an occupation provide at least some cue to the sort of people who *can* get into that occupation.

* Standard scores with mean of 100 and SD of 20.

SUMMARY STATEMENT

The process of using tests in educational and vocational counseling involves two main steps. First, the counselor must himself arrive at a sound interpretation of the significance of the test data. Secondly, he must communicate that interpretation to the counselee in such a way that the counselee's self-picture and plans come to correspond better with the realities of his abilities and interests.

Two somewhat different situations arise in the interpreting of test results. In one, the client expresses definite educational or vocational goals. The counselor must interpret the test results in relation to those goals. He must arrive at some judgment as to the likelihood that the goals can be attained and the probability that they will prove acceptable to the client if they are attained. The evidence by which the counselor is to reach this judgment is fragmentary and scattered. Some sources that may help him are suggested in the previous section.

In the second case, the client's goals are vague and undefined. The counselor must direct the counselee's attention to areas that look promising in terms of the test results. For most clients this type of guidance can be only in the broadest of terms because of the wide overlap in the abilities that different jobs require. Guidance as to general level of educational and vocational aspiration seems plausible, and counselees can be steered away from plans calling for abilities they lack. Positive suggestions should, however, be expressed in quite general and tentative terms.

The process of communicating test results also raises certain problems. If the test results are to be helpful, they must be presented in a way that makes it possible for the client to accept them. This is particularly difficult when the tests are less flattering than the client's previous self-picture.

Test results should usually be presented in rather general terms and with emphasis upon the interpretation and significance of the results. The interpretation should avoid overemphasis on exact test scores and should at the same time help the client to relate the tests to the plans to be made and the action to be taken.

QUESTIONS AND EXERCISES

1. If you were a counselor in a Georgia high school, how would you use a prediction equation such as the one for the University of Georgia shown on p. 593?

2. How specific is the vocational guidance that can be given on the basis of scores from a battery of ability and interest tests? What other factors should be taken into account in helping a student to formulate vocational plans?

3. What obstacles to communication is a counselor likely to encounter? What steps can be taken to overcome these?

4. In reporting test results to a counselee, how specific should a vocational counselor be?

5. What sort of validity data about an aptitude test would be most useful to a vocational counselor in giving guidance to a student? How should this information be organized and presented to the counselor for his use?

6. A boy got the following scores on the *Differential Aptitude Test Battery* and the *Kuder Preference Record* administered in the eleventh grade. What tentative plans seem suitable in the light of the test scores? How definite should these plans be at the present time? What further information should be sought?

DAT Subtest	Percentile	*Kuder* Scale	Percentile
Verbal Reasoning	95	*Scientific*	68
Numerical Ability	70	*Outdoor*	82
VR + NA	85	*Computational*	36
Abstract Reasoning	90	*Clerical*	43
Space Relations	80	*Literary*	72
Mechanical Reasoning	85	*Artistic*	45
Clerical Speed and Accuracy	60	*Musical*	38
Language Usage: Spelling	90	*Persuasive*	67
Language Usage: Sentences	95	*Mechanical*	35
		Social Service	18

7. In the same eleventh grade another boy had the following scores. What would be the objectives of counseling in his case?

DAT Subtest	Percentile	*Kuder* Scale	Percentile
Verbal Reasoning	15	*Scientific*	26
Numerical Ability	3	*Outdoor*	88
VR + NA	5	*Computational*	25
Abstract Reasoning	15	*Clerical*	58
Space Relations	30	*Literary*	12
Mechanical Reasoning	45	*Artistic*	28
Clerical Speed and Accuracy	40	*Musical*	62
Language Usage: Spelling	25	*Persuasive*	56
Language Usage: Sentences	10	*Mechanical*	75
		Social Service	55

8. How should a high school counselor use results such as those shown in Tables 10.3 and 11.4? What are the limitations on their usefulness?

9. What significance do the data in Tables 18.1 and 18.2 have for a high school counselor? How should such results influence his work with students?

10. What does Figure 18.2 tell about changes in occupational choice? How might a counselor use this kind of information?

REFERENCES

Bennett, G. K., Seashore, H. G., & Wesman, A. G. *Manual for the differential aptitude tests.* (4th ed.) New York: Psychological Corporation, 1966.

College Entrance Examination Board. *Manual of freshman class profiles.* New York: College Entrance Examination Board, 1965.

Flanagan, J. C. & Cooley, W. W. *Project Talent: One-year follow-up studies.* Pittsburgh, Pennsylvania: School of Education, University of Pittsburgh, 1966.

Gee, H. H. Differential characteristics of student bodies: Implications for the study of medical education. Paper read at the Conference on Selection and Educational Differentiation, Berkeley, California; May 1959.

Paterson, D. G., Gerken, C. d'A., & Hahn, M. E. *Revised Minnesota Occupational Rating Scales.* Minneapolis, Minnesota: University of Minnesota Press, 1953.

Regents of the University System of Georgia. *Normative data for the 1965–66 freshman class, University System of Georgia.* Atlanta, Georgia: Regents of the University System of Georgia, 1967.

Stewart, N. A.G.C.T. scores of army personnel grouped by occupations. *Occupations,* 1947, **26,** 5–41.

Thorndike, R. L. & Hagen, E. P. *10,000 careers.* New York:Wiley, 1959.

SUGGESTED ADDITIONAL READING

Baer, M. F. *Occupational information: The dynamics of its nature and use.* Chicago: Science Research Associates, 1964.

Bennett, G. K., Seashore, H. G., & Wesman, A. G. *Counseling from profiles: A casebook for the Differential Aptitude Tests.* New York: Psychological Corporation, 1951.

Berdie, R. F. et al. *Counseling and the use of tests.* Minneapolis, Minnesota: Student Counseling Bureau, University of Minnesota, 1962.

Campbell, D. P. *The results of counseling: Twenty-five years later.* Philadelphia: W. B. Saunders, 1965.

Goldman, L. *Using tests in counseling.* New York: Appleton-Century-Crofts, 1961. Chapters 4, 11–14.

Roe, A. *The psychology of occupations.* New York: Wiley, 1956. Chapters 6, 7.

Shartle, C. L. *Occupational information.* (3rd ed.) Englewood Cliffs, New Jersey: Prentice-Hall, 1959. Chapter 11.

Super, D. E. & Crites, J. D. *Appraising vocational fitness.* (Rev. ed.) New York: Harper & Row, 1962. Chapters 1 and 21 and Appendices A and B.

Tyler, L. E. *The work of the counselor.* (2nd ed.) New York: Appleton-Century-Crofts, 1961. Chapters 6, 7.

CHAPTER 19

Tests in the Selection and Classification of Personnel

ooooooooooooooooooooooooooooooooooooooooooooooooooooooooooooooooooooooooooooooooooooooooooooooooo

ONE major function that tests have come to serve in the United States is that of screening applicants for a training program or a job. Colleges and professional schools use standardized measures of achievement and aptitude as at least partial bases for deciding which applicants to admit. Vast numbers of civil service positions are filled on the basis of competitive examination. Industry selects men for many jobs in terms of their performance on tests of relevant abilities. All branches of the Armed Services have come to rely upon them to aid in the selection of men for entry into different types of technical schools and for assignment of men to different career fields. Such a selection program has as its objective maximizing the average level of achievement of those who are accepted for the training and the job and minimizing the occurrence of failures.

The school or employer that proposes to introduce a program of selection testing faces a number of issues. What is the best test to use, in terms of effectiveness versus cost? Should a single test be used or should it be supplemented by others? If more than one test is to be used, how should the tests be combined in order to produce the most efficient team? How should test results be combined with non-test data about the individual?

STEPS IN SETTING UP A SELECTION PROGRAM

The basic pattern of selection research is simple and straightforward. You decide what types of measures are promising as predictors of success in the training program or job with which you are concerned. You make a judgment as to what can best be accepted as an index of success in the training program or job. You buy or make the tests and administer them to a group of applicants. You get measures of success for these same applicants after they have had a period of experience in the training program or job. You determine the relationship of each predictor to the criterion measure of success. You pick the best predictor or predictors and use them to screen future applicants.

That is the basic pattern. There are, however, a number of issues that arise at each step in the proceedings. Some involve complex statistical problems that we cannot go into here. However, we shall consider the operations step by step and try to anticipate some of the recurring problems.

Picking Tryout Tests for Selection Research

How shall we decide what sorts of tests to try out as predictors of success in a given training program or job? Of course, we may have some hunches based on our familiarity with the school or job. The very fact that it is a school, for example, suggests that some type of scholastic aptitude test would be appropriate. But if we are to refine our crude original hunches, we can do it only by studying the school program or job duties. We carry out what has been called a *job analysis.* The term job analysis is a somewhat ambiguous one. It covers assorted techniques of studying jobs for one or more of a variety of purposes. The purpose may be to determine salary schedules, to improve safety procedures, to develop training programs, or to define ladders of promotion. It may also be to describe the tasks done on the job and to estimate what abilities and personal qualities are required to do those tasks well. The job analysis with which we are concerned focuses on this last type of information.

There is no special magic technique for job analysis. The analyst operates by going out and observing people working at the job, by talking to them about what they do, by examining the tools they have to use and the textbooks or instruction manuals they have to read, and by observing the conditions under which they have to work. His problem is to get a complete description of the job. From this and from his background of knowledge of human abilities, he organizes his hypotheses as to the abilities that are important for the job. These statements of job requirements are refined guesses based on scrutiny of the job.

Given a set of educated guesses as to the abilities important for a job, the next step is to translate them into actual test procedures. Often, the practical step will be to try some of the ready-made tests that appear to measure abilities much like those suggested by the job analysis. The sources suggested in Chapter 8 will identify available instruments and provide information about them.

In other cases, there may be no existing test that appears to fill the bill. It is then necessary to try to invent test tasks that will tap the functions whose importance was indicated by the job analysis. Test specifications must be prepared and tasks or items constructed. Many of the guide lines set down in Chapters 3 and 4 will apply, though tests of special aptitudes may differ quite a bit from tests of school achievement. Usually, it will be desirable to try out any new test on preliminary groups. Answers will be needed for such questions as the following:

1. Are the instructions sufficiently clear and detailed and are there enough practice items?

2. Are the time limits appropriate? If this is a speed test, are there enough materials to keep everybody busy? If the test emphasizes primarily power, are the limits long enough so everyone has a chance to try most of the items?

3. Are the separate test items satisfactory? Administration of the test to a preliminary group and analysis of the responses to each item by high- and low-scoring individuals is usually desirable as a means of eliminating items that fail to discriminate or that are too easy or too hard.

4. Does the test measure with at least moderate reliability? If reliability is very low, steps to improve it by lengthening the test or by revising and selecting items will usually be indicated.

Identifying a Suitable Criterion Measure

If we are to evaluate a test or some other type of predictor, we must have something against which to evaluate it. When we are dealing with success in college, professional school, or some type of training program, marks in courses or grade-point average are usually ready at hand. We tend to take them more or less for granted and use them as our criterion measure of success. This is good enough as far as it goes. We may have certain reservations about course grades as a standard of success, but the judgments they represent are at least a first approximation to the objectives of the educational program.

When our objective is to select persons for a job, as distinct from a training program, the problem of a criterion measure becomes much more troublesome. The novice in the field is likely to assume that he need only look and he will find ready at hand some suitable production record or fitness rating to tell him how good a worker each employee is. The truth of the matter is that existing records are rarely satisfactory and that better ones are hard to come by. One function of a job analysis is to explore and evaluate existing records that might serve as indices of job success and to look for other better procedures that might be substituted for them. Possible indicators of success that we may choose to use include (1) academic or training school grades, (2) proficiency tests, (3) performance records, and (4) ratings by supervisors or associates.

ACADEMIC GRADES. Grade in a training program provides a fairly simple and straightforward measure that is available with little delay and is usually of satisfactory reliabilty. The sad thing is that a summary of evidence to date (Ghiselli, 1966) indicates that there is often little correspondence between the tests that have high validity for a training criterion and those that predict success on the job itself. The tests of verbal, quantitative, and reasoning abilities that are good predictors of ability to learn are not comparably good measures of job performance. If the selection tests emphasize ability to absorb the training, they are likely to be relatively inefficient in picking persons who will later be judged to be good workers. Of course, when successful completion of a training program is a prerequisite for entry into the job, a certain type of administrative validity is automatically given to this type of criterion.

JOB PROFICIENCY TESTS. Suitable job proficiency tests are rarely available, and the preparation of a test measuring job competence represents quite an undertaking. In some jobs, accountancy for example, many of the knowledges and skills of the job can be reduced to test tasks. In others, such as selling, a test has quite limited possibilities. Often proficiency tests will need to be performance tests or performance checks. Thus, the competence of an airplane mechanic may be evaluated with some success by having a skilled mechanic observe the person being tested as he demonstrates various key procedures in plane maintenance and repair. A proficiency test can at best measure certain job knowledges and skills; it cannot tell how effectively the individual will apply them at work on the job. It may tell how well he *can* do certain tasks, but it cannot tell how well he *will* do them.

PRODUCTION MEASURES. The measure of job success to which one is always likely to turn first when seeking a criterion measure is some record of job output. The number of widgets produced per hour, the monthly sales of gilhickeys, or the number of defective whortlebugs per hundred seem like sound indices of the quality of a worker. In some cases, performance records can indeed be used to advantage. However, there are many jobs for which no simple performance measure can be found. The receptionist, the bank teller, the department supervisor, the plumber, and the teacher are doing jobs in which we can hardly find any product to count or score. The product is too varied or intangible to provide us with an acceptable criterion.

Even in those jobs in which there is some product to count or score, there are many pitfalls in using the product as a criterion measure. We may consider several briefly.

1. The product may depend upon other people. Thus, during World War II attempts to use bombing records as a measure of the competence of a bombardier broke down in part because where the bomb fell was affected by the way the pilot flew the plane. Again, the sales of an insurance agent may depend upon the type and amount of supervision and help he gets from the agency manager.
2. Outside conditions may vary from person to person. The quality of equipment may be important—new tools versus old, good maintenance versus poor. Prosperity of the neighborhood may be a factor in any measure of sales volume.
3. A sample of performance may be quite unreliable. Thus, accuracy of bombing by a single student showed wide variations from day to day. A limited sample of production or sales may be similarly undependable.
4. The performance measure may represent only a limited aspect of the job. Thus, for a life-insurance salesman the dollar volume of sales may be less important than the *permanence* of the sales. There is no profit in lapsed policies. It might be possible to keep a record of the output of dictation and typing for each of a group of secretaries, but this would take no account of dependability in remembering appointments or diplomacy in answering the phone.

An actual record of performance is undoubtedly an attractive candidate as a criterion of job proficiency. But performance records need careful scrutiny in terms of such considerations as those mentioned above. If the measure holds up under scrutiny, as it sometimes will, it can be used as a standard against which predictor measures can be appraised. But if no production records are available or if existing records are unsatisfactory for one reason or another, we shall have to look elsewhere for our criterion measure.

RATINGS OF JOB PROFICIENCY. In actual practice, the selection research worker is often thrown back upon ratings for lack of any more satisfactory criterion measure. It is almost always possible to arrange to get some type of rating, usually by instructor or supervisor. Ratings are applicable to almost any type of job. The fact that a rater can synthesize different aspects of achievement in one judgment and can make allowances for special external factors that may have favored or handicapped the worker is in some ways an advantage. However, the limitations of ratings as evaluations of competence are many. We have discussed them in detail in Chapter 13 and need not repeat that discussion here. It will suffice to say that the reliability of criterion ratings is often low, and they are frequently biased by factors not truly related to competence. Various of the techniques of analytical checklists or forced-choice judgments have been applied in an attempt to overcome these limitations. These procedures have some promise but are quite laborious. It is surprising, but true, that in personnel research obtaining good criteria of proficiency often calls for more skill and effort than developing predictor tests.

Administering Tests for Validation

Once tests have been selected for tryout and plans have been made to collect as good criterion data as circumstances permit, the tests should be administered to a group on a research basis. Ideally, tests are given to persons *before* they start on the job or training program. If the tests are given to individuals who are already on the job or who have already taken part of the training course, we cannot say how much of any relationship we find is due to actual experience in the job or training program. Thus, if we give a reading test at the end of the freshman year in college and find that those with high scholastic averages are good readers, we are never sure to what extent they did well in college because they were good readers to start with or to what extent they learned good reading skills as they worked effectively on their college courses. The motivation of applicants and of accepted students or workers may also be different, and this difference may distort the results.

It is always logically preferable to try out tests on a group that has yet to start on the job or training program. However, this procedure raises certain practical problems. Gathering data in this way is a slower process. There is always a delay of months, even years, while the persons tested are completing their training or getting well enough established in the job so that we can get a reasonable measure of their competence. Flow of new personnel into a job may be so meager that a long time is required to accumulate a sufficient sample of applicants. Reaching examinees for follow-up months or years later may be difficult. For these practical reasons, tests are sometimes tried out on groups already working in a job. But results for such a group must always be considered tentative when interpreted as evidence of the *predictive* effectiveness of the tests.

One problem that usually is serious in validating tests in a *job* context is that of getting groups of adequate size. The accuracy with which relationships can be established depends upon the size of the sample upon which statistics are based. The precision of the correlation coefficient is illustrated in Table 19.1 on page 622. Thus, if we have a sample of only 25 cases and the *true* value of the re-

TABLE 19.1 RANGE OUTSIDE OF WHICH SAMPLE CORRELATION COEFFICIENT WILL FALL 50 PERCENT OF TIME FOR SAMPLES OF DIFFERENT SIZES AND DIFFERENT VALUES OF TRUE CORRELATION

True Value of Correlation	Size of Sample				
	25	50	100	200	400
.00	−.143−+.143	−.098−+.098	−.068−+.068	−.048−+.048	−.034−+.034
.20	.058−.333	.104−.292	.133−.264	.153−.245	.167−.232
.30	.164−.425	.208−.387	.237−.362	.256−.343	.269−.330
.40	.273−.514	.315−.480	.341−.456	.359−.440	.371−.429
.50	.384−.600	.422−.570	.447−.550	.463−.536	.474−.525
.60	.500−.684	.534−.659	.555−.642	.568−.630	.578−.621

lationship in the *total population* of all cases is represented by a correlation of .20, we stand a 50-50 chance of getting a value that is either above .333 or below .058. The other entries in the table are to be interpreted in the same way.

Clearly, the larger the sample the more dependable our conclusions will be with respect to which tests to select as predictors. How large a sample do we need? This is the old question: How high is up? The only answer we can give is: The more the better. But there is probably a lower limit below which it doesn't pay to carry out statistical analysis of tests as predictors. At some point, our rational judgment based upon the nature of the tests and the nature of the job is probably more dependable than the empirical results from the small sample. We would judge that there is rarely any profit in computing predictor-criterion correlations for groups of 25 or less and that the value of analyzing groups of under 100 is often questionable. With samples as small as this, we can often put about as much trust in our judgment as in our statistics.

STATISTICAL ANALYSIS OF SELECTION TEST DATA

For the research worker analyzing several predictor tests in relation to a certain criterion of job success, the essential statistic is the correlation of each predictor with the criterion. The higher the correlation, the more effective is the predictor in identifying those who will do well on the criterion measure. We shall illustrate this point—and also a number of other issues that arise in using predictor test data—with a small set of actual data.

In the course of some research on electronics personnel, the decision was made to try out test materials dealing with (1) mathematics, (2) shop knowledge, and (3) electricity. The criterion measure in this case was a composite of grades received in an 8-month training program. Data are analyzed here for a sample of 99 students. Some were eliminated for academic failure before completing training, and these were assigned grades below the lowest of those graduating. Some of those who graduated had grades so low that they were designated as marginal. In all, 30 cases fell in this failed or marginally satisfactory group. The correlations of the three brief tests with the academic grades criterion were as follows:

Mathematics	.40	(20-item test)
Shop	.30	(10-item test)
Electricity	.58	(15-item test)

The numbers of unsatisfactory (failed or marginal) and satisfactory students at each score level are shown in Table 19.2 on p. 624. To see what these correlations mean in practical terms, let us consider two levels of cutting score. Suppose that we are setting cutting scores to eliminate (1) about one-third of the unsatisfactory cases and (2) about two-thirds of the unsatisfactory cases. Considering each test, what would be the *cost* in loss of individuals who would have become satisfactory graduates? The results are summarized below.

	Low Cutoff			*High Cutoff*		
	Min. Score	*Failures Elim.*	*Successes Lost*	*Min. Score*	*Failures Elim.*	*Successes Lost*
Mathematics	9	33.3%	14.5%	14	66.7%	37.7%
Shop	5	36.7	21.7	7	73.3	56.5
Electricity	7	30.0	8.7	9	76.7	24.7

This little table shows the relationship between the validity coefficient for the test and its practical effectiveness. The difference in the three selection tests shows up most clearly at the higher cutoff. At this point, using the electricity test, we could screen out 76.7 percent of the unsuccessful group at a cost of only 24.7 percent of our future successes. By contrast, the shop test screens out 73.7 percent at a cost of 56.5 percent. The greater efficiency of the electricity test is clearly evident, and if we could use only one test this is the one that we should keep.

COMBINING TESTS. When we have used several tests as predictors, a question that we often face is whether we should be content with the one best test or whether we should use more than one. If the decision is to use more than one, we must then decide how many to use and which ones. A full exploration of these

TABLE 19.2 NUMBER OF MEN RECEIVING SATISFACTORY AND UNSATISFACTORY GRADES IN ELECTRONICS TRAINING AT EACH SCORE LEVEL ON THREE SELECTION TESTS

	Mathematics		Shop		Electricity	
Score	Unsatis.	Satis.	Unsatis.	Satis.	Unsatis.	Satis.
1			1	1		
2			1	2		
3	1	1	7	3		1
4	2		2	9	1	
5	4		4	11	4	3
6	1	1	7	13	4	2
7	1	4	5	12	4	2
8	1	4	2	10	10	9
9	5	1	1	6	6	11
10		4		2	1	11
11	1	3				6
12	4	5				8
13		3				6
14	1	4				6
15	3	8				4
16	1	8				
17	3	12				
18	2	9				
19		1				
20		1				
Correlation	.40		.30		.58	

problems leads into complexities which we cannot consider here and, indeed, brings us face to face with some unsolved statistical problems. However, we can open up some of the main approaches to the problem.

In our illustration, the problem we face is whether to use only the electricity test or whether to give some weight to the mathematics and shop tests. The extent to which the math and shop tests will be useful will depend upon the extent to which they are measuring abilities *different from* those measured by the electricity test. If they are measuring essentially the same abilities as those tapped by the electricity test but not measuring them as effectively, there is no point in adding the extra tests to our battery. However, if they are measuring different components of our criterion, then pooling the several measures should give us more complete coverage of the essential abilities and, consequently, better prediction of the criterion.

To determine whether the predictor tests are measuring the same or different abilities, we must look at the correlations between them. These are:

Mathematics versus Shop	−.02
Mathematics versus Electricity	.37
Shop versus Electricity	.30

Thus, the electricity test shows some overlap with each of the other tests but not a very great overlap. There is most in common between the mathematics and electricity tests. The mathematics and shop tests are almost completely unrelated.

Is the overlap of electricity with each of the other two tests so great that they can add nothing of value to our prediction? To answer this question, we may compute a statistic known as the *partial correlation.* The partial correlation is a measure of the relationship which remains after the effect of one or more other factors is removed.* In this instance, it is the correlation of academic grades with math or with shop for students all of whom fall at the same score on the electricity test. These partial correlations are:

Math versus grades, electricity score partialed out	.25
Shop versus grades, electricity score partialed out	.16

Thus, we see that each of the other tests has some validity independent of the part held in common with the electricity test, though eliminating the part which they hold in common with the electricity test has reduced the validity of each.

THE VALIDITY OF A COMPOSITE. We must ask now how much we could gain in validity by using two tests or all three, combining them in the most advantageous way. For this we can compute the *multiple correlation.* The multiple correlation is the maximum prediction that can be obtained from an additive combination of scores on two or more tests.† In our example, the multiple correlations for combinations of two and three tests are as follows:

* The formula for partial correlation is

$$r_{12.3} = \frac{r_{12} - r_{13}r_{23}}{\sqrt{1 - r_{13}^2}\,\sqrt{1 - r_{23}^2}}$$

where $r_{12.3}$ is the partial correlation of variables 1 and 2, with the effect variable 3 removed.

r_{12}, r_{13}, r_{23} are the correlation of variables 1 and 2, 1 and 3, and 2 and 3, respectively.

† For two predictors the multiple correlation is given by the formula

$$r_{1.23} = \sqrt{1 - (1 - r_{12}^2)(1 - r_{13.2}^2)}$$

where $r_{1.23}$ indicates the multiple correlation of 1 with 2 and 3, and $r_{13.2}$ is the partial correlation of 1 and 3 with 2 held constant. The formula for more complex cases will be found in standard statistics textbooks.

Electricity and Mathematics	.615
Electricity and Shop	.596
Mathematics and Shop	.500
All three tests	.634

Thus, we see that the combined tests give a somewhat higher correlation (.634) with the criterion than does the best single test (.58) if the tests are combined with the most appropriate weights.

It may be possible to get a better intuitive feeling for partial and multiple correlation (though necessarily a mathematically inexact one) from a pictorial representation. Consider the diagrams in Fig. 19.1. These are designed to portray the relationships between the criterion score (C), the electricity test (E) and the mathematics test (M). Diagrams I, II, and III show the tests taken by pairs.

Thus, in diagram I, M represents what is measured only by the mathematics test, MC represents what is common to the mathematics test and the criterion, and C represents what is involved in the criterion score that is *not* measured by

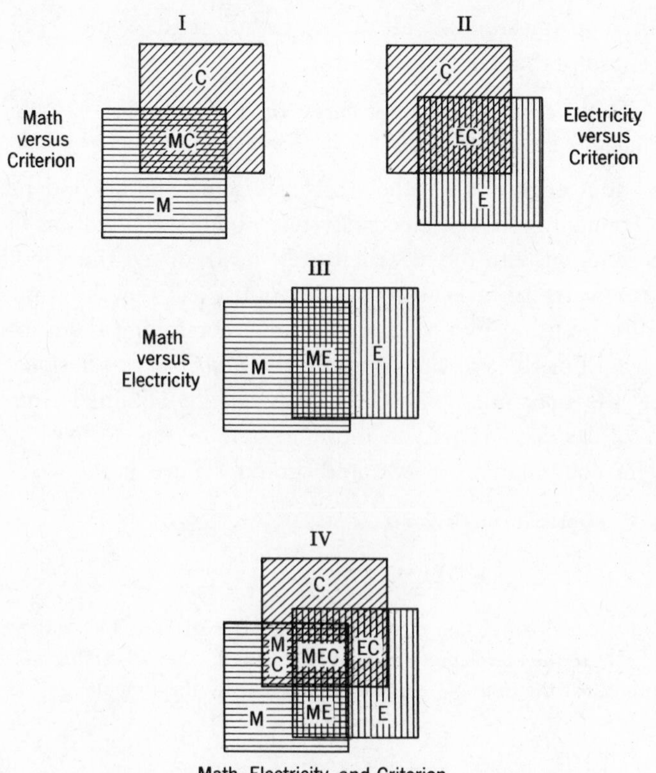

Fig. 19.1 Graphic representation of partial and multiple correlations.

the mathematics test. When comparing diagrams I and II, one can note that the area EC is larger than the area MC, corresponding to the larger correlation, that is, .58 for electricity and .40 for mathematics.

Now look at diagram IV. This shows all three tests at once. Note that a larger part of C, the criterion measure, is covered jointly by E and M than is covered by either of them separately. This larger area (MC + MEC + EC) corresponds to the larger *multiple correlation.* The area MEC can be thought of as the part of the criterion measure that is predicted by *both* M and E, a part for which the two predictors overlap and duplicate one another. The areas MC and EC represent the *unique* contributions of M and E, their *partial correlation* with C. Note that the area MC is quite small, corresponding to the rather small partial correlation between M and C. The partial correlation is small because much of what M and C have in common is also measured by E, that is, the part labeled MEC in the diagram. The diagram shows clearly that the gain from adding a new test to a selection battery depends upon the added test measuring some *new* aspect of the criterion that is not measured by the test or tests we are already using.

WEIGHTING TESTS. Our next problem is to determine the best set of weights. These are known as *regression weights.* They are best in the sense that they reduce to a minimum the errors in predicting the criterion score.* For our set of three tests the regression weights are, respectively,

Mathematics	.24
Shop	.17
Electricity	.44

These are the weights we should use if all our tests had the same standard deviation (for example, if they were all in standard score units). However, when the tests are in raw-score units, we must take account of the standard deviation. A test with a large standard deviation already receives a heavy weight just from the variability of its scores. The relative weights to be applied to raw scores are the regression weights *divided by* the corresponding standard deviations. For our example, we have the following:

* With two predictor variables, the regression weights to be applied to standard scores are given by the formula

$$\beta_{12.3} = \frac{r_{12} - r_{13}r_{23}}{1 - r_{23}^2}$$

$$\beta_{13.2} = \frac{r_{13} - r_{12}r_{23}}{1 - r_{23}^2}$$

The formulas and computing procedures for three or more predictors will be found in standard statistics textbooks.

	Standard Deviation	*Regression Weights*	*Raw-Score Weights*	*Integral Weights*
Mathematics	4.40	.24	.055	2
Shop	2.06	.17	.083	3
Electricity	2.76	.44	.159	6

The weights in the final column of the above table are simple integers that stand in very nearly the same ratios as the raw-score weights. They are more convenient to use than the decimal weights and are as good for all practical purposes. If we wish to combine our separate tests, we can use these integers as weighting factors to be applied to the scores on the three tests. Thus, we could take 2 times the mathematics score plus 3 times the shop score plus 6 times the electricity score as the composite score for each student.

We have calculated composite scores using the above multiplying factors. These composite scores were correlated with the criterion and in this instance the result checked perfectly with the predicted correlation of .634. To see what, if anything, we really gained by the pooling, we may prepare another table like Table 19.2. We have done this in Table 19.3. Repeating our calculations of cost and gain from two levels of cutting score, we find that we can:

Eliminate 23.3% of failures at a cost of 4.3% of successes, or
" 70.0% " " " " " " 20.3% " "

Comparing this accomplishment with that for the electricity test alone, it is hard to see any difference between them. In a sample of this small size the small

TABLE 19.3 NUMBER PASSING AND FAILING ELECTRONICS TRAINING AT EACH COMPOSITE SCORE LEVEL
(2 Math + 3 Shop + 6 Electricity)

Score	Unsatisfactory	Satisfactory
50–59	2	1
60–69	5	2
70–79	6	3
80–89	8	8
90–99	7	12
100–109	2	9
110–119		11
120–129		10
130–139		7
140–149		4
150–159		2

difference in correlation does not show up as any clear improvement in practical effectiveness. With a large sample, some improvement would presumably be noted.

PROBLEMS IN THE USE OF SELECTION TESTS

Two Ways of Using Two or More Predictors

In the last section, we showed how predictor tests could be used two or more at a time by multiplying each test score by an appropriate weight and adding them together to give a single composite score. Thus, using weights of 2, 3, and 6, a candidate who had scores of 10 on the mathematics test, 6 on the shop test and 7 on the electricity test would get a composite score of

$$2 \times 10 + 3 \times 6 + 6 \times 7 = 20 + 18 + 42 = 80$$

The same composite would result for a person who had a math score of 4, a shop score of 4, and an electricity score of 10, since

$$2 \times 4 + 3 \times 4 + 6 \times 10 = 8 + 12 + 60 = 80$$

This method of combining scores we shall call the method of *linear combination* since it is based on a simple linear equation * of the type a(Math) + b(Shop) + c(Electricity), or $ax + by + cz$. If we used this method mechanically, we would employ or accept for the training program those individuals with the highest scores, going down the line until we had enough to meet our quota.

Another way of proceeding would be to set separate qualifying scores for our separate measures and accept only those individuals who qualified on each hurdle. Thus, we might specify that each applicant must get at least the following scores:

Mathematics	5
Shop	3
Electricity	7

This procedure would screen out 10, or 33.3 percent, of the failures at a cost of 8, or 11.6 percent, of the successes. Higher minimum scores of

Mathematics	8
Shop	4
Electricity	8

* A *linear equation* is one in which each variable, in our example the scores on the three predictor tests, appears as a term of first degree. It contrasts with more complex relationships, such as a *quadratic equation* in which one or more factors is squared.

would eliminate 23, or 76.7 percent, of the failures at the cost of 16, or 23.2 percent, of the successes. In this illustration, the separate cutting scores represent little or no improvement over the electricity test alone, but neither did the single composite score.

In terms of statistical theory, the use of separate cutting scores usually seems less sound than the procedure of linear combination. The one exception to this is when some minimum level of a particular trait is absolutely essential for a job, but additional amounts are not of great importance. Furthermore, the cutting scores must be determined by an essentially trial-and-error process, and once they are set they are rather inflexible. The linear combination permits great flexibility, permitting one to accept as many of the applicants as are needed, starting from the top of the score distribution. However, application of the separate minimum requirements is probably simpler for an untrained person than is computing a combined score.

The real practical advantage of separate cutting scores comes when one of the predictor tests is expensive or time-consuming to apply. Then, a simpler and more economical test may be applied to the total group and part of the group may be screened out by this economical procedure. The more costly appraisal device need be applied only to the remainder. Thus, if a written test of subject-matter knowledge and a performance test of actual classroom teaching were being used in the selection of secondary-school teachers, it would be very reasonable to use the written test as an initial screening device and to use the performance test only with those who met minimum standards on the written test.

Selection Ratio and Test Effectiveness

The minimum scores that are set for the separate tests or for the composite score in any practical testing program will depend to a considerable extent upon the law of supply and demand. When applicants are few and vacancies many, lower requirements must be set; when applicants are many and vacancies few, the selecting agency can afford to be choosy. This ratio of acceptance to application is called the *selection ratio.*

The practical value of a testing program depends as much upon the selection ratio as it does upon the validity of available tests. In the extreme case in which we can afford to reject nobody, even the most valid test is of no value as a selection device. At the other extreme, if we need take only one applicant in ten, for example, the use of even a test with rather low validity will be quite beneficial. This fact is illustrated in Fig. 19.2. If the higher selection ratio is used, in which about 85 percent of the applicants are accepted, a good many potential failures are accepted even for the good test, in which proportion of successes changes

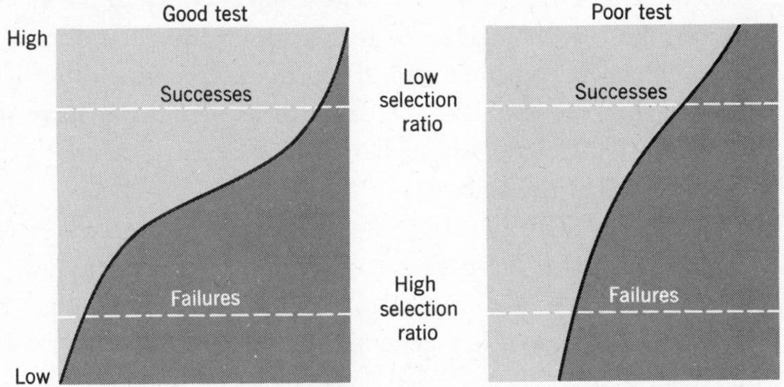

Fig. 19.2 Influence of selection ratio upon test effectiveness.

steeply as one goes from a low to a high score. If we can afford to use the lower of the two indicated selection ratios, the good test excludes almost all the potential failures and even the poor test improves our batting average markedly. In the numerical example that we used in the previous sections, if we had accepted only 10 out of our 99 applicants, even the shop test would have given us 9 successes, while at that same cutting score the electricity test would have yielded 100-percent successes. This compares with the 70 percent of the total group who were successful.

With a low selection ratio (few applicants accepted), a testing program gives promise of large practical gains. When the selection ratio is high (most applicants accepted), the practical gains will inevitably be much smaller.

Preselection and Test Validity

There is one factor whose influence on test validities we must mention here. The factor is a pervasive one that distorts the interpretation of tests in a good deal of personnel research. Again, the effect is a complex one that we cannot explore fully. The factor with which we are now concerned is that of preselection of the group on which we get criterion data.

In our illustrative example, suppose that a regulation had been in effect that no one with a mathematics test score below 10 would be admitted to the electronics technician training program. This requirement would have eliminated 26 of our 99 cases and among them 15 of our 30 failers. The spread of mathematics test scores within the group that remained would have been substantially less, and there would also have been less spread in grades. Under these circumstances, the correlation of test with criterion will normally be reduced. In this instance it drops from 0.40 to 0.15. Thus, if we had had a selection program in effect and had admitted only those with high math test scores, within the admitted group the math test would have appeared almost worthless. Its true value would not have been changed, but the evidence available to us would not have permitted us to see that value. Those who would have failed because of math deficiency would have been cut off at the source.

We cannot indicate in this discussion the mathematical procedures to correct for preselection. In practice, these cannot always be applied anyhow, because we may not fully know the nature and extent of preselection that has been operating. We can merely give a few general guiding principles.

1. When those admitted to a job or training program have been selected on the basis of score on some test, the apparent validity of that test for those remaining will be reduced.
2. The smaller the selection ratio (that is, the higher the cutting score), the greater will be the reduction in apparent validity.
3. Selection will also operate to reduce the validity of other tests that are correlated with the test used for screening.
4. In the correlated tests, the reduction will be in proportion to the correlation of the second test with the test used for screening. It will also be in proportion to the degree of selectivity.

If a school, military training program, or employer is installing a program of selection tests and must choose the best tests to use on the basis of validity statistics, it is important to try to appraise and allow for the effects of preselection in interpreting these statistics. A thorough discussion of both the logic and statistics of the problem has been supplied by Gulliksen (1950). For the present, it will suffice to point out the problem and warn the reader of its importance.

Rational Versus Empirical Bases for Weighting Tests

In preceding sections we have outlined procedures for deciding which tests to use and how much weight to give to each, basing the decision entirely on the empirical evidence from trying out the tests. For several reasons, however, it may not be desirable to be guided entirely by the validity data. The criterion measure will usually be imperfect, that is, incomplete or biased in some respects. The sample of cases may be rather meager. The empirical results may be distorted by the preselection effects discussed in the previous section. For these reasons, we may want to give some weight to our rational analysis of the situation as well as to the empirical evidence. Thus, in discussing selection tests for medical schools, Stalnaker (1951) said:

> While I should be unwilling to discourage anyone from correlating any two variables, I am neither impressed nor concerned when a low correlation is found between scores on a test in understanding modern society and grades in laboratory work in gross anatomy. I continue to favor selecting the men for the study of medicine who have some awareness of social sciences.
>
> If the average grades in first-year medical school do not correlate highly with a score which may crudely be representative of intelligence, I shall not conclude that a stupid M.D. is as good as a bright one as far as diagnosis of disease in my personal family is concerned.

In this example, limitations of the criterion are recognized. The writer is expressing his belief that rational analysis is as important in defining sound selection procedures as are statistical computations.

Combining Test and Nontest Data

In any program of personnel selection, consideration will usually need to be given to factors other than test scores. We have in mind such things as personal history data, educational or previous work record, and impressions or evidence gathered in a personal interview. In practice, this type of material is often used (1) without any systematic evidence of its validity and (2) in a rather haphazard and intuitive way. There is no real reason why personal data or work history items cannot be scored or rated, or why the impressions gained in an interview cannot be reduced to some quantitative estimate of probable success in the training program or value on the job. If this is done, the resulting scores can be evaluated in exactly the same way that test scores are evaluated. If they prove to have useful validity, they can be weighted in a composite score together with tests. That is, qualitative data can be first converted into quantitative terms and then pooled with other types of quantitative data. This would appear to be a sound extension of the research approach to personnel selection.

The Place of Clinical Judgment in Selection Programs

The procedures we have been proposing so far for the use of tests and even of qualitative data in personnel selection have emphasized uniform and essentially rigid procedures for pooling and evaluating the evidence on each case. This is likely to be offensive to the person who prizes his clinical judgment and would like to temper the decision in individual cases by that judgment. He is likely to feel that he can "beat the game" and make predictions that will be more accurate than those given by mechanical application of a set of regression weights.

Concrete evidence suggests that this is not generally so (Meehl, 1954). Where adequate empirical evidence is on hand to permit setting standard procedures for weighting and combining test results and other evidence, the mechanical combining usually gives more accurate prediction of a definite criterion than does an intuitive weighting, and persons for whom an exception is made on an intuitive basis do no better than their test scores indicated for them.

An intuitive appraisal of the individual, as by an interview, may serve a useful function as one of a team of predictors. As suggested in the previous section, this appraisal may be quantified as a rating on specific points, and the ratings may then be combined with other predictors. Again, as we indicated above, when empirical data are meager, rational and perhaps intuitive judgments may enter into original decisions as to the *weighting* of different aspects of evidence. But intuitive weighting of the evidence for each applicant seems justifiable only on the grounds of expediency and lack of any sound empirical evidence as to how different elements of information *should* be weighted.

THE OPTIMUM CUTTING SCORE

In any selection program, we face at some point the problem of deciding how selective to be. Shall we accept all but a few of the least promising applicants or shall we admit only a small group of the most promising? There are always practical limitations on how selective we *can* be, set by the number of applicants that it is possible to attract and the number of vacancies to be filled. However, there is some flexibility in the amount of recruiting done or in the speed with which vacancies are filled by the first individuals who appear as applicants.

In general, the more effort and expense we put into recruiting and testing, the higher we can set our cutting score and the more we can save in costs of training and efficiency of operation. Sometimes it may be possible to estimate the per capita cost of increasing the pool of applicants tested, on the one hand, and the per capita cost of training a new employee, on the other. Doppelt and Bennett (1953) report an analysis of costs and savings for several different employee-selection projects.

With food-store checkers, for example, the cost of testing an applicant was figured to be $2.00 and the cost of training a new employee to be $300. Basing calculations on the percent of employees at each score level rated as satisfactory, they calculate the per capita cost of obtaining a satisfactory employee. Thus, if the cutting score on the *Store Personnel Test* were set at 90, their data indicate that it would have been necessary to train 1.79 employees for each satisfactory one obtained and to test 3.89 in order to get the 1.79 to be trained. Using these figures and the costs of $300 to train and $2.00 to test, the cost per satisfactory employee became $544.

Similar calculations at each score level yielded the data of Fig. 19.3. Thus, insofar as the costs that have been considered give a true picture of *all* costs involved, the most economical procedure here would have been to set quite a high cutting score (about 110) and accept only those who fell above this score. In this particular instance, this would have meant accepting only the top 10 percent of applicants.

Such calculations as this are only partially realistic because it is almost impossible to determine either all the costs or all the gains. Thus, in our illustration we did not show the costs of recruiting a large group of applicants, and this might be substantial. At the same time, we did not show any long-term gains from having more efficient employees. The example shows the type of thinking

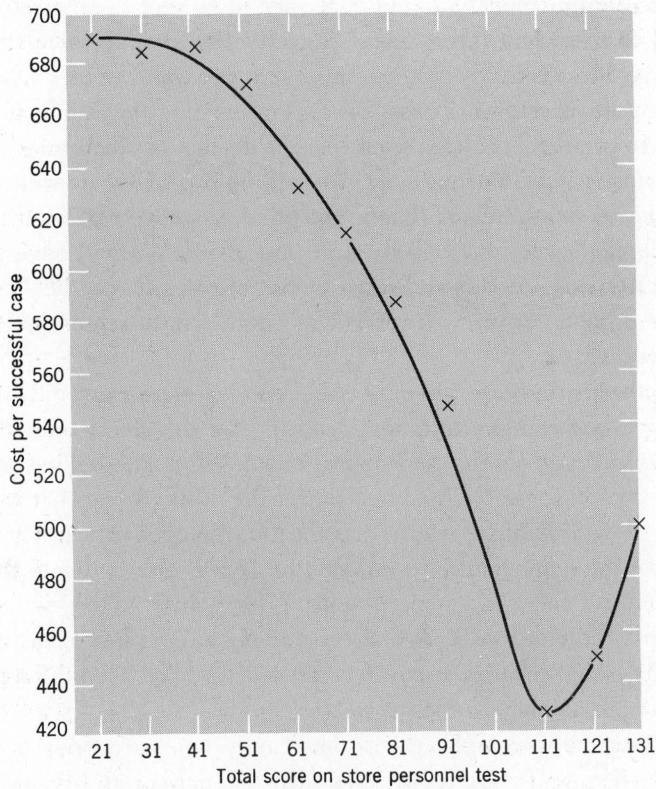

Fig. 19.3 Curve showing cost of producing satisfactory female checkers in a food-store chain. (From Doppelt and Bennett, 1953.)

that is involved in setting a cutting score. It is a balancing of one set of costs, tangible and intangible, against another, and setting a cutting score such that the most advantageous balance of costs and gains will be reached. However, it is rarely possible to reduce the solution to a precise matter of dollars and cents.

THE PROBLEM OF CLASSIFICATION OF PERSONNEL

So far in this chapter we have considered the problems of using tests and other devices in the *selection* of personnel for a single "job"—including in the term a single type of educational or training program. A more complex problem is that of *classification* of personnel into one of several training or job categories.

We shall illustrate the classification problem with the simplest version, only two assignment categories, set in a military context. Suppose that an Army Basic Training Center must meet a quota of 60 men to be sent to an electronics training school and 40 to a clerk-typist school. Exactly 100 men are available for assignment. The problem is to assign them in such a way that the men assigned to *each* school will be as successful as possible. This means that for each man we will need to be able to predict *both* how well he will do in the electronics school and in the clerk-typist school. Furthermore, we will be especially interested in whether he will do *better* in one school than in the other, since we will want to assign each man to the school where he will be more successful. We will have as difficult an assignment decision for Jimmy Brown whose test results predict high success in each of the schools, as we will for Willie Smith whose scores predict poor performance in each.

Faced with this problem, we must ask a good deal more of our predictor tests. We now need one or more tests that are valid for the electronics school and one or more that are valid for the clerk-typist school. What is more, we especially need tests that are valid for one school but *not* for the other. A test that is equally valid for both is of little help to us in a classification decision, since it will not tell us *which* school the man should be assigned to. It will only indicate that some men are promising for both and some promising for neither. Thus, we need to build up a team of predictor measures that collectively have comprehensive validity for each and all of our criterion measures and individually have differential validity for different ones of the criterion variables.

In our illustrative example, we assumed only two categories of assignment—electronics school and clerk-typist school. In practice, in an organization such as the army, the number of possible assignments is much larger than this. Thus, the demands upon a test battery become very great indeed. The battery of tests should make possible a valid forecast of prospects for success in each one of a number of different assignments, and it should separate as sharply as possible those who will be successful in any one assignment from those who will be successful in other assignments.

In its purest form, the classification problem can be expressed as follows:

Given: Jobs A, B, C, . . . K with quotas to be filled of a, b, c, . . . k individuals, and given a total supply of N = a + b + c + . . . k persons to fill the quotas.

Required: To assign the individuals to jobs in such a way that the total effectiveness or productivity of the organization will be a maximum.

The problem becomes very complex, because we now need to have a prediction of each individual's effectiveness in *each* job. The tests and other information must be sufficiently comprehensive to give a reasonably good prediction for each job, and must be combined in different ways so as to yield the several predictions. Furthermore, we cannot simply assign each individual to the one job in which *he* is predicted to be most likely to be effective, because we have quotas to meet in all the jobs, some of which may be small and some large. Paying attention to the individuals one at a time may fail to fill some quotas and give an excess in other job categories. Considering the group of candidates as a whole, a reconciliation must be worked out of abilities of candidates, quotas in different jobs, and the importance or priority of different jobs.

It turns out that under these requirements it is important that each test in the classification battery show relatively high validity for some jobs and low validity for others, and that tests have quite low correlations with each other. A battery of this type permits the computation of scores that have a good deal of *differential* validity, that is, high for one assignment and low for others, and these, then, become useful in making the decision between jobs.

The pure classification model that we have been describing is rarely encountered in personnel work. The nearest approach to it is in a military organization in which individuals are assigned to particular occupational specialties solely or primarily in terms of the needs of the organization. In industry, the individual usually applies for a *specific* job, or has very definite ideas as to the work that he wants to do, and so the employer's decision is one of accepting or rejecting for that job. However, there is a good deal of resemblance between the demands of a classification battery and of one that is to be used for vocational guidance. In vocational guidance, the counselor often wishes to be able to advise a client on his prospects for success or satisfaction in a wide array of different jobs or training possibilities. Here again, there is need for a team of predictors that have comprehensive validity over a wide range of possibilities. And here again, one would like to be able to make statements about the job areas in which the client would do relatively best, as well as statements about his absolute level of performance in each. A battery of tests is needed that provides for both comprehensive and differential validity.

SELECTION TESTING APPLIED TO ATYPICAL (DEVIANT, MINORITY) GROUPS

In recent years, there has been mounting concern about the appropriateness and fairness of selection tests, as these are used with groups that differ in some major respect from the main group upon whom the tests were standardized and validated and for whom any cutting scores were originally determined. The concern has developed as an offshoot of the civil rights movement, and has been focused on the use of selection tests with Negro job applicants with limited educational and cultural backgrounds. It is frequently asserted that tests, especially paper-and-pencil tests often heavily loaded with verbal abilities, are biased against and unfair to this group.

We must first try to clarify what should be meant by "unfair" and "biased." Then we can try to see what is known about the facts of the matter.

Any justifiable use of a selection test implies that there is an appreciable relationship between score on the test and some acceptable indicator of success on the job. If there is no such relationship, the use of the test is indefensible for *any* applicant. Bias must mean that the relationship is somehow different for the atypical group than it is for the general applicant population. The difference might be any one of the following.

1. Though a test had shown a significant relation to a criterion measure of success in the general applicant population, it might show essentially no relationship within the special group. That is, the test might be completely invalid within the special group.

2. Though a test had comparable validity for both the general and the special groups, a given score might correspond to a different average level of on-the-job performance in the special group than in the general group. Bias against the special group would mean that for a specific score, say 25 items right, the data would lead one to predict a higher criterion score for the special than for the general group, even without any special treatment of the members of that group.

3. The test might have comparable validity for both groups, but data might indicate that *if the special group were given some type of preparatory training,* the predicted performance would be higher for this group, score for score, than for the general group.

If the first situation holds, it seems clear that the testing procedure should not be used with members of the special group. If the second situation is characteristic, then it seems clear that an adjustment in test scores is called for in the special group to eliminate the discrepancy. In the third case, there may be a difference of opinion as to the responsibility that an employer has to provide special training to overcome the deficiencies that applicants bring with them as they apply for a job. This is a question of social philosophy rather than psychometric techniques.

Now we face the question of what we know in relation to the above three possibilities. The answer at the present time must be, we fear, not very much. There are several reasons for this. On the one hand, until very recently, pressure has been *against* identifying minority group members as such and treating them in any way differently from the white majority. Thus, companies have been forbidden to make a record of the race of job applicants, or to use this information in any way in connection with employment decisions. This has made it difficult to carry out separate validation studies for ethnic groups even if the companies had wished to do so. A second practical difficulty in many situations would be the limited number of Negroes who had either applied for or been employed in a specific job in a specific company. A third issue focuses on the criterion problem. We have already discussed (pp. 618–621) the general difficulties of getting satisfactory criterion measures. In ethnic group comparisons, we face the additional problem of getting criterion data that are themselves unbiased in relation to the groups that are being compared. Criterion measures have often been ratings by supervisors, and it is hard to be sure that these are free of bias * themselves, and therefore represent a uniform standard of performance against which test scores may be compared.

We have already discussed in Chapter 10 the evidence of bias in relation to academic success. We are able to cite only one group of studies that deal more or less directly with bias in relation to post-training criteria.

One recent publication (Kirkpatrick et al, 1968) reports five separate studies in which data for Negro groups are compared with those for whites. Unfortunately, each of the studies suffers from one or more shortcomings. Numbers of cases are often small, the two ethnic groups were sometimes trained or working in different schools or companies, and criteria sometimes related to training rather than job performance. As a consequence, the results that are reported are very difficult to interpret and to evaluate. It does appear that in some instances tests that are valid for whites are not valid for blacks, and vice versa.

* Ordinarily, one would think of the bias as being against, but one cannot dismiss the possibility of a "double standard" of rating that would be more lenient toward the less privileged group.

Instances can be found in the data in which average job criterion measures for blacks for a given test score are higher than those of whites with the same score, though this is not at all uniformly the case. One is at a loss to know whether the variations from one set of data to another are a reflection of the small number of cases (often no more than 30 or 40 in each ethnic group), or of some genuine differences in the job and the surrounding circumstances. About all one can conclude (and one could have said this in advance of the studies) is that ethnic group membership, together with whatever this implies concerning home background and education, *can* make a difference in both the validity of selection tests and in the level of job performance typical of a given score. The results are too meager and confused to permit a sound estimate of how frequent or how substantial the effects are.

SUMMARY STATEMENT

The basic pattern of personnel selection and personnel selection research is simple. Promising predictors are identified. These are related to a suitable measure of job success. On the basis of the evidence, the most effective predictors are selected, and procedures are set up for using the evidence from them, either jointly or in succession. When future students or employees are to be selected, the relevant evidence is gathered and combined by standard procedures, and those with the highest standing or those falling above specified minimum levels are accepted. However, many specific problems arise in connection with (1) discovery of promising predictors, (2) identification of a suitable measure of success, (3) the analytical procedures for studying predictor-criterion relationships, and (4) practical routines for using the evidence from predictors. Some of these have been considered in the present chapter.

Certain general viewpoints may be expressed in closing.

1. Any type of evidence, test or nontest, quantitative or qualitative, may appropriately be used in a selection program.
2. Qualitative material should be translated into quantitative form by either a scoring or rating system.
3. The validity of any type of evidence should be tested out empirically in terms of its relationship to criteria of job success.
4. The empirical evidence on validity should not always be followed slavishly in setting up standard procedures for using and combining test data. Rational judgment should be used to temper statistical evidence, and more weight should

be given to rational considerations when the empirical evidence is less satisfactory.

5. Once standard procedures have been set up, they should be used in a standard way. Subjective impressions may enter in as evidence but should not determine the way in which the evidence is applied to the individual case.

QUESTIONS AND EXERCISES

1. Think of some job you know fairly well. What measures might be used as a criterion of job success? What are the advantages and limitations of each?

2. Why is it important to have a large group of cases when studying the validity of a set of tests that have been proposed for use as predictors?

3. Why can combinations of tests generally predict better than a single test?

4. What advantages do you see in using two or more tests with separate cutting scores, rather than combining the predictors by a regression equation? Under what circumstances would separate cutting scores be most acceptable?

5. For a given validity coefficient, how does the selection ratio affect the value of a testing program?

6. Under what circumstances might one decide to deviate from a regression equation in weighting tests for personnel selection?

7. A test was originally tried out on an unscreened group of job applicants, and for them it was found to have a validity coefficient of .50. Then it was put into use and used to screen out 50 percent of applicants. What would you expect to happen to the validity coefficient in the group who were accepted? Is the change real, or is it a statistical artifact?

8. What considerations limit the use of results such as those shown in Table 19.2 to determine a cutting score?

9. What characteristics would make a test very useful for a *selection* program, but of little value for a *classification* program?

10. What kind of research evidence is needed to determine whether an aptitude test is fair to the culturally deprived? Outline the ideal study to provide evidence on this problem, if practical limitations could all be overcome.

REFERENCES

Doppelt, J. E. & Bennett, G. K. Reducing the cost of training satisfactory workers by using tests. *Personnel Psychology*, 1953, **6**, 1–8.

Ghiselli, E. E. *The validity of occupational aptitude tests.* New York: Wiley, 1966.

Gulliksen, H. *Theory of mental tests.* New York: Wiley, 1950.

Kirkpatrick, J. J. et al. *Testing and fair employment.* New York: New York University Press, 1968.

Meehl, P. E. *Clinical vs. actuarial prediction.* Minneapolis, Minnesota: University of Minnesota Press, 1954.

Stalnaker, J. Tests for medicine. In *Proceedings of the 1950 Invitational Conference on Testing Problems.* Princeton, New Jersey: Educational Testing Service, 1951.

SUGGESTED ADDITIONAL READING

Ghiselli, E. E. & Brown, C. W. *Personnel and industrial psychology.* (2nd ed.) New York: McGraw-Hill, 1955. Pp. 17–58.

Thorndike, R. L. *Personnel selection.* New York: Wiley, 1949. Chapters 1, 2, 5–10.

Tiffin, J. & McCormick, E. T. *Industrial psychology.* (4th ed.) Englewood Cliffs, New Jersey: Prentice-Hall, 1961. Pp. 75–109.

Glossary of Terms

Ability test	A test designed to measure what a person *can do.* Ability tests are subdivided into *aptitude* tests and *achievement* tests.
Abstract intelligence	The ability to deal effectively with *ideas* expressed in symbols such as words, numbers, pictures, or diagrams.
Achievement test	An ability test designed to appraise what the individual *has learned* to do as a result of planned previous experience or training, often that provided in school.
Age equivalent	A score conversion in which a test score is assigned the age value for which that score is the average score.
Age norms	A system of test norms based on age equivalents.
Alternate form reliability	An estimate of the accuracy or precision of a testing procedure based on the administration of two equivalent forms of the test and correlation of the scores on the two forms. The two forms may be given in immediate succession, in which case score differences arise primarily from the variation in sampling of tasks. If a time interval of some length comes between the two testings, score differences reflect variation both in the sampling of tasks and in individuals from one time to another.
Anecdotal record	A written report describing an incident of an individual's behavior. Incidents would usually be chosen

because they appeared significant for the understanding of the individual, either as being typical of him or as being unusual and surprising.

Aptitude — May be defined as "readiness for learning." This readiness depends, in unknown proportions, on the genetic characteristics of the individual and his whole life history of physical surroundings and previous learnings.

Aptitude test — An ability test designed to appraise what the individual *can learn* to do if he receives appropriate education or job training.

Arithmetic mean — The common average, obtained by adding together all of the scores in a set and dividing by the number of scores. The arithmetic mean of 12, 16, and 17 is 45/3 or 15.

Attenuation — Weakening or "watering down" of the relationship between two measures because of the unreliability of either or both.

Attitude — Feeling of favorableness or unfavorableness toward some group, institution, or proposition. For example, attitude toward the Chinese, toward the Supreme Court, or toward legalizing marijuana.

Average — A general term for the middle of a group of scores. A number of different averages have been proposed, but the common ones that are widely used in reporting test results are the *arithmetic mean* and the *median*.

Blueprint — A formulation of the design for a test, usually including specifications as to item content, difficulty, form of items, etc.

Bimodal distribution — A distribution having two distinct modes or points of high frequency.

Battery — A set of tests designed to be administered together. The tests in a battery have typically been planned and developed as a unit, with the objective of providing complete and efficient coverage of some domain of ability or personality. Usually the tests in a battery have norms based upon a common sample of cases.

Ceiling — The upper limit of measurement set by the items in a test. A test that had items practically all of which could be answered by the average fourth grader would have a ceiling at the fourth grade level.

Class interval — A grouping of several adjacent score values into a single category. A class interval of 3, 5, or some other number of points is often used in tallying data for a group of individuals.

Coefficient of correlation — See *Correlation coefficient.*

Construct validity — See *Validity.*

Content validity — See *Validity.*

Converted score — A score expressed in some type of derived unit, such as an age equivalent, grade equivalent, percentile, or standard score.

Correction for guessing — A test-scoring procedure, used primarily with true-false and multiple-choice tests, in which a fractional penalty is applied for wrong answers. The most commonly used correction is

$$\text{Rights} - \left(\frac{\text{Wrongs}}{\text{Number of answer choices minus one}}\right)$$

The procedure is based on the rationale that a person who guesses on this type of test will get a certain number of items right, and that it would be desirable to adjust for individual differences in readiness to guess.

Correlation coefficient — A statistical index expressing the relationship between two different measures within a group of individuals. The range of possible values is from +1.00 to −1.00. A correlation of +1.00 or −1.00 indicates a perfect relationship such that knowledge of a person's standing on one measure gives us exact knowledge of where he stands on the other, while a correlation of .00 represents a situation where the individual's standing on one measure gives us absolutely no indication of where he will fall on the other.

Criterion — Some indicator of performance on the job, or possibly in a training program, that we accept as showing how successful each person has been and use as the end result to be predicted by a test or battery of tests.

Cross-validation — The testing out of a set of items or a system of test weights derived from one sample of individuals upon a new sample, to see to what extent the procedure retains its validity with new and independent data. Cross-validation is especially important when items or test weights have been chosen from a large number of possible alternatives, and when the original sample was small.

Culture-free test — A test providing equal opportunity for success by a person who had grown up in any culture. Since any test is dependent upon the experiences of life, a culture-free test seems an impossibility, and the term culture-fair has sometimes been substituted, conveying the slightly different implication that different cultures provide equal preparation for the test.

Cumulative frequency — A sum of all the cases falling below a specified score. The *cumulative percent* is the accumulated percent of cases falling below a specified score.

Decile — Score value below which a specified number of tenths of the cases fall. The first decile is the score value below which one tenth or ten percent of cases fall. The fifth decile is the same as the median, or the 50th percentile.

Deviation — The difference between a score and some reference point, usually the arithmetic mean. If the mean is 25 and a score is 40, the deviation of that score from the arithmetic mean is +15.

Deviation IQ — A type of *standard score* in which the mean is set at 100 and the standard deviation is set at 15 or 16. These values were chosen because they corresponded approximately to those obtained on the Stanford-Binet using the ratio of mental age to chronological age.

Diagnostic test — A test that is sharply focused on some specific aspect of a skill or some specific cause of difficulty in acquiring a skill, and that is useful in suggesting specific remedial actions that might help to improve mastery of that skill. Diagnostic tests may be contrasted with *survey tests,* which give a general appraisal of an area of achievement.

Difficulty index — A numerical value used to express the difficulty of a test item. In the United States, the difficulty index (more logically called a "facility index") is usually the percent getting the item correct.

Discrimination index — An index to show how sharply an item differentiates between the more and less able examinees. Various indices have been used, but a simple index, which is practical for classroom teachers, is the difference in the percent passing the item among those in the top and the bottom quarter in total score on the test or on some other measure of the trait appraised by the test.

Dispersion — The degree to which scores spread out. The common measures of dispersion are the *semi-interquartile range* and the *standard deviation*.

Distractor — A term sometimes used to designate the incorrect response options provided in a multiple-choice item.

Distribution — See *Frequency distribution*.

Empirical key — A scoring key, typically for a measure of personality, in which the items to be weighted and the manner in which they are weighted are based on data on the extent to which the items do, in fact, differentiate different groups of individuals.

Equivalent form — One of two or more forms of a test that have been built to the same specifications to measure the same attribute or attributes, and that consequently have approximately the same statistical characteristics.

Error of measurement — The amount by which any specific measurement differs from the individual's hypothetical "true" score in the quality being measured. Since no measurement procedure is perfectly exact, each has included in it some component of error.

Evaluation — The complete process of identifying the objectives of an aspect of education and appraising the extent to which those objectives have been achieved. Evaluation is likely to use tests as tools, but also to include other informal types of evidence, and undertakes to integrate these into a value judgment of the effectiveness of an educational enterprise.

Expectancy table — A table showing, for each level of a predictor test, the frequency of different levels of success in some outcome variable.

External examination — An examination that is administered to students in a school system, over which the local school system has no control.

Face validity — The reasonableness or plausibility of test tasks, from the point of view of the person being tested in terms of what he considers that the test is measuring.

Factor — An attribute, inferred from the correlations among a set of tests, that is intended to provide a simpler explanation of what the tests have in common.

Factor analysis — A set of procedures for analyzing the complex set of relationships among a group of variables, usually shown through a table of the correlations of each one with each of the others. The purpose is to identify a small number of underlying "factors" that provide a relatively simple and meaningful "explanation" of the complete set of relationships.

Forced-choice (item) — A pattern, used in both self-description and rating of others, in which the individual is required to select one of a set of statements as most descriptive (and perhaps another as least descriptive). In preparing the sets of statements, the attempt is usually made to have all the statements in a set approximately balanced for acceptability or desirability, but quite different in what they signify about the person.

Frequency distribution — Arrangement of a set of scores for a group of individuals in which the possible score values are arranged in order from high to low, and the number of persons receiving each score is indicated. Sometimes the score values are grouped by three's, five's, or some other convenient grouping.

Frequency polygon — A graphic representation of a frequency distribution, in which the number of cases in each score category is plotted, and the successive points are connected with straight lines.

General intelligence test — A test of ability to deal with problems of various types involving ideas, symbols, and the relationships between them. Existing tests are primarily measures of *abstract intelligence.* Intelligence tests are usually considered measures of aptitude, and are contrasted with measures of special aptitudes on the one hand and with measures of achievement on the other.

Generosity error — As applied to ratings, the term refers to the tendency of raters, or of a specific rater, to assign consistently favorable or "above average" ratings.

Grade equivalent — A score conversion in which a test score is assigned the grade value for which that score is the average score.

Grade norms — A system of test norms based on grade equivalents.

Graphic rating scale — A rating scale in which the rater indicates his rating by making a mark at some point along a line. Selected points on the line are characterized by evaluative adjectives or descriptions of the quality of behavior represented.

Guess Who technique — A rating procedure in which pupils are nominated by their peers to fill certain roles or match certain descriptions, and the individual's score for a particular role or description is the number of times that he is nominated.

Guessing — See *Correction for guessing.*

Halo or *halo error* — As applied to ratings, the term refers to the tendency of raters to base evaluations of a person being rated upon general favorableness toward that individual and not to differentiate degree of possession of specific traits.

Histogram — A graphic representation of a frequency distribution in which the cases falling in each score category are represented by a bar whose size is proportional to the number of cases. Since each bar is the full width of the score category, the bars make a continuous "pile" showing the form of the frequency distribution.

Intelligence — Intelligence is a difficult term to define with any precision. The term, as used in testing, corresponds rather closely to general usage. Most tests are limited to *abstract intelligence,* that is, the ability to solve problems involving ideas and symbols.

Intelligence quotient (IQ) — An index for expressing the results of an intelligence test. The intelligence quotient is an indicator of the individual's standing in relation to his own age group. Originally, quotients were computed by the ratio

$$100\left(\frac{\text{Mental age}}{\text{Chronological age}}\right)$$

Currently, practically all intelligence quotients are *standard scores,* designed so that the average individual receives an intelligence quotient of 100, and the standard deviation in the group is 15 or 16.

Interest — A tendency to prefer or engage in a particular type of activity. Interest tests tend to focus on occupational and educational interests, and to assess them through the individual's selection of activities that he would like to engage in.

Internal consistency — Degree of relationship among the items of a test, that is, the extent to which the same examinees tend to get each item right. Measures of reliability based upon a single testing are really measures of internal consistency.

Ipsative test — A test yielding multiple scores, in which the sum of scores for all individuals is the same, so that an individual who is high on some scales of the test must be low on others. A test in which the individual's profile is expressed in relation to his own overall average, rather than in relation to some outside group.

Item analysis — Study of the statistical properties of test items. The qualities usually of interest are the difficulty of the item and its ability to differentiate between more capable and less capable examinees. Difficulty is usually expressed as the percent getting the item right, and discrimination as some index comparing success by the more capable and the less capable students.

Kuder-Richardson reliability — Reliability estimated from data available from a single test administration, using the average score on the test, its standard deviation, and difficulty indices for the separate items.

Mastery test — A test that is being used to determine whether a pupil or pupils have mastery of some unit that has been taught. In a mastery test, one is not really concerned about differences between individuals.

Mean — See *Arithmetic mean.*

Median — The score value that separates the upper half of a group from the bottom half. Exactly 50 percent of the group fall above the median, and 50 percent below.

Mental age — An age equivalent on an intelligence test. The mental age corresponding to a given score is the chronological age at which that score is an average score.

Mode — The score value that occurs most frequently in a given set of scores.

N — Symbol used to represent the number of cases in the group being studied.

Normal distribution — The frequency distribution corresponding to a particular mathematical model derived on the assumption that the final score is the result of many small independent contributing factors. The distribution is bell-shaped, that is, symmetrical with a piling up of cases in the middle, steep shoulders, and flat tails. The normal distribution is often assumed to apply to human abilities and achievements.

Normative test — A test in which the individual's performance is expressed in relation to that of some norm or reference group, as contrasted with an *ipsative test.*

Norms — Norms constitute frames of reference for the interpretation of test scores. They are based on the actual performance of groups of specified types. Norm groups are selected in terms of age, school grade, or occupational grouping, depending on the purpose for which they are to be used. The score for an individual is given meaning by expressing it as an *age equivalent, grade equivalent, percentile,* or *standard score.* (See these entries.)

Objective test — A test made up of items each of which has one, or at most a few, acceptable responses, and in which the acceptable responses have been agreed upon in advance so that they can be scored by machine, or by a routine clerk, from the answer key. Often, the form involves selection of the answer from alternatives that are supplied to the examinee.

Percentile — The score value below which a specified percent of cases falls. Thus, the 60th percentile on an examination is the raw score below which 60 percent of examinees fall.

Percentile band — A range of percentile values within which the true percentile for an individual may be expected to lie. Usually the band extends one standard error of measurement above and below the percentile rank corresponding to his obtained score.

Percentile norms — A system of norms based on percentiles within a specific reference group.

Percentile rank — For a given score value, the percent of cases falling below that value.

Performance test — A test, most often an intelligence test, in which ability is evaluated in terms of something the individual *does* rather than something he *says.* Tasks included are such things as mazes, form-boards, block-building, etc. Also includes performance measures of achievement, such as a typing test.

Personality test — Tests of personality undertake to appraise the individual's typical or habitual way of acting, as distinct from his *ability* to perform.

Power test — A test given with ample time, and designed to appraise how well the individual can perform, rather than how fast he can work.

Practice effect — The systematic change in scores on a test, ordinarily a gain, resulting from previous practice with the test.

Predictive validity — See *Validity*.

Proficiency test — Measure of current level of skill in some aspect of a job or of an educational program. The term is used with almost the same meaning as *achievement test*, but with somewhat more implication of a job-oriented skill.

Profile — Graphic representation of a set of scores for an individual, organized so that the high and low scores can be identified. In order for scores to be meaningfully displayed in a profile, they must be converted to some common score scale, such as standard scores or age or grade equivalents.

Prognostic test — A test designed to predict progress in achieving skill or knowledge in some area.

Projective test — A testing situation in which the individual perceives or manipulates some relatively unstructured stimulus material, and then a clinician makes interpretations of personality based upon the structure that the examinee imposes upon the material.

Quartile — A score value that separates one quarter of a group from the next. There are three quartiles. The first or lower quartile separates the lowest quarter of the group from the upper three-fourths. The second quartile is the same as the *median*. The third or upper quartile separates the top quarter of the group from the rest.

Random sample — A sample of cases drawn from some larger population in such a way that every member of the population has an equal chance of being drawn for the sample.

Range — The range of a set of scores is the difference between the highest and the lowest score in the set.

Raw score — A score expressed in the units in which it was originally obtained, that is, pounds, inches, or points earned on a test.

Readiness test — A test designed to provide evidence of the extent to which a pupil has the abilities to learn a subject if taught by the usual methods. The most widely used readiness tests are those for reading.

Reliability — The accuracy or precision with which a measure based on one sample of test tasks at one point in time represents performance based on a different sample of the same kind of tasks or a different point of time or both. Accuracy may be expressed by a *reliability coefficient* or by the *standard error of measurement.*

Reliability coefficient — The correlation coefficient between two equivalent measurements. The measurements may be two applications of the same test, or the application of two equivalent forms of a test.

Semi-interquartile range (Q) — One half of the difference between the upper and lower quartiles. The semi-interquartile range provides an index of the variability of a set of scores.

Situational test — A test based upon the simulation of a natural life situation. Usually there is some provision for observing and rating the examinee's performance in the test situation, though sometimes his performance may leave a permanent record that can be scored later.

Skewness — Tendency of scores to pile up at one end and stretch out at the other end of a distribution of scores.

Sociometric technique — Procedure for determining each individual's position within a social group such as a school class by analyzing the choices (and sometimes rejections) made by each group member with respect to the others in the group.

Spearman-Brown Prophecy Formula — Formula for estimating the reliability of a complete test from the correlation between equivalent halves of the test. The formula has been generalized to permit estimating the reliability of a test of any length if the reliability for some specific length is known.

Split-half reliability — Reliability estimated by dividing a test into two half-length tests, scoring these and getting the correlation between them, and then estimating correlation for the full-length test using the Spearman-Brown Prophecy Formula.

Standard deviation — A measure of the variability or spread of scores in a group. The standard deviation is the square root of the average of the squared deviations from the arithmetic mean of the group. The standard deviation provides the unit in terms of which *standard scores* are expressed.

Standard error of measurement — The standard deviation of the distribution of errors resulting from the application of a particular measurement procedure. A measure of the size of errors that are likely to result, expressed in the same units that were used for the original measurements.

Standard score — A score expressed in terms of standard deviations above or below the arithmetic mean of the group.

Standard score scales differ, depending upon the numerical value assigned to the mean and to the standard deviation. Thus, in a standard score system in which the mean was assigned a value of 50 and the standard deviation a value of 10, a score falling half a standard deviation above the mean would receive a value of 55.

Standard score norms — A system of test norms in which a test score is translated into a standard score within a specified reference group.

Standardized test — A test that has been published for general use. The most distinctive feature of a standardized test is a set of norms based on some general reference population, but other usual features include selection of the items on the basis of preliminary tryout and analysis, standard directions for administration, and a manual providing various types of statistical evidence about the test.

Stanine — The value assigned to an individual's score in a score system in which the mean is assigned a value of 5 and the standard deviation a value of 2. Stanine scores provide a single-digit *standard score* scale that is simple and convenient to use and that minimizes the apparent importance of small score differences.

Survey test — An achievement test that covers one or more major segments of the curriculum and describes general level of achievement. It can be contrasted with a *diagnostic* test that tries to probe into specific causes of poor performance or a *mastery test* that is concerned with mastery of certain specific and limited skills.

Temperament — A term used to refer to an individual's disposition, energy level, and social orientation. An aspect of personality.

Test-retest reliability — Reliability estimated by giving the same test on two occasions and finding the correlation between the scores for the two administrations. Since the test is unchanged, differences from test to retest reflect change or inconsistency of the individual from one occasion to another.

True score — The hypothesized underlying ability of an individual on the attribute measured by a test. An obtained test score is considered to result from this true level of ability modified by an error of measurement that characterizes that particular testing.

Validity

The effectiveness of the test in representing, describing or predicting the attribute that the user is interested in.

Content validity refers to the faithfulness with which the test represents or reproduces an area of knowledge.

Construct validity refers to the accuracy with which the test describes an individual in terms of some psychological trait or construct.

Criterion-related validity, or *predictive validity* refers to the accuracy with which the test scores make it possible to predict some criterion variable of educational, job, or life performance.

Variability

The extent to which the scores in a set of scores spread out from the average score in the group. Important measures of variability are the *semiinterquartile range* and the *standard deviation.*

APPENDIX I

Computation of Square Root

THE square root of any number can be determined quite rapidly by a series of successive approximations, as follows:

General Procedure	*Specific Illustration*
Problem: To calculate the square root of some number N.	What is the square root of 10.2703?
1. Pick a whole number that, when multiplied by itself, is close to the original number N.	$3 \times 3 = 9$
2. Divide the number N by the number you have chosen.	$3\overline{)10.2703}$ = 3.42
3. Add the divisor and quotient and divide by 2.	$\frac{3 + 3.42}{2} = \frac{6.42}{2} = 3.21$
4. Divide the original number N by the value obtained in step 3.	$3.21\overline{)10.2703}$ = 3.199
5. Add the divisor and quotient and divide by 2, as in step 3.	$\frac{3.21 + 3.199}{2} = 3.2045$
6. Repeat steps 4 and 5 until the result is stable for as many decimal places as you are interested in.	$3.2045\overline{)10.2703}$ = 3.2050 $\frac{3.2045 + 3.2050}{2} = 3.20475$

WHY THE PROCEDURE WORKS

We want to find the square root of the number N.

There is some number, call it X, that will give N, when multiplied by itself. That is

$$(X)(X) = X^2 = N$$

When we make an estimate, we pick a number that differs slightly from X. That is, we pick

$$(X - A)$$

where A is small in relation to X.

Dividing, we get

$$\frac{N}{(X-A)} = \frac{X^2}{(X-A)} = (X+A) + \left(\frac{A^2}{X-A}\right)$$

Since A is small relative to X, (that is, less than one half of X) $(A^2/(X-A))$ is still smaller relative to X. Now average $(X-A)$ and $(X+A) + (A^2/(X-A))$. The result is

$$X + \frac{A^2}{2\,(X-A)}$$

and this is still closer to X. Repeating the process of division, and dividing $N = X^2$ by $X + A^2/2\,(X-A)$, we get

$$\left(X - \frac{A^2}{2\,(X-A)}\right) - \left[\frac{A^2}{2\,(X-A)}\right]^2$$

Averaging

$$\left(X + \frac{A^2}{2\,(X-A)}\right)$$

and

$$\left(X - \frac{A^2}{2\,(X-A)}\right) - \left[\frac{A^2}{2\,(X-A)}\right]^2$$

we get

$$X - \frac{1}{2}\left[\frac{A^2}{2\,(X-A)}\right]^2$$

Since A is small relative to X, the last term, which involves the fourth power of A, is increasingly small relative to X.

With each successive approximation, our estimate differs from the desired value, X, by a smaller and smaller fraction of a higher and higher power of the small quantity

$$\left[\frac{A^2}{2\,(X-A)}\right]$$

and so the approximation gets better and better. The correct value always lies between the last divisor and the last quotient.

APPENDIX II

Percent of Cases Falling Below Selected Values on the Normal Curve

Deviation in Standard Deviation Units	Percent of Cases Falling Below	Deviation in Standard Deviation Units	Percent of Cases Falling Below
+3.0	99.9	−0.1	46.0
2.9	99.8	−0.2	42.1
2.8	99.7	−0.3	38.2
2.7	99.6	−0.4	34.4
2.6	99.5	−0.5	30.9
2.5	99.4	−0.6	27.4
2.4	99.2	−0.7	24.2
2.3	98.9	−0.8	21.2
2.2	98.6	−0.9	18.4
2.1	98.2	−1.0	15.9
2.0	97.7	−1.1	13.6
1.9	97.1	−1.2	11.5
1.8	96.4	−1.3	9.7
1.7	95.5	−1.4	8.1
1.6	94.5	−1.5	6.7
1.5	93.3	−1.6	5.5
1.4	91.9	−1.7	4.5
1.3	90.3	−1.8	3.6
1.2	88.5	−1.9	2.9
1.1	86.4	−2.0	2.3
1.0	84.1	−2.1	1.8
0.9	81.6	−2.2	1.4
0.8	78.8	−2.3	1.1
0.7	75.8	−2.4	0.8
0.6	72.6	−2.5	0.6
0.5	69.1	−2.6	0.5
0.4	65.6	−2.7	0.4
0.3	61.8	−2.8	0.3
0.2	57.9	−2.9	0.2
0.1	54.0	−3.0	0.1
0.0	50.0		

APPENDIX III

Calculating the Correlation Coefficient

THE correlation coefficient is an index that expresses the extent to which two variables (X and Y) go together. It indicates the extent to which high X scores go with high Y scores, and vice versa. But "high" and "low" must be expressed in some uniform terms from one set of data to another if the index is to have the same meaning for different sets of data. The standard framework for expressing "high" and "low" is the mean and standard deviation of the group. If each X or Y score is expressed as being so many standard deviations above or below the group mean, the product of these X and Y *standard scores* is calculated, and the average of these products is obtained, the result is the *Pearson product-moment* correlation coefficient.

This can be expressed by the following formula:

$$r = \frac{\Sigma z_x z_y}{N}$$

where r is the correlation coefficient.

z_x and z_y are standard scores in X and Y.

N is the number of cases.

This is a *definition* of the correlation coefficient. Now we must consider the steps in computing it. Below are outlined the procedures for computing the correlation coefficient from sets of raw test scores. The procedure is illustrated with numerical data from the reading and arithmetic tests shown in Table 5.1.

Step 1. Select class intervals for both of the variables.

In our illustration, both arithmetic and reading scores are grouped by 3's.

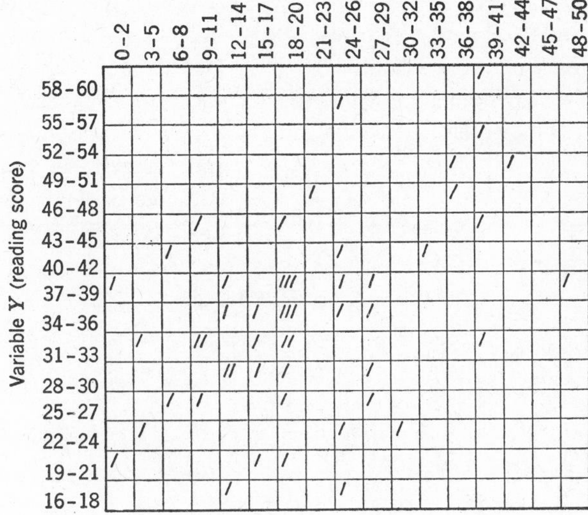

Fig. 1.

Step 2. Prepare a two-dimensional tabulation sheet, indicating class intervals for the X variable on the top and for the Y variable on the left of the chart. Cross-section paper or special tabulating sheets can be used with advantage.

The tabulation sheet is shown in Fig. 1. The X variable is the arithmetic score and the Y variable the reading score.

Step 3. Tally the data, entering each score as a tally mark in the cell corresponding to the X and Y score for that case. Count the number of tallies in each cell, and write in the frequencies in the upper part of the cell.

Tally marks have been entered in the tabulation sheet in Fig. 1. The frequencies are indicated in Fig. 2 on p. 662.

Step 4. Sum down each column and enter the totals on the bottom edge of the tabulation sheet. Sum across each row and enter on the right. These totals entered in the margin give the simple frequency distribution for X and Y, respectively.

Sums are shown in Fig. 2. The entries across the bottom are for the X (arithmetic) variable and those at the right for the Y (reading) variable.

Step. 5. Consider the values entered at the right of the table in step 4. They make up a simple frequency distribution of Y scores. Following Chapter 5 (pp. 149–151), carry out the steps for calculating the standard deviation. Determine N, $\Sigma fy'$ and $\Sigma f(y')^2$.

The values for y', fy', and $f(y')^2$ are shown in the three columns just to the right of the column of frequencies in Fig. 2. For this example, $\Sigma fy' = -7$ and $\Sigma f(y')^2 = 535$. (It may be noted that the Y variable is the reading test, and that these values are identical with the ones calculated for that test in Chapter 5.)

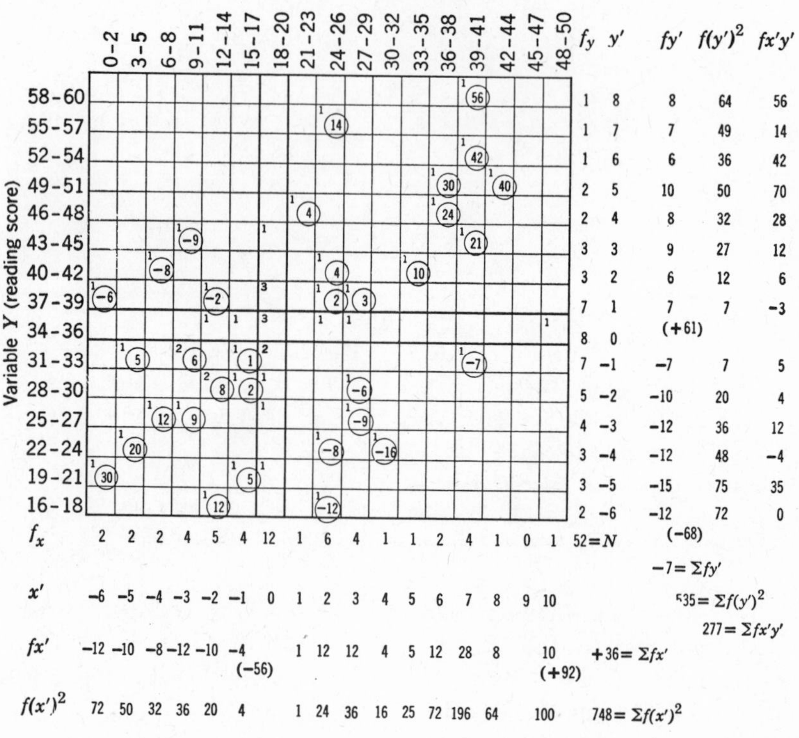

Fig. 2.

Step 6. Repeat step 5 for the frequencies of the X variable entered at the bottom of the table.

The value of $\Sigma fx'$ is $+36$; $\Sigma f(x')^2$ equals 748.

Step 7. Multiply the frequency in each cell of the two-way tabulation by the x' and the y' values for that cell. Enter this product, i.e., $fx'y'$, in the lower cor-

These entries have been circled in Fig. 2. Consider the row just above the heavy horizontal rules. Going right from the heavy vertical rules, we come

ner of the cell. This procedure will be easier if the column and row chosen for the arbitrary origin are enclosed in heavy rules, to show the zero point for each scale. The frequency in a cell must be multiplied by *both* the x' value for that cell and the y' value.

to a frequency of 1 in the second cell. For this cell $f = 1$, $x' = 2$, and $y' = 1$, so the product is $1 \times 2 \times 1 = 2$. For the next cell in the row $f = 1$, $x' = 3$, and $y' = 1$, so the product is $1 \times 3 \times 1 = 3$. Notice that in the upper left and lower right quarters of the table, the products are negative, because either x' or y' is negative. Also notice that all products for cells between the heavy lines are zero.

Step 8. Sum the $fx'y'$ values for all the cells. This gives $\Sigma fx'y'$, the sum of all the products of x' and y' values.

In the example, the values have first been summed across each row, and these sums entered in the column at the far right. This column has then been summed to give $\Sigma fx'y' = 277$.

Step 9. The formula for computing the correlation coefficient is

$$r = \frac{\dfrac{\Sigma fx'y'}{N} - \left(\dfrac{\Sigma fx'}{N}\right)\left(\dfrac{\Sigma fy'}{N}\right)}{\left\{\sqrt{\dfrac{\Sigma f(x')^2}{N} - \left(\dfrac{\Sigma fx'}{N}\right)^2} \times \sqrt{\dfrac{\Sigma f(y')^2}{N} - \left(\dfrac{\Sigma fy'}{N}\right)^2}\right\}}$$

Substitute the proper values in the formula and solve. (It should be noted that the two terms in the denominator are merely the formulas for the standard deviation of X and Y, respectively.

For our example, the solution becomes:

$$r = \frac{\dfrac{277}{52} - \left(\dfrac{36}{52}\right)\left(\dfrac{-7}{52}\right)}{\sqrt{\dfrac{748}{52} - \left(\dfrac{36}{52}\right)^2}\sqrt{\dfrac{535}{52} - \left(\dfrac{-7}{52}\right)^2}}$$

$$= \frac{5.33 - (0.692)(-0.135)}{\sqrt{14.38 - (0.692)^2} \times \sqrt{10.29 - (-0.135)^2}}$$

$$= \frac{5.42}{\sqrt{13.91}\sqrt{10.28}}$$

$$= \frac{5.42}{11.90}$$

$$= 0.46$$

APPENDIX IV

Section A

GENERAL INTELLIGENCE TESTS

California Short Form Test of Mental Maturity, 1963 Revision (CTMM)

California Test Bureau — *Testing time:* 40–45 min.
Range: Kindergarten–1.5, Grades 1–3, 3–4, 4–6, 6–7, 7–9, 9–12, 12–16

The *CTMM* yields three scores: (1) language IQ, (2) nonlanguage IQ, and (3) total IQ. Only one form of the test is available at each level. Some information is given in this edition of the nature of the factor scores. However, the factor scores are based on a relatively small number of items. The reliability of the nonlanguage subtest tends to be low. The artwork in the nonlanguage section is poor. The language portion of the test has a heavy emphasis on vocabulary. Predictive validity data are not given in the technical supplement but the language IQ and total IQ should have adequate correlations with academic achievement for the higher grades.

Chicago Nonverbal Examination

The Psychological Corporation — *Testing time:* 40–50 min.
Range: Age 6 and over

See discussion on pp. 307–309. The test is designed to minimize the English language factor in testing individuals and has been standardized with both verbal and pantomime directions. It is *not* a culture-free test, but does have value for testing deaf children or those with severe language deficits.

Cognitive Abilities Test (CAT)

Houghton Mifflin Company *Testing time:* 40–50 min.
Range: Kindergarten–1, Grades 2–3

See the discussion on pp. 294–295. The *CAT,* a group test using pictorial materials and oral instructions, is the primary level of the *Lorge-Thorndike Intelligence Tests.* Norms for the *CAT* were established by relating it directly to the *Lorge-Thorndike Intelligence Test, Multi-Level Edition* and samples for norming were drawn from the same schools and communities that participated in the norming of the *L-T.* Standard scores (deviation IQ's), age and grade stanines, and age and grade percentiles are provided. Reliability coefficients (K-R #20) range from .89 to .91 for each grade. Predictive validity data are not available since the test was published for use in September 1968.

College Qualification Tests (CQT)

The Psychological Corporation *Testing time:* 80–110 min.
Range: Candidates for college entrance

A series of three ability tests: (1) V-verbal, (2) N-numerical, and (3) I-science and social science information. Tests were developed for use by college admissions officers and guidance personnel. Form B of the test is restricted to colleges and universities. The test yields six scores including a total score for the entire test. The manual provides a number of different norms by sex, type of institution, and curriculum. Validity data for different courses of study in different institutions are provided in the manual and give evidence that test can be useful in the selection of students. Reliabilities are adequate, in the middle 90's for total score and ranging from the high 70's to low 90's for the subtests. The manual is excellent.

Cooperative Academic Ability Test (AAT)

Cooperative Test Division *Testing time:* 45–50 min.
Educational Testing Service
Range: Superior grade 12 students

Forms A and B of the test are also available as Forms IA and IB of *SCAT,* series II. The test consists of two subtests: (1) verbal analogies and (2) quantitative items requiring judgments of relative magnitudes. The test yields three scores: (1) verbal, (2) mathematical, and (3) total general ability. Standard scores and percentile bands are provided. Internal consistency reliabilities (K-R #20) for part scores are verbal, .88, mathematics, .92, total score, .94 for a 12th grade group. The mathematics test is speeded; therefore, the reliabilities are probably overestimated. No predictive validity data are given in the *Handbook.* Concurrent validity data against rank in graduating class show correlations of .49 for the verbal test and .50 for the mathematics. Normative samples are not fully described.

Cooperative School and College Ability Tests (SCAT)

Cooperative Test Division — *Testing time:* 60–75 min.
Educational Testing Service
Range: Grades 4–6, 6–8, 8–10, 10–12, 12–14.

SCAT yields three scores: (1) verbal, (2) quantitative, and (3) total. Manuals and interpretative materials accompanying the tests are excellent. Reliability coefficients are reported for only one form. The total score correlates well with measures of school success, but there is little evidence for differential prediction from the verbal and quantitative scores. Percentile and standard score norms are provided.

Henmon-Nelson Tests of Mental Ability, Revised Edition

Houghton Mifflin Company — *Testing time:* 30–45 min.
Range: Grades 3–6, 6–9, 9–12, 13–14

The tests designed for elementary and secondary schools yield a single overall score; the college-level test yields three scores: (1) verbal, (2) quantitative, and (3) total. The total score correlates well with other group tests of intelligence, with teachers' grades and with achievement test results. Reliability coefficients estimated by use of parallel forms range from .87 to .94 for the total score. Normative data for the elementary and secondary school levels and college freshmen are good but norms are lacking for other levels of the college edition. Only percentile norms are presented for the college edition.

IPAT Culture-Fair Intelligence Test

Institute for Personality and Ability Testing — *Testing time:* 20–30 min.
Range: Scale 2, ages 8–13 and average adults
Scale 3, grades 10–16 and superior adults

See discussion on pp. 315–316. The major claims made for these tests are that they have high saturation on general ability, g, and that they are relatively independent of environmental influences. Although there is some evidence presented that the test does appraise primarily the general ability factor, there is no convincing evidence that the test is culture-fair. Internal consistency reliabilities tend to be in the .70's and retest reliabilities are as low as .50 in some samples. Normative samples tend to be small and inadequately described. Predictive validity data are meager and the evidence that is reported is not impressive.

Kuhlmann-Anderson Intelligence Tests, Seventh Edition (K-A)

Personnel Press, Inc. *Testing time:* 25–60 min.
Range: Kindergarten; 1, 2, 3–4, 4–5, 5–7, 7–9, 9–12

The *K-A* consists of eight subtests at all levels. The lower levels yield a single overall score; the higher levels yield three scores: (1) verbal, (2) quantitative, and (3) total. Percentile norms and standard score norms (deviation IQ's) are available for each level. Reliability coefficients are generally satisfactory. The difference score between the verbal and quantitative subtests does not appear to have high enough reliability to be used. Data on concurrent validity are satisfactory, but there are few predictive validity coefficients reported in the technical manual. The subtests have very short time limits and, therefore, place heavy demands on the examinees for fast work and on the examiner for accurate timing.

Lorge-Thorndike Intelligence Tests, Multi-Level Edition (L-T)

Houghton Mifflin Company *Testing time:* 35–45 min.
Range: Grade 3 through college freshmen

For a description of the tests, see pp. 296–298. The *L-T, Iowa Tests of Basic Skills,* and *The Tests of Academic Progress* were normed together. Norming procedures were excellent. Standard scores (deviation IQ's), grade percentiles, and age equivalents are provided. Alternate form reliabilities range from .80 to .92 for the nonverbal battery with a median of .88. For the verbal battery the range is from .83 to .94 with a median of .90. Correlations of different forms given 1 to 3 years apart yield coefficients of stability from .49 to .74 for a 3-year interval and from .58 to .88 for a 1-year interval. Standard errors of measurement are provided for different score levels. Concurrent, construct, and predictive validity data are provided. Median predictive validity correlations against grades or rank in class are approximately .56 at the high school level for the verbal battery and .65 at the elementary school level. For the nonverbal battery, correlations average about .52 for elementary school grades.

Ohio State University Psychological Test, Form 21

Ohio College Association *Testing time:* No time limit
Range: Grades 9 to 16, adults

This is a power test designed primarily to predict success in college (correlations of about .60 with scholastic performance). Reliability is high. It emphasizes verbal ability. Norms are based on Ohio high school students and freshmen in Ohio colleges. A good scholastic aptitude test at the college level.

Otis-Lennon Mental Ability Tests

Harcourt, Brace & World, Inc. *Testing time:* 30–50 min.
Range: Kindergarten; 1–1.5; 1.6–3.9; 4.0–6.9; 7.0–9.9; 10.0–12.9

This series is a revision of the *Otis Quick-Scoring Mental Ability Tests* and closely resembles it. It has a spiral omnibus format and yields a total IQ. A very complete technical handbook is provided that describes procedures for constructing the test and gives complete data on validity, reliability, and standardization. Alternate form reliabilities with one or two week intervals range from .81 for age 5 to a high of .94 for age 14 with a median of .92. Split-half and K-R #21 reliability coefficients run slightly higher. Standard errors of measurement are reported for different score levels as well as over-all. Predictive and concurrent validity data are reported and compare favorably with those reported for other instruments. Deviation IQ's, percentile norms, and mental ages are provided.

Raven's Progressive Matrices

The Psychological Corporation *Testing time:* 30–60 min.
Range: Ages 5 and over.

The test is available in a black-and-white and colored form. It represents an attempt to appraise the general ability factor, Spearman's *g*. The tasks consist of designs with missing parts. The examinee chooses from the given options the design that best fits. Although the test is claimed by some to be "culture-fair," there is little evidence to support the claim. There are no time limits. Evidence on the reliability and validity of the test is inconsistent. Test tends to be extremely difficult for young children and reliabilities for the young age groups tend to be low. The manual for the test is inadequate. Normative data at best are sketchy. Most of the norms are based on British samples.

SRA Tests of Educational Ability, 1962 Edition (TEA)

Science Research Associates *Testing time:* 30–70 min.
Range: Grades 4–6, 6–9, 9–12

The *TEA* provides four scores: (1) language, (2) reasoning, (3) quantitative, and (4) total, and the lowest level yields an additional score, nonreading. However, the manuals suggest that only total scores be used and the evidence on validity is primarily in terms of total scores. The predictive validity data presented in the manual are for short-term (two months or less) prediction and should be interpreted with caution. The samples used to norm the test can be questioned both as to representativeness and size. Reliability of total scores is adequate. The technical manual is poorly written and difficult to understand. Conversion of the raw scores in terms of grade placement rather than age placement makes comparison with other tests difficult.

SRA Tests of General Ability (*TOGA*)

Science Research Associates *Testing time:* 35–45 min.
Range: Kindergarten–2, 2–4, 4–6, 6–9, 9–12

TOGA attempts to reduce stress on school-learned skills by presenting all test items at all levels in pictorial form. One subtest at each level is supposed to appraise reasoning and the other subtest is supposed to appraise information. Normative samples at all levels are small and *not* representative geographically. The reasoning subtest is claimed to be "culture-fair" but no evidence is presented to support this claim. Concurrent validity data presented indicate that *TOGA* appraises about the same functions as other commonly used intelligence tests and ranks students approximately in the same way. Total score reliability coefficients (split-half) range from .80 to .90 with a median of .87. Directions for administering the test are clear but permit the administrator of the test considerable leeway to alter timing particularly in the information test.

Section B

oooooooooooooooooooooooooooooooooooooooooooooooooooooooooooooooooooooooooooooooooooooooooooooooooooooooooooooo

APTITUDE TEST BATTERIES

Academic Promise Tests (APT)

The Psychological Corporation — *Testing time:* 90–120 min.
Range: Grades 6–9

The *APT* consists of four subtests: (1) abstract reasoning, (2) numerical, (3) verbal, and (4) language usage, which yield 4 separate subscores and 3 scores from combining the subtests. Reliability coefficients (internal consistency and parallel forms) are high. Predictive validity coefficients between test scores and grades are given. Percentile norms are provided for each grade. The tests should be useful in educational guidance and for sectioning and placing students.

The Dailey Vocational Tests

Houghton Mifflin Company — *Testing time:* 115–140 min.
Range: Grades 8–12 and adults

This battery, designed for noncollege-bound students, consists of three tests: the *Technical and Scholastic Test,* yielding seven subscores, a technical and scholastic score and a total score; the *Spatial Visualization Test,* and the *Business English Test.* Subtest scores of the *Technical and Scholastic Test* are quite short and unreliable. Normative data are incomplete and somewhat confusing. Validity data are largely limited to differences between high school curricular groups. Tests for students not headed for college are needed, but more information is required on this battery before it can be recommended for use.

Differential Aptitude Test Battery

The Psychological Corporation — *Testing time:* 300–330 min.
Range: Grades 8–12

See text, pp. 350–353, for discussion. This is a practical guidance battery for high-school use. It has an extremely full and well-organized manual. Extensive validation data are presented against educational criteria, but little against vocational criteria. Claims for validity are modest and realistic.

Flanagan Aptitude Classification Tests (FACT)

Science Research Associates — *Testing time:* 210–328 min.
Range: Grades 12–16 and above

This battery consists of nineteen tests and is essentially oriented toward vocational guidance rather than educational guidance. Each test is in a separate booklet and has a self-scoring answer sheet. Construction of test items appears to be very good. Reliability coefficients for separate tests tend to be low, but composite scores have adequate reliability. The greatest weakness in the battery is its lack of validity data to support many of the claims made in the manual and in accompanying materials. Until more validity data are available, it would probably be best to be extremely cautious in interpreting the meaning of the scores.

General Aptitude Test Battery

U.S. Employment Service — *Testing time:* 120–150 min. for group tests
Range: Grades 12 and above and adults

See text, pp. 353–357, for discussion of this battery. It is available only for use by State Employment Offices.

Multiple Aptitude Tests (MAT)

California Test Bureau — *Testing time:* 175–220 min.
Range: Grades 7–13

The battery consists of nine tests providing nine separate scores, which in turn yield scores on four basic factors. The word meaning, language usage, and arithmetic computation and reasoning tests have reliabilities in the high .80's or low .90's and are quite satisfactory; but the reliabilities for paragraph meaning, applied science and mechanics, and spatial relations tend to be only in the high .70's and this makes them somewhat less useful for individual guidance. Predictive validity data for school marks are given and tend to be disappointingly low. Concurrent validity for 42 different occupational groups is given showing differences in occupational profiles on the tests; however, these were obtained for groups that were already engaged in the occupation.

SRA Primary Mental Abilities, Revised (*PMA*)

Science Research Associates — *Testing time:* 65–75 min. (2–4)
Range: Kindergarten–1, Grades 2–4, 4–6, 6–9, 9–12 — 50–107 min. (4–6)
35–75 min. (6–9, 9–12)

Although this instrument, yielding 4 subscores as well as a total score (except in the form for grades 4–6, which yields 5 subscores), is promoted in terms of the differential information provided by the part scores, evidence of differential validity is scanty and most data are for the total score. Only one form is available, and for this test-retest reliabilities of total score are in the .80's or low .90's. Data on subtest validities, reliabilities, and norms are meager.

Section C

oooooooooooooooooooooooooooooooooooooooooooooooooooooooooooooooooooooooooooooooooooooooooooooooooooooooooo

READING TESTS

Davis Reading Test

The Psychological Corporation *Testing time:* 45–55 min.
Range: Grades 8–11; 11–12

The test yields two scores, (1) level of comprehension, and (2) speed of comprehension. Items on the test are well constructed and measure the subtler aspects of reading comprehension. The equivalent form reliabilities are in the high .70's or low .80's. Correlations between the scores on the reading tests and grades in English average about .50. Standard score norms and percentile norms are provided.

Diagnostic Reading Tests: Survey Section

Science Research Associates
Range: Grades 4–8 *Testing time:* 60–70 min.
Grades 7–13 175–200 min.

The level for grades 4–8 yields 5 scores: (1) word recognition, (2) comprehension, (3) vocabulary, (4) story reading, and (5) total. The level for grades 7–13 also yields 5 scores: (1) rate of reading, (2) story comprehension, (3) vocabulary, (4) comprehension, and (5) total. Manuals accompanying the tests are very difficult to comprehend and contain very little information on reliability and norming procedures. The manuals for administration are somewhat vague about time limits. Normative data are provided on separate mimeographed sheets with no description of the nature of the normative group. Although the tests have some interesting approaches to the appraisal of reading skills, the lack of reliability data, the inadequacy of the normative data, and the poor quality of reproduction would argue against wide use of the tests.

Gates-MacGinitie Reading Tests

Teachers College Press

Range:	*Testing time:*
Grade 1	40–50 min.
Grade 2	40–50 min.
Grade 3	50–60 min.
Grades 4–6	45–50 min.
Grades 7–9	45–50 min.

The *Gates-MacGinitie Reading Tests* provide a series of coordinated reading tests for grades 1 through 9. The tests for grades 1, 2 and 3 measure vocabulary and comprehension only; the tests for grade 4 and above measure speed, vocabulary, and comprehension. An additional test is available for grades 2 and 3; it measures speed and accuracy. Alternate form reliabilities (time interval not specified) for vocabulary and comprehension are in the .80's; the reliabilities for the number attempted scores are in the high .60's or low .70's. Split-half reliabilities given for the vocabulary and comprehension tests are in the high .80's and low .90's. Norms for the test were established by testing the same students in the fall and spring of the school year. Students in the normative samples were also given the *Lorge-Thorndike Intelligence Tests.* Tables are provided for interpreting the significance of differences between scores on the reading test and the intelligence test, of gain scores, and of differences between part scores. The tests have been carefully constructed and provide an easily administered appraisal of basic reading skills.

Primary Reading Profiles, 1967 Edition

Houghton-Mifflin Company — *Testing time:* 70–85 min.
Range: Grades 1.5–2.5, 2.5–3.5

The battery consists of 5 tests: (1) aptitude for reading, (2) auditory association, (3) word recognition, (4) word attack, and (5) reading comprehension. Test 1 is presented as a listening test and is recommended for use to indicate the level of reading achievement that could reasonably be expected from each student. Split-half reliability coefficient for Test 1 is .77 but for the other tests reliability coefficients (split-half) range from .90 to .96. Test 1 has correlations with the other tests of the battery of .45 to .56, and with mental age from the *Stanford-Binet Tests of Intelligence* of .53. Although the value of Test 1 has not been established, the three tests of reading skills appear to be adequate appraisals of reading at this level.

Stanford Diagnostic Reading Test

Harcourt, Brace & World, Inc.

Range: Grades 2.5–4.5 — *Testing time:* 160–180 min.

Grades 4.5–8.5 — 110–130 min.

The battery consists of tests of vocabulary, reading comprehension, and word recognition skills. The intercorrelations among the subtests range from .49 to .81 with an average intercorrelation of about .60. Split-half reliabilities average about .94. Standard errors of measurement are not provided by score levels. Data on validity are meager. The test could be useful to a classroom teacher to obtain leads as to the sources of reading difficulties.

Section D

ooooooooooooooooooooooooooooooooooooooooooooooooooooooooooooooooooooooooooooooooooooooooooooooooooooooooooo

ELEMENTARY-SCHOOL ACHIEVEMENT BATTERIES

Comprehensive Tests of Basic Skills (*CTBS*)

California Test Bureau *Testing time:* 240–260 min.
Range: Grades 2.5–4.9; 4.0–6.9; 6.0–8.9

The *CTBS* is the 1968 revision of the *California Achievement Tests.* The battery consists of 10 subtests: (1) reading vocabulary, (2) reading comprehension, (3) language mechanics, (4) language expression, (5) language spelling, (6) arithmetic computation, (7) arithmetic concepts, (8) arithmetic applications, (9) study skills using reference materials, and (10) study skills using graphic materials. The battery yields 15 scores, one for each of the 10 subtests, a total for each skill area, and a total battery score. The tests were normed with the *California Short-Form Test of Mental Maturity.* Except for tables of norms, description of normative sample, and analysis of content of each subtest, no technical data were available in January 1969. The absence of any reliability data in the manual for examiners and test coordinators is particularly troublesome. An examination of the normative tables indicates that each level of the test appears to be too difficult for the first grade of the level and too easy for the last grade of the level; for example, the level for grades 2.5–4.9 appears to be too difficult for the last half of grade 2 and too easy for the last half of grade 4. The subtests appear to be too short to appraise adequately the range of achievement that each is supposed to cover.

Iowa Tests of Basic Skills (ITBS)

Houghton Mifflin Company *Testing time:* 280–335 min.
Range: Grades 3–9

The *ITBS* uses a multilevel format, with a single spiral-bound reusable test booklet for all grades. Test level is controlled by starting and stopping at different points. The battery yields 15 scores: vocabulary (one score), reading comprehension (one score), language (four subscores and one total score), work-study skills (three subscores and one total score), arithmetic skills (two subscores and one total score), and composite score. The battery emphasizes the appraisal of functional skills needed by the child if he is to make progress in school. Reliabilities of the subtests are adequate and, of the total tests, are high. Procedures for norming the test were excellent. The *ITBS* and the *Lorge-Thorndike Intelligence Tests* were normed simultaneously and percentile norms by intelligence level are provided in a supplementary manual. In addition to general national norms, special percentile norms are provided for building averages, geographical region, large cities, and Catholic schools. The manuals are excellent—particularly the ones for the teacher and for the administrator. A modern mathematics supplement is available for use in addition to or to replace the arithmetic skills tests in the regular battery.

Metropolitan Achievement Tests, 1959 Edition

Harcourt, Brace & World, Inc.

Range:		*Testing time:*
	Primary I, grades 1.5–2.5	95–100 min.
	Primary II, grades 2–3.5	105–115 min.
	Elementary, grades 3–4	160–175 min.
	Intermediate, grades 5–6	250–280 min.
	Advanced, grades 7–8	260–290 min.

All of the batteries measure vocabulary, reading comprehension, and arithmetic skills. Word discrimination is tested in the three lowest levels; spelling begins in the *Primary II* battery and continues through the other levels. Language skills are added in the *Elementary* battery and continue through the other batteries. Language study skills, social studies information, social studies study skills, and science are parts of the intermediate and advanced batteries. The format of all the tests is attractive. Test content in the skills area appears to be adequate, and the test items, on the whole, are well written. Norming procedures are good. Reliabilities of total scores for all tests are adequate. A revised form of the *Metropolitan* is scheduled to be published for use in the fall of 1970.

Sequential Tests of Educational Progress (STEP)

Cooperative Test Division
Educational Testing Service
Range: Grades 4–6; 7–9

Testing time: 450–500 min.

The battery consists of six tests: (1) reading, (2) writing, (3) mathematics, (4) science, (5) social studies, and (6) listening. The tests are supposed to provide a continuous standard score scale to appraise growth in achievement from grade 4 through 14. Critics of the test have raised questions about the equivalence of the scale over the different levels. Norms are presented in terms of percentile bands. Manuals and handbooks for the battery are excellent. The battery is being revised and a new battery is scheduled to be published for use late in 1970 or early 1971. Preliminary plans for the revision indicate that the content of the tests will be changed considerably and that the listening test will be dropped.

SRA Achievement Series, 1964 Edition

Science Research Associates

Range:		*Testing time:*
	Grades 1–2	270–300 min.
	Grades 2–4	300–360 min.
	Grades 4–9	420–450 min.

The levels of the test designed for use in grades 1–2 and grades 2–4 are published as separate batteries; the one designed for grades 4–9 is published in a multilevel format. Reading and arithmetic skills are appraised at all levels; a subtest in language arts is added at grades 2–4 and all higher levels; and subtests in social studies and science are added at grades 4 and above. A test of work-study skills is provided as a supplement at grades 4 and above. The tests are very attractive and make good use of color. In the multilevel battery, answer sheets for different grades are color coded. The tests in science and social studies tend to emphasize recall of factual information. Vocabulary is appraised only in context of a reading selection. Reliability coefficients (K-R #20) are satisfactory but may be somewhat inflated. Grade equivalent, percentile, and stanine norms are provided at all grade levels. Procedures for norming, establishing the content of the tests, and determining reliability are inadequately reported.

Stanford Achievement Tests, 1964 Revision

Harcourt, Brace & World

Range:		*Testing time:*
	Grades 1.5–2.4	160–170 min.
	Grades 2.5–3.9	230–250 min.
	Grades 4.0–5.4	230–300 min.
	Grades 5.5–6.9	220–300 min.
	Grades 7.0–9.9	200–285 min.

The subtests included at each level vary, but reading, spelling, and arithmetic are included at all levels. At grade 4 and above, the battery can be purchased as a partial battery or complete battery. The complete battery includes subtests in social studies and science. Split-half and K-R #20 reliability coefficients are given and these tend to be satisfactory at all levels. No equivalent form reliabilities are given. Grade equivalent, percentile, and stanine norms are provided. Norms by stanine levels of performance on the *Otis Quick-Scoring Mental Ability Test* are given in the Technical Report and in the manual for administering the tests.

Section E

HIGH SCHOOL ACHIEVEMENT BATTERIES

Comprehensive Tests of Basic Skills (*CTBS*)

California Test Bureau — *Testing time:* 240–260 min.
Range: 8.0–12.9

This is the highest level of the same battery described in Section D. The range of grades to be covered by this level appears to be too large for a single, relatively short battery of tests. No reliability or other technical data were available for the tests early in 1969.

Iowa Tests of Educational Development (*ITED*)

Science Research Associates — *Testing time:* 330–540 min.
Range: Grades 9–12

The battery consists of 9 subtests: (1) understanding of basic social concepts, (2) general background in the natural sciences, (3) correctness and appropriateness of expression, (4) ability to do quantitative thinking, (5) ability to interpret reading materials in the social studies, (6) ability to interpret reading materials in the natural sciences, (7) ability to interpret literary materials, (8) general vocabulary, and (9) uses of sources of information. The battery yields 10 scores, one for each subtest and a composite total score based on the first 8 subtests. Predictive validity data and concurrent validity data are provided. Correlations between composite scores obtained in grades 10, 11 or 12 and grades in the freshmen year of college range from .40 to .71 with a median of approximately .60. Internal consistency reliabilities are satisfactory. Correlations between scores on the third edition and fourth edition taken one year apart are mostly in the .80's. Correlations among subtests tend to be high in the .70's; therefore, the value of the tests as a diagnostic instrument is questionable. Standard scores, percentiles, and percentile bands are provided.

Metropolitan Achievement Tests: High School Battery (*MAT*)

Harcourt, Brace & World — *Testing time:* 315–330 min.
Range: Grades 9–13

The battery consists of 11 subtests: (1) reading, (2) spelling, (3) language arts, (4) language study skills, (5) social studies study skills, (6) social studies vocabulary, (7) social studies information, (8) mathematical computation and concepts, (9) mathematical analysis and problem solving, (10) scientific concepts and understandings, and (11) science information. The language, mathematics, science, and social studies subtests are available as separate tests. Alternate form reliability coefficients (time interval not specified) for grades 10 and 11 combined range from .72 to .90 with a median of approximately .84. Split-half reliabilities for grades 10 and 11 combined are slightly higher with a median coefficient of about .86. Internal consistency reliabilities (K-R #20) for a single grade tend to cluster between .82 and .88. Percentile and stanine norms are provided for age-controlled samples at each grade level and for college preparatory groups at each grade level. Tables are also provided for comparing performance on the achievement tests with students who performed at different levels on the *Otis Quick-Scoring Mental Ability Tests: Gamma.*

Sequential Tests of Educational Progress (*STEP*)

Cooperative Test Division — *Testing time:* 450–500 min.
Educational Testing Service
Range: Grades 10–12; 13–14

See discussion of the battery in Section D.

Stanford Achievement Test: High School Battery (*SAT*)

Harcourt, Brace & World — *Testing time:* 320–350 min.
Range: Grades 9–12

The high school basic battery consists of 7 subtests: (1) English, (2) numerical competence, (3) mathematics, (4) reading, (5) science, (6) social studies, and (7) spelling. Supplementary tests in *Arts and Humanities, Business and Economics,* and *Technical Comprehension* are also available. The subject tests are also published in separate booklets. Percentiles and stanines are provided for total-grade groups, for college-preparatory groups by grade, and for groups having different numbers of semesters of study in a content area. Tables are provided for comparing performance on tests with the *Otis Quick-Scoring Mental Ability Tests: Gamma.* Internal consistency reliabilities for the different subtests are in the high .80's or low .90's.

Tests of Academic Progress (TAP)

Houghton Mifflin Company *Testing time:* 330–340 min.
Range: Grades 9–12

The battery consists of four overlapping tests, one for each grade, in the following six areas: (1) social studies, (2) composition, (3) science, (4) reading, (5) mathematics, and (6) literature. The tests are available in a single booklet or as separate booklets. Three types of norms are provided: standard score norms, grade-percentile norms for individual students, and grade-percentile norms for school averages. The tests were standardized in a coordinated program with the *Iowa Tests of Basic Skills* and the *Lorge-Thorndike Intelligence Tests.* Split-half reliability coefficients for the different grades are .85 or better except for the science subtest at grade 9 for which it is .83. The majority of the reliability coefficients are .89 or better. Standard errors of measurement are given for each subtest and for each grade for total score and at selected percentile-rank levels. *TAP* is a well-constructed, well-normed battery of tests that should be useful in a wide variety of secondary schools.

Section F

ooooooooooooooooooooooooooooooooooooooooooooooooooooooooooooooooooooooooooooooooooooooooooooooooooooo

INTEREST INVENTORIES

Brainard Occupational Preference Inventory

The Psychological Corporation — *Testing time:* 30 min.
Range: Grades 8–12; adults

The inventory covers six broad occupational fields: (1) commercial, (2) mechanical, (3) professional, (4) aesthetic, (5) scientific, and (6) personal service (for girls) or agriculture (for boys). Each occupational field is covered by twenty items which the respondent marks on a five-point scale ranging from "like very much" to "dislike very much." Data in the manual show that the instrument has moderate to low correlations with the *Kuder Preference Record–Vocational.* Scoring is simple. Evidence on validity is lacking.

Gordon Occupational Check List (*OCL*)

Harcourt, Brace & World — *Testing time:* 20–25 min.
Range: High school students not planning to enter college

The *OCL* is designed for use with individuals who have a high school education or less. The inventory contains 240 statements of job duties and tasks that are found in occupations at the middle and lower levels of skill and responsibility. The statements are classified into five broad occupational groupings. Top-level managerial and professional occupations are not included. Test-retest reliability data tend to be in the middle or high .80's. No norms are reported. Validity data are meager.

Kuder Preference Record–Occupational

Science Research Associates, Inc. *Testing time:* 25–35 min.
Range: Grades 9–16 and adults

The *KPR–Occupational* yields 50 scores for specific occupational groups and one verification score. The occupational keys were developed by comparing answers of men in specific occupations with men in general. Concurrent validity data only are reported in the manual. No predictive validity data are provided. Test-retest reliability data are scarce. The only test-retest data reported in the manual are over a one-month interval; the median correlation is .85. Correlations between *Kuder* scales and the corresponding scale of the *Strong Vocational Interest Blank* tend to be low to moderate. At the present time, more data on reliability and validity are needed.

Kuder Preference Record–Vocational

Science Research Associates *Testing time:* 40–50 min.
Range: Grades 9–16 and adults

See discussion in text, pp. 391–392.

Kuder Preference Record–Personal

Science Research Associates *Testing time:* 40–45 min
Range: Grades 9–16 and adults

Using the same pattern for items as the *Kuder Preference Record–Vocational,* this inventory appraises liking for five more aspects of life situations; being active in groups, being in familiar and stable situations, working with ideas, avoiding conflict, and directing others. The scores are fairly independent of each other and of those in the *Vocational* blank. The value of these scales for guidance purposes is less fully explored than that of the scales in the *Vocational* form.

Minnesota Vocational Interest Inventory (*MVII*)

The Psychological Corporation *Testing time:* 40–45 min.
Range: High school and adults

The *MVII* is an empirically-keyed inventory designed to appraise interests in nonprofessional occupations. It has been designed for use with noncollege-bound high school students or young adults who have had limited education or had a technical-vocational education. The inventory consists of 158 triads of brief statements describing the tasks or activities in a variety of trades and nonprofessional occupations. It yields scores for 21 occupational scales and 9 area scales that show the examinee's likes and dislikes for activities common to several occupations. Test-retest reliability coefficients for the occupational scales over a 30-day interval range from .64 to .88 with a median reliability of about .82. Validity data reported in the manual consists of differences in mean scores between "satisfied workers" and "dissatisfied workers" and the "percentage of overlap" between the criterion occupation and tradesmen-in-general. The inventory was published in 1965; therefore, it has not been as thoroughly researched and studied as have the *Kuder* and the *Strong*. However, the inventory serves the very important function of providing an interest measure suitable for use with noncollege-bound high school students and similar groups.

Strong Vocational Interest Blank for Men, Revised (*SVIB*)

Consulting Psychologists Press, Inc. *Testing time:* 30–60 min.
Range: Ages 17 and over

See discussion in text, pp. 388–391.

Strong Vocational Interest Blank for Women, Revised (*SVIB*)

Consulting Psychologists Press, Inc. *Testing time:* 30–60 min.
Range: Ages 17 and over

The *SVIB* for women is similar to the blank for men. This version has not been as thoroughly studied as the men's blank, nor does it seem to be as effective as the men's blank.

Section G

ooooooooooooooooooooooooooooooooooooooooooooooooooooooooooooooooooooooooooooooooooooooooooooooooooooooooo

ADJUSTMENT AND TEMPERAMENT INVENTORIES

California Psychological Inventory (*CPI*)

Consulting Psychologists Press, Inc. *Testing time:* 45–60 min.
Range: Ages 13 and over

The *CPI* has been developed for use with normal populations. It consists of 480 items to be answered "true" or "false." About one-half of the items on the *CPI* have been taken from the *MMPI*. The *CPI* yields 18 scores, three of which are check scales to determine test-taking attitudes. Items on 11 of the 15 scales were selected on their ability to discriminate contrasting groups. Test-retest reliabilities for high school groups over a year interval averaged .65 for males and .68 for females. Retest reliabilities for an adult group over a one- to three-week interval averaged about .80. Intercorrelations among the scores tend to be high, indicating that the scores are not as independent as the manual tends to imply. Separate norms are provided by sex for high school and college samples. Some of the validity data based on differences between extreme groups are questionable.

California Test of Personality, 1953 Revision

California Test Bureau *Testing time:* 45–60 min.
Range: Kindergarten to grade 3; grades 4 to 8, 7 to 10, 9 to 16; adults

This is one of the few personality inventories that have forms for use in the elementary school. Evidence on the validity of the scales is scanty. Reliability data indicate that only the total score and its two components, social and personal, are stable enough to use. The "right" answer to many of the questions seems obvious. At the elementary levels, the inventories require at least an average reading ability, limiting its usefulness with the low-achieving child. Suggestions given in the test manual for the use of the test results are questionable at best. In the hands of a person untrained in psychology, the suggestions could have disastrous consequences.

Edwards Personal Preference Schedule

The Psychological Corporation *Testing time:* 40–55 min.
Range: College and adults

This test has been designed to assess the relative strengths of 15 manifest needs selected from Murray's need system. Each need is represented by nine statements. The statements representing each need are presented in forced-choice format paired with a statement representing another need. The pairs of statements are supposed to be controlled for social desirability. Norms are provided for male and female college students and an adult sample. The representativeness of the adult sample is questionable.

Internal consistency reliability coefficients reported in the manual range from .60 to .87 with a median of .78, and one-week retest reliability coefficients range from .74 to .87 with a median of .83. The *Schedule* has been used extensively in research but consistent validity data are rather meager.

Gordon Personal Inventory

Harcourt, Brace and World, Inc. *Testing time:* 15–20 min.
Range: Grades 8–16 and adults

This inventory and the *Gordon Personal Profile* use the same format. Items are arranged in sets of four statements, two favorable and two unfavorable, from which the examinee is to select the one statement that is "most" like him and the one statement that is "least" like him. The inventory yields four scores: cautiousness, original thinking, personal relations, and vigor. Internal consistency reliability coefficients (split-half) of the four scales range from .77 to .84. Validity data consist primarily of correlations between scores on the subtests and performance criteria. However, since there is no theoretical basis for predicting either the direction or magnitude of the correlations, these data must be viewed somewhat skeptically unless they appear for several groups. Percentile norms are provided by sex for high school and college groups and for some occupational groups. The usefulness of the inventory is limited because of the lack of validity data.

Gordon Personal Profile

Harcourt, Brace and World *Testing time:* 15–20 min.
Range: Grades 9–16 and adults

The *Profile* yields four scores: (1) ascendancy–A, (2) responsibility–R, (3) emotional stability–E, and (4) sociability–S. Although the four traits were selected as being independent, the correlations between the A and S scales and between the R and E scales are .60 or higher. Reliability is adequate. Validity data reported in the manual include correlations between scores and peer ratings and counselor's trait ratings for college groups. Additional validity data are presented for groups in industrial and training situations. Percentile norms are provided for high school and college students, low and middle level employes, managers, salesmen, and foremen.

Guilford-Zimmerman Temperament Survey

Sheridan Supply Company *Testing time:* 50–60 min.
Range: Grades 9–16 and adults

See text, pp. 400–404. One of the best inventories for describing aspects of normal personality. Experience is needed to determine whether the dimensions are of practical importance for personal or vocational counseling.

The IPAT Anxiety Scale

Institute for Personality and Ability Testing *Testing time:* 5–10 min.
Range: Ages 14 and over

The *Scale* consists of 40 items that yield five part scores and a total score. In addition, the 40 items yield separate "covert" and "overt" anxiety scores. Construction of the *Anxiety Scale* was based on extensive factor analytic studies. The validity of the *Scale* is based on the factor analytic studies and external criteria. External validity is based on correlations of total scores with psychiatric ratings (range .30 to .40 uncorrected for attenuation); differences in mean scores between anxiety neurotics and the standardization population; and differences in mean scores among other clinically diagnosed groups.

Reliability coefficients for the part scores, based on subtests with as few as four items and a maximum of 12 items, are too low to justify the use of part scores with individuals. The *Scale* is probably most useful as a quick screening device for literate adults and as a research instrument.

Minnesota Multiphasic Personality Inventory (MMPI)

The Psychological Corporation *Testing time:* 30–90 min.
Range: Age 16 and over

For discussion see text, pp. 404–408. This instrument is oriented towards abnormal rather than normal groups, and is designed to differentiate between them. There seems to be some doubt that it does this very effectively. It is rather lengthy to use as a screening test. However, the profile based on the separate scale scores provides a good deal of material for interpretation by the sophisticated counselor or clinical psychologist.

Mooney Problem Check List

The Psychological Corporation *Testing time:* 20–40 min.
Range: Forms for grades 7–9, 9–12, 13–16, and adults

These check lists provide a systematic coverage of problems often reported or judged significant at the different age levels. Though the items are grouped by areas (health and physical development; courtship, sex, and marriage; home and family; etc.) and a count can be made of items marked in each area, emphasis is placed on using the individual responses as leads and openings for an interview. This instrument does not claim to be a test and the use proposed for it is the type that is probably most justifiable for a self-report instrument.

Omnibus Personality Inventory (OPI)

The Psychological Corporation *Testing time:* 50–70 min.
Range: College students

The majority of the items on the *OPI* have been drawn from other personality inventories, mainly the *MMPI, VC Attitude Inventory, Minnesota T-S-E Inventory,* and the *CPI.* The *OPI* was developed to assess the personality characteristics of college students, especially those who are intellectually superior. The inventory yields 14 scores. Internal consistency reliability coefficients (K-R 21) range from .67 to .89 for the separate subscores. Test-retest reliabilities with a three- or four-week interval range from .79 to .94 for 67 women at three colleges and from .84 to .93 for 71 upperclassmen at one college. Validity data consists primarily of correlations with other inventories and with ratings of various academic groups. Norms for the scales are based on 7,283 college freshmen from 37 institutions. At its present stage of development, the *OPI* should be used primarily for research purposes.

Sixteen Personality Factor Questionnaire (*16 PF*)

Institute for Personality and Ability Testing *Testing time:* 45–60 min.
Range: Age 17 and over

The *16 PF* has been developed to appraise a comprehensive range of traits. The construction of the instrument was based on extensive factor analytic studies and other research. The parent *16 PF* instrument has led to the development of inventories for younger age groups (*High School Personality Questionnaire, Children's Personality Questionnaire, Early School Personality Questionnaire*). The inventory yields 16 scores on primary factors and 4 second order factor scores. Split-half reliabilities of single factor scores from one form of the inventory tend to be low but the split-half reliabilities of the factor scores from pooling two forms of the test (Form A and Form B) are adequate. Norms are provided for college students and adults but normative samples are inadequately described. The *16 PF* is an interesting instrument that is potentially useful, but at the present time should be viewed primarily as a research instrument.

Study of Values, Third Edition

Houghton Mifflin Co. *Testing time:* 20 min.
Range: Grades 13 and over

The *Study of Values,* originally published in 1931, was designed to measure Spranger's six "value types": theoretical, economic, aesthetic, social, political, and religious. The second edition published in 1951 redefined the social value and added more discriminating items. The third edition, 1960, differs from the second edition only in providing more normatve data. The median reliability coefficients for different subscales are .82 (split-half) and .88 for test-retest with a one- or two-month interval. Split-half reliabilities are based on groups of 100 subjects and test-retest on groups of 34 and 53 subjects. Validity data presented in the manual consist primarily of demonstrating that the value patterns of various educational and occupational groups differ in the predicted ways. Norms are provided for college groups and for occupational groups that usually require some college education. The instrument has been criticized for lack of evidence on the unidimensionality of the scales, the problem of ipsative scoring, and the lack of generality beyond the college population.

Thorndike Dimensions of Temperament (*TDOT*)

The Psychological Corporation *Testing time:* 30–45 min.
Range: Grade 11 and above

For discussion see text, pp. 408–409.

APPENDIX V

Sources for Educational and Psychological Tests

American College Testing Program (ACT)
P.O. Box 168
Iowa City, Iowa 52240

None of the ACT tests are available to the general public, but descriptions of the tests and services provided, materials for students who plan to take the tests, research reports and other publications are available. Many are free.

California Test Bureau
Del Monte Research Park
Monterey, California 93940

Primarily achievement tests, intelligence tests, interest and personality inventories for elementary and high school. Best known tests are the *California Tests of Mental Maturity* and the 1968 revision of the achievement test series, *Comprehensive Tests of Basic Skills.*

College Entrance Examination Board (CEEB)
Publications Order Office
Box 592
Princeton, New Jersey 08540

None of the College Board tests are available to the general public, but descriptions of the tests, practice materials for students who plan to take the tests, research reports, books, and other kinds of materials are available. Some are free. A list of available publications can be found in *Publications of the College Board* available from the above address.

Educational Testing Service (ETS)
Cooperative Test Division
Rosedale Road
Princeton, New Jersey 08540

Publishers of the *School and College Ability Tests, Sequential Tests of Educational Progress,* the *Cooperative Achievement Tests* in various academic subjects, and the *Graduate Record Examinations.* Provides special scoring service for tests that it publishes. Other sections of ETS conduct special testing programs for professional schools and for other organizations. Also carries out test construction and administration of tests for College Entrance Examination Board.

The Evaluation and Advisory Service provides assistance on evaluation and testing problems. This section also publishes a series of booklets related to tests and use of tests suitable for the naive consumer. The booklets may be obtained at no cost.

Harcourt, Brace & World, Inc.
Test Department
757 Third Avenue
New York, New York 10017

Primarily publishers of achievement batteries and tests and general intelligence tests. Best-known tests are the *Metropolitan Achievement Tests, Stanford Achievement Tests,* special subject matter tests of the *Evaluation and Adjustment Series,* and the *Otis-Lennon Mental Ability Test.* Also publishes reading readiness tests—*Metropolitan Readiness Test* and *Murphy-Durrell Reading Readiness Analysis*—and prognostic tests for mathematics and foreign languages. Publishes very few personality or interest inventories. Has developed one of the few commercially available achievement tests for adults with limited education, *Adult Basic Learning Examination.* Provides scoring services for tests.

Publishes *Test Service Notebooks, Test Service Bulletins,* and *Test Data Reports* that discuss general issues and problems in testing and report research data on their own tests. These can be obtained at no cost.

Houghton Mifflin Company
2 Park Street
Boston, Massachusetts 02107

Publishers of achievement tests, general intelligence tests, reading tests and a few personality inventories. Best known tests are the *Iowa Tests of Basic Skills, Tests of Academic Progress, Cognitive Abilities Test, Lorge-Thorndike Intelligence Tests, Henmon-Nelson Tests of Mental Ability, Study of Values, Primary Reading Profiles,* and *Revised Stanford-Binet Intelligence Scale*. Provides scoring services for tests. Also publishes numerous books on testing.

Institute for Personality and Ability Testing
1602 Coronado Drive
Champaign, Illinois 61820

Publishers of *IPAT Anxiety Scale Questionnaire, Sixteen Personality Factor Questionnaire* and all of its derivatives, and the *Culture-Fair Intelligence Test*.

Personnel Press, Inc.
20 Nassau Street
Princeton, New Jersey 08540

Publishers of the *Kuhlmann-Anderson Intelligence Tests, Seventh Edition, Wisconsin Contemporary Tests of Elementary Mathematics,* and *Torrance Tests of Creative Thinking*.

The Psychological Corporation
304 East 45th Street
New York, New York 10017

Publishers or distributors of a wide variety of aptitude tests for schools, clinical tests, tests for industrial uses, and personality inventories. Best known tests are the *Differential Aptitude Tests, Wechsler Adult Intelligence Scale, Wechsler Intelligence Scale for Children, Wechsler Preschool and Primary Scale of Intelligence, MMPI,* and *Strong Vocational Interest Blank*. Provides test scoring service.

The Professional Examinations Division conducts special testing programs for a variety of professional groups and schools such as professional nursing, practical nursing, medical librarians, medical school admissions, and veterinary medicine. Publishes an excellent series of *Test Service Bulletins* that are available at no cost.

Sheridan Supply Company
P.O. Box 837
Beverly Hills, California 90213

Publishers of the *Guilford-Zimmerman Aptitude Survey, Creativity Tests, Guilford-Zimmerman Temperament Survey,* and other Guilford-Martin-Zimmerman tests and inventories.

Science Research Associates, Inc.
259 East Erie Street
Chicago, Illinois 60611

Publishers of *SRA Primary Mental Abilities, SRA Achievement Series, Iowa Tests of Educational Development, Kuder Preference Records,* as well as other achievement, general intelligence, aptitude, and personality inventories. Also publishes a wide variety of programs and materials for reading, mathematics, and guidance. Provides test scoring services.

Teachers College Press
Teachers College, Columbia University
525 West 120th Street
New York, New York 10027

Publishers and distributors of *Gates-MacGinitie Reading Tests* as well as other reading tests and practice materials in reading.

Index